FLOWERS ON THE ROCK

Flowers on the Rock

Global and Local Buddhisms in Canada

Edited by

JOHN S. HARDING, VICTOR SŌGEN HORI, AND
ALEXANDER SOUCY

McGill-Queen's University Press
Montreal & Kingston · London · Ithaca

© McGill-Queen's University Press 2014

ISBN 978-0-7735-4337-9 (cloth)
ISBN 978-0-7735-4338-6 (paper)
ISBN 978-0-7735-9048-9 (ePDF)
ISBN 978-0-7735-9049-6 (ePUB)

Legal deposit third quarter 2014
Bibliothèque nationale du Québec

Printed in Canada on acid-free paper that is 100% ancient forest free (100% post-consumer recycled), processed chlorine free

McGill-Queen's University Press acknowledges the support of the Canada Council for the Arts for our publishing program. We also acknowledge the financial support of the Government of Canada through the Canada Book Fund for our publishing activities.

Library and Archives Canada Cataloguing in Publication

    Flowers on the rock : global and local Buddhisms in Canada / edited by John S. Harding, Victor Sōgen Hori, and Alexander Soucy.

Includes bibliographical references and index.
Issued in print and electronic formats.
ISBN 978-0-7735-4337-9 (bound). – ISBN 978-0-7735-4338-6 (pbk.). –
ISBN 978-0-7735-9048-9 (ePDF). – ISBN 978-0-7735-9049-6 (ePUB)

    1. Buddhism – Canada. I. Harding, John S., 1971–, author, editor II. Hori, Victor Sōgen, author, editor III. Soucy, Alexander, 1968–, author, editor

BQ742.F56 2014   294.30971   C2014-902409-6
    C2014-902410-X

Typeset by Jay Tee Graphics Ltd. in 11/14 Minion

Contents

Conventions vii

Acknowledgments xi

Illustrations xiii

Introduction 3
JOHN S. HARDING, VICTOR SŌGEN HORI, AND ALEXANDER SOUCY

1 Buddhist Globalism and the Search for Canadian Buddhism 25
ALEXANDER SOUCY

PART ONE TAKING ROOT

2 Flying Sparks: Dissension among the Early Shin Buddhists in Canada 55
MICHIHIRO AMA

3 For the Benefit of Many: S.N. Goenka's Vipassana Meditation Movement in Canada 79
KORY GOLDBERG

4 Sitavana: The Theravada Forest Tradition in British Columbia 101
JAMES PLACZEK

5 Making a Traditional Buddhist Monastery on Richmond's Highway to Heaven 129
JACKIE LARM

6 Dharma on the Move: Vancouver Buddhist Communities and Multiculturalism   150
   PAUL CROWE

7 Buddhist Monasticism in Canada: Sex and Celibacy   173
   VICTOR SŌGEN HORI

   PART TWO   COMMUNICATING THE BUDDHADHARMA

8 Teaching Buddhism to Children: The Evolving Sri Lankan Buddhist Tradition in Multicultural Toronto   201
   D. MITRA BARUA

9 Reflections on a Canadian Buddhist Death Ritual   225
   ANGELA SUMEGI

10 Buddhist Prison Outreach in Canada: Legitimating a Minority Faith   245
   PAUL McIVOR

11 Correspondence School: Canada, Fluxus, and Zen   267
   MELISSA ANNE-MARIE CURLEY

12 Shaping Images of Tibet: Negotiating the Diaspora through Ritual, Art, and Film   287
   SARAH F. HAYNES

   PART THREE   BUDDHIST LIVES

13 Dhammadinna and Jayantā: Daughters of the Buddha in Canada   313
   MAVIS L. FENN

14 Thầy Phổ Tịnh: A Vietnamese Nun's Struggles in Canada   333
   ALEXANDER SOUCY

15 Leslie Kawamura: Nothing to Add, Nothing to Take Away   355
   JOHN S. HARDING

   Bibliography   385

   Contributors   421

   Index   427

Conventions

ROMANIZATION

The editors found it impossible to impose a consistent form of romanization on Chinese terms and names. For a very long time in Western scholarship, the standard system of romanization was the Wade-Giles system, and much scholarship was written with this system. In recent decades, scholars have switched to the Pinyin system. Numerous inconsistencies can thus occur. For example, an author who uses Pinyin may quote a passage from an older text that uses Wade-Giles. Or, such an author is sometimes forced by convention to mix romanization systems when writing personal names or the names of Chinese organizations that use Wade-Giles. In such situations, both Pinyin and Wade-Giles forms of romanization may occur on the same page. Throughout this book, we have tried to follow a policy of being faithful to the source. Quotations from other sources follow the system of romanization used in that original source. We use whatever romanization organizations or persons use for their own names. In the remaining situations, we use Pinyin.

USE OF DIACRITICAL MARKS

The editors also found it impossible to maintain a consistent policy on the use of diacritical marks. Scholars use terms from the many Buddhist languages using diacritical marks to indicate their pronunciation, but practising Buddhists use the same terminology usually without the diacritical marks. Complicating matters, many Buddhist terms have been accepted into the English language where they appear without diacritical marks. Complicating the matter even further, Buddhist organizations which once omitted diacritical marks have begun using them, thus Sākyadhitā began to use diacritical marks on its website, the Dharma Realm Buddhist Association uses diacritics for the name of its founder, Hsüan Hua, as does Shambhala for the name of its founder, Chögyam Trungpa. In this volume, we omit diacritical marks for those Buddhist terms which have entered the English language, as judged by the Concise Oxford English Dictionary (Eleventh edition). These include: Theravada, Mahayana, Hinayana, Pali, samsara, nirvana, prajna, vipassana, samadhi, sangha, dharma, sunyata, roshi, sutra, and others. We try to follow whatever convention a Buddhist organization has accepted for itself, whether that includes or does not include diacritical marks. But since the authors of the essays in this book are scholars with high standards of accuracy, they will use diacritical marks in rendering Buddhist terminology. This means that it is quite possible the same term could appear twice on the same page, once with and once without diacritical marks.

PALI AND SANSKRIT

Flowers on the Rock contains chapters written by scholars of Theravada Buddhism who base their scholarship on Pali primary texts rather than Sanskrit. In their chapters, they use Pali romanization. In those cases, after the first use of a Pali term, we insert the corresponding Sanskrit term, e.g., "*dhamma* (Skt. *dharma*)."

NAMES

Names of well-known places are written without diacritical marks, thus, Kyoto not Kyōto, Tokyo not Tōkyō.

Names of persons are written as the person himself or herself normally writes it or as normally appears on the person's publications. Usually diacritical marks are omitted. Thus, we write Hsing Yun not Xingyun; Cheng Yen not Zhengyan. An exception is Chögyam Trungpa, since this is the way his name appears on most of his publications. A special case is Thich Nhat Hanh. He publishes in English without diacritics and in Vietnamese with diacritics. In this volume, when he is mentioned in a Western context, we have left his name without diacritics, but in Soucy's opening chapter we have used diacritics for his name because he is being discussed in a Vietnamese context.

Japanese names are a particular problem. Our rule is that when the person in question is based in Japan, then his or her name is presented in Japanese order (surname first) with diacritical marks. Thus we write Ōtani Kōshin, Shaku Sōen. But if the person in question has immigrated to Canada, then the name is presented in Western order (surname last) and without diacritical marks. Thus we write Yutetsu Kawamura, Genjiro Mori, Orai Fujikawa. For both immigrants and those based in Japan, we use diacritics for Japanese titles such as *sōchō* (bishop).

Acknowledgments

The editors would like to acknowledge the support of Brian Nagata (US Office) and Yasuo Honjo (Canada Office) of the Bukkyo Dendo Kyokai (Society for the Promotion of Buddhism), otherwise known as the Numata Foundation, as well as the Social Sciences and Humanities Research Council. This volume is integral to the editors' larger project, "The Modernization of Buddhism in Global Perspective," which is funded by a five-year SSHRC Insight Grant. Other supportive institutions include McGill University, Saint Mary's University, and the University of Lethbridge for funding various stages of research. In addition to our home universities, we appreciate the support of the University of Victoria Centre for Studies in Religion and Society, which offered Victor Hori Visiting Research Fellow status in the summers of 2011 and 2012, and the winter of 2014. Similarly, we appreciate the support of the Institut d'études politiques d'Aix-en-Provence (Sciences Po Aix), France, which offered John Harding visiting professor status in June 2012.

We thank the organizers of the Tung Lin Kok Yuen Conference on Buddhism and Diaspora, University of Toronto, Scarborough Campus, for allowing us to organize an entire panel on Theravada Buddhism in Canada and for inviting Victor Hori as keynote speaker for that conference in May 2010. Similarly, we appreciate Professor Jessica Main of the University of British Columbia, who at our urging organized the *Buddhism in Canada: Global Causes, Local Conditions* conference in October 2010. Several of the chapters in this book originated as presentations at these conferences.

We are indebted to many individuals from Buddhist and scholarly communities who have assisted with research in innumerable ways. In particular, we acknowledge Thích Nữ Phổ Tịnh for her support and help with Alexander Soucy's research over the years. Dr Leslie Kawamura's contributions to Buddhism and Buddhist scholarship in and beyond Canada are deeply appreciated, as is his wife, Toyo's, assistance to John Harding in the chapter about Leslie Kawamura's life and contributions. Jonathan Crago and Ryan Van Huijstee were our editors at McGill-Queen's University Press overseeing the publication process. Copy editor Kate Merriman improved the volume in numerous ways. Additionally, we would like to acknowledge the anonymous readers for their insightful comments, which helped sharpen and shape this volume. Thank you to Victor Temprano, who helped with the index. We thank the many people from Buddhist organizations across the country who assisted us with this volume. We would also like to thank our family members and colleagues who offered perspective and support during the long process of bringing this work to fruition. Inevitably in a volume like this, there are numerous factual claims to be checked, numerous references to previous scholarship that have to be verified. For any mistakes or omissions, the editors take full responsibility.

John S. Harding, University of Lethbridge
Victor Sōgen Hori, McGill University
Alexander Soucy, Saint Mary's University

1 Group meditation at Dhamma Suttama, Montebello, QC, 2012. Photo by François Morin

2   Ajahn Sona, Sitavana Birken Forest Monastery, BC, 2011. Photo by Doug Hoyle

3   Sister Mon, Sitavana Birken Forest Monastery, BC, 2011. Photo by Doug Hoyle

4 Thrangu Monastery, Richmond, BC, 2012. Photo by Jackie Larm

5 Statue of Śākyamuni Buddha at Thrangu Monastery. Photo by Jackie Larm

6 Ling Yen Mountain Temple, Richmond, BC, 2013. Photo by Paul Crowe

7   Woman offering incense to Guanyin Bodhisattva, 2013. Photo by Paul Crowe

8 Lighting incense before the interment. Photo by Andrea Lorient

9 Eric Metcalfe, *New York Corres Sponge Dance School of Vancouver* (no date). Courtesy of Eric Metcalfe and the Morris and Helen Belkin Art Gallery (Vancouver, BC)

10   Anagarika Dhammadinna (Anna Burian) at ordination in 1964. Photo courtesy of Shirley Johannesen

11   Thầy Phổ Tịnh at the Great Pine Forest Monastery in 2006. Photo by Alexander Soucy

12   Rev. Dr Leslie Kawamura in Calgary, AB, 2008. Photo by Toyo Kawamura

13 Participants at the "Numata Symposium: Buddhist Studies in Canada" at the University of Calgary, 2009. Photo courtesy of the Numata Chair in Buddhist Studies at the University of Calgary

FLOWERS ON THE ROCK

石上栽花後　*Sekijō hana o uete nochi,*
生涯共是春　*Shōgai tomo ni kore haru.*

After you have planted the flower on the rock,
The days of your life will always be spring.
                                        ZEN VERSE

Introduction

JOHN S. HARDING, VICTOR SŌGEN HORI, AND
ALEXANDER SOUCY

The title of this book, *Flowers on the Rock*, is inspired by a story about the Japanese Zen monk Sasaki Sōkei-an, one of the first teachers of Zen to come to the West. Sasaki founded the First Zen Institute of America in New York City in 1930. When asked how long it would take before Zen Buddhism became established in the West, he replied that bringing Zen to America was like holding a lotus against a rock and waiting for it to set down roots (Fields 1992, 272).[1] Sasaki uttered those words in the first half of the twentieth century, before Buddhism had started to gain popularity. Since then, various forms of Buddhism from around the world have come to the West, and although many are still struggling to survive, flowers are indubitably starting to take hold on the rock. As in many other countries outside Asia, Buddhism is taking root in Canada.

The study of Buddhism in Canada is still in its infancy. Thus far, aside from a handful of master and doctoral theses, there have been only two full-length books devoted to the study of Buddhism in Canada as a whole: Bruce Matthews' *Buddhism in Canada* (2006) and our first book, *Wild Geese: Buddhism in Canada* (Harding, Hori, and Soucy 2010).[2] In addition, there have been a few studies dealing with specific groups, including Daniel Métraux's *The Lotus and the Maple Leaf: The Soka Gakkai Buddhist Movement in Canada* (1996) and Terry Watada's *Bukkyo Tozen: A History of Jodo Shinshu Buddhism in Canada 1905–1995* (1996). Finally, there have been three studies of different groups in Toronto: Janet McLellan's *Many Petals of the Lotus* (1999), Patricia Campbell's *Knowing Body, Moving Mind: Ritualizing and Learning at Two Buddhist Centers* (2011), and Suwanda Sugunasiri's *Thus Spake the Sangha: Early Buddhist Leadership in Toronto:*

Kwang Ok Sunim, Bhante Punnaji, Samu Sunim, Tsunoda Sensei, Zasep Tulku Rimpoche (2008). Our earlier book, *Wild Geese*, attempted to set in place the foundation stones upon which to base the study of Buddhism in Canada as a new field of academic enquiry. Thus, there were chapters devoted to the history of Buddhism in Canada, statistical analyses of the Buddhist groups in Canada, methodological examination of the concepts used for organizing the field, ethnographic studies of temples and meditation centres, and two biographies of Buddhist personalities. Inevitably, there were gaps in coverage. *Flowers on the Rock* addresses some of these gaps and continues laying foundation stones. The chapters in this book contribute several more historical studies, ethnographic field reports, and biographies of Buddhist leaders. In particular, more attention is paid to Theravada groups and to women in Buddhism. There are also field reports of West Coast Buddhist groups and greater attention to Vietnamese Buddhism in Canada. Although the study of Buddhism in Canada is only beginning, the two volumes, *Wild Geese* and *Flowers on the Rock*, are now a more complete and systematic foundation for the field.

THE PARADIGM

The theoretical stance of this book is expressed in the subtitle, *Global and Local Buddhisms in Canada*. *Flowers on the Rock* offers a critical reflection on the silent paradigm that underlies much writing in the field of Buddhism in the West. This paradigm assumes that the modernization of Buddhism is equivalent to the Westernization of Buddhism, that Asian culture is a relatively static repository of tradition incapable of innovation or renewal, and that the West will correct the long history of Asian cultural distortion of Buddhism and finally allow the truth of Buddhism to come forth. In the literature on Buddhism in the West, this paradigm is never set forth as an explicit theory, where it can be discussed, examined, and debated. Instead, it is implicitly contained in three sets of binary distinctions which Western writers impose on their subject matter: (1) Asian/ethnic and Western/convert; (2) traditional and modern; (3) inauthentic and authentic Buddhism. The first and second sets of distinctions are frequently treated as equivalent to each other, while the third is often implied as well. Without being aware, one is led to talking about Asian/ethnic Buddhism as "traditional" and inauthentic Buddhism, while Western convert Buddhism is implicitly associated with modern and authentic Buddhism. This counterintuitive association between the traditional and the inauthentic is particularly prevalent in popular discourse about Buddhism in the West, but these assumptions shape certain scholarly accounts as well. We need to critically examine the consequences of equating these three sets of binaries.

ASIAN/ETHNIC AND WESTERN/CONVERT

Most authors who write on Buddhism in the West use the terminology of the "Two Buddhisms," Asian/ethnic and Western/convert Buddhism, or some equivalent. As we argued in *Wild Geese*, this distinction is fraught with problems. First, the fact that there are no clear definitional criteria for "Asian" and "Western" leads to much ambiguity about who is an Asian/ethnic and who is a Western/convert. The generational issue brings this problem into clear focus. Second-generation Canadians are usually more Western than Asian, so if they attend an ethnic-Asian temple, classification becomes difficult: their hybrid identities are neither Asian nor Western, nor just a combination of the two. The children of converts who follow their parents in being Buddhist are not converts, but they are not Asian. The children of both Asian and Western converts will be Western-born Buddhists who are neither fully Asian/ethnic nor fully Western/convert. In the coming generations, not only will their numbers increase, they will likely constitute the single largest demographic of Buddhists in Canada. To recognize this intermediate group, Richard Seager has offered a three-part typology of (1) convert Buddhists (i.e., native-born Americans); (2) immigrant and refugee Buddhists, born and raised in an Asian Buddhist country; and (3) "Asian Americans, primarily from Chinese and Japanese backgrounds, who have practised Buddhism in this country for four and five generations" (Seager 1999, 9–10). Jan Nattier also has proposed three categories: (1) Elite Buddhists, who are wealthy enough to "import" their Buddhism; (2) Evangelical Buddhists, like Soka Gakkai, who "export" Buddhism through their proselytization practices, and (3) Ethnic Buddhists, who as immigrants bring Buddhism as part of their "cultural baggage" (Nattier 1998, 188–90).

Due to the definitional problems in trying to identify who is Asian and who is Western, Martin Baumann has argued that we should not try to identify groups of people but rather styles of Buddhist practice, which he labels "traditionalist" and "modernist." In "traditionalist" temples located in ethnic communities, ordained monks perform devotional rituals, promote practices to create karmic merit, and may even engage in selling protective amulets (Baumann 2002, 56–7). Meanwhile at "modernist" meditation centres, lay teachers eschew ritual and karma and focus instead on meditation, mindfulness, and rational understanding (Baumann 2002, 57–8). With this move, Baumann has avoided the nest of confusions associated with the binary Asian/ethnic and Western/convert, but as we shall soon see, the binary of "traditionalist" and "modernist" itself comes with its own difficulties.

In addition to such problems of definition, the terminology of Asian/ethnic and Western/convert also contains undesirable political nuances. Appearances to the contrary, the word "ethnic" is not a neutral, objective term taken from social science. François Thibeault points out that the idea of ethnicity presupposes a self/other distinction, with "ethnics" cast as the others. Specifically in regard to the way that scholars in the West have approached Buddhism, he writes, "convert Buddhists are non-ethnic, because ethnicity is usually conceived as a specific feature of those minority groups of individuals who have migrated to Western societies" (Thibeault 2006, 3). There is, therefore, a lack of recognition that Western/American culture is equally an ethnicity, rather than ethnic-neutral. As Shannon Hickey has pointed out, the term "ethnic" is applied only to groups that are not white. Yet, white groups also have ethnocentric cultural characteristics, although these are invisible from the position of white privilege (Hickey 2010, 14). Buddhism has been the cultural heritage of Asian countries for thousands of years, whereas Americans have discovered it only in recent generations. Nevertheless, many American practitioners think of themselves as the agents and principal actors in American Buddhism, while Asians are the "ethnics" and the "others." Helen Tworkov, the editor of *Tricycle* magazine, bluntly wrote in a 1991 editorial, "The spokespeople for Buddhism in America have been, almost exclusively, educated members of the white middle class. Meanwhile, even with varying statistics, Asian-American Buddhists number at least one million, but so far have not figured prominently in the development of something called American Buddhism" (Tworkov 1991, 4).

American Buddhism here is implicitly distinguished from ethnic Buddhism, which is usually depicted as community-focused, ritualistic, and heavily laden with "inauthentic" cultural form. If it is seen as an automatic and unreflective part of their culture, the Buddhism of ethnic Asians seems to lack the personal commitment and inner search which "converts" regard as constitutive of their own "practice" – one of the terms often used in favourable contrast to "religion." The silent implication is that the Buddhism of ethnic Asians is somehow less authentic.

TRADITIONAL AND MODERN

In addition to the standard trope of Asian/ethnic and Western/convert, much of the literature about Buddhism in the West imposes the typology of "traditional" and "modern" on the field. Quite aside from the question Soucy brings to these terms in chapter 1 – that they have a very specific cultural reference, constructed in opposition to one another in a way that is masked by assumptions of neutrality presumed in common speech – they carry unstated and erroneous meaning. As we saw in Baumann's distinction above, "traditionalist" Buddhism is the Buddhism of devotional ritual and irrational "superstition" – worshipping ancestors, praying for luck, and creating karmic merit – while "modernist" Buddhism often focuses on meditation, self-knowledge, and rational understanding. Baumann's typology is useful and more nuanced, but for less reflective observers the traditional vs modern binary is automatically mapped onto the Asian/ethnic vs Western/convert binary. That is, it is simply assumed that an Asian temple practises traditional Buddhism and a Western meditation centre practises modernist Buddhism. This conflation, however, does not bear out under close scrutiny.

Behind the ornate red and gold facades of the Chinese Fo Guang Shan temples in Vancouver, Toronto, Ottawa, and Montreal, the ordained nuns (usually the leader is a nun) teach Humanistic Buddhism. In the vision of Master Hsing Yun, the founder of Fo Guang Shan (FGS), Humanistic Buddhism deals with how people ought to act in this world, not with some future rebirth or other existence. Humanistic Buddhism is compatible with science and modern education; indeed, in Taiwan FGS operates its own schools and colleges, and in Los Angeles it operates an accredited school, The University of the West. FGS has a well-organized program to teach Buddhism through its temples to both children and adults; trained teachers use standardized textbooks (manga for children) and regularly administer tests. FGS knows that people today are juggling career, family, and the complexities of contemporary urban life, so it creates retreats and activities to fit in with their busy schedules, such as temporary ordination retreats, factory-based activities, and summer camps for children. Knowing that in times of disaster ordinary people want to pitch in and help, FGS organizes teams that put volunteers on site doing relief work within hours after earthquakes, typhoons, floods, and other natural disasters. FGS's own television station and media publications carry news of this work, not just locally but globally through its worldwide network of temples. FGS was one of the first organizations in Asia to use digital methods in compiling a Buddhist encyclopedia in 1988. It is currently involved in compiling a massive, completely online encyclopedia of Chinese Buddhism, to be available in both Chinese and English.[3] FGS is an Asian Buddhist organization but little about it fits the Asian "traditionalist" stereotype.

FGS is not alone in applying technology to modernist ideas of Buddhist activity in this world. The Buddhist Relief and Compassion Tzu Chi Foundation, based in Taiwan, is another Asian/ethnic organization, but as André Laliberté and Manuel Litalien illustrate in *Wild Geese* (2010), it is also thoroughly modern, very sophisticated, and global in its reach. Under the leadership of its founder, the charismatic Buddhist nun Cheng Yen, Tzu Chi has developed a worldwide network in more than thirty countries, including branches in Vancouver, Toronto, and Montreal. These are examples of well-known modernist, global Buddhist organizations with origins and headquarters in Asia.

The characterizations of traditional vs modern are also called into question by looking closely at groups that would normally be seen as representing "ethnic" Buddhism in the West. For instance, Vietnamese temples in North America, Europe, and Australia appear homogeneous, with ethnic Vietnamese members performing the devotional rituals that they have always practised in their homeland. However, many of the Buddhist monastic and lay leaders who established temples in the diaspora had been part of the Buddhist activist movements that produced people like Thích Nhất Hạnh. Consequently, while many of the practices were not significantly altered, the organization of the temples and many of the activities performed in them are significantly different. When Soucy visited Viên Giác Temple in Hanover, Germany in 2012, the abbot, Thích Như Điển, introduced him to the temple. The abbot showed him the office where the temple publishes its magazine, *Viên Giác*, available in both print and online editions.[4] A lay volunteer was using the main sanctuary at that time to introduce a university class to Buddhism. The temple's prayer book was written in Vietnamese and German, rather than in Sino-Vietnamese – a change similar to switching the Catholic mass from Latin to the vernacular. In a smaller sanctuary upstairs, the walls were lined with *thankas*, hung by a Tibetan Buddhist group that also uses the temple. While serving a Vietnamese community, and offering mostly Pure Land devotional services, this temple challenges the category of traditional. Most Vietnamese temples in Canada are similar in the complexity in which modernist reformist ideas have permeated their activities. Thiền Viện Linh Sơn on Hochelaga Street in East End Montreal performs the usual Pure Land rituals, but also holds meditation sessions and instruction in Vietnamese and French. Tu Viện Huyền Không, also in Montreal, is "traditional" in the sense that it performs Pure Land style rituals, but it is also working on building a retirement home to serve the older members of the Vietnamese community in Montreal. This sort of activism and community engagement is not something that would have existed in Vietnam a hundred years ago, despite the fact that all three of the examples just mentioned are temples that fall squarely within what is usually classified as "traditional" and "ethnic."

It is not merely that "Asian Buddhisms" are just as engaged in modernist discourses as "Western Buddhisms," but Buddhisms in Asia started modernizing long before there was such a thing as Western Buddhism. In Ceylon (now Sri Lanka) in the 1880s, Henry Steel Olcott (1832–1907) and Anagarika Dharmapala (1864–1933) reorganized Ceylonese Buddhism to protect it from Christian missionaries. The new Buddhism they created removed much "superstition" and ritual, rationalized Buddhist teaching so it could be easily taught (Olcott created a Buddhist catechism), and opened up Buddhism to a lay audience. Since their reorganization of Buddhism imitated many aspects of Christianity, some scholars have labelled their new product "Protestant Buddhism" (Gombrich and Obeyesekere 1988; Blackburn 2010; Obeyesekere 1972; Prothero 1996). The Japanese Zen monk Shaku Sōen (1860–1919) was in Ceylon during those turbulent times. Once back in Japan, he helped foster a movement calling for a "New Buddhism" (*Shin Bukkyō*) that was consistent with rationality and science, appealed to lay people, and permitted women to practice (Harding 2008; Snodgrass 2003; 2009b).

A generation later in China, the Chinese reformist monk Taixu (1890–1947) coined the term Humanistic Buddhism (*Renjian Fojiao*), and during the early years of the twentieth century called for a wholesale creation of a new Chinese Buddhism; the new Buddhism was to be less elitist, consistent with science, based on an educated monkhood, socially engaged, and so on (Pittman 2001). His vision influenced the reform movement in Vietnam starting in the 1920s (DeVido 2007; 2009) and triggered a chain of events which resulted in Thích Nhất Hạnh's "socially engaged Buddhism." By the time that the Beatniks in America became interested in Buddhism in the late 1950s, eight decades of modernist reform of Buddhism had already taken place in Asia. Many Western commentators have been so focused on modernization in the Western convert community that they have failed to recognize that Asian Buddhism coming into North America experienced modernization decades earlier. An important exception is David McMahan who, in *The Making of Buddhist Modernism*, is clear that "The modernization of Buddhism ... has in no way been an exclusively western project or simply a representation of the eastern Other; many figures essential to this process have been Asian reformers educated in both western and Buddhist thought" (McMahan 2008, 6; see also Lopez 2002 and Rocha 2012, 295). This book shares this view of the role of Asian reformers in the development of contemporary global Buddhism.

AUTHENTIC AND INAUTHENTIC BUDDHISM

Some writers on Buddhism in the West want to have it both ways, claiming that Buddhism in the West is simultaneously modernized by Western influence and yet is also truer to the intentions of the Buddha than most Buddhism that is practised in Asia. James William Coleman may be especially exuberant in his declarations, but his sentiment is representative of much writing about Buddhism in the West: "After fading out in the land of its birth centuries ago and teetering on the edge of twentieth-century extinction in Tibet and China, a new Buddhism is now emerging in the industrialized nations of the West. This Buddhism is fundamentally different from anything that has gone before, yet, in the best tradition of Buddhist logic, it remains at its core completely unchanged from the moment of Siddartha Gautama's great realization under the bodhi tree" (Coleman 2001, 3). While forthrightly calling it "New Buddhism," Coleman also makes the bold claim that this new Buddhism that is being created in the West is "completely unchanged" from the original Buddha's great enlightenment. In Coleman's eyes, the other forms of Buddhism that arose in Asia have been distorted by Asian culture. They absorbed "the Asian tradition of obedience and reverence for authority" (Coleman 2001, 85), the Asian religious rituals for "supernatural benefit" and similar "magical notions" (2001, 97), the "extreme sexism" of Asians (2001, 15), the "almost unquestioned authority, power and prestige the Asian teachers enjoy in their own traditions" (2001, 17), and so on.

Many writers on Buddhism in the West are not as extreme as Coleman. These more moderate writers take the position that Buddhism has the marvellous ability to adapt to quite different cultural environments without losing the true Dharma. In this view, Asian Buddhism and Western Buddhism are equally authentic forms of Buddhism. But the presence of this more moderate position highlights how extreme Coleman's views are. When Western writers claim that Western-inspired modernizations are going to correct the distortions to Buddhism rendered by Asian culture, we echo the errors of colonial, Orientalist scholarship.

This is the unspoken paradigm that underlies much writing in the new field of Buddhism in the West. The three binary distinctions of Asian/ethnic vs Western/convert, traditional vs modern, and inauthentic vs authentic are used in popular writing and some scholarship as if they were equivalent to each other. Judith Snodgrass insightfully points out, "The image of the Buddha seated in meditation beneath a tree provides the model for modern Buddhism's disproportionate emphasis on meditation ... and the basis for a certain arrogance among some western Buddhists who feel that the Buddhism of their practice is closer to Sakyamuni's teachings than that of traditional Asian practitioners" (Snodgrass 2009, 21). Without conscious assent, one smoothly moves into the assumption that the Asian/ethnic is traditional but somehow inauthentic, while the Western/convert is modern as well as authentic. *Flowers on the Rock* challenges this flawed paradigm.

We propose another paradigm that does not necessarily interact with the binaries of ethnic/convert, traditional/modern, or authentic/inauthentic. We believe that it is more helpful to organize and understand material on Buddhism in the West by using the interplay of global and local forces to better explore Buddhist transformations in, and beyond, Canada. These categories address central issues in understanding Buddhism in the contemporary situation: the way Buddhism has moved and is transformed in the modern period, with a strong emphasis on communication as a central theoretical concept. We turn now, therefore, to a discussion of the continuing impact of globalization on Buddhism.

GLOBALIZATION

In this volume, we characterize the development of modern Buddhism in terms of globalization because globalization cuts across the Asian/ethnic vs Western/convert dichotomy. Instead of getting caught in the misleading stereotype that positions Asia and the West in opposition to each other, we focus on globalization, which allows us to recognize that modernization movements first got started in Asia, and that modernization movements in Asia and modernization movements in the West are rooted in a similar modernist understanding of the world, the individual, and religion. Although modernization is clearly important for an understanding of how Buddhism has developed worldwide, at the heart of these changes are global interactions that often – but not always – put forward modernist ideas, not modernity. For this reason, we focus on the global processes that have brought about the significant, but not homogeneous, changes we are seeing in Buddhism at an international level. We, furthermore, contend that any understanding of Buddhism as it is developing in Canada must take into account the forces of globalization and the transnational linkages that not only inform but also propel these changes.

First, what do we mean by globalization? In the 1980s, the concept of globalization was introduced in an economic sense to describe and explain the worldwide spread of capitalism; it later broadened in scope to include the worldwide spread of peoples, technologies, and information. Because of its early economic use, for many people the term "globalization" has a negative nuance, connoting the spread of capitalism, the exploitation of underdeveloped countries by the advanced capitalist economies (the tragic Bangladesh garment factory collapse on 24 April 2013 comes to mind), and the imposition of the culture of McDonalds and Coca Cola onto local indigenous culture. In this view, economic globalization threatens to homogenize the world as a materialistic consumerism chokes out all native and indigenous traditions. Because of this earlier connection, some people consider "globalization" a new word for what used to be called colonialism.

Now scholars recognize that globalization is not merely economic but social as well. Giddens, for example, sees globalization in social terms as "the interlacing of social events and social relations 'at a distance' with local contextualities" (1991, 21). He continues, "globalisation has to be understood as a dialectical phenomenon, in which events at one pole of a distanciated relation often produce divergent or even contrary occurrences at another" (1991, 22). Elsewhere, he describes globalization as the "intensification of worldwide social relations which link distant localities in such a way that local happenings are shaped by events occurring many miles away and vice versa" (1991, 64). Globalization is as much social as it is economic (as if economics were not an intensely social activity in any case). When more and more local social events need to be understood against a global context, at some point a qualitative change occurs; from then on we need to speak not merely of local causes but also of "world systems," both economic and social. Globalization is not really a new process: it has been going on since humans started to wander. But beginning from the fifteenth to the seventeenth centuries, the network of international social and economic linkages has so intensified that today it deserves to be recognized as a qualitatively different "modern world system" (Vasquez and Marquardt 2003, 36).

Arjun Appadurai has isolated five of the flows, or "scapes" as he calls them, by which globalization exerts itself: (1) ethnoscapes, where people move; (2) financescapes, where capital moves; (3) technoscapes, where technology and communication move; (4) mediascapes, where information moves; and (5) ideoscapes, where discourses move (Appadurai 1996, 33–6). Importantly, Appadurai also shows that there are multiple centres and flows. Rather than going from west to east, north to south, urban to hinterland, these flows are multidirectional and unpredictable (Appadurai 1996, 29).

Globalization can have a liberating effect, allowing exploited peoples to resist their exploitation. Indeed, the many different groups opposed to economic globalization have skilfully used the internet to organize large-scale and well-orchestrated demonstrations against the World Trade Organization and other agents of economic globalization, thus showing that the anti-globalism movement is itself a globalizing phenomenon. Globalization is no longer just another name for colonialism; in the age of the instant, worldwide sharing of information, globalization denotes a new process of dialogue and encounter between cultures and civilizations that frees the local from parochialism (R. Robertson 2009).

It is difficult to ascertain all the ways in which globalization is reshaping religion. Religion is not simply reprising the role it played under colonialism. During the colonial period, as the Western powers extended their economic control of countries in Africa, Asia, and the Americas, Christian missionaries – with Bibles in hand – often preceded the soldiers holding guns and the capitalists looking for economic gain. The missionaries looked upon native peoples as savages who needed to be saved. The Christian church thus provided a religious and moral justification for the Western dominance of undeveloped countries. But probably because of that historical connection with colonial power, the Christian church today is much more wary of its current connection to globalization. In 2005, for example, Pope John Paul II cautioned against globalization: "New realities which are forcefully affecting the productive process – such as globalization of finance, of the economy, of commerce and of work – should never be allowed to violate the dignity and centrality of the human person or the democracy of peoples" (*The Globalist* 2005).

Nor is globalization fulfilling the predictions of social scientists following Max Weber – that as society became more modern, it would become more rational, and non-rational, pre-modern phenomena such as superstition and religion would of themselves die out. This is the well-known "secularization" hypothesis (C. Taylor 2007). In fact, not only has religion not died out, but with globalization religion is flourishing. Through processes that are not yet well understood, globalization seems to be simultaneously encouraging diverse religious developments from Pentecostalism to fundamentalist forms of Islam and Christianity as well as a more liberal and secular form of Buddhism. Buddhism is not merely a "world religion"; it is a "global religion" growing not in spite of, but because of the fact that it brings into interface different cultures and opposing ideas. Applying Appadurai to our understanding of Buddhism in Canada, we can say that the transformations taking place are not so much the result of Western influence as of the discourses emerging from multiple Asian meetings with diverse Western ideas. The transformations that we see are the results of multiple conversations that have arisen from particular historical encounters. As such, it is as important to understand the local as the global. Neither can be understood in isolation; both are part of the same process.

GLOBAL AND LOCAL BUDDHISMS

We use the term "Global Buddhism" to emphasize that Buddhism at the local level needs to be understood against its global background (as opposed to the term "Buddhist Globalism" that Soucy uses to identify the discourse that shapes "Global Buddhism"). A local Buddhist site is a creative bricolage of both local and global elements – ideas, persons, statues, incense, funding, rituals, texts, practices, robes, experiences, and more. Decisions made at any local Buddhist temple or meditation centre may be influenced by quite local issues (weather, neighbours, national holidays, municipal zoning laws, and so on) and by issues originating far away: Will the monk we are sponsoring get a visa? Is there funding from the head temple in Taiwan? When will the next initiation in the UK or the summer retreat in Korea or the ordination in Australia take place? In turn, the Taiwan head temple, the UK initiation, and the summer retreat in Korea are waiting to hear from the local Canadian branch. All forms of Buddhism are imbedded in global networks of shared information, persons, culture, and resources. Scholars seeking to understand these forms of Buddhism must pay attention to both these larger networks and each local constituent.

The drive to reform Buddhism first arose in Ceylon at the end of the 1800s, and in the ensuing century it developed in other countries, wherever traditional Buddhism underwent reform in its confrontation with the colonial Western powers. The modernizing Buddhisms often had similar features: they claimed to be consistent with science and rationality, they were open to lay people, women could participate, the basic practice was meditation, and so on. Aside from these features, the new Buddhism that was coming into being had a global spirit, a spirit that transcended the parochial urge to identify true Buddhism with one place. In 1891, Olcott offered a fourteen-point "Common Platform Upon Which All Buddhists Can Agree" to a meeting of Buddhist representatives from Ceylon, Myanmar, Japan, and Chittagong at Adyar, India (Prothero 1996, 116–33). In similar fashion, Christmas Humphries, a distinguished British lawyer and judge in the UK, drafted the document "Twelve Principles of Buddhism" in 1945 and presented it to a meeting of representatives of Buddhist groups from Ceylon, Thailand, Myanmar, China, Japan, and Tibet (Oliver 1979, 54). Many modernizing and transnational reform efforts were made by Asian Buddhists as well, such as Dharmapala and Taixu, whose efforts to form international Buddhist organizations were combined with attempts to bridge the gaps between religion and science on the one hand, and religion and social action on the other. These various early efforts did not bear much fruit, but the intention and vision were clearly global.

Thus, in our usage, Global Buddhism is not necessarily the same as "modern Buddhism." Global Buddhism understands itself as situated in a larger network and attempts to transcend the parochialism of local place and ethnic identity. Writers on modern Buddhism or Buddhism in the West frequently create a checklist of its characteristics: it is open to lay people and de-emphasizes monasticism, which is criticized as elitist and withdrawn from the world; it is open to women and eschews the sexism of patriarchal society; it is rational and consistent with science; its basic practice is meditation and it does not engage in hollow ritual; it is socially engaged; and so on. As we have noted, a Buddhism that can be so characterized developed in Ceylon in the 1880s, and spread throughout Asia before coming to the West. In spreading from country to country, in transcending the parochialism of local place, this Buddhism was global in spirit. But Buddhism with modern characteristics can also be used parochially. Coleman's concept of "New Buddhism," which claims that the characteristics of the New Buddhism are a product of specifically Western, not Asian, cultural influence on Buddhism, is one example. The ethnocentric privileging of Western Buddhism or New Buddhism over the Buddhism of Asia is clearly insular in thrust and does not exemplify the intercultural spirit often found in Global Buddhism. Hence, in chapter 1 Soucy moves away from attempts to create types with characteristics in favour of understanding Buddhist globalism as a complex and evolving discourse rather than a type, which, like the other types, risks reification of essentialist caricatures.

On the other hand, there are forms of Buddhism that are traditional and conservative in their characteristics yet global in intention. The Thai Forest Tradition consciously thinks of itself as returning to the traditional form of practice as set out by Śākyamuni Buddha. It forsakes the city and its materialistic culture for practice in the forest; it teaches that Buddhism is learned through personal experience in meditation, not through studying textual commentary; and it emphasizes strict adherence to the *vinaya* (rules of discipline). For example, its monks and nuns are celibate, are prohibited from handling money, and eat only one meal a day. Although this very conservative form of Buddhism is not meant for everyone, the Thai Forest

Tradition is increasingly making itself available around the globe. The network of the Forest Sangha now spreads far beyond Thailand and reaches the US, the UK, Switzerland, Italy, Australia, New Zealand, and Canada. In its intention to create Buddhism across the cultural divide between Asia and the West, it is clearly Global Buddhism. As James Placzek describes in chapter 4, the Thai Forest Tradition is not isolated in the forest, but navigating global issues as a result of its global spread.

Tibetan Buddhism has many different forms, but some forms are quite unmodern. The sophisticated philosophy of Mahayana emptiness is merged together with a pantheon of local gods and spirits; meditation is paired with long and elaborate ritual whose meaning is not obvious. Key aspects of Tibetan Buddhism have definitely not gone through the modernization process, yet Tibetan Buddhism may be the most global form of Buddhism today. Although it struggles to survive in Tibet, it thrives wherever the Tibetan diaspora has settled. In its intention to reach out beyond parochial ethnic boundaries, it is a form of Global Buddhism. This example also accentuates the fact that there is no single agent creating or constructing Global Buddhism. As Sarah Haynes points out in her chapter, both Tibetans within the diaspora and non-Tibetans outside the diaspora contribute to the construction of Tibetan Buddhism. Their visions may not be consistent but they contribute equally.

All forms of Buddhism are modernizing; that is, they are constantly in dialogue with the forces of modernist discourses and local pressures. Different forms of Buddhism interact with these discourses differently and are altered by local conditions. Some of the Taiwanese Buddhist movements have created successful new ways of practice for the busy urbanite. Many Western forms of Buddhism have provided meditation and other forms of Buddhist practice for lay men and women, but have struggled with sexual scandals. Modernist forms of Buddhism may exhibit a range of features that indicate the degree to which they are shaped by this discourse. In actuality, though, one form of Buddhism will possess some of these features and another form of Buddhism will possess others. They may be quite different, but because they share a "family resemblance" they can all be identified as modernist.

Global Buddhism grew out of these early reform movements and was influenced by modernist ideas of rationalism (but also, as McMahan points out, by romanticism; democracy and egalitarianism; stress on the individual and on experience; and other factors that emerged out of Western discourses [2008]), catalyzed by the colonial encounter, and perpetuated by global flows of people and information through technology. Rather than being identified with specific groups or movements who are "Global Buddhists" to the exclusion of other groups who are "traditional" or "local," most Buddhists, in our understanding, have been shaped to a lesser or greater degree by the discourses of Global Buddhism. Moreover, the forms of Buddhism which are most closely aligned with Global Buddhism also become localized as they accommodate local contexts, in a process that Roland Robertson has called "glocalization." This process of the local going global and then made local again is, in fact, "the constitutive feature of contemporary globalization" (R. Robertson 1995, 41).

THIS BOOK

Flowers on the Rock takes an overall local-global perspective and views local Buddhist developments on Canadian ground as connected to global developments of Buddhism in the world at large. Indeed, in a conference we held with Jessica Main at the University of British Columbia in 2010, we spliced the Buddhist concept of causes and conditions with globalization theory to produce the conference title "Buddhism in Canada: Global Causes, Local Conditions." In studying Buddhism in Canada, we are emphasizing that one cannot fully understand the establishment of a Thai Forest Tradition monastery in British Columbia, the career of a Vietnamese nun in Montreal, or a sex scandal at a Buddhist training centre in Halifax unless these cases are seen against the larger movements of Buddhism at the global level. And vice versa: one cannot understand the worldwide spread of Buddhism without studying the fascinating and ingenious changes, inflections, and adaptations Buddhism has made in every local culture in which it has set down roots, including Canada. Appropriately, the stance of *Flowers on the Rock* is non-dual, in that we consider every development of Buddhism in Canada to be part of the local religious landscape and at the same time an instantiation of trends in global Buddhism. Alexander Soucy, in his chapter "Buddhist Globalism and the Search for Canadian Buddhism," investigates these issues directly. In response to the question "What is Canadian about Canadian Buddhism?" he shows that, on the one hand, there are no criteria for a unique Canadian identity, and on the other hand, that the Buddhism developing in Canada looks very similar to the modern forms of Buddhism developing around the globe. In doing so, he introduces another approach, one that focuses on the forces that are exerted to varying degrees and in different ways on all forms of Buddhism today.

Part One of this book, "Taking Root," continues to fulfill one of our main missions: to provide a historical record of selected Buddhist groups, which have established themselves in Canada. In "Flying Sparks: Dissension among the Early Shin Buddhists in Canada," Michihiro Ama documents the internal strife which marked the Japanese Pure Land mission at the beginning of the twentieth century. In a tradition noted for peace and in an ethnic group noted for social harmony, there was surprisingly bitter disagreement at every level of organization, between ordained and lay people, between branch and headquarters, between the Higashi (East) Honganji and the Nishi (West) Honganji sects.

In "For the Benefit of Many: S.N. Goenka's Vipassana Meditation Movement in Canada," Kory Goldberg explains that S.N. Goenka created a secular, non-religious meditation method in order to appeal to as many people as possible. Although based originally in Burma (Myanmar), when Goenka took his meditation method international, he came first to Canada and France. Canada thus has a special place in the history of Goenka meditation, but the organization must be recognized primarily as international. James Placzek's chapter, "Sitavana: The Theravada Forest Tradition in British Columbia," documents the establishment of the first Thai Forest Tradition monastery in Canada and explores this tradition's stance on female ordination. In the history of Thai Buddhism, the Thai Forest movement, which got started at the beginning of the twentieth century, represents a return to early Buddhism. Thai Forest monks emphasize strict obedience to the precepts, monastic practice in the forest, and attainment of insight through meditation. It is important to realize, however, that despite its claim to return to Thai Buddhism's roots, the Thai Forest movement is another form of modernized Buddhism.

In "Making a Traditional Buddhist Monastery on Richmond's Highway to Heaven," Jackie Larm reflects on the Thrangu Tibetan Buddhist Monastery's claim to be "traditional." Among expected innovations, such as the use of English and new technology, the Tibetan monastery willingly organizes events to cater to its significant Chinese membership – a development that challenges the category of "ethnic" Buddhism. Paul Crowe's study, "Dharma on the Move: Vancouver Buddhist Communities and Multiculturalism," contributes an in-depth investigation of several Chinese Buddhist temples. It is noteworthy that they are surrounded by the large Chinese immigrant community in Vancouver and therefore do not feel a strong need to integrate and adapt to mainstream Canadian culture. He reflects on what this means for Canada's policy of multiculturalism. In his chapter, "Buddhist Monasticism in Canada: Sex and Celibacy," Victor Sōgen Hori recounts that Buddhist meditation centres in the West have a long history of sexual misconduct scandals that continue to the present. He contrasts the lay-oriented Buddhist meditation centre prone to sex scandals with the monastic-oriented Buddhist monastery where monks and nuns obey the precept to remain celibate. He asks what it is about Buddhist monasteries that prevents sexual misconduct and what it is about Buddhist meditation centres that permits it.

Peter Beyer, in his book on religion and globalization, reminds us that religion is not a private phenomenon enclosed within the consciousness of an individual; it is a social phenomenon built on meanings sent and received between people, meanings shared among people. That is, from a sociological perspective, religion is a kind of communication (Beyer 2006, 10). The chapters in Part Two, "Communicating the Buddhadharma," explore the many ways in which the Dharma is transmitted, missionized, and appropriated. Perhaps the most obvious example is teaching the Dharma to the younger generation. D. Mitra Barua, in his chapter, "Teaching Buddhism to Children: The Evolving Sri Lankan Buddhist Tradition in Multicultural Toronto," studies a new educational manual created by the Sri Lankan Buddhist temples in Toronto to teach *dhamma* to their young people. He shows that even as the new teaching guide strives to preserve the traditional Buddhist regime of spiritual development, it does so in the context of multicultural Toronto, recognizing the secular world view and religious pluralism of multicultural Canadian society. Communicating the Dharma can also mean adapting it to a different cultural context.

Angela Sumegi, who is both an academic scholar and a practising Buddhist teacher, recounts the decisions she made and the thought processes she went through in creating a Buddhist funeral in her chapter, "Reflections on a Canadian Buddhist Death Ritual." She wanted to invoke the meanings embedded in the 2,500-year-old Buddhist tradition and join them to the meanings that individuals of modern-day Ottawa bring to the mystery of death. Along the way, she explores the nature of ritual, which is at once so gripping to some and meaningless to others. Buddhism is also being communicated to those incarcerated in Canada's prisons. Paul McIvor, in "Buddhist Prison Outreach in Canada: Legitimating a Minority Faith," sets out the parameters of study for this new area of research. He begins by focusing attention on the Buddhist practitioners who visit the penitentiaries to give counsel to prisoners.

Elements of Buddhism can become separated from the Buddhist institution and take on a life of their own – think of vegetarianism, meditation, the shaved head, and the term "Zen" – yet these elements communicate Buddhism in a powerful way. In "Correspondence School: Canada, Fluxus, and Zen," Melissa Curley recounts the history of the Fluxus art movement, which was active in Canada during the 1960s and 70s. The Fluxus artists were not diligent practitioners of Buddhism but they were inspired by Zen examples of eccentricity, the Avatamsaka vision of an interconnected universe, and the Buddhist idea of a decentred self. Their art was goofy (it was called "vaudeville Zen") and perfectly in tune with the counterculture of the time. Finally, Sarah Haynes, in "Shaping Images of Tibet: Negotiating the Diaspora through Ritual, Art, and Film," describes how people in the Tibetan diaspora use art to construct their vision of their homeland. She analyses stage performances of Tibetan Buddhist dance, mandala construction, monks' debates, art exhibits, and film to identify the romanticized image of Tibet which they collectively help create.

The third and last section, "Buddhist Lives," includes biographies of four prominent Canadian Buddhist personalities who were charismatic in quite different ways. Mavis Fenn in "Dhammadina and Jayantā: Daughters of the Buddha in Canada" first gives us a valuable overview of the role of women in Buddhism and an introduction to the contemporary movement to restart the *bhikkhuni* (nun's) ordination lineage. She also tells us about Anna Burian, who took novice ordination in 1964 in Sri Lanka, and as Anagarika Dhammadinna returned to Canada in 1965 to begin teaching Buddhism. Dhammadinna, who was actively teaching before Buddhism started to become popular in the West, was not well known but she did start a lineage in Canada. Shirley Johannesen (Jayantā), the Canadian president of Sākyadhitā, the international organization of Buddhist women, carries on Dhammadinna's legacy.

Alexander Soucy's chapter, "Thầy Phổ Tịnh: A Vietnamese Nun's Struggles in Canada," paints a portrait of Thích Nữ Phổ Tịnh, for many years the dynamic leader of the Tam Bảo Temple in Montreal. Although well known for her enthusiasm, her education in a Canadian university, and her willingness to reach out beyond the Vietnamese community, her authority has been constantly challenged by the Vietnamese monastic institution and wider Vietnamese Buddhist lay community on the basis of her gender.

John Harding's chapter, "Leslie Kawamura: Nothing to Add, Nothing to Take Away," sketches Kawamura's contributions in two distinct forms of Buddhist dissemination. Buddhist studies within the Canadian academy have grown in the last forty years and Leslie Kawamura has carefully nurtured this field, both locally and globally, while also fostering new developments in Canada's oldest Buddhist school – Jōdo Shinshū.

Chapters from all three sections address gender and Buddhism. There are a number of important reasons for increased material about Buddhist women in Canada, not least to redress the lack of attention in *Wild Geese*. While many (though not all) leaders in reform movements and migrations of Buddhism to the West have been lay men (like D.T. Suzuki and Anagarika Dharmapala) and monks (like Thích Nhất Hạnh and Chögyam Thrungpa Rinpoche), women have quite often supported them. Dharmapala, for instance, would not have been successful without the financial support of Mrs Mary E. Foster of Honolulu, who provided funds for the efforts to reclaim Bodhgaya as a Buddhist pilgrimage site (Sangharakshita 2008). Women have been crucial to the globalization of Buddhism in these support roles and as notable leaders. Cheng Yen, the founder of the Tzu Chi Merit Society, and Chan Kong of the Order of Interbeing are two prominent international leaders. Women have also been influential in the development of Buddhism in Canada. Pema Chödrön is a prominent leader in Shambhala Buddhism and the abbess of Gampo Abbey in Cape Breton, Nova Scotia.

We decided not to have a separate section on women in Buddhism, but instead to integrate the material on women throughout the book. There are two chapters that highlight female Buddhist leaders. Mavis Fenn writes about Anagarika Dhammadinna, her successor, Jayantā, and female monastic ordination. Alexander Soucy discusses the role that Thích Nữ Phổ Tịnh has played in creating space for female leadership in Vietnamese Buddhism in Canada. James Placzek also discusses female ordination in the

Theravada tradition and the positions that male Buddhist leaders in Canada have taken. D. Mitra Barua discusses curriculum developed to teach Buddhism to children in Toronto, and while this fact is not elaborated, it is notable that a woman, Swarna Chandrasekera, developed the curriculum. As an "inventor" of Buddhism in Canada, the author of one chapter, Angela Sumegi, is an innovative Buddhist leader in Ottawa and she writes about her efforts to create Buddhist death rituals appropriate for Canadian mourners. These chapters illustrate some of the many ways that women are important participants in the localization of Buddhism to Canada.

Our first volume, *Wild Geese*, dealt inadequately with the Theravada tradition and with Vietnamese Buddhism, despite their importance in the Canadian Buddhist landscape. Regionally, British Columbia was underrepresented. The important current issue of women and Buddhism, as mentioned above, did not receive enough attention. These omissions provided the incentive and starting point for *Flowers on* tion for this volume, the three editors participated i two conferences to uncover ongoing research and t to do research in needed areas. As a result, *Flowers on the Rock* has four essays which focus on Theravada Buddhism, three chapters which focus on women and gender issues, and seven chapters dealing with Buddhism on the west coast of Canada. This volume contributes to our understanding of global and local Buddhisms in its own right and complements *Wild Geese*. These two volumes together provide a solid collection of papers for the study of Buddhism in Canada, but nonetheless do not represent an exhaustive treatment of this dynamic topic.

NOTES

1   His biography is appropriately called *Holding the Lotus to the Rock: The Autobiography of Sokei-an, America's First Zen Master* (Hotz 2003). Sasaki is making a literary allusion to the following verse:

石上栽花後　*Sekijō hana o uete nochi,*
生涯共是春　*Shōgai tomo ni kore haru.*

After you have planted the flower on the rock,
The days of your life will always be spring. (V. Hori 2003, verse 10.282)

Planting a flower on a rock requires long and patient effort. In the original verse, it symbolizes the great effort necessary to attain Zen awakening, but Sasaki uses it to mean the great effort to transplant Buddhism in the West.
2 We also have provided a chapter-length overview of Buddhism in Canada (Harding, Hori, and Soucy 2012).
3 http://chinabuddhismencyclopedia.com/.
4 Available at the temple's website, http://www.viengiac.de.

1

Buddhist Globalism and the Search for Canadian Buddhism

ALEXANDER SOUCY

During the 2012 federal New Democratic Party leadership race, one of the candidates, Nathan Cullen, stated: "I think as many New Democrats are making up their minds, they are making it up based on how we grow – or don't. And so, I feel somewhat Zen about this. I feel absolutely right with the campaign we have run" (*Globe and Mail* 2012). His appropriation of the Buddhist sect's name is not unique, or even unusual. It follows a widespread trend of evoking Buddhism, Buddhist symbols, and Buddhist ideas for purposes that range from calculated marketing, to frivolous posturing, to more sincere adoptions of Buddhist ideas and reverence of Buddhist figures. There are countless books entitled "Zen and the Art of ... " A new restaurant in Toronto, Buddha Dog, serves upscale "local food" hot dogs. Between 2000 and 2010 the Dalai Lama has been given honorary citizenships by Belgium, Hungary, Poland, France, Italy, and Canada (dalailama.com, n.d.). Many Canadians are citing non-violence and compassion as motivations for vegetarianism, and many non-Buddhists are meditating.

Some of these examples may seem trivial or unsavoury, but they signify the depth to which Buddhism has permeated Canadian popular culture. More importantly, they indicate how Buddhism has taken root in Canada, both among Buddhists, through the usual and expected avenues of transmission, and among non-Buddhists. As Melissa Curly and Angela Sumegi show in this volume, communication of Buddhism extends far past the usual forms of direct teaching through books, tracts, and dharma talks. The result is that Buddhism has become part of the multicultural fabric of Canadian society. It is no longer an exotic and fascinating foreign curiosity, but part of daily communication. If not completely naturalized, it is well on its way. How to understand this naturalization, however, remains unclear.

A debate has arisen over the degree to which a new form of Buddhism may be forming in Canada that could be called "Canadian Buddhism," corresponding to similar claims for an "American Buddhism." This new form would denote not just location but a distinct form expressing national cultural particularities. In *Wild Geese: Buddhism in Canada*, the first volume edited by Harding, Hori, and Soucy, we made the case that the developments we are seeing in Canada are part of a global process and not specifically Canadian. Furthermore, I argued that searching for a Canadian Buddhism would not ultimately move our understanding forward. I therefore concluded at the end of my chapter that "in the study of Buddhism in Canada, a greater contribution could be made by problematizing categories and definitions while shifting focus toward processes of global interactions" (Soucy 2010, 58). I intend to follow through with my suggestion here.

Following publication of *Wild Geese*, Jeff Wilson argued that the transnational nature of Buddhism in the modern world does not preclude the possibility of Buddhism in Canada developing into something uniquely Canadian. That is, it is possible for a "Canadian Buddhism" to emerge that has distinctive Canadian features while sharing commonalities with a more globalized Buddhism and participating in transnational processes and discourses. He writes, "Canadian Buddhism – meaning Buddhism that takes place in Canada, as well as Buddhism practised by Canadian citizens living outside of Canada – is perhaps more like a local idiom or accent than a whole different language" (Wilson 2011, 538). The ambiguity of this definition seems to suggest that "Canadian Buddhism" refers merely to Buddhism that happens to be in Canada or is practised by Canadians. But the title of his essay, "What is Canadian about Canadian Buddhism?" and the subsequent discussion, which links Canadian Buddhism to national identity, suggest that he is drawing parallels with the more extensive discussion of Buddhism in the United States, where an explicit distinction has been drawn between "Buddhism in America" and "American Buddhism." The latter refers to a new and unique form. Regardless of the definition, Wilson's aim is made explicit in the suggestion that there are five areas where we could search out a Canadian Buddhism: history, laws and policies, society and culture, the landscape, and international connections.

This essay continues the conversation with Wilson and others regarding the best way to approach the study of Buddhism in Canada, and in the West more generally.[1] Neither Wilson nor any other scholar has made a direct claim for a Canadian Buddhism, although he makes a call for scholars to search for it, paralleling the sustained claim for an American Buddhism. Therefore, my argument here is equally applicable to claims for an American Buddhism, an Australian Buddhism, or a Western Buddhism, built as they are on the same assumptions with only the national or cultural identity of the claims changing.

My argument builds on the one I developed in *Wild Geese* (see Soucy 2010). There I tried to show that the characteristics that have been put forward as making up "American" and, by extension, "Canadian" Buddhism,[2] have been falsely attributed to the West. These transformations originated in nineteenth-century Asian Buddhist reform movements that had come about in response to colonial hegemony and pressures from Christian missionaries. Henry Steel Olcott (1832–1907) and Anagarika Dharmapala (1864–1933) together spurred on a Buddhist revival in Ceylon (now Sri Lanka) that has been called Protestant Buddhism (Blackburn 2010; Gombrich and Obeyesekere 1988; Obeyesekere 1972; Prothero 1996). The Buddhist monk Shaku Sōen (1860–1919) spent three years in Ceylon and returned to Japan to reform Buddhism there in the face of Meiji persecutions of Buddhism as being backward and superstitious. He helped to foster a movement called "New Buddhism" (*Shin Bukkyō*) (Harding 2008; Snodgrass 2003; 2009b). In China, Taixu (1890–1947) influenced the development of a new Buddhism focused on this world, called Humanistic Buddhism (*Renjian Fojiao*), and he had an impact in Vietnam's reform movement starting in the 1920s (DeVido 2007; 2009). In Thailand and Cambodia a modernist movement called *Dhammayuttika Nikaya* (or *Thammayut Nikaya*), which began in the early twentieth century, became the Thai Forest Tradition (J. Taylor 1993; Tiyavanich 1997).

A Buddhism that had already been drastically altered to reflect Western constructions and sensibilities was then introduced to the West and embraced by counterculture Beatniks and Hippies, who mistook it for something foreign and exotic. In fact, they were attracted to their own cultural and philosophical tradition repackaged as Asian. As Sharf puts it, "Like Narcissus, Western enthusiasts failed to recognize their own reflection in the mirror being held out to them" (Sharf 1993, 39). The lack of a fixed tradition has meant that Westerners dissatisfied with their own religion have projected their ideal onto Buddhism. By the time the Beatniks became interested in Buddhism, almost a century of reform that involved intense transnational and transcultural communication had already taken place in Asia.

By unpacking the assumptions behind claims for a Buddhism that is uniquely "Canadian," "American," or "Western," and arguing for a refocusing of attention, I attempt once again to derail the notion of a Canadian Buddhism. I then present my current thinking on how to look at Buddhist trends in Canada, focusing not on categories and types of Buddhists, but on the process of transformation and the forces that interact in different ways with different groups and individuals. Vietnamese Buddhism provides a useful case study because its various guises, both in Vietnam and internationally, pose problems that demonstrate the weakness of Asian/Western or traditional/modern models. The problems are overcome by looking at larger global currents.

THE SEARCH FOR A CANADIAN BUDDHISM

I should be clear from the outset that I am not denying that there have been adaptations of Buddhism to the Canadian or Western context. Instead, I am questioning the usefulness and validity of the category of "Canadian Buddhism," and by extension "American" and "Western" Buddhism. Furthermore, I am arguing against the academic enterprise, as distinct from claims by practitioners, for such a thing. Whereas the former are supposed to be objective analyses (or at least reflexive about subjectivity), the latter should be understood as part of the communication of Buddhism in the West, and therefore treated as part of the religious phenomenon to be studied; that is, claims by practitioners should be taken by scholars as primary data, even though these claims are sometimes made under the guise of scholarship. The impulse to define a Buddhism based on national identity may be understandable, particularly for practitioners; however, scholars need to be circumspect about where this discourse arises and avoid participation, if only because it is ultimately unfruitful.

My objections to a "Canadian Buddhism" as a unique form that has arisen out of Canada's cultural, political, and historical circumstances, and the subsequent academic enterprise of searching for it, centre on the problems of reductionism, subjectivity, and the overall usefulness of the endeavour. To begin, we run into trouble as soon as we try to determine what constitutes a distinctly Canadian Buddhism. There are two instances of subjective bias that are of concern. (1) How do we objectively establish the Canadian cultural traits that might underlie a Canadian Buddhism? (2) How do we determine what constitutes a transformation that would be sufficient to make a claim for a new form of Buddhism that could be called Canadian?

What Is "Canadian"?

Without establishing qualities that are particularly Canadian, it is not possible to characterize Canadian Buddhism. But claims about Canadian national/cultural identity are fundamentally bound to nationalistic aspirations that arise from a drive to gain political advantage through the objectification of the "other" by which the self is measured. Frequently cited markers of Canadian identity include politeness, compassion, deference to authority, a laid back nature, the health care system, multiculturalism, nature, the arctic, hockey, and even Tim Hortons. These characterizations need to be recognized as constructions of the media, commercial advertising, and state propaganda. These constructions, in turn, have been adopted uncritically by popular culture. They do not stand up to close scrutiny. While Canadians may think of themselves as compassionate, for example, it is difficult to find a way to measure this. In what way? Compared to whom? One can certainly find support for this claim, but there is also evidence to the contrary. For example: the internment of Japanese Canadians during the Second World War; the residential schools; and the federal government's decision in 2012 to claw back health care for refugees, with immigration minister Jason Kenney's office claiming that "Canadians have been clear that they do not want illegal immigrants and bogus refugee claimants receiving gold-plated health care benefits that are better than those Canadian taxpayers receive" (Wherry 2012). Even multiculturalism as something uniquely Canadian exists mostly at a rhetorical level.[3]

All these characterizations are, at their root, reductionist stereotypes. Canada's national culture is an invented tradition and Canada as a nation is itself, to use Benedict Anderson's term (1983), an imagined community. The attempt to determine a uniquely Canadian Buddhism, therefore, is forced to rely on essentialized and subjective characterizations of a distinct Canadian culture that could significantly influence Buddhism. Determining this culture will remain elusive because it does not exist as anything more than an idealization.

What Constitutes Sufficient and Unique Change?

There are a number of parts to the question of what constitutes sufficient change. The first is that of comparison. In order to be able to call Buddhism Canadian, we have to determine that certain aspects are unique to Canada. In doing so, two comparisons need to be made. First, it must be established that Buddhism in Canada is sufficiently different from Buddhism in the countries of its origin (i.e., in Asia), and, second, that there are significant transformations to Buddhism in Canada that are unique (i.e., not the same as the transformations that have taken place elsewhere.) Moreover, Fields (1998), Hickey (2010), V. Hori (2010a, 37), Lin (1999, 134–6), and Tanaka (1998, 287–9) have documented the racist assumptions that have emerged due to the subjective way that determinations of a new, "American" Buddhism have been made.

Less recognized have been the nationalist or ethnocentric discourses behind the claims for American, Western, or Canadian Buddhism. For example, James Coleman's *The New Buddhism: The Western Transformation of an Ancient Tradition* (2001) exhibits a strong sense of triumphalism in its claim that Western Buddhism is closer to the original, and more authentic than Asian Buddhisms that have distorted the original meaning of the Buddha (Coleman 2001, 218). Coleman is not alone in this view, as Judith Snodgrass notes (Snodgrass 2009a, 21). Many scholars and practitioners have claimed that forms of Buddhism have emerged in the twentieth century that share sufficient commonalities to allow them to be categorized as a new form, termed Global Buddhism, New Buddhism, Western Buddhism, or more parochially, American Buddhism. These transformations have been mistakenly attributed to the West. In fact, for more than a century there have been reform movements in Asia that have more in common with this new Buddhism than they do with the "traditional," local Buddhist practices that continue to exist alongside them. These Asian-based organizations are international in scope in a way that still defies most Western-based organizations. Furthermore, most of the changes heralded as being

Western were brought from Asia and introduced to the West by Asian Buddhist missionaries like D.T. Suzuki, Thích Nhất Hạnh, and Chögyam Trungpa Rinpoche.

At the first Buddhism in America Conference in Boston in 1997, which brought together Buddhist teachers and practitioners, several participants identified the characteristics that they thought defined the new Buddhism being created in America (Rapaport and Hotchkiss 1998). Characteristics listed by subsequent authors include: an emphasis on lay over monastic Buddhism, a focus on the achievement of enlightenment through meditation, individualism, democratization, lack of hierarchy, gender equality, greater social activism, and a tendency toward eclecticism. Some of these characteristics, such as being non-hierarchical, appear to define essentialized characteristics of Western culture rather than of Buddhism in the West. Furthermore, the list of characteristics of this new, modern, Buddhism has changed over time. At the end of the nineteenth century, the claim that Buddhism was compatible with science drew on the theory of evolution, whereas today the same claim stresses similarities to quantum physics and neuroscience.[4] In other words, the process of determining the characteristics of an American, Canadian, or Western Buddhism is largely arbitrary.

Bias persists in supposedly critical scholarship because many of the scholars studying Buddhism in the West look at it in isolation from the wider context of Buddhist transformations in Asia and globally since the mid-nineteenth century. The consequent errors have been perpetuated in studies of Buddhism in the West: Ethnic communities have been ignored as innovators and instead viewed as conservative repositories of an ancient tradition, and their traditions have been criticized as more-or-less corrupted by cultural accretions and superstitions.

A further question is the extent of change required to establish that Buddhism in the West is fundamentally different. For example, early in my career I observed that external imperatives had brought about changes in the way a Vietnamese Buddhist temple operated in Montreal (Soucy 1994, 1996). These changes included alterations in gender dynamics when circumstances dictated that monks and nuns live together in one temple. Another change was the establishment of a board of directors in order to qualify for charitable status under Canadian law, which increased lay involvement in the running of the temple. Is either change sufficiently profound to justify claiming a new form of Buddhism? D. Mitra Barua in this volume shows how the language of multiculturalism is incorporated into pedagogical material developed by Sri Lankan Buddhists in Toronto. Is the adoption of the language and ethos of multiculturalism sufficiently profound (or unique) to make a claim for a new kind of Buddhism? My position is that these are not sufficient, but instead amount to superficial changes that do not alter Buddhist ideas or practices in any core way. However, my opinion is subjective, as would be the opinions of those who claim that these changes are sufficiently profound. Therein lies the difficulty. Ultimately, claims of change sufficient to warrant the label "Canadian" or "American" are subjective estimations that have too frequently been based on nationalist sentiment rather than objective observation.

In his call for a Canadian Buddhism, Wilson asks whether there has emerged a local version of Buddhism that could be called Canadian and that operates independently from large, global organizations. I think the answer would have to be negative. I have seen no convincing evidence that the Buddhism that we see in Canada is significantly different from Buddhism being practised in other places. There may be differences between the practices of some predominantly white groups (to use Fields' term)[5] and the practices of some ethnically homogeneous (Asian) groups in the West, but there are Asians in the West, and Buddhist groups in Asia that have emerged from Buddhist reform movements, who also share many of the practices and characteristics of so-called "Western," "New," or "Modern" Buddhism. For example, Thích Nhất Hạnh has both Western and overseas Vietnamese followers in his international organization. However, the internal differences in the way that his Vietnamese followers and Western followers in Montreal relate to and practise Buddhism is far greater than the differences between the way that his followers (Vietnamese or Western) practise in Canada versus in France.

Aside from the inherent dangers of nationalism and related cultural triumphalism, such discussions seem rooted in a nineteenth-century fixation with taxonomies. Buddhism is taken as a thing that has an essential nature that can be labelled according to genus and species. There is a presupposition of a core Buddhism that can exist without cultural influence. Change is seen as a turbulent period between stases, local variations as divergences from an original core. This model views change as a complication for our understanding of religion; but this is a misapprehension. It is precisely the process rather than the object that should be the focus of our attention. Therefore, in *Wild Geese* Harding, Hori, and I argued that this classificatory focus, which tried to isolate the distinguishing points of Canadian (or American) Buddhism, has been, thus far, a failure. Changes have been continuous throughout the history of Buddhism. Thomas Tweed made this very argument a decade ago, stating, "There is hybridity all the way down" (2002, 19), but it has not yet been sufficiently heeded.

Buddhism in any one country, be it Canada, Australia, America, or Great Britain, cannot be understood in isolation. I use the example of Vietnamese Buddhism as a case study (in two parts) to demonstrate the limitations of the categories and labels that have predominated in the study of Buddhism in the West.

CASE STUDY, PART ONE: VIETNAMESE BUDDHISM

Vietnamese Buddhism in the West has been largely viewed as "ethnic." As such, it has been taken as conservative, devotional (even superstitious), and "traditional." Furthermore, as a distinguishing point in opposition to so-called Western or American Buddhism, it has been seen as focused on the community rather than the individual. Researchers of Vietnamese Buddhism in the West – of which there are few – have generally not ventured beyond superficial descriptions. The underlying theme seems to be that Buddhism is a stable cultural reference that provides support for Vietnamese as they adapt to the West.[6] While this is certainly part of its function, and many practitioners view it this way, this vision of Vietnamese Buddhist temples that serve ethnically homogeneous communities as representative of Vietnamese Buddhism in the West is not entirely accurate.

First, there are problems with the construction of ethnic. Victor Hori raises an important point: "ethnicity is 'constructed,' that is, it is based less on objective connections of blood ties and more on a subjective sense of belonging to an imagined community" (2010b, 19). However, even putting this aside, the earliest appearances of Vietnamese Buddhism in the West do not fit the theoretical model of "ethnic" Buddhism. The first Vietnamese monk to settle permanently in the United States was Thích Thiên Ân. He went to Los Angeles in 1966 to teach at UCLA as part of a scholar exchange program and was asked by students to act as their guru as well as their professor. He started the International Buddhist Meditation Center, which was entirely made up of Western (i.e., non-Asian) Buddhists. He eventually ordained Western monks in the Lâm Tế (Japanese Rinzai) Vietnamese Zen lineage (although it is likely that what he actually taught was based more on his experience at a Rinzai Zen temple in Japan, where he studied in the early 1960s, than on his training in Vietnam.) In 1975 he published what was for many years the only English-language account of Vietnamese Buddhism,[7] but it deals with Vietnamese Buddhist history by describing early Zen lineages in Vietnam. In it he writes: "Zen comes closest to expressing the Vietnamese character, and as such, their attitude in all walks of life can best be described as a 'Zen outlook'" (Thich Thien An 1975, 27). As Nguyen and Barber note, his early death in 1980, coupled with not having a specific teaching, means that he did not have a lasting impact (1998, 131). Nonetheless, his meditation centre remains open and active, run by one of his first American (white) disciples, and is notable for housing monks from different traditions, including Theravada.

Thích Thiên Ân does not escape the ethnic label so easily, however, since he also opened the first ethnic Vietnamese temple in the United States. Called simply the Vietnam Buddhist Temple (Chùa Việt Nam), it was founded to support the refugees arriving in the late 1970s (see Farber and Fields 1987). The last five years of his life were dedicated to assisting with the refugee crisis. One of the people he sponsored was his lifelong friend Thích Mãn Giác, who became the head of the temple and of the first organization to unite Vietnamese Buddhists in the United States.

Another important figure that problematizes the categorization of Vietnamese Buddhism as "ethnic" is Thích Nhất Hạnh, now a world-famous Buddhist leader and author. He was also born in central Vietnam and went to school with Thích Thiên Ân. In 1966, while he was on a speaking tour in the United States, it became clear that he could not return home. Because of his neutralist peace activism, the government of South Vietnam accused him of being a Communist and the government of the Communist North Vietnam accused him of being pro-American (Chapman 2007, 304; Topmiller 2002, 123). He was to remain in exile until he returned to Vietnam for the first time in 2005, and again in 2007.

Until he settled permanently in France, his activities and notoriety centred on his activism rather than on Zen meditation or mindfulness, for which he would later become famous. In 1966 he wrote *Vietnam: Lotus in a Sea of Fire* (1967) to provide background on Vietnamese Buddhism and the Buddhist struggle for Western peace activists, to recruit the support of American war protesters for an American withdrawal from Vietnam, and to lay out a peaceful solution for ending the war. Thích Nhất Hạnh wrote in the introduction that "In the history of Vietnamese Buddhism, [Zen] is by far the most important sect" (1967, 4). As with Thích Thiên Ân's statement about the Zen outlook of Vietnamese Buddhism, it is at odds with the way that Vietnamese Buddhism is practised both in Vietnam and the West. Starting in 1973 he published a three-volume account of Vietnamese Buddhist history, *Việt Nam Phật Giáo Sử Luận* (History of Buddhism in Vietnam), under the pen name Nguyễn Lang (2000), which also misleadingly described Vietnamese Buddhism as Zen (C.T. Nguyen 1995, 82–3n5).

It is difficult to reconcile the characterization of Vietnamese Buddhism as "ethnic," "conservative," and "traditional" with the practices and teachings of Thích Thiên Ân and Thích Nhất Hạnh. Both insisted that Vietnamese Buddhism was Zen and largely dismissed or ignored Pure Land, devotional Buddhism. Their writings described Vietnamese Buddhism in a way that contradicted the devotional practices (chanting sutras, making wishes, and performing memorial rituals for the deceased) that I was seeing in Montreal in the early 1990s (Soucy 1994). What I saw in subsequent research in Hanoi, Vietnam from the mid-1990s to early 2000s was even more at odds with the written descriptions of Vietnamese Buddhism as Zen. Neither lay nor monastic Buddhists in Hanoi ever meditated. They directed their religious practice to a great extent toward the achievement of material gain in this life and improving one's fate after death (Soucy 2012). Another notable aspect was the way that Buddhism was fused with other elements that some would call non-Buddhist. For example, spirit possession rituals and mother goddess worship were a major part of the ritual life of Buddhist temples in northern Vietnam. Most of my Vietnamese informants explained that, if separate from Buddhism at all, these practices were complementary and necessary to their religious lives.

The Buddhism that Thích Thiên Ân and Thích Nhất Hạnh taught in the West was radically different from the traditional ritualistic-devotional Buddhism of Vietnam, but while they cannot be dismissed as "ethnic" Vietnamese Buddhists they also cannot be categorized as practising "Western Buddhism." The division between American, or Western, Buddhism on one side and Asian ethnic Buddhism on the other is inadequate. Thích Thiên Ân founded not only a Western group but also the first ethnic

Vietnamese temple in the United States, and he consistently presented himself as a Vietnamese Buddhist. His American followers were the first to go to refugee arrival camps in California to volunteer as chaplains and facilitators. Likewise, although Thích Nhất Hạnh's teachings are radically modern and stand at the forefront of what has been called "Western Buddhism," he has maintained his Vietnamese identity, writing books that draw on Vietnamese history and tradition. His followers have always included both Western converts and Vietnamese lifelong Buddhists, many of whom simultaneously chant sutras at "ethnic" Vietnamese temples.

The teaching of Thích Thanh Từ and his organization, Trúc Lâm, is yet another example of a modernized Global Buddhism. The roots of this new Zen can be found in the early Vietnamese Buddhist reform movement (Chấn hưng Phật giáo) that began in the mid-1920s. It is lay-oriented, stresses the need for comprehension of Buddhist teachings, and formalizes Buddhism as a religion through emphasis on initiation rites and other markers that delineate the Buddhist from the non-Buddhist. This is in stark contrast to the way that Buddhism is practised in most places and by most people in Vietnam, where formal statements of faith and boundaries of inclusion/exclusion are not common.[8] Trúc Lâm also stresses a teaching lineage that starts with the historical Buddha and links to the present through Kaśyapa, Bodhidharma, and the founding ancestors of the Trúc Lâm School. Thích Thanh Từ is based in Vietnam, but has been successful in expanding internationally. Today he has one monastery in Canada, one in France, five in Australia, ten in the United States, and seventeen in Vietnam (thuong-chieu.org, n.d.).

Thích Thanh Từ named his Zen movement "Trúc Lâm," after the only school of Zen supposedly indigenous to Vietnam, and he draws heavily from this nationalist symbolism for appeal. The movement, therefore, does not call itself new, but reaches back in Vietnamese history to create what Hobsbawm and Ranger have called an "invented tradition" – a tradition which appears, or is claimed to be, old but is in fact recent in origin and usually closely associated with nationalism or nationalistic movements (1983).[9]

Since the turn of the millennium, Zen has gained in popularity in Vietnam and among overseas Vietnamese. Furthermore, its popularity and construction have been heavily imprinted with notions that correspond to so-called Western Buddhist practices and sensibilities. Nonetheless, a scenario in which Western forms of Buddhism have made their way back to Vietnam via transnational overseas Vietnamese connections in what might be called a "pizza effect" is not convincing. The time-line is not synchronous and does not explain why both Thích Thiên Ân and Thích Nhất Hạnh so readily fashioned themselves as Vietnamese Zen masters in the West. Rather, Thích Thanh Từ's Trúc Lâm Zen movement should be seen as influenced by the Buddhist reform movements that cross-fertilized each other in Asia. The teachings of Taixu, D.T. Suzuki, and others were translated and circulated in Vietnam among reformist circles. Figures like Thích Nhất Hạnh were reading and absorbing the arguments, put forward by Japanese reformers, that Zen was uniquely suited to modernity.

Therefore, identifying a Canadian, American, or Western Buddhism does not help us understand the complexities that exist on the ground. Vietnamese Buddhism has come to Canada and has primarily been viewed as "ethnic," while at the same time groups like those founded by Thích Nhất Hạnh are popular across Canada and have been viewed as "Western" or "modern." Defenders of a Canadian Buddhism would have to undergo alarming contortions to claim that local Vietnamese temples across Canada are uniquely Canadian. Similarly, reducing Vietnamese neo-Zen movements to being Canadian, or indeed Western, is equally problematic, despite their participation in discourses that make them resemble other Western groups. The Canadian or Western typologies prove limiting for understanding the transformations, differences, and continuities of a transnational Vietnamese Buddhism. It is more useful to see global interactions as not being linear (i.e., Buddhism starts in Asia, comes West, and then influences Buddhism in Asia), but ongoing, so that transformations are seen as starting before the West became attracted to Buddhism and being continuous, multi-nodal, and interactive. In other words, in order to understand Buddhism in Canada and the West, we need a model for understanding Buddhism at a global level. That is, we need to think about the idea of a Buddhist globalism that interacts with and influences local Buddhisms.

BUDDHIST GLOBALISM, PAROCHIALISM, AND LOCALISM

I have chosen the term "Buddhist globalism" and bypassed terms like American Buddhism, Western Buddhism, Coleman's "new Buddhism"

(2001), Lopez's "modern Buddhism" (2002), and even Bechert and McMahan's "Buddhist modernism" (Bechert 1966, 1984; McMahan 2008), although all share some similarities. Indeed, I would go so far as to say that we are trying to describe the same phenomenon. However, by choosing the term "Buddhist globalism" I am trying to make explicit the fact that it emerges out of, and continues to be propelled by, global processes. That is, the phenomenon has been seen as the result of Buddhism's encounter with, and adaptation to, a Western modernity, but it is more fruitful to think of the phenomenon, following Tweed (2002), as a process of hybridity, deeply rooted in globalization. This ongoing process of hybridization is therefore neither Western nor Eastern, but dialectically something entirely new and truly global.

At the end of my chapter in *Wild Geese*, I called for a refocusing on processes rather than on types of Buddhism with specific characteristics. Therefore, "Buddhist globalism," unlike the terms "American Buddhism," "Western Buddhism," "modern Buddhism," or "global Buddhism," does not refer to a type of Buddhism with a set of characteristics, but to the processes, discourses, or forces that are exerted on Buddhists globally and that have an impact on the popular image of Buddhism internationally. Buddhist globalism has had an impact on virtually all Buddhists, both in Asia and in the West; even those who are seen as "traditional." I will discuss this force at greater length below, but for now it can be described as being roughly equivalent to what McMahan describes as "emerg[ing] out of an engagement with the dominant cultural and intellectual forces of modernity" (2008, 6). These discourses were manifested in Buddhist reform movements that started in the late nineteenth and early twentieth centuries and continue today.

While most Buddhist teachers and organizations in the West are influenced by Buddhist globalism, movements and organizations that originate in Asia have become internationalized and are also thoroughly infused with the same discourses. These organizations, like Fo Guang Shan and the Tzu Chi Merit Society (both discussed in *Wild Geese*), or the Vipassana movement (discussed in this volume by Goldberg), or Westerners' approach to the Thai Forest tradition (Schedneck 2011) have more in common with the characteristics commonly attributed to "Western Buddhism" than they have with the locally practised forms of "traditional" Buddhism in their homelands. Thus, Buddhist globalism is a relatively recent phenomenon,

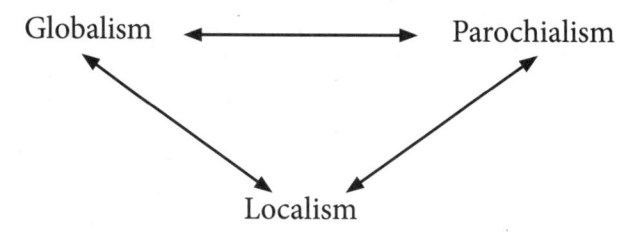

```
Globalism  ⟷  Parochialism
        ↘   ↙
       Localism
```
Relationship between Buddhist globalism, parochialism, and localism

having its inception in the Asian colonial encounter and influenced by ongoing development and globalization.

Buddhist globalism does not function in isolation, but in relationship with at least two other forces or processes. In opposition to the pressure exerted by Buddhist globalism is a phenomenon that I will call Buddhist parochialism. Parochialism here should not be understood in its pejorative sense as "backward" but as an inward looking or conservative predilection, neither better nor worse than the outward looking orientation of Buddhist globalism. This force is roughly equivalent to what has been called "traditional Buddhism" or "Buddhist traditionalism." It can be thought of as a form of perceived stasis in which people continue to appear to practise the same way they always have (although in fact there have been constant, unacknowledged changes). It is an inward orientation, centred on the community rather than on the outside. Thus, the small temple that I studied in Hanoi (Soucy 2012) was principally oriented in this parochial manner, not seeking to reform and often oblivious to the reformist discourses that surround it in Buddhist publications, Vietnamese academic descriptions of Buddhist purity, and state diatribes against "superstitious" practices.

On occasion, "Buddhist parochialism" can be practised more forthrightly and intentionally as a resistance to forces for change, such as those exerted by Buddhist globalism, but examples of this are rare. More often it has been a driving force in efforts to recreate, as when immigrant Buddhist communities in the West attempt to approximate the forms and practices that they remember from their homelands. Thus, Vietnamese Buddhism in Canada is shaped to a large extent by Buddhist parochialism. The main focus is inward and there is little attempt to engage with and learn from broader Buddhist communities that surround them. The term "traditional" is not helpful here, since the process of recreation of Vietnamese Buddhism in Canada does not replicate Buddhism in Vietnam, but instead creates a hybrid.

The final process or force is "Buddhist localism." This force is the situating of any form of Buddhism within its context. Where Buddhism is practised in largely traditional ways (in the sense of not intentionally reforming) in its traditional setting (say, Vietnamese practising Buddhism in a non-reflexive way in Hanoi), the parochial force and the localizing force work in tandem. However, where reformist Buddhism in Asia largely reflects the views and orientations of Buddhist globalism, it is at the same time under pressure to reflect local understandings and practices. Thus, Fo Guang Shan Buddhism at its home base in Kaohsiung, Taiwan, is a thoroughly internationalized and reformist organization in conversation with the discourses of Buddhist globalism. Nonetheless, it is also thoroughly Chinese – in the externalities of its material culture, art, and architecture; in its practices (mainly Pure Land Buddhist); and in the discourses in which they are engaged (Humanistic Buddhism, coming from the ideas of the Chinese reformer Taixu).

When Fo Guang Shan's international organization, the Buddha Light International Association, set up a temple in Toronto, we see how localism takes on a different connotation. The temple maintains its distinctive form, informed by Chinese Buddhist idioms as well as Chinese forms of the discourses of Buddhist globalism. Nonetheless, as Stuart Chandler (2004) shows, the organization intentionally localizes, and this force would be exerted regardless of intention. On the other hand, when Vietnamese Buddhists or Chinese Buddhists set up a local, parochial, temple in Montreal, with the intention of replicating a site where they can practise as they remember practising, there are still localizing pressures that bring about changes – some on the surface and others more fundamental. So, for example, on the surface, tax laws require that charitable organizations have boards of directors in order to be granted tax-exempt status, so management does not work in the same way in Canada. Partly as a consequence of this, but also because of a number of other dynamics, we also see more profound changes, such as lay-monastic tensions emerging over control of temples.

Let me turn now to a fuller description of Buddhist globalism. The ideological underpinnings of Buddhist globalism are extensive and should be understood as forming a constellation of similarities, or family resemblances, rather than a checklist of characteristics that must be ticked off to determine the dominant impulse of any one group, organization, or movement. There are, overall, four main thrusts to Buddhist globalism, which overlap somewhat, but are together responsible for the generation of many of the characteristics that have been attributed to Buddhist Modernism, Buddhist reform movements, and Buddhist transformations in the West. (1) Buddhist globalism is outward looking, concerned with international linkages, global communication, and dialogues with other Buddhist groups and other religions. (2) It is actively involved in constructing Buddhism as a World Religion. (3) It constructs Buddhism as a religion of modernity. (4) It stresses the individual and individual practice over the community. I stress that this is not a checklist to determine types of discourses, but a description of some of the important aspects of the globalist discourse.

Buddhism as an Outward Looking Religion

Buddhist globalism, from its inception, has been outward looking rather than principally concerned with the immediate requirements of the local community. It is therefore resolutely international in scope and communication. The reform movements in Asia were intentionally engaged in international conversations and imagined a larger Buddhist community. In Vietnam, the earliest journals that emerged in the 1920s from the reform movements reported on Buddhist events at a national and international level. Furthermore, DeVido has shown the extensive influence of Chinese reformer Taixu, which was fostered by ethnic Chinese transnational connections (2007; 2009). As a result of this outlook, organizations that sought to unite regionally, nationally, and internationally started to spring up. By contrast, in Vietnam there remain many parochial Buddhists, and Buddhist spaces, whose orientation focuses on community and family. The difference between Buddhist parochialism and Buddhist globalism can be best described as between an inward and an outward vision. Thus, awareness of inclusion in a greater international Buddhist movement is central, and conversely there is an abiding concern with delineating Buddhism from other religions and religious activities.

An outward vision prompted reform Buddhists like Anagarika Dharmapala, Shaku Sōen, and D.T. Suzuki, as well as later figures like Thích Nhất Hạnh, Thích Thiên Ân, and Chögyam Trungpa Rinpoche, to bring

Buddhism to the West. More recently, there have been large, internationalized organizations that have arisen in Asia and have maintained their bases in their home countries. These global organizations, like Fo Guang Shan, may still have constituents that are ethnically homogeneous for the most part, but their focus is global in scope and their intention is to extend beyond ethnic boundaries, though in practice this intention may not yet have been realized for various reasons.[10]

Another product of an outward orientation is the importance placed on communication. This has led a number of Buddhist organizations in Asia to set up television and radio stations, and others, most notably Soka Gakkai, to initiate missionary activities. Leaders such as Thích Nhất Hạnh, who engages in interfaith and ecumenical dialogue, and the Dalai Lama, in his discussions with scientists, demonstrate the centrality of communication to the outward orientation.

Buddhism as a World Religion

In *Religions in Global Society* (2006), Peter Beyer makes a compelling argument for the globalization of the concept of religion. He argues that in the modern period a dominant concept of religion has been formed and subsequently globalized, and that people have had to in some way frame their own beliefs and institutions in relation to it. Further, the very concept has been largely shaped by a Christian framework. Although religion is "no longer simply a Western, let alone Christian, notion" (Beyer 2006, 115), the forms that have come to be seen as constitutive of religions have been drawn from and continue to be shaped by Western, particularly Christian, expectations, which have become globalized. While some traditions (Confucianism, for instance) have rejected the label, Buddhists have largely bought into it and have, since the nineteenth century, sought to establish Buddhism as one of the "world religions."[11] In doing so, leaders of Buddhist reform movements often defined their religion in relation to Christianity, sometimes mimicking aspects of it. In Sri Lanka, for example, Buddhist schools that replicated Christian missionary schools were established, and Olcott wrote a Buddhist catechism.

This later delineation of core ideas of Buddhism reflects a Christian-derived concern for orthodoxy that was quite alien to Buddhism before the colonial encounter. However, with the creation of Buddhism as a religion it became important to draw boundaries about what could legitimately be called "Buddhism" and what could not. Thus, from the Asian reform movement to groups in the West today that are primarily influenced by the discourses of Buddhist globalism, there is a notable condemnation of practices and ideas that do not conform to what is deemed "authentic." What emerges is a distinction between true Buddhism and superstition or between what is truly Buddhist and what is merely cultural accretion.

In Buddhist globalism there is an imperative to practise an original and pristine Buddhism stripped of superstition and the heavy patina of culture (Lopez 2002, ix).[12] Correspondingly, activities like dharma talks and reading become more important. By contrast, at local temples in Hanoi where I do research, people commonly practise without consideration of, or interest in, the meaning of a ritual. Their concern is that the ritual be performed correctly. The effect, or fruits, of the ritual are not seen as contingent on faith. Sponsoring a ritual to get the buddhas' blessings, for example, will bring about good results, regardless of whether you fully believe or whether you even attend or participate (Soucy 2012).

Another notable result of this process of seeing Buddhism as a world religion has been the reimagination of the Buddha himself. Snodgrass has shown that emphasis on the historical Buddha as a founder and central figure in Buddhism is an invention of Western, orientalist scholars who sought to establish Buddhism as a religion comparable to Christianity (2009a). Before the mid-1800s, the Buddha was seen as only one of a succession of buddhas, and, while important, he did not take the position of founder and symbolic centre of Buddhism in a way that mirrors Christ's position in Christianity. One of the first tasks for Western missionaries and scholars was to establish a historically based biography so that Buddhism could be compared on an even footing with Christianity. Such a biography did not exist as a single text that "could be recognized as a biography: the life of the man from his birth to his death" (Snodgrass 2009a, 23).[13] Robert Spence Hardy, Wesleyan missionary to Ceylon, subsequently filled this gap in his books *Eastern Monachism* (1850) and *Manual of Budhism* [sic] (1853), which served as a basis for subsequent work by scholars like Rhys Davids (Snodgrass 2009a, 22–3). While the creation of a founder and symbolic centre for Buddhism served the needs of Western scholars, Christian missionaries, and colonial administrators, it ultimately also became a weapon of resistance, providing a legitimating narrative that aided Buddhist reformers in resisting colonial hegemonic pressures. As Snodgrass writes:

> Though they were not unaware of the deficiencies of the representation of their religion by Western scholars, modernizing Asians, particularly among the Western-educated elites who were leaders of the late nineteenth and early twentieth-century nationalist movements, found the work of the Pali Text Society, for example, extremely useful in their nationalist and anticolonialist campaigns. Its emphasis on the human historicity of the Buddha, Sakyamuni, might have been a distortion of tradition, but it fitted well with local movements toward the rationalization of the indigenous religion that had already begun with the momentum of creating modern Asian states. (Snodgrass 2009a, 40)

Buddhism as a Religion of Modernity

The globalist discourse is rooted in modernity, a movement that started in the West with the Enlightenment and the Reformation and has since spread around the globe, propelled by globalization. Thus, in the words of Charles Taylor, "Modernity is not that form of life toward which all cultures converge as they discard beliefs that held our forefathers back. Rather, it is a movement from one constellation of background understandings to another" (C. Taylor 1995, 24). Modernity is not a neutral movement away from tradition, but the imposition or adoption of a new set of ideas and understandings. Conversely, "tradition" is not a generalized pre-modern state, but a concept that emerges out of, and in relation to, the "modern." Tradition, as well as modernity, can both be said to be a new, and hegemonic, set of dispositions. Modernization and Westernization are not the same, although the ideas of modernity are in the first instance rooted in Western cultural understandings and developments. There are multiple modernities in the sense that globally different societies are doing different things with modernist ideas in a process called "glocalization," which refers to the re-localization of the global (R. Robertson 2005). Particularly when discussing religion in Asia, we can see that, for Buddhism, being modern usually means assuming Western/Christian modes of being a religion: setting up rationalized institutions, establishing Christian-like forms (e.g., being centred on a founder, stressing orthodoxy). However, what we see is not just wholesale adoption and conformity to Western modernist prescriptions, but creations of hybrids that are as much Asian as Western, and are often seen as culturally superior. The outcomes of this process are frequently labelled modern, as though modernity is culturally neutral, but this ignores the Western roots of the modernist understandings.

When I suggest that modernity is an important aspect of Buddhist globalism, I am saying that the discourses of modernity figure largely in Buddhist groups, and in the teachings of leaders, who are most influenced by Buddhist globalism. So, a notable difference between a parochial Vietnamese temple in Canada and, for example, the Order of Interbeing, is that the latter is part of an organization that is headquartered in France and has a recognizable leader (Thích Nhất Hạnh), whereas parochially oriented temples may nominally be part of a larger organization but were set up and operate independently. Modernist discourses lead to doctrinal orientations as well, most notably to the assertion that Buddhism and science are compatible and that Buddhism is fundamentally a system of psychology.[14] Thus, the Dalai Lama engages in discussions with scientists and has made the assertion that any truth revealed by scientific enquiry that conflicts with Buddhist doctrine should lead to Buddhism abandoning its position rather than holding to dogma (2005, 3).

Buddhism as an Individual Religion

Finally, Buddhist globalism stresses individualism, as one of "modernity's inescapable axioms" (McMahan 2008, 13), expressed primarily in the orientation toward personal spiritual growth (i.e., a pursuit of enlightenment) as the main goal of practice (Liogier 2010).[15] This may seem counterintuitive, and even contradictory, to Buddhism's central doctrine of *anātman* (no-self). Nonetheless, it is manifest as an orientation toward self-perfection, personal "practice" rather than group ritual, the goal of as-soon-as-possible enlightenment, and the idea that no one can assist you in attaining it. So, for example, whereas karma in Vietnam is commonly seen as transferable (for instance, in mortuary rituals which are done on behalf of the deceased to mitigate their punishment in hell and influence their subsequent rebirth), Buddhist globalism insists that each person is responsible for his or her own karma and spiritual development. The individualism of Buddhist globalism is emphasized particularly in the way that Buddhism has been constructed in the last century as a religion of personal choice, as part of the construction of Buddhism as a "religion." This idea of following Buddhism as a personal choice has led to the increased importance placed on initiation rituals and criteria for being Buddhist. In small temples in Hanoi in the 1990s I rarely heard about anyone performing a specific ritual in order to become Buddhist. Instead, people would follow the Buddha or not, participate or not, according to their own wishes. Being Buddhist was as simple as acting Buddhist. Lay Buddhists would don brown robes when chanting sutras, and this would mark them as Buddhist, but there was no ritual investiture. More frequently today I am hearing about rituals of taking precepts and taking refuge in the Buddha, Dharma, and sangha in order to "become" Buddhist. In some cases, I have heard lay Buddhists assuming Buddhist names as part of initiation – most notably in large organizations like Trúc Lâm.

Meditation is the central practice of most white Buddhists in the West, and it is increasingly important for Asian organizations who are most influenced by Buddhist globalism. In Vietnam there are several leaders who have risen to prominence, Thích Thanh Từ being the most famous, claiming authority as meditation masters (*thiền sư*). This growing trend toward meditation is predictable, since it is a technique suited to modernity because of its highly individualistic nature. Meditation, unlike chanting, is seen as a self-reliant technique for personal cultivation, with enlightenment as the goal. The technical, scientific way that meditation is presented decouples it from any notions of supernaturalism, as well as from other parts of the Eightfold Path. In asserting that meditation is the central, or only, way to be a Buddhist, a former monastic exercise has been laicized, mirroring transformations that took place in Christian Europe during the Reformation.

I have tried to introduce a new approach to understanding the forces at work in the transformation of Buddhism at a global level in the last century and a half. However, my primary reason for doing this is to present a way for better understanding Buddhism in Canada or elsewhere outside of Asia – one that goes beyond binary categorizations and typologies, like the ethnic/convert typology that has preoccupied scholars of Buddhism in the West for so long. I have proposed that there are three main forces at work: Buddhist globalism, which is outward oriented and reformist; Buddhist parochialism, which is conservative and inward looking; and Buddhist localism, which contextualizes all forms of Buddhism in accord with local circumstances. I have further discussed four of the main thrusts of Buddhist globalism: outward orientation, Buddhism as a world religion, participation in the discourse of modernity, and emphasis on the individual. It is from these features that most of the characteristics that scholars have identified as constituting Western or American Buddhism arise (e.g., lay emphasis, democratic structures, less hierarchy, gender equality, focus on enlightenment, pre-eminence of meditation and psychology, social activism, and so on).

CASE STUDY, PART TWO: A RE-EXAMINATION OF
VIETNAMESE BUDDHISM

Abandoning the enterprises of locating a Canadian or a Western Buddhism and categorizing types of Buddhism in Canada is a prerequisite for understanding Vietnamese Buddhism. Taking Vietnamese Buddhism in Canada as a transplanted, "ethnic" tradition does not give any explanatory room for the Zen claims of Thích Thiên Ân and Thích Nhất Hạnh. Their assertions that Vietnamese Buddhism is Zen could be seen only as fictitious (in the words of Nguyen and Barber [1998],) and their organizations, teachings, and writings as something other than Vietnamese Buddhism. We would also have to ignore their identification of themselves as Vietnamese. At the same time, it does not leave space for recognizing transformations in Vietnamese "ethnic" Buddhist communities as anything other than capitulation to external forces. Their agency is thereby denied, along with the ongoing process of transformation that was occurring before Vietnamese Buddhism was transplanted to Canada.

Vietnamese Buddhist Globalism and Localism

Thích Thanh Từ's Trúc Lâm Zen represents, in some ways, a bridge for understanding the gap between Thích Nhất Hạnh, who is heavily influenced by Buddhist globalism, and ethnic Vietnamese communities in Canada, who represent a mostly parochial expression of Buddhism. Unlike Thích Nhất Hạnh, whom even Vietnamese Buddhists describe as not traditional, Thích Thanh Từ does not present a radical break from what is understood as the Vietnamese tradition. Quite the opposite, he claims to be teaching a uniquely Vietnamese form of Zen and is now spreading it around the world. Nonetheless, his organization accentuates individual practice through meditation aimed at personal enlightenment, and de-emphasizes appeals to the supernatural for assistance. It is modernist, rational, and internationalist in scope and outlook. Thus, Thích Thanh Từ's Trúc Lâm is a link that demonstrates the continuities between Thích Nhất Hạnh and parochial Vietnamese Buddhism. Tracing the trajectories of monks like Thích Nhất Hạnh, Thích Thiên Ân, and Thích Thanh Từ shows that they were to varying degrees, and in slightly different ways, influenced by the discourses of Buddhist globalism. On the other hand, they fully participated in Vietnamese Buddhist discourses initiated in the reform period, rather than disconnecting themselves from Vietnamese Buddhism. Thus, while reflecting reform ideas, they were also influenced by the forces of localism. They expressed reformist ideas in Vietnamese cultural idioms, whether based in Vietnam (Thích Thanh Từ), France (Thích Nhất Hạnh), or the United States (Thích Thiên Ân).

Vietnamese Buddhist Parochialism and Localism

When Vietnamese Buddhists chant sutras or light incense on ancestor altars on a Sunday at a temple in Montreal, these may seem to be expressions of parochialism, and in many ways they are. These temples, at least for most of the participants, are inward looking. The temple focus is on the community, and many of the participants are primarily concerned with bringing benefit to their families (both alive and dead) through their practices. Often there will be future telling sticks and divination blocks that people use to tell their futures or assist in making life decisions. There is in most instances no interest in reform, in meditation, in ecumenical dialogue, or in removing beliefs and practices that are viewed by some as "cultural" rather than "Buddhist," or even as "superstitious." These worshippers want to continue practising Buddhism in the way they did in Vietnam. These people have been more or less dismissed as "ethnic" Buddhists and have not been seen as playing a significant part in the Western transformation of Buddhism. The framework of discourses described above, however, shows that no one group can be characterized as fitting entirely into a type. Nor is an individual leader or group entirely globalist or entirely parochial. Since these are orientations and discourses, any one group can be affected by all three forces to varying degrees and in specific contexts.

So, for example, while an ethnic-based temple in Montreal may be primarily parochial in orientation, the other forces are subtly at play as well. Many of the first generation of Vietnamese Buddhist monastic leaders in the West who started local Vietnamese temples were heavily influenced by the reform movement; disproportionately so. This is because most of the leaders of Buddhist activism in South Vietnam during the war had been taught, like Thích Thiên Ân and Thích Nhất Hạnh, at the Buddhist educational institutions established by the original reformers. In keeping with the international outlook of the reform movement and Global Buddhism, many also studied in universities overseas, following Western forms of rationalized education. Thích Thiên Ân studied at the main reform pagoda in central Vietnam before going on to get a PhD at Waseda University in Japan. After he died, Thích Mãn Giác, who had also studied in Tokyo at Toyo University, replaced him, becoming the leader of the first organization to unite Vietnamese Buddhists in the United States. These two, along with Thích Nhất Hạnh, who studied at Columbia University, were involved in founding the first Buddhist university in Vietnam (in Saigon), called Vạn Hạnh Buddhist University. They were classmates at Báo Quốc Buddhist Academy (a centre of Buddhist reform in central Vietnam). Furthermore, they, along with Thích Thanh Từ, were associated with Ấn Quang Temple in Saigon, which was the centre of the Buddhist protest movement during the 1960s and 1970s. Thích Huyền Vi, a prominent overseas leader who set up another international Vietnamese Buddhist organization of independent, parochial, temples before his death in 2005, was also associated with Ấn Quang and studied for his master's degree and doctorate at Nalanda University in India. Thích Thiện Nghị, who was the first Vietnamese monk in Canada and who set up one of the larger Canadian Vietnamese Buddhist organizations (see chapter 14 in this volume), was similarly involved at Ấn Quang and studied at Fo Guang Shan in Taiwan. Thích Quảng Ba, a leading Vietnamese monk in Australia, was educated at one of the reform institutions.[16] Many of the monks that lead largely parochially oriented temples in Canada and throughout the diaspora have been strongly influenced by globalist ideas, though the temples they run are not oriented in that way. Their activist involvement and international outlook compelled them to leave Vietnam and relocate around the world. Thus, it becomes clear that Vietnamese monks in the West do not represent conservative, "traditional" Buddhists, for which Vietnamese and other Asian Buddhists have too often been mistaken. Instead, they exemplify the complex Buddhist networks that have arisen out of globalizing forces. There has been a long and sustained history of transnational connections and communications among Buddhists in Asia and among Vietnamese Buddhists around the world.

Nonetheless, they usually set up temples that are distinctly local in character. They are parochial in the sense that they are rooted in a Vietnamese idiom and express a Vietnamese way of practising Buddhism. But, important for the understanding of transformations in the West, they are localized by having to adapt to their new contexts. Thus, they need to set up boards of directors, they need to think about attracting young people in a way that was not necessary in Vietnam, they need to bend schedules to conform to a Canadian rhythm of life, they need to interpret *vinaya* (Buddhist monastic rules) in a way that is suited to Canadian society, and so on.

CONCLUSION

Buddhist transformation is not taking place only in the West, inspired by Western Buddhists. Changes that we see in Canada, California, or Canberra are not the result of Buddhism's transformation to become suitable for practitioners in the West. Instead, they are local manifestations of a globalized or globalizing Buddhism. This process is not located solely in the West, nor is it temporally fixed in the 1950s when Beatniks started to be interested in Zen poetry or when the counterculture Hippies of the 1960s started to look east for answers to their spiritual questions. It is an ongoing process that is global and has been taking place for a century and a half. The primary dichotomy that should be drawn when looking at Buddhism in the West or around the world is not between Western Buddhism and ethnic/traditional Buddhism, but between Buddhist globalism and Buddhist parochialism. "Western Buddhism" has been assigned a single label because of the similarities shared by most Western Buddhist groups that override the particularities of the diverse traditions. However, we need to acknowledge that many of the new, or reform, Buddhist organizations and teachers in Asia have more in common with these Western traditions than they do with the local or "traditional" forms in the countries from which they have emerged. Trúc Lâm Zen interprets and practises Buddhism in a way more reminiscent of white Shambhala Buddhists in Halifax than of the neighbouring Vietnamese Buddhist temple not half a kilometre from their Zen centre in Hanoi.

The example of Vietnamese Buddhism demonstrates that the assumptions that ethnic communities are only recreating the religion that they brought from their homeland, and that any changes are superficial and externally driven by imperatives that compel adaptation to new surroundings, are false. These assumptions have emerged due to the methodological and theoretical preoccupations with locating a Canadian, American, or Western Buddhism. A more fruitful approach is to see Buddhism as communication, with the main orientations being Buddhist globalism and Buddhist parochialism, which never operate in isolation from one another. We can also see that a third process takes place that localizes all Buddhism to local contexts – whether globalist, parochial, in Asia, or in the West. These forces are dynamic and relational, and are fundamental for understanding Buddhism in Canada today.

NOTES

1 By "West" I am using shorthand to denote the Americas, Europe, Australia, and New Zealand, although countries like Israel may also be included, as it was in Prebish and Baumann's book *Westward Dharma* (2002).
2 No real attempt had yet been made to define a Canadian Buddhism, although Koppedrayer and Fenn suggested that Buddhism has not developed sufficiently in Canada to warrant the term "Canadian Buddhism" (2006, 73).
3 While the present Conservative government is implementing a program that deliberately pulls back from the generous spirit of multiculturalism by reforming immigration and refugee policies along more protectionist lines, some who have immigrated to Canada also disagree with multiculturalism. The Toronto Buddhist leader Suwanda Sugunasiri has, for example, written critically about multiculturalism (2001).
4 Thanks to Victor Hori for pointing this out.
5 I am using the term as shorthand to refer to non-Asian converts to Buddhism in the West, and their descendants if they have maintained Buddhist practices and/ or identities. Field consciously uses the term to underline the largely white, middle-class demographics of many Buddhist groups in the United States (1998, 197). It is an

admittedly inexact term, but it has the merit of bringing attention to latent racism in the way that Buddhism has been constructed and described in the West.

6 For examples of this in the United States, see Rutledge (1985, 74) and Hien Duc Do (Do 2006, 91–2); in Britain, see Law (1991, 57); in Australia, see Tuong Quang Luu (Luu 2011); and in Canada, see Dorais (2006, 136) and McLellan (1999, 128–32).

7 Not including superficial cultural manuals published by the US government during the war for strategic uses.

8 See Soucy (2012) for more on this.

9 Invention of tradition is not new. When the Chinese started developing new schools, they invented family lineage trees which connected the founder of their school with Śākyamuni.

10 For the Foguang Shan organization's difficulties in breaking the ethnic barrier, see Chandler (2004); for Tzu Chi see Laliberté and Litalien (2010). It should be noted that most groups in the West remain ethnically homogeneous, with the exceptions of Soka Gakkai and Thích Nhất Hạnh's Order of Interbeing. The latter has attracted both Vietnamese and white Westerners, though these groups appear in practice to operate as distinct sub-groups within the organization.

11 It is worth noting that many white Buddhists eschew the notion that Buddhism is a religion, perhaps because the idea of religion is associated with the religious traditions of their childhood from which they have turned away. While the contradiction is notable, this is not the place for further exploration.

12 Victor Hori points out, however, that many who view the new Western Buddhism as somehow closer to a core Buddhism intended by the Buddha ironically reject the central doctrines of karma and rebirth (2010b).

13 Whalen Lai (1982) also deals with the search for a historical Buddha that took place in Japan in the early twentieth century as a response to the claim by T.W. Rhys Davids and others that the Pali canon represented the true and original Buddhism.

14 For example, see the essays in Wallace (2003) that highlight the overlap between Buddhist and scientific ideas.

15 Raphaël Liogier has noted that this extreme individualism – what he calls "individuo-globalism" – is central to the reconstruction of Buddhism in the West, and that Buddhism in this form is at the centre of a new diffused global belief system (Liogier 2010).

16 Thích Quảng Ba, interview with the author conducted in Canberra in September 2011.

PART ONE

Taking Root

2

Flying Sparks: Dissension among the Early Shin Buddhists in Canada[1]

MICHIHIRO AMA

The Japanese workers who migrated to North America more than a century ago dreamt of earning a great deal of money and returning to Japan "dressed in brocade." They came to realize that the fulfillment of those dreams would require a longer timeline. Because of the difficulties in learning English and the anti-Japanese attitude of North American society, they longed for "home," the rural Japanese areas where they had grown up, and so they founded a Buddhist temple. Thus, during the early twentieth century, Jōdo Shinshū, the Pure Land school known as Shin Buddhism, became the major form of ethnic Buddhism in North America. In 1905, the Buddhist Mission of North America (BMNA), which began in San Francisco in 1898, extended its services to the Japanese labourers in Vancouver.[2]

The Honpa Canada Buddhist Mission (HCBM) was later organized and Buddhist temples began to be built where Japanese immigrants had settled. In western Canada, these included temples in downtown Vancouver, Maple Ridge, Fairview, Steveston, and New Westminster, as well as Royston on Vancouver Island, and Raymond, Alberta. Establishing Shin Buddhist temples in Canada was difficult. Financial crises, racial discrimination, and rivalry with Christianity plagued the management of local temples. Further, as Terry Watada (1996), Yutetsu Kawamura (1988, 1999), Shinjo Ikuta (1981), and Konen Tsunemitsu (1971) have observed, there were many conflicts within the American and Canadian Shin Buddhist organizations. The causes of the clashes and their characteristics are, however, unclear. A dearth of first-hand records, and the authors' insider status (Kawamura and Ikuta served as Shin ministers, while Tsunemitsu founded the *Bukkyō Times*), might account for the lack of discussion. And Japanese cultural ethos may have prevented them from disclosing their internal trouble, which would be seen as disgraceful.

This study sheds new light on the complexity of the Canadian Shin Buddhist organizations, primarily through an analysis of early records kept at the BCA Archives in the Japanese American National Museum which have heretofore been largely overlooked. It reveals the multiple levels of contention: between a local temple and its headquarters; between Canadian temples and the Japanese headquarters; within the two denominations of Shin Buddhism – Nishi (west) Honganji, represented by HCBM, and Higashi (east) Honganji; between clergy and laity in specific cases; and among ministers and parishioners in general. Conflicts of interest resulted in a schism within the HCBM and generated internal competition among its neighbouring umbrella groups. One such conflict led to the establishment in Vancouver of a Higashi Honganji organization. This chapter also explores how expectations of Buddhist ministers differed between the *issei* (first-generation Japanese immigrants) and the *nisei* (the second generation, children of the immigrants).

Buddhist organizations are not exempt from having to deal with internal rivalry. Conflicts result from members' various expectations of a Buddhist temple, reflecting differences in ethnicity, gender, language, spiritual orientation, and socio-cultural interests. Members of the congregation may find it hard to escape the hierarchy within the temple, created by seniority, generation gaps, the status of members, and the distinction between clergy and laity. These factors contribute to the forming of groups of like-minded people, triggering factions and hostility. In addition, the birthplace of the clergy and laity can account for internal Buddhist competition, and its significance should not be underestimated.

Wendy Cadge, for example, identifies birthplace as the key to classifying the terrain of Theravada Buddhists in America. She asks about the birthplaces of both the founders of the Buddhist centres and their congregants, as well as the lineage of those organizations. In her study, birthplace is not treated as a source of contention but discussed in relation to countries where Theravada Buddhism has been practised, such as Laos, Cambodia, Thailand, Burma, Sri Lanka, and the United States, as a means to highlight the differences between Asian immigrant Buddhists and Euro-

American converts (Cadge 2005b, 44–6). Concerning the experience of early Japanese settlers in Hawai'i, Yukiko Kimura writes: "Especially divisive were the provincial customs and dialects that had developed through centuries of feudalism in Japan. When the immigrants came to Hawai'i, they met for the first time their fellow Japanese" (Kimura 1988, xiii). The early Japanese immigrants had strong regional identities tied to their birthplace and formed prefectural associations for comradeship. The present study demonstrates the ways in which regional bonding among the *issei* Canadian Shin Buddhists led to conflicts in a temple.

A BRIEF INTRODUCTION TO SHIN BUDDHISM

Shinran (1173–1263) is known as the founder of Jōdo Shinshū. His teaching can be summarized as follows: "one who entrusts oneself to the Primal Vow and says the *nembutsu* attains Buddhahood" (Hirota et al. 1997, 1: 668). According to *The Larger Sutra of Immeasurable Life* (*Muryōjukyō* or *Sukhāvatīvyūhasūtra*), bodhisattva Dharmākara made forty-eight vows. Upon the fulfillment of those vows, he became Amida Buddha (Skt. Amitābha or Amitāyus) and established his Buddha-land, known as the Pure Land of ultimate joy. In the development of Shin Buddhism, the eighteenth vow of Dharmākara, known as the Primal Vow or the Original Vow (*hongan*), was the most crucial – those who, with a sincere heart, entrust themselves and wish to be born in the Pure Land, and who recite Amida's name (*nembutsu*) can attain rebirth in the Pure Land. In the case of Shinran, faith (*shinjin*) in Amida's Primal Vow was particularly important, and Amida Buddha directs both the *nembutsu* and *shinjin* toward sentient beings; hence, they represent Amida's activity in awakening unenlightened beings, causing them to seek birth in the Pure Land where they attain nirvana.

Shinran's followers structured his doctrine and practice by forming various organizations. Honganji became the most powerful Shin Buddhist order under the leadership of the eighth abbot, Rennyo (1415–1499). Mark L. Blum summarizes his contribution to Honganji's development in political terms.

Under his tenure many Shin communities achieved more economic and political independence than they had ever known, and some even instituted democratic systems of government at the local level. Rennyo was courted by daimyō for the size and commitment of his community, and a major part of his legacy was an institution in Honganji that seemed commensurate with that of a feudal domain in many of its functions, prompting some to see Rennyo himself as a daimyō. After Rennyo's death, Honganji only grew stronger, whereupon [Oda] Nobunaga sought its destruction as he had destroyed Mount Hiei, and yet it was the one domain he was unable to conquer. (Blum 2006, 4)

By the time of Rennyo's death, Honganji had become a formidable religious organization. The next generation of Honganji abbots fought and negotiated with national unifiers, such as Oda Nobunaga, Toyotomi Hideyoshi, and Tokugawa Ieyasu. With the establishment of the Tokugawa regime (1603–1867), Ieyasu divided the Honganji into two denominations – Nishi and Higashi Honganji – to weaken its powers.[3] The split was made for political reasons, not because of doctrinal differences. Since then, the two Honganji organizations have remained the dominant branches of Shin Buddhism.

The transmission of Shin Buddhism to the West commenced at the end of the nineteenth century. As Japan became modernized and internationalized, Honganji leaders foresaw the introduction of Shin Buddhism to the West on two levels. First, scholar-priests began to translate and circulate Shin texts in European languages. From Nishi Honganji, Akamatsu Renjō supported the translation of Shin Buddhist doctrine into English.[4] He wrote *A Brief Account of Shin-Shiu* (*Shinshū ryakusetsu*), which was published by the Buddhist Propagation Society (Akamatsu 1893). This work was sent to the World's Parliament of Religions in Chicago in 1893 along with several other theses, including *Outlines of the Mahayana as Taught by Buddha* (Kuroda 1893) and *The Skeleton of a Philosophy of Religion* written by Kiyozawa Manshi and translated into English for the parliament (Kiyozawa 2002).[5] Kiyozawa Manshi was Japan's first modern religious philosopher and also a Higashi Honganji priest. Other scholar-priests published Shin Buddhist texts in French and German. Second, because of the large number of Japanese workers in North America, Nishi Honganji initiated a full-scale campaign there, catering to their religious and social needs. In response to the requests of devout Shin Buddhist followers, the headquarters sent two priests to San Francisco in September 1899 and supported the founding of the BMNA. Shin Buddhism in Canada initially developed as part of the BMNA operation and the Canadian bishopric did not become independent until the 1930s.

TROUBLED PROPAGATION

In 1891, Kōbe Imin Kaisha recruited the first group of workers from Hiroshima to Canada. They arrived as contract labourers for the coal mining industry in Cumberland, British Columbia. Labour importation from Hiroshima and other prefectures such as Kumamoto and Fukuoka continued in Canada. In contrast to the Japanese workers in Hawai'i and California, however, which were dominated by migrants from Hiroshima and Yamaguchi prefectures, in British Columbia workers from Shiga and Wakayama prefectures outnumbered Japanese from other areas by 1912. Shiga and Wakayama eventually came to be known as "Let's all immigrate together prefectures" (*yobi yose imin ken*). Workers from Shiga frequently became contractors or foremen in the lumber business and kept strong connections with their birthplaces. More than half of the Shiga immigrants were *Gōshū monto*, referring to Shin Buddhists in the Hikone area (present-day Shiga prefecture) (Sasaki 1999, 70, 92). Shin Buddhism was, thus, the dominant Japanese religion in Canada. This situation was similar to Hawai'i and California, except that large numbers of *Aki monto*, referring to Shin Buddhists from Hiroshima, settled in those areas.

In the fall of 1904, Japanese Buddhists gathered at Yuichi Nagao's residence in Vancouver to discuss the possibility of constructing a Buddhist temple in Vancouver. They requested Nishi Honganji headquarters in Japan to send a minister. In response to their petition, Senjū Sasaki arrived in October 1905.[6] In 1906, Shin Buddhists formed a Young Men's Buddhist Association. Article 4 of its by-laws defines its mission: "The purpose of this association is [for its members] to take refuge in Buddha [Śākyamuni]'s teaching and become followers of [the doctrine of] the Two Truths and Two Practices, while nurturing and training the mind and body" (Sasaki and Gonnami 2000, 8:1302).

This statement implies the potential for conflicts among ideological categories that Canadian Shin Buddhists were obliged to observe, at least on a conceptual level. The doctrine of the Two Truths and Two Practices refers to Nishi Honganji's set of beliefs, namely the dual principles of observing spiritual and mundane rules: Shin Buddhists kept faith to themselves while outwardly conforming to secular rules. For the Canadian Shin Buddhists, however, each principle involved an internal conflict. Concerning the spiritual rules, keeping the precepts and moral principles were unnecessary for Shin Buddhists to attain birth in the Pure Land; however, by emphasizing the importance of taking refuge in the Śākyamuni Buddha's teaching, the Canadian Shin Buddhists endorsed the basic tenets of Buddhism, including the observance of the precepts and moral disciplines. Concerning the secular rules, the Canadian Shin Buddhists required themselves to observe both the laws of Japan and those of Canada. As Japan became an expansionist modern nation state, however, collisions between Japan and the Western nations, including Canada, were inevitable. In North America, state laws had already been hostile to the Japanese immigrants. This situation ultimately forced the Canadian Shin Buddhists – and Japanese immigrants in Canada for that matter – to choose their social belonging in either the sending nation or the receiving nation.

Apart from the doctrinal interpretation and a discussion of national identity, Canadian Shin Buddhists were on bad terms among themselves. The Honpa Canada Buddhist Mission (*Honpa kanada bukkyōkai*) suffered from internal conflicts for more than two decades after its founding. Senjū Sasaki, the first minister of the *Canada Bukkyōkai*, returned to Japan in February 1911 after successfully constructing a temple hall. Two ministers succeeded Sasaki, but Junichi Shigeno, who inaugurated the *Canada Bukkyōkai* in September 1913, could not get along with Gungai Kato, who had come to work there earlier. Although Kato left the temple, Shigeno's personal life continued to arouse controversy. In October 1920, a party of those who wanted to expel Shigeno collided with a group of laity who supported him. The former left the temple and formed another Buddhist association, the *Honganji Bukkyōkai*, which the BC provincial government recognized on 11 February 1921. The Nishi Honganji headquarters also supported this new organization by sending Takunen Nishimoto as its resident minister (Terakawa 1936, 425–7; Tsunemitsu 1973, 175–80; Watada 1996, 54–7).

The Nishi Honganji administrators tried to reconcile the two Shin organizations. Sasaki, the former minister in Vancouver, made the first attempt at reconciliation in February 1923, but without success. The conflict ended in September 1924 when the Japanese consul and two ministers of the BMNA office intervened (Tsunemitsu 1973, 180–2). The delegates of the two organizations agreed to consolidate and respect the decisions of the Kyoto headquarters, which would appoint the ministers. They named the merger of the two organizations the Honpa Canada Buddhist Mission (Watada 1996, 64). Although Shigeno and Nishimoto resigned as a result of the consolidation, discontent remained.[7] A group of parishioners who opposed the merger contacted Junjō Izumida, the head priest of Higashi Honganji in Los Angeles, in the summer of 1925. As a result, Izumida initiated Higashi Honganji's advance into Vancouver.[8]

Izumida had gone to southern California as an independent minister of the Nishi Honganji in Japan. In September 1904, he formed a nonsectarian Buddhist group called the *Rafu Bukkyōkai* in Los Angeles. Two more Buddhist organizations related to Nishi Honganji were established soon after. The Kyoto headquarters and the BMNA office made a major attempt to consolidate these three organizations in 1916. The unification, however, failed. Those who had opposed Izumida sought a settlement in a US court and Nishi Honganji in Japan excommunicated Izumida, who subsequently sought affiliation with the Higashi Honganji in Japan in order to maintain the *Rafu Bukkyōkai*. This incident formed a precedent for attempting to resolve splits in local Shin Buddhist temples in North America and introduced competition into Shin Buddhist organizations in the United States. Higashi Honganji had not planned to propagate on the North American continent, focusing its overseas expansion on Asia. Later, Izumida "acquired" those who broke away from Nishi Honganji in northern and central California, and established a Higashi Honganji organization in Berkeley in 1926 and in Parlier, California, in 1932. Re-establishment of the *Rafu Bukkyōkai* in Los Angeles as the centre of Higashi Honganji propagation thus became a potential threat to Nishi Honganji's operation in North America.

The Shin Buddhist denominational rivalry entered Canada in 1925. When a group of people sought to establish a Higashi Honganji organization in Vancouver, Izumida visited them on 31 July 1925, and he held a series of lectures in Steveston, New Westminster, Vancouver, and other places, thus increasing his influence. It appears that he even spoke at Nishi Honganji's West Second Avenue Buddhist Mission. Izumida sent a report about his activities to the Higashi Honganji headquarters in Japan, which sent Kendō Mito to Vancouver on 10 November as a resident minister.

Izumida and Mito held the inaugural service of *Ōtani-ha* (Higashi Honganji) *Bukkyōkai* on 15 November at 240 Alexander Street. In order to contain Izumida's advance to Vancouver, Nishi Honganji sent another minister, Gijin Taga, to the Honpa Canada Buddhist Mission in November 1925. Competition between the two Honganjis became keen: just one day after Higashi Honganji announced its gathering in the *Tairiku Nippō* – the local Japanese newspaper – HCBM announced the inaugural service of its Buddhist Women's Association. It also held welcome parties for Taga at various locations to demonstrate this increase in its ministerial personnel and its solidarity.[9]

Taga, however, became a cause for schism in the HCBM. He practised *o-fuse*, the Japanese custom in which family members make donations to the priest after he performs a memorial service. Since he kept the money for his own use, his income increased but the mission's revenue decreased (Ikuta 1981, 58). The president of the board petitioned the BMNA Advisory Committee to transfer Taga in July 1928. An advisory member who came to Vancouver in August 1928 agreed with the HCBM president's recommendation to send Taga back to Japan. Taga's situation worsened during the next two months. He and the other minister, Shōzen Naitō, who had come to the HCBM two years after Taga, could not get along. Taga was also said to be collecting donations from members to rebuild his home temple in Japan. Still, certain members supported Taga, and in January 1929 they insisted that the BMNA office allow him to remain in Vancouver.[10] Since the BMNA office did not carry out its original plan immediately, the president of the Honpa Canada Buddhist Mission, Eikichi Kagetsu, sent a reminder to the BMNA interim bishop in July 1929,[11] and the BMNA office finally removed Taga on 1 January 1930.[12]

While the Honpa Canadian Buddhist Mission was struggling internally, the Higashi Honganji's operation in Vancouver seemed to be successful. But the *Ōtani-ha Bukkyōkai* was suddenly closed at the end of May 1929. Before the unexpected and unexplained closure, Izumida and Mito had developed a systematic plan for the propagation of Higashi Honganji. They held Buddhist Women's Association meetings on the first Sunday at 2 p.m., Young Men's Buddhist Association meetings on the second Friday at 7 p.m., and the Young Women's Buddhist Association meetings on the third Sunday at 2 p.m. The minister delivered a Shin Buddhist sermon on the second and fourth Sundays at 2 p.m. and gave a lecture on basic Buddhism at 7 p.m., conducted a Shin study session on the third Wednesday at 8 p.m., and held Sunday school every Sunday morning at 9 a.m., which initially accommodated seventy children.[13] Moreover, the mission received pictorial scrolls of Shinran and Rennyo from Japan in July 1926, which may suggest that the arrangement of the altar had been completed by then. According to *Tairiku Nippō* in September of that year, the board discussed the possibility of purchasing land for a new building and of having an assistant minister. As a result, Shinjō Miura arrived in Vancouver on 4 October 1926, to assist Mito. Miura came from Shiga prefecture, the source of a large number of Canadian Shin temple members. The *Ōtani-ha Bukkyōkai* seemed to be flourishing, but just three years later, at the end of May 1929, it abruptly announced its closure, stating only, "The Higashi Honganji propagation center will be closed in the end of May [1929] because of circumstances."[14] Even Izumida seems to have been unaware of the *Ōtani-ha Bukkyōkai*'s situation. His letter to Miura during that time suggests only that the mission could no longer afford to keep Miura on its staff.[15]

In fact, the Canadian Japanese were in financial difficulty. After 1923, the Canadian government gave favourable treatment to fishermen who were "white British subjects" and cut fishing licences to Asians by 40 percent (Roy 2003, 108). This policy resulted in many Japanese fishermen losing their businesses. With financial assistance from the Japanese government, they took the government to the Supreme Court, which in May 1928 ruled in their favour. Discrimination against British subjects of Japanese origin was illegal. Although the Japanese won the case, by this time they had lost 54 per cent of their gill-net fishery. The legal costs came to $40,000, further adding to their financial difficulties (Roy 2003, 107–9; Sasaki 1999, 227). Although additional research is needed to identify all the causes of Higashi Honganji's closure, it is clear that the Canadian government's policy regarding fishing affected the Canadian Japanese economy and helped block the growth of the *Ōtani-ha Bukkyōkai*.

Gijin Taga took advantage of the closing of Higashi Honganji's activities to justify an extension of his stay at the Honpa Canada Buddhist Mission. According to his report, *Ōtani-ha Bukkyōkai* proposed to join HCBM after sending Miura home and returning the statue of Amida Buddha to the Higashi Honganji headquarters.[16] Taga seemed to want to end his career in Canada in crowning glory by unifying the two denominations and regaining Nishi Honganji's position as the sole Shin Buddhist authority in Vancouver. In his words, "Before I arrived at the Honpa Canada Buddhist Mission, Ōtani-ha was exerting its influence, damaging the HCBM diocese significantly. I felt it was urgent that we regain our control and exhausted myself completely in expanding the HCBM operation. Fortunately, my efforts paid off, when the activities of the *Ōtani-ha Bukkyōkai* came to a close. The minister returned to Japan and all congregations joined the HCBM."[17]

Taga's account reflects a sectarian rivalry; hence, his record of his "achievements," which borders on the ostentatious, should not be taken at face value. In all cases of intra-Shin Buddhist contests in the United States, the lay members were less concerned about the denominational differences between the two Honganji organizations than were the clergy. The dissensions were caused by conflicts of interests, not by differences in doctrine. Admittedly, by this time Kiyozawa Manshi's effort to redefine modern Shin Buddhism had encouraged Higashi Honganji followers to take a more subjective and experiential approach in their religion. While this movement could have affected the Higashi Honganji community in North America and separated it from the BMNA, this was not the case. Taking into consideration the patterns of Higashi Honganji's formation in North America and the split within a local Buddhist temple, the laity's attitude toward the two Shin Buddhist denominations in Canada turns out to be the same as its counterpart in the United States. What makes the Canadian situation unique is the flexibility of the laity (assuming that members of the *Ōtani-ha Bukkyōkai* proposed to join HCBM) and the restoration of Nishi Honganji's presence as the single Shin Buddhist authority in Canada.

In addition to the intra-Shin conflict, an ideological contest over the assimilability of the Japanese into the host society in Vancouver led to a confrontation between Japanese Christians and Buddhists. The religious quarrel accelerated when Japanese Christians preached "When in Rome, do as the Romans do," and the members of the Young Buddhist Association responded with "those who go to the Pure Land and those who go to Heaven cannot meet again." Further, the Japanese Christian clerics severely denounced the drinking, smoking, and gambling habits of the *issei* labourers who in return protested violently. The Shin clergy, however, tolerated such vices (Hayashi 2000, 329, 333) because of their understanding that all humans are ignorant beings filled with base desires (*bonbu*). At one point, the *nikkei* (people of Japanese ancestry) media was also divided, supporting one or the other religion: *Kanada Shinpō* sided with Christianity and *Tairiku Nippō* with Buddhism (Iino 2002, 54–5).[18]

Shin Buddhists were cautious about the Christian community as a whole. The members put construction of the Steveston Buddhist Church on hold because of concerns about the misconceptions of Anglo-Canadians, who might see Buddhism as an indicator of Japanese nationalism (Iino 2002, 56).[19] In Kelowna, two Christian priests opposed the Buddhist propagation initiated by Gijin Taga in 1927. However, Buddhist ministers and a group of over one hundred laity continued their efforts and established a *bukkyōkai* in January 1933 (Terakawa 1936, 451–3; Tsunemitsu 1964, 313–14).[20] Ironically, Christianity gave the Shin Buddhists an impetus to hold on to their religious heritage.

TROUBLES CONTINUE IN THE 1930S

Trouble among Canadian Shin Buddhist organizations continued during the thirties. Territorial disputes emerged when a local *bukkyōkai* sought independence from HCBM. In August 1930, those living in the area around Nanoose Bay and Comox on Vancouver Island petitioned the BMNA office to limit the jurisdiction of the Royston Bukkyōkai, which was attempting to extend beyond Nanaimo. According to the petition, Royston Bukkyōkai's propagation was related to the Royston Lumber Company's business expansion. Further, the resident minister of the Royston Bukkyōkai, Kōgyō Ōsuga, who was then also serving as a Japanese language teacher on Vancouver Island, breached an agreement made with a group of Japanese educators in Comox and tried to expand his operation.[21] The Nishi Honganji headquarters in Japan, however, did not respond to these accusations and recognized the Royston Bukkyōkai located at the lumber company (Terakawa 1936, 481).

The BMNA office recorded another territorial dispute between the Honpa Canada Buddhist Mission and one of its branch temples, the New Westminster Buddhist Mission. In 1931, the propagation zone of the HCBM was extended to the northern bank of the Fraser River, while that of the New Westminster Buddhist Mission ended at its southern bank.[22] On 30 April 1932, the board president of the HCBM reported to Bishop Masuyama[23] that Ryūzan Hayashi, the resident minister of the New Westminster Buddhist Mission, had rescinded this agreement and had begun to propagate in Steveston without the HCBM's consent. Although Hayashi made gestures toward Seishō Ishiguro of the HCBM to alleviate the conflict, he and the laity of New Westminster broke the agreement again and sought independence.[24] Further, there was a third case of contention, after which the BMNA office recognized the agreement made between the Steveston Bukkyōkai and HCBM regarding propagation zones – divided by the second bridge after Marpole along the Fraser River – on 6 December 1932.[25]

A series of disputes in Vancouver led to the opening of Nishi Honganji's Canadian District. When local Buddhist associations demanded independence, the clergy and laity of HCBM became concerned about losing their authority and financial sources in the British Columbia diocese. Because of the physical distance between British Columbia and San Francisco, where Bishop Masuyama and the BMNA headquarters were located, the BMNA office could not act promptly. Therefore, during the early 1930s the dissatisfied leaders of HCBM demanded that Bishop Masuyama establish a separate Canadian office within the mission.[26] In June 1933, the Kyoto headquarters and Masuyama recognized Canada Buddhist Mission as separate from BMNA with its own bishop's office (*Canada kaikyō kantoku jimusho*) housed in the HCBM building (Terakawa 1936, 421–2). Since the status of Honpa Canada Buddhist Mission was now elevated with a bishop's office and because of the Kyoto headquarters' financial support, Masuyama asked the board president to recognize the independence of local Buddhist organizations.[27] Masuyama initially doubled as the head of Canada Buddhist Mission, but on 8 April 1936, Zenyū Aoki took over this position and became the sole designated bishop in Canada (Tsunemitsu 1973, 183).[28]

In searching for the causes of the Shin Buddhist clashes, which occurred on multiple levels of personal and organizational relationships, the historical situation of the immigrants, the location of the temples, and the immigrants' cultural practice need to be taken into account. As Terry Watada surmises, a minister's personality and his mobilization of supporters were unlikely to be major factors leading to the schism of a *bukkyōkai*; such a generalization would place too much emphasis on his influence (Watada 1996, 65).

The Japanese in Canada experienced various transitions during the 1930s. First, the Gentlemen's Agreement, signed between Canada and Japan in 1928, restricted the annual quota of Japanese immigrants to 150, including relatives of those already living in Canada (Roy 2003, 88). The change in immigration laws limited the growth of the Japanese population.

Statistics from 1931 show that there were over 23,300 people of Japanese ancestry in Canada, almost one-third of them living in Vancouver. By 1934, approximately 2,000 Japanese immigrants lived in Steveston. Furthermore, by 1936 the number of the *nisei* and the *sansei* (the third generation) slightly exceeded that of the *issei*, indicating a generational change in the Canadian *nikkei* community (Adachi 1991, 122; Sasaki 1999, 226; Yesaki 2003, 83).

The number of Japanese immigrants was no longer increasing, the *nikkei* population as a whole reached a plateau, and the *issei* generation began to decline. Faced with this demographic shift, each Shin Buddhist organization tried to secure its current membership, prohibiting its members from moving to or joining another Shin organization. In Vancouver and its vicinity, the competitiveness and desire to demarcate membership was exacerbated by the large number of Shin Buddhist associations relative to the number of Japanese immigrants. In addition to the HCBM, there were at least four Shin Buddhist organizations in Vancouver (in West Second Avenue, Fairview, Marpole, and Kitsilano). Two missions were established outside Vancouver, in Steveston and New Westminster. Defining the propagation zone became necessary for a mission's smooth operation.

The Gentlemen's Agreement also affected the Japanese clergy who sought to enter Canada. Clergy were supposed to be sent by their sponsoring religious organization; hence, the Nishi Honganji headquarters in Japan was theoretically responsible for their ministers' salaries. The Canadian government, therefore, prohibited ministers from working as Japanese language teachers (although this had been a common practice) and limited their function to performing religious duties. If a minister received a salary from the local organization, he would be considered for immigrant status, but not for ministerial work.[29] In correspondence with Kyoto headquarters, Bishop Masuyama reported that non-immigrants in Canada could stay only one year with possibility of renewal up to a maximum of three years, making it difficult for ministers to propagate unless they decided to settle permanently. He asked the headquarters to contact the Ministry of Foreign Affairs in Japan to amend the conditions of ministers' visas in Canada.[30] The 1928 Gentlemen's Agreement made it more difficult for the clergy and the laity to develop a strong relationship and to agree to a mutual, long-term commitment.

Another major factor in Shin Buddhist competition was the *issei*'s cultural practice of religious confraternity (*kō*). In agrarian communities in

Japan, local religious gatherings remained autonomous. In some areas, a confraternity would hold religious services without including neighbouring associations, with some Shin Buddhist fraternities observing even *Hōonkō* (the most important annual ceremony commemorating Shinran's death) by themselves. While sharing the labour and responsibility equally among members, confraternities generally excluded outsiders. This practice points to the importance of maintaining the community's internal order and common ancestral worship (I. Hori 1962, 129, 154–5; Kodama 2005, 222, 236).

Shin Buddhists in Japan observed and engaged in ancestor worship. Exploring the connection between Shin practice and ancestor worship during the late Tokugawa period, Kodama Shiki argues that there was a religious gestalt of a Shin Buddhist "trinity" where followers equated Shinran with Amida Buddha and their ancestors, often calling Amida *oya-sama* (parents). Since enshrining Shinran also meant honouring their ancestors, there was no need to deify mortuary tablets of their deceased family members (Kodama 2005, 78–9). Because one of the confraternity's objectives was to honour the ancestors of its members, it is hardly surprising that Shin Buddhists in North America sought to establish a sense of belonging in their new location by making connections to the places from where they had migrated. The religious practice of combining ancestral worship and faith in Amida Buddha was arguably the strongest tradition that persisted in Shin Buddhist communities in Hawai'i and on continental North America.

Steveston provides an informative example. About half of the residents of the village of Mio-mura in Wakayama prefecture – locally known as "America town" (*Amerika-mura*) – moved to Canada, and most of them settled in Steveston. A survey was conducted in this village in 1951, which included interviews with those who had once lived in Steveston and had returned to Mio-mura. It describes the religious practice and ethos of Steveston. First, the religious environment was similar in both Mio-mura and Steveston. Residents performed various kinds of traditional religious rituals. Second, there was no Shinto shrine in Steveston, which would have represented their communal unity (*jien kankei*, literally "relationship to the place"), but the Buddhist temple signified the importance of keeping one's family lineage alive (*ketsuen kankei*). Third, the immigrants maintained the Buddhist rituals in their daily lives, including ancestor worship, and the majority refused to accept Christianity. Finally, according to a Shin priest in Mio-mura who was interviewed for this survey, those who had migrated to Steveston and returned to the village were more informed about Shin Buddhist doctrine than villagers who had never been abroad (Sasaki and Gonnami 2000, 10: 36, 309). When immigrants reinforced the values of their family religion (such as worshipping ancestors in the Pure Land) by emphasizing their connections to their homeland, strong regional identities emerged, as among the Japanese settlers in Steveston. And these identities might have been another way to define an organization's boundaries.

The management of a *bukkyōkai* was, in fact, affected by the regionalization of the *issei* workers. Two examples demonstrate the importance of prefectural identity, which was often promoted by prefectural associations (*kenjinkai*). When a group of the Fairview Buddhist Mission members demanded the resignation of the resident minister, Kakuya Tada, they requested that the BMNA office send a minister from Shiga prefecture as his replacement.[31] Gijin Taga became controversial at the Honpa Canada Buddhist Mission in part because of the rumour that he was collecting donations to rebuild his home temple in Shiga. Taga denied this charge but could not stop the members' spontaneous fundraising efforts.[32] It appears that Taga shared the same prefectural background with these members, whereas his rival minister, Shōzen Naitō, came from Fukui prefecture, whose association was much smaller.

Regionalization was not necessarily a peaceful process for the immigrants. Further localization within the same prefecture from which residents had moved to Canada may have added another layer of schism in the *nikkei* community. For instance, the aforementioned study of Mio-mura suggested that there had been two competing groups within the village divided by geography (Sasaki and Gonnami 2000, 10: 10, 232). Such local competition likely continued in Steveston. Another study indicates that immigrants from Hatsusaka-mura (on the eastern side of Lake Biwa in Shiga prefecture) created their own enclave in Vancouver. This is because the men who had migrated to Canada from Hatsusaka-mura married women from their home village and then returned to Hatsusaka temporarily, leaving their children there and returning to Canada. They continued to make remittances back to their families in Hatsusaka-mura (Sasaki and Gonnami 2000, 11: 162).[33] These studies point to internal rivalries within the *nikkei* community. Japanese nationals formed many different associations and clubs in Vancouver because of their places of birth in Japan.[34] The disputes within a Buddhist organization and among Buddhist organizations, therefore, need to be understood on this basis.

Unlike their parents, however, Canadian *nisei* Buddhists sought a collective identity as part of their cultural heritage. The national league of *nisei* Buddhists held annual conferences promoting the exchange of ideas among local organizations, published the journal *Kōgen*, sponsored various sport events, and organized the Sunday School Association, which by 1939 included 110 teachers and 1,200 students. Although Canadian Buddhists were no longer a part of the BMNA by then, the Young Buddhist Association (YBA) groups on the Pacific coast from Vancouver to California often held intercontinental conventions.[35] They also participated in the First Canada-Hawai'i-America Conference in San Francisco in 1932. In addition, local Canadian YBAs held an oratorical event annually. The majority of representatives, whose speeches were transcribed in *Otakebi* (published by the Fairview YBA as a special edition in 1930 to celebrate its ten-year anniversary) and *Butsuda* (by the Kitsilano YBA in 1935 for the same occasion), were concerned with preserving the *nisei*'s ethnic identity, represented by "the Japanese spirit" (*yamato damashii*), as a cultural ethos inherited from their parents' home country. They rarely discussed their understanding of Shinran or Sakyamuni's teachings, except for Hatsue Nishisaki's expression of joy at having faith in Shin Buddhism and Sutekichi Nishikawa's explanation of the practice of introspection.[36] For the majority of *nisei*, Shin Buddhist organizations became the centre of Japanese cultural activities.

CULTURAL AND RELIGIOUS NEEDS OF THE SHIN BUDDHIST TEMPLES

New findings have helped to clarify the laity's expectations of ministers in both cultural and religious terms. The Japanese fishermen who had settled near the mouth of the Fraser River were quite devout. Chitose Matsuba, a poet, described their lives in Steveston at that time.

> Dense fog over the ocean, while reciting the nembutsu,
> I suddenly hear my grandfather's voice catching salmon. (Shinpo 1996, 180)

Japanese fishermen, like others in this dangerous occupation, often drowned during storms, and part of the work of the Association of Japanese Fishermen was to search for the bodies and take part in arranging funerals. In October 1907, right after the Vancouver Riot, Sensuke Muto and Kosaburo Ono purchased a small Buddhist altar and formed a Buddhist Club (*bukkyō kurabu*) in Steveston. Members gathered on the second floor of a pharmacy, learned how to recite sutras from Fukumatsu Nakamura, who was known as *Amida-san*, and visited families of the drowning victims and conducted funerals. When a Buddhist minister later arrived in Vancouver, interaction between him and the followers of the Buddhist Club increased. In 1924, the members decided to build a Buddhist temple. By the spring of 1928, they had raised $8,000 and began construction despite a financial crisis in the Japanese community caused by the Canadian government's implementation of discriminatory policies that reduced the number of licences given to Japanese fishermen (Shinpo 1996, 179–82).

On 22 April 1932, the board president of the Steveston Buddhist Mission petitioned the BMNA bishop to assign a resident minister. In the petition he pointed to a possible connection between Steveston and Buddhism, since early Japanese fishermen used the kanji characters 須知仏恩 to sound out the town's name of "Steveston." The characters were read *su-chi-button* (Steveston) and meant "Truly to know our debt to Buddha."

Together with a history of the *bukkyōkai*, the board president of Steveston Buddhist Mission described the organization's general condition. The mission had a total of 324 members with an annual budget of approximately $1,000. Annual religious events included *Hōonkō* (commemoration of Shinran's death), *Ohigan* and *Higan-e* (services held during the spring and fall equinoxes respectively), *Eitaikyō* (the perpetual reciting of sutras as a memorial to deceased persons, which also aims to maintain the temple), and celebrations of Sakyamuni Buddha's and Shinran's birthdays. In addition to regular Sunday services, there were three or four wedding services and eight or nine funerals per year. The number of annual memorial services was 120 to 130 for which donations received by the minister were entered into the temple's accounts.

The board members also specified the requirements for a minister and his wife, as well as his remuneration. They requested that the minister be younger than forty years of age; healthy and married; determined to settle permanently and dedicated and active; eloquent and capable of dealing with new hot-blooded young immigrants; and interested in sports, such as Japanese martial arts, including *judō* and *kendō*. They expected his wife to be educated and mature enough to lead the Buddhist Women's Association or Young Buddhist Women's Association; acquainted with the Japanese arts, including flower arrangement and the tea ceremony; and versed in music, so that she could teach Buddhist hymns to the congregation. To compensate such a paragon of a human couple, the ministerial package was to consist of a monthly salary of $100 dollars, free housing with the utilities paid by the temple, and a total of $250 for moving fees, including travel expenses to Steveston. The board president promised a salary increase upon improvement of the economy.[37] In the minds of the Steveston Bukkyōkai board members, the performance of cultural activities was a necessity, whereas spiritual guidance appeared to be a formality. They sought the growth of Japanese cultural activities at the Steveston Buddhist Mission.

Another petition for a resident minister, made by the Raymond Buddhist Mission in Alberta on 20 July 1933, was, however, more religiously oriented. The board president sent a letter to the BMNA office when Shinjo Nagatomi[38] was forced to leave because his ministerial visa had expired. The board president strongly desired the continuation of the spiritual guidance offered by Nagatomi, who "had shown a white path of illumination in the darkness of ignorance."[39] He expressed regret that the *bukkyōkai* was unable to compensate Nagatomi enough for his dedicated work, which involved sharing his food and shelter with some members. The minister who would take over from Nagatomi needed to "leave behind all personal greed in order to complete the mission of guiding sentient beings." Interestingly, the board president preferred priests sent directly from Japan, and not those already working in the United States.[40]

Such *issei* religious attitudes had a positive effect on the spiritual development of some *nisei* followers. Takashi Tsuji, an active member of the national organization of Young Buddhist Associations, announced his intention to become ordained. His father, a devout Buddhist, was disappointed by the lack of Shin ministers; hence, he decided to have one of his sons serve at HCBM. Canada's first *nisei* candidate for ministry set off for Japan in 1938. Although Takashi's Japanese was limited, he survived at Ryukoku University with a subsidy from the HCBM. The headquarters ordained him with the Dharma name *Shaku Kenryū*. In November 1941, when diplomatic relations between Japan and the United States deteriorated, Takashi returned to Canada and assisted in the Sunday services for the first time in Vancouver (Watada 1996, 83, 100–3; Ikuta 1981, 83).[41] From 1968 to 1981, he served as the tenth bishop of the BCA (Buddhist Churches of America 1998, 1). Tsuji's case demonstrates a continuity of Shin Buddhist identity shared by parent and child, although lay members associated with a Shin Buddhist organization for a variety of reasons, from observing religious rituals to meeting their cultural needs.

CONCLUSION

The early Shin Buddhist community in Canada was far from harmonious. Causes of the clashes include the socio-political constraints forced upon the Japanese by the host nation, economic instability, conflicts of interest both at the individual and group levels, and cultural practices of the *issei* immigrants linked to their provincial identities. Delays in communication and miscommunication within the denomination frustrated the Canadian Shin Buddhists, since they needed to deal with the BMNA headquarters in San Francisco and the Nishi Honganji headquarters in Japan simultaneously, at least until the establishment of the Canadian bishopric.

On a micro level, the clashes paradoxically validate Shinran's teachings. Shinran considered himself a person "possessed of blind passion and ignorance" or a "foolish being" (*bonbu*) (Hirota 1997, 2: 187). The realization of his egotistical nature and the impossibility of liberating himself from his attachments by his own efforts led Shinran to entrust himself completely to Amida Buddha's compassion. He defines *bonbu* as

> *Foolish beings*: as expressed in the parable of the two rivers of water and fire, we are full of ignorance and blind passion. Our desires are countless, and anger, wrath, jealousy, and envy are overwhelming, arising without pause; to the very last moment of life they do not cease, or disappear, or exhaust themselves. When we, who are so shameful, go a step or two, little by little, along the White Path of the power of the Vow, we are taken in and held by the compassionate heart of the Buddha of unhindered light. It is fundamental that because of this we will unfailingly reach the Pure Land of happiness, whereupon we will be brought to realize the same enlightenment of great nirvana as Amida

Tathagata, being born in the flower of that perfect enlightenment. (Hirota et al. 1997, 1: 488)

The environment in which Canadian Shin Buddhists found themselves during the early twentieth century was very complicated. Strong political forces and institutional constraints, as well as various transnational restrictions, forced them to make decisions within a limited number of choices. The modern nation states of Japan and Canada pushed the *issei* into a peripheral position, where regional identity remained important to the Canadian Shin Buddhists, although forces of nationalization and centralization were affecting the lives of their counterparts in Japan during the same period. The dreams the early Shin Buddhists from Japan brought with them on their trip across the Pacific had to evolve and change with each passing year in Canada. The *issei*'s enduring provincial interests often overshadowed their spiritual concerns. In this combination of tensions, struggles, and constraints, sparks were bound to fly.

NOTES

1 This article is based on the author's recently published book *Immigrants to the Pure Land: The Modernization, Acculturation, and Globalization of Shin Buddhism, 1898–1941*. The author thanks John Harding, Victor Hori, Alec Soucy, Jessica Main, Peter Lait, and Ken'ichi Yokogawa for their suggestions and comments. The title is modeled after the rhetorical characterization of Shin Buddhist conflicts that George J. Tanabe Jr made when he read the original manuscript.

2 In 1944, the Buddhist Mission of North America changed its name to the Buddhist Churches of America.

3 However, within Honganji, there was a critical factor leading to the split of the organization. Whereas Kennyo, the eleventh abbot, signed the truce with Oda Nobunaga, Kyōnyo, Kennyo's eldest son, suggested entrenching at Ishiyama castle in Osaka and continuing to resist Nobunaga, knowing that Nobunaga had breached a peace agreement with Shin Buddhist followers in Ise Nagashima and killed them all. Later, Kyōnyo became the abbot of Higashi Honganji, while Junnyo, Kennyo's fourth son, became the abbot of Nishi Honganji. See Snodgrass (2003, 178).

4 Akamatsu Renjō was one of the earliest priests to envisage introducing Shin Buddhism in English (Amstutz 1997, 62–3, 206).

5   See Harding (2008, 105–6) for information about these three works sent to the 1893 World's Parliament of Religions.
6   By 1906, the laity had raised more than $5,600 for the establishment of the mission, which is equivalent to $100,000 today. The government of British Columbia recognized the *bukkyōkai* on 12 April 1909. For descriptions of the early establishment of Shin Buddhism in Canada, see Adachi (1991, 109–16); Iino (2002, 51); Watada (1996, 36–9); and Young and Reid (1938, 95–107).
7   The contributions of the two suspended priests to the development of the mission are worth mentioning. Nishimoto founded the YMBA within Honganji Bukkyōkai in 1920 and opened the first Sunday school in 1921. Shigeno "initiated" two Euro-Americans in 1913, Mr and Mrs Group with Dharma names *Shaku Kakuryo* (most likely *Kakuryō*) and *Shaku-ni Myokaku* (or *Myōkaku*), respectively. Although ordered back to Japan by the Kyoto headquarters, Shigeno did not return to Japan but continued his service at the mission on Franklin Street. He then moved to Toronto where he eventually died (Ikuta 1981, 38; Sasaki and Gonnami 2000, 8: 1320; and Watada 1996, 55, 58, 65).
8   Taga's letter to the BMNA office, dated 10 June 1929. (BCA Archives, Correspondence Files, box no.1.02.04). Also Izumida's progress in Vancouver is reported in "Izumida junjō-shi no Vancouver iri," *Chūgai Nippō*, 19 September 1925, 2.
9   *Tairiku Nippō*'s accounts in 1925 include "Higashi honganji bukkyōkai setsuritsu," 13 July, 5; "Izumida-shi kōen," 1 August, 5; "Izumida-shi kōen, nishi dainigai de," 5 August, 5; "Mito kendo-shi," 11 November, 5; "Kinkoku," 12 November, 5; "Kinkoku," 13 November, 5; "Taga kaikyōshi raiban," 26 November, 5; and "Seidai na kangeikai," 7 December, 5.
10 Naitō's and Taga's letters to the BMNA office, respectively (BCA Archives, Correspondence Files, box no.1.01.03, folder 1927–1928 16A); Yutaka Yasunaka's letter to the BMNA office (BCA Archives, Chronological Files, box no.1.01.02, folder 1926–1931).
11 The first letter was issued by Eikichi Kagetsu and others (BCA Archives, Chronological Files, box no.1.01.02), while the second was by Kagetsu himself (BCA Archives, Correspondence Files, box no.1.02.04). Kagetsu, a native of Wakayama prefecture, was a successful entrepreneur who founded the Deep Bay Logging Company in 1923 and also served as president of the Canadian Japanese Association (Takata 1983, 84–5).
12 BCA Archives, Correspondence Files, box no.1.02.04, folder 1929.
13 *Tairiku Nippō*'s accounts in 1925 include "Ōtani-ha bukkyōkai," 16 November, 5; and "Ōtani-ha bukkyōkai," 23 November, 5.

14 *Tairiku Nippō*'s accounts in 1926 include "Kyōkai tayori," 17 July, 5; "Ōtani bukkyōkai hōe," 7 August, 5; "Ōtani bukkyōkai tayori," 4 September, 5; and "Sakujitsu rainin shita Miura Shin kaikyōshi," 5 October, 5. Also "Miura-shi sōbetsu kai," 20 May 1929, 5.
15 Correspondence from Izumida to Miura, dated 23 May 1929, kept at Ryōtokuji, a Higashi Honganji temple in Hikone, Shiga prefecture.
16 Taga's correspondence to the BMNA office, dated 19 October (BCA Archives, Correspondence Files, box no. 1.02.03, folder 1927–1928 16A).
17 "Achievements" by Gajin Taga (BCA Archives, Correspondence Files, box no. 1.02.06).
18 Iino cites Kobayashi (1989, 83).
19 Iino cites Adachi (1991, 114).
20 There was at least one exception to the hostility of monotheistic religions toward Buddhism. When Buddhists in Raymond, Canada decided to found their church, James Walker, the Mormon bishop of the Raymond Second Ward, helped them purchase one of its old buildings for $5,000. Discrimination against the Japanese in Alberta was not as harsh as it was in British Columbia. In Alberta, Japanese-Canadian residents had the right to vote and served in provincial offices and the military. Because the Mormons and the Japanese established amicable relationships, this atmosphere of religious tolerance was later extended to the exchanging of spiritual fellowship between Japanese Christians and Buddhists in Raymond (Iwaasa 1978, 40, 44 [Iwaasa cites *A History of Forty Years of the Raymond Buddhist Church*]; Murai [1998, 57–8] [Murai cites *Raymond bukkyōkaishi*] and Harding 2010).
21 BCA Archives, Correspondence Files, box no. 1.02.05, folder Communication 1930 from District Temples K–S.
22 The agreement was reached between Kannosuke (or Hironosuke) Uenishi and Shintaro Toda, the board presidents of Honpa Canada Bukkyōkai and New Westminster Bukkyōkai respectively, (BCA Archives, Correspondence Files, box no.1.02.06, folder 1931 Communications from Districts T–Z).
23 Bishop Masuyama was a figure with influence far beyond his BMNA headquarters in San Francisco. During his term of office between July 1930 and February 1938, Masuyama vigorously admitted *nisei* and Euro-Americans to the BMNA.
24 The letter was signed and sent by Uenishi (BCA Archives, Correspondence Files, box no. 1.02.07, folder 1932).
25 The pact was made between Uenishi and Yosaku Yamashita (BCA Archives, Correspondence Files, box no.1.02.07, folder 1932).
26 Uenishi sent a petition (*shinseisho*) to Masuyama on 25 January 1932 (BCA Archives, Correspondence Files, box no.1.02.07, folder 1932).

27 Masuyama's correspondence to Eikichi Kagetsu, dated 30 July 1933 (BCA Archives, Correspondence Files, box no.1.02.07, folder 1932–1933).
28 However, Aoki resigned in June 1941 after which Bishop Matsukage of the BMNA served concurrently as Bishop of Canada (Y. Kawamura 1988b, 21–2).
29 Zesei Kawasaki's correspondence to Masuyama, dated 27 July. It seems that this letter was written between 1934 and 1938, reflecting his assignment in Vancouver (BCA Archives, Correspondence Files, box no.1.02.10).
30 Masuyama's correspondence to the Kyoto headquarters, dated 17 October 1933 (BCA Archives, Correspondence Files, box no.1.02.07, folder 1933–1934).
31 Seisho Ishiguro's correspondence to Bishop Masuyama, dated 11 February 1935 (BCA Archives, Correspondence Files, box no.1.02.09).
32 Gijin Taga's undated correspondence to the BMNA office (BCA Archives, Correspondence Files, box no.1.02.03, folder 1927–1928 16A).
33 The Shiga prefectural association in Vancouver was also divided into two groups in the late 1900s (Sasaki 1999, 208).
34 Ken Adachi states: "In the matter of a few decades, then, the Japanese built up a vast complex of associations and clubs, involving at least 230 units of secular and religious associations in British Columbia, of which 84 functioned in the Vancouver colony which contained, by the 1930s, nearly one-third of the province's Japanese population" (Adachi 1991, 122).
35 "Canada Young Buddhist League," *New Canadian*, 27 May 1939, 3; "*Bussei, Carry on!* National Meet Impresses Localities," *New Canadian*, 2 May 1941, 5; and Tsunemitsu 1964, 109–11. David Yoo has studied the ideas of the *nisei* Buddhist laity in the United States, who assumed the leadership at YBA meetings. For instance, Masao Kubose, who was later to be ordained at Higashi Honganji and founded the Buddhist Temple of Chicago in 1944, strongly believed that the *nisei* were capable of bridging the gap between Japan and the United States in the coming Pacific era. Manabu Fukuda stated that the Land of Buddha would serve as an alternative for those who could not be recognized in either Japan or the United States (Yoo 2000, 49–50).
36 See Fairview bukkyō seinenkai (1930) and Kitsilano bukkyō seinenkai (1935).
37 The Petition for Resident Minister signed by Yosaku Yamashita and five councillors of the *bukkyōkai* (BCA Archives, Correspondence Files, box no.1.02.07, folder 1932 Communications from District Temples T–Z).
38 This is the father of Masatoshi Nagatomi, the renowned professor of Buddhism at Harvard for more than four decades. See Harding (2010, 102, 144).
39 Correspondence from Yoichi Hironaka to Bishop Masuyama (BCA Archives, Correspondence Files, box no.1.02.07, folder 1933 Communications from Districts 1933 L–R).

For the activities of Hironaka, who contributed tremendously to the Raymond Buddhist Mission, see Y. Kawamura (1988a, 20–5, 156–61).
40 Correspondence from Yoichi Hironaka to Bishop Masuyama.
41 See also "Nisei Priest is Welcomed at Banquet," *New Canadian*, 7 November 1941, 5; and "Nisei Priest at Hompa Service," *New Canadian*, 21 November 1941, 5.

3

For the Benefit of Many: S.N. Goenka's Vipassana Meditation Movement in Canada

KORY GOLDBERG

In 1955, Satya Narayan Goenka, an Indian Hindu businessman born and raised in Burma (Myanmar),[1] learned the technique of Vipassana[2] meditation from Sayagyi U Ba Khin, a high-ranking Burmese government official and pioneering lay Theravada meditation master. With his teacher's encouragement, Goenka travelled to India in 1969 to disseminate Vipassana meditation in the country where the Buddha first discovered it. Since then, Goenka has established approximately 120 meditation centres worldwide, as well as one hundred other sites where ten-day silent, residential meditation courses are held. In 1979, Goenka travelled to Canada and France where he conducted the first of several ten-day Vipassana courses in Western contexts. Since the tradition's initial migration to Canada from India, regular Vipassana courses have been conducted all over the country by Goenka personally, or by his senior Canadian students. At present, three permanent centres have been established in Quebec, Ontario, and British Columbia, and two more are planned in Alberta and on Vancouver Island. To date, more than fifteen thousand people from all walks of Canadian life have attended these courses, and approximately 30 per cent have returned for at least a second course.

In this chapter, I identify the factors that account for the Goenka tradition's attraction and success. Particularly important, Goenka divorces the meditation practices from the religious aspects of Buddhism by depicting the Buddha's teachings as a secular, universal, and scientific technique consistent with the attitude of people in the modern world. To understand what draws Canadian spiritual seekers to Vipassana meditation and how Goenka's tradition has adapted to the multicultural Canadian context, I explore several avenues. I begin with a brief background description of Goenka's lay meditation lineage to highlight how his interpretation of the Buddha's teachings emerges from various interrelated global dynamics, from South Asian institutionalized monastic authority to Western colonial power and the aftermath of the Second World War. Next, I provide an overview of Goenka's ten-day, silent, residential course, followed by a discussion of common themes found throughout Goenka's teachings, practice, and organizational strategies that appeal to modern Canadian meditators: universalism, secularism, rationality, scientific objectivity, individualism, stress reduction, and egalitarianism. Steeped in an attitude of non-sectarianism, Goenka asserts that one does not need to convert to Buddhism to practise and benefit from Vipassana meditation. Following this discussion of how Goenka has reconceptualized the *Dhamma* (Skt. *Dharma*) to fit modern demands, I trace the development of Goenka's lay-oriented organization in Canada, briefly describing the principal locations where Vipassana courses are offered. I conclude by investigating cultural diversity and exchange at the centres as well as the challenges that arise when attempting to associate an identity with Vipassana meditators, especially in multicultural Canada.

BACKGROUND: S.N. GOENKA AND THE EMERGENCE OF A MODERN, GLOBAL TRADITION

Until a century ago meditation was practised primarily by ascetic, forest-dwelling monks in South Asia, whose secluded lifestyles were conducive to the cultivation of deep concentration. Sharf (1995) further argues that most of the practices of *bhāvana*, the Pali term used to denote meditation, consisted not of contemporary *vipassanā* or *zazen*, but primarily of chanting Buddhist texts, the aim of which was to accumulate merit rather than attain altered states of consciousness. However, in the beginning of the twentieth century a lay insight meditation movement began in Burma under the leadership and guidance of monks such as Ledi Sayadaw and U Narada, who authorized their advanced lay disciples to teach meditation (Vipassana Research Institute 1994, 82; Swearer 1989, 126). Shifting away from devotional practices and modifying meditation techniques to make them more suitable to lay practitioners, they place greater emphasis on the cultivation of insight (*vipassanā*) than on the cultivation of mental absorption (*jhānas*).³ Goenka, like his predecessors, stresses the importance of physical sensation (*vedanā*), the awareness of which can be maintained more easily during the quotidian life of a householder.

After the Second World War, the trend toward lay meditation became increasingly popular in Burma, resulting in the establishment of hundreds of centres, many operated by monks and a few by lay people. This sudden movement was fuelled by at least three factors: a desire to do intensive meditation, long frustrated by the institutionalized monopoly of the sangha; a new emphasis on lay-oriented methods; the stress stemming from the political aftermath of the war, Western colonial oppression, and the threats of Christian missionaries (Gombrich and Obeyesekere 1988; W. King 1980; Swearer 1989). King suggests that this "revolution" in access to meditation practice was more readily and widely effected in Burma than in Sri Lanka because of the ease with which the Burmese sangha may be entered, even temporarily for a few weeks, and left, at any age or stage (1980, 122–3).

The tradition of Vipassana meditation as taught by S.N. Goenka can be traced back to Venerable Ledi Sayadaw (1856–1923), the famous Burmese meditation master and scholar.[4] In his concern for all Buddhists to work toward their final salvation while there was time and opportunity, Ledi Sayadaw urged that everyone should at least begin meditation at their present level of spiritual development. The first lay Vipassana teacher was U Thet (1873–1945), a farmer who studied under Ledi Sayadaw for seven years, learning and perfecting his practice of the meditation technique. At the request of his teacher, U Thet began conducting regular Vipassana courses for his farming community. U Thet, or as he was later called, Saya Thetgyi,[5] quickly gained a reputation as a meditation master, and since his village was not far from Rangoon,[6] the capital of Burma, a number of government employees sought his teachings. One of these urban officials was U Ba Khin.

Sayagyi U Ba Khin began practising under the guidance of his teacher in 1937. On 4 January 1948, the day Burma gained independence, U Ba Khin became the nation's accountant general and for the next two decades worked in various capacities in the government, often holding two or more posts, each equivalent to the head of a department. U Ba Khin combined his responsibilities and skills as a civil servant with his strong commitment to the *Dhamma*. Webu Sayadaw, a monk revered throughout Burma, encouraged U Ba Khin to begin teaching meditation. In 1952, Sayagyi U Ba Khin established the International Meditation Center (IMC), two miles north of the famous Shwedagon Pagoda in Rangoon. At this centre, several Burmese and foreign students learned Vipassana meditation.

Despite his appreciation of the legacy of monastic institutions in Burma, which he acknowledged had preserved the *Dhamma*, U Ba Khin's pedagogical approach rarely referenced the traditional monastic world. Instead, his seminal lay institution was developed for intensive meditation practice by and for lay people.[7] Traditionally, monasteries in Asia neither taught laity the finer points of meditation nor offered them intensive residential meditation retreats. When U Ba Khin saw that lay people, like himself, sought serious instruction, he designed his ten-day course for modern individuals who wanted to engage with the Buddha's teachings on understanding and eliminating suffering. U Ba Khin retired from government service in 1967, and from that time until his death in January 1971, lived at IMC teaching Vipassana.

After experiencing severe migraine headaches that could be attenuated only by morphine, S.N. Goenka, a Hindu businessman born and raised in Buddhist Burma, decided to seek other, non-habit-forming remedies. A friend suggested that he learn Vipassana meditation from Sayagyi U Ba Khin. Goenka was reluctant to join, feeling that doing so would be a betrayal of his native religion. The Burmese teacher explained that Vipassana could be undertaken as a universal mind training exercise without converting to Buddhism. By the end of his first course with U Ba Khin, Goenka's migraines disappeared and he continued to practise under the tutelage of his teacher.

Fourteen years later, in 1969, Goenka emigrated to India, in part to take care of his ailing mother but also to fulfill his teacher's wish of returning the *Dhamma* to its country of origin. According to Goenka, U Ba Khin believed that doing so would serve as a means of paying the spiritual debt that Burma owed to India, where the Buddha's teachings had been lost. Moreover, this action would provide momentum for the second era of the Buddha's teaching (*sāsana*) which would spread around the world only after becoming established in India. Goenka asserts that his teacher's mission was not to convert people to Buddhism but to help people from all walks of life eliminate their suffering. U Ba Khin was eager to perform this task, but was unable to do so because the Burmese government did not provide passports to its citizens for foreign travel. Thus, he left the task to his Indian student (Goenka 1994, 20–1; 140–1).

During the first seven years of his tenure in India, courses were held at rented sites: schools, colleges, community centres, Hindu and Buddhist temples and monasteries, and mosques. Due to Goenka's universalist, scientific, and pragmatic approach to meditation, participants generally accepted his non-religious interpretation of the Buddha's teaching.[8] Goenka's vibrant teaching style included the strict discipline of a meditation master combined with lightheartedness and humour. His famous saying during the ten-day course is "be happy," and his discourses are laden with jokes, lively parables from the major Indian religious traditions, and colourful stories from his own personal experience to highlight how ordinary, secular, and religious lay people from all walks of life can benefit from the Vipassana technique.

In 1971, Goenka set up a trust known as the "Sayagyi U Ba Khin Memorial Trust" to give concrete shape to his teacher's goal to disseminate Vipassana in India. Soon the search began for a suitable site for the first Vipassana meditation centre. In 1974 a twenty-acre hilltop at Igatpuri, about 140 km from Mumbai, was purchased and Goenka named the centre *Dhamma Giri* (Hill of *Dhamma*). A handful of Goenka's students, including a few Canadians, stayed in an old building dating back to the British era, and meditated on the land as workers constructed the meditation hall, kitchen, dining hall, and residences. In a short time the courses at Dhamma Giri became increasingly popular and attracted spiritual seekers from around the world. Today, Dhamma Giri, the principal Vipassana meditation centre, where approximately one million people have taken courses of ten days or longer, is only one of forty-five centres in India.[9]

In 1979, Goenka travelled to Europe and Canada, where he conducted the first of several ten-day Vipassana courses outside India, and he returned to North America, Europe, and Australia regularly until the late 1990s. Since the tradition's initial migration to Canada from Burma and India, regular ten-day Vipassana courses have been conducted all over the country by Goenka personally or by his senior Canadian students. Goenka appointed his first assistant-teachers in late 1981 to conduct Vipassana courses via audio and videotape to help him meet the growing demand.[10] These assistants play Goenka's chanting,[11] instructions, and evening discourses and are responsible for guiding students in their meditation practice and overseeing the daily operations of the permanent centres and rented sites. These appointed assistants are dedicated students who have been meditating and volunteering on courses for many years. At present, there are approximately forty assistant-teachers in Canada, eight hundred in India, and twelve hundred worldwide.

Since Goenka began teaching globally with the help of his assistant-teachers, ten-day courses have been held at approximately 120 permanent centres in thirty different countries, as well as at rented sites in eighty-five countries. These courses are offered in thirty-one different languages. In Canada, the provinces of Quebec, Ontario, and British Columbia each have a permanent centre. Worldwide, Vipassana courses are now conducted for primary, secondary, and post-secondary students, prisoners, management trainees, police officers, bureaucrats, homeless people, and the visually impaired, indicating its potential force as a tool for both individual liberation and social transformation.

THE TEN-DAY COURSE

Buddhaṃ saranaṃ gacchāmi. Dhammaṃ saranaṃ gacchāmi. Sanghaṃ saranaṃ gacchāmi. "I take refuge in the Buddha. I take refuge in the *Dhamma*. I take refuge in the Sangha." With these words a student begins a ten-day Vipassana course in the tradition of S.N. Goenka. Recitation of the chant is known as taking refuge in the "Triple Gem" and is generally considered by Buddhists to be a declaration of being a Buddhist. However, Goenka (1987, 39–40) explains that this opening ceremony is not concerned with religious affiliation, but is instead an acknowledgment of one's aspiration to attain the quality of enlightenment as epitomized by the Buddha, to practise the universal teachings of the Buddha, and to express gratitude for and acknowledge the inspiration of the community of practitioners who have preserved the Buddha's teachings by attaining liberation themselves.

Goenka's teaching of Vipassana meditation is based on the Buddha's Noble Eightfold Path, a central doctrine accepted by most Buddhist traditions. The path is divided into three sections: morality (*sīla*), concentration (*samādhi*), and wisdom (*paññā*). To practise morality, Goenka's students vow to follow the traditional five precepts for the duration of the course: to abstain from killing, stealing, sexual misconduct, speaking falsely, and consuming intoxicants. For students who have taken one or more courses with Goenka or his assistant-teachers, an additional three precepts are included: to abstain from eating after midday; to abstain from bodily decorations and sensual pleasures; and to not sleep on high or luxurious beds. This simple code of conduct is said to prevent behaviours that agitate the mind, thus making it possible to perform the task of developing concentration and self-observation.

To develop concentration, students are taught *ānāpāna sati*, or observation of respiration. After three days of observing the breath and not speaking to anyone except the teacher to ask questions for clarification about the practice, the mind becomes focused enough to develop *paññā* (wisdom) through the practice of Vipassana meditation. In the technique taught by Goenka, Vipassana involves the development of awareness and equanimity toward all bodily sensations. By mentally scanning the body without generating craving for pleasant sensations or aversion toward unpleasant sensations, the meditator generates an understanding that all sensations have the same characteristic of arising and passing away (*anicca*). According to Goenka, this comprehension leads to insight into the two other characteristics of all phenomena: no-self (*anattā*) and dissatisfaction (*dukkha*). By realizing the transient nature of the body and mind, one comes to see that the sense of self or ego developed toward them is illusory and that any attachment to this self results in dissatisfaction. Direct realization of these three insights leads to the cultivation of wisdom and eventually to *nibbāna*, or liberation from existential suffering.

On the morning of the tenth day of the course, prior to breaking their silence, the students learn the technique of loving-kindness (*mettā-bhāvanā*). This practice entails the generation of loving-kindness toward oneself and sharing this feeling and the merits accrued during one's practice with all sentient beings. This aspect of the teaching initiates a harmonious integration back into the world.

RECREATING PRACTICE, RETHINKING DOCTRINE:
UNIVERSAL, NON-SECTARIAN, EGALITARIAN PRACTICE

In speaking with dozens of Canadian meditators,[12] I discovered several common themes that highlight the appeal of Vipassana meditation: a secular and "spiritual but not religious" approach, universally applicable ideas and practices, rational and scientific terminology used to explain the process of introspection, a sense of individualism and self-reliance, therapeutic benefits, and a feeling of egalitarianism. These themes, in conjunction with sentiments of disappointment with the Judeo-Christian monotheistic traditions in which most Canadians are born, and a feeling of disillusionment with Western materialism, are indicative of the shift toward a lay-oriented meditation practice that has influenced, and been influenced by, Western conceptions of modernity. Goenka has reconceptualized Buddhist doctrine, history, and practice as a secular, universal, and scientific process for understanding the relationship between the mind and body. This modernist interpretation enables Goenka, who is not a Buddhist, to assert that one does not need to convert to Buddhism to practise and benefit from Vipassana meditation.

When he began teaching Vipassana in India, especially to modern, secular, middle- and upper-class Indians, as well as Western spiritual seekers, Goenka quickly realized that he needed to shift away from the religious dimensions of the practice common in Burma,[13] if it were to successfully attract people. Goenka's caution toward framing the *Dhamma* in religious terms is also meant to eliminate the various misperceptions of the Buddha in India.[14]

Goenka's innovation of secular insight meditation practice has instigated a wider trend in Western meditation circles since the 1970s.[15] Distinguishing between "Buddhism" and "the teachings of the Buddha" or the "*Dhamma*," Goenka maintains that the former is an organized and sectarian religion; the latter is a universal, scientific practice aimed at understanding the interaction between mind and matter. Stephen Batchelor (1998) articulates this type of divergence by drawing a contrast between "religious Buddhism" and "dharma practice," or as he puts it "Buddhism without Beliefs." This agnostic approach to spiritual practice acknowledges a strong tendency toward secularization in the re-rendering of Buddhism in culturally appropriate terms for Westerners who, from the 1970s, began to practise meditation seriously in significant numbers. In confronting Western modernity, Goenka, influenced by his teacher, has instigated a global trend in reinterpreting canonical texts and encouraging serious practice of meditation as the key to the *Dhamma*. He dismisses rituals as accretions on the original teaching. While respectful of monastic authority, he has not hesitated to question received traditions and has urged a focus not only on academic study but also on practice. "Vipassana," as Goenka asserted in his talk at the United Nations Millennium World Peace Summit, is not an organized religion and "involves no dogma, rites, rituals, conversion." Vipassana, which he labels a form of "universal spirituality," is not a religious organization aimed at converting people to its sect. He states, "The only conversion is from misery to happiness, from bondage to liberation, and from cruelty to compassion" (Goenka 2000). Thus, the majority of Vipassana practitioners in North America with whom I spoke insist that Vipassana is a "technique" or "way of life" quite distinct from "religion," including various forms of Buddhism whose ritual, hierarchy, and dogma are not dissimilar to the Judeo-Christian traditions that they have left behind. In keeping with the notion of a universal and nonsectarian practice, as well as to emphasize the qualities of enlightenment rather than a specific person, none of Goenka's centres displays images of the Buddha.[16] As one meditator from Ontario stated, "there's no bowing down to any invisible gods or exotic statues ... you don't need to change your name, your clothes, or your friends." While some meditators, especially those from Buddhist backgrounds or those who possess a natural inclination toward language, may feel a calling to learn more on their own about Goenka's Pali chanting, most in North America do not.

Despite the skeptical attitudes toward religion that many meditators express, it is not uncommon to find devout adherents from most major religious traditions present at centres in North America. Laity as well as religious specialists such as Roman Catholic monks and nuns, Protestant preachers, Jesuit priests, Muslim imams, Jewish rabbis, Buddhist *bhikkhus*, and Hindu *sannyasis* have found Goenka's adaptation of the Buddha's teaching to be a useful tool in their lives that is not incongruent with their religious beliefs. In many cases these religious practitioners have implemented Vipassana meditation within their own respective systems. The universal presentation of the practice has constructed a bridge whereby ideological differences can be crossed over without fear of conversion. Goenka writes: "This can be practiced by one and all. The disease is not sectarian, therefore the remedy cannot be sectarian: it must be universal. Everyone faces the problem of suffering. When one suffers from anger, it is not Buddhist anger, Hindu anger, Christian anger. Anger is anger ... The malady is universal. The remedy must also be universal" (Goenka 1994, 108).

Novice students often approach the technique as a therapy or self-help method that will enable them to cope with the daily pressures of modern life and help them understand how they are responsible for their own happiness or suffering. Veteran practitioners who possess theoretical insight into the practice also understand Vipassana as highly therapeutic, although they do not reduce it solely to stress reduction.[17] For most of these "old students," as anyone who has taken at least one ten-day course with Goenka is called, Vipassana is articulated in terms of the Four Noble Truths framework that analyses the ways in which the mind possesses the potential to create or eradicate existential dissatisfaction and lead to ultimate liberation from psychological defilements.

Egalitarianism is another important feature that has helped many of Goenka's students to deepen their commitments to both the practice and the organization. The individualistic and self-reliant approach of Vipassana enables meditators to progress in the practice according to their own capabilities, not the directions or pressures of an external source. The experience is direct and immediate, and is not mediated by some authority figure.

The practice is also egalitarian in that it remains accessible to anyone regardless of race, gender, religion, political affiliation, or economic status. The number of spaces available for men and women is roughly equal, although in some centres in North America there are a few more spaces available for women because the demand for courses by women is approximately 30 per cent higher. The number of men and women assistant-teachers and trust members is approximately the same. Most of Goenka's assistants teach only to their gender and, in the rare instances where a single person conducts courses, that person is often a woman.[18] Courses are also increasingly made available for those who are incarcerated.[19] The features of self-reliance and open access provide equal opportunities for people to explore themselves in ways that may have been previously absent in their lives.

Courses are also offered free of charge, including the cost of food and accommodation, and entry is permitted on a first-come-first-serve basis, thus making the teaching accessible to all economic groups. With the exception of ongoing administrative duties and maintenance, where a small number of old students may receive a stipend depending on need, courses operate solely by the work of volunteers who guide the meditation, coordinate the courses, cook the food, clean the centre, ring the gongs, and attend to the needs of students. This non-commercial attitude requires all assistant-teachers and trust members to have livelihoods independent from their *Dhamma* work. In addition to the organization's cultural diversity, as I discuss below, occupations of the old students range widely: doctors, lawyers, teachers, computer programmers, farmers, writers, construction workers, graphic designers, administrators, and so forth. All course expenses are met by donations from people who, having completed at least one ten-day course, believe that they have felt the benefits from the practice and wish to give others the opportunity to experience the same.

Egalitarianism is further expressed by the institution's organizational structure, and is not dissimilar to what Prebish (1999; 2002) refers to as the "democratization" of the sangha. While Goenka has established strict guidelines for teaching Vipassana, he encourages the individual centres to manage themselves independently. A team of assistant-teachers who transmit the teaching of Vipassana[20] directs each of the centres and a board of trustees manages the daily operations. Decisions among both groups are generally reached through dialogue and consensus. Gender, racial, social, and class differences may be evident, although these distinctions do not shape the power dynamics of the organization.

The centres operate independently from one another, although assistant-teachers from the different centres periodically meet to discuss common challenges. The centres also maintain some connection to Dhamma Giri, the principal centre in India, by sending annual reports to Goenka and his senior deputies. Some senior students and assistant-teachers also travel to India to meet with Goenka to receive guidance and to take part in advanced courses at the larger centres.

VIPASSANA MEDITATION IN CANADA: AN OVERVIEW

The third course given personally by Goenka outside India was in Montreal, Quebec. Twenty years later, in September 1999, after numerous courses conducted in rented locations either by Goenka or one of his assistants, a thirty-four acre conference/retreat centre was purchased in Sutton, Quebec, becoming the first Vipassana meditation centre in Canada (see illustration 1). Goenka named the centre *Dhamma Suttama*, or Excellence in Dhamma, and since its inception, it has been holding regular ten-day courses and other courses in English and French for up to fifty students at a time (with approximately 120 applicants per course). Occasional eight-day, three-day, and one-day courses are offered to returning students, as well as one-day courses designed for children and adolescents.[21] Since the early 1980s, Goenka's students have organized periodic courses at rented sites all over Canada. In 2003 enough funds were amassed to purchase a 140-acre boy-scout camp in Alliston, Ontario. As in Quebec, *Dhamma Torana* (Gateway of Dhamma) holds a variety of courses for up to seventy-three students at a time.[22] In 2000, a group of Goenka's students bought a forty-acre plot of land in Merritt, British Columbia and constructed a custom-designed meditation centre to hold courses for fifty-two students at a time. As with the other centres, demand for courses at *Dhamma Surabhi* (Fragrance of Dhamma) has exploded and the numbers on the waiting list are more than double the number of available spots.[23] In other words, the organization cannot keep up with the demand for ten-day courses in Canada as approximately six hundred applicants are turned away from these centres on a monthly basis. To date, more than fifteen thousand people have attended ten-day Vipassana courses in Canada.

The centres in Ontario and British Columbia offer courses primarily in English, whereas the courses in Quebec are conducted in English and French. All these centres have recorded translations available in thirty-one languages, and it is not uncommon for centres to offer individual instructions to students on personal CD and MP3 players, especially in Ontario where courses often occur in five different languages. In these instances, the students must have a working knowledge of English (or French in Quebec) to communicate with the teacher. Every year, the BC centre also offers bilingual courses in English-Hindi, English-Farsi, and English-Burmese, while the Ontario centre also offers these, as well as courses in English-Cantonese-Mandarin, English-Khmer, and English-Russian-Polish.[24]

To date, each of these centres has welcomed approximately five thousand students, while thousands more have been turned away due to a lack of space. Courses at all these centres are usually booked within five days of the course offering (four months in advance) and the course that happens over the new year is generally booked within twenty-four hours of the opening of registration, with people beginning to register at midnight in the hope that they will secure a space. Recently, in February 2011, a former boarding school was purchased near Montebello, Quebec, and courses for one hundred students began in May 2011. Two years later the main building has been expanded to accommodate 150 students. Land for a second centre in British Columbia has been donated on Vancouver Island and land in Alberta has been purchased, which the organization hopes will ease the long waiting lists at Dhamma Surabhi.

Vipassana courses are also now being offered at the Po Lam Buddhist Association in Chilliwack, British Columbia. The Venerable Sik Yin Kit, abbess of this ethno-religious hybrid nunnery, is both a disciple of Venerable Sing Yat, ninth patriarch of Weiyang House of Chan in Hong Kong and an assistant-teacher of S.N. Goenka.[25] In addition to her ritual and social responsibilities as abbess of a Buddhist Chan temple, since 2006 she has organized and conducted three ten-day Vipassana courses and six one-day courses per year. These courses were offered in Cantonese, Mandarin, and English, and were restricted to women. The abbess is expanding the convent's facilities, which will eventually permit up to ten courses per year for sixty people. The Vipassana courses are strictly funded by donations from students who have taken at least one ten-day Vipassana course, in line with Goenka's guidance that Vipassana courses should be funded entirely by sincere old students.

The six nuns at Po Lam not only study and chant Mahayana *sutras*, but they also take at least one ten-day course per year and practise Vipassana every day for a minimum of two hours as part of their spiritual training. Approximately 60 per cent of the two hundred congregation members[26] also practise Vipassana and consider themselves Buddhist. Po Lam is unique, not only because of its blending of "religious Buddhism" and "dharma practice," to borrow Batchelor's (1998) terms, but also in the way it has found inspiration in a lay movement to further its monastic agenda. Modern Buddhism, as discussed earlier in the chapter, is often characterized as a transition from monastic-based practice to lay practice; however, in the case of Po Lam, the opposite holds true.

Po Lam is also a good example of what many scholars, such as Bodhi (2009b), Bond (1996), S. King (2005), and Queen (2000), as well as Buddhist leaders such as the Dalai Lama, Thich Nhat Hanh, and Sulak Sivaraksa, refer to as "Engaged Buddhism." Beyond serving the Chinese community's ritual and contemplative needs, Po Lam also operates the Compassionate Centre for Health which strives to provide emotional and spiritual counselling in Cantonese, Mandarin, and English to the elderly, the ill, their family members and caregivers. The volunteers consist of Po Lam's nuns, as well as approximately fifty lay devotees, many of whom have recovered or who are recovering from cancer. These volunteers, most of whom are also Vipassana meditators, visit patients and their families at home or in hospitals and chant sutras on their behalf, listen to their stories, offer advice, and in some cases, meditate with them.

WHO IS A VIPASSANA MEDITATOR?

While determining the number of Buddhists in Canada is difficult due to imprecise census statistics (Beyer 2010), providing an accurate number of Vipassana meditators is impossible. Of course, one may determine the number of students who have taken a course, but the number of people who continue the practice must be estimated by the number of old students who return for at least a second course. However, this approach is problematic because there is not a precise definition of what it means to be a "Vipassana meditator." Does the definition include anyone who identifies as a meditator? Or is the definition limited to those who follow Goenka's guidelines of practice, i.e., those who maintain the five precepts in their daily lives, practise formally for at least two hours per day, and take at least one course of ten days or longer per year?[27]

Moreover, it is not possible to classify Vipassana meditators in Canada because they do not fit into any of the typical categories for identifying Buddhists in the West (see Harding, Hori, and Soucy 2010; Nattier 1998; Prebish 1979, 1999, 2002; Tweed 1999). Just as the terms "ethnic," "Asian," "Western," "import," "export," "evangelical," "elite," "convert," or "night stand" used by these scholars are imprecise when describing Buddhists in Canada, they are even more problematic when discussing Vipassana meditators who hail from diverse backgrounds. In general, Canadian meditators either identify themselves as secular and non-religious, or still hold on to the liberal branches of the religious traditions in which they were born. Very few identify as Buddhists unless they were born into that tradition. Most of the people taking courses are similar to what Tweed (1999) refers to as "sympathizers." Among Vipassana meditators there is no claim toward the formation of a "sangha" either in the traditional sense of a community of monks and nuns, or in the modern sense that encompasses lay people. At best, it is a loosely knit group of people who get together to share something that they have in common. Old students often gather to meditate together for one-hour, half-day, or full-day meditation sessions. Old students in most major cities throughout the world organize these gatherings through the closest Vipassana centre. At present, there are five cities in Quebec, eleven in Ontario, six in British Columbia, two in Alberta, one in Saskatchewan, one in Manitoba, and one in Nova Scotia hosting such gatherings. These sessions provide meditators with the necessary support to deepen their practice while dealing with the vicissitudes of daily life. For many, joining weekly gatherings, participating in trust meetings and committee work, and attending courses at the nearest centre (or abroad in India) often create feelings of allegiance and unity, sustain individuals' practice, and help the community of meditators to flourish, albeit in a loosely knit and general manner.

Every Goenka centre around the world offers identical courses, yet their specific cultural and geographic positions result in local particularities (see Wilson 2009). Goenka's universalist and secular position has created the conditions for the emergence of a multilingual, multicultural, and transnational community of meditators. Canada's multicultural and multilingual situation has created a demand for bilingual and trilingual courses. More than half of the participants on these bi and trilingual courses come from the community associated with the additional language(s). Several months before the course, old students from the given community organize information sessions at community centres, schools, or homes where a video is shown introducing Vipassana and questions about the technique are answered. These courses are also coordinated and conducted by assistant-teachers and other volunteers from these communities, enabling a smoother process of spiritual and cultural translation that is genuine and comfortable.

These multicultural and multilinguistic courses also enable intercultural experiences. People from diverse backgrounds not only learn to meditate together but they often share their experiences at the end of the course once the silence is broken, and in some cases, exchange coordinates to meditate and socialize together. Moreover, old students who volunteer for ten days on a course intimately learn from other volunteers about cultural world views different from their own. The communal and intercultural experience is integrated into one's routine at the centre as awareness is catalyzed through outward activity. These courses, as well as the management of the centres,[28] allow for cultural differences to be acknowledged and accepted and a sense of belonging and unity to be fostered.

Food is another way in which intercultural experiences occur at the centres.[29] Unlike centres in countries with less cultural diversity, where the food is representative of a single group (for example, in India, Thailand, Japan, Italy, or Mexico), North American centres serve a global, cosmopolitan, vegetarian fare: rice and steamed vegetables, spaghetti with primavera sauce, tofu steaks, stir-fried noodles, veggie burgers, tortillas, stews, salads, etc. Most centres in North America also feature an "Indian"" day, an implicit nod toward the tradition's relationship to India. The Ontario centre, with its high number of Indo-Canadian meditators, usually has multiple Indian food days. On the bi- and trilingual courses food is prepared by old students from the targeted communities.

The Vipassana meditation movement changes as it adapts to the local Canadian conditions and the local contexts change as Vipassana centres become established. In this manner, globalization and localization are not discordant and, as Harding, Hori, and Soucy (2010, 8) write, "Every adaptation is both an example of the global becoming local, and the local going global." Goenka's organization has adapted itself to the cultural, linguistic, and, as evidenced at Po Lam, religious needs of meditators.

Contemporary Vipassana practice in Canada has not been tailored specifically to the Canadian context; instead, it addresses whatever local issues may arise. Goenka's Vipassana movement is not, and never has been, a static or rigid entity, but is rather a dynamic and evolving tradition that emanated from Asia and is now unfolding everywhere around the globe. The way the movement has adapted to the multicultural Canadian context and accommodates to students coming from various backgrounds is indicative of its flexibility. The development of Vipassana meditation in Canada is simply one link connected to an expanding global chain of centres and practitioners.

CONCLUSION

By analysing the way Goenka has reconstructed the history, doctrine, and practice of the *Dhamma* as a secular, universal, and scientific process of understanding the relationship between mind and body, I have shown some of the changes a contemplative tradition undergoes as it crosses geographical, ethnic, cultural, and religious borders.

Vipassana is a modern, transcultural movement that cannot be categorized by race, ethnicity, or nationality. However, its Burmese-Indian hybrid manifestations inevitably change as it penetrates human boundaries. The unique features of Vipassana in Canada have to do not so much with the practice but with the tradition's ability to adapt on an organizational level to the issues that arise in a multicultural environment. At the same time, these changes are not sufficient to label the movement *Canadian* Vipassana, and I am unsure that even exploring this question is a useful endeavour (see Soucy 2010).

Attempting to understand the Vipassana movement purely from a cultural standpoint is limited and the conclusions derived, as demonstrated by earlier studies of Buddhism in the West (see Harding, Hori, and Soucy 2010), would be simplistic and fallacious. As these authors argue, isolating a tradition from its earlier historical and cultural expressions disguises the profound changes that practice of the Buddha's teachings in Asia experienced as a response to Western hegemonic rule. In this way, the adaptation of Vipassana to Canadian culture is not simply a unique event in modern history but is a part of an evolving global manifestation of the way the *Dhamma* is practised, which began in the nineteenth century when Buddhism first collided with Western colonial powers. As Soucy (2010) and V. Hori (2010a) contend, there are no "pure" forms of Buddhism, or any other tradition for that matter. Constant adaptation and renewal are common for any religious movement. From this perspective, Vipassana as a global phenomenon can be understood only in relation to its historical experience in Burma and India, as well as to its local manifestations in Canada and elsewhere. Moreover, in a diverse country such as Canada, the movement can be understood only in its specific locality because, as I have demonstrated, it has quite distinct developments in different parts of the country due to regional and demographic differences.

From a cultural perspective, Vipassana both influences the evolution of Canadian culture and is also influenced by it. On the one hand, Vipassana plays a role in the formation of people's world views as Canadians as they integrate their spiritual insights into the ways in which they behave as social, economic, and political actors. As Canadians increasingly use this introspective tool, their values, beliefs, and behaviours shift away from, or in some cases, expand upon, their existing world views. On the other hand, public and personal perception of Vipassana continues to evolve as it interacts with other technologies available in the West. The internet and audio-visual technologies have contributed to the wide dissemination of the practice. Scientific research and analysis also provide new mediums for communicating and evaluating the effects of Vipassana on the individual and society, and postmodern and feminist praxis have provided space and opportunity for women practitioners and teachers.

The Vipassana movement is not creating a separate fabric in Canada, but is becoming part of the rich, complex, and evolving tapestry. As centres develop and expand, as meditators from different backgrounds unite to support each other's practices, and as Vipassana practice integrates into public spheres in flexible, non-elitist, and non-exclusive ways, it becomes increasingly clear how and why Canadians are drawn to this paradigm. As long as people are not required to self-identify as "Vipassana members" or to let go of existing beliefs and traditions, and as long as they experience tangible, therapeutic benefits, Vipassana will continue to flourish in our landscape.

NOTES

1 In 1989 the military government officially changed the country's name to "Republic of the Union of Myanmar." Many local opposition groups and countries (including Canada) still refer to it as Burma.
2 In this chapter I write *vipassanā* to refer to the Pali term for "insight" and use Vipassana to refer to both the meditation practice and tradition of S.N. Goenka.
3 For a detailed explanation of these meditative paths, see Gethin (1998); Gunaratna (1985); W. King (1980); and Sole-Leris (1986).
4 The background presented here is based on Ahir (1999), Goenka (1987, 1994, 2006), Hart (1987), Ledi Sayadaw (1999), Vipassana Research Institute's publications (1994), as well as conversations with some of Goenka's senior students.
5 *Saya* means "teacher" and *gyi* is a suffix denoting respect.
6 Present-day Yangon.
7 With that said, many monks and nuns learned meditation from U Ba Khin. Similarly, Goenka's courses have also been embraced by both Theravada and Mahayana monastic communities all over Asia. Many of Goenka's assistant-teachers in Myanmar, Thailand, Sri Lanka, Cambodia, India, Mongolia, Taiwan, and Hong Kong are monks

and nuns. An increasing number of courses are also being held exclusively for the monastic community.

8   There have been a few cases of Brahmin priests and Buddhist monks resisting Goenka's courses for religious-political reasons, but none was able to garner sufficient support to impede Goenka's *Dhamma* mission. See note 14 below.

9   Advanced twenty-day, thirty-day, forty-five-day, and sixty-day courses are offered at Dhamma Giri and other large centres in Jaipur (Dhamma Thali), Hyderabad (Dhamma Khetta), and Gujarat (Dhamma Sindhu).

10 The audio-visual technology allows every course given around the world to be the same. This standardization enables students to receive identical instruction wherever they are and in their mother tongue since Goenka's Hindi and English teachings have been translated into twenty-nine other languages by his senior students.

11 Every morning students hear Goenka chant both traditional Pali verses and his own Hindi couplets. These compositions express homage to the Triple Gem, request spiritual protection, and project Goenka's feelings of goodwill toward all beings (*mettā*). The chanting is believed to provide a congenial and supportive atmosphere in which Vipassana can be practised. Translations are not available to students during courses but those who are interested have access to Goenka's *The Gem Set in Gold: Dhamma Chanting from the Ten Day Course in Vipassana Meditation* (2006) at the end of the course and may purchase it online from various Buddhist book suppliers.

12 Since 1997 I have informally interviewed and observed dozens of Canadian, American, and Burmese meditators from diverse social, economic, and cultural backgrounds at Goenka's centres in Canada and India.

13 In Myanmar, Goenka's five established centres serve as a place of practice for thousands of students who identify themselves as Buddhist. Western and Indian students, however, identify with the assertion that one does not need to be Buddhist to practise Vipassana meditation.

14 There has been much hostility toward Buddhism in India for two primary reasons. First, after the eighth century, Hindus appropriated the Buddha into their religious culture by portraying the Buddha, who was critical of Brahmanic authority and ritual practice and whose community enjoyed royal patronage from the third century BCE to the eight century CE, as a divine charlatan. The *Buddhavatara Puranas* (popular myths describing the lives of the gods) depicts the Buddha as an avatar of the god Vishnu and born from the mouth of Brahma. The purpose of his incarnation was to lead the wicked and demonic away from the truth in this age of degeneration (*kali yuga*). This attitude has created highly ambivalent feelings toward Buddhists to this day (see Holt 2004), and Goenka, who sees the Buddha neither as a devil nor a god,

but a great human contributor to the Indian intellectual and contemplative tradition, wishes to derail these Brahmanical assimilations and representations. Goenka's primary methods of doing so are through his courses, writings, televised discourses, and the construction of the Global Pagoda, the world's second largest pagoda (after Shwedagon Pagoda in Yangon) and largest hollow dome. Visitors to the pagoda can receive meditation instruction and learn about the Buddha's life, according to a critical reading of the Pali texts, through multimedia technologies. Second, political association with the modern Ambedkarite Dalit movement that has embraced Buddhism as a tool of resistance against systemic caste-based prejudice and oppression has created a one-sided image of Buddhism in the middle- and upper-caste Indian imagination (see Doyle 2003).

15 Several contemporary Vipassana teachers affiliated with the Insight Meditation Society (IMS) network such as Joseph Goldstein, Sharon Salzberg, and Daniel Goleman took courses with Goenka in the late 1960s and early 1970s. The ten-day models used by these teachers and others who teach under them are inspired by Goenka's course framework.

16 However, in the South Asian Buddhist countries, where explicit devotionalism is built into the culture, Goenka has permitted the centres to build a shrine room where students may express their devotion in front of the statues after or between courses. The meditation halls, however, do not have images.

17 By freeing the mind from the yearnings and memories of the past and hopes, fears, and expectations of the future, and allowing it to rest in the present reality as it is, certain therapeutic actions have the potential to develop within the meditator. Fleischman (1999, 38) writes that these actions include:

> increased self-knowledge, deepened human trust and participation, integration with and acceptance of one's past, deepened activation of one's will, an increased sense of responsibility for one's own fate; greater concentration, deepened ethical commitments, firm yet flexible life structures and disciplines, fluid access to deeper streams of feeling and imagery, expanded historical and contemporary community; prepared confrontation with core realities such as time, change, death, loss, pain leading to an eventual diminution of dread, anxiety, and delusion; fuller body-mind integration, decreased narcissism, and a fuller panorama of character strengths such as generosity, compassion, and human love. (Fleischman 1999, 38)

18 In India, the situation is generally the opposite since more men attend courses. It is also not unusual for a man to conduct a course for both genders whereas it is unheard of for a woman assistant-teacher to do so. These differences have less to do with gender discrimination within the organization and more with Indian social

norms. In the West, on the other hand, this practice prevents sexual misunderstandings and inappropriate situations, not uncommon in Western spiritual centres (see Edelstein 2011; Kramer and Alstad 1993).

19 See Donnenfield (1997) and Menahemi and Ariel (1997).
20 These assistant-teachers tend to have their closest association with the centre nearest to their place of residence, but they are not bound to any one centre and often travel to teach in different parts of the world.
21 In 2010, the centre held 21 ten-day courses attended by 1,128 students, 2 eight-day courses for 70 students, four three-day courses for 204 students, 4 one-day courses for 127 students, and 5 youth courses for 709 students. A total of 258 old students volunteered on these courses.
22 In 2010, Dhamma Torana held 20 ten-day courses attended by 1,304 students, 2 eight-day courses for 79 students, 2 three-day courses for 118 students, and one twenty-day course for 34 students. Two hundred and eighty-seven old students volunteered on these courses.
23 In 2010, Dhamma Surabhi held 21 ten-day courses attended by 900 students, 2 eight-day courses for 88 students, 3 three-day courses for 103 students, and 5 youth courses for 108 students. Two hundred and thirty-eight old students volunteered on these courses.
24 Depending on the demand, the English-Hindi course and English-Cantonese-Mandarin courses are usually offered twice a year. Dhamma Sikhāra, the centre in Dharamsala, India, has the largest multilingual courses in the world. The average course is conducted in nine different languages and it is not uncommon to observe up to thirteen languages in use such as Hindi, English, Marathi, Gujarati, Hebrew, Japanese, Russian, Polish, French, Spanish, German, Portuguese, Italian, Cantonese, and Mandarin.
25 The abbess is considered an outstanding leader for both men and women in the BC Chinese community, as well as for Chinese Canadians and Americans who practise Vipassana meditation (she conducts most of the Cantonese-Mandarin-English courses in North America). Since 2006, she has also taught meditation and provided counselling to a dozen women in a BC correctional institute.
26 Of Po Lam's members, 70 per cent are Chinese and 70 per cent are women.
27 Or, is the definition even more narrowed down to "serious old students" who follow the five precepts, practise at least two hours per day for two years, have taken at least five ten-day courses, and one special eight-day course based on the *Satipaṭṭhāna Sutta*, and have volunteered on at least one ten-day course? These students have access to advanced courses ranging between twenty to sixty days.

28 For instance, the board of trustees for the Ontario and British Columbia centres include meditators with Indian, Chinese, Burmese, Sri Lankan, Russian, Iranian, and Western European backgrounds.

29 All food at every centre is strictly vegetarian.

4

Sitavana: The Theravada Forest Tradition in British Columbia[1]

JAMES PLACZEK

This chapter looks at Sitavana Birken Forest Monastery,[2] a Buddhist temple-monastery near Knutsford, British Columbia. The chapter attempts to evaluate the subtle degrees of historical adaptation of two Theravada Buddhist traditions (those of Sri Lanka and the Thai Forest Tradition) to the Canadian culture and environment as found in the lower mainland and central region of the province. A related issue, which came to a head in 2009, is a lineage controversy over attempts to revive female ordination in Theravada. The controversy raises questions about the historical and contemporary mechanisms of rule change in Theravada, as reflected in the Thai Forest Tradition. This chapter argues that Birken has been gravitating toward this tradition as part of its process of cultural adaptation. The arguments are based on the premise that the way in which a Buddhist group relates to the Buddhist rules of discipline (*vinaya*) defines whether it is Theravada or not.

BIRKEN FOREST MONASTERY: A BRIEF HISTORY[3]

The antecedents of Sitavana lie in the Birken Forest near Pemberton, BC. This was an area favoured by Tom West, an accomplished musician and a married man who has a deep reverence for what he has called "the healing power of the forest" and an appreciation of the benefits of solitary life in the forest, the life of a hermit (see illustration 2).

Around the years 1985–86 he was living in a hermitage in Birken Forest, which he affectionately (or accurately) called "the shack." This was the first phase of Birken, usually called "Birken I." He then travelled to the Bhavana

Society in West Virginia and lived as a supporter there. Eventually, he took ordination as a Theravada Buddhist monk with Bhante Gunaratne,[4] a famous Sri Lankan monk who had been teaching in the United States since 1968. He was given the Pali name Sona,[5] and around 1990 as Bhikkhu Sona he travelled to Thailand and spent three-and-a-half years at the monasteries of the famous meditation teacher Ajahn Chah, where he developed strong friendships with the senior Western monks in the lineage.

In January 1994 he returned to Canada and stayed at the Sri Lankan Buddhist temple in Surrey for some time before returning to the Shack, accompanied by Bhikkhu Piyadhammo, a Theravada monk originally from Germany. The two Western monks gradually gathered support from local Canadian Buddhists and from some Sri Lankan and Thai families and individuals, and eventually Ajahn[6] Sona was able to re-establish the monastery with a residence and retreat centre on some land near Princeton, BC. He retained the name Birken Forest Monastery (now called "Birken II").

While Ajahn Sona was at the Princeton location, opportunity and donations coincided, allowing the purchase of a plot of land and a building in a rural setting on the shore of a marshy lake near forests outside Kamloops, BC. This new location (now "Birken III") is about 40 kilometres from the nearest urban centre (Kamloops) and some 10 kilometres or so from a resort at nearby Roche Lake. This is about five hours' drive from Vancouver and other cities on the coast.

When Ajahn Sona and his few followers moved in, the building structure was complete but unfinished. Over the years the siding has been completed, the basement finished as a meditation space and library, outbuildings have been added as needed, and the property has been landscaped. Birken now looks complete. Current projects have made Birken as environmentally efficient as possible.

Milestones along the way have been the ordinations of four Canadian monks and one American monk, none of whom were Sri Lankans or Thais. Another milestone was the establishment of Abhayagiri Forest Monastery near Redwood Valley, in northern California, and the development of a close relationship between Ajahn Sona and the monks there. Abhayagiri monks are among the most senior members of the Ajahn Chah lineage, and Ajahn Pasanno, the current abbot there, has authority from the Thai National Elders Council *(mahãatheerá samaakhom)* to perform ordinations, one of nine Westerners in the Ajahn Chah lineage so honoured. Ajahn Pasanno is a Canadian, and he came to Birken to perform the first ordinations there (2003); the next round of Birken ordinations was performed at Abhayagiri in 2008.

By 2012 Birken was widely recognized as a disciplined and serious monastery with high standards of training and teaching.

SRI LANKAN ORIENTATION AT BIRKEN

Ajahn Sona has retained his link with and his respect for his original Sri Lankan preceptor, Bhante Henepola Gunaratne. In fact, in 2009 he took on his teacher's duties in West Virginia during Bhante Gunaratne's leave to write a book, which Ajahn Sona later helped edit.[7] Aside from this enduring link, the contact with Sri Lankans seems to be fading.

Kirti Senaratne, who had worked tirelessly to bring Theravadin Buddhists together, strongly supported Ajahn Sona in his time at the Sri Lankan temple in Surrey in 1994 (Madanayake 2010, 135). Another strong supporter was Punyah Sahabandu. For a while the Sri Lankan community depended on Ajahn Sona for its regular Buddhist rituals, but eventually Ajahn Sona returned to his hermitage at Birken I. A strong movement toward Sri Lankan cultural identity among the community at the Sri Lankan centre in Surrey was probably a factor in his decision to return to the forest.

In the early days of Birken I, a small group of Sri Lankan supporters made the long trip out to the "shack monastery," among them Gamini Randini, who remains today a director of the legal society that manages the monastery. Overall, however, the original Sri Lankan influence was reduced as Ajahn Sona moved further away from metropolitan Vancouver, where the majority of Sri Lankans live. He is still respected by the BC Sri Lankan community and visits them from time to time. A few Sri Lankan families still travel to Birken III, usually coming as a group to offer food and supplies. Presumably, this would be on a day trip or overnight stay. There is a good Sri Lankan presence whenever Ajahn Sona gives talks or retreats in Vancouver, and he has made trips to Sri Lanka in 2006 and 2012. So the Sri Lankan link remains, but it is attenuating as the years go by and as Ajahn Sona moves further into the role of trainer of monks, none of whom (so far) have been Asian.

THAI ORIENTATION AT BIRKEN

During the Birken I phase, the number of Thai supporters increased. The numbers were never great, but Thais have an "unerring radar for monks" ("Birken Forest Monastery 2005," 4) and began to support Ajahn Sona while he was still in Surrey. Most were women with a particular interest in meditation and the *Dhamma*. They included, among others, Matchima Noikumpha, Edie Seger, Pom Khamchata, Pu Duangjan, Dr Anat Iamarun, and Pia Phibulsarawut, as well as Tik (Nikki) Barkasy, who has also served as a director of the legal society.

During later phases, Piriya (Tom) Novak, a Thai woman from Burnaby, BC also became an active supporter. Along with Jackie Balfour, Piriya arranged a Kathina event in 2009, the first time such an event had been held at Birken. Two carloads of Thais attended and presented robes. Some stayed on to help with the traditional dyeing of the robes by the monks. Piriya and others also arranged an annual weekend retreat in the Vancouver area for Ajahn Sona, and this event has become the most continuous connection to local Thais, although many of those who attend are non-Thai. Responsibility for these annual events seems, at the time of writing, to be spreading across a network of supporters, many of whom are not Thai.

Achara Sunti, who lives in the Seattle area, has also been a good Thai supporter over the years. There are also some Thai families who live in Kamloops who will attend important annual feast days at Birken and offer food and supplies, and the Thai restaurant in Kamloops is sometimes used as a more convenient shipping address for Birken. Despite these continuing links with the Thai community, contacts with the city-based Thais are gradually fading, as they did with the Sri Lankans. While this process continues, Ajahn Sona's links to one movement within Thai Buddhism seem to be strengthening. This is the link to the Thai Forest Tradition of Ajahn Chah.

The Thai Forest Tradition was revived in the twentieth century but has roots going back to the *araññavasi*[8] practitioners of early Buddhism who emphasized wearing only robes made of rags and living simply in the forest. This tradition is often contrasted with *gamavasi* or "town-dwellers" associated with textual study. It is also closely identified with the thirteen *dhutangas*[9] or ascetic practices, and the notion of *kammaṭṭhāna* (literally "basis of work"), a general ascetic approach to monastic life focused on uprooting greed, hatred, and delusion. The *kammaṭṭhāna* approach complements the *dhutangas* and indeed the words are interchangeable or compounded in Thai (Maha Boowa 2004, ix, 490). Within Thailand the Forest Tradition fell out of favour during the nineteenth and early twentieth centuries as the nation modernized along European lines. During the reign of the Fourth King (Mongkut, r. 1851–1868) of the present Chakri dynasty, there was a strong trend to eradicate folk beliefs and local superstitions, and focus on textual study and rational debate. He established the Thammayut sect as agents of this reform. They were part of his successful effort to convince predatory colonial-era missions to Bangkok that the Siamese were not barbarians. His successor, the Fifth King (Chulalongkorn, r. 1868–1910), modernized the country technologically and bureaucratically, centralizing the monastic hierarchy and bringing it under government control (see P. Jackson 1989; Tiyavanich 1997, 2007).

Despite this trend, there were always monks who chose the ascetic forest life. They were respected by the local people for their courage, living in forests full of fierce tigers or in charnel grounds among the ghosts and decomposing corpses. Among the few famous forest monks, the career of a remarkable monk, Ajahn Man Phurithat (1871–1949), stands out. He is known to have practised seven of the thirteen *dhutangas* consistently almost all his life into old age, and is reported to have regularly conversed with angels and devils. When cremated, his ashes were said to contain many gem-like relics, which were taken as a sign of his great spiritual advancement. His reputation and stature have contributed greatly to the revaluation and re-establishment of the practice of the itinerant ascetic monk in Thailand. According to Justin McDaniel, "The modern lineage of forest monks is seen as beginning with Phra Ajahn Man Bhuridatto [Phurithat from the Thai] and Phra Ajahn Sao Kantasilo. Scholars sometimes portray these and other Thammayut monks as symbols of pure Buddhist simplicity. They are described as straight-talking monks for the people – monks who do not sully themselves with excessive textual scholarship, monastic examinations, the practice of protective magic, or elaborate rituals. They lead the ideal monastic life in the forest, meditating, teaching, and not harming trees" (2006, 105).

McDaniel goes on to portray Ajahns Man and Sao as agents of the religion-reforming Thai nationalists, pointing out that the first monasteries of the Thai Forest Tradition (from 1853) were built by the monarchy and then the government. While there is truth to this point, it is also true that the forest monks were practitioners of the Buddhist *Dhamma* in a kind of raw form, and were particularly effective in spreading Buddhism and at the same time turning villagers in very remote areas away from their beliefs in ghosts, protective spirits, and shamans. This made them perfect counteragents against the wave of millenarian uprisings that had resulted from the bureaucratic reforms and the 1902 Sangha Act (Tiyavanich 1997, passim). These reforms denigrated local customs and disempowered local elites and shamans. In general, forest monks did not deal with political and social trends but may have been willing participants in these government programs since their own lives and methods were not affected: they would simply continue to do their thing. Indeed, they benefited from reduced prohibitions against wandering and cessation of the official vilification of their "vagabond" lifestyle (Tiyavanich 1997, 229, 372n39).

In the 1950s Thailand again took a violent turn to military government, and respected monks in Bangkok who had been advocating meditation were threatened or jailed. Once again monks in the Forest Tradition were vilified as nothing but vagabonds and Communists. Ajahn Man had died by this time, and surviving forest practitioners felt compelled to remain in their home monasteries. Eventually the practice revived again in public awareness in part due to the expanding numbers of foreigners who were travelling to Thailand in the 1960s and 70s and seeking out the remaining masters. The forest monk who was most successful in this regard was Ajahn Chah (the founder of Ajahn Sona's Thai lineage). Prestige still accrues to any Thais who had a connection to Ajahn Man and, although Ajahn Chah was not a disciple of Ajahn Man, he did meet him.

The connections between Birken and the Ajahn Chah lineage can be seen in the photo displays on the monastery walls. About six years ago (see Placzek and De Vries 2006), in the main building at Birken there was a sequence of photographs, starting with Ajahn Man and moving to Ajahn Chah, and then to Ajahn Sumedho (Ajahn Chah's first Western disciple and long-time senior monk of the International Branch of the Ajahn Chah teaching lineage in England). At the end of the line was Ajahn Sona's photo. This sequence of photographs explains the teaching lineage of Ajahn Sona, but also serves to legitimize his training and his knowledge, consciously or not. Note that in this lineal depiction there was no place to record Ajahn Sona's Sri Lankan link. The Sri Lankan link is still frequently mentioned and is very real, but since it is increasingly focused on Bhante Gunaratne, it does not supply a readily presentable and demonstrable progression as the Thai Forest Tradition does.

By 2010, I found that the direct lineage display of photographs had somewhat dispersed, and the individual photos were now found in the *sala* or main meditation hall, in the monk's dining and meeting room, in the hallway, and in the basement walking meditation area. Bhante Gunaratne is now prominently displayed in two locations. Ajahn Man and Ajahn Chah, the two most revered Thai monks, are prominently hung beside the entrance to the main meditation hall (inside). Next to Ajahn Chah is a photo of Ajahn Liem, the Thai successor of Ajahn Chah as the abbot of Wat Nong Pah Phong in Thailand (and the overall head of the Ajahn Chah teaching lineage). There is still a direct sequence of Ajahns Chah-Liem-Passano (senior lineage monk in North America)-Sona, so it could be argued that the lineage is still visibly displayed, with Ajahns Liem and Pasanno added and Sumedho moved elsewhere. Overall, however, the collection of photos is more dispersed, and there are many more photos of the senior Western monks of the Ajahn Chah lineage, including Ajahns Sumedho, Amaro, Sucitto, Chaiyasaro, Pasanno (two places), Viradhammo, and Tiradhammo (the last three being Canadians). The net result is to downplay the direct lineage but to emphasize the connection to the Thai Forest lineage as a whole. Another exception to this trend is a photo in the hallway to the monks' dining room. This is a photo of Anagarika Dhammadinna, a pioneer Theravada nun in the BC lower mainland (see chapter 13 in this volume). The overall effect, I would argue, is that it is not the general Thai connection that is valued at Birken, but rather it is the Ajahn Chah lineage, and in particular the Western branch of that lineage.

The Thai Forest Tradition features a training monastery for Westerners in Thailand (Wat Pah Nanachat) and an overseas headquarters in England (Amaravati). So in fact the Thai Forest Tradition has itself become internationalized. The lineage also has a branch monastery, Wat Abhayagiri, in northern California, with a branch hermitage in Washington State. There is an ongoing exchange of monks between Birken and Abhayagiri, with the result that Birken is drawn further into the organization and the culture of the teaching lineage of Ajahn Chah.

While neither Ajahn Sona nor the former Birken steward Linda Furrow (resident seven years to 2010) saw any sudden or rapid change in this relationship, my impression is of an increase in the connection to the Thai Forest Tradition. There is more on this connection below.

CULTURAL ADJUSTMENTS AT BIRKEN: TRADITION VERSUS ADAPTATION

When any major religious tradition comes to a new cultural territory, there is always some give and take, some preservation and some adaptation. Ajahn Sona views his role in this overall process as dealing with the basic physical requisites of Theravada monks and "the challenge of making 2500-year-old teachings useful to contemporary Westerners" (Birken Forest Monastery 2005, 1). At the same time he summarizes his goals as follows:

> I consider there to be one and only one main purpose in taking formal ordination as a monk: to attain full enlightenment as soon as possible. All other aspects of the monk's life– and there are many – are secondary to this purpose. I had deliberately sought out teachers and groups who maintained this ideal in accord with the historical teachings of the Buddha as found in the Theravada tradition.
>
> I had a strong conviction that if this "Buddhism in Canada" experiment was to go well, it must begin well, with a dedication to the proper lifestyle for a monk, and not to immediately abandon the rules of discipline out of a desire for trivial convenience. The theme of adhering to the spirit, and in many cases the letter, of the historical Buddha's code of discipline (*vinaya*) has stood me in good stead throughout this decade, as it has the dozen or so other Western Theravada monasteries around the world. (Birken Forest Monastery 2005, 2)

The relative isolation of Birken makes some traditions such as the morning alms round impossible. Yet Birken is sustained by generous donations from supporters.

Although Ajahn Sona spent considerable time in Thailand, his fundamental vision of living simply and frugally in the forest was already established before his Asian contacts. Thus, for him training in Thailand is not a necessity for individual development or for the ultimate goal – enlightenment. He explains that Westerners ordained abroad learn to live mentally far from their home cultures. Having gained new perspectives, "they can never go back."[10] Ajahn Sona jokes about the "independent kingdom of Birken" where the culture is more Buddhist than it is the culture of any ethnic or national grouping. He prefers the word "cosmopolitan" in the sense in which it was used by Diogenes, being "beyond culture." But he quickly adds that "culture remains" as one of the main areas of uncritical mental habits that need to be examined in the ongoing practice of a Buddhist monk, and indeed of any Buddhist.[11]

Ajahn Sona mentions a book by John Raulston Saul, in which Canada is described as a result of compromise, negotiation, and intermarriage. In a parallel way, the monks of Birken are "spiritually mixed," and Ajahn Sona will emphasize teachings or stories from a range of traditions, despite his adherence to the Theravada discipline.

The landscaping of Birken is Japanese while the interior decoration has a folk quality, with large hanging quilts. The main building is generally "modern" in appearance; that is, it has no particular ethnic style. The main Buddha image is Thai, but it has an un-Thai plain wooden supporting structure, and Birken steward Linda Furrow noted that, when it was ordered from Thailand, a "long Western nose" was specified. The environment at Birken could be summarized as "Buddhist eclectic" with a strong element of Canadian or at least Western culture.

THE STATUS OF BIRKEN WITHIN THE AJAHN CHAH LINEAGE

Birken has been affiliated with the Ajahn Chah lineage organization since 1994. In the lineage there are about five affiliated *wats* (monasteries) like Birken. Ajahn Sona is often asked "What is an affiliate?" and the status is not really clear to many members of the lineage itself. He attended the last several "world abbots" meetings at considerable cost and inconvenience, while some official branch abbots do not go regularly. Ajahn Sona has known some of these monks for twenty years.

In 1993, after the death of Ajahn Chah and the resignations of several senior Western monks, the lineage decided that there should be no more expansion for the time being, especially no more formal branches. Nevertheless, when the opportunity arose for a new branch in the United States (Abhayagiri) that had strong local support, that branch was established.

Because the lineage had already spread into many countries from its headquarters in England without any branch in North America, I consider Abhayagiri the "beachhead" of the American lineage.

Ajahn Sona lists the benefits of being an official branch. First, personnel can be shared: monks can go and stay in other branches, and vice versa. Second, standards, annual cycles, and even daily routines will be the same or very similar. Third, at the annual abbots' meetings, leaders can discuss problems and solutions, relying on seniors' experience. This can be especially helpful with intractable issues of far-reaching consequence.[12] In 2009, when Ajahn Sona was called to help his preceptor Bhante Gunaratne in West Virginia, some senior monks came from Abhayagiri to spend the winter in Birken. This freed him up to perform a service for his own teacher, and gave the Birken monks more experience. After that, Ajahn Pavaro, the most senior monk ordained at Birken, went to stay at Abhayagiri after passing his five-year "probation" period. So even though Birken is not formally a branch monastery, it is able to share in the strengths and mutual assistance of the lineage.

Although group discussions at world abbots meetings can be useful in major, protracted issues, the results of these discussions must be applied to all wats in the lineage, with potential for bureaucratic delays in sometimes critical decisions. When he was invited to raise the level of Birken's participation in the lineage to branch status, Ajahn Sona asked himself, "Do we need another level of bureaucracy?" The final decision, made by Ajahn Sona with input from his monks and regular supporters, was that they did not need to become an official branch, having been successful in affiliate status.[13] The decision might have surprised the international lineage leaders in England.

BHIKKHUNIS, OR FEMALE MONKS

The status of women was bound to be an issue in the adoption of Buddhism in the West (see Placzek 1981). In the time of the Buddha there was a female monkhood, with specific additional rules laid down by the Buddha himself. However, the ordination lineage of the female monastics died out in Theravada Buddhism some centuries ago. In Sri Lanka and in Burma it ended in the eleventh to thirteenth centuries, but in Thailand, it had already died out when the first Thai kingdoms were set up in the thirteenth century, because a *bhikkhuni* tradition in Siam/Thailand has never been recognized by any Thai kingdoms or modern governments.[14] A female monkhood does survive in Mahayana Buddhism (in China, Taiwan, Vietnam, Korea, and Japan) but many Theravadins see this branch of Buddhism as outside their own branch, and thus not acceptable as a source of senior *bhikkhunis* to conduct a proper female ordination, as specified by the Buddha himself.[15] In this view, *bhikkhuni* ordinations can *never* be valid, since the required validly ordained senior Theravada *bhikkhunis* will never be available.

In the later centuries, it has become a tradition in Thailand for women who are interested in Buddhism (usually older women with reduced family obligations) to take a less formal ordination. This involves taking five to eight basic precepts, shaving the head, and wearing white robes. It is a level of commitment often adopted by both men and women temporarily, usually during festival days or other events such as a funeral. This level of commitment became a fixed traditional option for women under the label of *mâe chii*. In modern day Thailand, there are some *mâe chii* who are recognized as well advanced in the *Dhamma*, and they are respected for their achievements, including teaching meditation. Others are popular social activists with their own television shows. But a large number of *mâe chii* live in monasteries, do much of the cleaning, cooking, and even organizational work, and are given very little respect or status. Often they are seen as servants of the monks. In other cases, women in *mâe chii* robes may set up a small shrine on a busy market lane and collect donations. These *mâe chii* are seen as little more than beggars. Even though the Thai government has consistently resisted a legal monastic status for *mâe chii*, individuals and foundations have been working to establish colleges and monastic centres[16] where *mâe chii* are brought into a more widely shared and more unified discipline, and this may soon affect the public perception of *mâe chii*. Ironically, this improved *mâe chii* status is sometimes seen as a rival by those dedicated to the revival of the *bhikkhuni* lineage in Thailand, but *bhikkhuni* ordination should be seen as an optional path within the reforming *mâe chii* institution, not the required goal for all *mâe chii*.

In the Ajahn Chah lineage in the West, initially in Britain, some women who had advanced in the training felt the need for a status somewhat distinct from that of *mâe chii* and of ordinary new postulants, both male and female, all of whom wore white. In a process over decades, in close consultation with the elders of the lineage in Thailand, Ajahn Sumedho, the most senior Western disciple of Ajahn Chah, developed a status of ten-precept, dark-robed women called *sīladharās*.[17] This was basically an attempt to deal with the strong restrictions on women which go back to the Buddha himself, are found in the Pali canon *vinaya* monastic rules, and are therefore inviolable in the Theravada tradition. These restrictions have to be accommodated to the cultural values of equality that have taken deep root in modern Western society. Crucially, this *sīladharā* innovation at Amaravati in England had clear approval from the conservative Thai ecclesiastical authorities. It was a relatively daring innovation for the Thai elders, and demonstrates the trust they had in Ajahn Sumedho.

Despite these compromises, which were in fact stretching the bounds of what is central and essential to the Theravada identity, the *sīladharā* women continued to express some dissatisfaction. The problem seemed to lie with the overt and unmistakable lower status of the most senior *sīladharā* compared to that of the most recently ordained male *bhikkhu*. This dynamic is similar to what Alexander Soucy explores in chapter 14 of this volume. The dissatisfaction probably came from the newer *sīladharās*, who found it painful to see their own highly respected teachers so flagrantly disrespected every time there was an event which brought the *bhikkhus* and *sīladharās* together. At Amaravati and the other larger central wats in England this happens every day. Of course, the disrespect was more in the positioning and priorities of the formal rituals, rather than in the *bhikkhus*' attitudes. Given their rigorous and isolated training in Thailand and the male bonding that ensued, there must have been some sexist attitudes among them, but it is their job to watch their own minds for such cultural or social inputs, and neutralize them.

In some ways the problem was minimized; for instance, when a sermon was required or someone was needed to lead a ritual, the senior monk had the option of inviting a senior *sīladharā* to fill that role. Despite this, grumbling among the *sīladharās* persisted, along with the complaint that the communication channels between *bhikkhus* and *sīladharās* were weak or non-existent. Ajahn Sumedho declared a moratorium on *sīladharā* ordinations until he could find a solution to the problem (Western Elders Council 2009).

In the end, he asked the *sīladharās* to reaffirm their position within the Theravada tradition by accepting the Five Points, four of which were based on the Buddha's own rules for *bhikkhunis*. The fifth point was that the *sīladharā* form was not some kind of preliminary *bhikkhuni* status, but rather was a complete system of training in its own right. The Five Points became a flash point in the *bhikkhuni* controversy, in part because they were perceived as introduced without sufficient consultation.

Ajahn Sumedho offered two further initiatives. One was to appoint a *bhikkhu*, approved by the *sīladharās*, as a liaison officer. Another was to provide increased separation of the communities, so that the daily display of apparent disrespect was reduced. Eventually, Aloka Vihara, an exclusively *sīladharā* monastery, was established in northern California near Abhayagiri Monastery. Two of the three original *sīladharās* there decided to ordain as *bhikkhunis* and the focus of the monastery changed, although they still welcome *sīladharās*.

Although the current international leadership of the lineage acknowledges that there is a cultural gap here, and further that Ajahn Sumedho's compromise of *sīladharā* status for Western women does have its problems, these leaders probably share a sense that this is the correct way for a Theravada lineage to adapt to a new environment: keep the core teachings of the Buddha, especially the *vinaya* rules; adapt in ways that do not violate those teachings and only if there is a clear and persistent need perceived that adaptation is absolutely necessary. These monks are Westerners too, and they appreciate the sometimes deep cultural divide between their training in Asia and Western cultural values. But their goal is to rise above these cultural distinctions, even the fundamental gender distinctions. This careful and measured response is their way of building a bridge to resolve that contradiction.

Some *bhikkhus* and *sīladharās* within the tradition, however, were not content to wait for an unspecified amount of time for higher ordination for women, and thus the great *Bhikkhuni* Ordination Crisis of 2009 came about.

AJAHN BRAHM AND THE *BHIKKHUNI* ORDINATIONS OF 2009

Ajahn Brahmavamso is an Englishman who was ordained in 1974 by Chao Khun Brahmagunaporn, abbot of Wat Saket in Bangkok. In recent years the Chao Khun has become the acting Supreme Patriarch, and wields considerable influence within the Thai monkhood. Eventually, Ajahn Brahm went to train in the Ajahn Chah lineage. In 1981 he was invited to help develop the Bodhinyana monastery near Perth, Australia, and sometime after that he became the abbot of the monastery.

Ajahn Brahm is a charismatic speaker and has inspired many Buddhists and non-Buddhists alike with his humour and his profound observations about modern life and its obsessions. He was, thus, widely accepted as a senior monk in the Thai Forest Tradition and a scholar of Buddhism in his own right, although he plays down the scriptural emphasis.

Despite this, Ajahn Brahm can also be seen as somewhat independent-minded, with only a loose connection to the international branch of the Ajahn Chah teaching lineage (headquartered in England), and its hierarchical senior body, the lineage headquarters at Wat Nong Pah Phong in Thailand. Some find him egotistical, since the charisma and confidence can be interpreted that way. His rock-star status in Australia, Singapore, and Malaysia adds to this perception.

In 2009 Ajahn Brahm received encouragement from the Buddhist Society of Western Australia to assist in the ordination of four women as *bhikkhuni*. Ajahn Brahm's assistance in this rite follows a recent worldwide trend where female ordination has been revived with support from Mahayana *bhikkhunis*, mostly Taiwanese and Western. In 1988, there were mass ordinations in India, and recently there have been as many as a thousand ordained *bhikkhunis* in Sri Lanka, the heartland of Theravada. This is partly explained by the fact that Sri Lanka has a long history of *bhikkhunis* and no official national body of conservative monks to resist such a movement. Leadership resides in the various monasteries and there are many intellectually independent abbots who have strongly supported the movement.

The opposite set of conditions applies in Thailand where there is a national body of conservative monks and no communal memory of *bhikkhunis*. So the small movement toward Thai *bhikkhuni* ordination has so far received no official acceptance from the National Elders council or the government. In fact, *bhikkhuni* ordination in Thailand remains illegal by a 1928 law.

When Ajahn Brahm informed the Western lineage leaders that the ceremony was to be carried out within a matter of weeks, their reaction was swift and negative. The lineage elders felt that Ajahn Brahm had not properly informed them. Since they had only recently accepted a Thai

National Elders Council resolution not to support female ordinations, Ajahn Brahm knew they would not accept his participation in the ceremony. In their view he had been not only uncollegial, but also deceitful. He had turned down an open discussion of the issue and the process of reaching consensus, which are the essential bases of communal harmony, as taught by Ajahn Chah himself.

At the later full meeting of the lineage elders (both Thai and Western), Ajahn Brahm refused to promise straightforwardly not to ordain other *bhikkhunis* (see Wat Pa Nanachat Sangha 2009a, 2009b, and 2009c). There were also some details of the ordination ritual that could be faulted as incorrect[18] along with the major concern that the senior *bhikkhunis* involved in the ritual were not Theravadins; thus the ordination was deemed invalid. Ajahn Brahm's monastery was de-listed as an official branch monastery of the Ajahn Chah lineage, although his status as a Buddhist monk was not changed. He retained his ranking within the Thai National Elders Council (since that is a royal appointment) but lost his status as *upajjhāya* with the right to ordain new monks, since that was part of his standing within the Ajahn Chah lineage.[19]

Ajahn Brahm says that he had been assured that the Thai National Elders council has no authority beyond the borders of Thailand, and that his ritual was true to the spirit and intention of the original rules in the Pali canon. It was also as close to the letter of those rules as one could get in the twenty-first century. By his account, he had clearly promised not to assist in any more *bhikkhuni* ordinations. There probably was a language problem, since the proceedings were conducted in Thai and Ajahn Brahm's Thai is limited, as confirmed by three senior Western monks, all fluent in Thai, who attended the meeting. So Ajahn Brahm's view is that the issue comes down to the validity of the ordination, not a lack of openness or refusal to stop assisting such ordinations (see Brahmavamso 2009a, 2009b).

The controversy can be seen as a step along the way to the development of a genuinely Western sangha (community of monastics), one that stays true to the teachings of the Buddha, but allows for specific local cultural emphases. For example, when Buddhism spread to China, it developed a special emphasis on filial piety and social duty because of Confucian influence. In the West there is an expected adjustment for principles of democracy and gender equality (see Placzek 1981). Thus, Ajahn Brahm's *bhikkhuni* ordination controversy can be seen as inevitable, in the sense that the issues it raises would occur somewhere eventually, even if he had not participated in that particular event. And these controversies will recur as Western Buddhism continues to develop, mature, and adjust to fundamental components of local cultures.

EFFECT OF THE *BHIKKHUNI* CONTROVERSY ON BIRKEN

Ajahn Sona attended the 2009 Western elders' meeting a month after Ajahn Brahm's monastery was de-listed from the Ajahn Chah lineage. At that time he emphasized to the Thais that, when it comes to public media, "if they react to Ajahn Brahm they won't get any sympathy; he will."[20] That is exactly what occurred when one senior Thai monk stated in an interview that they would like to "take back" Ajahn Brahm's wat in western Australia, this despite the considerable support from local lay Australians. As Ajahn Sona predicted, it was a media disaster in Australia. The general Thai view would be that Wat Bodhinyana had been established because of the reputation of Ajahn Chah, his training of the Western monks, and the generosity of Thais both in Thailand and locally. The view of the lineage elders would be that Wat Bodhinyana was offered to the lineage as a branch. If difficulties arise, the abbot may be moved, but the wat remains as part of the lineage. However, such arguments are not convincing in the West where strict laws controlling charities apply. This incident provides potential for a rupture of the lineal succession in the Ajahn Chah teaching tradition.

One positive sign is the fact that in October 2011 Ajahn Brahm met with Ajahn Amaro (successor to Ajahn Sumedho at lineage headquarters in England) and another senior monk and discussed the issue. Genuine efforts were made to repair some of the social damage, even if the fundamental views could not be unified. Ajahn Brahm agreed to accept status as a "visiting monk" (*agunduka*), but he declared himself satisfied to remain outside the lineage (Bramavamso 2011). There are also other independent monks, such as Ajahn Sujato in Bundanoon, New South Wales, and some in England. As long as they remain separate individuals, or even together do not claim official title to the teaching lineage of Ajahn Chah, there will be no schism.

Many of the Thai National Elders council members were ordained as poor boys from rural areas. Now as successful senior monks, they socialize with the country's elite: the generals, the bankers, and sometimes even the royal family. Therefore, they tend to be very conservative. Ajahn Sona feels that they fear the rise of Western influence in their religion. They are not used to being pressured, even by local Thais such as the reformer Sanitsuda Ekachai of the *Bangkok Post*. There was recently an unsuccessful movement among Thai monks to have the fierce *lèse majesté* laws protecting the royal family extended to apply to the monkhood. As noted above, there is still a 1928 law on the books in Thailand forbidding the ordination of *bhikkhunis*. So the conservative side in Thailand's power structure seems a formidable obstacle, but it is mostly inert rather than active.

Ajahn Sona describes how, in the meeting in Thailand about Ajahn Brahm, the monks took three days to think about the impact of the decision and were very careful with their language. Ajahn Sona pointed out to the monks that both sides, from their own perspectives, were being reasonable. He reports that the Thai elders and the lineage leaders were shocked by the explosive media reaction. They needed a year or so to comprehend what had happened.

The Western Buddhist world has been waiting decades for *bhikkhuni* ordination. In 2007 there was a great meeting in Hamburg, Germany, attended by the Dalai Lama and all traditions. There was a clear consensus that *bhikkhuni* ordination is a goal. But after the meeting no clear steps were taken. Some of the more activist monks, such as Ajahn Sujato and Ajahn Brahm, began to wonder if such advancements would happen in their lifetimes.

These factors led to Ajahn Sona's understanding of Ajahn Brahm's tactics in this event. Ajahn Brahm has highly developed social skills. He knows when to be diplomatic, when to be determined, and is careful in handling the media. If his participation in the ordination had been accepted, the precedent would have been set for the modern Thai Forest Tradition in the West. Ajahn Brahm probably did not expect the strong reaction from the Thai and Western elders.[21] I suspect that additional factors were Ajahn Brahm's relative independence, his extreme popularity, and his tendency to emphasize other controversial topics such as studies of reported memories of past lives. These are the stuff of cults, and other monks see them as danger signals. I heard similar criticisms of (now disrobed and discredited) Ajahn Yantra when he visited the lineage centres in England in 1993. Especially for the reserved forest monks, Ajahn Brahm's strong self-confidence can be interpreted as egotism. So it seems that the reaction was as much against him personally as it was against his support for *bhikkhuni* ordination in Australia.

As discussed above, at Birken there are a number of framed photos of leading Western disciples of Ajahn Chah. When asked why there are no photos of Ajahn Brahm, Ajahn Sona pointed out a second photo of Bhante Gunaratne. "That used to be Ajahn Brahm." His photos and books were removed from the monastery after his exclusion from the lineage. Ajahn Sona notes that later he received a phone call reminding him that Birken's website still included talks by Ajahn Brahm. This illustrates the nuanced stance of Ajahn Sona in this controversy. Despite his having declined official branch status and his energetic arguments for flexibility in interpretation of the monastic rules, he still holds the rules as the foundation of the Buddha's teaching for regulating Sangha society. There is no contradiction here. It is a question of practicality, common sense, and an approach that is very careful, unhurried, and attuned to preserving the essence of the teaching, the ultimate Theravada value. Although he remains a personal friend of Ajahn Brahm, he also goes along with the judgments of the lineage elders and has removed the works and references to Ajahn Brahm from Birken.

Finally, how do the women at Birken view the controversy? *Mâe chii* Mon was a long-time resident of Birken in the early days (see illustration 3). A Thai national, she was ordained as a *mâe chii* at Birken and has a following among local Buddhist women. Currently, she has returned to Birken from Thailand. Ajahn Sona asked her for her view of this controversy. Her reply expressed confidence that the senior monks would find a compromise. This indicates that at least some of the women in full Buddhist practice were not overly concerned by the controversy.

The controversy affects all monasteries in the lineage, in fact all Thai monasteries. Monastic life in Thailand is very much male-centred. After living for some years in Thailand, I was quite confused when I met *sīladharās* in England, and despite that experience, confused again at meeting Korean *bhikkhunis* years later. It comes as a shock to realize that this monk is a *woman!* I have several times heard Thai women speak disparagingly of *bhikkhunis* as "women who want to be men." That is how strong the connection between "monk" and "male" is in the Thai culture. It will not be overturned quickly. Still there is a small but growing *bhikkhuni* movement in Thailand which attracts male as well as female supporters through its discipline and competent teaching.[22]

WHY CAN'T WE JUST MODERNIZE THE RULES? *VINAYA* AS THE CORE OF THERAVADA

The Vinaya *and Rigidity*

The principles of the *vinaya* guide the monastic community when it is faced with unclear or novel cases. It is one of the three main books or "Baskets" (*pitaka*) of the Pali canonical texts. The actual rules are known as the *pātimokkha*, and are recited by the monastic community every fortnight. There is some scholarly debate about the canonical status of the *pātimokkha*. It is in an ancient commentary called *sutta-vibhaṅga*, which most scholars consider to be an integral part of the *vinaya pitaka*, but some as "para-canonical" (Dutt 1957, 76). Over the centuries, different *vinayas* have grown up in the different branches of Buddhism, and this has also sparked much debate, but all branches share the basic rules, and the core rules are basically the same. In Theravada the *bhikkhu vinaya* has 227 rules while that of the *bhikkhunis* has 311.

> The Buddhist monastic discipline, called Vinaya, is a refined training of body, speech and mind. This discipline is not an end in itself, but a tool which, when applied in conjunction with the spiritual teachings (*Dhamma*), can help foster maturity and spiritual development.
>
> Apart from the direct training that the Vinaya affords, it also serves to establish a supportive relationship between lay people and renunciates [i.e., monastics], which is an essential aspect of the Theravada tradition. Within the context of this relationship Buddhist monastics give up many ordinary freedoms and undertake the discipline and conventions of Vinaya in order to focus on the cultivation of the heart. They are able to live as mendicants because lay people respect their training and are prepared to help to support them. This gives rise to a sense of mutual respect and co-operation in which both lay person and samana [i.e., monastics] are called upon to practice their particular life-styles and responsibilities with sensitivity and sincerity.
>
> Many of the Vinaya rules were created specifically to avoid offending lay people or avoid giving cause for misunderstanding or suspicion. (Tisarana Forest Monastery, n.d)

Ajahn Sona tells the story of an incident when he was walking in Surrey, BC and got caught in a rare snowstorm. He was offered a ride, but he had to refuse it because it was offered by a lone female, and that would have broken a strong *vinaya* rule that forbids a monk from being in a confined space with a woman. "What could I do? The rules were not to be trifled with. They free one from so many complications, and are the lifeblood of the religion" (Birken Forest Monastery 2005, 2).

There are some areas where the *vinaya* rules are especially rigid, such as in interaction with members of the opposite sex, or are generally agreed upon, such as in bans on growing one's own food, or officiating at marriage ceremonies. The rationale for these rules is given in scriptural accounts in which the Buddha, faced with a specific incident among the monastics, created a rule to define proper behaviour. As a generalization, there are three areas in which Theravada becomes quite rigid in its interpretation of the *vinaya*. The first concerns cases which could call into question the fidelity of a lineage (or of a practice) to the *vinaya* itself. Wearing shoes in Canada is not one of these. But relaxing restrictions on sexual contact or carrying money are more serious. The second area is in the validity of ordination. If a monastic's ordination is questioned, he or she could be expelled or at least forced to re-ordain, losing all seniority. In fact, there are historical cases where just such a device was used to destroy the political and economic power of the monkhood when it threatened the authority of the kings of Pagan in thirteenth-century Burma (Myanmar). The monks' ordinations were criticized and they were sent off to Sri Lanka to be re-ordained. The king of Pagan then was able to confiscate their considerable properties (K. Taylor 1992, 166–7). The third area of inflexibility is where the symbiotic relationship between the monastics and the lay community is threatened. Some examples are given below.[23] In other areas, however, there is a range of flexibility.

The Vinaya *and Flexibility*

Over the centuries, and as Buddhism spread to different cultures, preserving the original *vinaya* became more and more impractical. "Therefore, without changing the letter of the law, the monks discovered ways and means of overcoming the difficulty by interpreting the law without compromising themselves. These interpretations and decisions ... are known under the term *palimuttaka-vinicchaya*, i.e., decisions not found in the original canonical texts. These are tantamount to amendments or new rules, though they are not considered as such" (Rahula 1978, 62-3). These "outside" (non-canonical) decisions survive in a text called *pālimuttaka-vinayavincchaya*, compiled in Sri Lanka in the thirteenth century. Although it has not been used since then, it has become central in discussions of the rules in American Theravada communities since the mid-1990s (Prebish 2003, 61–2).

Ajahn Tiradhammo has reviewed the particular approach to the *vinaya* taken by Ajahn Chah, calling his approach very strict "but not rigid." Ajahn Chah saw the *vinaya* as "a support for spiritual practice, most particularly to help increase mindfulness and encourage communal harmony. For example, it requires a fair degree of wisdom and much awareness of body, speech and mind in order to keep *Vinaya* in a relaxed and skilful way rather than through fear or repression" (Prebish 2003, 63–4).

Ajahn Sona talks of the Mahapadesa, the "great standard," a scripture-based way of handling new situations (see also Prebish 2003, 64). If future conditions are similar to those of a *vinaya* rule, the rule will apply to those new conditions. He gives the example of polyester cloth. This certainly did not exist at the time of the Buddha and is not listed as approved cloth for robes. Should modern monks accept polyester robes? One way to judge is by the fact that polyester is common in the clothing of ordinary men and women. Therefore, it should be acceptable as robe material, as this parallels the kinds of cloth approved by the Buddha.[24] Ajahn Chah relied considerably on the Mahapadesa.

The Buddha in two cases gave permission to change minor rules (see also Sujato 2007). But in the entire history of Theravada, no Great Councils have officially changed a single rule (Rahula 1978, 62). Ajahn Sona gives an example, from many, of an informal adaptation: the *vinaya* specifies that a monk should bathe no more often than once in two weeks. This was probably a rule against luxurious behaviour. But in hot climates where people take baths at least twice a day, this rule has been relaxed.[25] Typically "relaxed" implies there is general consensus among senior monks in that community. Such consensus is called *katikāvata* in Pali (Prebish 2003, 62).

Notice that there are restrictions on the allowance of flexibility. Usually sheer impracticality or health and safety concerns are the motives behind the change. If the motive is mere inconvenience or if the change leads to vices that are the target of the specific rule, no flexibility is tolerated. Some cases are controversial. For example, some Thai wats in Los Angeles have allowed their monks to drive cars (Prebish 2003, 66). This is shocking to conservative Thais. Another example is the handling of money. In general, forest monks do not handle money. In contrast, it is common for "mainstream" or city-based Thai monks to carry cash, credit cards, and to receive cash donations specifically for their personal use. This, of course, complicates the lives of city monks in ways that forest monks do not have to deal with. It also reduces the differences between the monks and the laity, inevitably reducing the respect and the support of the laity for the monks and the monastic institution. For this reason, the "driving monks" of Los Angeles are restricted to driving only on monastic or *Dhamma*-related business, and one of the abbots there has explicitly stated the importance of preserving the interdependent relationship between monks and laity (Prebish 2003, 67–8).

Another area of widely differing interpretation even within Thailand is the restriction on eating after midday. In general, monks are required to eat between dawn and midday (1:00 p.m. during daylight saving time), and to eat only those foods that are offered to them. The only things they may ask for are plain water or medicine. They cannot store food for the next day (although lay supporters or postulants may do so for them). This leads to a major difference between Theravada and Mahayana. The dependence upon the generosity of the laity, often very poor peasant farmers, along with these restrictions on requesting specific foods, leads Theravada monks to eat meat. Of course, in a settled monastic environment the laity will learn that they should bring only vegetarian foods, but the monks can never refuse food which has been appropriately offered.

Theravada monasteries allow drinks such as tea or coffee at an evening meeting. Sugar candies and chocolates are allowed at some monasteries (including Birken) probably under a category of items which have a "tonic or reviving quality (such as tea or sugar)" (Tisarana Forest Monastery, n.d., 4).

The Forest Tradition counts milk, including malted drinks such as Ovaltine, as a food; thus, these should not be consumed in the evening. However, some monasteries allow cheese, which seems strange. Cheese is rather exotic in Southeast Asia, where most ordinary people are lactose intolerant. So perhaps as an exotic foreign food it was seen to fit the special category of "pharmaceutical medicines, vitamins; plant roots such as ginger, ginseng; herbal decoctions such as chamomile; beverages such as tea, coffee and cocoa" (Tisarana Forest Monastery, n.d., 5). Ajahn Sumedho joked that some forest masters were "cheese-eating," but other forest masters were "non-cheese eating." New monks simply followed the senior abbots and teachers in such matters.[26] Overall, Prebish finds that these relaxations have fit well within the system outlined above of non-canonical reinterpretations based on consensus (2003, 65).

Thus, it is clear that in some areas there is a range of interpretations, but these are seen as non-essential areas or are justified by looking at the underlying motives of the rule. This kind of gradual innovation is supported by meetings of the elders and their considerations of such changes. However, when core issues such as sexual temptation or the validity of ordination are involved, change is not an option.

All cultures have literalist and liberal extremes. Since in practice many rules are relaxed out of necessity, Ajahn Sona feels it is "against the Buddha to be inflexible." Thus, in his view an extreme literal interpretation of the *vinaya* is a violation of the teaching.[27] He talks about his own first teacher, Bhante Gunaratne, who was mystified by the attachment in the West to the tradition of the "rains retreat." It is a very important part of the Theravada tradition and its beginning and end are major festivals of the annual cycle. However, it doesn't make sense in a country without a rainy season. Bhante Gunaratne saw the observance of the rains retreat in northern countries as an inflexible attachment to rules and rituals. Birken observes a winter retreat almost by necessity, since the heavy snows of central BC restrict travel and outdoor movement, much as the rains do in Monsoon Asia.

Mahayana followers might see Theravada as wholly absorbed in frivolous details of rules and regulations. However, in the Theravada perspective, attention to rules is inevitable given the focus on the *vinaya* as the glue that holds everything together (see Prebish 2003, 60 for another view of *vinaya* as glue). But there are also ways and systematic approaches to tolerating practices that do not conform to the rules. However, this process is ponderous, involving extensive consultation and consensus among the elders. No monk or council wants to be seen as arrogant enough to try to "improve" on the *vinaya* of the Fully Enlightened One. So accommodation to the realities of new societies and to the changing modern world will have to be accomplished by compromise and the kinds of pragmatic "tolerances" of the rules that are described here. For those activists intent on change, however, this is unacceptable.

Flexibility and Bhikkhuni Ordination

The senior *bhikkhunis* who have been conducting Theravada *bhikkhuni* ordinations were ordained in Mahayana lineages. This is a serious obstacle for Theravada *bhikkhuni* ordination because the elders of Thailand see the use of Mahayana *bhikkhunis* for Theravada ordinations as invalidating the ordinations. Therefore, this dispute may find no resolution and the danger of schism increases, something that would be a historic tragedy for Theravada Buddhism and would rob both its Asian and Western branches of the mutual benefits of the cross-cultural interaction experienced by the first generation of Westerners to ordain in Thailand and other Theravada centres. In a sense, there is a crucial cross-cultural window here, carried by this first generation of Western Theravada monks. It is up to them to find bridges and accommodations within the *vinaya* as received on the *bhikkhuni* issue. In their eyes, if they abandon the *vinaya* they are no longer Theravada, and the essential teachings of the Buddha, preserved at great cost by 2,500 years of devotees, will have been lost. Worse, this loss will have occurred on their watch. Ajahn Sumedho has developed the *sīladharā* ordination as one bridge. Some women have accepted it, some have refused it.

Bhante Gunaratne organized a *bhikkhuni* ordination in West Virginia over twenty years ago, but there was too much controversy at that time. His disciple Ajahn Sona sums up the *bhikkhuni* crisis in the lineage: "We don't criticize, we accept. Let go of the critical mind, rationality. We have to live with this [the contradictions] ... We are prepared to let it go a century or two."[28]

Note that he does not exclude the possibility of *bhikkhuni* revival. The fact remains that there are no mechanisms within Thai Buddhism or within Theravada (a much more amorphous entity) to make such a change. It can come, but will require a change in thinking not only among the monastic leadership (equally amorphous "consensus among the elders") but also within the societies of the Theravada nations. And because of the sanctity of validity of ordination, it will have to overcome the ancient divisions between Theravada and Mahayana, which are based on millennia of separate development in sometimes widely different societies. One bright light here is the rapidly shrinking world of modern communication, travel, and scholarship. Closer interaction and deeper understanding between the branches is happening daily, and the great gap between branches could be overcome within a century, or even within decades.

Ajahn Sona points out that one of the worst offences in the Pali canon *pātimokkha* (ritually recited rules) is to cause a schism. There has never been a schism in the history of Theravada (over two thousand years). The controversy over *bhikkhuni* ordination could cause just such a historic split but only if the differing sides want to force the issue. As noted above, there has been at least some meeting of the minds between Ajahn Brahm and the Western leaders of the lineage. This is a hopeful sign.

THE FUTURE OF BIRKEN

Where is Birken going? Ajahn Sona repeats what he has been saying for the past several years, that the monastery is well funded and he is very grateful for that. The property is almost paid off, and the routines have become stable, allowing for some innovation, such as the move to solar power and getting off the grid. The "wild fragile" period is now over. The monastery is developing its own traditions; for example, it has developed a style of monastic coat for the severe winters in this area. Ajahn Sona sees the monastery as a "rich and precious resource in a fraying and stressed society."[29] It is, and will continue to be, an island of sanity in this society.

Those who were ordained at Birken but later disrobed still remain in touch and most are lay teachers. Ajahn Sona now concentrates on the teaching and the practice. His focus is on the individual, since each seeker is unique and there is no simple progression from one level or stage to another: "Some go one way, some another."[30] As for his own practice, Ajahn Sona was on solitary retreat for a year starting from 5 April 2013.

Will the decor of Birken become more Thai, or develop a unique design? In terms of the landscaping and the interior decoration, Ajahn Sona consciously tries for a mix of traditions. This is not a Thai wat or a Sri Lankan monastery, nor is it a purely Western creation. The goals of the blend are a "serene mind, a sense of proportion, beauty, simplicity."[31]

The Thai Forest Tradition is taking root in the West, and is now established in British Columbia. So far, and as long as Ajahn Sona is in charge, what grows up in BC will be heartwood (see Cadge 2004), that is, a centre for genuine Buddhist practice in the West.

NOTES

1 Thanks are due to the Tung Lin Kok Yuen Foundation for organizing a conference on Buddhism and Diaspora at the University of Toronto in 2010, where this chapter was first presented as a paper. Thanks are also due to those whom I have had the opportunity to interview, including Ajahn Sona, *Bhikkhus* Dhammavaro, Suvaco, and Subharo at Birken, and Ajahns Sumedho and Tiradhammo. Matchima Noikumpha, Piriya Novak, Ranjit Da Silva, Jessica Main, Brian Ruhe, and Edward Lewis also contributed information. All errors in the manuscript are, of course, my own responsibility.
2 The common name is Birken Forest Monastery, here called "Birken" for short. "Sitavana" means "cool forest" and was added in 2007. This name was probably added to conform to the Ajahn Chah lineage tradition wherein all monasteries (*wats* in Thai language) receive names in the Pali language.
3 Much of the information here is from the booklet "Birken Forest Monastery."
4 Gunaratne is also romanized Gunaratna or Gunaratana.
5 There are fourteen famous monks listed under "Sona" in various Buddhist dictionaries (http://www.palidictionary.appspot.com/zh_CN/browse/s/sona).
6 The Thai word "Ajahn" comes from the Sanskrit word *ācāriya*, "conductor; leader; teacher." In Pali texts its equivalent is never used as a title, except in specific contexts where a monk qualifies as a teacher. The Thai word is used as a title meaning "teacher" in general lay contexts, and has become a term of respect for monks who are generally senior. In the Pali contexts where it means "teacher," one qualification is ten years' seniority. In Western contexts, monks in the Thai tradition are referred to as "Ajahn" automatically after ten years of seniority. See Sujato (2010a) for full details.
7 Bhikkhu Sona, interview with author at Birken Forest Monastery, 23 April 2010.
8 Also *vanavasi*.
9 These thirteen *dhutangas* are undertaken voluntarily or assigned by teachers to correct a particular attachment. Also note that the living locations are options and cannot all be used at the same time. The thirteen are
    1 wearing only robes made of discarded cloth
    2 wearing only the three principal robes, no others
    3 going on almsround every day without fail

4   not omitting any house on almsround
5   eating only one meal per day
6   eating all food directly from the almsbowl
7   not accepting food offered after the almsround
8   living in the forest
9   living at the foot of a tree
10 living in the open, not under a tree or any roof
11 living in a cemetery
12 accepting any bed or resting place that is available
13 sitting, standing, or walking, but never lying down. (Maha Boowa 2004, 490)

10 Bhikkhu Sona, interview with author at Birken Forest Monastery, 23 April 2010.
11 Ibid.
12 Ibid.
13 Ibid.
14 There is some recent literature on the apparent survival of a *bhikkhuni* tradition in northern Thailand and other outlying areas of the Thai/Tai cultural area. These include local mythic histories and legends, as well as some Western observations of ochre-robed women in Ayutthaya, the regionally dominant Thai capital from 1350 to 1767. None of these references, including sculptures and inscriptions in various provincial locations, as well as mural paintings on royal wats in Bangkok, is emphasized in contemporary descriptions or cultural tours. Monks are taught that there has never been a *bhikkhuni* lineage in Siam. See Tathaaloka (2007).
15 For a strong counter argument, see Sujato Bhikkhu (2010), indicating clear Theravada roots of the Chinese and Taiwanese *vinaya*.
16 For examples, see Lindberg Falk (2008).
17 Most information here is from Western Elders Council, Forest Sangha. There is a comparable tradition well established in Sri Lanka called Dasa Sil Mata (or Matha). It was brought to Sri Lanka in 1905 by a Sri Lankan nun who had trained in Burma (Weeraratne 1998). The *sīladharās* formally observe ten traditional precepts from the Pali canon *vinaya*, but their training involves a great number of other requirements. This is part of the basic compromise of the *sīladharā* status.
18 For example, how many novices are ordained at one time by one *bhikkhuni*? See Thanissaro Bhikkhu (2009), and for a response Bodhi Bhikkhu (2009a). Ajahn Thanissaro emphasizes that the important thing is not only the source of one's *vinaya*, but whether the *vinaya* is used as the core of the tradition and is actually followed in the way that it is in the Theravada Forest Tradition.
19 Ajahn Tiradhammo. Personal communication, 2 May 2011.

20 Bhikkhu Sona, interview with author at Birken Forest Monastery, 23 April 2010.
21 Ibid.
22 For an overview of the history of this issue and its ramifications in Thailand, Sri Lanka, and worldwide, see Placzek 2011.
23 Paul Numrich has a similar three-fold overview of Theravada *vinaya* rigidity, focused on the factors of preservation of monastic life, practicality, and the achieving of consensus (cited in Prebish 2003, 68).
24 Bhikkhu Sona, interview with author at Birken Forest Monastery, 23 April 2010.
25 Ibid.
26 Ajahn Sumedho. Personal communication, 28 June 2010.
27 Bhikkhu Sona, interview with author at Birken Forest Monastery, 23 April 2010
28 Ibid.
29 Ibid.
30 Ibid.
31 Ibid.

5

Making a Traditional Buddhist Monastery on Richmond's Highway to Heaven

JACKIE LARM

Thrangu Monastery Canada, a large and opulent Tibetan Buddhist monastery of the Karma Kagyu lineage, opened its doors to the public in July 2010 (see illustration 4). Reportedly the "first Kagyu Monastery in the Pacific Northwest," the centre was built along Richmond, British Columbia's famous stretch of Number 5 Road known as the "Highway to Heaven." Thrangu Monastery Canada thus became the newest neighbour to the highway's string of religious organizations, which includes two Protestant churches, a mosque, a Vedic centre, a Sikh gurdwara, a Jewish school, and two other Buddhist centres (one Chan monastery and one Pure Land temple). Thrangu Monastery Canada, the first Tibetan Buddhist representative on the highway, is, according to the monastery's website, a place where "students can come to study and practice under [Thrangu Rinpoche's] direction in a traditional Monastic setting." The careful positioning of this Buddhist centre, as one that belongs under the spiritual leadership of Thrangu Rinpoche, and as one that claims to offer a "traditional" repertoire and setting, is an attempt to advertise the monastery's uniqueness amid the plethora of religious, including Buddhist, institutions occupying Richmond's diverse religious marketplace.

My first encounter with Thrangu Monastery Canada was over the Internet – an obviously modern mode of communication by which Thrangu Monastery advertises itself as traditional. My fiancé and I registered online for two empowerments/initiations (Tib. *wang/dbang*; Skt *abhisheka*) and for Thrangu Rinpoche's week-long teaching on Gampopa's treatise *The Jewel Ornament of Liberation*. We went to the appropriate website to add to our (virtual) shopping cart and pay for our upcoming empowerments and teachings. I remember feeling a bit uneasy about adding my spiritual practice to cyber shopping carts because I had not expected my initial experience of a so-called traditional monastery to be in the form of a web purchase. Then it occurred to me that I should think about what "traditional" signifies, what it designates, and how it applies to a new Tibetan Buddhist centre in Canada. More specifically, I wondered: to what does the word "traditional" point, what are the limits of this term, and who or what determined whether this monastery from its inception was actually traditional or not?

This chapter has two purposes. The first is simply to describe, offering some early observations of the new but traditional Thrangu Monastery in Canada. The first half of the chapter gives background information on the monastery and then discusses how the sense of traditional is evoked. The second purpose is to explore the concept of being "traditional," its connotations, its boundaries, its applicability, and its utility. This section also examines how the term is connected to questions of a centre's legitimacy and authenticity. This chapter concludes with a suggestion about how the word "traditional" may be usefully conceived and applied, that is as a framework rather than as a simple and limited adjective with a prescribed set of connotations. This chapter is based on the researcher's ongoing communications with monastery representatives and on her frequent visits to Thrangu Monastery Canada from July 2010 to May 2012. Data collection was through participant-observation and semi-formal interview techniques.

THRANGU MONASTERY CANADA: A BRIEF OVERVIEW

The Very Venerable 9th Khenchen Thrangu Rinpoche, a recognized *tulku* (reincarnated teacher or *lama* of high rank) in the Karma Kagyu lineage, opened Thrangu Monastery Canada on 25 July 2010. This was the newest and most ambitious addition to the group of Thrangu Rinpoche's Canadian dharma centres as well as an expansion of the vision for his earlier Vancouver centre, which had been operating under one of his dedicated monks, the Venerable Lama Pema Tsewang, who arrived in Canada in 2003.[1] The new, large monastic complex has quarters to house and train several monks; living quarters for both the head of the monastery, Thrangu Rinpoche, and the head of the Karma Kagyu lineage, His Holiness the

Karmapa; retreat and teaching facilities; administrative offices; a library; a donation collection centre; a kitchen/dining hall; a small shop area; and a large, colourful, and ornate main shrine room with a massive Śākyamuni Buddha statue in the centre (see illustration 5), thousands of smaller gilded deity statues lining the temple walls, and dozens of *thangkas* (wall hangings), mandalas, and murals along the ceilings and walls.

As stated on its website, the monastery serves as Thrangu Rinpoche's seat in North America, the home base where "Rinpoche can continue his teaching activities in the West." Its importance for Thrangu Rinpoche and his students cannot be overemphasized. Thrangu Rinpoche has centres throughout the world, but Thrangu Monastery Canada is the first of his monasteries built outside Asia.[2] This monastery is an extension of his network of monasteries and abbeys, used for training his monks and nuns and for teaching Tibetan Buddhism to lay community members. It is the main North American centre for the 9th Thrangu Rinpoche and presumably for his future rebirths as well. In Buddhist terms, Thrangu Monastery is notable because it represents the spread of Thrangu Rinpoche's activity. Its pamphlets and websites state that "a monastery provides a stable part of the external environment so that it can propagate the dharma for several generations" and as such, operates as a "means to accumulate merit for the world." In addition, it is hoped that "Thrangu Monastery may help spread the genuine Dharma in many lands, thus quelling the misfortunes of epidemics, famine and war in this world and helping peace, education, and prosperity to flourish."[3]

As evidence of this monastery's regional importance for the larger network of Karma Kagyu practitioners and thus its importance even beyond the circle of Thrangu Rinpoche's students, the monastery hosted the Second North American Kagyu *Monlam* (Great Prayer) Festival in June 2011. Its grand opening was a significant event for Thrangu Rinpoche, his followers, and for the city of Richmond, which is already noted for its cultural and religious diversity.[4] Hundreds of people, including lay practitioners, government representatives, media, and individuals and leaders from other Tibetan Buddhist organizations and local religious groups, attended the opening. The fanfare included a ribbon cutting, speeches from municipal and federal government representatives, speeches by Thrangu Rinpoche and Khenpo Karthar Rinpoche,[5] a lama dance, ceremonial rituals and prayers, and a free vegetarian lunch for all attendees. Lama Pema, the Vajra

Master and administrative head of the monastery, credits the monastery's completion to his positive karma, his determined intention to help as many beings as possible, and his good fortune in meeting dedicated supporters after arriving in Canada. Two main local sponsors, Eva Lau and her daughter, Margaret Lee, donated undisclosed but certainly sizable sums of money and time to the project. Thrangu Rinpoche also delegated many artists, ritual specialists, monks, and lamas from his monasteries in India and Nepal to Canada for the construction process, and many local volunteers and a construction company contributed to the building efforts.

As of May 2012, the monastery had a regular *sādhanā*, teaching, and ritual practice schedule. It has held regular seminars on Tibetan Buddhist philosophy and texts, Tibetan language and art classes, meditation sessions, and instruction and empowerment sessions for various Tibetan Buddhist practices. Weekend and week-long prayer retreats occur frequently throughout the year, with ten to thirty participants. The ordained sangha members perform additional prayer and empowerment ceremonies in response to lay community requests or to world problems (for example, conducting prayers for the victims of the March 2011 earthquake in Japan). Some events, like weekend meditation instruction, are free of charge while others, like empowerments and teachings, are not. The monastery houses nine of Thrangu Rinpoche's monks, who are at the time of writing all Tibetan from Nepal, Bhutan, and India. With some exceptions, the monastery's resident monks lead all of the monastery's regular practice and teaching sessions, but volunteers help perform other daily tasks (administrative, legal, translation, housekeeping). The participation of the monastery's lay followers ranges from those who only attend empowerments to regular *sādhanā* and course attendees, and thus it is difficult to ascertain with certainty the number of people affiliated with the monastery.[6] From my observations, however, 150 to 500 people are present for empowerments depending on who conducts the ceremony (more attend when Thrangu Rinpoche gives the empowerments personally), and about two to three dozen typically register for the lamas' and *khenpo*'s weekend teachings. For Thrangu Rinpoche's 2011 ten-day course, more than one hundred lay students attended each day of teaching. The monastery is open to visitors throughout most of the week and is promoted by the city of Richmond as a tourist destination. From casual observation, the monastery attracts mostly Chinese, Indian, and non-Asian sightseers.

The lay followers' socio-economic and cultural backgrounds are diverse, but it is the latter, its intercultural aspect, that is unique. The monastery serves local lay Tibetans, who are usually present in larger numbers during special occasions and empowerments. However, the majority of the lay community are Chinese individuals originally from Hong Kong, Taiwan, or mainland China. A handful of members are from South East Asia. Early interviews have shown that among Chinese individuals, most hear about the monastery from friends, and a few informants have credited one of the monastery's sponsors, Eva Lau, for being influential in this regard. There is also a substantial component of Canadian and American-born followers, who are both of Asian (including Japanese and Chinese) and non-Asian (including British, Western European, and African-American) descent. A few continental Europeans are regular attendees at the monastery as well. Representative of the cultural diversity, the monastery's working languages are Mandarin (Chinese), Cantonese, and English, although the monks often use Tibetan (Lhasa dialect) and Nepali among themselves and with individuals from the Tibetan community. Because of the diversity, intensive teaching courses, such as Thrangu Rinpoche's ten-day teachings, are delivered first in Tibetan and then translated into English and Mandarin by monks or lay people. Most of the on-site resident monks have obtained working knowledge of English and Mandarin in order to communicate effectively with lay members. Lay volunteers regularly teach the monks English and Mandarin for this purpose.

For regular *sādhanā* practices, there are generally more Chinese practitioners than members from other ethnic groups, but the overall participant numbers remain small. Usually fewer than one dozen people attend *sādhanās*, although it depends on the practice itself. On the other hand, Tibetan and Chinese people attend empowerments *en masse*. In fact, for many, empowerments might be the only time(s) they come to the monastery. One Tibetan Buddhist practitioner compared these irregular visitors to "Christmas and Easter Christians," and another monastery member thought these individuals were not sincerely interested in learning more about Tibetan Buddhism or in partaking in any of the other practices, stating that they attend empowerments only because they want the blessings they assume or hope the teacher and the ritual will bestow. They believe that Thrangu Rinpoche's high rank within the Kagyu lineage guarantees powerful blessings and protection. One attendee said, "I phoned my friend in Hong Kong to ask about this *lama*. She told me he was high up there, even the teacher of the top person. She said I had to go [to the empowerment], even being in his presence was a blessing." Unlike the attendees at either *sādhanā* or empowerment ceremonies, 30 to 40 per cent of those who attended Thrangu Rinpoche's 2011 teachings were white, and most were or had been affiliated with Shambhala International, with which Thrangu Rinpoche is connected (he is the appointed abbot of Gampo Abbey, a Shambhala monastery in Cape Breton).[7]

BUILDING THE IMAGE OF TRADITIONAL

Thrangu Monastery Canada's websites and brochures emphasize its traditional character. It advertises itself as "the first traditional Buddhist monastery in the Pacific Northwest" that serves as a place where "students can come to study and practice under (Thrangu Rinpoche's) direction in a traditional Monastic setting." One pamphlet (no date) states: "Under the direction of Thrangu Rinpoche, the Monastery will follow the practice of the Kagyu Lineage in accordance with the Dharma teachings of the 17th Gyalwang Karmapa, the spiritual leader of the Kagyu lineage. Thrangu Monastery will uphold Traditions of Tibetan Buddhism and practices through offering teachings, meditation, and short and long term retreats." "Traditional" here signifies that the monastery (1) belongs within a verifiable Tibetan Buddhist (Karma Kagyu) lineage, (2) affirms the lineage's globally recognized leader (i.e., the Karmapa), (3) and remains under the direction of a reputable Tibetan Buddhist scholar (i.e., Thrangu Rinpoche). Furthermore, these references to being traditional relate to the monastery's preservation of history, culture, and authenticity in its teachings, rituals, and leadership. As will be discussed, both the monastery's form (its architectural design and its artwork) and its content (its ritual proceedings and its leader) help to demonstrate the monastery's traditional image.

Traditional Form

Advertisements for Thrangu Monastery Canada state that the building's structure and form are rooted in antecedent traditional Indian and Tibetan Buddhist monasteries, buttressing the Canadian monastery's traditional as well as sacred character. Thrangu Rinpoche, who is credited with creating the overall architectural design of his Canadian monastery, reportedly based the style on the structure of the Nalanda Monastic Institute, a historic Buddhist monastery near Bodhgaya. He is also said to have incorporated design elements from a mandala principle and used many historical rituals and prayers during the monastery's construction, which is suggestive of the monastery's inherent sacredness. The building design even connects some students to Thrangu Rinpoche's current projects in Asia. One German student reported that Thrangu Monastery Canada mirrors his institutes in Nepal and India, which have all been built recently. She claimed, "his Namo Buddha monastery and the one in Canada look exactly the same ... They are not different." In addition, the extensive Tibetan Buddhist artwork and sculpture that adorn both the interior and exterior of the monastery reinforce the sense of the traditional at Thrangu Monastery Canada. Lama Pema said the main shrine's Śākyamuni Buddha statue was evidence that the monastery was traditional, because the statue had been designed and constructed according to the strict mathematical proportions, techniques, and ritual procedures developed long ago in Tibet.

The continuity of form evokes a sense of the traditional, connecting this new monastery to a sacred and ancient heritage. Like some of Thrangu Rinpoche's current projects in Asia, the monastery building's architecture and artwork are displays of religious preservation with respect to construction method and final product.

Traditional Content

Many of the practices and rituals appear to be stable through time because of their authorized transmissions between lineage holders. Practice and ritual stability strengthen the monastery's claim to being traditional. Again, the appearance of preservation and genuine transmission of knowledge and practice is key, and, therefore, language, costume, texts, and teachings that are tied to the practices must seem to conform to historical precedent. For example, while some Tibetan Buddhist centres in English-speaking countries use English for their prayers and chanting, Thrangu Monastery retains the use of Tibetan in all its ritual chanting, prayers, and empowerment ceremonies. Also, Thrangu Rinpoche's monks in Canada have stated that they follow the same morning practice routines that they would in Tibet, continue to rely on relatively unchanged Tibetan dharma texts for practice and ritual, and emphasize that the instructions they give to lay students are those they had received from their own teachers. It is not surprising that continuity and maintenance of lineage, which they trace to Śākyamuni Buddha and/or to later Buddhist masters, are continuously stressed during rituals, during teachings, and during more formal ceremonial functions.

Students' perception of Thrangu Rinpoche's character as traditional likewise contributes to the perception that his monastery is traditional. Several of Thrangu Rinpoche's students in Canada and in the United Kingdom described their teacher as "very traditional. Very, very traditional." Some explained further, saying that they were referring to Rinpoche's own traditional training in Tibet in the 1930s and 1940s, his strictness, his teachings (which they thought tended to be similar to material taught in Tibetan monasteries), and his training methods. Others stressed the type of ceremonies Rinpoche was willing to conduct or the manner in which he conducted them, as well Rinpoche's and his monks' mode of dress (for example, they wear traditional monks' robes and they don traditional ritual hats during important ceremonies). During the opening teachings, Thrangu Rinpoche even described himself as "old" and the presentation of his teachings as not very new or interesting, maybe even "boring." This admitted lack of innovativeness has helped to confirm students' suspicions that he is a traditional type of teacher delivering traditional teachings and rituals in a traditional setting, while making Tibetan teachings accessible to Western students. Therefore, from the students' perspectives, Rinpoche's appearance, teaching method, and teaching content appear rooted in authentic Tibetan Buddhism from an older Tibet, where preservation of history is a necessary component.

INNOVATION AND MODERNITY WITHIN TRADITION

Despite its claims to uphold tradition, Thrangu Monastery has integrated numerous "untraditional" elements into its design, practices, rituals, and function – that is, into the very elements that are crucial to building its image of traditionality. The monastery is fitted with modern technological conveniences, and monks employ modern tools to run the centre. Online donations are taken using PayPal, and for some teachings and rituals, participants can join via online streaming or Skype. The monks carry cell phones and iPads and respond to current salient issues, such as lay members' concerns respecting ethics or world events. Innovation, adaptation, and modernity are part of this traditional monastery. Observations from Thrangu Monastery support earlier academic research on tradition showing that tradition includes innovation and adaptation (Hobsbawm and Ranger 1983).

In one of its brochures, the monastery is described as "A Miniature Tibet You Should Visit in Richmond, British Columbia," as though part of Tibet and its undefined essence have been transported to, replicated, and preserved in western Canada. Apparently, the monastery seeks to "be a place of peacefulness and compassion where visitors will have the opportunity to rejuvenate both mind and body in the midst of this busy urban setting." Yet the notion that monasteries in Tibet are places of peace and refuge is, for the most part, both romanticized and inaccurate. Researcher Sherab Gyatso states: "The term 'Buddhist monastery' has become a cliché in the West, fodder for bland conversation. Evoked when someone expresses a half-hearted yearning to 'get away from it all,' the trite image is of a haven of peace and tranquility, somewhere where one can sever links with matters mundane and devote oneself to a simple, contemplative existence. It is hard to imagine a ruder challenge to such romantic notions than the large Tibetan monasteries. The atmosphere is likely to be noisy, boisterous and very much that of centres of (rather than retreats from) activity" (Gyatso 2003, 218–19). Gyatso's statement suggests that Thrangu Monastery Canada's advertising itself as a place of rejuvenation draws on the invented Western cliché of peaceful Buddhist monastery getaways. Thrangu Rinpoche's centres in Nepal and India, some of which house hundreds of nuns or monks at a time, cannot be places of quiet retreat. Moreover, Tibetan Buddhist monasteries were neither static nor uniform through space and time. Therefore, this "traditional" Thrangu Monastery Canada cannot be simply a replica of any Tibetan Buddhist counterpart, nor does it have a completely traditional setting or function. That it is a place of peacefulness for rejuvenating mind and body must be an adaptation to a new cultural setting – leaders have identified that they need to appeal to members of the Canadian public seeking solitude away from their busy urban lives. The invention of the traditional, in this case a peaceful retreat monastery in Canada, serves certain ideological ends (cf. Grieve and Weiss 2005, 1).

Innovation is integral to Thrangu Monastery Canada's operations, where adaptation and invention occur alongside the attitude of preservation.

Perhaps one of the most intriguing innovations to date is the introduction of the Official Membership scheme, which requires a monthly donation of money and/or service from an individual or a family to the monastery. Membership is voluntary and non-membership does not theoretically impede one's access to the monastery since one does not have to be an official member in order to join events, teachings, or practices. Members are, however, given special privileges, such as discounts on events or classes. Different membership levels are said to provide different types of offerings, such as flowers, food, or candles to the Buddha or the sangha, but the membership scheme was implemented principally to support the cost of running the monastery, both in terms of its mundane affairs, like paying its electrical and heating bills, and in terms of its religious practices, like providing art supplies.[8] According to Lama Pema, this is one way for the monastery to generate donations from its followers, who are living in a historically non-Buddhist society and are therefore not accustomed to supporting the sangha as extensively as is required for a monastery of this size. This new scheme is approached with an attitude of preservation of Buddhist teachings, apparent when leaders frame membership in terms of the Buddhist virtue of generosity. Lama Pema said during a private interview, "I hope people can get much merit from [giving to the monastery]. I want it to be good for them." The introduction of the Official Membership program demonstrates that the monastery's leaders are willing to be innovative as they face the challenges of operating a Tibetan Buddhist monastery in Canada.

Other non-traditional elements reflect the multicultural heritage of the lay community. Language is one of the most obvious. Teachings are usually given in Mandarin and English, and written material (posted signs, books, pamphlets) are usually in Chinese (classical script) and English (some material is in Chinese only). The distribution of *lai see* (Cantonese)/*hong bao* (Mandarin)/red pockets or lucky money for money collection, especially during long teachings and during empowerments, is clearly an incorporation of a useful Chinese custom. More substantial changes are observable in the monastery's ritual program, where rituals have frequently been added to accommodate the community's requests. In 2011, the monastery held celebrations for both Chinese and Tibetan New Year (*Losar*). Also, monks performed a Chinese Tomb-Sweeping Ceremony, an annual ritual honouring deceased ancestors. Moreover, as a response to the community's businessmen who wanted "better prosperity for 2011," at the beginning of the year the monastery offered an empowerment for yellow Zambhala, who is a Tibetan Buddhist deity often associated with wealth. Thus, while neither ritual is in itself a new phenomenon created by the monastery's leaders, the former has been adopted from Chinese cultural practices into a Tibetan Buddhist cultural setting, and the latter, although a Tibetan Buddhist ritual formerly, was performed strictly as a result of requests from a particular cohort within the lay community. In fact, when my fiancé, currently a university student, asked Lama Pema whether he should attend the empowerment ceremony as a blessing for the new year, Lama Pema laughed and said that he should not bother making the trip to the monastery. "[The Yellow Zambhala empowerment] is because the businessmen wanted it, so they could have fortune in 2011. We don't normally give for New Year ... Maybe it's not necessary for you. You don't need it now."

This Tibetan Buddhist centre is a community comprising "ethnic" members (Tibetan origin) and "convert" members (all others from a variety of cultural backgrounds), which in itself is unusual – this was neither the norm in Tibet nor the norm for Buddhist centres in North America or Western Europe.[9] I expect that this monastery will face many challenges as it tries to serve and appeal to an ethnically and culturally diverse lay community, which includes those born into Tibetan Buddhism and those who have adopted these practices in their adulthood. I would therefore expect the monastery to make several more adaptations to ritual programs and events as a result, even though it is unlikely all changes will be palatable to everyone. For example, several non-Asian individuals have commented that they found red pocket distribution, which has often been insistent, off-putting, causing potential tension within the lay community. One man also stated that he initially found the temple's display of wealth, such as the gold Śākyamuni statue, off-putting. Thrangu Rinpoche, Lama Pema, and the rest of the resident monks must also address the needs of various community members, as different cohorts of practitioners seem to be interested in slightly different events. Chinese and Tibetan people are typically more involved during empowerments, and some Chinese people request particular ceremonies, but teaching/studying programs tend to be more ethnically diverse. Further challenges relate specifically to language; the resident monks speak English and Mandarin but not all are fluent. As a result, many English speakers have left for other centres in search of Buddhist teachers with a better command of English. Similarly, both Mandarin and Cantonese speakers in the lay community will go to one or all of the many Chinese Buddhist centres in the greater Vancouver area because they seek a native Chinese-speaking teacher.

It is unclear why there are so many Chinese people at Thrangu Monastery. Two monks from different Kagyu centres thought that the high number was due to the fact that "Asians are more familiar with Buddhism so they just believe; they don't doubt so much like Westerners." Certainly, the significant Chinese population in Richmond and the Vancouver area is helpful, and the nearby Chinese Buddhist centres draw potential adherents to the vicinity. On the one hand, this proximity may mean that Thrangu Monastery must compete with these centres for members, but, on the other hand, the proximity is useful. One individual at Thrangu Monastery says he also goes to the Chinese Buddhist centres in the area for his "spiritual weekends," depending on their schedules. For example, he would participate in a morning *sādhanā* at Thrangu Monastery and then participate in an afternoon meditation session at the neighbouring temple. Obviously, this individual's intention was to practise and learn about Buddhism regardless of the different forms and lineages the centres represented.

Thrangu Rinpoche has centres in Hong Kong and Taiwan, but preliminary data suggests that at Thrangu Monastery Canada, most individuals heard about Thrangu Rinpoche from friends while in Canada, not Asia. All the individuals interviewed so far have been in Canada for fifteen years or more, which indicates that they are not new immigrants, and thus were not necessarily seeking belonging to a Chinese community when they started to attend the centre. Martin Baumann's observation, that "a traditionalist temple's aim is to provide a home away from home and to serve the religious and cultural needs of the transplanted community" (2001, 31), is challenged here, especially since this traditionalist temple serves not just one transplanted community but several.

The effects of foreign political pressures on membership are similarly unclear at this point. One practitioner stated that the People's Republic of China's sixty-year history of hostility toward all religions accounts for the small number of Mainland Chinese practitioners in the centre. However, this statement is unfounded, and I believe inaccurate. With regard to Chinese practitioners from other areas, Victor Chan has noted that the Dalai

Lama has been welcomed in Taiwan (2003, 106), but Chan's acquaintances in Hong Kong have refused to talk with him about the Tibetan situation or its exiled leader; "They have a lot to lose and they will not rock the boat. They will, as usual, take the easy way out: they will simply pretend Tibet does not exist." Many of the Chinese practitioners at Thrangu Monastery are certainly in different social conditions from Chinese people in present-day Hong Kong – they do not live under the jurisdiction of the Chinese government, and they have been residents of Canada for decades. But it may be worthwhile to note that (1) I have yet to hear any mention of Chinese/Tibetan politics at the monastery, and (2) the head of Thrangu Monastery's lineage, the 17th Karmapa Orgyen Trinley Dorje, was officially recognized and sanctioned by the Chinese Communist government when he was a child. It may also be worthwhile to note that H.H. the 14th Dalai Lama's picture is not in the shrine room or in the monastery's public hallways.

WHY TRADITIONAL?

Both "traditional" and "untraditional" Tibetan Buddhist teachers and lineage holders can be recognized – by their own students and by other Tibetan Buddhist teachers – to possess verifiable qualifications for transmissions of blessings and teachings. Yet in choosing particular Kagyu centres and teachers, practitioners and seekers often link concerns of legitimacy and authenticity to a centre's traditional image (or alternatively, the centre's lack of traditionality.) Fieldwork data from Kagyu centres from the United Kingdom and Canada (Shambhala, Samye Ling, Diamond Way, other Thrangu Rinpoche centres, Mangalashri) suggests that at one end of the spectrum are those attendees who are attracted to and believe in a Tibetan Buddhism minus the Tibet. For them, their place of worship and their teachers are legitimate because they represent "true, essential" Buddhism, a Buddhism without any cultural influence or, as one practitioner put it, "baggage." One visitor to Edmonton's Shambhala centre commented, "Some places I've been to just had too much of that cultural crap, and I couldn't get into [Buddhism]." Another individual in Calgary said, when speaking of her teacher, Ole Nydahl of the Diamond Way organization, "The first time I met him, I was just blown away ... He gives us Westerners the essential teaching, takes Buddhism right out from its Tibetan culture and teaches us the core, the *true* meaning of Buddhism. *He understands the Western culture so well*" (speaker's emphasis). One individual at Thrangu Monastery was forthright in his preference for Shambhala's presentation of Buddhism, which was Buddhism without Tibetan aesthetics, adornments, ritual, and colourful temples. He stated that he enjoyed being able to practise at Thrangu monastery (as well as all the other Chinese Buddhist centres in the area), but thought that Shambhala taught a pure form of Buddhism.

On the opposite end of the spectrum, practitioners and seekers believe that a particular Buddhist teacher/centre is authentic because it is "traditional" in multiple ways, including its appearance, ritual, language, function, organizational structure, and teachings. As Sandra Bell observes about four Theravada monasteries in Britain, the appeal of British Buddhist monasteries "is charged with references to antiquity and to tradition" (2000, 21). For practitioners preferring the traditional, the careful preservation of all the elements of the dharma, whether they be interpreted as cultural or not, is what ensures the correctness of the teachings and/or transmissions received. Several followers expressed their desire for continuity with an ancient Tibetan heritage, in whatever way that continuity was demonstrated and the heritage was constructed. One woman at Thrangu Monastery said recently, "I had never seen the procession to welcome the Karmapa like that before and I've been to lots of dharma centres. This is the tradition. This is real." When asked whether this ritual had been performed in Tibet, she said with certainty, "Oh yes, it's the same."

This same woman mentioned on another occasion that she felt Chinese Buddhism had incorporated too many cultural elements and beliefs from other religious traditions. In her opinion, Tibetan Buddhism had remained "correct" about the original Indian teachings, although she did not speak or read Sanskrit or Pali, and did not have extensive education in Buddhist philosophy. Her interpretation was likely somewhat romanticized. Bell has observed that "Western disciples have a tendency to romanticize the Tibetan 'tradition' (S. Bell 2000). One should note that the student mentioned in my example was a Chinese woman who had immigrated from Hong Kong more than twenty years ago, so she is both a "Western" and an "Eastern" disciple. Similarly, another member at Thrangu Monastery Canada said, "I went to Shambhala and some other places but I prefer more traditional places. I like saying, doing the practices in Tibetan, and everything like that. It just seems more comfortable." Giddens observes that tradition gives actors a sense of self-identity, "a continuity and form to life" (2002, 45, 47), which was perhaps attractive to these practitioners. For them, being in a traditional place was crucial for their sense of belonging.

In fact, change may be resisted if it appears to be new. One of Thrangu Rinpoche's teaching monks mentioned that Tibetan Buddhist converts often comment, after different melodies to chanting are introduced, that they prefer the "old, traditional" tune rather than the "new" one. He said that practitioners apparently fail to realize that melodies are frequently changed within Tibetan Buddhist practice, and that melodies are chosen simply to sound nice and pleasant so are not integral to the prayer itself. Moreover, prayer leaders may simply be reverting back to a historically older, previously used melody. In other words, it would seem that some practitioners not only place great importance on what teachers have deemed inconsequential for practice (that is, a tune of the chant), but they may also believe that their current practices are completely "traditional." Edward Shils's research noted that variations occurring before or during the handing-down process may become part of the tradition itself (1981, 14), but it is important that the observer believes that the essentials were transmitted and are recognizable, or that no substantial change occurred. In the case of chanting at Thrangu Monastery, practitioners believed that they had received an essential traditional tune, making change undesirable.

An intriguing example from outside Tibetan Buddhism and Thrangu Monastery Canada confirms that some sets of Buddhist practitioners prefer the traditional over modernity, however traditional is connoted. Louise Connelly's research on virtual Buddhism discusses "traditional" Buddhist temples in Second Life, an online virtual world where one can construct both oneself and his/her surroundings (private conversation, October 2010).[10] Some practitioners have expressed their desire for such temples to be traditional (apparently in form and function) because they are better suited for their spiritual needs. "Traditional" is not the most applicable adjective for a Buddhist temple that exists only in cyberspace. Yet clearly, it is their mental projection and the conviction that their meditation and worship space is inarguably traditional, i.e., that it belongs to an older time and place, that resonate with practitioners who use the virtual world to meditate. In other words, despite the unconventional location of their temples, practitioners still want their temples to feel traditional. Tradition and the traditional become interpretive categories to refer to thoughts, practices, and people that coalesce around particular visions of social, religious, and/or historical continuity and rupture (Carbine 2005, 145–6). The concept of being "traditional" must therefore appeal to practitioners on an emotional level, offering comfort and a hold on seemingly timeless wisdom.

Therefore, many Tibetan Buddhist centres describing themselves as "traditional" will continue to appeal to a particular group of practitioners. This supports both Grieve and Weiss's (2005) and S. Bell's (2000, 3) separate findings that particular value judgments are made about tradition, associated with the old in contrast to the new. The image of traditionality is desirable, marketable, or appealing because it attracts and retains members, offering them a sense of security and continuity in the face of modernity. I have yet to hear members of the monastery discuss change and the monastery's methods of adaptation to its new context – that is, how it is "not traditional." Perhaps this is because the integration of new cultural elements or practices is seen as either inconsequential or non-existent. Innovation at Thrangu Monastery may be perceived as superficial, inessential to the perceived core elements of Tibetan Buddhism being taught there and the core traditional elements being retained and preserved. On the whole, however, it is too early to tell how potential and existing members will think about innovation with respect to their teacher or their monastery, or how their perceptions and practices of Buddhism have been, or will be, influenced by the monastery, which for the moment upholds an image of being traditional. The perception and effects of innovation would best be observed over several more years. I am not suggesting that the debate between "traditional" and "modern" is pertinent to all practitioners at Thrangu Monastery Canada, but certainly questions of traditionality and authenticity will continue to arise.

BEGINNING TO UNDERSTAND "TRADITIONAL"

Observations on the use of the word "traditional" at Thrangu Monastery support the findings of previous scholarly research – that tradition integrates adaptation, innovation, and modern developments. Despite innovation and incorporation of modern technologies, this traditional monastery represents what has been handed down from generation to generation (Shils 1981, 12; Despland 2005, 19), connecting actors into the past (usually with a reverence for the past) and into a diachronic community (Grieve and Weiss 2005, 3). Traditionalism and modernization are, in a sense, responses to each other, and tradition may be valued where modernity feels threatening or ambiguous (Berkwitz 2003, 59; Hughes 2005, 54). Consonant with Grieve and Weiss's work in Nepal (2005), tradition can then only exist with modernity because "the maintenance of the traditional as an apparent remnant from an earlier age becomes valuable" in a contemporary setting.

For the study of Buddhism outside of Asia, Victor Hori's observation should be kept in mind: "Part of our problem in understanding Buddhism in the West is that we are quick to assume that ethnic Buddhism is 'traditional,' a survivor from a pre-modern world ... In this assumption, we are implicitly associating Asia with the traditional and the West with the modern" (2010a, 30). He points to a particular set of problems arising from the ethnic/convert dichotomy used in the study of Western Buddhism. The traditional is often blindly equated with a sense of the pre-modern, which in turn is associated with ethnic as opposed to convert Buddhist communities. Although Thrangu Monastery advertises itself as traditional, it neither represents a pre-modern Tibetan Buddhist world nor fits well into the ethnic/convert paradigm (all non-Tibetan are converts, and this includes Asians! Also, the monastery looks after both ethnic and convert Tibetan Buddhists.)

For practitioners, seekers, and onlookers, "traditional" is associated with the degree of continuity, retention, and static-ness of what they see as essential elements in the tradition. Any unchallenged changes seem to be interpreted as non-threatening to the centre's overall usefulness and legitimacy, or are unobserved. For this Tibetan Buddhist monastery, traditional often relates to the lack of incorporation of what they consider Western elements, the lack of innovation and innovativeness (especially on the part of the teacher), and the retention of what they see as historically bound, essential Tibetan Buddhist rituals, presentation, methods, costumes, artwork, organizational structure, language, performance, and teachings (and thus retention of the centre's authenticity and legitimacy).

"Traditional" can be usefully thought of as a type of framework, a seemingly old framework that points to a particular tradition and offers a structure into which we can place the monastery's appearance, rituals, teachings, and teacher. The traditional framework can connect actors into the past, the present, and the future, in addition to connecting them to a diachronic community, as Grieve and Weiss have observed. Consequently, the parameters that maintain a tradition and the boundaries that signify the traditional are neither vital nor concrete. For example, in the case of Thrangu Monastery, members are unconcerned about whether monks are driving cars or walking on grass (which in former times were considered a breach of vows) because of the implicit belief that traditionalism is the monastery's modus operandi. The structure of the traditional is already in place even though the boundaries that separate the traditional from the modern are not fixed. Here, the meaning of the boundary – that it separates the traditional from the modern – is more significant than the boundary itself (see Anthony Cohen 1985, 12). The monastery's highly pragmatic teachers and leaders are not concerned about discerning whether the monastery is traditional or not. Their greatest challenge at the moment is trying to manage a diverse lay following while maintaining their personal religious responsibilities.

Being traditional is a result of the monastery's intent as well as a result of the students' expectations. In this sense, the monastery is extremely contemporary, a product of contemporary people, contexts, and concerns. The monastery's leaders are acutely aware of, and responsive to, contemporary issues and problems, and are generally seen as being highly engaged in helping their global and local communities. In addition, the monastery reflects the shared present-day desire to have an institution that can symbolically stand for Tibetan Buddhist history and culture, whether imagined or real.

Because of its groundedness in social reality, the boundaries defining the framework of traditionality are neither solid nor immovable. As discussed above, changes in rituals and practices, modification to the building's design, and accommodation to non-Tibetan cultures have already been introduced at Thrangu monastery. I assume that additional adaptations of teachings or innovation in other areas can likewise occur unnoticed in the future. As long as the changes remain either plausible within, or inconsequential to, the framework of traditionality, the monastery will continue to be able to successfully project its "traditional" character. As Anthony Giddens reminds us, endurance over time is not a distinguishing feature of being traditional (2002, 41). He states that "the traditional way means defending traditional activities through their own ritual and symbolism –

defending tradition through its internal claim to truth" (2002, 43). A traditional framework provides structure around activities such that it offers the reflective capacity for internal claims to truth to be made.

The majority of the framework's components seem to be passed down from generation to generation such that newness and place of origin largely go unquestioned. New innovations, like the Official Membership Program, and additions of another culture's traditions, such as the Chinese Tomb-Sweeping Ceremony, are woven into the traditional framework such that members can access an age-old Tibetan Buddhist tradition and an age-old Tibetan Buddhist community through these innovations. This demonstrates why adaptation of Thrangu Monastery Canada, or any other Buddhist organization in Canada, is crucial; it adapts in order to be relevant to its context. One of the chosen methods for its adaptation to the Canadian environment is through instilling a sense of the traditional.

CONCLUSION

Thrangu Monastery Canada has for the time being repeatedly reinforced its image of being a "traditional Tibetan Buddhist monastery" by emphasizing those elements, such as artwork and architecture, ritual, and hierarchical structure, that evoke most strongly a sense of historicity. Certainly more factors, such as organizational structure and hierarchy, could be discussed, but these examples provide a springboard for thinking about a traditional monastery. Thrangu Monastery Canada projects an image of preservation and historicity, which attracts some practitioners and deters others seeking an authentic Buddhist experience. Practitioners, some of whom may leave boundaries of the "traditional" largely uncontested but for whom it is a component in deciding which Tibetan Buddhist organization they would like to join, will likely continue to raise issues of legitimacy, authenticity, and the traditional.

Thrangu Monastery Canada provides an interesting case study for thinking about how researchers, practitioners, and leaders of institutions conceive and employ the term "traditional." At its simplest, "traditional" is a type of framework into which most elements within a place, in this case the practices, teachings, rituals, architecture, and teachers at Thrangu Monastery, seem to belong. It is a normative outline that allows pieces of a puzzle to fit together with the sense of connecting to an older, maybe wiser, past.

It may just be a place where adding Gampopa empowerments to my Internet shopping cart can become an authentic part of my traditional Tibetan Buddhist experience.

NOTES

1   As of January 2011, Thrangu Rinpoche had one centre in Edmonton and another near Toronto. Some research and photography on his Ontario site have been produced by John Negru (Karma Yönten Gyatso). See Negru (2009).
2   As of May 2012, Thrangu Rinpoche's other monasteries and abbeys were in Tibet, India, and Nepal.
3   I have not heard Thrangu Rinpoche or any of his monastics distinguish between what they would perceive as genuine versus false dharma. Several practitioners on the other hand have spoken about "charlatans," people who propagate false dharma. For them, charlatans often lack proper spiritual qualifications (not having lineage-verifiable teachings and training, having broken lineage transmissions) and motivation (for example, they want to make money instead of helping people).
4   Richmond's cultural and religious diversity was praised numerous times during the Grand Opening. With respect to Buddhism, Placzek and De Vries noted that the number of Buddhist adherents in Richmond more than tripled between 1991 and 2001, and several Buddhist centres of various traditions had made their homes in Richmond prior to the opening of Thrangu Monastery Canada (Placzek and Vries 2006, 17). For example, Richmond is home to Dharma Drum Mountain Vancouver Center (Chan), Steveston Buddhist Temple (Jōdo Shinshū), and the immense International Buddhist Temple, also known as the Kuan Yin Temple (Chinese Mahayana).
5   Khenpo Karthar Rinpoche is the abbot of Karma Triyana Dharmachakra (KTD), the North American seat of the Karmapa (head of the Karma Kagyu lineage), in Woodstock, New York.
6   As of January 2011, 675 recipients were registered on the monastery's email list. Certainly, this gives no indication as to the number of affiliates, or their degree of affiliation or participation in monastery events. It does not indicate the number of Canadian Buddhist practitioners who profess being students of Thrangu Rinpoche. It simply shows the number of people (visitors, practitioners, other interested parties) who requested information through email.
7   In 1990, Thrangu Rinpoche founded Söpa Chöling, Gampo Abbey's three-year retreat centre, and he has continued to be involved in the teaching and training of the retreat

participants. More recently, his involvement has been from a distance. For example, in 2011 at Thrangu Monastery Canada, he gave a group of future retreatants all the empowerments they would need for their upcoming three-year retreat.

8 Similarly, charging attendees for empowerments and for teachings was introduced recently. It was done to cover the monastery's operating costs.

9 Because the monastery serves non-Tibetans and Tibetans, Thrangu Monastery challenges the "ethnic" versus "convert" model, and any permutation thereof.

10 According to the researcher, practitioners use these online Second Life temples to supplement their personal practices, for example, simultaneously meditating at home and in their virtual space.

6

Dharma on the Move: Vancouver Buddhist Communities and Multiculturalism

PAUL CROWE

INTRODUCTION

Academic reflection on immigrant religious communities often, and justifiably, focuses on the flux of religious forms as they take shape in their new Canadian social context. A related assumption is that religion conceived of as *sui generis*, a trans-social or trans-historical unity, is, at the very least, unhelpful. Religious life, based as it is on social and cultural solidarity and the complex dynamics of constant institutional and congregational renegotiation, is always in transformation. These foundational methodological assumptions predispose us to view immigrant religious communities through the lenses of adaptation and integration. Accordingly, in *Religion and Ethnicity in Canada*, editor Paul Bramadat observes: "religious ideas, texts, rituals, symbols, and institutions are in the end redeployed by newer Canadians in a uniquely Canadian way. Another way to put it is to say that religion is never relocated (like baggage), but rather is always re-created" (Bramadat 2005, 13).

In line with Bramadat's observations, Terry Watada describes the adaptive reflex of Japanese Canadians reacting to increasing racial tensions in British Columbia during the 1920s, '30s, and '40s. He notes that "Shin Buddhists responded to this concern by self-consciously 'Christianizing' their Buddhist practice" (Watada 2010, 67). Rather than Buddhist temples there were churches with pews and hymnals. Communal practice involved Sunday services and Sunday school. The assuming of a less jarring public profile is evident in early Chinese immigrant communities beginning in the late nineteenth century, when newcomers were forced to close cultural ranks and retreat to the safety in numbers represented by early Chinatowns in cities such as Victoria and Vancouver. Indeed, so low was the profile of Chinese religious expression through the pre-war period that we have virtually no information on the number and nature of these institutions. David Chuenyan Lai, Jordan Paper, and Li Chuang Paper speculate that prior to 1970 there were only two Chinese temples built in Canada and both were in the oldest Canadian Chinatown, in Victoria (Lai, Paper, and Paper 2005, 95). Tam Kung (Tan Gong 譚公) Temple was located in a single-storey house likely rented by a Hakka society and officially dedicated on 21 January 1876 (D. Lai 1988, 193). The second was Laat Sing Kung (Lie Sheng Gong 列聖宮), established in 1885 when a shrine was installed on the top floor of the Chinese Consolidated Benevolent Association (D. Lai 1991, 67).[1] In a social climate fraught with racial tensions, assuming a lower profile was a reasonable adaptive response aimed at survival through avoidance of confrontation.

While reading the institutional history of immigrant religious groups through the lenses of adaptation and integration remains a valuable approach, the current situation of Chinese religious Buddhist organizations in the Lower Mainland of British Columbia warrants considering that another perspective – one that allows a discourse of continuity, orthodoxy, and cultural solidarity – is equally important and may sometimes be in tension with that of integration. This chapter is based on interviews and participant observation conducted primarily between 2006 and 2009 for a chapter on Chinese religions in *Asian Religions in British Columbia* (Crowe 2010a). During the interviews, whenever the subject of adaptation arose, the response was more complicated than a recounting of ways in which groups were trying to fit into their respective geographic and sociocultural contexts. This chapter foregrounds these responses and raises some questions about their implications for immigrant religious communities and for Canada's multiculturalism policy and public philosophy, given changes to the language associated with multiculturalism currently being instituted by the federal Conservative Party. In this time of increased global migration, the official discourse of multiculturalism plays a powerful role in mediating public perception of the nature of integration, and need for it. On balance, Canada's multiculturalism public policy and philosophy have served Canada well, providing a public realm in which cultural continuity can be safely pursued in the context of a strong Canadian civil society. As migration sources have shifted dramatically from Europe to Asia, multiculturalism continues to serve to maintain a national context of appreciation for diversity, which has for centuries been the reality for Canada.

New Canadians of Chinese heritage do not frame their efforts to maintain continuity, orthodoxy, and cultural solidarity in the language of rejection – rejection of Canada and its social and political institutions. Rather, they tend to speak more positively of maintaining the integrity of community belief, praxis, and identity. Discussion of the need for integration can cause tensions to surface because such discussion is necessarily bound up with a tacit assumption that the "adapter" is at a distance from the elusive "mainstream" of Canadian society, which implies doubt regarding the subject's claim to a Canadian identity and disregards the fact of their multiple subjectivities. Questions concerning adaptation, integration, identity, and even orthodoxy are, of course, raised within a broader context of social forces – in particular, demographic shifts occasioned by immigration trends emerging in British Columbia in the 1980s and accelerating since 2000.

A QUESTION OF INTEGRATION

In the course of interviews and observation conducted for the book mentioned above (De Vries, Baker, and Overmyer 2010), a standard questionnaire was used at locations where Chinese religious groups met and practised. The internal dynamics of the various groups was one important focus. How were they organized? What sorts of divisions existed within groups? Did these divisions follow gender, age, or formal religious rank? Much time was spent on the kind of activities conducted at each centre, on their respective histories, and on the events that members understood to be of great significance within those histories. We also discussed how members believed people beyond the immediate horizon of their own religious cohort perceived them. Did people understand who they were and how they were seeking to adapt their practices, teachings, and organization to a new social and cultural context?

It came as something of a surprise to learn that the questions about perceptions and adaptation, in contrast to those about history, teachings, mission, and organization, were received with a mixture of puzzlement, vague references to needing to provide translation at dharma talks, and emphatic assertions that adaptation was not needed. Further, adaptation, it seemed, could represent a potential problem since it might lead to compromising the orthodoxy on which was based the validity of the practice and identity of a group's tradition.

Lotus Light Temple (Hua Guang Lei Zang Si 華光雷藏寺) was established on East Hastings Street, on the periphery of Vancouver's Chinatown, by Master Lianci 蓮慈 in 1996, at the urging of "living Buddha" Lu Shengyen 盧勝彥. It is one of more than forty temples constituting the network of the True Buddha School (Zhenfo zong 真佛宗), including ten in Canada.[2] At Lotus Light Temple, a monk responded to my questions concerning adaptation by stating with obvious pride that whether you walked through the door of a sister temple in Taiwan or this one in Vancouver the experience would be indistinguishable. He noted one difference: that non-Chinese visitors tend to prefer watching the weekly ceremony whereas those of Chinese heritage are more likely to join in. A book with ritual proceedings, mudras, descriptions of *qi* 氣 exercises, and chants, which included English and Taiwanese-style phonetic rendering of the Chinese text chanted by devotees, illustrated the "traditional" nature of the practice and an element of linguistic adaptation.[3]

A similar response was evident at Gold Buddha Monastery located roughly three kilometres south of Chinatown. The founder of the Gold Buddha Monastery, Ven. Master Hsüan Hua (Xuan Hua 宣化),[4] was born in 1917 in the county of Shuangcheng 雙城, Jilin province. The master travelled to famous Caoxi 曹溪 in northern Guangdong where he took up residence at Nanhua Monastery (Nanhua si 南華寺) under the guidance of Elder Master Xü Yün 虛雲.[5] In 1962, in his mid-forties, Master Hsüan Hua "brought the Proper Dharma to America" (Dharma Realm Buddhist Association 1996) where, in 1974, land was purchased to establish the present headquarters of the Dharma Realm Buddhist Association at the City of Ten Thousand Buddhas in Ukiah, California. In 1982 a lay Buddhist group in Vancouver made up of Chinese immigrants invited Master Hsüan Hua to consider opening a "Way Place" (*daochang* 道場)[6] in Vancouver. In December 1983 Gold Buddha Monastery was opened on Gore Street in the old Salvation Army building.

When I asked the head nun at Gold Buddha Monastery, a Caucasian American ordained more than forty years ago, about the need to adapt, she explained that the temple continues to teach the "orthodox dharma" (*zheng fa* 正法). Thus, the fact that the temple operates in a "Western" context in no way compromises the continuity and integrity of the teaching it provides. She clarified that Gold Buddha Monastery adheres strictly to the rules of monastic conduct, maintains correct ritual, and is not "contaminated" by folk religious tradition. Further, the monastery and its teachings represent the "Catholic Church of Buddhism." At a later date, in a seminar at Simon Fraser University, two young Taiwanese nuns from the same monastery provided details of their rigorous daily schedule confirming how committed they were to the "orthodox" monastic code of conduct.

Beyond what could arguably be described as a cautious, conservative attitude toward adaptation and accommodation in praxis and teaching, the broader social circumstances for Gold Buddha Monastery also appear to be moving in a direction away from integration. The head nun explained that in the early days it was principally Americans with no Asian heritage who took leadership roles. With their move in 1983 to Canada's west coast, two young Caucasian monks, Heng Sure (Heng Shi 恆實) and Heng Chau (Heng Zhao 恆朝), found themselves serving a mostly Cantonese immigrant membership. In the years since its establishment, Chinese nuns from Taiwan have assumed leadership.[7] The nun I interviewed is the only non-Chinese monastic now residing at Gold Buddha Monastery, and her busy schedule keeps her away from the Vancouver monastery for extended periods.

Gold Buddha Monastery has been offering the "orthodox dharma" in Vancouver for nearly three decades. During my several visits over the past three years, it has become evident that these many years of activity have not led to integration, if that implies a mixed congregation. Virtually all the participants attending weekend celebrations, dropping in during the week, or sitting down to vegetarian lunches on the weekend are Chinese and their first language continues to be Cantonese or Mandarin,[8] though regular translation for Vietnamese members is also available.

Ling Yen Mountain Temple (Ling Yan Shan Si 靈巖山寺) is located in Richmond, a municipality to the south of Vancouver (see illustrations 6 and 7). Established in 1999, it is linked to a monastery of the same name in central Taiwan, constructed in 1984. At the time of my visit, in March 2006, I was told that the temple served more than six hundred families. I was fortunate to participate in a formal vegetarian lunch complete with a dharma talk in a hall with numerous lay followers and the forty-nine nuns currently in residence. All participants appeared to be of Chinese heritage and the proceedings were carried out in Mandarin. I asked one of the head nuns how the temple has had to adapt as it has become established in Canada. Rather than receiving an explanation of the ways the temple leadership has sought to adjust to suburban Richmond, I was told how tolerant Canada is and how groups are free to maintain their own cultural identity:

> What makes Canada a place that people honour and love is precisely its multiculturalism; its ability to embrace ethnic minorities and religions. Owing to the fact that Canada is a country of immigrants, ethnic minorities, and religions, it is a great melting pot. Everyone in Canada is able to manifest and develop their own traditions and customs. Together we paint its multicoloured and multifaceted diversity. Therefore we can say Ling Yen Mountain Temple truly has no difficulty with what you call adaptation because it is itself part of Canada.
> 加拿大最令人尊敬及可愛的地方，就在於它對多元文化、民族及宗教的包容性。由於加拿大是移民國家，本身就是文化、民族及宗教的大熔爐，加拿大的每一份子都能夠盡情展現其傳統風格，共同描繪出加拿大多采多姿的多元風采。所以說，加拿大靈巖山寺並沒有所謂『適應』的問題，因為它本身就是屬於加拿大的一部分…[9]

As expected, the language barrier was mentioned, although it seemed the barrier was more likely to be between Chinese dialects than between English and Chinese.

Indeed, not only did it appear that adaptation and accommodation were not primary concerns or motivating forces behind temple activities; on the contrary, their main concern was the full expression of their own religio-cultural identity and solidarity with the Chinese immigrant community. This is indicated most obviously, or publicly, by the aspirations of Ling Yen Mountain Temple's members to expand their already impressive facilities to four times their current size at an estimated cost of 40 million dollars.[10] In sharp contradistinction to the early Jōdo Shinshū groups in British Columbia, who housed themselves in churches, members of Ling Yen Mountain Temple approached Richmond city council for zoning concessions for construction of a building higher than any other in the municipality that would house a 30-metre-tall gilded Buddha. These plans have caused no small measure of bluster in the local media, which has characterized the proposed development as a "Buddhist Disneyland."[11] An initial proposal was put before Richmond city council in 2005 but neighbouring residents raised concerns about parking and the shadow they believed would be cast eastward over Highway 99 by the approximately 43-metre-tall main building.[12] As a result, the temple withdrew its application. A second attempt was made late in 2010, but a decision was put on hold since time was needed to review the Agricultural Land Reserve policy. The temple is now putting forward a revised development proposal for consideration by Richmond residents and city council. Plans were exhibited at an open house in the South Arm Community Centre in Richmond on 26 June 2013. The tallest building has been reduced from 43 to 30 metres and the main site has been moved much further back from the adjacent roadway. The new plans include provisions for no net loss of land from the Agricultural Land Reserve. The antipathy and delays have not diminished the hopes of temple leadership and the more than ten thousand members who, it is claimed, depend on and support the temple. This tenacity shows just how much the dynamics of Chinese immigrant religious expression have changed. Accommodation and "keeping one's head down" have been replaced by an unapologetic determination to forge a strong, visible presence in a community that, in some quarters at least, appears emphatically resistant to such intentions.

Another development related to the question of integration has been that of parallel congregations. Here I am not speaking of the thoroughly discussed and problematic divisions of ethnic vs convert Buddhists or those referred to by Suwanda Sugunasiri as "Ethnic-Buddhist" and "Euro-Buddhist" (Sugunasiri 2006, 111–14). Those groups are parallel in a much wider sense than is intended here. At the Tung Lin Kok Yuen Canada Society temple (Jianada donglian jueyuan 加拿大東蓮覺苑) on Broadway at Victoria Drive in Vancouver, for example, meditation and discussion groups are held behind the Ancestral Hall in a building adjacent to the main worship or Buddha Hall. These meetings cater to English speakers interested in Zen meditation and are led by a Caucasian monk who spent thirteen years in a Japanese Sōtō Zen monastery before returning to Canada and assuming teaching duties at Tung Lin Kok Yuen. Upstairs in the main hall, large groups of Chinese-speaking lay devotees participate in Pure Land rituals led by nuns. The two constituencies do not interact but maintain their respective modes of practice within this single temple.

The Canadian missionary work of Dharma Drum Mountain (Fagu shan 法鼓山), a Chan Buddhist organization established in 1989 in Jinshan 金山 Township, Taibei County, Taiwan, provides another example. The principal teacher was Jiangsu native Master Sheng Yen 聖嚴, who left home to become a monk at age thirteen. After conscription into the Nationalist Army he moved to Taiwan and, ten years later, undertook a six-year period of solitary retreat after returning to study with his teacher Venerable Dongchu 東初 at Nung Chan Monastery (Nongchan si 農禪寺). In 1969, at the age of thirty-nine, he took up studies at Rissho University in Tokyo, where he obtained a doctorate in literature. He began teaching in 1975. After Master Sheng Yen's visit in 1994, space was first rented at the Marpole-Oakridge Community Centre in south Vancouver. When the Master visited again the following year, the Vancouver group was holding regular chanting and meditation sessions three times per month and occasional lectures on Buddhist teachings. In 2007, I attended the first anniversary celebrations of the inauguration of the new Dharma Drum Mountain Vancouver Centre. In contrast to other Chinese Buddhist buildings, the simple lines and colours of the new Dharma Drum centre might be seen as reflecting a greater concern for blending in, though the organization's website explains that the intention is to exemplify "the quality of nature, being simplicity and stability" (Dharma Drum Mountain Vancouver Center, n.d.). Roughly three hundred people, including local politicians and representatives from other Buddhist organizations, attended the celebrations. The vast majority of attendees were of Chinese heritage.

As with Tung Lin Kok Yuen Canada Society, there is a gradual coalescing of two distinct constituencies within this organization. Two meditation teachers, originally from Taiwan, are dedicated to developing practice and study for non-Chinese speaking students who do not share the cultural interest in, for example, Pure Land repentance ceremonies. The group's meetings are conducted in English and focus on meditation and discussion of Buddhist philosophy. With the registration of a new organization under the Society Act in British Columbia, the distinction between the two groups has taken institutional form. As of 11 June 2008, the group became known as the "Chan (Zen) Community of Canada Association" (CZCCA). Its head teacher is Venerable Guo Jun 果峻,[13] a dharma heir of Master Sheng Shen. The idea of establishing CZCCA was discussed with and approved by Master Sheng Yen in 2006 and was also approved by the Taiwan headquarters of Dharma Drum Mountain. A separate public identity was thought to be more conducive to attracting students who would otherwise not become participants in the main Dharma Drum assembly. By branching out, the organization can reach beyond institutionalized boundaries in a way that does not challenge the relative homogeneity and continuity expected by a majority of members who are most comfortable in a Chinese Buddhist cultural and linguistic milieu. Master Sheng Yen had a great interest in reaching across cultures and, as with Gold Buddha Monastery's translation efforts, dedicated much energy to inclusivity by making the Buddha dharma accessible to those who cannot read or speak a Chinese dialect. It would seem, however, that a parallel organization is required to realize these intercultural ideals.

A final example reflects an altogether different response to the question of integration. Vancouver's Universal Buddhist Temple (UBT) (Shijie fojiao hui 界世佛教會) is the oldest active Chinese Buddhist temple in Vancouver. It was established by a group of lay Buddhists from Hong Kong who were making their new home in Canada. The group coalesced around the figure of Mr C.C. Lu (Lü Luojiu 呂雒九) (1899–1982), a Taiwan-based businessman with family origins in Sichuan. He provided the principal financial support needed to rent a space for the temple, from 1968 until 1977, above the Chinese Freemasons at 116 East Pender Street in the heart of Vancouver's Chinatown. The temple is now located at 49th Avenue and Fraser Street in what was originally a church, though that fact is no longer apparent due to the adoption of more conventionally Chinese architectural features. While monks and nuns are contracted to offer Buddhist teachings and officiate at weekly ceremonies, the leadership is in the hands of a core group of lay devotees who are resolutely non-sectarian in orientation.[14] This arrangement is certainly a departure from the more common institutional dynamic in which leadership is in the hands of monastics. This change is partly necessitated by legal requirements for incorporation of a religious organization which specify that there be a board of directors and bylaws. But this relationship between lay congregants and monastics preceded concerns related to incorporation. It was adopted in a self-conscious effort to preserve the flexible, non-sectarian orientation of the temple in accordance with the intentions of Mr Lu and the founding group.

Many of the members UBT serves migrated to Canada up to forty years ago. Given this fact, a problematic dynamic emerges when a more recent immigrant to Canada, the present Caucasian author, asks a "Chinese" UBT leader about their position on integrating into mainstream Canadian society and the effect of such efforts on their institution. The response to this inquiry was one of frustration: this particular question was not new to the interviewee. The response was that UBT members *are* Canadian and that the question should not be about adaptation or integration but rather about how they have been contributing to Canadian society as Canadians since the 1960s. This pointed response from a Buddhist community leader brings to light the power dynamic implicitly present in such a question: "*You*, as a Chinese Buddhist, need to find your way into *my* society." This inside/outside, me/other duality raises difficulties similar to those associated with the term "ethnic." Victor Sōgen Hori includes in the opening chapter to *Wild Geese: Buddhism in Canada*, a quotation of François Thibeault's incisive observation that "ethnic identity is a social construction that implies self- and other-observation'" (Hori 2010a, 19). The same can be said of "our" expectations of integration and adaptation. While the language used to frame such questions is problematic, it remains true that religious communities do cohere around their own customs, habits of comportment, food preferences, language, and shared geographic origins.[15] The question is whether such self-expression need imply distance or separation from an imagined essential or core national community that is Canada. While visits to the Universal Buddhist Temple confirm that there is a high degree of homogeneity to the group, as with all the groups discussed above, it is also clear that there is no active resistance to including those who do not share the traits that sustain group solidarity. The reality is, though, that a certain insularity naturally tends to result. So then, what of the question concerning integration?

A LOOK AHEAD IN BRITISH COLUMBIA

It is obvious to those who do field work at Canadian Buddhist institutions populated by Chinese-speaking congregants that language serves a dual purpose. It provides a strong internal bond among participants but it also reduces the social permeability of the groups, restricting access for would-be participants lacking the requisite language skills. The barrier is not consciously constructed, but the consequences are undeniable. If, by integration, we mean that more culturally and linguistically blended congregations will emerge, then, at least in British Columbia, we should be prepared to be disappointed. Veritable islands of religious discourse have already taken shape and are likely to remain substantially monolingual for an indefinite future. Ordinarily, one might expect that first-generation immigrants would rely heavily on their first language, which would carry with it a degree of isolation from the English- or French-speaking "mainstream" while preserving strong communal ties with fellow migrants. Their children and the subsequent third generation would lose their family's first language and, through the process of participation in educational institutions and other social activities outside the family, integrate much more fully into society beyond the boundaries defined by the first language. These expectations, however, appear not to be supported by data from Statistics Canada. Two major trends need to be acknowledged: first, the considerable shift in migration dynamics and, second, the apparent change in intensity of first-language transmission evident from 1981 to 2006.

Migration Dynamics

Immigration statistics show a dramatic turn occurring from 1971 through 2006. In 1971 European migration to Canada eclipsed that of Asia at a ratio of 5:1. By 1981 the ratio was almost 1:1 and by 2001 the number was inverted to nearly 1:5. That ratio has altered little in the 2006 census (Chui, Tran, and Maheux 2006).[16] The 2006 Census enumerated 6,186,950 foreign-born persons residing in Canada, which represents the highest level in seventy-five years (Chui, Tran, and Maheux 2006).[17] Thus, we have entered an unprecedented period in our multicultural history, with major implications for Chinese Buddhist communities in terms of their sense of identity and ability to integrate. Returning to the specific case of Chinese migration, as of 2006 the census recorded 1.2 million Chinese in Canada (Statistics Canada 2006).[18] While this number is significant, it still represented only 4 per cent of the total population (31.2 million) (Statistics Canada 2006). How can such a relatively sparse population provide sufficient cultural and linguistic critical mass to sustain Chinese Buddhist communities as "linguistic islands" in British Columbia? The answer becomes clearer if we consider the distribution of Chinese migrants in Canada. Of the 1.2 million Chinese who, by 2006, had chosen Canada as their home, two cities received a disproportionately high number. In 2006 Toronto's Chinese population numbered 486,330, while in Vancouver the number was 381,535 (Statistics Canada 2006). First, it is very significant that 867,865 or more than 72 per cent of Canada's Chinese immigrant population had chosen to live in two urban centres. Second, in the case of Vancouver, while the net numbers are lower than those of Toronto, the proportion is considerably greater; while the total Census Metropolitan Area (CMA) population of Toronto in 2006 was slightly more than 5 million, the figure in Vancouver was only 2 million (Statistics Canada 2006). Thus the Chinese populations constituted nearly 20 per cent of the total Vancouver population in 2006 while in Toronto the figure was less than 10 per cent. Another factor is the size of the respective cities. Toronto occupies 630.18 square kilometres while Vancouver occupies only 114.71 square kilometres. The variance in population density is significant at 3,972.4 persons per square kilometre in Toronto and 5,039 in Vancouver (Statistics Canada 2006).[19] Thus, Vancouver and surrounding districts, most significantly the municipality of Richmond, include areas of higher immigrant concentration than other major urban centres. Richmond has the highest concentration of immigrants of all municipalities in Canada, with the 2006 census indicating that 57.4 per cent of the population are immigrants. Of these, 49.8 per cent are from Hong Kong and the People's Republic of China (*Hot Facts* 2008, 3). A high proportion of Richmond residents speak Cantonese or Mandarin and a large number of "Chinese malls" make it possible to dine, access medical and dental care, do one's banking, purchase car insurance, organize holidays, and obtain virtually any other service without using English.[20]

What of the future? A Statistics Canada CMA report released on 9 March 2010 indicates that by 2031 the visible minority population in Vancouver could double: "The largest visible minority group in Vancouver would be the Chinese, as it was in 2006. Their population could double from 396,000 to 809,000 over the next two decades. As a result, their share of Vancouver's population would rise from 18% in 2006 to 23% in 2031" (Statistics Canada 2010). The immigration profile of British Columbia will continue to be shaped by trends that gathered momentum in the early 1980s and show no sign of slowing for at least another generation. This poses interesting questions for those studying Chinese Buddhist communities in the Lower Mainland of British Columbia. It may not be reasonable to anticipate the usual process of integration among immigrant communities as subsequent generations are born and mature. The historical arc of these communities may turn out to be very different from that of Canada's Jōdo Shinshū congregations. Chinese youth are often immersed in their first language both at home and even at British Columbia's post-secondary institutions; there are also numerous Chinese daily newspapers, magazines, and radio and television stations.

Language is a major factor in sustaining more homogeneous religious communities. What can we expect concerning the transmission of immigrant first languages in the above-described context? Given the circumstances outlined, one would anticipate a relatively high rate of language transmission and this, in turn, should help preserve the cultural insularity and, one could add, integrity of the communities considered.

Language Transmission

A Statistics Canada report on immigrant-language transmission prepared by René Houle compares the intergenerational transmission of the mother-tongue from mothers to children under eighteen years of age, based on figures from the 1981 and 2006 long form of the census which represents a sample of 20 per cent of the total Canadian population (Houle 2011). The report shows that while some languages have experienced relatively low rates of intergenerational transmission (Dutch, Italian, Creole, and Tagalog at 20 per cent), other languages are maintaining significantly higher rates (Armenian, Punjabi, Chinese, Persian, Turkish, Bengali, and Urdu, all either at or exceeding 70 per cent) (Houle 2011, 3–5). A broad survey of all immigrant languages compared between the two populations (1981 and 2006) shows that in 1981, on average, immigrant languages were passed on to Canadian-born children at a rate of 41 per cent. This number increased significantly by 14 per cent, to 55 per cent, by 2006. What factors are contributing to this long-term trend? According to Houle, a significant factor in intensity of language transmission is immigration flow (2011, 11), which has been high in British Columbia and, as already stated, has been heavily weighted on Asian immigration since the early 1980s. Globalization, with its attendant increased ease of communication and mobility, has also been a factor, as has the rise of the Internet, global telecommunications, and access to satellite television programming (Houle 2011, 12). When these extra-local factors are added to the migration flow, with its associated increase in opportunities for social interactions in a first-language context (including at Buddhist institutions), the combination yields a much stronger impetus for transmission.

These factors are evident in Chinese Buddhist organizations on the Lower Mainland: the monastic leaders, usually from Taiwan or Hong Kong, provide religious services to congregations that are fed by a steady stream of migration from those regions. Chinese Buddhist organizations are connected both locally, to the families who constitute their congregations, but also globally through members travelling across the Pacific, particularly during the lunar New Year, and an often well-developed presence on the internet. Monks and nuns also visit Canada in larger numbers for special occasions, providing personal connections to their counterpart institutions in Asia.

An obvious final point, of course, is that Canada has maintained a policy of multiculturalism since 1971, and the weight of this policy increased with the 1982 Charter of Rights and Freedoms and the Constitution. This was followed by the official and legal adoption of the Canadian Multiculturalism Act under the Mulroney Conservative government on 21 July 1988. As Houle observes, "the Canadian Multiculturalism Act and the preamble to the Official Languages Act state that Canada should encourage the preservation of foreign languages and enhance their status and use" (Houle 2011, 1). This fact is not lost on Chinese Buddhist institutions such as Ling Yen Mountain Temple, where this encouragement and the freedoms it entails are celebrated as an officially endorsed opportunity to develop their institutions in a way that honours continuity, orthodoxy, and a unity of communal expression.

MULTICULTURALISM AND FEARS OF FRAGMENTATION

While many Chinese Buddhists in British Columbia are embracing this nationally sanctioned opportunity for institutionalized social solidarity and cultural preservation, there has been no shortage of hand-wringing in the popular media and among scholars concerning the fragmenting possibilities that accompany legally enshrined cultural freedoms. One expression of this concern relates to supposed legal ambiguities around freedom of cultural practices.

A subject that serves to highlight these dangers is violence directed to women in communities of new Canadians. The violence can take the form of tradition-based constraints on women's conduct or more direct and shocking forms such as physical violence. An article in the *Toronto Star*, titled "Multiculturalism Policy Falling behind the Times," addresses the former. Lynda Hurst refers to the intent of multiculturalism policy: "Between the lines, what the policy also said to newcomers and ethnic groups already here was two things: 'You do not have to assimilate. But we would like you, in time, to integrate into all aspects of Canadian society'" (Hurst 2007). Thus, people were free to keep what Hurst calls their cultural "celebratory trappings" and by doing so not disappear into a homogeneous "Canadian culture," but were still expected to "integrate into all aspects of Canadian society." The problem, as Hurst and others she quotes see it, is that the second message has simply not been conveyed. Thus, groups of new Canadians may interpret their multicultural freedoms as extending into domains of political or legal self-determination where they do not apply: "As it stands, some minorities wrongly assume that, if Quebecers have self-governing rights, then under the multiculturalism act, they can too, and that their religious rights supersede all other Charter provisions" (Hurst 2007). The article cites the example of "a red flag test in 2004" in which Muslims in Ontario attempted to apply sharia law to the settling of family disputes. Before the dispute entered the formal legal arena, then premier Dalton McGuinty stated that "We believe that no matter where you come from or how long you've been here, we are all to be held accountable by the same law" (Hurst 2007). The fear associated with this kind of concern is, one must suppose, that the Canadian legal system might be fractured by calls for religiously based approaches to the management of life within groups that retain a high degree of cultural identity.

An example of the second kind of violence is found in another *Toronto Star* article titled "When rights collide with freedoms" (Diebel 2007).[21] The article sets the tone from the outset with the following statement: "True story: man kills wife, stabbing her in the neck 19 times with a steak knife, is convicted of first-degree murder and appeals on basis that she was unfaithful and, as a devout Muslim, he was protecting family honour." The article closes with a statement by a Muslim woman, Alia Hogben, president of the Canadian Council of Muslim Women: "Tell people what to expect in this country. Tell them that women's equality is fundamental in Canada. Hitting may be part of one's culture but we don't permit it here ... Sorry, hitting women is not allowed in Canada" (Diebel 2007). Despite the thrust of the opening and closing statements, the article does not simplify the "multiculturalism problem" and Diebel does a good job, in a very brief piece, of giving space to a variety of voices on the issue at hand. At one point, Ratna Omidvar, executive director of the Maytree Foundation, advises that we should be cautious in avoiding a simplification of the challenges we face in attempting to incorporate cultural tolerance into civil society. "Don't position women's rights versus multiculturalism. There's too much baggage in that term, and it should never be either/or" (Diebel 2007). The question, as Omidvar sees it, should instead be "how do we protect the rights of women in an inclusive and diverse society?" This is a helpful corrective to what can, in the popular media, quickly deteriorate into a polarized discussion. It would, though, have been more helpful to conclude the article with the above statement rather than placing it in the middle. The article may leave the impression that it is indeed a battle between intolerant immigrant cultures and Canadian respect for gender equality.

It is all too easy to blame multiculturalism for creating loopholes that permit abuses of many kinds. However, while it would be naive to think that such abuses do not occur, if multiculturalism is to be judged on these terms, we need solid evidence of seriously corrosive consequences over the past forty years rather than judgments in the popular consciousness fed by anecdotes and sensational flashpoints highlighted in newspapers and on newscasts.[22] We also need to consider the role of our legal framework, including our constitution, in mitigating or, indeed, eliminating the kinds of threats to civil society that occasionally rise to the surface of public discourse. Such episodes are to be expected in this national experiment in acceptance of diversity. Is it reasonable to suppose that our criminal code is seriously threatened by multiculturalism?

A more tangible threat to social stability is the debate itself, drawing as it often does on stereotypes or caricatures and a lack of grounding in social scientific research (Garcia 2008, 154).[23] After conducting a thorough review of Canadian academic literature presenting the anti-multiculturalism position, Joseph Garcia observes, "There is a tendency for the postulators to comment on the fragmentary effects of multiculturalism public philosophy and public policy more on the basis of what they believe, rather than on the basis of facts produced by any systematic research and analysis. Moreover, generally, the postulators do not concede that producing facts either on the fragmentary or unifying effects of multiculturalism is very difficult, if not impossible, due to the challenges of establishing clear causal relationships and producing reliable measurements" (2008, 154). When specific laws are challenged or when violence occurs, these specific cases can be examined. However, caution is needed when making pronouncements on the causal correlations between the already ill-defined concept of multiculturalism and the gradual decay of civil society or the fragmentation of that other abstraction, the Canadian nation. Much of this "informed" opinion is simply rhetoric, but rhetoric can mobilize public opinion in some quarters against those constructed as the potential problem. This can quickly become a discourse that isolates the other and levels misplaced blame.

CONSEQUENCES

Those who research Chinese Buddhist groups in areas where there is a strong flow of immigration need to be self-conscious and self-critical about expectations concerning adaptation and integration in accounts of these institutions. It is easy to shift subtly in the direction of tacit judgment in describing groups that are linguistically and culturally homogeneous. It is possible to inadvertently feed a public narrative that sees "those people who come here but do not want to be part of Canada" as a potential threat to national pride and unity. On the national political stage, we are seeing a disturbing and regrettably influential example of the poorly grounded rhetoric described by Garcia.

In a March 2009 speech to students and faculty at Huron College, University of Western Ontario, Minster of Citizenship and Immigration Jason Kenney referred to the positive dimensions of diversity but then moved on to refer to some recent publications.[24] Significantly, he noted some of Andrew Cohen's observations in *The Unfinished Canadian* where the author "deplores the way Canada is becoming, in the words of novelist Yann Martel, 'The greatest hotel on earth.' Cohen believes that Canada is becoming a residence of convenience that expects virtually nothing in return for one of the easiest passports in the world to acquire" (Kenney 2009). Kenney followed this by quoting from an op-ed piece written by a student of journalism at Ryerson University: "It is a good thing if Canada does not have a specific identity. Canada is so multicultural and this prevents us from having a fixed identity, and that's a good thing" (Kenney 2009). Minister Kenney then referred to co-founder of the Dominion

Institute Rudyard Griffiths' note of caution in his 2009 book, *Who We Are* (which Kenney made a point of recommending), in which Griffiths laments the post-national position which sees virtue in lack of pride in national symbols and institutions. Kenney then erroneously cites a review, which he takes to be of Griffiths' book, that refers to how "many see Canada as the perfect rooming house, a peaceful, accommodating post-nation State or as a soul-less railway terminus, a place that demands little of its citizens."[25] He continues, "But we need to take this metaphor of 'Hotel Canada' very seriously, warns Rudyard Griffiths, because it's undermining the very strengths and underpinnings that have made Canada a great country." This, he concludes "is potentially disastrous."

What are these "underpinnings" that have made us great? Cohen observes that in the "early years" there were no Japanese, Norwegians, Russians, or Chinese and beyond native peoples "there were only the English, the French, and later, the Americans" (Andrew Cohen 2007, 12). It is they, he concludes, who have made us what we are (2007, 12). Given that the first Chinese landed at Nootka Sound, BC in 1788, one wonders how long they should have been in Canada before they might be recognized as more than second-class contributors.[26] Why should we accept the retrograde nineteenth-century language of "Empire" and "Dominion" and deny that "who *we* are" is constituted by a rich diversity of peoples who have contributed to our nation building over the past two centuries? In addition to Canada's indigenous peoples, Japanese, Chinese, and Indo-Canadians know well the bitter consequences of such narrow provincial views.

Cohen elects to describe the perils of multiculturalism in rather dire and inflammatory terms: "And so we worship the deity of diversity. To some in Canada, multiculturalism is a fetish. It is not seen as a means to a unified society of universal values but an end in itself. The danger is that ethnic nationalism will trump civic nationalism, instead of the other way around" (2007, 162).

We must remain vigilant concerning the potential consequences of such charged and polarizing rhetoric, which can contribute to the isolation of groups who maintain communities that are insular in their institutional dynamics – groups who could easily be viewed as those who merely reside temporarily in "hotel Canada." When we read the history, organization, and social dynamics of immigrant religious communities through a hermeneutic of adaptation and integration, we risk creating their stories in terms that assume a distance between "those communities" and "the rest of us" and contributing to the polarizing language currently affecting public discourse in this country.

Monolingual, unintentionally closed Buddhist groups can be viewed from another perspective that does not see such religio-cultural enclaves as damaging to Canada. Two notions are helpful. The first is common space as described by Kamal Dib, Ian Donaldson, and Brittany Turcotte (2008). Rather than seeing linguistic and cultural islands as potential threats, they suggest focusing on the daily journeys of exploration and participation that these island inhabitants undertake: "Contrary to some public and media discourse that multiculturalism is divisive and perpetuates enclavism and separate identities, this article describes a variety of multicultural common spaces wherein Canadians of all backgrounds interact and together contribute to an evolving, shared identity" (2008, 161). They argue for a bottom-up view of identity in which lived experience in shared multicultural spaces gradually and organically shapes our sense of belonging through interaction. This is a more viable and realistic approach than policy informed by top-down, abstract conceptualizations referring to historical notions and symbols that provide an essentialized Canadian identity as the ultimate reference point. A shared sense of who we are beyond our respective islands (and we all inhabit them) comes from gathering in shared geographic spaces to cheer, lament, work, complain, vote, be entertained, and celebrate. We share common workplaces, join the same political parties, attend the same schools, live in the same cities, use the same public transit systems (Dib, Donaldson, and Turcotte 2008, 163). This flow of life in shared public space instills our sense of shared experience beyond the particularities of the specific and sometimes more exclusive groups to which we all belong. This focus on public space brings with it a much more complex sense of how we shape each other and form real bonds through common experience. This understanding is in stark contrast to the "two-way street" metaphor in which "the host or mainstream society has a duty to accommodate, welcome, and respect immigrants and minorities, the latter have a duty to integrate and embrace elements of the society" (2008, 163). It is precisely this language of accommodation that is now being used to characterize the ideal functioning of Canadian multiculturalism. At first hearing, the two-way street metaphor sounds a friendly note, but we should be alert to undeclared assumptions. It situates communities of new

Canadians in an oppositional role to those who are likely also from immigrant backgrounds but who can claim to have arrived earlier or can rely on "appearing more Canadian."

The notion of shared space can be complemented by another consideration. Given the vastness of Canada, the reality is that we will never actually meet most of our fellow citizens. It is here that Benedict Anderson's idea of "imagined community" can play an important part in articulating the potential contributions of Chinese religious groups to our national story. Anderson, whose mother was English and father was Irish, grew up in China, studied in England and the United States, and did research in Indonesia and Thailand (Anderson 2005). In a 2005 interview conducted at the international literature festival, "Kapittel 05," Anderson muses on his experience as a young man at Cambridge, where he witnessed his fellow Englishmen beating up Sri Lankan students for protesting the role of Britain in the Suez Crisis. This, he says, made him feel ashamed of England and this very shame was to him an expression of nationalism. He identified with a national ideal that was being compromised. His shame, as an expression of nationalist sentiment, came not from government policy or a legal framework but from his participation in a shared set of values constituting part of his imagined nation. The strength of Anderson's position on nationalism as imagined community is that it extends the notion of space and defies the binary simplicity of the two-way street. It expands the domain within which sometime inhabitants of cultural islands can participate in creating a nation. Built into this observation is the notion that the "imagined" nature of a particular nationalist conception means that it is formed by us in public discourse, particularly through the media, and not found or discovered.[27] Thus it behooves us to form it with self-conscious caution and care.

CONCLUSION

Chinese Buddhist institutions in British Columbia find themselves in a demographically unusual space without historical precedent. Constituted by members of a large and growing immigrant population, it may well be that these institutions will not conform to expectations of integration. Increased intensity of language transmission may reasonably be expected to continue to support relatively homogeneous religious communities.

This fact needs to be considered in light of Buddhist community leaders' claims to a self-conceptualization that is not founded predominantly on a group narrative of integration. Rather, the language of cultural and institutional integrity and continuity is seen as vitally important and as something Canada's constitution and multiculturalism legacy not only permits but, historically at least, encourages. For Buddhist organizations, this ideal of continuity supports claims to orthodoxy and legitimacy of leadership, which in turn appeals to new Canadians arriving from various parts of Asia including Hong Kong, Taiwan, or the People's Republic of China.

A recent shift in the approach to multiculturalism being promoted by Citizenship and Immigration Canada and, more particularly, by the minister, adopts language that harks back to nineteenth-century language of the Dominion by drawing on popular and nostalgic imagery constituting the well-circulated opinions of Cohen and Griffiths. Given that national identity is made and not found, Chinese Buddhist institutions in BC may well find themselves located within a public discourse made less tolerant of the language of cultural continuity. As their numbers and profile increase over the coming generation, will charges in the popular media such as "Buddha Disneyland" fade from memory or be renewed? In the interest of reducing social antagonism and intolerance, we must challenge simplistic polarizing narratives of multiculturalism shaped by their attendant "moral obligation" to integrate. By expanding our sense of how we all participate in continual national identity formation and transformation, we will find the space to engage our fellow Canadians, who happen to be Chinese Buddhists, in mutually supportive conversation about our future together.

NOTES

1 Beyond the "temples" mentioned, it is very likely that from the late nineteenth century, early Chinese communities in Canada included shrines to deities associated with clan villages in China in their association meeting spaces. This is common practice today in Chinatowns in Canada. These religious sites, both past and present, are largely invisible to people who are not directly involved in the associations.
2 See T. Liu (2005; 2010). Noah Casey, prepared a detailed report on the True Buddha School (2002). Also reviewed for this chapter is an unpublished article by Jackie Ho (2012).

3   The sixteen-page book is titled *True Buddha School: Cultivation and Meditation Booklet* (True Buddha School, n.d.).
4   The history recounted in this opening section is taken from a personal interview with a female Dharma master on 26 January 2006; a publication of the monastery, *Red Lotuses Abound in the Valley of a Thousand Mountains*; and *Xuanyan zhengfa: Wanfo cheng*宣演正法萬佛城 (Propagating the Dharma: The City of Ten Thousand Buddhas).
5   I encountered the name of this Chan teacher in my interviews and research at the Po Lam convent (Baolin xuefo hui 寶林學佛會) in Chilliwack where the abbess, Ven. Sik Yin-kit, explained that her teacher Sing Yat (Sheng Yi 聖一) in Hong Kong had been a student of Master Xü Yün.
6   A *daochang* 道場 is a place (*chang* 場) where the Way or Dao 道 is taught. In this context *dao* is synonymous with *dharma* (*fa* 法) or the Buddhist teaching. Thus a *daochang* is a place where the Buddha dharma is taught.
7   The reason for this change of personnel is not clear but there is no indication that it stemmed from an untenable situation. Heng Sure continues to play a leadership role as director of the Berkeley Buddhist Monastery and gives frequent lectures on Buddhhist teachings and veganism. I have no information on Heng Chau.
8   When I participated at Gold Buddha Monastery, the chanting was in Mandarin with both characters and phonetic transcription included. The fact that Mandarin is used most of the time does not deter readers of Chinese from following the proceedings.
9   This answer is taken from a series of written responses to questions posed in an interview conducted at Ling Yen Mountain Temple in Richmond on 4 April 2006. The translation of the Chinese text is my own.
10 This is according to K.M. Chen, the architect in charge of the 233,500 sq. ft. development (Bennett 2010).
11 The Sunday edition of a major Vancouver daily expressed citizens' concerns in an article that included a photograph of Ling Yen Shan Temple covering the entire front page (B. Lewis 2010, A8–A9).
12 These concerns are mentioned in a letter dated 28 August 2005 from the developer Khevin Development Services Ltd to Terry Burnette in the City of Richmond's Planning Department.
13 Venerable Guo Jun, in addition to serving as head teacher for the Chan (Zen) Community of Canada Association, is abbot of the Mahabodhi Monastery located at 8 Lorong Kilat in the Upper Bukit Timah area of Singapore.
14 Much more detail on Universal Buddhist Temple can be found in Crowe (2010b).

15 Beyond obviously religious communities, this type of solidarity (based on place of origin), is evident in North America's Chinatowns where clan associations have perservered for over a century, binding families from the same four counties in the Pearl River delta.
16 See Figure 2, "Region of birth of recent immigrants to Canada, 1971 to 2006," http://www12.statcan.ca/census-recensement/2006/as-sa/97-557/figures/c2-eng.cfm.
17 See Figure 1, "Number and share of the foreign-born population in Canada, 1901 to 2006," http://www12.statcan.ca/census-recensement/2006/as-sa/97-557/figures/c1-eng.cfm.
18 See "Visible minority groups, 2006 counts, for Canada provinces and territories and census metropolitan areas and census agglomerations – 20% sample data," http://www12.statcan.ca/census-recensement/2006/dp-pd/hlt/97-562/pages/page.cfm?Lang=E&Geo=CMA&Code=01&Table=1&Data=Count&StartRec=1&Sort=2&Display=Page.
19 See "Population and dwelling counts, for Canada and census subdivisions (municipalities), 2006 and 2001 censuses – 100% data." Catalogue no. 97-550-XWE2006002. Released 12 July 2007. http://www12.statcan.gc.ca/census-recensement/2006/dp-pd/hlt/97-550/Index.cfm?TPL=P1C&Page=RETR&LANG=Eng&T=301&S=3&O=D.
20 I do not know the number of "Chinese malls" in Richmond although David Chuen-yan Lai, a geographer at the University of Victoria, conducted a survey (unpublished) in 1998 and related to me that he counted forty-nine malls built on the eastern side of No. 3 Road from Park Road to Capstan Way. He has since given up counting.
21 Both articles appeared as part of a series on multiculturalism in Canada.
22 A thorough, well-balanced, and carefully reasoned examination and critique of the arguments against multiculturalism is found in Phil Ryan, *Multicultiphobia* (2010).
23 In making this point Garcia cites Jean Burnet (1979).
24 See Ryan's discussion of Minister Kenney's approach to negotiating the public rhetoric of multiculturalism in chapter 12 of his book.
25 In fact, the quotation to which Kenney refers comes from a review of Noah Richler's book titled *This Is My Country, What Is Yours?* The review, titled "Noah Richler: In Search of Nowhere," was written by Brian Bethune in *Maclean's*, 6 September 2006.
26 While it must be noted that significant numbers of Chinese did not arrive until seventy years later, one wonders why their contributions to the building of Canada should be ranked below those of the Americans.
27 Richard Rorty provides a useful discussion of this notion (1999, xvii).

7

Buddhist Monasticism in Canada: Sex and Celibacy

VICTOR SŌGEN HORI

On 2 July 2011, the Zen Studies Society of New York City sent out to its email list the transcript of an unusual and special announcement (Zen Studies Society 2011). In that announcement, Eido Shimano Roshi, the Zen Master and long-time teacher of the Zen Studies Society, formally stepped down and transferred teaching authority to his student, Roko Sherry Chayat Roshi. Shimano had finally acceded to demands that he resign as Zen teacher. An extended campaign on the Internet had accused him of a long history of sexual impropriety stretching across decades and involving numerous women.[1] The events of that day fit a pattern that, over the last three decades, has become quite familiar. In 1983, the board of the San Francisco Zen Center forced the resignation of its teacher, Zentatsu Richard Baker Roshi, after it was revealed that he had been sexually involved with his students (Tworkov 1989, 199–252; Downing 2001). Very soon after, in 1984, the students at the Zen Center of Los Angeles forced their teacher, Taizan Maezumi Roshi, into a detox clinic for treatment for his alcoholism. Subsequently his sexual liaison with one of his senior students became public knowledge.[2] These revelations triggered major crises at both the San Francisco Zen Center and the Zen Center of Los Angeles. Many students left, feeling their teacher had betrayed them. The Tibetan Buddhist teacher Chögyam Trungpa was well known for outrageous behaviour, which included much drinking and sex with his students, but since he did this without any attempt to conceal, the students accepted his behaviour as examples of his "crazy wisdom." Trungpa died in 1987 and his long-time student, Thomas Rich, succeeded him as Vajra Regent. In 1988, it became known that Rich had AIDS but had concealed the fact and knowingly had sex with a male student, thus transmitting his infection. The ensuing crisis rent the Shambhala organization into factions and eventually forced it to totally reorganize its leadership.[3] In the following years, several other Buddhist teachers were exposed for having had sex with their students, usually triggering a major crisis with devastating consequences at the meditation centre involved.[4]

In response, some Buddhist organizations have adopted codes of ethics, such as the *Teacher Code of Ethics* of the Spirit Rock Meditation Center (Spirit Rock 2012) and *The Diamond Sangha Teachers Ethics Agreement* (Zen Center of Denver n.d.). The San Francisco Zen Center has created an Ethics and Reconciliation Council (San Francisco Zen Center n.d.) and the Insight Meditation Society of Barre, Massachusetts has created an ethics committee to receive complaints of misconduct by teachers and staff (Insight Meditation Society n.d.). The sexual misconduct of Buddhist teachers became the theme of many articles in Buddhist magazines such as *Tricycle, Shambhala Sun, Buddhadharma,* and *Turning Wheel*. Books were published devoted to the topic.[5] Despite the scandals, the adoption of codes of ethics, and the publication of books and articles, teachers at meditation centres continue to engage in sex with their students.[6] Why is that?

While our attention remains riveted on these scandals, far out of sight of the public eye another option in Buddhist sexual behaviour has been developing – celibacy. The celibacy option has become available in tandem with a new (for North America) kind of Buddhist institution: the Buddhist monastery. As Buddhism has become established in North America, it has developed three different kinds of institutions. First came Buddhist temples, initially built by the Japanese community at the start of the 1900s and later by many other immigrant communities since the change in immigration laws in the late 1960s. Then from the 1960s came Buddhist meditation centres, usually serving a Western lay membership. Most recently, we have seen the opening of Buddhist monasteries, which may serve either a Western membership or an immigrant community. Far fewer in number and attracting far less attention than lay-oriented meditation centres, Buddhist monasteries have been created by, and maintained for, formally ordained monks and nuns. These are communities of men and women who have taken vows of obedience to the precepts; they shave their heads, wear the Buddha's robe, have no home except the monastery, and dedicate virtually every act in their daily lives to Buddhist practice. The vows they have taken include the vow to maintain sexual celibacy. This development – of strictly celibate Buddhist monastic communities – is equally as significant as, but nowhere near as sensational as, the sex scandals at Buddhist meditation centres.

For scholars, the development of Buddhist monasteries provides a methodological opportunity; it is now possible to compare Buddhist meditation centres with Buddhist monasteries and ask what it is about the meditation centre that permits sexual misconduct, and what it is about the Buddhist monastery that prevents it. In this chapter, I argue that the Buddhist monastery has internal checks and balances for restraining sexual behaviour; these are absent from Buddhist meditation centres and this absence opens the field for sexual misconduct. The Buddhist monastery differs from the Buddhist meditation centre in three ways. First, the Buddhist monastery is usually a single-sex community of either men or women, where contact between the sexes is deliberately kept to a minimum. By contrast, the Buddhist meditation centre is usually a mixed community in which men and women freely mingle, thus creating the opportunity for heterosexual relations to occur easily. Second, in Buddhist monasteries, monks and nuns take vows to live a life of ascetic discipline, a life in which precepts regulate every aspect of daily life, including sexuality. In Buddhist meditation centres, on the other hand, rules of behaviour regulate only limited parts of practice life; they basically set out the ritual form to be followed in the meditation hall or the meditation retreat and do not regulate relations between the sexes. Finally, Buddhist monasteries of East Asia have a peer-pressure social dynamic of "mutual polishing" in which monastics teach and learn from each other; their life of discipline is not imposed top-down by the teacher but is self-imposed by the group onto itself. Buddhist meditation centres in North America lack this strong group structure where members monitor each other's behaviour, with the result that Western Buddhist meditation centres, ironically, have a much stronger culture of top-down hierarchy than do Asian Buddhist monasteries. This makes students at a meditation centre much more vulnerable to the actions of an irresponsible teacher.

Some caveats before I launch into more detailed discussion. First, I will not be concerned in this chapter to discuss the other institution, the Buddhist temple. In my rough definition, a Buddhist temple has three defining features: it is led by ordained monastics; it includes a ritual space such as a Buddha hall; and it serves the ritual needs of a local Buddhist community. These definitions are rough and approximate. I recognize that many

Buddhist sites that call themselves "temple," "monastery," or "meditation centre" do not fit my definitions precisely and that there can be cases where a single site fits more than one definition. But we need some such rough definitions in order to recognize the fact that the Buddhist institutions which have developed in North America have important differences of structure and function.

Second, this volume is devoted to Buddhism in Canada and some may say that the issue of sexual misconduct has nothing especially to do with Buddhism in Canada. In response, I would cite the fact that perhaps the first recorded case of sexual misconduct by a Buddhist teacher in North America took place in Canada. During the 1960s and 1970s, Montreal was a lively site for Buddhist activity. Chögyam Trungpa arrived in Montreal in 1969 from Scotland to await permission to move to the United States; the Korean monk Samu Sunim was in retreat there from 1968 to 1971; Philip Kapleau came up from Rochester to teach at the local Montreal branch of his Zen Center. And then there was Tyndale Martin. Tyndale Martin established the Greatheart Buddhist Monastery in 1969 on Mountain Street in Montreal. Male disciples were housed outside, but Martin lived in the Monastery house, which also contained the quarters for the female disciples. The Internet blog *Coolopolis* reports that he fathered ten children with seventeen unofficial wives before the monastery shut its doors in 1990. Local newspapers were accusing it of being a cult.[7] In another case, Zenson Gifford, a successor to Philip Kapleau, was the leader of the Toronto Zen Centre until his sexual involvement with one of his students was exposed. He left the centre and was replaced by Sunyana Graef, another Kapleau disciple, in 1996. The dramatic story of Chögyam Trungpa and Thomas Rich, mentioned earlier, has a Canadian connection since Trungpa's organization, Shambhala International, is headquartered in Halifax. Despite the claims that "Canada is not the United States," the shared public attitudes toward sexuality and the shared structure of Buddhist meditation centres mean that the sexual misconduct of Buddhist teachers with their students is also a shared problem.

WHAT IS A BUDDHIST MONASTERY?

What is the difference between a Buddhist monastery and a Buddhist meditation centre? In my definition, a Buddhist monastery has three defining features: it is a resident community; the community consists of ordained monks or nuns; and together they live a "consecrated life." Meditation centres differ on all three counts. First, meditation centres are not usually resident communities. Many meditation centres are just informal groups of people who meet in the home of one of the members. The more established meditation centres may have a few permanent members who live on site but the greater membership lives in their own homes, have occupations usually unconnected to Buddhism, and gather together only when there are activities at the meditation centre. On the second point, some meditation centres may have a leader who has taken vows and is formally ordained, but this is not a necessary condition; there are many meditation centres where everyone, teacher and student alike, is a layperson. Third and most importantly, monastics in a Buddhist monastery together live the "consecrated life" whereas members of a meditation centre do not.

I will discuss the term "consecrated life" in more detail later, but briefly, one of the features of the consecrated life is that the ordained monk commits his entire life to the practice of his religion; the ordained nun devotes herself totally to religious practice and has no secular interest. Ordained monastics give up self-direction over their lives. By contrast, the members of a lay-oriented meditation centre have secular interests outside of meditation. Instead of making themselves servants of their religion as ordained people, they continue to lead a secular life working at a job and maintaining a family. Having said this, I recognize that the line between the lay and the ordained is not sharp; many people live some variation of a part-lay and part-ordained life.

In this chapter, I discuss in detail the Thai Forest monasteries[8] and Chinese Buddhist monasteries in Canada but I do not discuss Gampo Abbey. Connected with Shambhala International headquartered in Halifax, Gampo Abbey is probably the best established and best known monastery in Canada. I am deliberately ignoring it because in our previous volume on Buddhism in Canada, *Wild Geese*, three chapters discussed Shambhala International.[9] It is time to focus attention on other monasteries in Canada that are less well known.

In Canada, there are three monasteries associated with the Thai Forest tradition: Sitavana Berkin Forest Hermitage near Kamloops, British Columbia; Arrow River Forest Hermitage south of Thunder Bay, Ontario; and Tisarana Buddhist Monastery near Perth, Ontario. In addition, there is Sati

Saraniya Forest Hermitage near Lanark, Ontario, for women practitioners. Ayya Medhanandi, a nun who trained in the meditation practice of Thai Forest monks, founded Sati Saraniya, but because she herself is not recognized as a *bhikkhuni* (ordained nun) in the Thai tradition, her monastery Sati Saraniya hermitage is not officially considered part of the Forest Sangha.[10] Although each of these monasteries practises Buddhism in the Thai Forest tradition, they are not "ethnic churches" (Mullins 1987) serving a Thai immigrant congregation. They have all been created by Western teachers primarily for Western practitioners. See James Placzek's chapter in this volume for an account of the evolution of the Birken Forest Monastery. In its early days, it had strong ties with the Sri Lankan and Thai immigrant communities but over the years it has become more and more a centre for Western practitioners.

MEN, WOMEN, AND THE LIFE OF PRECEPTS

The Buddhist canon, the *tipiṭaka* (Skt. *tripiṭaka*; literally "three baskets"), divides into three sections: *vinaya*, the rules regulating the sangha monastic community; *sutta* (Skt. *sūtra*), the teachings of the Buddha; and *abhidhamma* (Skt. *abhidharma*), commentary on the words of the Buddha. The *vinaya*, the body of rules and regulations of the Buddhist monastery, explicitly regulates sexual behaviour.[11] The *Pāṭimokkha* (Skt. *Pratimoksha*) is the actual text which lists the rules. It divides the body of rules into eight categories according to severity of offence. (The following discussion presents the *vinaya* for monks; there is a parallel set of *vinaya* rules for nuns.) The first category of rules, called *pārājika* (literally "defeat"), lists the most serious offences, the punishment for which is expulsion from the sangha. The first of the four *pārājika* rules is as follows:

> Should any *bhikkhu* engage in sexual intercourse, even with a female animal, he is defeated and no longer in affiliation. (Thanissaro 2007)

The next most serious offences are the thirteen *saṅghādisesas*, precepts so grave that when a monk commits one of these offences, the act triggers a meeting of the entire local sangha community to pass judgment and decide punishment. The thirteen offences include five offences dealing with sexuality:

1. Intentional emission of semen, except while dreaming,
2. Being overcome by lust, with altered mind, engaging in bodily contact with a woman,
3. Being overcome by lust, with altered mind, addressing lewd words to a woman,
4. Being overcome by lust, with altered mind, speaking to a woman ministering to one's own sensuality and alluding to sexual intercourse,
5. Conveying another man's intentions to a woman or a woman's intentions to a man, proposing marriage or paramourage, even if only for a momentary liaison. (Thanissaro 2007)

Very important is the prohibition outlined in the *Aniyata* ("Indefinite") rules section which prevents a monk from sitting privately with a woman on a secluded seat; any monk who does so is to confess the transgression (Thanissaro 2007). This rule has traditionally been interpreted to mean that a monk may not be alone with a woman in any secluded space. Applied to the modern urban and technological context, monastics today understand this precept to forbid a monk or nun being alone with a person of the opposite sex in an elevator, taking a ride with a lone person of the opposite sex in a car, or sleeping under the same roof with a person of the opposite sex (Brahmavamso 1997).

In her study of celibacy, Elizabeth Abbott has divided the major world religions into sex-positive and sex-negative categories, and placed Buddhism into the sex-negative category (Abbott 1999). In this chapter, I cannot discuss the question of why early Buddhism had such a negative attitude to sexuality[12] except to note that this negative attitude contrasts with the liberal attitude of many Western practitioners of Buddhism that sexuality is a natural urge, not to be repressed but properly expressed in a healthy manner. My concern in this chapter, rather, is with the question of how the Buddhist attitude to sexuality was implemented in daily sangha life. Pardon the generalization, but I think the traditional Asian attitude is that the sexual urge is so strong that one cannot expect men and women living in community together to maintain celibacy; they would inevitably engage in sexual relations. Or as Richard Baker put it in more idiomatic English, "Once you have men and women, you have fucking" (Tworkov 1989, 220). One obvious way to live in obedience to these precepts is for men and women to live segregated lives where they would not normally encounter each other. Thus, in the Asian world, Buddhist monasteries have implemented the Buddhist *vinaya* by creating separate communities for the sexes. Men train in all-male monasteries under male teachers and under rules which prevent them from coming into contact with women; women train in all-women monasteries under women teachers and under rules which prevent them from coming into contact with men. In Asian Buddhism, it is highly unusual for a male Buddhist teacher to be surrounded by a mixed community of men and women, the situation that has become so common in the West.[13]

In his book, *The Mind of Clover: Essays in Zen Buddhist Ethics*, Robert Aitken noted that in the Western Zen centre, men and women sat, ate, worked and sometimes bathed together. He commented, "Though there are many problems, I think the overall effect of such proximity is beneficial to the practice ... Fantasies about sex are still present, but surely are less fierce than they might be if there were no chance to experience the humanity of the other in the give and take of cooking, gardening, and reroofing together" (Aitken 1984, 40–1). The Japanese Zen monk, Nishimura Eshin, in his review of Aitken's book, took a different tack. "Aitken dwells on the merit of male and female Zen students living and practicing together in Western Zen centres, a situation which he says results in a deepened understanding of the other sex. It may be that I am wrong and simply behind the times, but I feel obliged as a Japanese student of Zen to say that I personally find it hard to believe that true Zen practice is possible under such circumstances" (Nishimura 1987).

Segregation of the sexes was once a much more prominent practice in Western culture; even now on old school buildings, one can see the words "Boys" and "Girls" cut in stone over separate entrances. But in the last several decades, liberalizing influences in mainstream culture have insisted upon the equal acceptance and integration of women in schools, businesses, government institutions, and in practically all social institutions. It is therefore difficult to suggest that Buddhist meditation centres in the West be segregated by sex. There are exceptions, of course. Below I discuss the Friends of the Western Buddhist Order (recently renamed the Triratna Buddhist Community) which has developed single-sex communities. But in general, women are suspicious that in gender matters, "separate" does not mean "equal" and thus will not agree to segregation of the sexes in Buddhist meditation centres.[14]

In the Buddhist meditation centres that have attracted a Western convert following, the Buddhist teacher faces a mixed body of students, but the Buddhist monasteries now developing in Canada follow the traditional Asian example of separation of sexes. Although women have access to the monastery, the ordained male monks of the Thai Forest monasteries in Canada live in what is intended to be primarily all-male communities. Although men have access to the monastery, the ordained nuns of the Chinese Avatamsaka Monastery in Calgary live in an all-female community. In contrast to Buddhist meditation centres, the new Buddhist monasteries in Canada are following the traditional segregation of sexes.

Sociological evidence seems to affirm that the long-term stability of a community is related to the regulation of the sexual relations among its men and women. Rosabeth Moss Kanter studied the hippy communes of the 1960s and the religious communes of the late nineteenth century, many of which explicitly controlled sexual relations between men and women. She observed, "Two-person intimacy poses a potential threat to group cohesiveness unless it is somehow controlled or regulated by the group" (Kanter 1972, 86). That is because when a couple forms, the affection the partners feel for each other is stronger than the loyalty they feel toward the group. To prevent this erosion of loyalty toward the group, some nineteenth-century communes imposed celibacy as the rule and other communes imposed enforced free love. In enforced free love, men and women were allowed to have sexual relations with each other but were required to change partners at frequent intervals to prevent long-term attachments. From the sociologist's perspective, enforced free love is thus equivalent to celibacy because both regulate intimacy in order to prevent the formation of couples who are more attached to each other than to the group. And this in turn enhances the long-term stability of the group (Kanter 1972, 87). The lesson applied to modern Buddhist organizations is that a Buddhist community that does not control sexuality among its members is likely to be less stable than a community that does.

The solution to one problem, however, can exacerbate another problem. One organization, the Triratna Buddhist Community, formerly the Friends of the Western Buddhist Order (FWBO), has developed same-sex communities which, it is observed, provide the basis for stable friendship because they are same-sex. "What has been discovered is that the single-sex arrangement tends to provide for the most stable spiritual friendships.

Moreover, it has been discovered that single-sex chapters and residential communities tend to allow both males and females to become more truly androgynous. No one is entirely sure why this is so, but Alex Kennedy, alias Subhūti, has surmised that this segregated arrangement encourages people of both genders to develop for themselves characteristics that are stereotypically associated with the other gender" (R. Hayes 1995, 6). The creation of single-sex communities, however, also increases the possibility of sexual relations between people of the same sex, especially if the community encourages its members to develop the characteristics of the other gender. During the 1970s and '80s, the FWBO itself suffered from a dramatic sex scandal in which, among other charges, a member alleged that he was manipulated into having a homosexual affair with Sangharakshita, the leader of the FWBO (Bunting 1997). Recall also that the medieval monasteries of Japan were all-male communities that included young boys, who became the sexual targets of the older monks. In the Buddhist countries of Asia, people often suspect that the creation of all-male communities attracts gay males and that living in such a community brings out homosexual tendencies which otherwise might remain latent. The creation of same-sex communities reduces misconduct based on heterosexual relations but it is not a panacea for all sexual misconduct.

THE ASCETIC ATTITUDE

In my definition, in a Buddhist monastery monks and nuns live the "consecrated life." "Consecrated life" is a technical term taken from the vocabulary of Roman Catholic monasticism. It is the life of ascetic self-discipline. The paradigm of those who live the consecrated life are Catholic monks and nuns who have taken the three vows of "chastity, poverty, and obedience" and reside together in a community withdrawn from society. Virtually every hour of their day is ritualized to symbolize the fact that their entire lives are committed to religious practice. The Buddhist version of the consecrated life is the sangha, the monastic community of those who have "gone forth" into homelessness. In the very early days before the rules of the *vinaya* were compiled, the Buddhist equivalent of the three vows of chastity, poverty, and obedience was the four *nissayas* ("necessities"): begging for food, wearing rag robes, lodging at the foot of a tree, and using only urine for medicine (Freiberger 2006, 245). As the sangha developed into permanent resident communities with more and more ordained monastics, the four *nissayas* developed into the full *vinaya* with its hundreds of rules.[15]

At this point, an objection may arise. Not just Buddhist monasteries but Buddhist meditation centres carry on ascetic practice. During retreats, members of a Buddhist meditation centre often spend long hours in meditation, cutting back on sleep and depriving themselves of comfort. They keep a rule of silence; they endure great pain in the body, especially in the legs; the sitting may be conducted under the regime of a head monk who carries a stick; the windows may be open to the cold. This certainly resembles the asceticism of a Buddhist monastery. In what sense then is the ascetic practice of the consecrated life a defining feature of Buddhist monasticism and not of the meditation centre?

First, there is difference in degree. Ascetic discipline in a meditation centre is partial and limited while ascetic discipline in a Buddhist monastery is total. In the life of an average lay member of a centre, practice means sitting in meditation and perhaps some ritual chanting. This typically takes up a few hours in a week, but the greater part of that person's day and the greater part of that person's week is otherwise taken up with secular activity. By contrast, practice for ordained monastics in a Buddhist monastery includes not just sitting in meditation but all the day-to-day tasks of living in a monastery – cooking and eating, sweeping and cleaning, ritual and ceremony, teaching and learning. There is no break. There is no secular activity. All activity is undertaken as a matter of religious self-discipline.

Then, there is difference in kind. In most Western meditation centres, it is assumed that Buddhist practice is meditation, not morality. True, most members think that deeper meditation leads to a more moral life in some way, but the immediate practice is focused on sitting meditation, not on ethical behaviour. This is quite different from, for example, the lay person at a Chinese Buddhist temple who participates in a retreat by first taking a vow to uphold the five precepts. For that person, the immediate practice is focused on ethical behaviour and secondarily on meditation. It is true that there is an ascetic element in a Buddhist meditation centre but it is usually not strong enough that members feel they should be ascetic in their private relations. Thus, it is quite possible for a member to strictly follow the rules of posture in sitting, of formal eating of meals, of chanting – and yet still feel no compunction when it comes to sexuality.

Because ordained monks and nuns in a monastery have explicitly taken a vow of celibacy, they talk about the issue of contact with the other sex. This is a major difference in the cultures of the monastery and the meditation centre: in a monastery, it is possible to talk about sex whereas in the Buddhist meditation centres that suffered sex scandals, there was usually a culture of silence about sex. The members of a Buddhist monastery often explicitly question the appropriateness of their relation with the opposite sex. If you are an ordained monk, can you accept a ride from a lone woman driving a car? (As Placzek describes in his chapter in this volume, Ajahn Sona of the Birken Forest Monastery was once caught in a heavy Canadian snowstorm and determined that he had to refuse a ride offered by a woman because she was alone in the car.) If you are an ordained monk in an elevator and a woman enters, have you violated the precepts? If ordained monks and nuns are staying in the same temple, can they be given sleeping quarters on the same floor? Can you shake hands with a member of the opposite sex? What about hugging? And so on. Ordained monks and nuns are constantly judging whether their behaviour is, or is not, too intimate with the opposite sex and discussing such matters openly. Contrast this with the culture of denial in a Buddhist meditation centre. If two people are sexually intimate, the other members feign ignorance. Observers who see what is happening may privately talk to each other but will not make a public issue about two people being sexually intimate. The culture of denial covers up the presence of sexual problems, allowing them to fester and become worse.

In Buddhist monasteries, the ascetic attitude constitutes one of the checks and balances which help prevent ordained monastics from engaging in improper sexual behaviour. The absence of such a check in Buddhist meditation centres opens the field for sexual relations.

MUTUAL POLISHING

The ordained monastics in the Chinese Buddhist monasteries of Canada organize themselves in a unique way to help each other maintain the precepts. First, we need a little background on Chinese Buddhist temples in Canada.

The Cham Shan Temple, founded in Toronto in 1973, was the first Chinese Buddhist temple built in Canada. Since then it has created an impressive network of branch sites (temples, a library, a seminary) both within Toronto and in several smaller cities throughout southern Ontario (T. Liu 2005; 2010). A similar site is the Ling Yen Shan temple in Richmond, British Columbia, on the southern edge of Vancouver. (Paul Crowe discusses this temple in his chapter in this volume.) Although it was begun only in the late 1990s, the temple on No. 5 Road has grown into a large complex of temple buildings, prayer halls, imposing statues, and peaceful courtyards. In addition to serving the religious and ritual needs of their Chinese communities, both Cham Shan and Ling Yen Shan are monasteries. At any given time, Cham Shan has a sangha community of about twenty ordained monks and nuns. According to Crowe, at the time he did a field visit in 2006, Ling Yen had forty-nine nuns in residence. However, not enough scholarly research has been done on these two monasteries for us to be able to make any detailed statements about their monastic lives.

We know a good deal more about the Avatamsaka Monastery in Calgary and the Gold Buddha Monastery in Vancouver because they are part of a network of monasteries known collectively as the Dharma Realm Buddhist Association (DRBA), founded by the Chinese Tripitaka Master Hsüan Hua (宣化 Xuanhua; 1918–1995). This charismatic Buddhist leader and his devoted disciples have attracted the attention of both scholars and public media (Fields 1992, 339–46). Hsüan Hua first came to the United States in 1962. Although today the DRBA looks like a network of "ethnic churches" based in Chinese immigrant communities, in the beginning Hsüan Hua was largely ignored by the Chinese community. Instead, he attracted the attention of a small but committed group of white Americans. Overcoming differences in language and culture, he inspired a generation of young Westerners to commit themselves to lives of Buddhist asceticism and devotion. The power of his inspiration can, for example, be seen in the "Three Steps, One Bow" pilgrimage undertaken by two of his monks, Heng Sure (Christopher R. Clowery) and Heng Ch'au (Martin Verhoeven), who made a "three steps, one bow" pilgrimage for world peace, walking the shoulder of the highway from South Pasadena to Ukiah, California, a distance of 800 miles. They took turns, one person walking and bowing while the other stood guard to alert drivers on the highway. After walking forward three steps, the monk would bow and prostrate on hands and knees. The pilgrimage took two years and six months, from 1977 to 1979.[16] Although Hsüan Hua passed away in 1995, his organization, the Dharma

Realm Buddhist Association, continues on. It now includes more than a dozen monasteries (located mainly in cities in the United States, but there are several branches in Malaysia); an educational system including elementary school, secondary school, and university; and a translation institute. The headquarters monastery is the City of Ten Thousand Buddhas in Ukiah, California. Canadian branches include the Gold Buddha Monastery in Vancouver and the Avatamsaka Monastery in Calgary, Alberta.[17] The Gold Buddha Monastery in Vancouver was created in 1984. The first monks to lead the new Canadian monastery were Heng Sure and Heng Ch'au, the two monks who had become well known for their "three steps, one bow" pilgrimage. Since they gave dharma talks on the weekends in English, they at first attracted a young Western audience as well as Chinese immigrants. The Avatamsaka Monastery in Calgary was begun in 1985 in a building which soon became too small for its many members and activities; it moved into larger quarters in 1996. It is now in the midst of a major expansion project that will add three more storeys to the present building.

Hsüan Hua was noted for the strictness of the discipline in his monastery. Rick Fields describes it thus:

> Life at Gold Mountain Monastery and at the City of Ten Thousand Buddhas follows the most severe practice of all American Buddhist communities. Bhikshus and bhikshunis live apart and adhere closely to the Vinaya. They rise at 3:40 in the morning for a program that includes bowing, chanting, services, meditation, language study (Mandarin Chinese, Sanskrit and European languages) and work. They eat one vegetarian meal a day, and many of them sleep in the meditation posture at night. ("Difficult for your legs for the first year or two," says Bhikshu Heng Lai, "but it's really beautiful. Your head is clear all night long.") These "bitter practices," as they are called, are an important part of the training under Master Hua, who succinctly sums up their value in the saying, "Bitter practice, sweet mind," and though at first they seem impossible, many who undertake them find that with time they become quite natural. (Fields 1992, 342–3)

This observation suggests that Chinese Buddhist monasteries are as strict in discipline as the Thai Forest monasteries. The Avatamsaka Monastery website notes that for monks and nuns at the monastery, a "normal day" begins at 4 a.m. and ends at 10 p.m. (Avatamsaka Monastery n.d.). However, in addition to possessing the same ethos of ascetic discipline, Chinese Buddhist monasteries also possess a highly developed group dynamic which enhances monastic practice – what I call "mutual polishing."

Monasteries in China, Korea, Japan, and Vietnam all absorbed the family structure characteristic of Chinese ancestor worship. In this structure, the master of the monastery is the father figure; indeed, his title *shifu* literally means "teacher father." The monks are sons to the father; they treat their master with great respect and loyalty – the monastic equivalent of Confucian filial piety. The monks themselves, like sons in a family, are organized in terms of seniority; all related to each other as older brother or younger brother. In any monastery, the monks think of themselves in terms of generations descended from a monk who is their first ancestor. Each such first ancestor himself represents a branch of a great lineage tree that traces itself back to the first ancestor of all Buddhism, Śākyamuni Buddha. On ordination, many monks assume a new surname *Shi* 釋, the first character of *Shi-jia-mo-ni-fo*, the Chinese pronunciation of Śākyamuni Buddha. In each generation, the most important responsibility of the master of a monastery is to transmit his understanding of Buddhism to a worthy successor who then becomes the next generation's master of the monastery.[18]

In the image that many Westerners have of Asia, Asian social structure is an authoritarian hierarchy. Maybe so, but in an Asian monastery there are two kinds of authority at work – vertical and horizontal – which complement and balance each other out. First, there is the vertical top-down authority of the master over his monks and of older brother over younger brother. Many Westerners automatically assume that authority implies authoritarianism, that a master treats his monks cruelly, that an older brother monk lords his authority over a younger brother monk. Things are not so simplistic. Granted, the master is treated as a figure of great authority. His attendants cook his food, wash his laundry, clean his room, write his thank you notes, serve tea to his guests, place a new flower in his room every day. Monks in the presence of the master remain silent unless spoken to. Even when spoken to, monks keep their eyes pointed down and do not look him in the face. Before the master can touch a door, one of his monks will open it for him. After he steps out of his shoes, someone will straighten them for him. And so on. In addition, there is a rhetoric with a very long history that says the master of a Zen monastery has the same awakened mind as the Buddha himself. According to legend, the Tang period Chan monk Deshan Xuanjian (德山宣鑒 Te-shan Hsüan-chien, 780–865) would visit Chan temples urging the monks to tear down the Buddha Hall since the presence of a living Chan master made it unnecessary to have a wooden statue of the Buddha (Yifa 2002, 74).

But in actual practice, the Asian master of a monastery does not flaunt his authority. Because it is good training that monks assume responsibility for their own practice, the master transfers much decision-making power over day-to-day matters to his monks in a chain of authority that begins with the head monk, passes through the senior monks and the middle-ranking monks and then finally ends with the novices. At every level, in day-to-day teaching and learning, practice and ritual, in a large monastery a monk does not usually turn directly to the master for instruction; he expects to get instruction from the senior monks above him. In turn, he is required to give instruction to the junior monks below him. In addition, the other authority relation – between older brother and younger brother – is not so authoritarian. In Asian society, the older brother is taught that he has a moral responsibility to look out for the welfare of the younger brother. If the younger brother commits some transgression, it is the older brother who should be reprimanded. Furthermore, when the older brother actively teaches a lesson to the younger brother, he needs to learn that lesson thoroughly himself. Older brother must set a good example in his own behaviour. Thus even though older brother must be obeyed, the presence of the younger brother exerts a kind of moral pressure on the older brother. The Western stereotype of Asian society is that it is a tyrannical hierarchy, but hierarchy is not simply a one-way street where the higher-ranking person has free rein to abuse the lower-ranking person.

Monks in a monastery in East Asia understand that they mutually assist each other in their practice, regardless of hierarchy and status. The metaphor that monks use to describe this socially mutual aspect of practice is that of stones in a bowl. Rough stones are placed into a stone bowl and then mixed around and around. Each stone knocks the rough edges off the other stones; the mixing action eventually smoothes the surface of all the stones. I call this "mutual polishing" (for more detail, see V. Hori 1994a). A variant of this image is "washing potatoes." Potatoes are put into a tub with water; they are then mixed around so that mutual friction removes their skins.[19]

The nuns at the Avatamsaka Monastery in Calgary have all undergone a period of precept training before ordination and on ordination, they undertake explicit vows to keep precepts just as do the monks of the Thai Forest tradition temples. The nuns do not eat meat or drink alcohol; they do not eat after the noon meal; they avoid handling money; they will not ride in a car with a lone male; and so on. But they live the life of precepts as a group and their group dharma practice is a clear example of mutual polishing (Verchery 2013). They sleep in shared quarters, cook together, do errands together, and only very rarely do any activity alone. When an individual nun has an errand to do alone, she attempts to finish the task quickly in order to rejoin the group. The nuns are quite clear on the rationale for group practice. With the other nuns always watching, no one nun will break precepts. This constant and mutual monitoring is not felt as a burden; rather, group life is understood to be a compassionate practice that makes keeping the precepts easier, not harder. One person alone would find it extremely difficult to maintain such a high standard of discipline, but when every person helps the others, then all members can keep temptations at bay, be strict in the maintenance of precepts, keep the mind clear of distractions, and concentrate fully on dharma practice.

"THE AUTOCRACY OF THE ZEN MASTER"

In an Asian monastery, the daily horizontal pressure of the peer group influences an individual practitioner's actions much more strongly than the vertical top-down authority of the master. But in the 1960s, when Zen Buddhist meditation centres opened in the West and implemented their version of Buddhist teacher-student relations, they reversed this structure. The Westerners assumed a Zen master had the authority of Buddha to which students were to bow in complete submission. They had no knowledge that the sangha community itself was a repository of authority which counterbalanced the master's authority. They created only vertical, top-down authority and totally omitted horizontal, mutual polishing. Years later when abuses of authority came to light, this authority structure was called "the autocracy of the Zen master" (Tworkov 1989, 149). Critics blamed the autocracy of Asian culture when really it was made in California.

American Zen centres assumed that in Asia all authority is autocratic and that Zen practice implied complete surrender to it. This was the imagined model to which they thought they had to conform.[20] Zen students were quite willing to make that surrender because they also subscribed to the romantic image of an omniscient and omnicompetent master. Everything that the Zen master said and did was taken as an example of enlightened mind.[21] They practised literal guru worship, a guru worship far more extreme than in the original Asian model. Everyday conversation was laced with "Roshi said this ...," "Roshi said that ..." as student members strove to ensure their every act conformed to Roshi's enlightened rule. In Japan, I talked with a Zen priest who had spent two years assisting the Roshi at the Mount Baldy Zen Center. He said that whenever he tried to show the American Zen students the proper zendo way to do anything, immediately he was challenged: "Did Roshi say that, or is it just you saying that?" There was no other source of authority beside "Roshi said."

While creating a regime where the Zen master exercised far more direct power than was the case in Japan, American Zen centres failed to create peer-pressure authority to balance out top-down authority. They did not understand the nature of mutual polishing in a group and thus did not realize that horizontal social interaction and peer pressure could be applied to promote dharma practice. But when I have asked Zen practitioners at Zen centres how open they would be to giving and receiving practice instruction from fellow students, the common answer I have received is "I don't tell anyone else what to do and they don't tell me what to do." This radical individualism prevents the creation of mutual polishing, prevents the creation of a horizontal peer authority, to balance out the top-down authority of the Zen master. Whereas in an Asian monastery, each practitioner has some sort of teacher-student practice relation to every other member of the group (student to every senior member, teacher to every junior member), in a Western Zen centre, each practitioner has a teacher-student relation to one and only one person: the Zen master.

Helen Tworkov's description of the leadership of Richard Baker Roshi, the first Zen teacher to be accused of sexual misconduct, makes clear that the exaggerated guru worship set the stage for abuse of authority. In her account below, *dokusan* is a private one-to-one meeting between teacher and student, usually where a monk presents his insight into the kōan which has been the focus of his meditation.

At Zen Center, dokusan became the place where students discussed their marital problems, affairs, unwanted pregnancies, alcoholic parents, abused childhoods, and so on. The disclosure of personal details is not where the intimacy of Zen practice resides, but Baker got caught in the entanglements of giving advice, making suggestions, and often telling people what to do. "I can have something to say on almost any topic. And if people ask me something, I just answer. It was just advice. But it was hard to make it just advice."

Where Baker lacked the confidence required to define the parameters of his teaching qualifications, the students willingly filled in the blanks ... Baker was told things that people didn't tell each other, contributing to psychological dependencies that he was not trained to handle. He became the sole arbitrator of personal decisions and what actions did or did not hurt others or the community. Case by case this may have had its merits, but as a strategy for community harmony it became a disaster. In addition to spiritual omniscience and paternalistic jurisdiction, it also invested him with the very potent power of private information. This blocked open communication, making it less accessible by placing Baker on an ever-higher pedestal. The more students invested in him, the more perfect he had to be in their eyes to justify that investment. (Tworkov 1989, 232–3)

In an East Asian monastery, two kinds of authority function as check and balance to each other. But at the San Francisco Zen Center, members were explicitly discouraged from talking to each other and no horizontal authority could develop to offset top-down authority. A practitioner recalls, "Richard kept us all apart because it was easier for him to deal with us individually" (Downing 2001, 144). A senior monk was once quoted as saying, "Anything one talks about in public isn't very important" (Tworkov 1989, 233). An ethic of heroic silence meant that members could not come together as a group to confront the issues they faced individually.

Ironically, Zen meditation centres in the West thought that they were copying Japanese tradition. In the Zen monasteries of Japan, despite his ritually exalted position, the Zen master is not the object of cult worship. His monks do not expect him to be omniscient or omnicompetent. He is respected for his dedication to his students, his sincerity, and his determination to be a good teacher, but he is considered a human being with his own set of strengths and weaknesses.

Zen students in the West have believed themselves to be recreating Japanese tradition on Western soil, but it would be more accurate to say that the Japanese Zen tradition provided a screen on which they projected their (Western) religious longings and yearnings. The modern life, with its assumption that science tells us what objective reality is, contains within it a source of dissatisfaction: where is that enchantment of old, that experience of feeling connected to the cosmos, that sense of oneness with the universe? To many, the religions of the West were long ago institutionalized, leaving no ground for spirituality. When Zen arrived, practitioners in the West used the opportunity to fashion a religion that conformed to their spiritual longings and yearnings otherwise frustrated by modernity.

In a recent article on the Internet, Dosho Port wrote, "It seems to me that the traditional, feudal power models that the Japanese Zen pioneers brought with them served to rapidly establish practice, enlightenment and institutions in the West AND led to serious abuses of power" (Port 2013). This statement blames the abuses of power on the traditional feudal power models of Japan. This is quite mistaken. Sexual misconduct in the Western Zen centre is a Western phenomenon. The Zen master's sexual liaison with his students resembles Catholic monks' sexual misconduct with children in their charge, football and hockey coaches' sexual exploitation of their players, President Bill Clinton's sexual intimacy with Monica Lewinsky. Wherever there is a powerful male in a position of strong authority, there is the potential to sexually exploit that power differential. The American version of the Zen master unfortunately failed to incorporate the checks and balances built into the original Asian system and thus created in the name of Zen just another male authority exploiting a position of power. So long as critics continue to blame Zen in Japan, there will never be a recognition of where responsibility lies and never a resolution to this ongoing crisis.

CONCLUSION

Beginning in the 1980s, Western Buddhist meditation centres have been rocked by sex scandals; these scandals continue right to the present. The continuance of these scandals raises the question of what it is about the Buddhist meditation centres and their leadership structure that makes them prone to sexual misconduct. What is now clear is that early Buddhist students, quite ignorant of how power is actually used in a monastery, believed the stereotype that authority in Asia is absolute and tried to create an American version of submission to absolute authority. Much more thoughtful was Sangharakshita, the leader of the (then) Friends of the Western Buddhist Order, a monk who had actually lived and practised in Asia. In reflecting on the many crises of leadership within Western Buddhism, Sangharakshita has suggested that the key failure of most Buddhist leaders has taken the form of placing far too much emphasis on vertical guidance (such as the disciple's loyalty and devotion to a teacher or a lineage of teachers) and far too little emphasis on horizontal friendship (simple fellowship among disciples) (R. Hayes 1995, 5).

This early insight did not seem persuasive at the time, but in recent years, Buddhist monasteries have been created in the West by ordained monastics who practise celibacy. A comparison of the Buddhist monastery with the Buddhist meditation centre shows us that indeed good horizontal social relations between peer disciples does much to avoid the negative imposition of vertical authority.

In this chapter, I have identified three elements within the Buddhist monastery that help prevent sexual misconduct and are absent from the Buddhist meditation centre. (1) Buddhist monasteries are same-sex communities, whereas Buddhist meditation centres are usually communities where the sexes freely mingle. (2) In Buddhist monasteries, the ordained monks and nuns have committed themselves to living their lives according to the precepts. This self-discipline is not a mere matter of behaving according to ritual form; it is a personal commitment through which the monastic strives to cultivate a better self. This ascetic ethos is much weaker in a Buddhist meditation centre. (3) In East Asian monasteries, there is a group dynamic of mutual polishing in which peer pressure is used to support dharma practice. This horizontal peer pressure to a large extent displaces the top-down authority of the master. Buddhist meditation centres often have the opposite structure. The master is invested with all authority and there is no group dynamic of mutual polishing. The absence of these checks and balances opens the door to sexual misconduct.

The Buddhist meditation centre is a modern invention. Unlike more traditional Asian social structures in which the group is a source of identity and authority, in Buddhist meditation centres in the West, there is no such group authority. This absence leaves the teacher in an extremely strong position where his authority remains unchecked and sexual misconduct can easily occur. This has nothing to do with Asian hierarchy. The sexual misconduct of Buddhist teachers with their students looks very much like the sexual misconduct of priests with parishioners, schoolteachers with students, doctors with patients, psychotherapists with their clients, Bill Clinton with Monica Lewinsky in that in all of these cases a person with great authority exploited a person with little authority.

Writers who try to define "American Buddhism" or "the new Buddhism" or "modern Buddhism" frequently declare that the new Buddhism being created in the West will be lay-oriented rather than monastic-oriented, thus correcting the "elitism" of traditional monastic Buddhism (Coleman 2001). It seems to me that this judgment is in danger of throwing the Buddha out with the bath water. To date, most of the Buddhist places of practice in North America have been meditation centres, not monasteries (although they may have described themselves as monasteries). Now that actual monasteries are being constructed, we have an opportunity to compare them. With real examples in front of us, I believe we will learn the following lessons. First, the example of Buddhist monasteries, with their commitment to celibacy, shows that it is possible to construct a place of practice which is not prone to sexual misconduct. Second, the example of Buddhist monasteries will show that the dichotomy "monastic – lay" is not an either-or choice. The strength of one does not imply the weakness of the other. In fact, I predict that the growth of Buddhist monasticism in the West will strengthen the growth of lay Buddhism as well. Third, the growth of monastic Buddhism will remind us that the Three Treasures of Buddhism are Buddha, Dharma, and Sangha, not Buddha, Dharma, and Psychotherapy.

A stream within current Buddhism in the West associates Buddhist practice with psychotherapy. Practitioners in this stream are apt to think that the goal of Buddhist practice is insight into the contents of one's own mind and resolution of the consequent problems they find there. But the rise of the Buddhist monastery reminds us that Buddhist practice is not carried on in solitary aloneness; it is carried on in a social context, in a sangha. The sangha is one of the Three Treasures of Buddhism. Peter Harvey has said, "Buddhists invented monastic life" and "no other human institution has had such a long-lasting continuous existence, along with such a wide diffusion, as the Buddhist sangha" (Harvey 1990, 73). Before summarily dismissing Buddhist monasticism as elitist, it is worthwhile asking if there are lessons to be learned about the monastic way of practice.

NOTES

1 Stories of Shimano's conduct with women had been circulating for years, but the publication in May 2010 of Robert Aitken's letters held at the University of Hawai'i Manoa Library Archives documenting Shimano's behaviour since 1984 provided conclusive evidence. See Lachs and Vladimir K. (2010). For further articles and blogs which added to the momentum to force Shimano to resign, go to the Sweeping Zen website, http://sweepingzen.com/?s=eido+shimano&cat=s&Search=Search.

2 The crisis at the Zen Center of Los Angeles was captured in a documentary, *Zen Center: Portrait of an American Zen Community*, written and produced by Anne Cushman, and directed by Lou Hawthorne. Anne Cushman was a senior at Princeton University who arrived at the Zen Center of Los Angeles to film her documentary at exactly the moment when it was revealed that Taizan Maezumi Roshi had been sexually involved with a senior student. In an interview with Cushman, Maezumi Roshi says, "being alcoholic, I really don't know how many immoral things I have done" (Cushman 1987). At one time, this video was available from Zen Center Video Stockpile, 159 Peralta Ave, San Francisco 94110, but that company no longer exists. See the review of this video documentary by Stephen Bodian (1989, 90).

3 For references, see the chapters by Eldershaw, Haynes, and Soucy, *Wild Geese* (Harding, Hori, and Soucy 2010).

4 Regarding sex scandals at Buddhist meditation centres in North America, see S. Bell (2002); Boucher (1988); Buddhist Peace Fellowship (1991); Butler (1983); Coleman (2001); L. Friedman (1987); Lachs (1994; 2002); Sidor (1987); Tworkov (1989).

5 In 2002, Michael Downing wrote *Shoes outside the Door: Desire, Devotion, and Excess at San Francisco Zen Center*, a detailed examination of the Richard Baker affair. In 2004 Natalie Goldberg wrote *The Great Failure* when she learned that her Zen teacher, Dainin Katagiri, had had sexual liaisons with several of his meditation students. In 2011, Scott Edelstein published a more analytical book, *Sex and the Spiritual Teacher*.

6 At the time of this writing, another controversy was building on the internet about the longtime sexual misconduct of Sasaki Jōshu Roshi, the centenarian teacher of the Mount Baldy Zen Center and Rinzai-ji of Los Angeles (see Sweeping Zen n.d.).

7   At the time of this writing, *Coolopolis* had three mentions of Tyndale Martin: part 1 on 24 December 2009 at http://coolopolis.blogspot.ca/2009/12/quiz-whos-guy-on-left.html; part 2 on 26 April 2010 at http://coolopolis.blogspot.ca/2010/04/more-tyndale-martin-and-his-greatheart.html; and part 3 on 26 August 2010 at http://coolopolis.blogspot.ca/2010/08/tyndale-martin-pt-3_26.html). Newspaper stories of the time describe his organization as a cult (B. Hayes 1967, 10; Bagnall 1981, 1), although there are exceptions. See *Saturday Citizen* (1975, 29).

8   To date, there has been little academic research on the Thai Forest tradition monasteries in Canada. See the chapter in this volume by James Placzek. Jack (Yunchang) Liu gave a paper on the Thai Forest tradition monasteries at the *Buddhism in Canada: Global Causes Local Conditions* conference, 16 October 2010 (Y. Liu 2010). Amy Binning, an undergraduate student at McGill University, has written an honours thesis on Sati Saraniya (Binning 2012).

9   Soucy (2010); Shiu (2010); Eldershaw (2010).

10 For the Forest Sangha, see Forest Sangha (n.d.). For Sati Saraniya, see Binning (2012).

11 There is more than one version of the *vinaya*. The Theravada *vinaya* followed throughout Southeast Asia contains 227 precepts for monks and 311 precepts for nuns; the Mulasarvāstivāda *vinaya* of Tibet, Mongolia, and Nepal has 253 rules for monks and 364 rules for nuns (although there is no female lineage in Tibet). The Dharmaguptaka *vinaya* followed in East Asia contains 252 precepts for monks and 348 precepts for nuns. See Holt (1981); Prebish (1975; 1999), Wijayaratna (1990).

12 Interested readers could start with the essays in Cabézon (1992).

13 There are exceptions. The Rinzai Zen monastery of Sōgen-ji in Okayama, Japan has a large membership of both men and women training under Harada Shōdō Roshi.

14 Where in theory women were to have separate and equal practice centres, in fact, support for women's monasteries was historically far weaker than it was for men. Monks flourished; nuns "vanished." See Falk (1989, 155–65).

15 I cannot discuss here the very interesting question of the Buddhist attitude to ascetic practice. In the well-known biography of the Buddha, Siddhartha engaged in extreme ascetic practice for many years without attaining awakening. He finally came to the conclusion that the proper path of practice was "the Middle Way," between self-indulgence and self-mortification. For a general discussion of Buddhist asceticism, see Holt (1981). For a good list of citations of relevant passages from Pali texts, see Anālayo (2003, 34–9).

16 A photo album of the pilgrimage can be found at http://www.urbandharma.org/udharma7/3steps.html. Rick Fields discusses the Three Steps One Bow pilgrimage in Fields (1992, 343–6).

17 I am indebted to Lina Verchery, who gave me a preliminary report entitled "Avatamsaka Buddhist Monastery in Calgary, Alberta" at the colloquium on *The Consecrated Life in Canada: What Is the Future?* held 24 August 2011 at McGill University.

18 John Jorgensen has written an illuminating account of how the Chan school absorbed Confucian ritual and ancestor worship during the Tang period. See Jorgensen (1987).

19 The Korean Son teacher Samu Sunim once used this image in a dharma talk precisely to illustrate how a group of practitioners mutually assist each other in practice. Lina Verchery reports that the nuns at Avatamsaka Buddhist Monastery use this same image to describe the social nature of Buddhist practice (Verchery 2013).

20 "The autocracy of the Zen master has its counterpart in surrender as an ideal form of spiritual practice. In Japan surrender to the master is taken for granted not just for the attainment of Zen teachings but for the attainment of harmony with the entire universe. It has existed between Zen master and disciple with no more urgency or virtue than between warlord and samurai, feudal landlord and serf, mistress and maid, or boss and employee" (Tworkov 1989, 149).

21 In the 1973 documentary *Sunseed*, directed by Frederick Cohn (1973), a Zen student describes the way Suzuki Roshi eats an apple leaving only a core that is matchstick thin. This is the way an enlightened master eats an apple. The portion of the film which deals with Shunryu Suzuki has been excerpted and is available at the Shunryu Suzuki Digital Archive: shunryusuzuki.com (minute 8:00 to 8:30).

PART TWO

Communicating the Buddhadharma

8

Teaching Buddhism to Children: The Evolving Sri Lankan Buddhist Tradition in Multicultural Toronto

D. MITRA BARUA

We will inevitably end up having to rethink our conceptualizations of Buddhism as a translocal tradition with a long and self-consciously distinct history but which is at the same time a tradition dependent on local conditions for the production of meaning.

CHARLES HALLISEY 1995, 51

Migration to a new land may ignite rethinking and reinterpreting within a tradition; the emergence of a new generation in that land may become a justification for such endeavours. A religious tradition like Buddhism comprises a set of beliefs and practices that are socially embodied and historically extended, and those beliefs and practices establish the integrity or identity of the tradition. On the other hand, the impulses to rethink and reinterpret testify to the viability of tradition. This perennial effort to maintain both identity and viability animates a religious tradition. The process of religious education in a new cultural setting, which facilitates a dialogue between two generations shaped by two cultures, illustrates how the identity-viability interplay unfolds. This essay examines how that identity-viability interplay has played out within the Sri Lankan Buddhist tradition in Toronto, as the tradition itself is transplanted in a new sociocultural setting and transmitted to a new generation. It does so through an analysis of *Teaching Buddhism to Children* (Chandrasekera 2001), a Buddhist educational manual developed and adopted by Sri Lankan Buddhists in Toronto. I contend that *Teaching Buddhism to Children* brings multicultural themes embedded in the Buddhist tradition to the fore as Sri Lankan Buddhists strive to transmit their cherished religion to their Canadian-born and/or raised children.[1]

I explore what *Teaching Buddhism to Children* tells us about Sri Lankan Buddhism in the diaspora, specifically in the Canadian context. First, I briefly discuss the history of *Dhamma* education, showing that a moral tone has characterized Sri Lankan Buddhism in modern times. In the second section, I briefly explain how *Dhamma* education has been transplanted in Toronto, and why it has become the most sought out temple service within the community. Next, I provide an in-depth analysis of *Teaching Buddhism to Children* in three sections, focusing on the purpose, method, and contents of the manual. The "purpose" section shows that Toronto's multicultural and multireligious milieu prompts Sri Lankan Buddhist leaders in Toronto to rethink and redefine their inherited tradition. They do so as they strive to pass Buddhism on to their Canadian children. The "method" section delineates how the Buddha's gradual teaching method has been used to program *Dhamma* education. The manual thereby remains faithful to Theravada Buddhist conceptualizations of spiritual development as a step-by-step process of cultivating confidence, morality, concentration, and wisdom. The "content" section illustrates how Sri Lankan Buddhist leaders in Toronto have incorporated ambient secular world views and multicultural values into their presentation of Buddhism to Canadian-born children. In the final section, I propose that the teaching manual signifies an immigrant religious community's response to ambient social realities, including religio-cultural diversity and the Canadian multicultural policy. In that response, Sri Lankan Buddhism reconfigures itself by highlighting the aspects that resonate with the ambient social norms and principles.

DHAMMA EDUCATION AS MORAL ARGUMENT IN SRI LANKAN BUDDHISM

Dhamma education in Sri Lankan Buddhism denotes formal Buddhist religious education designed for children and youth. In the late nineteenth century, *Dhamma* education emerged as a reactionary movement against Christian evangelism, on the model of Christian Sunday schools in colonial Sri Lanka (Bartholomeusz 1994, 61; Bond 1988, 48–52, 85–8,

111, 117–18; Gombrich and Obeyesekere 1988, 205, 211, 235; Prothero 1996, 101–6). Indigenous sources confirm that C. Don Bastian, a local artist, established the first Buddhist Sunday school in 1872 (Nanakirti Himi 2008, 3). However it was American civil war veteran and Theosophist Colonel Henry Steel Olcott who provided organizational, financial, and educational leadership for *Dhamma* education.

In 1881 Olcott wrote *The Buddhist Catechism* for Buddhist religious education. This first handbook for Buddhist students shaped the content, tone, and purpose of Buddhist education throughout the twentieth century. Its legacy of cognitive formation of Buddhist laity is still felt in Sri Lankan Buddhism. Olcott's organization, the Young Men's Buddhist Association (YMBA), financed and systematized *Dhamma* education. The YMBA introduced a set of examinations on the Buddhist tradition in 1920 that established an internal structure and standards for *Dhamma* education (Pannasiha 1995, 4; Susila Himi 1995, 23). The All Ceylon Buddhist Congress, an offshoot of the YMBA, strived to mobilize and implement those standards throughout Sri Lanka, but met with less success. Only with the state's assistance did *Dhamma* education become an institutional practice associated with Buddhist temples in postcolonial Sri Lanka in the 1950s and 60s.

Dhamma education is an integral part of the Buddhist temple. From the beginning of the nineteenth-century reform movement, the temple has been the base for *Dhamma* education. Currently, almost every Buddhist temple (except some of the forest hermitages) in Sri Lanka administers a *Dhamma* school. Furthermore, *Dhamma* schools, like all educational institutions, comprise a rational and hierarchical structure that includes a principal, vice-principal, teachers, student leaders, a student body, and a volunteer group. These internal organizational features are strengthened by an external governing body that connects an individual *Dhamma* school to other *Dhamma* schools across Sri Lanka. *Dhamma* education in Sri Lanka has been loosely institutionalized through official registration, annual examinations, nation-wide *Dhamma* school competitions, accreditation, and textbooks. Access to political power in postcolonial Sri Lanka finally enabled Buddhists to transform *Dhamma* education into an institutionalized practice.

Dhamma education has also become a tradition-defining practice that lays out the fundamental presuppositions about the content (what constitutes the tradition) and the purpose (formation of Buddhists) of the tradition. By defining the identity and illustrating the function of Sri Lankan Buddhism in modern times, it shapes two important aspects of tradition (Asad 1986, 7, 14). In other words, *Dhamma* education in Sri Lankan Buddhism is founded on a moral argument that seeks to construct Buddhist moral agents by inculcating Buddhist knowledge, developing Buddhist attitudes, and cultivating cultural and moral skills. To achieve these educational objectives, *Dhamma* schools advocate a set of practices that includes memorizing Pali chanting, studying Buddhist history and philosophy, performing Buddhist rituals, and so on. These are historically derived practices, taking different forms and meanings depending on when, where, and by whom they are performed. *Teaching Buddhism to Children* illustrates how the tradition-defining practices mentioned above are taking new forms and meanings to redefine what Sri Lankan Buddhism is and what it means to be a Sri Lankan Buddhist in a new location, namely Toronto, Canada.

DHAMMA EDUCATION IN TORONTO: *TEACHING BUDDHISM TO CHILDREN*

In Toronto, *Dhamma* education has become the most sought-out temple service, in part because of its focus on the intergenerational transmission of Buddhism. For example, the survey that I conducted in 2008 indicates that 74.5 per cent of Sri Lankan Buddhists in Toronto rated *Dhamma* education as the "most liked" temple service. Every other temple service, such as protective chanting, full-moon day precept observation, or weekly sutra studies, scored lower than *Dhamma* education. With the absence of the extended family and ambient Buddhist cultural environment, first-generation Sri Lankan Buddhists depend on *Dhamma* education as a primary, and at times sole, means to pass Buddhism on to their children. Many Sri Lankan Buddhist temples across North America, except the few that serve Caucasian Buddhists, administer some sort of *Dhamma* education. Three of four temples in Toronto provide weekly *Dhamma* school services to socialize children and youth of the Sri Lankan Buddhist community. The fourth temple, a representative of the Sri Lankan forest tradition (*Asapuwa*), does not conduct a formal *Dhamma* school, but it offers a monthly meditation practice geared toward youth and children. The Toronto Mahavihara *Dhamma* School in Scarborough was started in

1978 and, at the time of my fieldwork (2009), it maintained a list of over 135 registered students. The West End *Dhamma* School in Mississauga, founded in 1992, has the largest student body, with nearly 300 registered names. The Mihindu *Dhamma* School in Brampton, established in 2007, is the most recent. These *Dhamma* schools illustrate the emphasis Sri Lankan Buddhists place on formal Buddhist education in Sri Lanka and in the diaspora.

The Mississauga West End *Dhamma* School stands out in a few ways. It has been identified as the largest Sri Lankan *Dhamma* School in North America (Wijesundara 2008, 16; Attygalle 2009, 8). In 2008, it launched an annual *Dhamma* School Day and introduced a *Dhamma* school song and flag. Although its student body is made up of a majority of descendants of Sri Lankan immigrants, a few Theravada Buddhist immigrants from Bangladesh, India, and Singapore also send their children to this *Dhamma* school. Its 2009 *Dhamma* School Day celebration displayed the Indian and Bangladeshi flags beside the Sri Lankan and Canadian flags. More importantly, the West End *Dhamma* School has adapted a new *Dhamma* school curriculum that demonstrates the transition within the Sri Lankan Buddhist tradition in multicultural Toronto.

After four years of experimenting with the *Dhamma* education project at the West End *Dhamma* School, in 2001 Swarna Chandrasekera, a Sinhalese specialist in the field of education, wrote *Teaching Buddhism to Children*. In the process of designing the curriculum, a committee comprising monks, lay *Dhamma* teachers, parents, and youth met to discuss the content of the prospective curriculum. The monastic leadership had the final say with respect to the contents while Chandrasekera was responsible for the format. Chandrasekera acknowledges that "In writing this book I have benefited from the cumulative knowledge of the *Maha Sangha*, my colleagues and students; and a host of resource persons who came from diverse disciplines to make their individual contributions" (Chandrasekera 2001, 4). She gives credit to Bhante Punnaji, the most senior monk within the community, for clarifying Buddhist terms and concepts (Chandrasekera 2001, 4). Thus, the book itself represents a number of diverse voices, including those of monks, men, women, teachers, parents, and youth of a Buddhist temple.

The book's foreword, issued by all resident monks of the temple, recognizes that the ambient social reality of religio-cultural diversity in Toronto requires them to culturally adapt their inherited tradition to their new location. The monks assert, "We are not impervious to the demands of the 'religio-cultural' diversity we see around us. It is, indeed, the environment in which our children will have to grow up. Therefore we believe cultural adaptation to be the regular norm. Our teaching methods ... should allow for such openness and ingenuity as to be capable of intelligent adaptation where necessary ... Swarna's book and the curriculum go a long way in fulfilling our own vision about the propagation of *Dhamma* in the Canadian context (Chandrasekera 2001, 2)." In unpacking the preceding statement, a few important issues come to the fore. Monks identify themselves as cultural interpreters of Buddhism, a historical role that has been challenged by lay movements in modern times. They understand that cultural adaptation is normal, implying that they are simply following the pattern found in their tradition. They also confidently assert that what they are doing is right and intelligent. More importantly, they rationalize their action by highlighting the presence of second-generation Buddhists in Toronto. Chandrasekera's book represents the so-called "intelligent adaptation."

The subtitle of the book – "a curriculum guide to *Dhamma* School Teachers" – suggests that Chandrasekera prescribes what to teach and how to teach Buddhism to children. Exploring the nature of a curriculum, Kieran Egan states that a curriculum should "address the *what* and *how* questions together" (Egan 2003, 15). The "what" question refers to the contents (what should be taught) and purpose (what the contents are for) of a curriculum. The "how" question (how should things be taught) details method(s) of teaching (Egan 2003, 12, 14). Chandrasekera explicitly addresses both types of questions. Therefore, the book provides a method of teaching and also recommends a specific form of Buddhism. The foreword, as discussed above, suggests that *Teaching Buddhism to Children* also addresses the "why" (why the recommended form of Buddhism should be taught in the recommended method) question. By analysing the ways in which the *what, how,* and *why* questions are addressed, it is possible to discern something of how a Buddhist tradition evolves in a new cultural setting.

Purpose: Intergenerational Transmission of the Sri Lankan Buddhist Tradition

Teaching Buddhism to Children intends to pass on an inherited Buddhist tradition to Sri Lankan Buddhist descendants, particularly in Toronto, but also in other places in Western countries. The monks at the West End Buddhist Centre hope that *Teaching Buddhism to Children* "will serve as a beacon of light to all the teachers of Sunday *Dhamma* Schools in the West ... in fulfilling his/her responsibility of imparting to the children of the community with joy, the '*sanantana* – the eternal – *Dhamma*,' the hallowed religion of their forefathers, in all its beauty and splendour!" (Chandrasekera 2001, 2). Thus the teaching manual represents an intergenerational transmission of a Buddhist tradition in a new location. Echoing the monastic voice, Chandrasekera also states that she intends to provide "a rational and coherent synthesis ... of the Buddha *Dhamma* in respect to its morality and values in the light of today's fast-track society which our children have to contend with" (Chandrasekera 2001, 6). The first-generation Sri Lankan Buddhists trust that the Buddhist concepts, practices, attitudes, and values that they have cherished can be passed on to their children in such a way that the latter find their inherited tradition viable and useful in the current socio-cultural setting. They expect *Dhamma* education to facilitate the socialization of Canadian-born children into Buddhism. Accordingly, Chandrasekera identifies three learning objectives of *Dhamma* education: gaining knowledge of Buddhism, developing certain skills by applying what is learned in everyday life, and cultivating attitudes so that students embody desirable values.

The contents and method of transmission are historically grounded. For example, the Sri Lankan Buddhist tradition has a history, and Sunday *Dhamma* school as an institutional practice is situated within that history. Sri Lankan Buddhists in Toronto have revisited the tradition and reconceptualized its practice of *Dhamma* education for a Canadian-born generation. These efforts point to continuity of a religious identity along with fluidity and maintaining both the integrity and viability of a tradition. The identity and integrity ground a tradition in the past; however, fluidity and viability validate a tradition in the present and generate hopes for the near future. For instance, Chandrasekera explains that her book contributes to the formation of Buddhists as well as to good Canadian citizens. She claims that her book imparts, "an education as well as a complete formation to children so that they will be better equipped intellectually, morally and emotionally to tackle today's hurdles and face tomorrow's challenges as Buddhists and as good citizens of this great Canadian nation of ours" (Chandrasekera 2001, 6). Thus, *Teaching Buddhism to Children* stands for the conscious endeavour of a first-generation immigrant community to merge its inherited Buddhist identity with its adopted Canadian identity. They understand, however, that both identities are inheritance for their children. They combine both so that their Canadian-born and/or raised children will be simultaneously Canadian citizens and Buddhists within the Sri Lankan tradition.

The first-generation Sri Lankan Buddhists envision that Buddhist norms and values such as respecting the Triple Gem (the Buddha, *Dhamma*, and Sangha), following the five precepts, taking care of elderly parents, and being a caring and compassionate person, will nurture their children to be better Canadians. By this they mean that the Buddhist cultural values mentioned above do not contradict Canadian values, especially the appreciation of religious and cultural diversity and peaceful coexistence. For instance, one of the learning objectives in *Teaching Buddhism to Children* states that "Students will develop and demonstrate respect for other religions so that they can appreciate Buddhist values they may observe among their non-Buddhist peers ... [so that they] will develop skills in living and sharing in a multicultural/multireligious milieu" (Chandrasekera 2001, 15). Chandrasekera believes that as students learn and practise Buddhism, they will develop the ability to care for and respect Buddhism, as well as other religions. In other words, her book encourages *Dhamma* students to recognize, respect, and relish their own cultural norms, values, and practices as well as those of others who are religiously, culturally, and ethnically different.

In fact, this multicultural and multi-religious value has been emphasized from the very beginning of *Dhamma* education in Toronto. Referring to Buddhist education in Toronto during the mid 1980s, K.S. Gunaratne emphasized that, "When we attempt to enlighten the child with regard to ideas and beliefs gathered by him during his association with children of other faiths, we should take the precaution not to speak in a manner derogatory of other religions. *We should advise the child to respect all religions, even though they are different from his own*" [emphasis added] (Gunaratne 1986, 11–12). This has become an overtone of *Dhamma* education from its early beginning in multicultural and multi-religious Toronto. Such a harmonious perspective mitigates the confrontational traits expressed in the term "Protestant Buddhism" (Gombrich and Obeyesekere 1988; Obeyesekere 1970; Prothero 1996) that has been used to refer to the modern interpretation of Buddhism in Sri Lanka. What we see in *Teaching*

Buddhism to Children is not a new invention. It is, rather, a reconfiguration of Sri Lankan Buddhism by the discursive synthesis of aspects from its history, making it feasible for a new generation living in a new culture. Thus, *Teaching Buddhism to Children* interprets the inherited Sri Lankan Buddhist identity and tradition for the Canadian-born generation, and it does so by remaining faithful to the Theravada Tradition in its method.

Method: *Teaching* Dhamma *in Gradual Steps*

Chandrasekera, in her introductory chapter "Thematic Notes," describes the Buddha as a model teacher in the teaching of Buddhism to children. She introduces the Buddha as a "unique teacher" who, even at his final breath, encouraged his disciples to learn *Dhamma*. She briefly recalls incidents where the Buddha reached out to children to help them. The stories of Sōpāka and Sāmaṇera Rāhula refer to the Buddha's emphasis on individual and collective commitment to children's needs. The "Buddha held that children should be given priority in all matters and their interest should always prevail and be protected" (Chandrasekera 2001, 7). Despite the hyperbole, this statement indicates that children are increasingly the priority in the diaspora since the intergenerational transmission of Buddhism can no longer be taken for granted. "Buddhism and Children" is an emerging academic area in Buddhist studies (Sasson 2012).

In order to illustrate the Buddha's effective teaching methods, Chandrasekera recalls events from the Buddha's life story. Chullapanthaka was ridiculed when he failed to memorize a four-line stanza. However, the Buddha, with his "practical and homely methods," helped Chullapanthaka to realize the *Dhamma*. The story of Angulimāla highlights the importance of compassion and empathy in teaching, and conversation as an interactive teaching method (Chandrasekera 2001, 7–8). Chandrasekera suggests that the Buddha used a "social case work method" and a "field-trip method" in teaching *Dhamma* to Kisāgōtami and Buddha's own stepbrother Nanda respectively (Chandrasekera 2001, 9). Kisāgōtami, a mother devastated by her infant's death, begged the Buddha to bring her infant back to life. The Buddha asked her to bring some sesame seeds from a family where no death had occurred. She went in vain from house to house, only to realize that death is inevitable and incurable. The story of Nanda illustrates another instance of the Buddha's skilfulness. Nanda was infatuated with his lover Janapadakalyāni. The Buddha took him to one of the heavenly realms and promised that rigorous meditation would enable him to be with angels who are far more beautiful than his lover. With the Buddha's meditation instructions, Nanda became an enlightened individual (*arahat*) free from infatuation. These references highlight the need for diverse means in explaining Buddhist teachings to children.

Since the book is designed as a teaching manual, Chandrasekera lays out the basics of teaching *Dhamma*, including a list of the qualifications a *Dhamma* teacher should possess. She also gives a ninety-minute lesson plan and practical advice on lesson preparation and presentation. A list of relevant scriptures in the Pali canon and a redefined glossary of Pali terms are provided for teachers' reference. Two evaluation sheets are included; one is for students and the other for teachers. The core of the book is a curriculum of Buddhism for the weekly West End *Dhamma* School.

Above all, Chandrasekera recommends and implements "*Anupubba Dēsana*" or "gradual preaching/teaching" of *Dhamma* in progressive steps. She argues that "gradual teaching" intimately connects with the gradual character transformation of *Dhamma* practitioners/students (Chandrasekera 2001, 7). This "gradual teaching" method characterizes *Teaching Buddhism to Children* in multiple ways. Chandrasekera organizes the curriculum into five steps by arranging the contents according to child growth and spiritual development in Theravada Buddhism. Steps One (age 3 to 6) and Two are called *saddhā* (Appreciation of Goodness). Although the Pali term *saddhā* is translated as "appreciation of goodness" in the curriculum, more generally, it refers to a Buddhist practitioner's confidence in the Buddha, *Dhamma*, and Sangha. In Theravada Buddhism, *saddhā* is considered the initial step in spiritual development. Step Three (age 9 to 12) is *sīla* (self-control); Step Four (age 12 to 15) is *samādhi* (calm and purity); and Step Five (age 15 to 18) is *paññā* (wisdom). *Sīla, samādhi,* and *paññā* are Three Leanings derived from the Eight-fold Path. In Theravada Buddhism, spiritual growth is often conceptualized as a progressive development of four qualities, namely confidence, morality, concentration, and wisdom. The Pali terms for these concepts are used to name the five steps, by classifying the first and second steps under confidence.

Each step contains twenty-three lessons. The author recommends one lesson for two Sundays and eleven lessons for the entire academic year (September to June), which means that a student is expected to spend two years at each step. Thus, if a student enrols at Step One, she or he would take ten years to graduate from the West End *Dhamma* School. This lengthy Buddhist religious educational program is designed for students between the ages of 3 and 18. Although students advance in progressive steps, the progression is more spiral than linear. First, Chandrasekera briefly introduces a concept or practice, and in the next step, she returns to the same issue with new information. For example, at Step One she introduces what *Vesak* is (Chandrasekera 2001, 28), in Step Two she explains why Buddhists celebrate *Vesak* (Chandrasekera 2001, 33), and in Step Three she illustrates how a Buddhist celebrates *Vesak* (Chandrasekera 2001, 37). A similar pattern is used in illustrating the life story of the Buddha, which runs across Steps One to Four.

In terms of teaching techniques, the author recommends that storytelling be predominant, with the morals related to the everyday lives of the students. Through Steps One to Four, *Jātaka* stories dominate. Chandrasekera invokes the Buddha as an exemplary storyteller who imparts Buddhist knowledge, practices, and values.

> The Buddha, the great teacher, selected the popular "storytelling" method as a teaching tool to address the masses who were lovers of stories. This method consisted of *Dana Katha* (Stories of "Giving"), *Sila Katha* (Stories of Moral Restraint), and *Sagga Katha* ([stories] of other dimensions of existence according to *kamma* [Skt. *karma*]): *Dana Katha* ... exemplify benefits of "giving" and "giving up of self." *Dana Katha* ... help develop virtues of compassion, concern for others and above all, detachment from worldly things; *Sila Katha* [promote] self control and helping the practice of virtues of justice, fairplay and equality, etc.; *Sagga Katha* ... exhort devotees to do good and lead lives of purity for the purpose of evolving into higher levels until one reaches *Nibbana*. (Chandrasekera 2001, 9)

Here, too, the author emphasizes the gradual method of teaching in her selection of the order of stories. Sri Lankan Buddhists commonly believe that the Buddhist way of life evolves in sequence or a logical order. One starts with giving. Through the practice of giving, the student gradually becomes interested in ethical practices. Ethics is considered a prerequisite for success in contemplative practices (*bhāvana*).

Similarly, Sri Lankan Buddhists think that cognitive knowledge of the Buddha's teachings preconditions the practice and experience in Buddhism. This understanding in fact necessitates and rationalizes the practice of *Dhamma* education. Chandrasekera explains, "We begin by instructing and establishing the students in … the theoretical aspects of Buddha's entire teaching (*Pariyatti*) to help them achieve that experiential understanding (*pativedha*) of the Buddha *Dhamma* which can only come about through individual practice [*patipatti*]" (Chandrasekera 2001, 6). Although the claim to instruct the "Buddha's entire teaching" is unrealistic, the preceding quotation invokes a sequential development of one's spirituality in Buddhism. One first studies (*Pariyatti*) what the Buddha taught, then practises (*Patipatti*) the teachings so that s/he gains experiential understanding (*Pativēdha*) of the *Dhamma*. By relating individual spiritual development to teaching *Dhamma*, Chandrasekera invokes a Buddhist perspective of religious education, which highlights the involvement of co-agency, the importance of practice, and the emphasis on experiential understanding. In *Dhamma* education, teachers and students are co-agents. *Dhamma* teachers present knowledge of Buddhism to students, but students must practise what they have learned to gain experiential insight. Thus, the Buddha's gradual teaching method has become emblematic in *Dhamma* education. By adopting it, *Teaching Buddhism to Children* sheds new light on the content of the curriculum.

Content: The Evolving Sri Lankan Buddhist Tradition in Relation to Multicultural and Secular World Views

Chandrasekera includes many aspects of Theravada Buddhism in *Teaching Buddhism to Children*, including concepts, principles, norms, values, and practices. She arranges them as answers to what, why, and how questions. In lower grades, concepts like *kamma* are introduced casually: for example, "If you give love you get love" (Chandrasekera 2001, 34). In higher grades, the term is philosophically introduced along with a story of a monk who lost his eyes as a result of intentionally blinding someone else in one of his previous lives (Chandrasekera 2001, 43). In the final grade, a complete lesson is dedicated to the concept along with twelve classifications of *kamma* (Chandrasekera 2001, 51). To embody the teachings, students memorize Pali chants, such as the three refuges, the five precepts, the salutation to the Triple Gem, and the discourse on loving-kindness. Instructions about how to perform certain practices are provided. For example, the steps required to develop mindfulness on breathing (*ānapānasati*) and to cultivate loving kindness (*mettā* for oneself and others) are laid out. Above all, what is emphasized is how people behave when the teachings are fully practised and embodied in characters. For that, Chandrasekera discusses in detail the life of the Buddha, Jātaka stories, and spiritual biographies of monastic and lay sangha.

All these aspects of the Theravada tradition (concepts, stories, and practices) are included to varying degrees in all steps, but the proportions and levels of sophistication differ. The first two steps are more about relationships, and they emphasize the appreciation of goodness in oneself, parents, teachers, friends, and others. Step Three highlights sacred Buddhist sites in Sri Lanka, and it includes many spiritual biographies of monks, nuns, laymen, and laywomen of the Buddha's time. In Step Four, numerous celebrated virtues and values are introduced along with some stories. In Step Five, Buddhist philosophical concepts are explained with an emphasis on meditation. A few lessons are dedicated to Buddhist history, other religions, and Canadian culture. All the lessons, regardless of grade, end with meditation or chanting.

Teaching Buddhism to Children advocates a Theravada Buddhist identity. Memorizing basic Pali chanting (the three-refuge formula, the five precepts, and salutation to the Buddha, *Dhamma*, and Sangha) strengthens this identity. Pali, being a language of liturgy across all Theravada communities, underscores a common Theravada Buddhist world view whose attitudes and practices constitute individual and group identity. Thus, Pali represents a pan-Theravada Buddhist identity, although this common Theravada identity will have a particular flavour depending on the particular history of a Theravada Buddhist community. The manual insists on taking refuge in the Buddha, *Dhamma*, and Sangha (an expression of general Buddhist identity) in the Pali language. For instance, its two lessons entitled "I am a Buddhist" define Buddhist identity in the first-person and clearly lay out what makes a person Buddhist. They emphasize taking refuge in the Triple Gem: "*Buddham Saranam Gacchami*' (I take refuge in the Buddha)" and "Obeisance to the Triple Gem (*Ti-sarana*)" (Chandrasekera 2001, 26, 36). The lessons also relate the observance of the five precepts to Buddhist identity, and students commit to memory the relevant Pali chanting. The worship (praising the virtues of the Buddha, *Dhamma*, and Sangha), rituals (offering flowers to the Buddha), and "habits" (implying that all the above practices need be turned into habits) are highlighted, suggesting that these practices play significant roles in forming a religious identity. In a typical Sunday *Dhamma* school, teachers, students, and parents take refuge in the Triple Gem and observe the five precepts in Pali. They bow to the Buddha and offer flowers and other items to him. All these actions illustrate the traditional way of establishing a Theravada Buddhist identity, preferably a life-long one. The textbook used for the lessons reads, "As long as I live, I adore the Buddha. I follow the *Dhamma*. I respect the Sangha" (Nanayakkara 1997, 35).

Moreover, a more particularized Theravada identity stands out as Chandrasekera describes Buddhist sacred places. The lessons on "The Vihara (Monastery)" give a Sri Lankan flavour of Theravada Buddhism (Chandrasekera 2001, 26, 36). They highlight "Pagoda, Bodhi Tree, Shrine Room, [and] Monks" as the integral parts of the Sri Lankan Buddhist temple (Chandrasekera 2001, 26). The monks' presence is crucial to make a Theravada temple, as the Pali term for temple, "*vihara*," itself means "the residence." The other parts are honoured as symbolic presence of the Buddha. The Bodhi tree, under which the Buddha is believed to have realized awakening, is a distinguishing feature of a Sri Lankan Buddhist temple. The temples in Toronto manage to maintain Bodhi plants indoors. This brings a sense of completeness. It also reminds students that *Bodhipuja*, honouring of a Bodhi tree as a symbol of the Buddha, is a central practice in Sri Lankan Buddhism, although the practice has diminished in the diaspora.[2] Moreover, in these lessons, Chandrasekera introduces two Buddhist places of worship with great historical significance: Swarnamali Maha Thupa and Samādhi Buddha Statue in Anuradhapura (Chandrasekera 2001, 36). These references to important places highlight the connection between Buddhism and Sri Lanka as a place. Consequently, what we see in the manual is a "Sri Lankan Buddhist identity" opposed to a "Sinhala Buddhist identity." Unlike the latter, the former does not imply an exclusive connection between Buddhism and the Sinhala ethnicity.

Chandrasekera emphasizes how Buddhist children relate to their parents and friends. The first generation worry that the individualistic culture of North America may diminish the Sinhala Buddhist cultural emphasis on honouring, respecting, and, more importantly, taking care of elderly parents. If parental anxiety related to old age is a future concern, their more immediate concern is the influence of peers on their children. They are vigilant about whom their children associate with, and what kind of influences they bring. Parents expect *Dhamma* education to make the younger generation understand the importance of parents and elders, and how much influence friends have in one's life.

Correspondingly, Chandrasekera highlights the parent-child hierarchical values in numerous lessons: "I Love My Parents (Honour your parents), Respect and Listen to the Elders" (Chandrasekera 2001, 26), and "My Precious Parents" (Chandrasekera 2001, 37). A teacher involved in *Dhamma* education since the mid 1990s claims that *Dhamma* school shapes "a generation who respect elders, specifically parents and teachers." Students in lower grades commit to memory two specific Pali verses dedicated to parents,[3] and they are encouraged and expected to bow at the feet of the parents before going to bed. Students annually perform this ritual by bowing at the feet of their parents at *Dhamma* school on the Sunday closest to the traditional Sinhala New Year in April. In addition, Chandrasekera warns students that "Peer group and friends can influence you favourably or unfavourably" (Chandrasekera 2001, 37), and to choose friends wisely. Many youth reveal that issues related to friendship and dating often cause disagreements with their parents. Reflecting on these concerns, Chandrasekera dedicates a few lessons to cultural tensions (Chandrasekera 2001, 41, 46). She lays out a Buddhist emphasis on mutual duties in the children-parents relationship and advises *Dhamma* students to maintain "respect for parents and elders in the family" (Chandrasekera 2001, 41). She also puts the Buddhist concepts of "good" and "bad" friends in the context of Canadian culture (Chandrasekera 2001, 46). The discussion of who a Buddhist is and how s/he relates to parents invokes numerous classical Buddhist ideals: the prospective buddha (*bodhisatta;* Skt. *bodhisattva*) with ten progressive practices (*dasa pāramitā*) (Chandrasekera 2001, 36), the good person (*satpurusa*) with a sense of gratitude (Chandrasekera 2001, 34), and the devoted and duty-bound male and female householders (*upāsaka* and *upāsika*) (Chandrasekera 2001, 52). These ideals demonstrate the Buddhist identity that the first generation would like their children to uphold. At the same time, Chandrasekera presents some Buddhist concepts, stories, and practices in a way that would reflect the Canadian multicultural context.

Multiculturalism is a social reality in Toronto. In 1971, Canada became the first country in the world to adopt an official policy of multiculturalism.

Like other social realities, multiculturalism keeps changing and evolving, and different dimensions have been added to the relevant policy. A 2010 Canadian government report on the policy identifies four stages of multiculturalism, identifying a decade for each stage since 1971 (Kunz and Sykes 2010, 21). Currently, multiculturalism policy has been identified as "a means to an inclusive and equitable society" (Kunz and Sykes 2010, 5). In order to achieve this noble goal, the policy promotes a multicultural discourse that celebrates ethno-cultural diversity, encourages cultural sensitivity, envisions employment equity, implements social inclusiveness, and promotes dialogue and mutual understanding.

This multicultural discourse of social harmony and peaceful coexistence has influenced ideas about how to be Buddhist and Sri Lankan in Canada, permeating different levels of the curriculum. In lower grades, it surfaces in the morals of stories. The moral of the *Swarna Hansa Jātaka* says "Live, let live and help live." In the story, the *bodhisatta* (the Buddha in one of his previous lives) was born as a swan with golden feathers who helped a poor family. He gave a feather to the family every day, and the family met their everyday needs by selling the feathers. One day, the greedy head of the family caught the swan and plucked out all the feathers. Since the feathers were plucked out against the swan's will, they ceased to be golden. The moral of the story could be read as the virtues of contentment and gratitude, but instead, the lesson in the curriculum highlights the importance of peaceful coexistence, which is further strengthened by insisting that "We are not living alone. Others are important. We should care for them; sharing through exchange, cooperation and team work" (Chandrasekera 2001, 32). This teaching reinforces the spirit of multiculturalism as much as that of Buddhism. The implied multicultural theme becomes obvious when we read the lesson in the context of the author's emphasis on Toronto's multicultural and multi-religious context discussed above.

In higher grades, intercultural themes are overtly developed in full lessons, i.e., "The Value of Buddhism in Canadian Life and Cultural Conflicts" (Chandrasekera 2001, 41), and "Relevance of Buddhism in Canadian Life" (Chandrasekera 2001, 46). These lessons contextualize Buddhism in Toronto. They provide a Buddhist perspective on certain virtues related to social ethics, such as responsibility, honesty, concern for others, expression of love and care. Chandrasekera encourages students "to respond rationally instead of reacting emotionally and irresponsibly" (Chandrasekera

2001, 46). She also relates Buddhism to "fair exchange and trustworthy relationships with others" and highlights "charity, social service, and ... making a contribution to society" (Chandrasekera 2001, 46). These concepts remind students that Buddhism can help them enrich their social life in multicultural Canada. They are the conceptual tools used to integrate young Buddhists into the wider Canadian society. They promote multicultural values such as mutual respect, sympathetic understanding, and peaceful coexistence.

Teaching Buddhism to Children has made a more substantial effort to coalesce Buddhism and multiculturalism by redefining the Buddhist Eight-fold Path as follows:

1. Harmonious Perspective (*Samma Ditthi*)
2. Harmonious Visualization (of goal) (*Samma Samkappa*)
3. Harmonious Speech (*Samma Vaca*)
4. Harmonious Action (*Samma Kammanta*)
5. Harmonious Lifestyle (*Samma Ajiva*)
6. Harmonious Practice (*Samma Vayama*)
7. Harmonious Attention (*Samma Sati*)
8. Harmonious Equilibrium (*Samma samadhi*) (Chandrasekera 2001, 50).

Here, the term *samma* is translated as *harmonious* instead of *right*, the common English translation. The word *right* carries a spiritual arrogance along with a truth claim. That is, if one says Buddhist living or perspective is right, it implies that other lifestyles or other perspectives are wrong. The statement carries a self-asserting assumption and other-denying rhetoric, which may induce religious intolerance and interpersonal tension and impede inter-religious enquiry, respect, and understanding. From a broader perspective, the term "harmonious" embodies the comprehensive meaning of the "Middle Path," a synonym for the Eightfold Path. Generally, the term "Middle Path" envisions a life of balance that transcends two extreme modes of living, namely extreme sensual gratification and self-torture or self-denial. The term "harmonious" demonstrates Sri Lankan Buddhists' sensitivity to the pluralistic society of Toronto. It endorses a Buddhist way of life in a pluralistic society, but it does not necessarily nullify other ways. This context-sensitive interpretation is noticeable in other parts of the teaching manual.

Chandrasekera states that she employs the Buddha's method of "gradual preaching" for her book because the method induces "a gradual (trans) formation of the character of the listener" (Chandrasekera 2001, 7). Chandrasekera refers to gradual spiritual development in a way that invokes both this- and other-worldly ontology. One can read the above reference as "a gradual transformation" and/or "a gradual formation." The former implies that *Dhamma* students who could be as young as three years old have been formed even before they enrol in *Dhamma* school. This reading alludes to the Buddhist concept of rebirth and *saṃsāra*: the current life is just one link of a long chain of many lives that precede and follow this one. Accordingly, *Dhamma* students, like everyone else, carry predispositions or character traits linked to previous lives, which need to be transformed. However, the term "formation" does not relate to such religious ontology. Instead, it invokes a secular view of human beings with no reference to previous births or lives after death.

Secular world views give priority to humanity and human agencies. They tend to establish parameters that people can verify. Although Theravada Buddhism highlights the importance of human agency, its world views go beyond verifiable parameters. Karma and rebirth are integral parts of Buddhist ethical teachings. They, however, remain obscured in Chandrasekera's treatment of the five precepts, the basic Buddhist moral guidelines: "The Five Restraints (*pañcasila*) are the beginning of goodness. Goodness is the beginning of peace and happiness ... If you neglect moral restraint, you will be injuring or harming both yourself as well as others. Moral restraint should be based on *consideration for others as well as oneself*. It is based on Universal Goodwill (*Metta*), and not on the belief in *punishment* and *reward* [emphasis added]" (Chandrasekera 2001, 47).

Here, a secular discourse overrides a religious one. Certainly, the context and the Pali words maintain that the five precepts constitute Buddhist moral behaviour. Nonetheless, the preceding definition describes the five precepts as secular ethics, as opposed to religious ones. The difference is that the former prioritizes a this-worldly orientation. Its rationality is based on ordinary, commonsensical, and verifiable principles. What is verifiable by human faculties constitutes the parameters of secular ethics. In contrast, religious ethics are not confined to verifiable parameters, and transcend this-worldly reasoning. More importantly, the otherworldly rationality of religious ethics distinguishes it from its secular counterpart. The term

"Universal Goodwill" in the above quotation invokes a transcendent principle; however, it is not necessarily referred to as an otherworldly goal. The implication is that one should follow the five precepts not simply because they are prescribed by the Buddha and/or they have otherworldly benefits, such as pleasant births, but because they are socially conducive to a peaceful and happy society. In other words, the five precepts are reworked as interpersonal ethics.

This definition overshadows any religious necessity or urgency for strict commitment to the precepts. Instead, it leaves room for the practitioners' creative engagement with the precepts. It highlights social responsibility and benevolence based on this-worldly rationality and self-judgment. The preceding definition emphasizes that one should follow the five precepts because they derive from a universal truth, and "not on the belief in punishment and reward." Here, as with secular world views, external authority is put to the side while human authority is centralized. The definition locates agency in the individual self and encourages one to realize a transcendental goal: "Universal Goodwill." In so doing, the definition distinguishes the five precepts from other ethical systems that are based on divine punishment and rewards.

In the context of religious pluralism, the new curriculum's emphasis serves to establish a non-theistic Theravada Buddhist identity. At the same time, it indicates the influence of secular world views on Buddhism. The manual minimizes the otherworldly religious language of Buddhism. The multi-layered Buddhist heavens and hells are mentioned nowhere in the teaching manual except in occasional references to "*Sagga Katha.*" The latter term literally means stories related to heavens. However, Chandrasekera defines the term as stories of "other dimensions of existence according to karma," and she highlights their ethical purpose. For example, she asserts that the heavenly stories are meant to encourage the "devotees to do good and lead lives of purity for the purpose of evolving into higher levels until one reaches *Nibbāna*" (Chandrasekera 2001, 9). Moreover, the references to religious concepts like *kamma* and rebirth are followed by scientific comments. In a lesson on the concept of rebirth, a phrase noting "case studies of rebirth from Sri Lanka and other countries" is added. This implies that the concepts of *kamma* and rebirth are not merely religious concepts. They are, rather, explanations of what is happening in society; therefore, the concepts could be and should be taught with reference to the accounts of rebirth.

CONCLUSION

The way in which *Teaching Buddhism to Children* is constructed informs us about the nature of Buddhism, particularly Sri Lankan Buddhism in Toronto, Canada. The preceding analysis of the purpose, method, and contents of Chandrasekera's book illustrates the issues that trigger, if not demand, adaptations and how in fact those adaptations are rationalized and carried out within an inherited tradition in resettlement. Although *Teaching Buddhism to Children* illustrates a Sri Lankan Buddhist response to multicultural social reality in Toronto, its implications certainly go beyond Sri Lankan Buddhism in Toronto. More importantly, the book exemplifies how local social realities, such as cultural diversity, national policies like multiculturalism, and communal concerns related to intergenerational transmission influence an immigrant religious community.

As noted above, *Dhamma* education has become the most popular temple service among Sri Lankan Buddhists in Toronto. Like all other immigrant Buddhists in Western countries, Sri Lankan Buddhists realize that they cannot take the transmission of their religious tradition to their children for granted. As Victor Sōgen Hori observes, "'How will we transmit our culture to our children ...?' is perhaps the most important issue in every ethnic community" (1994b, 50). The transmission of Buddhism to children is increasingly becoming a concern because the children are influenced by the ambient non-Buddhist culture, which often challenges, and in some cases contradicts, the religio-cultural practices and values of Asian immigrant Buddhists. Sri Lankan Buddhists in Toronto are privileged to have an institutional practice (i.e., *Dhamma* education/school) in place in their religious tradition that directly addresses the transmission concern. Often what we see in resettlement, particularly during the time of the first generation's leadership, is an abridged version of the same Buddhist tradition in their respective countries of origin. Janet McLellan (1999, 2008) observes that pre-migration experiences and the migration process shape how Buddhists in Toronto recreate and redefine their religious traditions. I would add that, as the transplantation of *Dhamma* schools indicates, the ways Asian Buddhists pass on their tradition to their children are also closely related to the Buddhism that they have practised before migration.

To put it differently, the existing institutional practices of a particular tradition are transplanted in the diaspora during the time of the first generation. *Dhamma* education, being an institutional practice in Sri Lankan Buddhism, secured its place in the diaspora. At the same time, it also directly addresses one of the greatest concerns of many immigrant Buddhists, namely the intergenerational transmission of Buddhism in settlement. These two issues, combined, have made *Dhamma* education a very important service for Sri Lankan Buddhists. The urgency and enthusiasm for *Dhamma* education among Toronto-based Sri Lankan Buddhists derive from their own formation in the context of *Dhamma* education in Sri Lanka. They find that raising children with Buddhist values and attitudes in a non-Buddhist cultural environment is a challenge. They consider *Dhamma* education, an institutional practice in Sri Lankan Buddhism, to be an invaluable tool in meeting this challenge, but not before adapting the tool to the present circumstance.

The "gradual method" adopted and adapted in the teaching manual echoes one of the earliest discourses in the Pali canon. The back cover of *Teaching Buddhism to Children* directly quotes from the canon. The Buddha in the *Pahārāda Sutta* in the *Anguttara Nikāya* explains, "Even, Paharada, as a great ocean deepens gradually, slopes gradually, shelves gradually with no abruptness like a precipice, even so, Paharada, in this Teaching and Discipline there is a gradual doing, a gradual path, with no abruptness in the penetration of profound knowledge" (Chandrasekera 2001, back cover). This citation legitimizes the use of "gradual method" in *Dhamma* education in Toronto. Moreover, Chandrasekera's sequential use of the Pali terms, i.e., *saddhā* (Appreciation of Goodness), *sila* (Self-control), *samādhi* (Calm and Purity) and *paññā* (Wisdom), to name the stages of curriculum should not be overlooked. Through this terminology, I suggest, she connects the educational method adopted in the manual to the Theravada claim that spiritual maturity takes place in a gradual process.

Moreover, the gradual method also echoes the historical development of Theravada Buddhism. George Bond identifies the Asōkan and Pali Commentarial Theravada Buddhism, the second of three widely known developmental phases of Theravada Buddhism, as the gradual path (1988, 22–33). It was preceded by Pali canonical Buddhism of the third century CE and followed by modern Theravada Buddhism commencing in the late nineteenth century. Bond argues that Buddhism was interpreted as a gradual path "to meet the needs of all kinds of people" (1998, 25). Although this interpretation shares post-canonical textual roots, it was fully developed in the famous Pali commentator Buddhagōsa's *Visuddhimagga*, written in ancient Sri Lanka in the fifth century CE. Within this gradual path interpretation, the realization of *Nibbāna* was conceptualized "as a distant goal at the end of an immensely long, gradual path that the individual had to ascend over the course of many lifetimes" (Bond 1988, 26). According to Bond, "[t]his [gradual] path ... represents the hallmark of traditional Theravada" in premodern times (1988, 26). This otherworldly Buddhist religiosity, however, has been significantly challenged by some modern Theravada Buddhists who argue for and aspire to realizing *Nibbāna* in this life. Nevertheless, the gradual path still resonates with the religious aspirations of many Theravada Buddhists. By adopting the gradual teaching method, Chandrasekera situates the manual in the long history of Theravada Buddhism. The historical connection legitimizes the author's re-examination of the tradition in a contemporary socio-cultural context.

As noted earlier, the context of *Teaching Buddhism to Children* redefines the Buddhist Eight-fold Path. The text replaces the adjective "right" with a new adjective, "harmonious," to describe the practice. By doing so, the manual invokes a positive sentiment in Buddhism. One may argue that the term "harmonious" captures the popular Western image of Buddhism as a religion of peace, non-violence, and non-confrontation (Shiu 2010, 108). Like the gradual teaching method, the term "harmonious" resonates with scriptural authority, namely the *Madhupindika Sutta* in the *Majjhima Nikāya*,[4] one of the early middle-length doctrinal discourses in the Pali canon. In this particular discourse, answering the questions "What does the recluse [the Buddha] assert, what does he proclaim?" the Buddha utters, "Friend, I assert and proclaim such [a teaching] that one does not quarrel with anyone in the world with its gods, its Maras, and its Brahmas, in this generation with its recluses and brahmins, its princes and its people; such [a teaching] that perceptions no more underlie that brahmin who abides detached from sensual pleasures, without perplexity, shorn of worry, free from craving for any kind of being" (Nanamoli and Bodhi 1995, 201). The Buddha's reply illustrates that what the Buddha taught promotes external and internal harmony. Words like "gods," "princes," and "people" imply that the Buddha's teaching advocates harmony at religious, political, and social levels. In the second section of the answer, the Buddha highlights that his teaching also brings harmony at psychological and spiritual levels. This internal harmony derives from the detachment of sensual pleasure, mental worries, and latent craving. This canonical definition of Buddhism resurfaces in a Buddhist curriculum guide to teach Buddhism to children who are born and/or raised in multicultural and multi-religious Toronto.

Teaching Buddhism to Children identifies that Toronto's diverse cultural environment and the Canadian-born generation necessitate cultural adaptation. It shows us that the emergence of a new generation and encounters with a new culture often induce changes within a tradition. The challenge is to accommodate changes yet not lose the integrity and identity of a religious tradition. Chandrasekera's book illustrates how a tradition reconfigures itself by sifting through its own resources and distilling them so that they resonate with the ambient cultural sentiments. By doing so, it creates new meanings and maintains the viability of tradition, yet it does not disrupt historical ties that validate a tradition. The manual addresses the questions that Buddhists, like all other immigrants, face in Toronto. It attempts to harmonize the Buddhist tradition with powerful discourses like multiculturalism and secularism that shape the public and official projection of Toronto and Canada at large.

Moreover, *Teaching Buddhism to Children* indicates that one cannot ignore the socio-cultural context in which Buddhist agents live. As noted above, Chandrasekera and her fellow educationists do not intend to make Buddhism Canadian. But they re-examine their inherited tradition in the context of Canadian social realities and public policies to nurture a young generation who identify themselves as Canadian. Moreover, the Buddhism that emerges in this re-examination looks qualitatively different from its predecessor. Gananath Obeyesekere (1970) and others characterize the late nineteenth- and twentieth-century Buddhism reformation in Sri Lanka as "Protestant Buddhism," which protested against colonialism and Christian evangelism by taking as its model Protestant Christian norms, principles, rhetoric, and organizations such as Christian Sunday schools. Sunday *Dhamma* schools persist in Toronto, but with a different tone, and teaching manual that capitalizes on the popular perception of Buddhism as a "gentle, non-violent, 'nice,'" religion (Shiu 2010, 108). As we strive to understand how Buddhism is perceived and practised in Canada, we need to consider the local as well as global impulses within Buddhist communities, as Harding, Hori, and Soucy's *Wild Geese* (2010) urges. At the same time, we need to understand what we observe in Buddhist communities in Canada within the histories of respective communities. Charles Hallisey observes, "We will inevitably end up having to rethink our conceptualizations of Buddhism as a translocal tradition with a long and self-consciously distinct history but which is at the same time *a tradition dependent on local conditions for the production of meaning*" [emphasis added] (1995, 51). Thus, Chandrasekera's *Teaching Buddhism to Children* illustrates how a religious tradition in the diaspora evolves by incorporating historical and contemporary impulses and responding to local and global discourses. In doing so, it strives to maintain the integrity and viability of the Sri Lankan Buddhist tradition.

NOTES

1 The data used in this essay derive from the author's doctoral research (conducted from September 2005 to December 2009) on Buddhist practices, particularly those related to the transmission of Buddhism to second-generation Buddhists at two Sri Lankan Buddhist temples in Toronto, Canada. The research included analysis of Buddhist educational curricula and textbooks, participant observation, group and individual interviews, and two separate surveys (one for each generation).

2 In March 2010, I witnessed a rare but intact *Bodhipuja* performed by a recently arrived monk.

3 The verses are translated as follows in an assigned textbook: "You brought me up with loving care; Introducing me to important people everywhere; You have wonderful qualities, which are so rare; To me, you have always been very fair; So my dear father, I kiss your feet and say: 'To displease you, I'll never dare'" (Nanayakkara (Step One & Step Two) 1997, 52).

"For ten long months you bore me; Risking your own life; Fed me, nursed me, showering with love; Throughout day and night. You were always behind me, Never letting me out of your sight. You taught me more than anyone else; What really is proper and right. So my dear mother, Lovingly kissing your feet, I say: 'As before, please show me the way'" (Nanayakkara (Step One & Step Two) 1997, 53).

4 This Pali discourse is referred to as MN 18 (Pali Text Society).

9

Reflections on a Canadian Buddhist Death Ritual

ANGELA SUMEGI

In this chapter, I explore the challenges and advantages of constructing a Buddhist death ritual peculiar to local conditions. The local conditions in this case constitute a small Ottawa Buddhist community and their non-Buddhist friends and family. To qualify the ritual as "Buddhist" is to call upon a tradition that spans some 2,500 years and encompasses numerous cultural expressions, most of which are mere curiosities for the majority of Canadians. How, then, to invoke the meanings embedded in the tradition and join them to the meanings that individuals of this place and time bring to the mystery of death? What are the dynamics involved in a meeting between a global tradition and a specific cultural instance that results in meaning felt, acknowledged, and enacted? How can we appreciate, in Catherine Bell's words, "the ways in which people manipulate traditions and conventions to construct an empowering understanding of their present situation" (C. Bell 1998, 217)? Such are the questions that have inspired this piece.

Within the larger context of the transformation of Buddhist rituals, the focus here is on Tibetan rituals since these are the ones with which I am most familiar. This chapter does not address the transformation or modification of rituals by monastic religious authorities who seek to make a particular cultural construction suitable for an alien environment. The purpose here is to consider the transformation of ritual by local agents as a direct response to community needs. To do this, I examine a funeral ritual composed by a lay Buddhist Canadian with the intent to make it a Canadian Buddhist ritual. The term "Canadian" is used here as a dominant cultural signifier and not with any reference to ethnicity. I created the death ritual in question for my husband's memorial service in June 2010. It was the fourth end of life ritual that I had conducted for Canadian Buddhists since 2007. I should make it clear that I function as a Buddhist practitioner, teacher, ritual guide, and devotee, as well as an academic whose task it is to query and problematize the theories and practices of Buddhists – my own included – which places me in the double role of both "observing scholar" and "performing native."

In order to examine this ritual, which I constructed and performed in my role as a Buddhist guide and practitioner, I had to look to an unfamiliar methodology: autoethnography. I use this term with caution, but in the academic world, this was the closest I could come to a legitimate voice with which I could express my interest in analysing the activity of creating Buddhist ritual within a local context, the data for which happened to be self-generated. Deborah Reed-Danahay characterizes the autoethnographer as a boundary-crosser who assumes the role of a dual identity (Reed-Danahay 1997, 3). She also notes that "autoethnographers possess the qualities of often permanent self-identification with a group and full internal membership, as recognized both by themselves and the people of whom they are a part" (Reed-Danahay 1997, 5). There is, however, an emphasis in current autoethnography on subjectivity and narrative that can result in writing that does not go beyond a descriptive storytelling exercise. I will, therefore, align myself with those who have made efforts to link subjective experience and self-reflexivity with social scientific methods of qualitative inquiry and data analysis. Among them, sociologist Leon Anderson proposes the term "analytic" autoethnography in contradistinction to "evocative" autoethnography, which, in his words, "seeks narrative fidelity only to the researcher's subjective experience" (L. Anderson 2006, 386). He argues that in its "analytic" form, autoethnography, which has been thus far appropriated and promoted as a poststructuralist rejection of realist or traditional ethnography, can be comfortably situated within the genre of analytic ethnography: "The purpose of analytic ethnography is not simply to document personal experience, to provide an 'insider's perspective,' or to evoke emotional resonance with the reader. Rather the defining characteristic of analytic social science is to use empirical data to gain insight into some broader set of social phenomena than those provided by the data themselves" (L. Anderson 2006, 386–7).

Based on the distinction in the scholarly literature between evocative and analytic autoethnography, this chapter can be regarded as an exercise in the latter. It should be noted, however, that this qualitative inquiry takes place in retrospect, since the funeral rituals were initially created and conducted in response to community need without recognition of their possible use as an occasion for scholarly research. As a last methodological comment, with regard to ritual, this chapter draws on performance theory in the sense that I am less interested in the ritual as a re-enactment of a set script, even an adapted set script, and more in the significance or meaning of the ritual activity itself – how the words and actions of the ritual, as Bell writes, "produce a culturally meaningful environment as opposed to simply communicating ideas or attitudes" (C. Bell 1998, 208).

REFLECTIONS ON RITUAL

Since this chapter is in part a conscious self-exploration of my role in the re-creation of a Buddhist funeral ritual, perhaps a few words about my own practice and position in the Buddhist community of Ottawa would not be out of place. I came to Buddhism in the late 1970s through the academic study of texts and philosophy. Buddhist religious practice and ritual were of no interest to me until 1981 when I took up a fellowship in Mysore, south India, and encountered Pema Norbu Rinpoche, the abbot of Namdroling, a nearby Tibetan monastery. During the subsequent five years that I spent with my family in south India, I entered into a teacher-student relationship with him that has endured until today. I cannot say that I underwent any kind of conversion experience during my time in India or since. Even many years after my return to Canada, I found myself unable to answer a simple question put to me by a Buddhist monk: "Are you Buddhist?" While I easily answer yes to that question now, I would not be able to say exactly when or why or how my self-identification became Buddhist. In 1996, I founded a charity in support of the children housed at Namdroling monastery, and out of that grew a local meditation community and dharma centre.

As the director of the Ottawa Palyul Centre, which is affiliated with a traditionally ritual-laden school of Tibetan Buddhism, the Nyingma, I am often asked about the meaning of ritual – in a general sense, that is, of what is the necessity or the point of ritual. Patricia Campbell's study of a Zen Buddhist temple in Toronto (Campbell 2010) confirms my own experience that Canadians who explore Buddhism as a spiritual path are more than likely drawn to its mind-training aspects – meditation, taming the mind; or its "way of life" aspects – compassion, patience, letting go of negative mind states; or they are drawn to its intellectual, academic aspects. Tibetan esoteric ritual practices, which can involve long periods of chanting unrecognizable Tibetan syllables while making offerings of food and drink to the deities and visualizing oftentimes fearsome or erotic images, are much more problematic for newcomers. To be sure, many Canadian Buddhists find great meaning in the tantric rituals, and there are those who become entirely proficient at ritual practice. However, for others, such rituals are a distraction from the explanations and prescriptions relating to Buddhist views on meditation, philosophy, psychology, or the problems of daily life. These types of discursive "teachings" are understandable and have a perceivable meaning for their daily lives – meaning that cannot be accessed through the rituals without much study of Indo-Tibetan culture and symbolism.

In our dharma centre, more people show up for the meditation and dharma talk sessions than show up for the twice-monthly ritual liturgical practices. This is a different scenario than, for example, might be found in a dharma centre in Taiwan, where the monks are ritual specialists and people have faith in the benefits (mundane and supramundane) of the *puja* (ritual worship). It is my experience that in the day-to-day running of a Western dharma centre, introducing Tibetan Buddhism to Canadians as well as constructing or reconstructing Buddhist ritual in a local Canadian context involves accounting for the relevance of ritual, and requires an intellectual pedagogical orientation that would not necessarily be emphasized in a Tibetan or Asian cultural context.

Tibetan ritual practice can be viscerally and personally experiential; the sound of the drums and bells and horns and chanting, the stylized hand gestures, the specialized dress, all can induce an effect without any explicit meaning attached. Of course, the ritual *is* imbued with meaning or significance, but what it signifies is not necessarily apparent to an outsider and explanations are often not much help because they, too, are culturally constructed. For example, one website provides this quotation in explanation of the ritual feast offering to the deities called *tsok*: "The Tibetan word 'Tsok' means 'gathering' or 'accumulation.' The Tsok Ceremony is a sacred event which completes the four gatherings of male and female practitioners, offering substances, wisdom deities, and merit. Tsok provides us with an opportunity to purify our obscurations, restore our spiritual commitments, and create merit for ourselves and all living beings" (Lama Chhimi Kinley, n.d.). Such an explanation, steeped as it is in Tibetan Buddhist discourse, would not be easily comprehensible to someone new to Buddhism. In other words, there is a need for Buddhist religious language to be made accessible to the personal understanding of North Americans. Those in the field of psychology and psychotherapy have recognized this and made good use of Buddhist ideals and meditation practices such as mindfulness, translating them into the language of North American culture for the purpose of promoting social and personal well-being. The language of Tibetan Buddhist ritual, however, is not so easily translated, first because it cannot be abstracted from its specific cultural context and second because it draws on a devotional dimension that is equally embedded in a specific cultural context. Without faith or devotion, there is no link between the meaning of the ritual and the meaning of a person's ordinary life, a disconnect that renders ritual at best an interesting curiosity and at worst a waste of time.

In the North American context, ritual can be fascinating, inspiring, emotionally satisfying, and even mysteriously fulfilling, but for many, religious ritual is associated with meaningless words and actions, childhood coercion, and institutional hypocrisy. There are Western Buddhist authorities for whom ritual is extraneous to true Buddhism and associated with cultural adaptations that belong neither to original Buddhism nor to our culture. For example, Upasaka Culadasa, a Western Buddhist meditation teacher, states that the original rituals of Buddhism consisted only of taking precepts and taking refuge, and that "the forms of Buddhism that follow most closely upon the Buddha's original teaching keep rites and rituals to the absolute minimum" (Culadasa 2010). Culadasa is not unique in his views. Indeed, the fact that from its inception, whatever we might identify as "Buddhism" (including the earliest reported words of the Buddha) is inseparable from cultural construction has not prevented "original" Buddhism from being keenly sought.

The globalization of Buddhism involves a trend toward isolating the active ingredient of enlightenment; what is the essential Dharma distinct from cultural accretions? For example, the Tibetan lama and film director Khyentse Norbu Rinpoche states in an interview with the *Shambhala Sun* magazine: "From the moment Buddha taught, the essence of the teachings hasn't changed, and it shouldn't change. Anyone who tries to modernize buddhadharma is making a grave mistake. It's important to make a distinction between the culture and Buddhism ... Dharma is the tea and culture is the cup. For someone who wants to drink tea, tea is more important than the cup. The cup is also necessary but it is not the most essential" (Jones 2008). The notion of an unchanging Buddhadharma is the Buddhist discourse that allows for the idea of true or original Buddhism that is the same regardless of the cup in which it is presented. Cultures themselves, however, are ever-changing complexes continually responding to other ever-changing institutions and thought processes; similarly, the recorded and received teachings of the Buddha have never been a de-cultured or fixed entity that can be discovered or recovered in its purity. The varying nature of the ways in which Buddhist doctrines and practices have been assimilated, owned, and expressed through time and across cultures is an ongoing process to which the following investigation aims to contribute some analysis.

CANADIAN BUDDHIST FUNERALS

I was first asked to conduct a funeral service by a Canadian Japanese member of the small Ottawa sangha that I lead; June's husband, Eiji, had died very suddenly in the fall of 2007. Although June was an active member of our Buddhist community, her husband and grown children were not Buddhist; they could be described as secular Canadians with an affinity for Buddhist thought. In speaking with the family, I came to realize that they were looking to me to provide a ceremony that was recognizably Buddhist, but not necessarily compliant with a Japanese cultural form, which would not be familiar or particularly meaningful to the family, especially the younger generation. As studies have shown, Japanese identity in Canada (let alone Japanese Buddhist identity) is an extremely complex sociological phenomenon. In her examination of five Asian Buddhist communities in Toronto, Janet McLellan reports: "Within Japanese-Canadian communities across Canada, three distinct subgroups developed, each with different sociocultural referents, generational identity, and wartime experience. They are the *issei* or first-generation Japanese immigrants, *nisei* or second-generation children, born in Canada, and *sansei* – third-generation children, of *nisei* parents. Additional subgroups today include the *yonsei* or fourth generation, and the *shinijusha*, the new immigrants from Japan since 1960" (McLellan 1999, 36).

That, however, is not the whole story. McLellan goes on to distinguish a total of eight subgroups, including the mixed parentage children of third-generation (*sansei*) Japanese who have a 90 per cent rate of intermarriage with non-Japanese (McLellan 1999, 36–7). Even then, the reality on the ground is that people do not always fit into the neat categories used for identification or analysis. June would be *nisei/sansei* born to an *issei* father and *nisei* mother. Eiji was born in Japan and so *issei*; their children, then, are third/fourth generation and, in a sense, represent all the categories of *nisei*, *sansei*, and *yonsei*. They also follow the third-generation demographic of intermarriage, so June's grandchildren are *yonsei* with Japanese and non-Japanese parents.

As Victor Hori demonstrates, the complexity of so-called ethnic identity calls into question the ways in which scholars identify Buddhist practitioners as ethnic-born Buddhists or Western converts.

> When we confront the Buddhism practised by the next generation, it becomes increasingly difficult to say just what it is we are trying to distinguish. Asian/ethnic Buddhism, for some people, implies a socially oriented devotion to ancestors tinged with belief about karma and rebirth, while Western/convert Buddhism implies an individually oriented practice of Buddhism based on meditation aimed at clear self-understanding. With the terms "Western/convert" and "Asian/ethnic," are we trying to distinguish groups of people regardless of what kind of Buddhism they practice? Or are we trying to distinguish two styles of Buddhism, regardless of the ethnic and cultural origins of the people who practice them? (V. Hori 2010a, 17)

Although there is not space in this chapter to enter into the debates surrounding these categories and how they relate to Buddhism in Canada, I would like to highlight a few aspects of the problem before continuing. For example, instead of focusing on the types of persons who practise Buddhism, whether Asian/ethnic/immigrant or Western/convert, Martin Baumann draws his distinction based on concepts held and practices followed. He proposes the terms "traditionalist" and "modernist," which contrast devotional, ritual, and merit-making practices related to monasticism and concepts of rebirth with modern movements led by lay practitioners that emphasize meditation, textual study, and rational thought (Baumann 2002, 57–8).

However, while such a division may work well for Buddhist forms such as Theravada and Zen, it would not apply to certain Tibetan Buddhist centres in the West, which practise devotional and merit-making rituals in a traditional Tibetan temple setting, yet actively promote a modernist approach involving meditation and rational inquiry. Alexander Soucy argues that the very hybridity of religious systems makes it a pointless exercise to seek out a "Canadian Buddhism" or to focus scholastic efforts on determining what does or does not constitute any kind of ethnically defined Buddhism. He concludes that a greater contribution can be made by focusing on the effects of global interactions and transformations that inform the various expressions of Buddhism (Soucy 2010, 57–8). While I agree with Soucy that a search for an essentially Canadian Buddhism may be off the mark, nevertheless, to be Canadian has meaning not only for the nation but for individuals, and I believe that the constellation of any religious system shifts according to the identities of the peoples engaging with it. So the questions then would be: How do Canadians engage with Buddhism, and are there any shared characteristics to which we can point that speak to a Canadian style of engagement?

Apart from the members of our sangha, the participants at Eiji's funeral included members of his golf club, professional associates, family, and friends – very few, if any, of whom were Buddhist. The situation of a Buddhist funeral requested by the deceased's family, which served a congregation of mourners, the majority of whom were non-Buddhist, was to repeat itself throughout all the services that I conducted. Eiji's funeral service, however, in which a non-Japanese officiant performed a non-traditional ritual for a mixture of Japanese Buddhists, non-Japanese Buddhists, and non-Buddhists, underscores the argument made by Victor Hori that categories which link ethnic Buddhism with Asians and Western Buddhism with converts are untenable as analytic tools. In my experience, the concept of conversion, with its proselytizing missionary associations of turning around in the seat of one's soul, does not apply to those who come to our meditation centre seeking to learn more about Buddhism. Very few, if any, of our members would identify themselves as "converts" from another religion. A number maintain membership both in our Buddhist sangha as well as in other religious systems, while others, although active and supportive, would hesitate to take on the label "Buddhist."

The second funeral service I conducted took place only a few months later when a close member of our sangha died very suddenly of a brain tumour. Her sister and family flew in from Scotland and Halifax to care for her in the time she had left, which was about eight weeks. They were not Buddhist but were well aware of her affiliation with our group, and were very open to our involvement with her last days. They requested that I perform a Buddhist funeral service for her, as she would have wished. The participants at this service included many of our sangha, but the majority consisted of the deceased's non-Buddhist friends, family, and work associates.

On the third occasion, in February of 2010, I was asked to provide a funeral service for a woman whom I did not know. She was not a member of our sangha, but identified herself as Buddhist, and her non-Buddhist family, therefore, was looking for someone to conduct a ceremony that would honour her religious beliefs. This service was the only one held in the presence of an open casket, since the family intended to bury her body rather than cremate as the others had done. Finally, the fourth occasion was a service conducted for my husband who died on 30 May 2010.

LOCAL OTTAWA FUNERAL SERVICE

The details of the service will be explained further below. In general, the ritual that was performed began, in all cases, with a welcome to the participants and some opening remarks followed by my personal prayers. Next came group recitation of a refuge prayer, incense offering prayer, the Heart Sutra, and an excerpt from the Mettā Sutta. The chanting was followed by a brief dharma talk on the meaning of death in Buddhism; then family members were invited to give the eulogy. After the eulogy, we spent a few minutes in silent reflection accompanied by music. Closing prayers included a prayer from the Tibetan Bardo Thodol (familiar to Westerners as the "Tibetan Book of the Dead"), and a dedication of merit.

All the services were held at a local funeral home in a generic, ecumenical-type chapel or, if attendance exceeded its capacity, in one of their larger halls. The location reflected a number of concerns, among them the fact that our traditional shrine space would be too small to accommodate the congregation. But beyond that, the setting allowed me to establish a more generic Buddhist feeling for the ceremony and to tone down the distracting "strangeness" of Tibetan Buddhism by eliminating the distinctive iconography and using only an image of Sakyamuni Buddha, recognizable to all. A simplified Tibetan-style altar was set up with a central image of the Buddha and the seven traditional Tibetan offering bowls (holding water for drinking, water for washing, flowers, incense, light, scented water, food, and music) laid out in front of it. A picture of the deceased, candles, and flowers were also on the altar.

The ceremony took approximately one hour. This time period was chosen to conform to the expectations of the funeral home where it was held and for the convenience and comfort of the participants. It was preceded by a period dedicated to greeting the family and followed by food and drink at a reception, again following a format proposed by the funeral home and accepted by the family. No monastics were present – I was regarded by the funeral home as the clergy and, therefore, given the certificate of a funeral performed there for my records. In all cases, the majority of attendees were non-Buddhist, reflecting the fact that Canadian Buddhists practise in a predominantly non-Buddhist environment.

The content was chosen, first, to suit the one-hour time period. In one case, the service was slightly longer due to the requirement of an interment, which included a procession to the plot where the urn was placed in the ground (see illustration 8). Prayers at the place of interment included a prayer from the Bardo Thodol and a prayer to be reborn in Buddha Amitābha's Pure Land. Second, but more importantly, the content was chosen (1) to establish the self-consciously Buddhist context of the service – this was not to be a humanist, "can fit any religion or none" type of service, and (2) to allow the non-Buddhists in attendance to participate in the service, not just observe a culturally interesting but essentially foreign ritual performance.

In the opening remarks, I introduced myself and shared with the participants my double identity as Buddhist practitioner and religion scholar. I also acknowledged that the service to come would not be found in any Buddhist text or service book, but that the parts and pieces had a long history in the Buddhist tradition, some prayers having been chanted by different peoples for many centuries and others being newer Western expressions of the Buddhadharma. Following the welcome and introduction, I requested the indulgence of the congregation while I turned my back to them in order to pay my respects to the altar and to recite my own ritual prayers. After bowing to the altar, I took a few minutes to chant some mantras and prayers in Tibetan that focused on devotion, purification, and offering. The sangha members who were present accompanied me in reciting these prayers. These few minutes were the only time that the entire congregation was not included. This was an intuitive decision based on the feeling that the prayers were specific to the Tibetan cultural context, therefore, requiring much more explanation than I could give in the time frame. Also, from an insider perspective, they were deeply devotional and not to be recited out of mere politeness or conformity. The distributed program included all the remaining prayers in English, and everyone was invited to recite them along with me. For each prayer, I offered a brief comment, explaining its significance in the service and in the Buddhist tradition.

We first recited a refuge prayer, which I pointed out is the basic distinguishing feature of a Buddhist ritual in that the only requirement to be a member of the Buddhist community is to sincerely take refuge in the Buddha, the teacher; the Dharma, the teaching; and the sangha, the community of those who realize and embody the teaching.[1] The next prayer, accompanying the offering of incense, I explained in terms of the six *paramitas* (the "perfections" or qualities that are to be developed on the Buddhist path – generosity, virtue, patience, perseverance, meditation, and wisdom) as representing the belief that all the blessings we receive are directly related to our capacity for giving. The incense, then, functions as a symbol of our wish to develop a mind of generosity and our wish to be of unceasing benefit to others.

I acknowledged to the congregation that the next recitation, the Great Heart of Wisdom Sutra, representing the foundational wisdom teaching of the Mahayana tradition, is notoriously difficult to understand, even for long-time Buddhists, but that it was important to include it because it is traditionally recited at Buddhist funerals and because it is one of the most revered and widely used texts in the world of Buddhism. In a nutshell, I could only comment that this short scripture points to the basic Buddhist teaching that nothing whatsoever is permanently real or exists in a totally independent manner – all things are constantly changing due to their dependence on constantly changing causes and conditions, and are therefore empty of any permanent or fixed reality. I concluded my explanation with the thought that a deep appreciation of this idea brings freedom from all fixations and relieves the suffering caused by ego, by attachments, and by our resistance to change and loss.

We then moved to a more universally apprehensible text, the Mettā (Loving-kindness/friendliness) Sutta from the Pali canon, which evokes the mental state of loving kindness extended to all beings. I took this opportunity to comment on the Buddhist view of the role of mind and mental states in our perception of the world in which we live. Family members were then invited to give the eulogy and to call on any who wished to come up and share memories of the deceased. I then gave a brief dharma talk in which I spoke on the Buddhist view of death. This included some simple explanation of the Buddhist doctrines of impermanence, karma, and rebirth. The dharma talk was followed by a few minutes of silent reflection with music during which I encouraged people to simply relax and allow the mind to be peaceful. Then we recited a prayer taken from the Bardo Thodol, which I pointed out was a Tibetan text traditionally read for the deceased for forty-nine days. Finally, we recited a closing prayer and the dedication of merit, which is the standard ending of a Buddhist ceremony. I explained that although the notion of sharing good karma goes counter to the doctrine of reaping the results of one's own actions, good or bad, it has remained an enduring and important element in Buddhist ceremonies, both as a symbol of generosity and the intent to benefit another, and as a bulwark against self-cherishing and the desire to hold on to what is good for oneself alone.

In the prayers, I looked for translations that were as simple and as religiously jargon-free as possible. Similarly, in my explanations and talk, the aim was to provide an opportunity for the participants both to understand the Buddhist context and to be able to blend their own meaning with what we were doing there. It seemed to me that a ceremony that was to appeal to both Buddhist and non-Buddhist participants needed to provide a space where the ritual was not so much enacted as embodied. By that I mean that in a traditional ritual, as in the forty-ninth day ceremony discussed below, the ritual is enacted by specialists who invite the participants at certain points in the ceremony to join in the action of the ritual, whereas my intent was to create an occasion where participants could experience the meaning of the ceremony not in the watching or doing, but in whatever feeling, whatever insights, whatever mental states were generated in themselves.

As far as evaluating how successful these services were in satisfying the needs of the population for whom they were intended, I can only say that based on expressions of gratitude and satisfaction, it appeared to me that what I had set out to do was accomplished: that is, to provide a formal ritual space in which Buddhist Canadians could reaffirm their understanding of the religion, and a non-Buddhist Canadian congregation could access and find meaning in Buddhist liturgy and practice.

A comparison between the Canadian Buddhist ritual that I conducted for my husband and the traditional forty-ninth day ceremony carried out for him at a Tibetan temple in upstate New York reveals substantial differences.

TIBETAN FORTY-NINTH DAY RITUAL

Before I discuss the comparison between the Tibetan forty-ninth day ceremony and the Canadian service, some background on Tibetan Buddhist theory and practice relating to death is necessary. From the Tibetan perspective, contemplation on death serves to underscore three indisputable facts: (1) that death is certain; (2) that the time of death is uncertain; (3) and that at the time of death and after, spiritual practice is the only help. In this framework, the certainty of death underscores the Buddhist teaching on impermanence, but impermanence also feeds uncertainty – not only uncertainty regarding when death will come but also regarding what happens to the person after death, and the relationship of the deceased to the living. The only refuge is Dharma, which refers to the person's spiritual/mental state before death and at the time of death, as well as to the rituals and practices carried out after death. Tibetan Buddhist death rituals, therefore, convey both the uncertainty of the living relatives and the deceased person, as well as the certainty of the Dharma that overcomes all doubt. Upon death, an extensive and elaborate complex of ritual actions is set in motion. It includes: the ritual of *powa* (transfer of consciousness) intended to bypass the intermediate state between death and rebirth (*bardo*) and transfer the deceased's consciousness directly to a Pure Land (the field of activity created by a Buddha that offers the most perfect conditions to attain enlightenment); and the ritual of casting the death horoscope to determine the day and time of disposal and to provide an indication of the deceased's next rebirth. There might also be the reading of various texts that guide the deceased through the *bardo*, a period that is traditionally said to take forty-nine days. Familiar to Westerners as the Tibetan Book of the Dead, the Bardo Thodol (Liberation upon Hearing) is one such text. However, as Brian Cuevas has shown, the title Bardo Thodol refers not so much to a specific text as to a genre of texts that are intended to assist the deceased in negotiating the frightening *bardo* states and to guide the person away from rebirth in places of great suffering (Cuevas 2003, 211–12). For our comparison, I am interested here, however, only in the post-disposal rituals, which are concerned with purification of the dead person's karma in order to ensure a good rebirth as well as protection of the living from the negative forces that surround death. In her study of Tibetan death rituals, Margaret Gouin discusses the use of the name-card in rituals of purification for the deceased. "The idea is that the consciousness of the deceased is easily distracted and flung about because of their disembodied state, so by giving them a 'body' (in the form of the name-card), they are enabled to stay in one place and pay attention to the rituals being conducted for their benefit, until the officiating lama tells them to leave" (Gouin 2010, 100).

Another post-disposal ritual is the feeding of the deceased, one form of which is the *sur* ritual, in which food is ritually burnt and the scent offered for the nourishment of the deceased and all other spirit beings, as well as being an offering to the Buddhas. Merit-making activities by the living also constitute an important part of the rituals since the merit accumulated can be dedicated to the good rebirth of the dead person. Meritorious activity can include sponsoring religious art or construction, dispensing food and/or alms to the poor, feeding monastics and making monetary offerings to the temple and the officiating lamas. Finances, as Gouin notes (2010, 123–4), is a major factor in the length and complexity of death rituals, which can range from the full seven weeks to a few days or a few hours; but whether short or long, the forty-ninth day is generally marked by an especially elaborate ceremony that effectively closes the cycle of funeral ceremonies.

Compared to the Canadian service, the Tibetan ritual was longer, taking two hours. This time frame reflected in part a condensed ritual performance adapted to a Western context, and the fact that it was only one aspect of the traditional death rituals mentioned above that would be performed from the time of death. The setting was a traditional Tibetan temple constructed by monastic authorities. With regard to officiants, several ordained lamas conducted the Tibetan ritual; a single lay practitioner conducted the Canadian ritual. Participants in the Tibetan ritual were all devotees committed to this particular cultural expression of Buddhism, compared to the large proportion of non-Buddhists attending the Canadian ceremony. With regard to content, the Tibetan ceremony included a number of distinct rituals. Among them was the ritual worship of Amitābha Buddha associated with the Pure Land and the *sur* or ritual burnt food offering to nourish the continuing consciousness of the deceased through scent. For this ritual, I had been asked to prepare platters of food (fruit, nuts, cookies, sweets, juices) and was invited, along with a few close friends, to take the offerings to the fire. In the end, many Tibetans and others unknown to me joined the line to receive the merit of transporting the offerings and placing them in the fire. Another separate ritual involved the calling down of the consciousness of my dead husband into the name-card, a small block-printed placard which acted as the physical support for his consciousness and was placed along with his photograph in front of the officiating lama. Since at the time I was not acting as a researcher, I am unsure of the exact nature of some of the rituals that took place. The subsequent ceremony could have been a *powa* (transfer of consciousness to the Pure Land) ritual or some form of posthumous initiation (empowerment of the disciple to recognize his innate wisdom) ritual in which I was required to act as a proxy for my husband and offer the required three prostrations to the Buddha. Finally, there was the burning of the name-card and the picture of the deceased. This act has various symbolic meanings: severing the deceased's connection with this life, and the attachment of the living relatives to the dead; releasing the deceased's consciousness to hopefully take a good rebirth; or symbolizing the attainment of the Pure Land (Gouin 2010, 102).

All elements of the Tibetan ritual essentially focused on the continuing welfare of the deceased in the after death state – no part of the ritual was directly concerned with the participants, except insofar as participation in the ritual is considered to be of direct benefit to the participant. By contrast, the Canadian service, although generally dedicated to the benefit of the deceased, was much more participant-oriented. It provided an opportunity for the participants to bring their own understanding of death into the ritual. In other words, there was no imposition of an after death scenario into which the participants were required to enter. This is a difference that, I would say, highlights an open-ended approach that is part of the Canadian cultural environment and that is difficult to maintain in a context where one is required to accept a specific religious paradigm. For example, in the Canadian service I pointed out that the prayer to be reborn in the Pure Land can be understood cosmologically, but it also can be understood symbolically or metaphorically. This open-ended approach, which allows people to recognize similarities between their own thinking and modes of thought that on the surface are quite alien, I think, is reflected in the very strong interfaith movement that is prominent in many Canadian cities, especially Ottawa. Finally, the relationship of the participants to the deceased in the Canadian ritual was much more past oriented – related to remembering what the person was like in life, celebrating what the person did in life. The Tibetan ritual was present and future oriented – where is the deceased now? How can we help him now? How can what we do now assist in ensuring a good future for him? I should perhaps point out that in the Canadian context, other rituals had been carried out that would conform to the esoteric aspect of Tibetan Buddhism involving only sangha members, e.g., reciting the Bardo Thodol, mantra recitation, and *powa* practice. The funeral service, therefore, represented an exoteric public aspect.

In general, the Canadian ritual followed the external format of generic Christian funeral services that most participants would likely have attended before. They would be familiar with the funeral home chapel setting, the greeting of the family, the sitting in pews, an officiant at the lectern or pulpit, a sermon, the reception afterward. Attendees have commented, however, that despite the cultural familiarity, they felt that they had attended a Buddhist funeral. Apart from the overt liturgical and pedagogical elements, the features identified as contributing to the Buddhist ambiance were the altar, and especially the few minutes of Tibetan chanting at the outset, about which many people commented. Although it was unintelligible to most, according to one person, the Tibetan chanting created a sense of the sacred that set the tone for the rest of the service. Other comments were that it provided a sense of authenticity and a feeling among the people listening that they were engaged with an established tradition and not, as one person put it, some "made up" ritual. Ironically, the ritual was indeed made up of a combination of various prayers and chants taken from various Buddhist traditions. However, such a comment points to the widespread belief that ritual is stipulated, that authenticity and authority reside in the chain of actions, words, and meanings prescribed by a tradition that links the present through the past to a changeless, timeless, ultimately significant moment. Using many different lenses, ritual studies scholars have explored in great detail the religious activities that we would identify as ritual. Some of their conclusions may be fruitful for understanding the way in which local transformations fit into the larger context of Buddhist ritual.

In his article on ritual and meaning, Axel Michaels argues that there are good reasons why rituals are "intrinsically bound up with this notion of changelessness" (Michaels 2006, 260): first, because of the importance of transmitting through set patterns the solution to existential problems of being human; second, to maintain the transmission without the burden of rational choice at each and every occasion; and third, because they offer a way for people to resist change and death by identifying with the timeless. Interestingly, Michaels notes that this does not mean that rituals are changeless but that "they are altered without giving up the claim of being invariable" (Michaels 2006, 260). In the context of globalization, the notion of invariability is under pressure as Buddhist theories and practices are undergoing some radical changes, as for example, the Thai practice begun in the 1980s of ordaining trees or performing long-life rituals for rivers to aid in environmental protection. Although the monk who performed the first ordination ceremony used an adaptation of an image consecration ritual and not a monastic ordination text, Susan Darlington's study of the phenomenon (Darlington 2009, 192) implies that such modification is not always the case. Various texts are used, chosen by the officiating monk, and in one ceremony she reports that the ordination ritual followed the basic structure of a *bhikkhu* ordination. The trees are wrapped in orange monastic robes and the local population regards them as not only sacred but "ordained." The villagers, therefore, bow in respect to them as they pass, just as they would to a human monk (Darlington 2009, 192). On the other hand, Michael Blum has shown how completely at odds these practices are with normative Buddhist theory. He points out that "ordaining trees is inconceivable within ancient, medieval, and even pre-modern forms of Asian Buddhist orthodoxy or orthopraxy" (Blum 2009, 210). Blum argues that such changes are the result of global interactions, and in the case of the Thai monks, specifically the interaction with American Transcendentalism. Despite the rationale of the environmentally concerned monks, ordaining trees is problematic for the keepers of the tradition who recognize the lack of a past established Buddhist authority to which the ritual can be linked. Nevertheless, as Darlington reports, "While their work is not publicly condoned by the sangha leaders ... environmental monks have won over their superiors ... by introducing and translating new ideas through careful Buddhist interpretation" (Darlington 2009, 204).

It seems to me that the ability to provide and support a Buddhist interpretation is an important aspect in the various successful transformations in Buddhism that are taking place today; perhaps it has always been so. In his discussion of authenticity, Jay Garfield identifies the root of Buddhist interpretation when he says that rather than thinking in terms of texts, doctrines, or ritual practices, it is "more faithful to Buddhist hermeneutical practice, to focus on insights, on realizations" (Garfield 2009, 101). So whether we consider the non-traditional rituals of the Thai environmentalist monks or the feminist movement for gender equality and the restoration of the *bhikkhuni* (female monastic) ordination ritual in Tibetan Buddhism, the success of their activities depends in large part on the ability of the key players to demonstrate that their interpretations are based on realizations and insights that flow from the teaching of the Buddha. Perhaps this is what Ursula Rao means when she says, "ritual is a domain that invites negotiations" (Rao 2006, 158). She argues that rituals are distinguished from other actions through "social framing," that is, social activity that sets the context and determines the "sense" in which an activity is understood (Rao 2006, 159). Following this line of thinking, then, although the funeral rituals I conducted did not follow any established form and were constructed non-traditionally from a variety of Buddhist elements, these facts, perhaps, were not as important as the interpretations offered and the sense of authenticity generated in the participants, which in turn served to imbue the ritual with that all-important feeling that, for the period of the ritual, the inconstancy of the present is consumed in a timeless moment.

CONCLUSIONS

Could my construction of a Buddhist death ritual in a Canadian context be construed as an adaptation or reconstruction or transformation of Tibetan Buddhist ritual or any Buddhist ritual? I would say not, since such an explanation implies a traditional ritual form that is modified or changed in some way. Many Tibetan lamas perform such reconstructions in their attempt to adapt and assimilate their rituals to Western culture. However, the Canadian service was not based on an original; it represented a self-conscious individualistic creation, constituted of a bricolage of Buddhistic and Canadian cultural elements in response to local needs. Where or how could this service, then, be situated within the religion? Certainly, it would not belong to the "great tradition" of Tibetan Buddhism, text-based, watched over by the religious hierarchy, whose rituals are authenticated by genealogy and carried forward by lineage. Yet, if we think in terms of the "little tradition," folk religion,[2] that is everywhere marked by specific local conditions and carried out by local authorities in response to local needs, then it could be said that it functioned as a Buddhist ritual that provided religious meaning for those particular people at that particular time.

In closing, I suggest that rites of passage are situated differently in our psyche than rituals of worship. When the object of worship is devalued, worship naturally loses its importance in a society, but rites of passage are not so easily foregone because they have a history as markers for one's life story. Many people cling to baptism or naming rituals much more out of a sense of social custom than any deep religious conviction. Rituals of marriage are being transformed, remade to suit the couple's sense of how they want to mark this moment in their lives. I suggest, however, that rituals of death have an even stronger hold over us than other rites of passage; they are not easily tampered with or abandoned. It is not uncommon in a secular society that a child is born but not baptized; and more and more Canadians live with a partner without the ritual of marriage; but when a person dies and the body must be disposed of, there is a very deep need in human beings that calls for ceremonial social recognition of this passage. Yet, where do we find such a ritual without religion? Secular funerals do exist, but rituals of death are still firmly in the grasp of religious institutions that generally require or assume certain beliefs of the participants. This can create conflict for those who participate in a funeral not for the sake of the doctrine, but for the sake of the ritual. Doctrine presents us with definitive content that invites belief or disbelief, proof or disproof, whereas ritual provides an opportunity for meaning to be discovered, in all its indeterminacy and intimacy. Ritual invites our attention and creativity. Although the Canadian ceremony was constructed from a Buddhist vantage point, it possessed a self-consciously multivalent quality that allowed for a space in which the participants could immerse themselves in the overtly expressed Buddhist meaning and at the same time invest the words and actions with their own value and consciousness of death, thereby appropriating for themselves a significance that was not imposed but instinctively self-generated.

Finally, although I would not claim that the service examined here represents Canadian Buddhism, since the parameters of that category are still debated, nevertheless, it does represent an aspect of Buddhism in Canada.

NOTES

1 I am aware that the reference here to "Buddhist community" draws upon an ideal concept, and that the notion of refuge as the hallmark of Buddhist identity is a somewhat more complex matter than described. However, in the context of the service and in the interests of simplification for a general audience, such issues are not addressed.
2 Regardless of how odd it may seem to categorize a Canadian funeral service along with Thai spirit cults or Vietnamese ancestor veneration as "folk religion."

10

Buddhist Prison Outreach in Canada: Legitimating a Minority Faith

PAUL MCIVOR

Buddhist outreach to, and practice within, correctional systems is an under-researched area of contemporary Buddhism. Much of what we know about the Buddhist prison outreach work in Canada is still tentative and subject to correction as research continues. At this point, our understanding, to borrow terminology from biology, consists of taxonomy of such outreach as well as anatomy and function. In order to gain a sense of how Buddhism operates in Canada's prison system, we need to know the characteristics of that system because, to a great degree, they determine what forms of practice and outreach are possible.

This chapter examines several important factors shaping Buddhist outreach in Canada's prisons – inmate characteristics, correctional structures (physical, legal, and administrative), as well as the religious environment (including the ways in which chaplains work) within correctional facilities. It then reviews the ways in which outreach is typically provided, including the forms it takes and its use of Buddhist literature. Finally, it examines the volunteers who deliver the services in the Canadian correctional system, the overwhelming majority of whom are unpaid. Noticeably absent from this discussion is the inmate experience; this is the subject of future research. Readers interested in this aspect of Buddhism in prisons are directed to inmate narratives and recent documentaries that have chronicled prison programs in the United States.[1] The present discussion focuses on the experiences of Buddhist volunteers and how the corrections environment shapes the outreach they provide. In part this stems from my own continuing experience as a Buddhist prison volunteer. For the past four years I have volunteered at Maplehurst Correctional Complex in Milton, Ontario. This is a medium to maximum security men's facility that can house up to 1,500 inmates. I regularly counsel inmates, support the facility chaplains on Buddhist matters, and have previously run meditation sessions for inmates.

Based on these, admittedly constrained, lines of inquiry, we may move toward a theoretical understanding of two areas of Buddhist prison outreach: what motivates volunteers to provide such services, often at significant cost with no obvious reward, and what is the value of such outreach for Buddhism as a spiritual tradition in Canada, both within the currents of contemporary Buddhism and in the context of Canada's broader faith community.

THE VOLUNTEER ENVIRONMENT

Volunteers serve an inmate population characterized by low education, substance abuse issues, and the prevalence of mental illness.[2] Inmates are overwhelmingly male (just 11 per cent of those confined in a provincial or territorial facility and 4.7 per cent of those in the federal system are female) and young, between the ages of twenty and thirty-nine. Most declare a Christian faith at the time of admission. Volunteers work in noisy, crowded places. Privacy is at a minimum; most acts, including spiritual practice, are conducted under the eyes of other inmates. Facilities for spiritual practice may be limited, depending on the physical layout of the facility or its security level.

While religious rights and freedoms are enshrined at the highest levels of Canadian law, correctional facilities legislation often overrides these, so that religious practice is subject to "such reasonable limits as prescribed for protecting the security of the penitentiary or the safety of persons."[3] On an official policy level this sometimes takes the form of restricting group gatherings by limiting group size or preventing intermingling of inmates from different units within a facility. On an informal basis, it can perhaps take the shape of correctional officers disposing of religious materials during a cell search or rejecting some religious literature because it advocates intolerance. Inmates, then, are free to believe what they wish, but their practice – and the forms of outreach volunteers are able to offer to them – is defined by the security needs of the institutions in which they are confined.

Many inmates, faced with the challenges described above, find solo Buddhist practice a daunting task within the prison system. They may turn to the facility chaplain, who although "multi-faith-competent," is not usually equipped to support non-Christian spiritual practice beyond the delivery of reading materials, coordination of religious services for specific holy days (if applicable), and ensuring some form of access to volunteers. He or she is also likely to be extremely busy – for example, there are two full-time chaplains at Ontario's Maplehurst Correctional Complex, yielding a ratio of one chaplain for 650 inmates.

Inmates must, then, rely on volunteers to meet their spiritual needs and support their practices. In the past, the federal correctional system used paid external contractors – one for each of its administrative regions (Pacific, Prairie, Ontario, Quebec, and Atlantic). This means that these resources are stretched thinly. Kelsang Donsang of the Kuluta Buddhist Centre held the contract for the Ontario region. His location in Kingston was practical, given the constellation of federal facilities near there.[4] He functioned as a Buddhist chaplain, providing pastoral care to inmates. However, other institutions are further afield, such as the Grand River Institution, a federal women's facility, which is located in Kitchener, 350 kilometres away from Kingston. Contractors in areas like the Prairie region were even more challenged by such distances. The Prairie region of Correctional Service Canada also engaged James Mullens of the University of Saskatchewan to advise on Buddhist matters.[5]

In 2012 Corrections Canada eliminated most of its contract chaplain positions in an effort to cut costs. This measure was, to a degree, amended in early 2013, with some contractors rehired. Corrections Canada has since indicated that it will restructure chaplaincy services under the umbrella of a single contractor. The details of this new policy remain unclear, as do the implications for the provision of non-Christian chaplaincy services (Quan 2012).

In the face of such uncertainty, and with limited paid resources now available, federal facilities rely on Buddhist volunteers. Provincial and territorial corrections systems similarly rely on volunteers because they have no budget for non-Christian chaplains. The number of volunteers is approximately between 150 and 200, based on the fact that there are 100 volunteers active with Freeing the Human Spirit (an outreach organization that is not explicitly Buddhist) [6] and 53 Canadian members of the

Prison Dharma Network (a US-based coordinating organization) (Prison Dharma Network n.d.) and that there are likely to be some who volunteer independently of any organization.

These volunteers must navigate a complex system with its own internal logic, negotiate access, balance rules and religious freedoms, devise and execute outreach methods that do not conflict with the operating environment, and tailor them to the capacities and interests of the inmates they serve, all the while remaining cognizant of the often threat-filled world of prison in which the Buddhist prisoners practise. A seemingly simple one-hour meditation class to be held every two weeks on the remand side of the Maplehurst Correctional Complex required extensive discussions with chaplaincy staff to obtain approval to bring up to ten inmates together in one room. Room availability had to be ensured, since it was a multifaith room used for chapel and other services. Posters needed to be distributed to communicate the program to inmates. At the start of each session, correctional officers had to be asked to collect the participants and at the end to unlock the room to enable us to leave. Aside from these mechanics, the program needed to be delivered differently each time since the participants changed frequently due to the remand nature of this side of the facility.

Support activities of volunteers follow a scale of intensity. At the most informal, a volunteer may correspond with an inmate. This may be occasional or regular letter writing, covering a wide range of Buddhist and related topics as well as the application to a prison environment. A volunteer may also provide literature to an inmate by coordinating its delivery or by arranging for a correctional facility to receive book donations from organizations like the Corporate Body of the Buddha Educational Foundation in Taiwan. Volunteers may also run meditation groups within prisons, which can be either explicitly Buddhist or non-Buddhist. For example, since 2004 the Freeing the Human Spirit organization has been running combined meditation and yoga programs in twenty-one federal, provincial, and territorial facilities.[7] Volunteers may also advise chaplains and prison administration on matters of religious accommodation, such as diet. At its most intense, volunteers may counsel inmates in a Buddhist equivalent of pastoral care. This is a blend of support for spiritual practice and counselling such as that delivered by psychotherapists.

MECHANICS OF OUTREACH

The discussion that follows is, as mentioned earlier, based on my own experiences in prison outreach as well as conversations with both volunteers and prison staff (principally chaplains).

The structures of the prison environment, to a great degree, shape outreach work. For example, although a volunteer might wish to implement a disciplined, graduated reading program in Buddhism, the lack of texts in the prison library or the circulation system used may mean that an inmate does not have access to the requisite texts or may access them only haphazardly. The physical configuration of the facility and the security classification of the inmates may also prohibit group meetings. The rules-based world of corrections, which seeks to apply common regulations for the treatment of volunteers, functions as a limiting factor reducing the opportunity for many forms of outreach common outside prison walls, for example, retreats. In practical terms, the nature of the corrections system and the specific facility narrow the options available for outreach. More imaginative initiatives run against the grain of the systems and require a forceful personality, sympathetic prison administration, and the persistence to press for them. The vast majority of outreach, therefore, involves smaller groups or individuals. For example, prior to my arrival as a volunteer at Maplehurst Correctional Complex, the Freeing the Human Spirit organization operated a combined yoga and meditation program for sentenced inmates. Freeing the Human Spirit is a Toronto-based prison outreach group founded by Sister Elaine MacInnes (who trained in the Sanbo Kyodan lineage of Zen); it relies on volunteers to deliver its programs. The perception of prison staff was that the program had been initiated through the tenacity of participating volunteers with the support of prison chaplain personnel and that it had later been discontinued due to a lack of continued volunteer participation. Outreach efforts, therefore, seem to follow an arc starting with initial work to establish programs (sometimes overcoming resistance) and continuing to be maintained for as long as there is volunteer capacity to support them.

Volunteers typically work autonomously, whether corresponding with inmates or visiting them. If the outreach is in person, volunteers (following a security screening and orientation process) devise programs and determine scheduling in concert with a volunteer coordinator and/or a chaplain. However, best intentions are tempered by prison realities; it is correctional officers who coordinate the movement of prisoners and entry into facility rooms. Volunteers need good relationships with the facility's security in order to maintain access to the prison. While running a meditation group at Maplehurst, I developed a rapport with a correctional officer, which resulted in her appreciation of the value of such a class. Her respectful attitude toward meditation as a regular prison program helped prevent inmates who participated in the program from becoming the subject of mockery by their peers and also enabled timely access to the (locked) room we used for practice.

At the time of writing, although there undoubtedly were Buddhists with a high degree of knowledge and long histories of practice behind bars, there was no indication of a significant inmate-to-inmate Buddhist prison program formally existing in the corrections system. The majority of Buddhist support still comes from outside the prison walls through volunteers who visit and/or run programs.

Volunteers may pursue another avenue and meet individually with inmates, following standard visitation procedures. In such cases no prior screening or training would be required. In general, such a visitor would sign in during regular facility visiting hours and see the inmate in the designated visitor area. Such visits are short and confined to a visiting room or hall, which may be private or semi-private. The security level of a facility will also determine whether the volunteer is in the same room as the inmate or not. In this model, some sort of prior relationship or external connection with a faith group would likely exist in order to allow for the volunteer to visit.

Volunteers also interact with inmates through correspondence and, less frequently, by telephone. Correspondence is most often an individual "pen-pal" relationship such as those facilitated by the Prison Dharma Network (PDN) from its offices in the United States. In this circumstance an online clearing house enables the PDN to post inmate requests and volunteers to select an inmate they believe is a good match. Volunteers commit to correspond with inmates for one year. Volunteers may also facilitate the supply of books and other reading materials to inmates, either sending them directly or, where regulations require, coordinating direct delivery from a bookseller or publisher.

Supporting the multi-faith mission of paid chaplains also forms part of the work of many volunteers. This may take the form of advice on the Buddhist tradition and sourcing and provision of texts for dissemination to inmates. Most prison libraries rely on donations to stock their shelves. Mainstream faith traditions and those with a missionary approach often supply prisons with a large volume of literature. The uncoordinated nature of Buddhist prison outreach means that most prisons rely on individuals to collect and supply Buddhist books. In some circumstances, such as the PDN's Books Behind Bars program, prisons (usually through a chaplain) may request Buddhist books. Books Behind Bars relies on donations from Buddhists. The PDN collects books of all sorts from individuals and then ships a selection to those facilities that have requested Buddhist books. In other circumstances, volunteers themselves may source reading materials.

Buddhist texts used by volunteers to support their work fall into four categories – "sacred," explanatory, personal narrative, and improvised text. Sacred texts include sutras, instructions, commentaries, and devotional literature. Explanatory texts encompass a vast literature from all Buddhist traditions, pre-modern and modern, Eastern and Western. Personal narratives include works by inmates and former inmates (such as Jarvis Jay Masters and Calvin Malone) as well as other accounts that resonate with inmates (such as Claude Anshin Thomas's life story as documented in his book, *At Hell's Gate: A Soldier's Journey from War to Peace*) (Thomas 2004). Improvised texts typically consist of a volunteer's personal selection of sutras, poems, and extracts from larger works. They are usually produced in small quantities and distributed directly to inmates.

There are several texts written specifically for use in prison. Bo Lozoff's *We're All Doing Time* (1985) is likely the most recognizable book in this category, having been published in 1984 and now in its seventeenth printing. Fleet Maull's personal narrative of his experience with prison and Buddhist practice inside, *Dharma in Hell* (2005), is available to prisoners through his organization, the Prison Dharma Network, which also donates copies of Kobai Scott Whitney's practical manual, *Sitting Inside: Buddhist Practice in America's Prisons* (2002).

There are a number of factors shaping the sort of literature used: the spiritual tradition of the volunteer or organization and that of the inmate served, the inmate's reading ability and level of Buddhist knowledge, and, perhaps the most significant influence, the availability of purchased or donated texts. I have served inmates who requested materials specific to the Tibetan tradition, books by notable spiritual teachers such as the Dalai Lama or Thich Nhat Hanh or simpler books. Recently, I struggled to overcome a Vietnamese inmate's low level of literacy in both English and Vietnamese, resolving this problem with a copy of Thich Nhat Hanh's *A Pebble for Your Pocket: Mindful Stories for Children and Grown-ups*. Material in Asian languages is often difficult to obtain. I have found myself purchasing Vietnamese and Korean language materials simply because none was otherwise available. A significant portion of the Buddhist population passing through Maplehurst Correctional Complex is Vietnamese. In those cases where an inmate has little or no reading skill in English, I have sourced Buddhist texts from Vietnamese temples in Mississauga and Toronto and also purchased them directly from a Vietnamese language bookshop in Toronto that stocked Thich Nhat Hanh's books.

Volunteers differ not only in their choice of texts but also in how they use them. While proselytizing is prohibited in prison, there is room for bias to enter. A volunteer familiar with a particular tradition may stress characteristics of that tradition (quite naturally); Western Buddhism, for example, places a great emphasis on meditation practice, something that is less important in other traditions such as Shin Buddhism. Volunteers may supplement the content of a prison library by providing books directly to inmates (typically routed through the chaplain), using specific texts in services and counselling, quoting from texts in correspondence, creating their own "chapbooks" containing selected texts, or arranging for an organization to send books directly to an inmate.

Volunteers also bring secularized or modified Buddhist teachings into prisons. At the time of writing, there have been two attempts to initiate Vipassana programs (the organization described by Kory Goldberg in chapter 3) in Canadian correctional facilities, as well as programs delivered by volunteers from Freeing the Human Spirit and individual efforts to teach mindfulness-based stress reduction (MBSR).

On the practical level, Buddhist prison outreach can take many forms. I will give four examples to show the wide variance in delivery of outreach. In many cases volunteers may perform some or all of these activities at the same time; in others, volunteers may limit themselves to a single form of outreach because of personal interest or capabilities (e.g., a volunteer unable to arrange transportation to a prison may be limited to correspondence).

A volunteer wishing to correspond with an inmate contacts a clearing house such as the Prison Dharma Network and requests contact information for an inmate who has expressed an interest in corresponding. My first involvement in prison outreach began in precisely this manner; I was connected by the PDN with an inmate in Pelican Bay State Prison, a supermax facility in California, and corresponded with him for almost five years. The volunteer typically writes an introductory letter and then, much like a conversation, the letter writing continues (sometimes for years). Physical location is not a factor; in some cases, Canadian volunteers correspond with US-based inmates. Letters may respond to specific requests for guidance on moral dilemmas, practice issues, and details as well as for information about Buddhist principles or the doctrines of specific traditions. I have corresponded with inmates about Buddhist sexual morality, responses to violence, and adaptation of Buddhist principles to prison life. In all cases, one must be aware of the potential consequences of advice offered and respectful of the inmates who must try to live by Buddhist principles in a correctional environment. Letters may also be simply conversational, maintaining a form of human contact. Such long-distance pastoral care seldom follows a structured model, responding instead to the specific situation and needs of each inmate.

A volunteer working to coordinate a group within a prison, such as a meditation group, would first discuss the idea with the facility volunteer coordinator and chaplaincy staff to determine its feasibility (in some cases the request for such a group may come from the administration to the volunteer or group). In the case of the meditation group run at Maplehurst, the interest came from one of the facility chaplains who thought it would be helpful to the inmates under his care. Along with another volunteer, Taigen Henderson (roshi of the Toronto Zen Centre), we established a routine and schedule. Program feasibility is determined by the nature of the facility, the population, previously expressed inmate interest, and the volunteer's capacity to support such a program for an extended period of time. If deemed acceptable, a schedule would be drawn up and the group would be promoted within the facility. The volunteer would arrive at the specified time and work with correctional officers to access the space for the program (often a multi-use room) and collect the inmate participants. The actual program may be structured or fluid. It may follow a defined agenda (e.g., yoga first, followed by three ten-minute sitting sessions) or it may adapt to the needs of those inmates attending on the given day. When running the Maplehurst meditation program, I usually began by determining the level of the participants' experience with meditation. If they were novices, we would begin with short, five-minute "sits" but if they had participated before, or done meditation elsewhere, we would extend the periods to ten or twenty minutes. The meditation session ended not at a specific time but when the majority of participants felt they had practised enough.

A volunteer providing more intimate pastoral care and seeing inmates for "one-on-one" visits would usually either have an existing relationship with an inmate or be connected to prospective inmates through the chaplaincy staff. He or she may be provided with a list of inmates who declared themselves Buddhist upon intake into the facility. The volunteer would meet inmates for a short assessment of their interest in receiving further one-on-one visits. The volunteer would typically request that correctional officers bring such individuals to the specified visiting area where the pastoral care session would occur. These sessions are highly variable in nature: they may take the form of detailed discussions of doctrine, practical tips for practice on the inside, what may be termed "psycho-social care," or informal listening to enable an inmate to have a sympathetic outlet for dealing with the frustrations of prison life. The precise amount of Buddhist discussion depends on the relationship of the volunteer and the inmate and the specific circumstances of the visit.

Finally, chaplaincy staff sometimes ask volunteers to assess the authenticity of an inmate's claim to be Buddhist. This would involve a personal visit with the inmate and a detailed review of his faith commitment (or conversion, if that is the case) and request for special consideration. The volunteer must decide whether she feels it is an authentic expression of spirituality or perhaps an attempt to get special privileges (such as a special diet). The volunteer would then advise chaplaincy staff, who in turn would factor that advice into their decision. In my experience this has always begun with an inmate requesting a special diet for religious reasons – vegetarian or vegan – which prompts a request by a chaplain to review the matter and provide a recommendation. The issue is usually straightforward and, after having met personally with the inmate, I have usually concluded that an inmate is a genuine Buddhist or an interested explorer of the tradition and thus deserving of dispensation.

It should be plain, then, that in practice Buddhist prison outreach is not as clear-cut as it might seem. Just how explicitly Buddhist it may be will vary significantly, as can its formal processes. The lines between Buddhist practice and tenets and the secularized Buddhist elements such as meditation and mindfulness (including mindfulness-based stress reduction) are in many cases blurred.

VOLUNTEER MOTIVATIONS

Given what we know about the prison environment and its practical challenges for delivery of Buddhist outreach, it is initially difficult to imagine why someone would choose to be a prison volunteer. Although I have not yet conducted confirmatory research, my impression is that Buddhist prison outreach is a trans-national phenomenon and that the motivations for this outreach are shared among, at least, Western Buddhists. I shall assume this while examining American Buddhists involved in such work.[8] In my pool of research informants there were three Canadians who were also active in outreach in the United States.

An obvious element of volunteer motivation is what Bo Lozoff terms "the public fascination with prisons."[9] Prisons, as portrayed in films such as *Dead Man Walking*, *The Green Mile*, and the television series *Oz*, are dramatic, dangerous places. Volunteering in such an environment could be seen as conferring an aura of something approaching heroism, which bolsters self-esteem. Imagining themselves as similar to Sister Helen Prejean (portrayed in the film *Dead Man Walking*), some volunteers noted that the rescue role was their first rationale for volunteering in prison. "I believe my ideas about saving people who are victims of the 'system' was my initial motivation," an informant told me.[10]

Self-esteem is indeed a motivator for volunteer work. Sociometer theory contends that an individual will behave in a way that prevents "relational devaluation" (i.e., rejection) within the communities to which he belongs, whether these are familial, work-related, temple or practice centre sanghas, or the broader, loosely connected community of people involved in prison outreach. We act to enhance "relational value in others' eyes and, thus, improve ... chances of social acceptance" with the group to which we belong or with which we wish to identify (Leary 1999, 33). In sociometer theory, the key aspect in the case of Buddhist prison outreach is the public nature of the act – "events that are known (or potentially known) by other people have much greater effects on self-esteem than events that are known only by the individual" (Leary 1999, 33). Prison outreach involves work in a symbolic institution – the prison – long held in Western culture as an icon of repression and injustice (as is obvious in the representations of prisons in much of Western literature and cinema). Prison outreach also involves working with inmates who are metaphorically represented in Buddhist literature in the figure of the murderer, Angulimala, who had a close relationship with the Buddha and whose presence in the literature gives criminals (and the possibility of their rehabilitation) a prominent place in early literature and later Buddhist thought. Outreach also involves taking on a teaching role. This last is important since Buddhism typically lends great weight to teachers and guides; being perceived as a teacher could go far to add to the credentials of an individual as a "serious" Buddhist practitioner. Outreach is thus tailor-made as a public, or "known," act that would support self-esteem by enabling opportunities to convey one's bona fides to an audience of peers within the Buddhist community, whether that consists of a temple or group to which one belongs, an online group in which one participates, or a blend of both. This could also be augmented by efforts to communicate one's actions through an article in a Buddhist publication, for example.

There are, in addition, practical benefits of outreach that would motivate volunteers. In particular, one's own Buddhist practice can be strengthened and enhanced by such work. One informant called this "reciprocal practice,"[11] indicating that the value given to inmates was equalled or exceeded by the benefit received. Such benefit could take the form of encouraging one's own practice outside of prison (i.e., if inmates can meditate in their environment then someone on the outside has no excuses for not meditating). Teaching the core elements of Buddhism and responding to questioning may enable a volunteer to critically examine this spiritual tradition, question assumptions, and pursue deeper study. Outreach in prisons can also involve engagement with, and reflection on, Buddhist understanding of issues such as sexual abuse, violence, and addiction; these may be matters not often faced by a volunteer in her own life, offering opportunity to apply Buddhist teachings beyond the usual sphere of understanding. I once corresponded with a transgendered inmate who had difficulty balancing his Buddhist beliefs, his sexual orientation, and his presence in a prison for men. Much of this was foreign territory for me and was initially outside of my understanding of Buddhism. Helping him manage his sexual interests, his Buddhist precepts, and his personal safety required careful consideration and consultation with other Buddhists before any advice could be given, especially since he would have to live with the consequences of any action, not I.

Fully half of Canadians believe prison conditions are too easy for inmates; a third of Canadians believe that the purpose of a corrections system is to punish offenders (Roberts 2005, 3-4). Buddhist prison volunteers are thus working at odds with beliefs of the majority of Canadians, helping to support inmates and possibly assist in their rehabilitation. Going beyond bolstering self-esteem and deepening one's practice, there is another explanation of the motives of Buddhist prison volunteers.

Durkheim[12] argued that religion serves to stimulate social action. Marx posited that religion and religious action are precursors to mature political opposition (Raines 2002). However, the experience of the Buddhist informants with whom I spoke stands Marx's evolutionary idea on its head and adds a preliminary component to Durkheim's model. In the case of the majority of informants I interviewed, a radicalization process occurred, either during the 1960s and 1970s or during the later period of confrontations in the early 2000s. I interviewed a woman who had been active in the anti-war movement of the 1970s and another woman who had been inspired by the anti-globalization actions during the World Trade Organization protests in Seattle in 1999. At the same time, spiritual explorations took place, often spurred by casual encounters with Eastern spiritual traditions. Robert Bellah has observed this, finding that the spiritual traditions of the 1960s counterculture were largely derived from Asian sources. For many informants, the idea of social action as a necessary corollary to religious practice makes perfect sense. They would concur with long-time Buddhist activist Alan Senauke: "part of what happened in '68, '69 and '70 was feeling there's this spiritual yearning on one hand and then there are these radical yearnings on the other and they don't mesh. And when I began to explore anew I felt 'of course they mesh'"(Senauke 2008). What we see is the following model:

political sensitization/radicalization → encounter with
Buddhism → Buddhist social action

Very few informants were active in social outreach prior to taking up Buddhism, although many were involved in oppositional acts such as civil disobedience and protest. Several informants had, for example, been arrested for civil disobedience. They, therefore, did not share a common "charitable sensibility" that pushed them all toward social action, regardless of their religious affiliations. Nor is it likely that prior exposure to religious charity was a factor. Most informants had desultory religious educations as children, ranging from near-atheism to frequent shifts in church denomination. This seems to undercut the idea that social action, common in many Christian churches (for example), was engrained in informants through early religious exposures.

One element of informants' sense of identity is derived from this political radicalization, which provided the initial impetus leading to Buddhist prison outreach. Volunteers differentiate themselves by a continuation of their resistance to the state. Outreach is thus more an act of opposition than of charity. They oppose the practical deleterious effect of the current corrections system on inmates, its practices as well as its symbolic nature as a surrogate for the politically conservative government of Canada and the dominant political ideology of the nation (as evidenced in public opinion about corrections). All informants objected strenuously to the notion of the role of corrections as punishment and questioned the sincerity of the government's commitment to rehabilitation, especially in light of its "tough on crime" stance. In essence, by opposing the correctional system, condemning the ideology that supports it, and working to mitigate its impact on inmates, they oppose the conservative factions of Canadian political life and the conservative political perspectives that continue to dominate (and indeed to grow). Interestingly, while condemnation of the system as an abstract entity was universal among informants, on a more concrete level, there was little criticism of administrative personnel or chaplains and only occasional disparagement of correctional officers.

Another aspect of the sense of identity is derived from the way in which volunteers manifest dissent while still maintaining an image of Buddhist pacifism. This portrait is important to serious Buddhists, given the qualities ascribed to Buddhists generally and the "gentle" public personae of leaders such as the Dalai Lama and Thich Nhat Hanh. Indian scholar Ashis Nandy points out how such a balance has been struck by subjects of the colonial system. His model offers insight into the case of Buddhist prison outreach. Nandy explains that the colonized have several options available to them. They may follow a path of servile imitation of their "masters." They may collude with or join the oppressive structures. They may rebel, either as "ornamental dissenters" or as serious opponents (Nandy 1988, xiv). Or they may be "neither a player nor a counter-player" (Nandy 1988, xii) but a non-player. The non-player refuses to abide by the conventions that govern the game. He or she refuses to "fight the victor according to the victor's values, within his model of dissent" (Nandy 1988, 111). Buddhists involved in prison outreach are formulating their dissent in explicitly Buddhist terms, which shifts the quality of that dissent from a purely secular and political realm (e.g., the conventional left wing of Canadian politics) to a moral one based on spiritual principles. It may, in fact, prove more effective, as Nandy suggests when he writes of the slaves' cognition of the master as a human being as a view superior to that of the master, who views the slave as a thing. Buddhist principles such as non-duality do not permit such a radical differentiation between self and other. This is a very different model of dissent from that commonly used by secular opponents of the corrections system. It is also a model that positions these Buddhists behind a stereotypical image of peaceful, non-confrontational figures, an image that can be used to screen their dissent, giving them what Nandy calls a position of "perfect weakness" (Nandy 1988, 111) from which to oppose the prison system and yet still navigate successfully between the corrections enterprise, anti-prison activists, and the inmates themselves. It is, after all, difficult to oppose Buddhist compassionate action on the grounds that such altruism is in fact critical of the corrections system.

This non-player oppositional stance helps to build an identity as a political progressive, which, as we have seen, appears to be the original impetus for social action. On a spiritual level, social action helps construct an identity as a "serious" Buddhist, committed to the spiritual tradition by engaging in "off the cushion" practice. It augments other markers of commitment, such as length of time practising as a Buddhist or leadership roles. The view among a little more than half (ten of nineteen) of informants was that social action of some sort was helpful both in showing one's bona fides as a serious Buddhist and in maintaining that status.

If we accept that there are between 150 and 200 people in Canada involved in Buddhist prison outreach out of a total Buddhist population of 300,345 (Statistics Canada 2001), then 0.05 per cent of Canadian Buddhists volunteer. This is a very small minority of Canada's total Buddhist population. One may obviously be Buddhist but not involved in any form of Buddhist outreach. For those inclined to Buddhist social action in Canada's prison system, there are obvious impediments: a criminal record would bar one from many ways of volunteering in corrections; a lack of transportation would be a major barrier to in-person visits, given that many facilities are located away from urban centres; inflexible work and/or family schedules could also prevent one from finding time to volunteer in person. As Murray Milner Jr puts it, "People have agency but only to the degree that they have power and resources to make a difference in social outcomes" (Milner 1994, 6).

The benefits prison outreach offers may also be available from other social outreach activities, such as working with the homeless. Ethnicity sometimes plays a role in determining one's attitudes to outreach, as could one's previous exposure to, and familiarity with, the corrections system (as a former inmate, corrections officer, or a relative of one of these, for example). Theories of behavioural change, such as Prochaska's transtheoretical model, (Prochaska 1997), can help explain how some individuals progress from awareness of such outreach efforts to actual participation in them. The transtheoretical model posits six stages of change from precontemplation (unawareness of desire or need for change, unwillingness to change) through to maintenance (sustaining and supporting a change in behaviour). The moral development of Buddhist volunteers could be analysed in this way as well.

There is also the nature of inmates with whom one must work. I have worked with a Vietnamese Buddhist who, disconnected from his birth faith and only barely familiar with its external rituals, wished to return to it and draw strength from it. Another was an eclectic, curious spiritual seeker, uncommitted to Buddhism and exploring many spiritual paths at once, reading the *Tao Te Ching* as well as Buddhist texts. Another "hated God" and wanted a non-Christian sympathetic ear to hear his grievances. The notion that Buddhist outreach is provided to "serious" and experienced Buddhist practitioners is quickly dispelled. Volunteers may be dismayed at this. I know of one volunteer who had a leadership position and several advanced students outside of prison. He found the contrast between the experienced Buddhist students outside and the inexperienced, incarcerated students to be frustrating and eventually withdrew from prison outreach to concentrate on those students outside of corrections. The nature of the prison population may also cause frustration; volunteers running meditation groups at remand facilities will find that attendance is highly variable due to inmate turnover and that, as a result, one usually teaches only the rudiments of meditation, over and over again. Volunteers must also spend time with individuals accused or convicted of a range of crimes. Providing Buddhist counsel to someone accused of possessing child pornography, for example, will challenge one's notion of *karuṇā* (compassion). All these considerations may militate against one's commitment or desire to volunteer in a prison setting.

PRISON OUTREACH AS LEGITIMATION

Buddhist prison outreach in Canada exists in two contexts. The first is within the community of Buddhists. The second is the community of faith groups present in the country. Both are highly influenced by trends occurring beyond Canada and by discourses shaping faith development.

Canadian Buddhists participate to a great degree in the broader currents of Western Buddhism. They are informed by the viewpoints and moral actions of key figures such as Thich Nhat Hanh and the Dalai Lama, as well as Buddhist media outlets such as *Tricycle* and *Turning Wheel* and a plethora of online media sources. Transnational organizations that are (or have been) active in Buddhist prison outreach have a presence here, such as Shambhala, the Buddhist Peace Fellowship, and the Prison Dharma Network. Whether termed engaged Buddhism or Buddhist social action, forms of outreach – and their applicability or necessity for twenty-first-century Buddhism – have become a subject of much discussion and debate within these organizations and in journals, at conferences, and on websites. Christopher Queen, an American scholar of Buddhism, propagates Ambedkar's view that social action constitutes a fourth *yana*, or vehicle, following the turning of the wheel of Buddhist development, in which "Buddhist activists attempt to bring their mindfulness into situations of great complexity or conflict" (Helbling 2004). Whether this is indeed a fourth *yana* or not, prison outreach is a part of a larger trend in Western

Buddhism, along with eco-activism, championing of human rights, anti-war efforts, and outreach to the homeless.

"One of the sexiest things to do in our culture is to do good deeds," says Rob Bergman, youth pastor at Windsor Crossing Church in Missouri (Bergman 2011). For faith groups, this emphasis on good deeds is often focused on prisons. There has been an increase in prison outreach among several faiths in the last decade. Some Christian groups consider prisons to be significant "spiritual harvest fields" (Van Auken n.d.) and have expanded efforts to reach incarcerated populations. Criminon, established in 2000, seeks to use the principles of Scientology to rehabilitate prisoners, thereby extending the reach of that spiritual path (Criminon International n.d.). Lisa Miller of the *Wall Street Journal* noted a decade ago that "prison ministry has become a sophisticated and competitive business" involving many faiths (Miller, 1999, B1). A Canadian prison chaplain advised me that "prison work is fashionable right now" for faith groups.[13] The growth and maturation of Buddhist prison outreach in the West in the 1990s and the 2000s, including Canada, can be seen as part of this increased general interest in such social service.

In such contexts, Buddhist prison outreach works to legitimate "off the cushion" Buddhism (whether termed Engaged Buddhism or described as Buddhist social outreach or something similar) within the wider Buddhist community and to legitimate Buddhism within the broader Canadian society. The choice of a prison environment for such legitimation is not new; in the early 1970s the Transcendental Meditation movement (a quasi-religious organization based on the teachings of Maharishi Mahesh Yogi and with an emphasis on meditative practice) attempted to obtain such legitimation through a short-lived program at the La Tuna federal prison in Texas (Orme-Johnson and Moore 2003). Similarly, Jon Kabat-Zinn and others offered mindfulness-based stress reduction (derived from Buddhist practices) to inmates and staff in the Massachusetts correctional system between 1992 and 1996 (Samuelson et al. 2007). So, too, have Vipassana practitioners in Washington state and Alabama[14] sought to demonstrate the legitimacy of their practice through prison outreach. There have been efforts to bring Vipassana programs to several Canadian prisons but none has been offered to date. In all cases what prison experience delivers to a spiritual tradition (or therapeutic technique) is symbolic capital. The symbolic capital is generated through acceptance by the state through the agency of the various correctional authorities. Practically, this takes the form of inclusion in policy and in programming opportunities (such as meditation programs or consultation on matters of faith). Such inclusion gives Buddhism parity with other spiritual practices, being accredited not only in principle but also in practice within the corrections environment.

Prison outreach also offers opportunity to demonstrate the relevance of Buddhism, its utility and applicability in difficult circumstances, as has been described above. That relevance is built on Buddhist responses to some of the challenges of prison life – loss of control over one's life, regret for past actions, fear of the future, despair, and depression. Meditation's value as a calming agent can account for the prevalence of that form of Buddhist spiritual practice in prison and its value as an example of Buddhism's relevance. But there are other aspects of Buddhism that help construct this relevancy. The emphasis on the present moment as exemplified in *sammā-sati* (right mindfulness) is of practical value for inmates who are sometimes tormented by thoughts of past actions or suffering anxiety contemplating the possibilities of an imprisoned future. So, too, is *sīla*, or ethical conduct, which has practical value in supporting or justifying behaviour in prison. These are immensely practical aspects of Buddhism that can work to define its utility in a prison setting, addressing real challenges and thereby helping to define its relevance and ultimately contribute to a legitimation of the Buddhist spiritual path.

There is more to Buddhism's legitimation than practical value. The sociologist of religion Peter Berger contends that one of the principal purposes of religion is to ground an individual's life in some sort of meaningful order in the face of an "out of balance" and ever-changing world (Berger 1990, 5). In essence, a believer may anchor himself in an eternal present in order to survive the tumult of the ordinary (or "earthly") present. The solution offered by Buddhism is not one of creating an eternal cosmological order out of time in opposition to the temporary "in time" nature of this world. Rather it stands this idea on its head, positing a solution grounded in a profound recognition and acceptance of the transitory nature of all conditioned phenomena – *anicca*. What is important here is not whether the Buddhist solution to this question is satisfactory or adequate for inmates but the fact that Buddhism has an answer – a formal response to the issue of a person's relationship to the cosmological order, whether an eternal order or one defined by constant flux.

Berger also claims that the strength of a religious tradition lies in its response to what in philosophy and religion is often termed the problem of evil. Berger borrows the term "theodicy" to mean an explanation of suffering that defines it in a way that supports the sense of cosmological order. Once again, prison, by the nature of the mental and physical suffering inherent in the system, is a proving ground for theodicies. A religious tradition, if it is to have relevance in prison, must put forward a meaningful and satisfactory explanation of suffering. Berger goes further, advocating that "Every society is, in the last resort, banded together in the face of death. The power of religion depends, in the last resort, upon the credibility of the banners it puts in the hands of [men and women] as they stand before death, or more accurately, as they walk, inevitably, toward it" (Berger 1990, 51).

To legitimate a spiritual tradition, one must, therefore, put forward a convincing explanation of suffering and, by extension, death. Buddhism begins with the First Noble Truth, setting *dukkha*, or suffering, as a central plank. The rest of the Noble Truths elaborate on the nature of such suffering and the way to escape from it. Thus, unlike Jewish, Christian, or Islamic theodicies, Buddhism sidesteps the dilemma posed by the simultaneous existence of the divine and suffering, and instead focuses on a blueprint for encountering and responding to suffering: "the bodhisattva cultivates the capacity to live within the raw reality of suffering on the ground and transform life's adverse circumstances into a path of awakening" (Preece 2009, 3). As with Buddhism's response to the cosmological question, it is less important whether or not this is compelling for inmates than that a response to suffering exists within the Buddhist spiritual tradition.

The prison environment demands not only that Buddhism be useful to inmates – providing concrete guidance and benefits from practices such as meditation – but that it include spiritual responses to humanity's place within the cosmological order as well as an explanation of suffering. Buddhism succeeds on these points. The prison setting provides opportunity not only to explicitly illustrate these features of the tradition but also to demonstrate their utility, thereby supporting the claim of relevance for Buddhism and working to legitimate it as a spiritual tradition in Canada. That this happens in an environment commonly perceived as harsh and extreme only heightens the legitimation.

CONCLUSION

We must be honest about what we do know: the nature of the prison outreach environment, the framework of religious freedoms in Canadian prisons, the portrait of Canadian prisoners, and the forms of outreach possible. We know, too, how prison outreach typically works, how the Canadian correctional systems are integrating a minority faith such as Buddhism into spiritual care commitments for inmates. But we must also be clear about where knowledge is lacking. What factors determine the selection of prison volunteer work in addition to, or instead of, other forms of social action? What do Buddhist prison practices look like from the inmates' perspective? What is the experience of conversion to Buddhism behind bars?

Based on what we do know, it is possible to construct working hypotheses about the motivations of volunteers engaged in this work. We can also suggest the value of prison outreach as a tool for the legitimation of Buddhism in Canada. If, as I suggested earlier, Buddhist prison outreach is a trans-national phenomenon, then (drawing on my research in the United States) we can see that, on a micro level, Buddhist prison outreach is an act of resistance on the part of volunteers against a monolithic and highly symbolic institution representing repression and the state, contributing to the construction of individual Buddhist identities. At the macro level, Buddhist prison outreach serves to legitimate Buddhism as a spiritual tradition, elevating it alongside other traditions with longer histories of prison outreach, such as Christianity.

NOTES

1. See, for example, Malone (2008), Masters (1997), Maull (2005), and Phillips (2008).
2. Inmate statistics in this section are drawn from Calverley (2010, 2, table 9).
3. Government of Canada, Section 25, Corrections and Conditional Release Act, 1992, c 20.
4. Kelsang Donsang, telephone interview with the author, 10 September 2010.
5. Deborah Tanasiecuk, Regional Chaplain, Prairie Region, Correctional Service Canada, telephone interview with the author, 27 September 2010.

6   Cheryl Vanderburg, Program Director, Freeing the Human Spirit, email message to author, 21 December 2010.
7   Vanderburg, email message to author, 21 December 2010.
8   In 2008 and 2009 I surveyed nineteen informants using qualitative and quantitative methods to document their backgrounds, involvement in Buddhist prison outreach in the United States, and their motivations for doing so.
9   Bo Lozoff, telephone interview with the author, 8 March 2009.
10 Informant "KD," email message to author, 19 December 2005.
11 Informant "L," telephone interview with the author, 18 February 2008.
12 Durkheim (1912) argues that religion is both a product of the social milieu and an influencer of social action. For him religion is most emphatically social.
13 Chaplain "A," 22 December 2010.
14 See Parks et al. (2003) and the documentary film, *The Dhamma Brothers*.

11

Correspondence School: Canada, Fluxus, and Zen

MELISSA ANNE-MARIE CURLEY

There was no doubt at that time, really I think the impetus for the actual creation of *The Eternal Network* has come from these people in Canada – now of course it has spread world-wide, and it is the way we have to create, to be creative outside or without the advice, or opinion, or concern even at times of the media, or the art establishment.

ROBERT FILLIOU, 1977; cited in Shea 2001

The artists examined in this chapter – a small group of Canadians associated with the Canadian arts collectives Image Bank and the Western Front and with the transnational artistic movement known as Fluxus – were not faithful Buddhists. There were members of Fluxus who were diligent Buddhist practitioners, foremost among them Robert Filliou, whose remark about "these people in Canada" I have taken as the epigraph for this chapter, but Filliou was French, not Canadian. This makes the connection between this essay and the others in this volume a fragile one: if this is a book about Buddhism taking root in Canada, why devote space to folks who, if Buddhist, were not Canadian, and if Canadian, were not explicitly Buddhist?

My argument is that the artists I will consider here were, in a somewhat idiosyncratic way, culturally Buddhist. I take my cue from studies of the Japanese poet Bashō (1644–94). It is a commonplace that Bashō was a Zen poet whose work is suffused by "the spirit of Zen" (Suzuki 1938, 264; Dumoulin 1979, 83). Bashō was not a priest, but, Dumoulin insists, there "can be little doubt ... that he had a natural openness toward Zen and that his mind was able to deeply grasp essential elements of the Zen way" (Dumoulin 2005, 350). Lucien Stryk suggests that despite his lack of formal affiliation, Bashō "considered himself a Zennist" (Stryk 1985, 15); Shinkichi

Takahashi asserts that Bashō "mastered Zen" during his brief tenure as the lay disciple of a Rinzai teacher (cited in Ueda 1983, 364). In fact, however, there is good evidence that Bashō did not consider himself a Buddhist at all, instead defining himself against the tradition and its norms (Barnhill 1990, 274–5). If the spirit of Zen is at work in Bashō's poetry, so too is the spirit of folk religion (Barnhill 1990, 286) and the spirit of neo-Confucianism (Thornhill 1998, 341ff). As Arthur Thornhill puts it, Buddhism constituted "only part of [Bashō's] literary heritage," and his literary praxis ought not to be confused with a meditative praxis (Thornhill 1998, 354). Nonetheless, Bashō moved in a Buddhist culture, and Thornhill allows that his "aesthetics ... undeniably embody Buddhist values" (Thornhill 1998, 354). This opens up the possibility of reading Bashō as a Zen poet by looking for the resonance between his aesthetics and Zen ethics, without struggling to establish Bashō's bona fides as a Zen master – to read him, in other words, as culturally Buddhist.

The artists I take up in this essay were obviously not operating within a majority Buddhist culture. They were, however, working out of a subculture on which Buddhism exerted a significant influence: Buddhism was, in other words, part of their aesthetic heritage, and the language of Zen was a language they felt entitled to use. In the pages that follow, I try to demonstrate that, as a consequence, their aesthetics likewise express Buddhist values and show us something interesting about the shape those values might take outside the precincts of an orthoprax Zen centre.

BUDDHISM IN FLUXUS, OUTSIDE CANADA

The subculture I'm discussing here is the 1960s counterculture out of which Fluxus emerged. Fluxus was a global, self-consciously cosmopolitan art movement, with participants in Europe, Asia, and North America. As is evident from the name, the movement was animated by an interest in contingency, transformation, and impermanence. Artists associated with the movement tended to emphasize process over outcome; Fluxus pieces very often took the form of instructions to be carried out or scores to be interpreted, and rarely culminated in the production of a stable, saleable object readily recognizable as an artwork. Indeed, Fluxus was characterized by a certain contempt for galleries and museums as artwork distribution systems, pushing instead for a radically egalitarian approach to art through which, it was hoped, art would ultimately become indistinguishable from life. It is not easy to discern all the lines of transmission that brought Buddhist ideas into circulation within Fluxus, but if we were to try to list them, we might begin with three major figures: John Cage, Ken Friedman, and Robert Filliou.

John Cage (1912–1992) was a musician, composer, and music theorist; he was a major figure in the American avant-garde in general and a kind of unofficial patron for Fluxus in particular. Hannah Higgins observes that those artists who came to Fluxus through Cage tended to share Cage's interest in Zen, and to have "a more Zen or experiential sense" of what Fluxus meant (Kaplan et al. 2000, 9). Cage had attended D.T. Suzuki's lectures on the Avataṃsaka Sūtra at Columbia University in 1952 and seems to have taken special interest in the Huayen vision of the three thousand worlds interpenetrating in a single thought-moment: "I like to think that each thing not only has its own life but its own centre and that that centre is each time, the exact centre of the universe. That is one of the principal themes I've learned from my studies of Zen" (cited in Doris 1998, 123). Music has the potential to demonstrate an "ecologically balanced situation … A situation in which each thing and each sound is in its place, because each one is what it is" (cited in Katz 1999). This is recognizable, I think, as a way of talking about dharma positions in Buddhism. The artist's own ego (or taste) interferes with the dharma position of things; much of Cage's work thus revolves around developing techniques for muting himself so as not to impose upon the music that things make when left to their own devices. One example of this is his strategy of chance composition, which used repeated castings of the *Yijing* to determine which notes to play, at which tempo, for what duration, and so on. Another is his famous silent piece *4'33"*, first performed in 1952, the score for which instructs the performer to take up his or her instrument without playing it, for four minutes and thirty-three seconds. The music, in this case, consists of the various sounds of the performance space, over which neither the composer nor the performer can exert any control. Cage conceived *4'33"* as, on the one hand, stripping away the agency of the artist and, on the other hand, drawing the audience's attention to naturally occurring sound in the environment which is usually, paradoxically, rendered silent by a restless desire for music. Jonathan Katz has argued that Cage's interest in Zen silence also had a political element. Cage was gay, but resolutely silent on the subject of his sexuality; this silence was self-protective, but, Katz suggests, "also ... a chosen mode of resistance" (Katz 1999). From Zen, Cage picks up the notion of an expressive, communicative silence, a notion he could not extract out of "our religion" or "our society" (Katz 1999). This Zen silence offered "freedom from meaning [that] was also freedom from domination, definition, and control in a very real world sense" (Katz 1999). In Cage's work, then, we see the wedding of a Zen aesthetics characterized by silence with a Zen ethics characterized by an effort to decentre the self, and a politics of resistance characterized by a refusal to contribute to oppositional power structures – Cage sought "not to challenge power, but to escape it" (Katz 1999).

Ken Friedman (1949–) takes Cage's Zen silence and explores it within the ambit of Fluxus. Friedman has held faculty positions at the Norwegian School of Management and the Danish Design School, and is currently dean of the Faculty of Design at Swinburne University, Melbourne, Australia; he is both a major artist within the movement and one of the movement's most important archivists. Friedman the scholar makes frequent reference to Zen in defining Fluxus, telling us that "In every respect the heritage of Japan and of Zen Buddhism has influenced the development of Fluxus" (K. Friedman 1990, 2) and identifying the foundations of Fluxus as "music, Zen, design, and architecture" (K. Friedman 1998, 237). Friedman the artist deals with silence in pieces like the *Zen for Record* variations: a defective phonograph record with no sound, a series of empty phonograph record sleeves, a set of records spray-painted so that the grooves would no longer produce sound when played, and so on. And he deals with the decentring of the artist in many of his event pieces, which consist only of a score for someone else to interpret and perform, like his 1966 *Thirty Feet* ("Find a piece of paper 30 feet square. Inscribe a large circle on the page. Send it to John Cage") (K. Friedman 2009, 76) or his 1965 *Anniversary* ("Someone sneezes. A year later, send a postcard reading: 'Gesundheit!'") (K. Friedman 2009, 43). Friedman also comes to emphasize a goofy or unserious quality less immediately apparent in Cage's aesthetics. He coins a term, "Zen vaudeville," to "capture both the meditation and the humor in Fluxus pieces" (K. Friedman 1990, 2). *Zen Vaudeville* is also the title he gives to a 1966 event score, the instructions for which read simply "The sound of one shoe tapping" (K. Friedman 2009, 80). In its vaudeville aspect, Fluxus art becomes something to laugh at – or, as David Doris puts it, laughter becomes "an important index of understanding" (Doris 1998, 129). Where seriousness serves to reinforce the professional artist's "position of mastery and privilege," unseriousness undermines the notion of artistic mastery and transmits the status of artist to everyone (Doris 1998, 119). And where seriousness serves the interests of a hierarchy in which art and life are set in opposition to each other, unseriousness destabilizes that hierarchy and attempts to reframe art in terms of quotidian life.

This impulse to remove the boundary between art and life is explored most fully in Robert Filliou's notion of the eternal network. Filliou (1926–1987) was trained as an economist and worked for the United Nations in South Korea before deciding to pursue art full-time. He was on the verge of completing a three-year retreat at a Tibetan Buddhist centre in Dordogne when he died. Filliou began to develop the idea of the eternal network in the mid-1960s, partnering with Cage's former student George Brecht to open a "non-shop" called La cédille qui sourit (The smiling *cedille*) in the town of Villefranche-sur-Mer. La cédille was intended to serve as "an international centre of permanent creation," based on the injunction "whatever you do, do something else; whatever you think, think something else" (cited in Perkins n.d.). The phrase translated here as "permanent creation" is *la Fête permanente*, which plays on the sense of creative making or doing (*fait*) and the sense of a party or shared enjoyment (*fête*), making art an event to which everyone is invited, and so joining artist and audience "in a common creation" (Perkins n.d.). But Filliou and Brecht themselves proposed a less literal translation of *Fête permanente*, rendering it instead as Eternal Network. When they eventually shut down La cédille, Filliou and Brecht mailed out an announcement that the physical place of La cédille was now to be superseded by a deterritorialized network of creative activity.

Filliou would go on to use the notion of the eternal network to capture a number of overlapping ideas. On one level, the eternal network was intended to replace the avant-garde. In a talk at the Nova Scotia College of Art and Design, Filliou explained, "I would propose that there is not one single artist nowadays who knows all the advanced research in art that goes on, and if this is true, I propose that the concept of the avant-garde is obsolete. That you cannot know who is in front, if you don't have all the knowledge of what goes on. You don't know who is in front or in back or anywhere – and I think that a more useful concept would be that of considering each and every artist as part of an Eternal Network" (Filliou 2004,

255). On another level, the eternal network was intended to point to the artist's necessary participation in the non-art world, the "wider network [of things] going on around him all the time in all parts of the world," and to recognize such ordinary events as "private parties, weddings, divorces, lawcourts, funerals, factory works, trips around towns in buses" as performances (cited in Perkins n.d.). Ultimately, the eternal network described the totality of ceaselessly changing conditions in the world: "There is always someone asleep, and someone awake, someone dreaming asleep, someone dreaming awake, someone eating, someone hungry, someone fighting, someone loving, someone making money, someone broke, someone travelling, someone staying put, someone helping, someone hindering, someone enjoying, someone suffering, someone indifferent, someone starting, someone stopping – only the Network is eternal'" (Filliou 2004, 255).

For Cage, the task of the artist was to refrain from imposing his own taste on things and so allow each thing its own subjectivity, or individual dharma position. For Filliou, the task of the artist was to realize all the ways in which things array themselves in relation to each other, or the interdependence of individual dharma positions. Tusa Shea characterizes this as intersubjectivity – a positing that "reality results from a process of interpretation and communication about the world between subjects" (Shea 2001, 28) – but we might also recognize it as the fundamental Buddhist teaching of interdependent coorigination. The work Filliou produced out of this apprehension of interdependence took the form of "conceptual tools" (Dezeuze 2004) designed to illuminate the constant reconfiguring of the network itself. In a 1965 piece, he describes the "secret" to participation in the *Fête permanente* in terms of meditative practice: "aware of self / wide awake / SITTING QUIETLY / DOING NOTHING" (cited in Thompson 2011, 59–60). For Filliou as for Friedman, then, performance art and Zen meditative practice were intimately related: in the Fluxus context, the more you applied what Fluxus founder George Maciunas called "Zen method," the better your work would be (cited in Doris 1998, 127).

In thinking about Buddhism as read by Fluxus, then, I would like to focus on three key features. The first is an interest in using silence to subvert language and express difference; because language is associated, for these artists, with mind, silence also becomes a way of rooting their work in the body, and, by extension, in the natural world. Correctly or not, this silence is explicitly understood as Buddhist – as Dick Higgins puts it, "When I think about Zen, it's very much about thinking outside of a verbal framework ... There's a possibility for thought in all these other sensory zones" (cited in Kaplan 2000, 11). The second is an emphasis on the virtues of decentring the self, or depersonalizing one's work. Silence supports this kind of decentring. So do modes of creative activity in which the artist's agency is obstructed. This can be done in a number of ways: by forcing critical choices to be made collectively rather than by a single author, or leaving those choices to chance operations; by taking measures to hamper, limit, or undermine the artist's skilful self-expression; or by undertaking work in a spirit intentionally opposed to purposefulness or meaningfulness. Artists working with Fluxus explicitly understood such creative activity as resonating with Buddhist ideas of curbing the ego and allowing things to assert themselves spontaneously. The third, following from this interest in egoless activity, is a repositioning of the generative locus of creative activity from the inner world of the artist's unconscious to an external network of relationships with other people and things. Artistic production thus becomes a way of concretizing or objectifying the principle of interdependent coorigination. This idea is given its clearest articulation by Filliou, who clearly understands it as expressing a truth not just about art but about life, to be realized through silent meditation. I take these to be the defining features of Fluxus-style Buddhist culture.

TRANSMISSION TO CANADA

Canada proved to be an exceptionally fertile ground for Fluxus. Filliou made his first Canadian tour in 1973, framing it as an opportunity to research the eternal network. By that time, a sprawling project engaging the notion of networks was already underway. Some years earlier, Vancouver artists Michael Morris, Vincent Trasov, and Gary Lee-Nova had established Image Bank, a mailing list through which participating artists could request items from others on the list (for example, a 1972 request card from Mexican artist Pedro Friedberg asks for images of "Ludwig II King of Bavaria. Ronald Firbank. All kinds of royal palaces"). In 1971, Ken Friedman had had his own contact list absorbed into the Image Bank directory, bringing it up to some fourteen hundred names in total. And in 1972, the Toronto arts collective General Idea began publishing FILE *Magazine* (or *Megazine*), issues of which included the Image Bank directory and request lists as an insert. Image Bank published its own International Image Exchange Directory the same year. In the summer of 1973, while Filliou was in Nova Scotia, Image Bank was wrapping up an event at the Museum of Modern Art in Paris: they ran an on-site image request bureau as part of the museum's exhibition of Canadian art. Filliou had initially planned to visit only the east coast, but Morris persuaded him to travel to Vancouver and spend some time at the alternative, artist-run centre the Western Front, which Morris and Trasov co-founded along with collaborators Kate Craig, Glenn Lewis, Eric Metcalfe,[1] Mo Van Nostrand, Henry Greenhow, and Martin Bartlett.

This turned out to be the first of many productive trips to Vancouver for Filliou. During his first stay at the Western Front, he and his Canadian hosts began planning an event for the following year, to mark the tenth anniversary of Filliou's 1963 piece *Art's Birthday*. Art's Birthday: the Decca-Dance was held in Los Angeles in 1974; it proved to be the largest eternal network event ever, and *Art's Birthday* remains to this day "a high holiday on the Front's cultural calendar" (Friz 2007). Over the course of the 1970s, Canada established itself as a world centre for mail art (Welch 1993, 188) and for artist-run alternative presses (Shea 2001, 1). Filliou credited Canadian artists with driving the creation of the eternal network, and so did Friedman, who called Canada "a powerhouse and beacon in helping to promote and develop what the Canadians called 'eternal network' consciousness around the world" (cited in Shea 2001, 124).

Why did the notion of the eternal network prove so attractive to these Canadian artists? The answer, I think, is probably overdetermined. One factor we might consider is timing. It happened that a number of lines of thought were converging in British Columbia in the 1970s, which together made Filliou's Buddhist-inspired eternal network easy to think about. Because of the strength of federally funded alternative, artist-run centres during this period, Canadian artists were in a position to build strong relationships nationally, and international artists associated with Fluxus (including Filliou himself) were able to spend time in Canada pursuing their own projects. Asian Buddhist aesthetics – understood somewhat eclectically – had also been filtering into contemporary Canadian art through the work of psychedelic artists. We know, for instance, that Lee-Nova was interested in expatriate American artist Jack Wise (Watson n.d.), whose mandala paintings depicting intricately connected worlds-within-worlds were informed both by his studies with *thangka* painters in India and his own sense of himself as working "in the spirit of what the Zen artists call *muga* (it is not I that is doing this)" (cited in Woodcock 1975–76, 8). And at Simon Fraser University, theorist Anthony Wilden was asserting that across disciplines, the intellectual movement of the moment was a "radical change in the theory of knowledge ... from aggregate to whole, from heap to structure, from part to system ... in a word, from atom, to system, and thence to ecosystem" (Wilden 2001, 241; Sava n.d.). We might say, then, that the time was ripe for the arrival of Filliou's eternal network.

At the same time, there are several reasons why the eternal network might have had particular appeal to these artists. It offered a way of overcoming geography. Filliou's eternal network is decentred; this follows directly from his understanding of the network itself as the only permanent thing, and reflects Cage's understanding of each thing as constituting its own centre. Any artist working in Canada during the 1960s and 1970s was in some sense working at the periphery of things, far from the art centres of New York, Paris, and Berlin. This was perhaps doubly the case for artists working in Vancouver, who were at a distance even from the centre of the Canadian art world (Shea 2001, 80). Morris recalls having the sense "that Vancouver was an outpost, a frontier, and that we had to re-invent everything – including, and most importantly, a context for ourselves and our work" (cited in Jacob 2002). In that work, we can see these artists attempting to articulate what it means to be at the edge of things, and feeling out alternative networks. In a 1971 photo essay for *artscanada*, Lee-Nova explores what he calls "Our beautiful west coast thing," opening with a quote from the San Francisco Renaissance poet Jack Spicer: "We are a coast people / There is nothing but ocean out beyond us."[2] This is one concrete reason for Canadian artists generally and West Coast artists especially to be drawn to Fluxus – it promised a situation in which "there is no more art centre in the world" (cited in Shea 2001, 80) and held out the possibility of attaining "a level of collective visibility within the international artworld" (Arnold 2008).

It also offered a way of queering identity. As suggested above, for Cage, Zen provided a language for expressing his sexual difference differently, that is, without reliance on an antagonistic relationship between the (straight) self and its (gay) opposite. More generally, the Fluxus conception of identity as mutable and performative resonated with a queer sensibility that emphasized irony and camp. Not every artist associated with Image Bank and the Western Front identified as gay, but many did; unlike Cage, they were living and working in a milieu in which it was possible to be out as gay, but like Cage, they would find that their difference would be tolerated only if they also allowed themselves to be subordinate and did not challenge the hierarchical binary construction of sexual identity. When as part of a performance piece Michael Morris, as his persona Marcel Dot, was crowned beauty pageant queen Miss General Idea, he understood himself to be committing "career suicide": he had "always been out," Scott Watson tells us, "but now he had flaunted it" (Watson 1992). Watson explains that this kind of flaunting – that is to say, the open defiance of stable, normative identity – led to a "homophobic backlash" culminating in an unsigned article in the Vancouver weekly *The Grape* accusing the artists involved with the network of both "parad[ing]" and "[s]hitting on their own homosexuality" (Watson 1992). Faced with conservative critics on the right and doctrinaire critics on the left, "they had nothing to stand on but their aestheticism and in some cases their Buddhism" (Watson 1992). This, then, is another concrete reason for the West Coast artists at least to be drawn to Fluxus – it could accommodate and give expression to an understanding of the self as mutable and pluriform.

Finally, Filliou's sense of the place of the self within the network may have resonated in some productive ways with a Canadian sense of national identity as relatively unstable – in other words, Canadian artists might have been well-disposed, as Canadians, to consent to an understanding of identity as contingent and arbitrary. Friedman and Maciunas conceived of the State of Flux as "a country whose geography was a figment of the communal imagination, whose citizenry was transient" (cited in Saper 1998, 147); their 1977 collaboration *Visa TouRiste* provides a passport to this imagined country. An editorial in the Vancouver poetry magazine *Tish* declared that "Canada does not exist except as a political arrangement for the convenience of individuals accidentally happening to live within its arbitrary area" while "the community of poetry is a universal thing" (cited in Shea 2001, 48). That the boundaries of the nation-state have an arbitrary quality is a fact for every nation, but to have an acute sense of that fact reflects a Canadian sensibility. Critical theorist Linda Hutcheon proposes that Canada produces its fragile national identity out of "*regionalist* impulses: the ex-centric forces of Québec, the Maritimes, the west," making Canada's history "one of defining itself against centres" (Hutcheon 1988, 4). This gives Canadians "a firm suspicion of centralizing tendencies" (Hutcheon 1988, 3) and makes resistance to the idea of a stable Canadian identity itself a feature of Canadian identity. Hutcheon argues that this makes Canadians natural postmoderns; I would propose that it may have given Canadian artists a special affinity for Fluxus.

The artists of Image Bank and the Western Front shared a sense of themselves as geographically, nationally, culturally, and sexually marginal. Through Fluxus, and the Fluxus appropriation of Zen, they found a way to reconceive the margin as a decentred position of strength. What kind of artwork did they produce as a result? I now consider three projects pursued by Vancouver's network artists: mail art, the Mr Peanut mayoral campaign, and Colour Bar Research.

CORRESPONDENCE SCHOOL (I): MAIL ART

Mail art was the primary pathway for exploring and extending the eternal network. A mail art piece began with the artist mailing a request, a response, or an object to somebody else, drawing the recipient into the artist's network. The focus was not so much on the item mailed, but on the act of mailing and the artist's negotiation with the distribution system: as Nam June Paik put it, if the Marxist imperative was to seize the means of production, the Fluxus imperative was "Seize the distribution-medium!" (cited in Saper 2001, 133). Many Fluxus mail art pieces thus sought to illuminate the otherwise obscure workings of the postal system. Some projects played with the idea of mass mailing, like Friedman's Sock of the Month club. Others tried to enlist the participation of postal workers in their pieces, as in Ben Vautier's *Postman's Choice*, a postcard with two identical sides, requiring the postman to decide which is the address and which the return address; or a piece from Switzerland's Cabaret Voltaire, which attempts (successfully, it turns out) to mail a matzoh cracker sealed in clear plastic to New York using only two artist-made stamps.

Canadian artists turned out to be very good at mail art, which is unsurprising given that mail art gets better the further one is from the centre of things. Image Bank was intended to "propel network relations" (Gangadharan 2009, 289) by providing "a structure for setting up extending stabilizing and reinforcing correspondences, creating a network using the postal system as a means for communications" (cited in Sava 1996, 90). It played a major role in giving Canada pride of place in the mail art network. So did the activities of the New York Corres Sponge Dance School of Vancouver,[3] a "cross between correspondence and choreography dealing with meetings, mailings, and events" (cited in Sava 1996, 90). Spearheaded by Glenn Lewis, the Dance School handled "the personal, informal, and social aspects of the members of the Western Front and the Eternal Network" (cited in Sava 1996, 90). So, too, did the support of federal agencies: the National Gallery sponsored a cross-country exhibition of the Image Bank postcard show (displaying more than five thousand artist-created postcards), and the National Research Council commissioned a piece conceived by Lewis and produced in cooperation with the Dance School, the Great Wall of 1984. Installed in the National Science Library of Ottawa, the Great Wall was made up of some 365 Plexiglas safety deposit boxes, into which were deposited – over a period of many years – items solicited from or volunteered by members of the Image Bank network.

Michael Morris's praise for the Great Wall – "the most anarchistic yet democratic and intelligent manipulation of official bureaucracy to date" (cited in Watson 1992) – reflects the particular political bent of the mail artists. In Canada as elsewhere, mail art was driven by a utopian desire to establish a territory in which everyone was equal. Participating artists conceived of the mail art network as "an alternative to the hierarchical, commodity-oriented, mainstream art world and to the impersonal, information and communication-saturated, bureaucratic society" (Gangadharan 2009, 280). Coming out of the 1960s, it was still faintly possible, as Friedman puts it, "to believe that art and the postal system could reshape the world" (cited in Ferranto n.d.). For this reason, Friedman understood the Image Bank as "an act of social responsibility" (cited in Ferranto n.d.), a move toward establishing what he describes elsewhere as "a world in which it is possible to create the greatest value for the greatest number of people" – an aim consistent with "many of the central tenets of Buddhism" (cited in Thompson 2011, 59).

This politics interacts with mail art aesthetics in two related ways. First, it informs the adoption of a number of methods that decentre the artist. It calls on participants to mute their own taste and accept all submissions as they come, to leave the selection of materials to the collective, and to work anonymously. We see this in Glenn Lewis's call for materials for the

Great Wall, which asks only that people choose the box number they prefer and indicate when they plan to mail their submission; he is willing, from the outset, to include everything, and to refrain as much as possible from imposing himself on the work. Second, it shifts the aesthetic focus away from the individual art object toward the working of the network itself – we are here to "judge works of art according to the human interrelations that they comprise, produce or cause" (Gangadharan 2009, 284). If our aesthetic response to the Great Wall is based only on the miscellaneous objects actually deposited in Lewis's Plexiglas boxes, we may be unlikely to find it beautiful; if, on the other hand, our aesthetic response is based on the ways in which the Great Wall represents the working of a network that bring artists into intimate contact with each other (and with us) across spatial and temporal borders, we might find it moving and even, as Morris does, somehow thrilling. For some participants in the mail art network, this aesthetic shift proved unmanageable, and they reacted by recentring themselves – Lee-Nova, for example, recalls that he "got a lot of garbage and threw out most of it … It was so shallow and poorly put together I just couldn't take it seriously" (cited in Shea 2001, 120). He ultimately left the network in 1973. But others found in the network aesthetic something they could sustain. Vancouver-based mail artist Anna Banana, for instance, stuck scrupulously to the network's "unwritten rules" – "no rejections, no returns and documentation to all participants" – and never threw anything away (Banana n.d.). Shea suggests that for Banana, "the concept of the Eternal Network superseded aesthetic quality" (Shea 2001, 121), but I would propose instead that the network offered a different kind of aesthetic satisfaction for those artists who were able to mute their own taste successfully.

CORRESPONDENCE SCHOOL (II): MR PEANUT

In 1969, the same year Image Bank was founded, Vincent Trasov made himself a Mr Peanut costume, mimicking the top-hatted, monocled mascot for Planters (see illustration 9 for a rendering of Mr Peanut by Eric Metcalfe, signed with his usual pseudonym, "Dr. Brute"). While travelling for Image Bank events and collaborations, Trasov would sometimes put on the costume and pose for photographs in Canada's scenic places, inserting Mr Peanut into the landscape as a kind of fetish object. Mr

Peanut appeared on the cover of *FILE Magazine* in 1972 and made a series of public appearances in Vancouver the same year, as part of an effort to create "the atmosphere of an 'art city'" (Trasov n.d.). The Mr Peanut performances reached a peak in 1974 when, at the urging of sculptor John Mitchell, Mr Peanut threw his hat in the ring as a candidate for mayor of Vancouver. His campaign slogan was "Elect a nut for mayor," and his major campaign promise was that if elected, he would establish "lending libraries for umbrellas and galoshes" (Mitchell and Trasov n.d.). Trasov never spoke while in costume; he communicated only by tap-dancing, backed by his official chorus line, the Peanettes (artists associated with the Western Front); Mitchell, his campaign manager, interpreted Mr Peanut's dancing for the press. Although Mr Peanut ultimately lost the election, winning just 3.4 per cent of the vote, his campaign was considered a great artistic success (Mitchell and Trasov n.d.).

As Mr Peanut, Trasov faced criticism for his intervention in the mayoral race, with some of the more conventional candidates charging him with "undermining the seriousness of the democratic process" (Antliff 2005). This seems like a fair assessment. Indeed, it is echoed in the author William S. Burroughs' official endorsement of the Peanut candidacy: "Since the inexorable logic of reality has created nothing but insolvable problems, it is now time for illusion to take over. And there can only be one illogical candidate – Mr. Peanut" (cited in Trasov n.d.). In Fluxus terms, the Mr Peanut campaign is an outstanding example of Zen vaudeville, working at the intersection of meditation and laughter. Mr Peanut's own silence and his efforts to communicate outside a verbal framework, using his "body" and the bodies of the Peanettes, serve to interrupt the ritual speech of the serious candidates, their debates and press conferences. Like other Zen vaudeville performances, the Mr Peanut campaign functions as "an interruptive art that questions the power and pretensions of both frame and framer" (Doris 1998, 119). Where Friedman's vaudeville typically interrupts the art world, Mr Peanut interrupts the political world. This interruption prompts laughter from an audience trained to attend politely and obediently to the usual political rituals, and this laughter subverts the ritual by calling its authority into question. So Mr Peanut's mayoral campaign really does undermine the seriousness of the democratic process. On the other hand, as Doris has explained above, in the Fluxus understanding seriousness is a virtue only insofar as it reinforces the professional's position of mastery and privilege. When professional politicians insist that the democratic process be taken "seriously," then, they are implicitly asking their audience – in this case, the citizens of Vancouver – to respect that mastery and privilege by leaving politics to the professionals. The "democratic process" here is actually undemocratic. Mr Peanut's silent, comic presence saps that process of its power, returning power to the people in the form of explosive laughter. The campaign then, like Lewis's Great Wall, is anarchic (insofar as it undermines the seriousness of the democratic process) but also genuinely democratic (insofar as it traffics in a carnivalesque laughter that gives voice to the people).

This carnivalesque quality is amplified by the variety of border crossings that Trasov plays with as part of his performance. As an extension of the "art city" effort, it crosses the line separating art from politics, and as an appropriation of the commercial mascot for new purposes, it crosses the line separating art from commerce. The figure of Mr Peanut himself is of course a hybrid – both person and peanut. Trasov's donning the costume adds another layer to this, as a person dressed up like a peanut dressed up like a person. The interest in hybrid forms here owes a debt to Filliou and his eternal network, which offers a way of rethinking the self once the atomistic self-contained ego has been decentred.

CORRESPONDENCE SCHOOL (III): COLOUR BAR RESEARCH PROJECT

Border crossing is also at the heart of the Colour Bar Research Project. In the early 1970s, Morris, Trasov, Mick Henry, and Carole Itter purchased a property on British Columbia's Sunshine Coast, which they christened Babyland. One project Morris and Trasov undertook toward border crossing was Colour Bar Research. Together, they produced thousands of colour bars – wooden blocks painted in various colour spectrums – and placed them in the landscape. The infinite number of possible arrangements of the colour bars ("as ziggurat patterns on fields, let loose on streams, and floated on a lake" [Jacob 2002]) unfolded in parallel with the infinite number of possible arrangements of the bodies of Babyland's human visitors. Over the course of several years, Colour Bar Research explored and archived "the activities and interactions by an ensemble cast of naked performers with thousands of hand-painted colour bars that were floated on lakes, tossed into the air, and released down streams to randomly re-form – by the elements of nature and chance – into a series of endless paintings" (Rosales n.d.). Videos taken during this period capture the staging of Babyland as a pastoral Eden, in which visitors return to nature, and to their bodies.

One of the ideas being tested at Babyland was the possibility of overcoming "the binary fault line, nature/culture" (Watson 1992) and so restoring paradise through a reintegration of nature and culture. The Colour Bar Research Project sought to introduce artificial colour – culture – into the landscape and thereby cue the eye to notice colour in the landscape itself – nature. The project thus leveraged audience interest in culture in order to generate interest in nature. Morris and Trasov would insist that the project "marks the (visual and material) differences between nature and culture and the fluid boundary that lies within this relationship" (Morris and Trasov n.d., 2); what we see in Colour Bar Research, they say, is a form of "cultural ecology" (Morris and Trasov n.d., 2). In this respect, Colour Bar Research responds to a suggestion from the German Fluxus artist Joseph Beuys that the work of Fluxus must be to "continue along the road of interrelating socio-ecologically all the forces present in our society until we perform an intellectual action which extends to the fields of culture, economy, and democratic rights" (cited in Adams 1992, 28) and resonates with Anthony Wilden's understanding of ecology as a logic of non-compartmentalization. For the West Coast artists, it also reflected an understanding of the self in relation to environment that came naturally to them: working in Vancouver, "situated at the edge of the Pacific Ocean along a coastal mountain range, the question of political and artistic alternatives to mainstream culture were frequently shaped by the imposing presence of the natural environment" (Sava n.d.).

This is something quite different from the kind of deep ecology more often associated with American Buddhism, which emphasizes the preservation of pristine, wild nature and is resolutely non-anthropocentric – we might think here, for example, of Gary Snyder's call for "an immediate reduction of population, of human population" in service of the goal that "every animal that was here 200 years ago should be here now" (cited in Sale 1986, 32). Morris and Trasov's cultural ecology is much closer to social ecology, which understands nature and culture as mutually constitutive. Social ecology thus identifies ecological problems as arising from the same structures of domination that produce social problems; it therefore rejects the preservation of nature from culture that deep ecology seeks, and instead proposes that (interlinked) social and ecological problems be addressed through the creation of what Murray Bookchin describes as "a nonhierarchical cooperative society – a society that will live in harmony with nature because its members live in harmony with each other" (Bookchin 1987, 2). Social ecology has been overshadowed by deep ecology to such an extent that the contemporary reader might not recognize social ecology as a form of environmentalism, but it is clear that for Morris and Trasov the Colour Bar Research Project was an action intended to liberate both environment and participant.

Colour Bar Research explores Filliou's notion of the network in its focus on Babyland as a space in which the coming together and drifting apart of people and things can be observed and documented. Morris and Trasov explicitly appeal to Filliou's sense of the eternal network as dismantling the category of art and reintegrating art with life (Friz 2007) when they say that through the research, "Transported by the art, we will attain life. Life, which is the opposite of Art" (Trasov cited in Rosales n.d.). This, in fact, describes a situation in which the opposition of life and art has been overcome, in which life is "saturated" by art. The overcoming of this opposition was to arise interdependently with the overcoming of other oppositions – between artist and audience and between nature and culture. In this respect, the baby in Babyland might represent a return to the beginning of things, before the arising of a separation between self and other. A romantic vision of returning to a childlike state of innocence in which there is no estrangement from the body or from nature is blended here with an East Asian Buddhist vision of return to primordial non-duality and the recovery of one's original self.

The project also explores Zen silence through its effort to locate other sensory zones through which to think. The earthiness and frank eroticism of the project reflect Morris and Trasov's notion that Colour Bar Research takes "touch" as its object and "people and paintbrushes" as its materials (Trasov, cited in Rosales n.d.). In a 2009 exhibition in Germany, curator Grant Watson paired archival material from the Colour Bar Research project with nineteenth-century illustrations of Indian ascetics (Rosales n.d.). This might strike us as a strange choice, if we take the goings on at Babyland to be a form of self-indulgence. But for Morris and Trasov, the aim of Colour Bar Research was to transmute the body; they were not returning to an animal state of nature, but seeking instead a more absolute form of expression through the body. In this respect, the baby in Babyland might represent a return to a prelinguistic, polymorphously perverse state through which it becomes possible to discover new sensory zones and new modes of expression.

A SPACE FOR FLUXUS

A single gesture informs each of the projects we have considered here. This gesture points to an understanding of identity as generated between interrelated objects rather than secreted away within an independent subject. Sharla Sava describes the motive behind this gesture as follows: "Being attentive not only to things but to the space in which they came together, and perceiving individuals not as such but rather as shifting sites of intersubjective consciousness, seemed to offer a sense of life that was more attuned to the real" (Sava n.d.). Sava is talking about art and ecology here, not Buddhism, but Fluxus artists themselves understood this sense of the self as a site of intersubjective consciousness as derived from Buddhism, and where they found ways to successfully communicate it, they understood themselves as communicating in the language of Zen. It would be difficult if not impossible to make a case for the artists we have talked about here as serious Zen practitioners. Nonetheless, Zen was a formative influence of the West Coast artists working in correspondence with Friedman and Filliou, in the lineage of John Cage.

If we grant that their work had a Zen dimension, and include them in our history of Buddhism in Canada, what do we gain?

On the one hand, their inclusion draws our attention to the contributions of Buddhist thought to Canadian culture outside of the frame of multiculturalism and ethnographic studies. A common way of narrating the transmission of Buddhism to North America is in terms of a somewhat unidirectional process of adaptation, in which Asian cultures and values are reshaped and transformed in a North American setting. One effect of this, it seems to me, is that it gives the impression that Buddhism is perpetually arriving in North America for the first time – Buddhists coming to North America encounter a non-Buddhist culture, no matter whether they arrive in the nineteenth, twentieth, or twenty-first century. But in fact, Buddhist ideas have been in circulation in North America for close to two hundred years, and during this time, North American interpretations of Buddhist ideas have also been recirculated into Asia. Including the Fluxus artists in our study of Buddhism in Canada highlights the complexity of the networks through which Buddhist ideas travel. Recognizing the multiple ways in which Buddhist ideas would have been available to and incorporated by the West Coast artists in the 1970s helps us to see, I think, that the cultural shift Wilden describes from atom to ecosystem was not simply (by happy coincidence) *like* Buddhism in its outlook: it developed, in part, because people living in the same milieu as Wilden found in Buddhism a compelling set of concepts open to appropriation and redeployment.

On the other hand, it draws our attention to a moment in the history of North American Buddhism when Buddhism was different from itself. It seems to me, for instance, that scholarship on Buddhism and the queer community typically takes 1980 (the year San Francisco's Gay Buddhist Fellowship was founded) as a kind of starting point;[4] in this version of North American Buddhist history, the contributions of artists like Morris and Trasov (and Cage before them) are left out. This leads to a situation in which scholars of religion have to ask "what American Buddhists can learn from the gay liberation movement" (Storhoff and Whalen-Bridge 2010, 8) and queer theorists can conclude that "the strongly binarist gender system of Buddhism is resistant to" a queer understanding of identity, "especially if queer is taken to mean 'to fuck with gender'" (Yip 2010, 138). The fact that Buddhism was an intellectual resource for artists who were among the first to articulate a notion of queer identity is elided here, and as a result, so is the fact that somehow a great transformation has taken place unseen, from a moment in the 1970s when it seemed obvious that Buddhism could be deployed in support of a queer politics, to the present moment when Buddhism is understood as just beginning to recognize the existence of queer practitioners. Including Fluxus in our account of Buddhism in Canada brings that transformation to our attention, and allows us to wonder why it might have happened.

Similarly, both deep ecologists and social ecologists have tended to tie Zen to deep ecology, such that deep ecologists like Arne Naess and George Sessions identify Zen (as transmitted to them by Alan Watts and Gary Snyder) as a key influence on their thought. And a social ecologist like Bookchin likewise identifies Buddhism as one of a number of sources informing his opponents: "Deep ecology," he writes, "has parachuted into our midst quite recently from the Sunbelt's bizarre mix of Hollywood and Disneyland, spiced with homilies from Taoism, Buddhism, spiritualism, reborn Christianity, and in some cases eco-fascism" (Bookchin 1987, 3). Lost here is the memory of the articulation of a cultural ecology in Vancouver and Victoria during the 1960s and 1970s, its use of a conception of the network influenced by Fluxus (and via Fluxus, by Zen), and the many projects like Colour Bar Research that sought to contest "the assumed border between culture and nature" and realize utopian spaces (Sava n.d.). Including Fluxus in our history of Buddhism in Canada allows us to emend the historical record, and opens up new possibilities for Zen ecology in the present.

In Japan, Zen has cultivated a complicated self-representation – it is strict and severe, but also irreverent and iconoclastic. In its strictness and severity, it seems to resonate with American Protestantism: "the American ethos, with its promise of advancement based on initiative and hard work, is one in which Zen is at home" (Kjolhede 2000, 389). This was not at all the ethos of the Canadian West Coast in the 1970s. It was instead an ethos that privileged ex-centricity over advancement, free and easy wandering over initiative and hard work. And yet, the success of Fluxus suggests that this ethos, too, was one in which Zen, in its irreverent, iconoclastic aspect, could be at home.

NOTES

1 See illustration 9.
2 Available online at vancouverartinthesixties.com/archive/428.
3 This was spun off of Ray Johnson's New York Correspondence School, the key centre for mail art in the United States, and features in Metcalfe's rendering in illustration 9. Johnson dissolved the Correspondence School in 1973, re-establishing it the same year under the name Buddha University.
4 For example, see Cadge (2005a, 139–52); Corless (2000, 269–79); Prebish (1999, 79–81).

12

Shaping Images of Tibet: Negotiating the Diaspora through Ritual, Art, and Film

SARAH F. HAYNES

In 1950, after decades of tension between Tibet and China, China invaded Tibet and subsequently incorporated the country into the People's Republic of China. In response, a teenaged Dalai Lama assumed early leadership of Tibet; in 1959, he fled to India. Since then, thousands of Tibetans, following his example, have made their own journey into exile, eventually settling in India, Europe, and North America. At the request of the Dalai Lama, Canada began welcoming groups of Tibetan refugees in 1968, settling them in communities in Ontario, Quebec, Manitoba, and Alberta. Today, the largest of these communities is found in the Parkdale neighbourhood of Toronto.[1]

Tibetans began the process of adapting to their new geographical space and creating a new identity as Tibetans in exile immediately upon their arrival. Although many younger Tibetans have never been to Tibet, Tibetans in diaspora continue to identify with the Dalai Lama and their country of origin. In the process of creating this new diasporic identity, they re-imagine Tibet and its culture. This chapter examines the ritual and artistic processes through which Tibetans, both within and outside the diaspora, re-imagine Tibetan culture and religion, paying particular attention to the mechanisms involved. Specifically, it highlights three artistic media – painting, movies, and monastic performance – that span the traditional-modern divide. Tibetans in diaspora in Canada and wherever they are around the world, participate in the re-imagination of Tibetan religion and culture.

First, I argue that the use of ritual and art provides exiled Tibetans with a "space" to more easily negotiate identity and create an image of Tibetan religion and culture. Ritual and art serve as a means to create identity, albeit not always a homogeneous one, that allows Tibetans in exile to move beyond boundaries and to gain a degree of control over their political situation and status as refugees. Second, ritual and art enable non-Tibetans to join in this process of image creation. In other words, members of the Tibetan diaspora are not solely responsible for re-imagining Tibet. Furthermore, the re-imagination process does not result in a unified representation of Tibetan religion and culture. It is important to recognize that exceptions to a static symbolic representation of Tibet do exist. Finally, this process of re-imagining Tibet is not unique to Canada but is part of a larger global culture where images are constantly being created by the media, popular culture, etc. There is no one individual responsible for the re-imagination of Tibet and what it means to be Tibetan.

DELINEATING TERMS: DIASPORA, RITUAL, AND ART

The Tibetan diaspora has received a significant amount of attention from the academic world in the last twenty years, but little attention has been paid to the thriving Tibetan communities in Canada.[2] Since the Canadian government began accepting Tibetan refugees in the late 1960s, small but vibrant communities have developed, with major growth occurring in urban areas during the last ten years. The largest and most active of these communities is located in the West Toronto neighbourhood of Parkdale. While the Parkdale community is the most visible Tibetan community in Canada, there are exile communities of significant sizes in both urban and rural locations across the country. However, this chapter focuses on events in the communities in Toronto and Calgary.

It is not easy to define what characterizes the Tibetan diaspora. For over fifty years Tibetans have been negotiating borders, politics, and religion, typically all at the same time. Therefore, to speak of the Tibetan diaspora, and how one dwells both mentally and physically within it, as a uniform experience is to paint a wholly inaccurate picture. How an exiled Tibetan living in Nepal or India perceives her identity, religion, and culture may differ markedly from how an exiled Tibetan living in Toronto does, and what it means to be Tibetan varies from one individual to another.[3] Yet, by and large, the Tibetan community puts forth a uniform representation of itself. It is the uniformity of its representation that motivates this research.

While this chapter takes up issues related to diaspora, culture, and tradition, it does not provide restrictive definitions of these terms or outline definitive theories. With that caveat, the terms are employed as follows:

"diaspora" in the context of Tibetans typically refers to those dwelling outside the Tibetan Autonomous Region (TAR). This includes Tibetans living in South Asia (primarily India and Nepal), North America, and Europe. Specifically, the term "diaspora" is used in line with William Safran's six criteria that distinguish diaspora from other movements of peoples.

> (1) They, or their ancestors, have been dispersed from a specific original "center" to two or more "peripheral," or foreign, regions; (2) they retain a collective memory, vision, or myth about their original homeland – its physical location, history, and achievements; (3) they believe that they are not – and perhaps cannot be – fully accepted by their host society and therefore feel partly alienated and insulated from it; (4) they regard their ancestral homeland as their true, ideal home and as the place to which they or their descendants would (or should) eventually return – when conditions are appropriate; (5) they believe that they should, collectively, be committed to the maintenance or restoration of their original homeland and to its safety and prosperity; and (6) they continue to relate, personally or vicariously, to that homeland in one way or another, and their ethnocommunal consciousness and solidarity are importantly defined by the existence of such a relationship. (Safran 1991, 83–4)

The terms "exile," "exiled Tibetan," and "refugee Tibetan" are used interchangeably with "diaspora" and "diasporic Tibetan."[4]

The term "tradition(al)" is used to identify a collectively held understanding of what it means to be authentically *Tibetan* and/or representative of Tibet. Furthermore, what is considered "traditional" and "authentic" in the diaspora is often linked with pre-1959 Tibet. As Robertson notes, "The primary goal of Tibetan existence in exile today remains much as it did sixty years ago: the preservation of Tibetan culture 'in its pure form' before an eventual return to the homeland. This should be understood not only to mean the observable manifestations of culture (language, music, dress, religious practices, festivals and the like) but the deeper significance behind them, the 'essence' of culture itself, a sense of Tibetanness" (J. Robertson 2011, 48).

The preservation of Tibetan culture was an immediate concern of the Dalai Lama upon his arrival in India in 1959. The Tibetan Dance and Drama Society, the predecessor to what is now the Tibetan Institute of Performing Arts (TIPA), was the first institution to be set up in the exile community of Dharamsala. With the creation of TIPA the process of cultural preservation in exile began. However, it can also be argued that the process of adaptation began simultaneously. The moment traditional dances and artistic styles were performed and recreated in their diasporic contexts, adaptations occurred. These recreations were, and are, based on the need to preserve what the Dalai Lama identifies as external culture. Singer notes the Dalai Lama's distinction between *internal culture* and *external culture*. For the Dalai Lama, *internal culture* refers to the compassion and non-violence that he sees as the heart of Tibetans, while *external culture* refers to what Robertson calls the observable manifestations of culture: folk songs, dances, art, etc. (J. Robertson 2011, 48). This distinction is of interest because, "In the case of the Dalai Lama, he expresses and represents seemingly contradictory views on these subjects. While the Dalai Lama personally emphasizes the superior significance of internal culture, in Dharamsala, where he lives in northern India, and for many around the world, he is the most prominent symbol of external Tibetan culture" (Singer 2003, 234). As a religious figure he is employed in the diaspora in multiple ways – as political symbol, as teacher, as god, and for Westerners and Tibetans alike, as representative of all Tibetans. In fact, many view him much like they do the pope, as the head priest of an entire religion.

The Dalai Lama, held up as a universal icon for all Tibetans, is an example of what Jane Iwamura calls the Oriental Monk figure.[5] She writes: "The term Oriental Monk is used as a critical concept and is meant to cover a wide range of religious figures (gurus, bhikkhus, sages, swamis, sifus, healers, masters) from a variety of ethnic backgrounds (Japanese, Chinese, Indian, Tibetan). Although the range of individual figures points to a heterogeneous field of encounter, all of them are subjected to a homogeneous representational effect as they are absorbed by popular consciousness through mediated culture" (Iwamura 2011, 6). According to Iwamura the Dalai Lama is increasingly used as the model for the Oriental Monk figure (Iwamura 2011, 163). The Dalai Lama's narrative presents the characteristics of the standard Oriental Monk story: he is a solitary spiritual figure; he acts as a bridge of wisdom or a transmitter of knowledge to other cultures; and he represents hope. Yet this image of the Dalai Lama is being shaped and shifted by internal and external forces.

The perception of Tibet has gone through a similar process, although the media's image has yet to move beyond stereotypes. Early perceptions of Tibet were greatly affected by the Shangri-la image presented by early twentieth-century movies and books, especially *Lost Horizon* by James Hilton, published in 1933. This novel depicted Tibet, at that time a largely isolated country, as a mystical utopia. This idealized and romanticized presentation was perpetuated in early academic work on Tibet and exacerbated by research premised on Orientalism. This research is largely Eurocentric in nature, favouring distinctions between the "Orient" and "the Occident" – an "us" versus "them" approach. The Orientalist perspective created further assumptions that fed into the idea of Tibet as a mysterious, mystical, spiritual country, associated with Shangri-la. Ironically, this romantic image was being disseminated to North Americans and Europeans at a time when things were less than ideal or utopian for Tibetans.[6] This image has been slowly disappearing from academic work but continues to be perpetuated in the media, where the stereotypical image of the mystical enlightened monk is commonly presented as the uniform identity of Tibet.

It is this image that most non-academics associate with Tibet – the compassionate monk like the Dalai Lama. The struggle to control this image reflects real political conflict. Whereas in the past, non-Tibetans were responsible for presenting an essentialized and stereotypical image of Tibet – i.e., a uniform image that ultimately reduces something, in this case Tibet and what it means to be Tibetan, to a number of attributes that define it and come to represent its "essence" while ignoring the complexities and multidimensionality of individuals – currently, the stereotypical perception of Tibet is upheld by Tibetans. In addition to this reverse Orientalism, one needs to consider the attempts by the Chinese government to put forward an opposite stereotype about the Dalai Lama, the Tibetan people, and Tibet.

DANCING IN THE DIASPORA: SACRED PERFORMANCE AND CULTURAL PRESERVATION[7]

Tibetan Buddhist monastic dance (*'chams*) dates back to the eighth century and the legends of the great Padmasambhava, the individual responsible for taming the demons of Tibet at the behest of King Trisong Detsen.[8] Padmasambhava removed the evil forces through his great tantric powers and allowed for the spread of Buddhism in Tibet, beginning with the building of Samye monastery. Padmasambhava initiated the construction of the monastery by performing a dance to the powerful tantric deity Vajrakilaya (Pearlman 2002, 18). The connection between dance and Padmasambhava, arguably the most important figure in Tibetan Buddhist history, established the importance of ritual dance in Tibetan Buddhist practice.

Several scholars have studied the historical development of 'chams, yet little is definitely known.[9] Monastic dance appears in conjunction with several important figures in Tibetan history and in its earliest appearances is associated with the Nyingma school, often linked to Padmasambhava. The performance of monastic dance preceded the assassination of King Langdarma in 842 CE, an event in Tibetan history that is often seen as making possible the re-blossoming of Buddhist teachings (Kohn 2001, 156). Several hundred years later, 'chams appears in the written works of the Fifth Dalai Lama (1617–82); specifically, a 'chams yig or dance manual is attributed to him. Regardless of the less than concrete historical sources for monastic dance, it clearly remains an integral part of the mythic-historical memory of Tibetan Buddhism. Its connection to significant events and individuals provides it with legitimacy as an important cultural tradition. Since my concern is with monastic dance in the creation of Tibetan identity in diaspora, I will only briefly detail traditional 'chams performances before shifting to an examination of its adaptation for North American audiences.

Traditional monastic dances were created to serve multiple purposes. A 'chams performance often takes place over several days and involves the attendance and participation of hundreds of people. A performance may be undertaken in honour of a deity, as a tantric initiation (*dbang*), or as a celebration or blessing. Traditionally, the performances would take place in a monastic setting, temple, or within a village. Significantly, despite an apparently loosely structured ritual practice, these performances are considered sacred performances or rituals within the control of religious specialists. Observers often incorrectly assume that these dances are done for the benefit of the lay practitioners; in fact, the primary purpose of 'chams is the meditative advancement of the dancer.[10] These dances are in fact tantric practices. As in tantric ritual, a monastic dance moves through three stages – introduction or preparation, generation or fulfillment, and conclusion – each stage more complex and detailed than the previous. The dancer is expected to be an advanced meditation practitioner with the ability to visualize *yidams* (tutelary deities) and intricate mandalas during the generation and fulfillment stage. Wisdom beings descend upon the dancer during the creation stage, as the dancer generates the *yidam* from his stability of mind, and then visualizes his body as the *yidam*, his speech as mantra, and his mind as clarity, emptiness, and luminosity. After the dancer visualizes himself as the *yidam*, he visualizes the *yidam* in front, looking back at him. During the phase of the dance when the *yidam* is invoked, practitioners assume the disposition of the deity, whether wrathful, semi-wrathful, or peaceful (Pearlman 2002, 59). The dance is not about the footwork, detailed as it is; the focus should be on the meditative reality being created during the performance. As Schrempf indicates, the movement together with the meditative state and visualizations transform the dancer and the ritual space (Schrempf 1994, 108).

Although present in North America and Europe prior to 1959, it is only within the last twenty years that *'chams* has risen to prominence and taken on entirely new dimensions. The monastic dances that are typically seen in North America are amalgamations of traditional Tibetan, secular, and religious dances. These dances are altered to fit a shortened time frame and are performed outside their intended context. Having observed many performances in both Canada and the United States by different dance troupes, I can attest to the similarity among them. Currently there are several monastic troupes that travel across North America performing for large audiences comprising both Tibetans and non-Tibetans.[11] The most prolific of these troupes, sponsored by Richard Gere's production company, is based in Atlanta, Georgia at the North American branch of Drepung Loseling.[12] The troupe tours under the title *The Mystical Arts of Tibet*, and each stop on the tour usually includes an evening of monastic dance and the creation of a sand mandala over a period of several days.

The commonalities among the monastic performances are far greater than their differences. For instance, the black dance, the yak dance, and various invocations and multiphonic chants are always performed. Typically, there is an introductory statement about Tibet, the performers, Buddhism, and the Tibetan political situation, but very little commentary about the performances. Some performances include short explanations about each dance; others include this material in the program handed out at the entrance to the theatre. The major distinction of note between performances is the inclusion of monastic debate by the Mystical Arts of Tibet troupe. Monastic debate is a distinctly religious, specifically monastic, practice that falls outside the boundaries of traditional entertainment. Furthermore, the inclusion of monastic debate as performance is an odd choice since it is done entirely in Tibetan language and with no translation.

The first monastic performance I attended was by the monks of Gaden Tsawa Monastery at the downtown branch of the Calgary public library in June 2005.[13] My only previous experience with Tibetan Buddhist monks performing on stage had been a brief encounter at a Beastie Boys concert in Toronto in 1994, an experience similar to that described by McMahan in the opening scene of his book *The Making of Buddhist Modernism* where Tibetan Buddhist monks took to the stage of a hip nightclub in a college town.[14] When walking into a monastic performance by a group of monks, one always sees the same general scene. As at a rock concert, merchandise is sold in the lobby – CDs, prayer flags, Free Tibet paraphernalia, incense, reprints of *thangkas* (wall hangings), mandalas, and other symbols associated with Tibet and Tibetan Buddhism. But I realized, after attending several more performances, that the Calgary performance was unique. The performance itself was not different: the audience was. Calgary has an active Tibetan community whose members constituted a very large presence in the crowd, in contrast to other monastic performances I have attended where the Tibetan presence is small. In addition, the Calgary community is involved in raising awareness about Tibet's political situation and supporting the Tibetan community as a whole. The Calgary Tibetan community is actively engaged in the larger community, where one often sees them protesting outside the Chinese consulate, and encounters them as an influential group at the University of Calgary. In contrast, at another performance I was sitting two seats away from a young Tibetan man, a former monk turned academic. There were few Tibetans present that evening and as we left the theatre the young Tibetan man laughed at what he had just witnessed. He commented to our group, "This was not authentic. It was not what monks do." In fact, without knowing my area of research, he declared, "Someone should study this." The major difference between this performance and the one in Calgary was the composition of the audience. The Calgary audience was largely Tibetan. The second performance was held in conjunction with an academic conference. Therefore, although it was open to the public, few Tibetans were present and the audience was mostly academics from around the world.

Regardless of the reaction of the audience and the ritual adaptation that occurs, such performances are responsible for creating an image of Tibet and Tibetan Buddhism that resonates with many Tibetans and non-Tibetans alike. While skepticism was evident in the former monk turned academic, these performances have served as a successful means of advocating a certain political position and positing an understanding of what it means to be Tibetan.

> Practitioners, performers, and audiences need not agree on the meaning of a ritual in order to agree that a ritual is important. It is important that participants consider their ritual important but not that they agree upon, or even know, the meanings of their actions. By agreeing that a ritual is crucial, people define themselves as part of a group whose members share the experience and knowledge of that event … alterations of ritual practices into performance or art, changes made to meet the expectations of a specific audience, and commodifications of rituals all imply statements about who people are or wish to become. (Dubois et al. 2011, 49–50)

Ultimately, the monastic performances employ the symbols of Tibetan Buddhism, the culture of Tibet (which for many are inseparable), and the current political situation as a way to negotiate identity in the diaspora. One only needs to look at the stage at a monastic performance to understand how this works. The *Mystical Arts of Tibet* tour has minimal props on stage during the performance. When one walks into the theatre and looks at the stage, one sees traditional Tibetan instruments – horns, cymbals, and drums. However, what immediately attracts one's attention is the backdrop and the altar that sits directly in front of it. The backdrop is a huge mural of the Potala Palace, the Dalai Lama's former winter residence in Lhasa. The image of the Potala Palace is iconic, symbolic of the past and what once was. The palace is named after the location where the bodhisattva of compassion, Avalokiteshvara, dwells, another important symbol for Tibet and Tibetan Buddhism (the Dalai Lamas are said to be reincarnations of Avalokiteshvara.) The image of the Potala sits behind a sizable altar that holds an image of His Holiness the 14th Dalai Lama. The photo is draped with a *khata*, a white silk ceremonial scarf symbolizing purity and compassion and often given as a blessing. Also on the altar and elsewhere on the stage are other iconic symbols associated with Tibet and Tibetan Buddhism. A large Tibetan flag with the snow lion hangs in one corner of the backdrop; in the other corner is the five coloured flag associated with Buddhism.

On this stage, through the props and the performance, an idealized past and an idealized Tibet are recreated. The monastic performances help create an identity that reinforces a romanticized understanding of Tibet and Tibetan Buddhism.[15] Under the guise of preserving cultural and religious traditions, the monastic performers are actively engaged in creating an image of what it means to be Tibetan (see Dorjee and Giles 2005). This image and this process of negotiation are reminiscent of the Orientalizing process that Westerners were guilty of decades ago. Western scholars, missionaries, and government representatives created an essentialized and static image of the Orient that politically justified the Western colonization of Asia (Said 1979). In negotiating the diaspora, the political situation, and what it means to be Tibetan today, a reverse Orientalism has occurred where Tibetans in the diaspora are presenting a static, essentialized notion of what it means to be Tibetan. To complicate matters further, the Chinese government attempts to create an image of Tibet and the Dalai Lama that counters the reverse Orientalist perspective.

The Parkdale area of Toronto is home to a large Tibetan community for whom the preservation of Tibetan culture is a priority. This is evident in the number of cultural events hosted by the community, and specifically in the involvement of students of all ages in Tibetan music and dance programs. Tibetan students are able to take classes in traditional Tibetan instruments and dance styles, often forming youth performance troupes and giving public performances. In describing Tibetan youth performance troupes in Toronto, Robertson notes:

> Here lies an example of the multiple representations of Tibetanness. Was it a Tibetan performance framed in multiculturalism, multiculturalism framed in a Tibetan performance, or something else? Were the performers primarily presenting their culture to the outside world, or rather to the geographically inside world (Parkdale), or was its goal

Tibetan cultural transmission to other Tibetans, and all else is peripheral? It seems from my own observations that in this performance, like all Tibetan performances, a variety of frames were being employed as Tibetans attempted to negotiate their identity both for themselves and for others. (J. Robertson 2011, 139)

There are obvious differences between the monks who do the monastic performances and the children who perform in youth troupes. But the same process of negotiation occurs. On the one hand, monastic performances are done for audiences composed primarily of non-Tibetans, whereas the Parkdale youth performance was for a largely Tibetan audience. However, the performances by both are marked by the need to present an image of what it means to be Tibetan in the diaspora and what is authentically Tibetan and representative of Tibetan Buddhism. "The creation of a pre-1959 Tibet on the stage where the Dalai Lama is openly displayed is an attempt at preserving what it means to be Tibetan." Earlier, Robertson comments:

It is argued here that for many émigré Tibetans the performance space might be where the "real" Tibetan world is recreated, and the staged performance the vehicle through which that world is experienced. For the performers themselves, the rehearsal space is where the Tibetan world is structured, with the stage the place where the world is performed ... When the properly framed performance moves fully to the front (the physical stage) and is accepted by the audience as authentic (authenticity being dependent upon the frame and the performance itself), it becomes a definite sign of Tibetanness and, for many, a fulfillment of the *raison d'être* in exile. (J. Robertson 2011, 120)

Here we see that cultural preservation, specifically *external culture*, becomes the reason for existence for some diasporic Tibetans. While the Dalai Lama upholds the superiority of *internal culture*, here we see *external culture* and symbols of Tibetanness strengthening the yearning for the homeland which defines diasporic existence.

The Parkdale community has the highest concentration of Tibetans in Canada. However, the site of many community events is the Tibetan Canadian Cultural Centre (TCCC) in South Etobicoke, in the western suburbs of Toronto.[16] The mission of the TCCC is "*to preserve, foster and share the rich and distinct Tibetan culture in Canada.* In today's increasingly diverse and multicultural Canadian society, our mission will be met in a spirit of co-operation and harmony among people of different cultures. We will work on developing and fostering community spirit by promoting anti-oppressive practices through civic engagement, adult education, elder care, social service, athletics, arts, recreation, Tibetan system of medicine, astronomy and astrology, moral education and other community endeavors [italics mine]" (http://www.tcccgc.org/mission/). Additionally, the TCCC website outlines the vision and goals of the community centre:

> To be the premiere centre in Canada to develop and build community engagement for the promotion of moral values, peace and religious harmony by sharing the value of distinct Tibetan arts, culture and heritage ... To create awareness and understanding of the unique Tibetan culture and tradition within Canada's multicultural and inclusive society, to promote harmony and friendship in our diverse society ... To serve newcomers by offering a variety of service including settlement service such as job development service, referral services; youth programs such as language classes, music & dance classes, *thangka* painting classes; and health and wellness programs such as meditation classes, Tibetan medical counseling camps, and yoga classes. (http://www.tcccgc.org/mission/)

The TCCC, in conjunction with the Parkdale community, is engaging in cultural preservation initiatives that extend beyond the youth troupes. Performing arts classes are offered on the weekends to children up to the age of 18, as are lessons in traditional Tibetan instruments and Tibetan language. A special program for seniors offers a variety of lessons and workshops related to Tibetan culture, and educational resources on life in Canada. The TCCC's programs clearly focus on the preservation of Tibetan culture. A large portion of its website is devoted to showcasing traditional Tibetan art, dance, and music, but there are also links to documentary footage about life in the Tibetan diaspora in Canada and a Tibetan language short movie written by a local Toronto director.

BREAKING FREE OF TRADITION: ART IN THE TIBETAN
DIASPORA

The relationship between art, politics, and religion has been well attested in all cultures throughout history; one only needs to look at protest songs, street art, and paintings like Picasso's *Guernica*. While traditional Tibetan Buddhist artistic styles, such as *thangka* painting (wall hangings) and sand mandalas, are used by artists in exile, one also sees exiled Tibetan artists breaking free of tradition to express what it means to be Tibetan beyond the stereotypical caricature of a Tibetan Buddhist. Two Tibetan artists who have transcended the stereotype through their art are Gonkar Gyatso and Ang Tsherin Sherpa.

The Toronto Tibetan community held its first, and what it is hoped will be annual, *Art for Tibet Canada* gallery show in October 2011. Modeled after the successful *Art for Tibet* I and II shows in New York, the *Art for Tibet Canada* show was sponsored by Students for a Free Tibet Canada, who used the event to raise money through a charity auction. The show highlighted contemporary art related to Tibet, by both Tibetan and non-Tibetan artists, in a variety of artistic styles, including photography, traditional Tibetan painting, and modern interpretations of traditional Tibetan styles. The call for submissions stated that "Art plays a vital role in Tibetan culture, and has long been a profound tool for social and political change" (Art for Tibet Canada Benefit Event Committee 2011). While all of the art shown was worthy of discussion in its own right, what is interesting here is the use of traditional and anti-traditional artistic styles in the negotiation of identity.

Ang Tsherin Sherpa is a Nepali-born contemporary Tibetan artist now living in California who has exhibited work in Toronto. The homepage of his website bears the title "For the Preservation of Thangka Art" below which are seemingly traditional representations of Tibetan deities (Sherpa n.d.). At the bottom of the page is the option to view "contemporary" art and it is here that one sees anti-traditional representations of Tibetan art. The painting Ang Tsherin Sherpa displayed in Toronto was titled "Things That Pop in My Head." The image is reminiscent of traditional Tibetan Buddhist representations of a mandala and a deity, yet the head of the individual is replaced with an array of images related to Asian religions, popular culture, modernity, and so on. According to Sherpa, "In

California, being Tibetan often means being depicted as a 'Shangri-la being'[17]... Sometimes I come across people who think everyone from Tibet is enlightened. That puts a lot of pressure on someone like me, because I feel I am as ordinary as anybody else. This piece [Things That Pop in My Head] tries to show that, with pop icons 'popping' in my head and is a self-portrait of sorts."[18] Instead of representing himself, as a Tibetan, by using traditional art or culture, he has infused his representation of himself with modern representations of popular culture. Sherpa has used his art as a way to turn the stereotypical and essentialized representation of what it means to be Tibetan on its head.

Another example of a Tibetan artist moving beyond an essentialized notion of Tibetan identity is UK-based artist Gonkar Gyatso, who was also involved with the Art for Tibet project. Gyatso is a Lhasa-born artist trained in Beijing and London. While still in Tibet, Gyatso, together with a group of artists, engaged "in heated discussions about the future of Tibetan culture and their paintings acted as catalysts in the debate about modernity and Sinicization. Their stated aim was to produce a new type of art which was both specifically Tibetan (rather than Chinese) and explicitly anti-traditionalist in form" (Harris 2006, 702). Upon arrival in Dharamsala, Gyatso experienced a sort of backlash against his attempts at innovation and modernization of Tibetan art. Harris writes:

> By the 1990s what I have termed the "preservation in practice ethos" of the exile government held sway in Dharamsala and a religio-cultural definition of Tibetan-ness was paramount. The Sinicization and secularization of Tibet itself led the exiles to see themselves as the custodians of Tibetan traditionalism and in this, artists were key players. They produced murals of the exilic replication of monasteries, *thangka* for the commemoration of the dead and figures of the Buddha to be placed in every orphanage and office throughout the refugee community. As the living embodiments of long-standing artistic lineages, they were revered by other Tibetans for providing a link to the past and for activating in visible form the Tibet of their memories. Both exilic art and artists, therefore, had a claim to authenticity of a sort Gonkar Gyatso could not compete with and in the conservative atmosphere of Dharamsala he rapidly became caught in the no man's land of conflicting conceptions of who or what was truly Tibetan. (Harris 2006, 703)

The issue of what and who is authentically Tibetan arises in different contexts among diasporic Tibetans. Tensions exist within the exile community regarding Tibetans from Tibet appearing Chinese and not reflecting the representation of Tibet that is upheld in exile communities. Reflecting on her own experiences in the diasporic community and the lack of a unified understanding of what is authentically Tibetan, Emily Yeh notes that the "staged performances of 'Tibetan culture' ... fracture the imagined unity of a seamless diasporic community" (Yeh 2007, 649).

In navigating the diaspora through his art, Gyatso has used traditional imagery and symbolism associated with Tibetan Buddhism, but like Ang Tsherin Sherpa, he has pushed the boundaries. A series of digitally altered photographs titled "My Identity" question what it means to be Tibetan, to be a representation of a religion, a culture, and a political situation. Regarding his own work, Gyatso notes:

> As my own experience has been one that reflects a kind of hybridity and transformation my work also holds this quality. We are all repositories of our time and place and I think the work can not help but reveal the politics and cultures that have shaped me. In this way my work has a spatial and temporal component to them; where time and place collide into each other. While in the past I have not intentionally been overtly political, I have explored political themes. And just as the identity of my motherland, Tibet, can not be separated from religion and politics, I think my own sensibility has been shaped by the undeniable bond between the two.[19]

Without rejecting politics and culture, Gyatso has moved beyond the essentialized presentation of what it means to be Tibetan. Art has allowed him to explore issues related to politics and religion, yet in a way that has enabled him to gain control of what it means to identify with Tibet and not fall back on a static understanding. Both Gyatso and Sherpa are examples of exiled Tibetans who are anti-traditional, in that they do not represent the stereotypical version of a Tibetan, even though they may employ traditional Tibetan artistic techniques. These two artists offer only token concessions to those who argue for homogeneity within diasporic art. In fact, they are exceptions to the diasporic construction of a unified identity and image of Tibet.

MODERN MEDIA AS A METHOD OF PRESERVATION AND MEANS OF RE-IMAGINATION: FILM IN THE TIBETAN DIASPORA[20]

The Canadian film community has long had an interest in movies on the subject of Tibet.[21] In recent years a number of documentaries have been made about the Tibetan diasporic community in Toronto. The Canadian Tibetan Association of Ontario has sponsored the production of several videos of the Dalai Lama's visits to Toronto, including "The Power of Compassion"; in addition, a documentary titled "Champion of Compassion" was made by Endless Knot Films, a company devoted to preserving Tibetan culture through the making of movies, music videos, and photography.[22] The last few years have seen a slew of video footage from a Toronto-based Indie filmmaker named Tharchin Y. Goenpo. Goenpo hosts a YouTube channel in conjunction with Tibetwood Films Canada that streams footage from around Toronto's Tibetan communities. Included in these videos are cultural performances, hunger strikes, and meetings from the TCCC. Goenpo has also made a short movie about Tibetans living in the diaspora called *My Precious Si*.[23]

The most active organization in the production of film related to Tibet has been and continues to be the National Film Board of Canada (NFB). Over the last twenty years the NFB has sponsored seven documentary films related to Tibet.[24] All deal with the diaspora in one way or another, covering a range of topics related to Tibetan Buddhism, including the performance of the *Tibetan Book of the Dead* in a Ladakhi community in northern India, narrated by Leonard Cohen.

The earliest of the NFB films, *A Song for Tibet*, opens with two monks performing the Black Hat Dance, often included in the monastic performances in North America. The film then moves to a man singing a traditional Tibetan song while playing the Tibetan lute. He narrates an account of his involvement in the creation of TIPA and his subsequent journey to life in exile in Canada, where he teaches the cultural traditions of Tibet to those living in exile. The film then follows a young exiled Tibetan woman from Canada back to India where she visits Dharamsala, the heart of the exile community. Her arrival in Dharamsala is marked with the performance of traditional Tibetan folk song and dance. *A Song for Tibet* thus makes the connection between religion, politics, and culture very clear.

Three of the seven NFB films deal with important Tibetan Buddhist teachers. The 2009 film *Tulku* focuses on the son of Chögyam Trungpa Rinpoche, the teacher responsible for the development of the Halifax Shambhala community (Mukpo 2009). A *tulku* (Tib: *sprul sku*, Skt: *nirmānakāya*) is literally an "apparitional body" and refers to the reincarnation of a high-ranking lama. The lineage of the Dalai Lama is a notable example of a *tulku* lineage. *Tulku* follows Trungpa's son Gesar Mukpo as he deals with the difficulty of being recognized as the reincarnation of an important Buddhist teacher. The film examines the issues regarding the recognition of *tulkus* outside Tibet, many of whom are non-Tibetan, and the struggles these individuals face as they try to navigate their lives in the modern world as the recognized reincarnations of Tibetan Buddhist masters.

Words of My Perfect Teacher is probably the best known of the NFB films related to Tibet. The film follows Dzongsar Khyentse Norbu, the monk/film director responsible for *The Cup* (Norbu 2002) and *Travelers and Magicians* (Norbu 2005). The film details the daily life of Khyentse Norbu and his students as he journeys across Europe, Canada, the United States, and Bhutan, all the while getting involved in activities not typically associated with monks (Norbu 2005). The popularity of the film has, no doubt, to do with the popularity of Khyentse Norbu himself, but also with its more lighthearted nature and the appearances of numerous celebrities.

It is clear that the National Film Board of Canada has been supportive of films related to Tibet and Tibetan Buddhism for the last twenty years. What is worth further discussion is the use of film as a means of negotiating politics, religion, and culture. Immediately after 1959 Tibetans began using traditional performance styles as tools of resistance against their political situation (Ahmed 2006, 151). Today we see modern technologies, such as the films of the NFB, as tools of resistance.[25] The NFB films are used to bring awareness of the political situation of Tibetans and to highlight the cultural traditions and current status of Tibetan Buddhism in the diaspora. These movies simultaneously support the romanticized view of Tibet and present individuals within the diasporic community questioning its traditions.

The NFB films raise the question of who are the agents responsible for the re-imagining of Tibet. More specifically, one can ask this question based on geography. Who are the agents responsible for shaping the image of Tibet in the West? Who is responsible for alternative images? How does

China figure into the re-imagining of Tibet and the Dalai Lama? Until now, it appears that the Tibetan diaspora has been solely responsible for this process of re-imagining within the West.[26] However, the filmmakers involved in these movies include Tibetans and non-Tibetans. Therefore, it is not just the Tibetan diaspora that is responsible for creating images about the Tibetan diaspora.[27] While these movies involve a working relationship between those within the diaspora and those outside in creating an image of Tibet, this is not the only instance of this occurring. For instance, Richard Gere's production company is the force behind the *Mystical Arts of Tibet* monastic troupe. Furthermore, one sees those within the diaspora working together with those outside the diaspora in Students for a Free Tibet, a group that is very influential in shaping images of Tibet.

POLITICS, RITUAL, AND CULTURE IN THE TIBETAN DIASPORA

The negotiation of identity within the Tibetan diaspora is compounded by several factors, politics being the most significant. However, one cannot ignore how the Western fascination with Tibet and Tibetan Buddhism has impacted this process of negotiation. As has been well-documented, Western interest in Tibet, its culture and religion, resulted in the perception of Tibet as a Shangri-la. Recognizing the Western fascination with Tibet and using this to their advantage, neo-orientalist strategies have been employed by the exile community to aid the Tibetan cause, both political and cultural.[28] As Harris notes, "An exilic elite of religious figures and artists, writers, performers and musicians has been at the forefront of the promotion of what is in fact an invented tradition of what it means to be Tibetan after 1959: an invention defined in terms of the imagined communities of Tibetan Buddhism and neo-nationalism" (Harris 1999, 42-3). The Tibetan exile community has consciously used ritual and art as a means of negotiating what it means to be Tibetan, although it is not alone in this task. Through the creative process, of both ritual and art, the Tibetan diaspora and Westerners have put forth an idealized and nearly uniform understanding of Tibetan identity. However, by using ritual and art as a means of negotiating identity and presenting a particular image of Tibet to the outside world, diasporic Tibetans are dealing with the current political situation in a way that allows them a modicum of control. Not only are they using media such as art, ritual performance, and movies that appeal to Westerners but they are also employing methods that allow for the manipulation of powerful symbols and icons.

The use of the Dalai Lama as an icon of the Oriental Monk figure symbolic of Tibet and Tibetan Buddhism, or the appropriation of Buddhist ideas for use in the political arena lends weight to what is identifiably Tibetan. As Grimes notes, "icons span the domains of media and ritual. The term icon refers not only to tiny pictograms on computer desktops but also to ritually executed, liturgically venerated images of saints and divine beings. In ritual circumstances, icons do not merely refer or point to something; rather, they incarnate or embody it" (Grimes 2011, 15–16). The symbolism of Tibet as Shangri-la and the Dalai Lama and Buddhism as indicative of what it means to be Tibetan points toward the attempt to unify the diaspora. Even though the Chinese government has attempted to fracture this unity, ritual and art are able to unify past, present, and future. As Kertzer writes, "ritual helps give meaning to our world in part by linking the past to the present and the present to the future ... by repetitively employing a limited pool of powerful symbols, often associated with emotional fervor, rituals are an important molder of political belief" (Kertzer 1996, 340; see also 344). The majority of monastic performances, art, and movies attempt to preserve a pre-1959 understanding of Tibetan culture.

Through ritual and art, diasporic Tibetans have indeed engaged in inverted Orientalist strategies, but in a way that allows them to take partial control of the representation of Tibet to the outside world and to have some control over their liminal status. In his discussion of Tibetan protest, Schwartz notes the ability of ritual to help overcome powerlessness and provide a sense of cohesion or *communitas*. "Through protest Tibetans are able to overcome their objective powerlessness, and experience both solidarity and equality as they mutually acknowledge their common nationhood ... ritual is a way of solving problems, of resolving, in the form of a drama of symbols, conflicts and contradictions in social life that admit to no real solution" (Schwartz 1994, 20–1). I argue that the same process is occurring in the diaspora through the romanticization of Tibet and the use of the Dalai Lama and Buddhism as powerful symbols. These symbols not only create a uniform representation of Tibet to the outside world but also attempt to bring cohesiveness to the exile community. As noted in Robertson's study of the Toronto Tibetan community, one of the most valued aspects of this community is the cohesiveness they share in comparison to others (J. Robertson 2011, 3n9). The cohesiveness within the diasporic community continues to grow stronger despite the Chinese government's ongoing protests and rhetoric. The Chinese consistently present the Dalai Lama as a separatist who is working to undermine the government and stability within the Tibetan Autonomous Region instead of as a peaceful symbol of Tibet and its religion and culture.[29]

Finally, it must be acknowledged that the uniform representation of Tibet and what it means to be Tibetan is not entirely accurate. Ultimately, the mechanisms that create images of Tibetan culture and religion are not located in one particular country or one group of individuals. Stereotypical images of Tibet are a result of decades of oversimplification of complex issues related to religion, culture, and politics. Furthermore, journalism, broadcast media, and the Internet perpetuate these stereotypical images in a way that ignores these details and complexity. In the age of the Internet, where images and stories go viral, a uniform presentation of Tibet is even more of a challenge. The media tends to present one side, the side that presents a memorable story, and not the multidimensional truth behind the history of Tibet and what it means to be Tibetan. This chapter has shown how this global process has manifested in Canada.

The complexity of the re-imagining process is not unique to Canada. As Diehl notes, "an extended stay with Tibetan refugees taught me that public representations of Tibetan-ness and the lives of Tibetans have tended to grossly smooth over the striking unevenness of experiences encompassed in refugee lives" (Diehl 2002, 20). In her study of music in Tibetan refugee communities, Diehl observed the creation of an essentialized Tibetan identity does not speak to the range of opinions, beliefs, and identities recognized by Tibetans. In fact, there are diasporic Tibetans who are negotiating identity in different ways. Recognizing that the perception of a "Shangri-la being" is dominant in the West, artists, musicians, and performers are bending the rules of traditional Tibetan practices. This will only continue as the Tibetan diaspora moves into third and fourth generations.

The conscious efforts of the Dalai Lama and other diasporic Tibetans to preserve cultural traditions in a way that highlights a pre-1959 idealized and essentialized Tibet has allowed the community to succeed in raising awareness about Tibet's political situation. However, one cannot ignore the fact that an inverted Orientalism is occurring in this process, not to mention how China attempts to affect the re-imagining process. As Diehl notes, "traditions are selected and ever changing. A number of important publications have problematized the notion of 'tradition' by revealing it to be selective, invented, and/or symbolically constructed" (Diehl 2002, 3). As the fight for the preservation of Tibetan external culture continues, whether it be through painting, movies, or monastic performance, the Tibetan diasporic community is going to have to recognize that traditional culture is being constantly adapted: therefore, one can question what "traditions" are actually being preserved.

NOTES

1 In 1997 the Canadian Tibetan Association of Ontario (www.ctao.org) identified 133 individuals in the Toronto Tibetan community. In 2004 the number of Tibetans in Toronto was approximately 3,000 to 4,000. Official statistics estimate the number at 4, 275 by 2006. However, John Robertson notes that the Tibetan community claims that there are 10,000 members. If true, the Toronto Tibetan community is the largest in North America, surpassing the community in New York (J. Robertson 2011).
2 Exceptions include Logan (2010), McLellan (1999), and J. Robertson (2011).
3 For detailed discussions of the distinctions regarding what it means to be "Tibetan," see Dorjee and Giles (2005), Houston and Wright (2003), and Yeh (2007).
4 The use of these terms is worth further consideration in another paper. This categorization becomes more problematic since exile communities of Tibetans are now into the second generation. However, I argue that the terms remain employable since the Tibetan diasporic community continues to hold onto the notion of return.
5 See Iwamura (2011). Specific mention of the Dalai Lama occurs in her conclusion.
6 The early twentieth-century construction of Tibet as Shangri-la is much more nuanced than covered here. The most comprehensive work on the subject is Donald S. Lopez Jr's *Prisoners of Shangri-la* (1998). While this image of Tibet was being perpetuated, Tibet was facing growing tension and opposition from China.
7 See Haynes (2013) for further discussion of monastic performance in North America.
8 See Yeshe Tsogyel (1978) for further information regarding the importance of Padmasambhava.
9 See Hansen (1996), Kohn (2001), Pearlman (2002), Ricard (2003), and Schrempf (1994) for detailed histories and characteristics of *'chams*.

10 It is worth noting that different types of *'chams* exist, including those (*'chams gar*) that are done in secret for the benefit of the lamas.
11 Monastic performance troupes are found in other Buddhist traditions, including Korean and Chinese.
12 Drepung Loseling is a monastery built in Lhasa in the fifteenth century. After 1959, monks from Drepung rebuilt the monastery in Mundgod, Karnataka in South India. A North American branch was built in Atlanta, Georgia in 1991.
13 The monks from this troupe are affiliated with the Gaden Monastery in Mundgod, Karnataka, India.
14 This is worthy of a paper in itself. See McMahan (2008, 3) for a description of this experience.
15 See Donald S. Lopez Jr (1998), for a detailed examination of the romanticization of Tibet.
16 http://www.tcccgc.org. In 2004, while in Toronto for the Kalachakra, the Dalai Lama blessed the development of the TCCC. In 2008 the Tibetan community acquired the site in South Etobicoke.
17 See Huber's discussion of the reinvention of a modern Shangri-la image (2001, 358).
18 Painting and quotation can be found at http://www.flickr.com/photos/tentseringc/6252302700/in/photostream.
19 http://buddhismwoot.weebly.com/gonkar-gyatso.html
20 Another use of media that would be an interesting study is Radio Tibet Toronto, an FM stationed launched in 2007.
21 It is worth noting that the Toronto Tibetan community, sponsored by the Canada Tibet Committee and Students for a Free Tibet Canada, has been hosting the Toronto Tibet Film Festival beginning in 2005. The festival screens movies related to Tibet, its culture, religion, and history and movies that showcase Tibetan filmmakers. The festival often includes appearances by individuals associated with the Tibetan political cause, including activists and journalists. The festival does not limit its selections to Canadian filmmakers, but tends to include films produced by the National Film Board of Canada (NFB).
22 http://www.endlessknotfilms.com/ekf/welcome.html
23 The movie can be found on YouTube.
24 A search of the NFB collection results in the following titles related to Tibet: *A Song for Tibet* (1991), *Tibetan Book of the Dead: A Way of Life & The Great Liberation* (1994), *Spirit of Tibet: Journey to Enlightenment, the Life and World of Dilgo Khyentse Rinpoche* (1998), *Words of my Perfect Teacher* (2003), *What Remains of Us* (2008), *The Trap* (2008), and *Tulku* (2009).

25 Other modern technologies are employed in preservation and awareness efforts. For instance, the Dalai Lama is an active Twitter user, and there are Facebook pages for different chapters of Students for a Free Tibet and for different lamas popular in the diaspora.
26 While China attempts to present a certain negative image of the Dalai Lama, it has been relatively unsuccessful in gaining supporters for this perspective in the West.
27 One only needs to look at the involvement of influential Westerners such as Richard Gere as an example.
28 See Anand (2000) for a discussion of neo-Orientalist strategies and Borup's (2004) discussion of an inverted Orientalism.
29 See official press releases from the Chinese government's official web portal: http://english.gov.cn/2012-11/13/content_2264613.htm and http://english.gov.cn/2012-10/19/content_2247692.htm.

PART THREE

Buddhist Lives

13

Dhammadinna and Jayantā: Daughters of the Buddha in Canada

MAVIS L. FENN

The history of women in Theravada Buddhism may be characterized as one of opportunity and ambiguity. This is especially true for Buddhist nuns. Ambiguity regarding the role of women, both lay and ordained, continues to the present, but in the twentieth and twenty-first centuries, opportunities for women have increased, including full ordination as nuns. These changes, begun in Asia, continued with the exportation of Buddhism to Europe and North America. Western women who went to study in Asia, some of whom ordained, returned to their home countries where they were instrumental in establishing Buddhism in the West. While Theravada Buddhism was slow to take root in the United States, it was established early in Canada due to the pioneering efforts of Dhammadina (Anna Burian), a German-born Canadian, and Jayantā (Shirley Johannesen), who, as a lay teacher, has extended and developed Dhammadina's legacy. If we are to understand the magnitude of their contributions, we must first understand the historical circumstances from which Theravada Buddhist women emerged.

In India, while there had always been isolated female ascetics, it was not until the establishment of Jainism and Buddhism (sixth/fifth centuries BCE) that religious communities for women were created. Indeed, the Buddhist account in the Pali canon (*Cullavagga* X) shows the Buddha as initially reluctant to establish a formal order for women (*bhikkhuni sangha*), an event that occurred about five years after the establishment of the male order (*bhikkhu sangha*). The nuns' order was eventually established through the mediation of the Buddha's long-time attendant and cousin, Ānanda. He appealed to the Buddha on two grounds. The first he phrased as a question: If women follow the same path as men, can they attain perfection? The

Buddha replied that they can, and Ānanda replied that, if they can, they should be allowed to have an order of nuns. Then he reminded the Buddha that Mahāpajāpatī took over the role of his mother when his own died. The Buddha agreed but stipulated that ordination would require Mahāpajāpatī to accept eight rules. These eight rules, in effect, placed the nuns and their order under the supervision of the male order.

How can we account for the Buddha's seeming reluctance? This is not the place to discuss the composition and redaction of the text or to wonder whether the Buddha actually said these things. Suffice it to say that they are accepted as the words of the Buddha and taken as authoritative. We can provide a number of explanations, but at the root of them all is the notion that women are inferior to men naturally and spiritually. This notion may be grounded in ancient blood taboos which appear in many cultures. Even now women may be isolated from family during their menstrual period, forbidden to cook, and denied access to sacred sites. In short, they are considered to be unclean or polluted due to menstruation and childbirth. At the time of the Buddha, women were thought to need constant supervision and were subject to their fathers in youth, husbands in middle years, and eldest sons when widowed. While Indian society has never been uniform in opinion, and cultural values have changed over time, rebirth as a woman has generally been considered a lesser birth, indicative of negative deeds in former lives.

Many monks and lay people would have considered the admission of women into the sangha a major breach of monastic purity. Since the sangha relied on the alms of the community for its very existence, there was undoubtedly an economic fear as well (Bailey and Mabbett 2003). It is not that women in India received no respect. Lay women were respected as mothers of sons, including future kings and buddhas. And they received respect as donors. As household managers, lay women were primarily responsible for meeting the daily needs of the monastic community, a fact that remains true today. Even this could be problematic, however, since the lay women also represented the world the monks had left behind.

The establishment of an institutionalized religious life for women provided them with an opportunity previously unavailable, and the Buddha's strong endorsement of female spiritual capacity encouraged many to become ordained. The *Therīgathā*, a text of verses possibly composed by enlightened women, gives numerous reasons why women took up the religious life. Of course, women pursued enlightenment for the same reason that men did, to put an end to suffering. In addition, they sought to escape abusive husbands, to not marry, and to be free from social expectation. They exercised their freedom through following the Buddha, their lives a refutation of the notion that they were of inferior capabilities.

This opportunity and ambiguity followed women even while they played an integral role in the establishment and dissemination of Buddhism throughout India and Southeast Asia, as well as in China, Korea, and Japan. Nuns were at a disadvantage in all these cultures due to the belief that females were less worthy than males. Donations of the necessities of life – food, shelter, clothing, and medicine – to the monastic community by the lay community were, and are, believed to generate merit (*puñña*) for the laity. Merit is a spiritual capital that aids in producing positive karma which, in turn, produces a better rebirth. The amount or quality of the merit produced is dependent, in part, on the purity of the recipient. Donations to nuns were believed to produce less merit for the donor. Some scholars hold that this was one reason why the nuns' order struggled and died out in India before the monks' order (Falk 2001).

Before Buddhism died out in India it was transmitted to Sri Lanka, where the Theravada tradition took shape. The nuns' order appears to have been quite successful and active. They were patronized by kings and the wealthy. They travelled to China in the fifth century and established the order of nuns there. And yet, in the eleventh century both the male and female orders died out in Sri Lanka. The male order was re-established from Burma but there do not appear to have been attempts to restore the female lineage (Bartholomeusz 1994, 21). This state of affairs continued to the late nineteenth and twentieth centuries with the modernization of Theravada Buddhism in Sri Lanka. Colonialism eroded the relationship between the state and the sangha not only financially but also in social matters such as education. The state, or king, had been the traditional overseer of monastic values, keeping the sangha pure, that is, orthodox. The British colonial authority coerced the king to cease the sponsorship of Buddhism, leaving the Buddhists stranded and directionless. Lay people moved in to fill this vacuum. This led to greater lay involvement in temple affairs, and internal reforms such as the creation of new monastic lineages and a forest hermitage movement. The Buddhism that arose in this context is sometimes referred to as Protestant Buddhism because it took the position that liberation or salvation is possible for all Buddhists and should be pursued by lay people as well as monks. Women played an important role in this process. Many lay women put on robes and taught publicly, laying the basis for the institutionalizing of what Bartholomeusz calls the "lay nun" (Bartholomeusz 1994, 27).

Bartholomeusz's use of the term "lay nun," while dated now, is an apt description of the first stage of a movement that would eventually lead to a call for the re-institution of the *bhikkhuni* sangha in Theravada Buddhism. Central to the Buddhist revival in Sri Lanka was the idea that women, due to their role in the family, would be at the forefront of the rejuvenation of Buddhism. Schools were established to educate women, and some young women took the ten precepts and donned robes, a declaration of renunciation and also a novice ordination. An American convert, Countess Canavarro, established the first school-nunnery in 1898; a Western-educated Sri Lankan Christian convert, Catherine de Alwiss (given the Buddhist name Sudharmacari), founded the second in 1907 (Bartholomeusz 1994, 101). Unlike the American countess who believed she was ordaining women into full *bhikkhuni* or nun status, de Alwiss was clear that her goal was the rejuvenation of a tradition of a community of *dasa sil upāsikā* or *dasa sil mata*, lay women who keep the ten precepts (Bartholemeusz 1994, 94).[1] De Alwiss understood that under monastic rules a quorum of fully ordained nuns (ordained by male and female sanghas under 311 monastic rules) was required to reinstitute the *bhikkhuni* order. That requirement could no longer be met since the female order had died out in Burma and Sri Lanka and had never reached Thailand. Full ordination would have to wait until the next Buddha, Maitreya. The community founded by her was composed not only of young women but also of older women, some destitute. As well as providing for these women, the community taught underprivileged children (Bartholomeusz 1994, 97).

These schools, supported by upper class and Western donors, provided not only education but also validation for women who wished to follow the religious path seriously, and gave them some status in society. For a variety of reasons, including the coming of Sri Lankan independence, such support did not continue, (Bartholomeusz 1994, 126–7). The revival of Buddhism had been part of the resistance to colonization, and with independence elites turned to politics directly. Gradually, the composition of the *dasa sil mata* changed, including women who adopted the life more to escape disadvantage than from religious calling, and its status declined. While they had renounced lay life, many members found themselves still performing lay duties such as tending to children or the elderly. In a pattern repeated across the Himalayan Buddhist regions, in order to support themselves many nuns spent their time doing devotions for lay donors and had little time for education or personal religious development. This lowered the status of female renunciation overall. Both the government and the religious community itself took steps to correct this (Bartholemeusz 1994, 149).

To this mix was now added a few Western women who came to Sri Lanka to learn meditation and whose knowledge of Buddhism was gained primarily through books and reading the Pali canon. While their Sri Lankan counterparts generally focused on devotion, the Western nuns focused on meditation. The latter tended to be educated elites and they never questioned the right of women to full ordination. Probably the best known of these was Ayya Khema, a German-born Theravada nun and one of the founders of Sākyadhitā (Daughters of the Buddha), the International Association of Buddhist Women, along with Lekshe Tsomo, an American-born Tibetan nun, and the Thai lay woman Chatsumarn Kabilsingh (now Dhammananda). Having taken the novice ordination in 2001, Kabilsingh took full ordination in 2003, setting off a storm of controversy that continues today. There was general agreement that the living and educational conditions of the *dasa sil mata* needed improvement. However, there was some dispute about whether they needed, wanted, or were able to take full ordination under the Theravada *vinaya*. Many religious women accepted the idea that they must wait for the next Buddha to re-establish a full order. Others did not want to become fully ordained since that would then place them in a subordinate position to the monks. Finally, many simply did not care about the matter since for them religious practice was a personal matter not dependent on institutional structures. These arguments against full ordination for women also can be found within the Tibetan monastic community (Mrozick 2009, 360–78).

Initially, support for the re-establishment of the *bhikkhuni sangha* came from Western-educated women and monks who worked in North America. Bartholomeusz notes that Asian monks recognized that if Theravada Buddhism was to compete with other forms of Buddhism in the religious marketplace of the West, it would be unlikely to draw women without the option of full ordination (Bartholomeusz 1994, 186–90). On technical grounds, the argument was that, since China had received its nuns' *vinaya* from Sri Lanka, this line had never been broken, and that ordination in that *vinaya* (Dharmaguptaka) was quite acceptable. Many Theravada elders rejected this argument, countering that, while the Chinese *vinaya* is one of the schools contemporary with the Theravada, it was not the Theravada *vinaya*. They argue further that the Chinese schools are Mahayana and thus are not acceptable to the Theravada tradition. They also reject the argument that since the Buddha spoke of a Fourfold Sangha of male and female religious specialists and male and female laity, Theravada Buddhism is incomplete without a re-instituted order.

In 1987 Ayya Khema, Chatsumarn Kabilsingh, Lekshe Tsomo, Jampa Tsedron, and others convened a conference for nuns in Bodhgaya, India. Opened by His Holiness the 14th Dalai Lama, the conference was convened in order that nuns from the various religious traditions could discuss their mutual challenges: lack of economic, educational, and social support; and the absence of full ordination in the Theravada and Tibetan traditions due to *vinaya* issues. A considerable number of lay women and some men also attended, and in a debriefing meeting at the end of the conference, the attendees decided that the lay women and the monastic women should come together to found an organization for all Buddhist women, Sākyadhitā or Daughters of the Buddha. Since that time, there have been thirteen international conferences with a fourteenth planned for Indonesia in 2015. In 2008 the organization was institutionally reconfigured, due to its growth, but the aims of the organization have remained consistent over the years with few changes.[2]

The primary focus of Sākyadhitā is to create an international alliance of Buddhist women who will advance Buddhist women's spiritual and secular welfare and promote gender equity within the tradition. Sākyadhitā organizes biannual conferences in Asia where academic papers are interspersed with workshops on more practical issues such as parenting, health, gender issues, and meditation. Meal times provide an opportunity for cross-cultural conversation, an exchange of ideas, and networking. The influx of large numbers of people, especially from non-Asian countries, puts pressure on local and government authorities in the host country to pay attention to the issues raised at the conference – proper education, living conditions, the lack of financial and social support for nuns, and the issue of ordination. The conferences have provided fertile ground for the creation of new projects and the promotion of existing ones.

Those who attend these conferences and follow the development of a revitalized *bhikkhuni* sangha in Sri Lanka agree that the model to follow is that of the Taiwanese nuns. They are highly educated, well financed, and socially esteemed for their dedication and hard work. The nuns of Fo Guang Shan, for example, run large temples around the world and are heavily involved in education and social service. Tzu Chi Merit Society, a major relief organization run primarily by female laity, was founded and is run by Taiwanese nun Cheng Yen. They, their activities, and the opportunities they have provided for women, grew out of a reform Buddhism begun by the Chinese monk Taixu and further developed by his disciples in Taiwan. This style of Buddhism focuses on the relevance of Buddhism for everyday life, combining personal religious development and social service.

The Sākyadhitā argument is that education and training for Buddhist women, combined with the status of full ordination, will improve the lot of women by providing a respectable career path, and will enhance the quality of life in Buddhist societies, as it has done in the Taiwanese case and others such as Korea. But that still leaves the technical problem. The International Congress on Women's Role in the Sangha was convened in Hamburg, Germany in 2007. It brought together high-level monks, nuns, and scholars from around the globe to discuss technical issues of *vinaya* in the Theravada and Tibetan traditions. While not directly a Sākyadhitā event, numerous Sākyadhitā members and sympathizers participated. The congress concluded that there were means provided in the *vinayas* themselves to allow for the re-institution of the female order in Theravada and Tibetan Buddhism.

All these threads – women's monastic engagement with Theravada, moves to improve the circumstances of the *dasa sil mata*, the involvement of Western women in Buddhism both in Asia and North America, and the development and growth of Sākyadhitā – come together in most interesting ways in Canada. Dhammadina (Anna Burian) travelled through parts of Asia and returned to Canada to establish the Theravada presence on the West Coast and in Alberta.

DHAMMADINNA: AN EARLY CANADIAN BUDDHIST PIONEER[3]

Anna Burian (1913–1990) was among those Western women who, especially in the 1960s and 1970s, travelled to Asia on a spiritual journey. She was born in Austria in 1913. She and her students were pivotal influences in establishing Buddhism in Western Canada and in shaping the form it took. Anna Burian lived through two world wars. A child during the First World War, she was in England studying to be a nurse when the Second World War broke out, making it impossible for her to return to Austria until 1947. In 1951 she immigrated to Canada with her teenage son, settling in British Columbia. She worked as a nurse, taught drawing and sculpture at the Vancouver School of Art, and also pursued an avid interest in philosophy, mysticism, and hatha yoga.

In a brief biography for the first Yoga Association of Alberta Conference in 1981, held at the University of Calgary, she notes that from an early age she had questions that her Roman Catholicism could not answer. In her late forties, she embarked on a spiritual quest to India. She stayed in South Asia for about seven years. She travelled alone, a challenge in the late 1950s and early 1960s, visiting various ashrams, temples, and hermitages. Initially she explored the Hindu tradition. She studied Vedanta with HH Swami Sivananda and took *sannyasi* (renouncer) vows with him. In 1964 she travelled to Sri Lanka and studied at the Verdant Monastery in Kolatenne, Bandarawala province. She studied Pali, doctrine, and specialized in *vipassana* and *abhidhamma*. It was here that she took the novice ordination from the Venerable C. Nyanasatta Mahathera, a Czechoslovakian-born scholar-monk. This ordination conferred on her the status of a *dasa sil mata*. She was given the religious name Anagarika Dhammadinna (see illustration 10). The title "*anāgārika*" (homeless one) is a designation introduced by the Sri Lankan Theravada reformer Dharmapala in the latter part of the nineteenth century.[4] Her religious name, Dhammadinna, is a reference to a nun noted in the Pali canon for her teaching ability.

In Asia *dasa sil mata* wear white robes, but on her return to Canada in 1965, Anagarika selected modified brown *bhikkhuni* robes.[5] She settled in a community near Nelson, BC, across the road from a yoga centre run by a German *sannyasi*, Radha. While she lived a quiet life, she began to teach, and taught for almost thirty years before her death in 1990.

When Anagarika began to teach in the mid-1960s there was little in the way of Buddhist meditation available in North America. The first Zen centre in North America (San Francisco Zen Center) was established in 1962. Many of the Japanese-trained Zen masters, such as Philip Kapleau and Jiyu Kennett, the first woman *rōshi* (master), did not return to the United States until the late 1960s or early 1970s. It was not until the 1970s that Tibetan Buddhism began to spread. Interest in Theravada was slight, and it only began to make inroads in North America after the modern Theravada style *vipassana* movement began to take hold in the 1980s. As Buddhist scholar Victor Hori notes, "Considering the almost total absence of Buddhism in Canada at that time, Anagarika Dhammadinna really was a pioneer."[6] Dhammadinna lived on the same street as Swami Radha and, through her, Dhammadinna met Shirley Johannesen, who studied yoga with Swami Radha. In 1974, when Johannesen and other members of the fledgling Yoga Association of Alberta were looking for someone to lead a retreat, one of the board members suggested they contact Anagarika Dhammadinna.

Dhammadinna taught methods of meditation and *abhidhamma*, traditionally reserved in Asia for monastics. *Abhidhamma* can be quite dry and is not a mainstay of teaching in the West. But because Anagarika was excited about it, so too were her students. Johannesen remembers her pleasure at filling countless notebooks with hurriedly jotted notes. Dhammadinna taught *abhidhamma* to her students to help them understand the experiences they had while meditating. She supervised their meditation, organized retreats, conducted study sessions, encouraged her students to begin their own study groups, and inspired the establishment of several centres, some of which are discussed below. As her reputation grew, she travelled to various places in the lower mainland of BC and finally settled in Half Moon Bay. She also taught in Calgary and Edmonton in Alberta and was instrumental in producing students and encouraging the establishment of Buddhism there as well.

In 1981 she returned to Kanduboda, Sri Lanka, for further study with *vipassana* master Sumatipala Nyaka Mahathera, an expert in the Burmese style of *vipassana*. On this trip she also met with Venerable Nyanaponika Mahathera, a well-known German-born scholar-monk and one of the founders of the Buddhist Publication Society; the late Egerton C. Baptist of the International Buddhist Society, himself the author of numerous books on aspects of Buddhism; and the Venerable Nyanasatta Thera of

Banderawela. She imported books for her students and invited eminent monks to teach *abhidhamma* or lead meditation retreats and give *dhamma* talks in Canada. From Sri Lanka came Venerable Ananda Maitreya Maha Nayaka Thera, first principal of Nalanda College and one of the founders of the Buddhist Publication Society, and the Venerable Piyadassi Mahathera, a teacher who travelled extensively and who was the editor of the Buddhist Publication Society until his death. From Thailand came Achan Sobin Namto, who taught extensively in Southeast Asia and the West and became the first abbot of the first Thai temple in Los Angeles, California. There can be no doubt that Anagarika Dhammadinna was in the forefront of the expansion of Buddhism to the West. Her own teaching in Canada and her invitations to the monks noted above, who travelled extensively and wrote and taught in English, show a determination to make Buddhism, including *abhidhamma* and *vipassana* meditation, accessible to those outside Asia.

The inclusion of Venerable Ananda Maitreya in this list is notable. A highly respected senior monk, he was one of the monastic hierarchy who opposed the re-establishment of the nuns' order in Sri Lanka. Still, the record is clear he and others respected Anagarika, and she sponsored their trips to Canada so that her mostly Canadian students could benefit from their teachings. Anagarika Dhammadinna also invited Ayya Khema, one of the founders of Sākyadhitā and an ardent supporter of full ordination. Shirley Johannesen states that in all her years with Anagarika Dhammadinna, the subject of full *bhikkhuni* ordination never came up. There are several possibilities for why this is, but given the deaths of all concerned, we cannot conclusively establish Anagarika's thoughts on the matter. Perhaps her status as a *dasa sil mata* was considered irrelevant to their mutual spiritual interests.[7] They certainly accepted that Anagarika Dhammadinna could play an important role in propagating Buddhism. The technical status of Anagarika Dhammadinna was clearly irrelevant, if known at all, to her students. Johannesen notes that Dhammadinna was respected for the seriousness of her own study and practice, and known as a compassionate and energetic teacher who expected her students to practise and study seriously and to integrate the teachings into their daily lives.

Dhammadinna's impact can be seen in the legacy she bequeathed, the organizations she inspired and, most importantly, the students she taught. Kirthi Senaratne, one of Dhammadinna's students, organized a joint effort between the Sri Lankan Buddhist community and the Burmese community to construct a Buddhist temple in Surrey in 1993. The success of the temple and its rapid growth led to the creation of two separate communities, the Buddhist Vihara Society and the Manawmaya Theravada Buddhist Society. Theravada Dhamma, a Theravada Buddhist Society established in BC in 1979, although dormant for a while, is again offering retreats. Light of the Dhamma, established in Edmonton in 1984, also continues to provide retreats. Dr Eddie Bernstein, another former student, is a family physician who has practised insight and mindfulness meditation since 1977. He is a meditation instructor at the Center for Mindfulness and regularly gives courses on mindfulness-based stress reduction at Cascadia Retreats in Robert's Creek, BC. Through their efforts, British Columbia and Alberta have provided a stable and longstanding presence for Theravada Buddhism that serves both immigrant populations from Sri Lanka, Burma, and Thailand and those who wish to access Buddhist teachings and meditation techniques through non-sectarian retreats. The Calgary Theravada Meditation Society was founded in 1976 by Shirley Johannesen and continues to meet regularly under the direction of Anne Mahoney. Johannesen (discussed below) also established Stretch Awareness and teaches yoga and meditation in Calgary. She is also linked with Abhayagiri monastery in Red Wood Valley, California, which is the only Ajahn Chah lineage monastery in the United States.

Dhammadinna's few American students have created international programs through their innovative use of technology in Buddhist teaching and outreach. Gregory Kramer, who has been teaching since 1980, is one of the founders of the Metta Foundation. His website lists a variety of programs provided by the non-profit foundation, including the development of a Buddhist inspired practice called Insight Dialogue, Relational Dhamma Distance Learning Programs, and *mettā* (loving kindness) programs for children. Kramer's website biography notes that he has written several books, has a PhD in learning and change in human systems, and is a visiting teacher at the Barre Center for Buddhist Studies. Jacqueline Kramer is the founder of the Hearth Foundation, another online organization and community that focuses on Buddhism for parents. It was founded in 2006. The website states its mission as "supporting home based spiritual practice through information sharing and community building" (Hearth Foundation n.d.). Kramer is the author of *Buddha Mom – The Path of Mindful Mothering*, and in 2007 she received an Outstanding Women in Buddhism Award.

While many of the organizations listed above mention Buddhism, they do not offer the same training in *abhidhamma* as Dhammadinna did. Their focus is more on *sati*, mindfulness meditation, cultivating an awareness of one's body, feeling, mind, and mental objects. Some teachers offer mindfulness-based stress awareness programs. And while Dhammadinna certainly urged her students to take this awareness into daily life, there are more specific areas of concern to which it is applied; the environment and raising children are only two examples. Dhammadinna's teachings have provided the basis for innovation. We will discuss this in more detail in the section on Shirley Johannesen.

While most of the teachers invited to Canada by Anagarika Dhammadinna were from Sri Lanka, she has also had an impact on the Thai Forest Tradition of Ajahn Chah in Canada. Ajahn Sona (see illustration 2), the founder and abbot of Birken Forest Monastery, met Dhammadinna when he travelled to BC to establish a mountain hermitage. Of her, he states,

> At this time I encountered, as well, one of the real pioneers of Theravada in the West, and also of women's spirituality. Her name was Anagarika Dhamma Dinna. I was quite surprised and pleased to meet a Westerner who had many years before – it was still a very, very rare experience – gone off to Asia to study meditation in a very serious way. She had become a nun in Sri Lanka and practised with the meditation monks, had returned to Western Canada, and as a true pioneer she taught various forms of mindfulness and insight meditation. She was also an enthusiastic importer of famous Sri Lankan missionary monks. She was most happy to introduce Canadians to such luminaries as Ven. Ananda Maitreya, Ven. Piyadassi, Ven. Punnaji and Sister Ayya Khema. Many Canadians who encountered these inspiring teachers in the 1970s have continued to practise to this day. (*Ehi Passiko*, 13)

Ajahn Sona and the Birken Forest Monastery receive a full discussion in chapter 4 of this volume, so there is no need to restate the details here. The compelling forest tradition is both well rooted in Canada and attracting Canadians for ordination. Birken Forest Monastery in BC is connected with Thai Forest Tradition monasteries in the United States, Thailand, Mexico, and Africa as well as Perth (Tisarana Monastery), Thunder Bay (Arrow River), and Lanark (Sati Saraniya), Ontario.

The world-wide Forest Sangha monasteries and the Thai Forest monasteries in Canada are quite involved in the *bhikkhuni* ordination issue. The *bhikkhuni* lineage never reached Thailand and so there have never been fully ordained nuns in Thailand. Women who renounce are referred to as *mâe chii*. Their status has generally been extremely low and many have lived in extreme poverty. The Thai religious hierarchy is firmly against any attempt to ordain nuns. However, the Birken Forest Monastery includes a *mâe chii*, Sister Mon, as one of its members (see illustration 3).[8] To have a *mâe chii* live in a temple to do the cleaning is not uncommon in Thailand, but to have one studying with monks in a monastery as *mâe chii* Sister Mon does is a very modern and Western situation. It will be an interesting development should she wish to become ordained since the Ajahn Chah lineage does not provide full ordination for women. The Sati Saraniya Hermitage, founded by Ayya Medhanandi, is a monastery for women. She received full *bhikkhuni* ordination in Taiwan, an ordination which is not accepted in Thailand. The innovations at Birken Forest Monastery and the existence of Sati Saraniya Hermitage are perhaps suggestive of a move toward a more inclusive Theravada tradition in Canada. This issue is explored more fully in Placzek's chapter in this volume.

The production of a strong lineage is not a chance occurrence. In the case of Anagarika Dhammadinna, the primary contributing factors appear to have been her monastic training and enthusiasm for *abhidhamma*, her personal charisma, and the seriousness of her students. By passing on her monastic training to her lay students, she gave them a strong foundation and respect within the Theravada tradition. As a teacher, she provided them with a model to emulate. The teachers she produced, whether ordained or lay, have been active for decades, a testament to their commitment. One such student, who continues to make a significant contribution to the development of Buddhism in Western Canada and also internationally, is Shirley Johannesen.

JAYANTĀ: SHIRLEY JOHANNESEN

Born in British Columbia, Johannesen notes that, like her teacher Dhammadinna, she had questions about the purpose of life and death from an early age. Although very involved in student life in high school in Quesnel, BC, president of the student council, active in sports, on the Honour Roll, she still felt "not connected" because of questions concerning the meaning of life and why there is suffering and death, questions that others did not seem to ask and for which there seemed to be no satisfactory answers. After a move to Montreal in the 1960s, where she graduated from the Canadian Society of Radiological Technicians of Quebec, she discovered yoga. Always interested in anatomy and human movement, she notes that, from the first class, she "felt a peacefulness and calm I had not experienced before."[9] She studied Iyengar Yoga with B.K.S. Iyengar at his ashram in India, and with senior teachers in both Sivananda's and Krishnamacharya's lineage. She holds advanced certificates from Dona Holleman in Italy and Orit Sen-Gupta in Israel and a Bachelor of General Studies with a kinesiology major from Athabasca University. She is a founding member of the Yoga Association of Alberta (YAA), the Yoga Centre of Calgary, and the Canadian Iyengar Association.

Johannesen encountered Buddhism and her teacher through yoga. In 1974 she invited Anagarika Dhammadinna to lead a meditation retreat for the YAA. She became a student of Dhammadinna at that retreat, and remained so until Dhammadinna's death in 1990. At that time she thought, "This is the end of my searching for a spiritual path. This is the path I want to follow."[10] Her ordination name is Jayantā. Through Dhammadinna, she trained in *vipassana* and *abhidhamma* and was encouraged to start teaching classes and retreats. She studied with both Sri Lankan meditation masters and those from the Thai Forest tradition, including Venerables Ajahn Pasanno, a Manitoba-born monk, Ajahn Amaro, an English monk who was co-abbot with Ajahn Pasanno of Abhayagiri Monastery in California until 2010, and Sobin Namṭo (noted above). While visiting Amaravati monastery in the United Kingdom, she met Ajahn Viradhammo, now the abbot of Tisarana Monastery in Perth, Ontario, and Ajahn Pasanno. Later Ajahn Pasanno asked if she would consider training as a lay minister for Abhayagiri monastery in Red Wood, California, the only Ajahn Chah monastery in the United States. She was the only Canadian participant in the four-year study program and is now a member of the Community of Abhayagiri Lay Ministry, which meets regularly and acts as a bridge between the lay people and monks. This institution of highly trained lay people who take on a monk-like role is an innovation generally found in non-Asian Buddhism. The strict monastic/lay distinction found in Asia is not a good fit for Western culture. In the West, there are few monastic teachers, and Buddhism tends to be lay led. Recognizing some lay Buddhists as "lay ministers" or "senior students" serves two functions. First, it is a means of marking lay leaders who can provide solid guidance for those who have little access to an ordained teacher, and second, it provides a way of marking one's progress in spiritual life.

In 1987 Anagarika Dhammadinna suggested that Johannesen invite Ayya Khema, a German-born Theravada nun, to Canada to lead a meditation retreat. Ayya Khema had just come from the international conference of Buddhist nuns in Bodhgaya, India that had been convened to discuss common problems and concluded with the founding of Sākyadhitā International. Ayya Khema, excited about the prospects for Sākyadhitā, asked Johannesen if she would be the Canadian representative to the new organization. She agreed, although she admits that she was uncertain precisely what was entailed in this. Johannesen has attended nine Sākyadhitā International conferences as well as two in the United States convened to discuss issues specific to Western nuns and women. From her first encounter, Johannesen has played an active role at these conferences. She has presented papers, organized and run workshops, and staffed the registration desk. She is well suited to bridging the gaps between people: monastic training makes her comfortable discussing issues with nuns; her experience as a teacher allows her to answer questions about Buddhism or practice; and the fact that she is a lay woman enables her to understand that perspective as well. Sākyadhitā has grown considerably in the past twenty-five years and in 2008 it was restructured along more formal legal lines, adopting a branch system of organization. Johannesen successfully applied to the international organization for accreditation, and in 2009 Sākyadhitā Canada became a registered not-for-profit association, receiving charitable status in 2011. The board of directors is made up of both laity and monastics. As a branch of Sākyadhitā International, Sākyadhitā Canada is able to pursue the goal of developing an organization that can connect Canadian Buddhist women with each other for the purpose of supporting both the few nuns that exist outside the Asian context, and laywomen who are not connected with a practice community.[11] This goal can more easily be accomplished under the well-known banner of Sākyadhitā International, which also supplies other forms of support such as assistance with a website, and expertise in organization and publicity.

Sākyadhitā Canada continues its support for the objective of increasing the material and spiritual welfare of Buddhist women internationally.

Sākyadhitā Canada now produces a newsletter and has a well designed and maintained website which publicizes local and international events and encourages participation and donations. This should provide increased opportunities for expansion east of Ontario, a goal for the near future.

Johannesen is ideally suited to the task of heading the first Canadian branch of Sākyadhitā. She brings with her not only four decades of experience in Buddhist doctrine and practice but the institutional memory of the organization itself. Already her efforts are bearing fruit. The Calgary-based branch held a week-long fundraising retreat on Salt Spring Island that raised sufficient funds to send one nun to the twelfth Sākyadhitā Conference (2011) in Bangkok, Thailand. More recently, a one-day miniconference was held in Calgary, Alberta (2012).

As president of Sākyadhitā Canada Johannesen has the opportunity not only to represent Sākyadhitā but to build its membership base in Canada and facilitate increased interaction between Canadian Buddhist women from Asian and non-Asian Buddhist traditions. The appointment, at her suggestion, of Sister Thich nu Tinh Quang of Hamilton, Ontario to the Sākyadhitā board represents one of these possibilities. Sister Tinh Quang is a Caucasian nun ordained in Vietnam by Thich Nhat Lien, who was ordained in both the Theravada and Pure Land traditions.

Sister Tinh Quang is bilingual (Vietnamese and English) and has established a Zen centre, Little Heron Zen Hermitage, in Hamilton. This is atypical for traditional Vietnamese Buddhism, so it is not surprising that the members of the centre are Western. She has adapted some rituals for her non-Asian students and has created new rituals for them as well. She incorporates her previous training in psychology to offer Gestalt workshops and dream workshops. The creation of new rituals and the inclusion of insights from other fields and traditions are also characteristics of Buddhism in the West.

Sister Tinh Quang assists the local Vietnamese temple in its relations with the broader community, is active in fundraising for the orphanage associated with her home temple in Vietnam, and is a member of Buddhist organizations in Toronto as well (Fenn 2008, 124; 2013, 198–9; 2012 online). Her involvement will undoubtedly raise the profile of Sākyadhitā in Ontario with both Asians and non-Asians and encourage networking.

Over the course of the past four decades, Johannesen has organized yoga retreats and workshops, including the 1981 Canadian Yoga

Conference discussed above. As well, she established Stretch Awareness in Calgary, which provides retreats and instruction in yoga and meditation. Johannesen is an innovative teacher. Her teaching combines yoga with mindfulness training, an approach that teaches practitioners to focus their awareness not simply on the body but on the feelings and thoughts that arise, to see their tendencies in regard to "like" and "dislike" and thus be able to make choices that are productive for them.[12] She established the first yoga teacher-training course for the Yoga Association of Canada, and subsequently developed yoga and meditation teacher training courses for Stretch Awareness. While comfortable with giving traditional *dhamma* talks, the majority are non-sectarian in nature and focused on the practical things of daily life. This practical approach allows her to better communicate with those who may not be Buddhist or indeed religious at all.[13] She has taught extensively in the western provinces of Manitoba, Saskatchewan, Alberta, and as far west as Salt Spring Island, BC. She has also taught in Quebec, Ontario, and internationally. She has taught yoga to a broad spectrum of individuals, the business community, sports groups (the National Hockey League's Calgary Flames, and various equestrian groups), and offered courses for educational (University of Calgary) and medical institutions. Johannesen believes that her ability to be innovative in teaching and practice is only possible because of her sound grounding in *vipassana* and *abhidhamma*. Innovation is a way to honour Dhammadinna's dictate that students must bring their awareness into their daily life. Just as Dhammadinna was at the forefront of bringing Theravada to Canada, Shirley Johannesen and the other students have been at the forefront of the movement to make Buddhist insights and practice more broadly accessible. They also highlight the fact that teaching is predominantly done by lay teachers trained in traditionally monastic practices.

CONCLUSION

Little notice has been given to the important role played by Canadians in the expansion of Buddhism beyond Asia. Canadians have been major participants in the development of Theravada outside Asia. Anagarika Dhammadinna set the stage for a Buddhism that stresses meditation and includes the more technical aspects of *abhidhamma* required to analyse its workings in consciousness. Fully ordained or not, Anagarika established a monastic style of Buddhism for laity in Western Canada. Some of her students have gone on to use this technical training to establish a strong forest tradition in Canada and the United States. Other students have combined this Buddhist training with Western psychological insights to produce a series of meditational and spiritual approaches to personal development and social harmony.

Shirley Johannesen has done more than continue the tradition instituted by her teacher. She has extended and developed it in multiple ways. As well as teaching meditation internationally, she has forged Canadian links with European and American forest traditions. Her work with Abhayagiri monastery in the United States is part of the expansion of lay Buddhism in the West, providing services traditionally provided by monastics, such as teaching meditation, and services that were not traditionally done by monastics, such as pastoral services and counselling.

One of Johannesen's most important contributions to Canadian Buddhism has been her role as a historian. Having been present from the beginning of Theravada in North America, she carries the institutional memory of those times and those individuals with her. Because of her we know how early on Canada adopted Theravada Buddhism and how it has grown, adapted, and spread. Her memories of Anagarika Dhammadinna serve as a reminder that the Theravada tradition has room for strong female teachers. Her long involvement with Sākyadhitā provides evidence of how the organization has grown over the past twenty-five years, the progress that has been made, and the distance left to go. Especially in a country that frequently forgets its past, it is good to know about Canada's early experiences with Buddhism and how it has developed.

Buddhism made a change in the cultures of the countries to which it was exported and it too changed in the process. Theravada Buddhism will change in Canada as well. The voice of the early Asian monks who felt Theravada would not flourish in the West without offering women the chance for full ordination appears to be being heard to some extent. We see some evidence of that in the recent research of D. Mitra Barua, who is also featured in this volume. Barua's research at two Theravada temples in Toronto shows, in part, the adoption of a more egalitarian position regarding the education of the young. Most of those involved in dharma education in Toronto are lay women in contrast to the situation in Sri Lanka, where monks predominate. It will be interesting to see whether or not such innovations will be exported back to Sri Lanka and Thailand (Barua 2010a; 2010b).

The push to re-establish the *bhikkhuni* ordination lineage will continue, but it will continue to be contentious. This is an issue that is front and centre for Sākyadhitā as part of their goal to improve the conditions for Buddhist nuns. The organization has accomplished a great deal, but there are multiple tensions: the tension between those who wish to ordain and those who do not, between Asian and Western cultural perspectives, between the needs of lay and ordained women, the need to provide financial support to both Asian and Western nuns, and the inevitable tensions inherent in running a large, volunteer-staffed organization. The Canadian branch is too young to have to deal with such issues yet, but as they grow, they can expect issues to arise.

From the beginning, the history of women in Buddhism has been one of opportunity and ambiguity. Progress has varied according to historical and cultural conditions, but there has been progress. Canada's position as a multicultural nation provides an excellent vantage point for the scholar to mark that progress.

NOTES

1 The *dasa sil mata* or *dasa sil upāsikā* is held to have been created after the first Sri Lankan female converts took the ten precepts and lived in common while they waited for nuns to arrive from India to fully ordain them.
2 The website lists these as: to establish an international alliance of Buddhist women; to advance the spiritual and secular welfare of the world's women; to work for gender equity in Buddhist education, training, institutional structures, and ordination; to promote harmony and dialogue among the Buddhist traditions and other religions; to encourage research and publications on topics of interest to Buddhist women; to foster compassionate social action for the benefit of humanity; to promote world peace through the teachings of the Buddha (Sākyadhitā n.d.).
3 Many thanks to Shirley Johannesen for providing the information about Anagarika Dhammadinna and her students, and for her remembrances of their time together. Thanks also to Kay Koppedrayer who read an earlier draft of this chapter.
4 This is a title that is rarely used. It denotes an individual who is not a fully ordained monk or nun but who has renounced family life for full-time pursuit of religious

objectives. But this is something all *dasa sil mata* do. However, in 1964 when Anagarika Dhammadinna ordained, it is unlikely that many *dasa sil matas* of Sri Lankan heritage would have been heavily involved in *vipassanā* and *abhidhamma* (philosophical) study. *Anāgārika* would be a more appropriate title for a novice monk awaiting full ordination. Without direct evidence in this matter, one can only speculate that this title was an acknowledgment of the depth of her studies.

5   According to Johannesen, her preceptor gave permission. E-mail communication with the author, 14 July 2013.
6   Victor Hori, e-mail communication with the author, 11 December 2011.
7   This is the most likely explanation, as Bartholomeusz quotes the Venerable Ananda Maitreya as stating that if the *das sil mata* kept the 311 *vinaya* rules for nuns, they would be regarded as nuns although they were not technically fully ordained (Bartholomeusz 1994, 169).
8   See the website, Sitavana Birken Forest Monastery, Resident Monastics, http://birken.ca/resident_monastics.
9   Johannesen, communication by phone with the author, 13 July 2013.
10 Ibid.
11 Sākyadhitā is open to all women in Canada who are Buddhist regardless of ethnic background. Most Asian nuns, however, are connected to a community that supplies their needs. This is generally not the case for non-Asian nuns who often are isolated or who have little or no financial support. See Fenn 2014.
12 Johannesen, communication by phone with the author, 13 July 2013.
13 Ibid.

14

Thầy Phổ Tịnh: A Vietnamese Nun's Struggles in Canada

ALEXANDER SOUCY

I first met the Venerable Thích Nữ Phổ Tịnh (henceforth Thầy Phổ Tịnh) when we were undergraduates at Concordia University in the late 1980s.[1] She and Thích Thiện Nghị (her uncle and the abbot of a prominent Vietnamese Buddhist temple in Montreal, Tam Bảo Temple)[2] were taking courses at this secular institution in order to further their understanding of comparative religion and to increase their cultural and linguistic literacy in their new Canadian environment. Due to his lack of English fluency and pressures from his ambitious projects to establish Vietnamese Buddhism in Canada, Thích Thiện Nghị soon abandoned his attempts, but his niece remained, finally attaining a master's degree in religion.[3]

Her inner strength and determination were immediately obvious to all her classmates. She persevered despite the difficulty of studying in a language in which she was not fluent. She was also challenged by the restrictions of her monastic discipline, which meant that she could not travel alone to class and had to attend her evening classes long after her last meal of the day, at noon.

Since the early 1990s, when I started to do research at Tam Bảo Temple, Thầy Phổ Tịnh has been largely responsible for its daily operations and providing instruction to the novice monks and nuns resident there. She has always been incredibly active, taking a hands-on approach, and well regarded in her temple. She is dynamic and charismatic, with a quick wit and a ready smile (see illustration 11). Victor Hori relates one incident he witnessed that illustrates her sense of humour and strong character: "I once heard her translate for her uncle giving a dharma talk. Thích Thiện Nghị would say a few sentences and then pause to allow Thầy Phổ Tịnh to translate. At one point, when he stopped to allow her to translate, she paused and smoothly said with a large grin 'I already translated that last time.' She definitely has charisma."[4]

While her uncle was highly respected, he kept a regal distance as a figurehead of authority. One young monk at Tam Bảo Temple described the difference between uncle and niece this way: "Oh, she's serious, but she has more sense of humour. My older master, sometimes he is very funny too. But when it comes to serious stuff, he's serious."[5] Another monk described her as "like a mother: easy to talk to." A lay Buddhist from Quebec City told me in 2006 that he considered her exceptional and revered her as his teacher. He was to be married in a month and he and his fiancée had asked her to conduct the wedding.

In the early 2000s, after having a stroke, Thích Thiện Nghị moved to Brisbane, Australia, to convalesce, making Thầy Phổ Tịnh functionally the head of both her temple and the pan-Canadian organization (the Unified Buddhist Church of Vietnam in Canada – *Giáo Hội Phật Giáo Việt Nam Thống Nhất Tại Canada*) that her uncle had founded. Female leadership at Tam Bảo Temple was a major innovation and also a factor that led to division and the consequent multiplying of Vietnamese Buddhist institutions in Canada. Her leadership – indeed her very presence – at Tam Bảo Temple has been contested from both within and from outside. Nonetheless, some lay Buddhists at the temple are fiercely loyal to her. Her story brings important insights into the challenges women face as leaders within ethnic-based Buddhist communities in Canada, as well as the dynamics and difficulties for the Vietnamese community as it adapts to Canada.

Biographical accounts of women in Buddhism are scarce and, as Shneiderman (1999) points out, even rarer are those that deal with non-Western Buddhists.[6] In the years since her essay was published, little has changed to rectify this situation. There are a number of reasons for this. First, there are few prominent women Buddhists in Asia[7] since many of these countries tend to revere monks over nuns and provide women with few opportunities to advance or gain renown. Studies of Buddhism in the West have tended to focus on prominent women who are Western, perhaps because of lack of linguistic competency on the part of investigators, or perhaps because of a subtle bias against those who have been deemed "ethnic" Buddhists, and are presumed to be doing no more than replicating the Buddhism from their homeland.[8] However, while Shneiderman's essay is commendable for pointing out that Western Buddhism has been privileged, leaving Asian women and their understandings of their practices behind, she is somewhat mistaken in seeing Asian Buddhist women as only passively upholding a "traditional" Buddhism and its institutions. This essay shows that Asian women are active agents in reworking their position within their traditions. Further, despite the challenges, the transnationalization of Buddhism – in this case Vietnamese Buddhism – has opened spaces and provided opportunities for dynamic and intelligent Asian women leaders to do so.

I should be clear that the material on Thầy Phổ Tịnh's life and the challenges that I describe are based on a series of interviews I conducted with her between the early 1990s, when I was doing my master's thesis research on her temple (Soucy 1994), and in the summer of 2006, and are therefore largely from her point of view. I have not tried to validate what she told me by discussing her views with others – particularly those whom she has seen as opposing her, although I have interviewed many of them.[9] In short, I am more interested in her voice and perceptions as a female monastic leader than I am in establishing a factual record of events, which is likely not possible in any case. I begin with a brief description of Vietnamese Buddhism's coming to Canada then give a biographic sketch of Thầy Phổ Tịnh and describe her role at Tam Bảo Temple and in her organization. Finally, I discuss the challenges that she faces.

VIETNAMESE BUDDHISM COMES TO CANADA

Vietnamese Buddhism is a latecomer to the Canadian Buddhist scene. The first Vietnamese arrived in Quebec in the 1950s as students, supported by scholarships provided by the Canadian government.[10] However, it was not until the fall of Saigon (now Ho Chi Minh City) in 1975, and subsequent reunification of North and South Vietnam, that enough Vietnamese arrived in Canada to form religious institutions. The Vietnamese refugees came in waves, with the first arriving in 1975, evacuating just before the defeat of South Vietnam. This first wave was a precursor to the much larger exodus that came in the late 1970s and early 1980s with the crisis of the "Boat People." Following the fall of the south, the Communist government imposed a radical restructuring of southern Vietnamese society (P. Taylor 2001, 26–7). Religious activity was curtailed, land was confiscated and redistributed, and many who had been involved in some way with the regime in the south during the war (or had worked with the Americans) were sent to re-education camps. Many southerners found the situation intolerable and fled by whatever means they could find and afford, most famously on rickety fishing boats that drifted in the South China Sea, which, they hoped, would carry them to Malaysia, Indonesia, or Thailand.

Many boats – ill-equipped and poorly prepared – foundered on the open sea or drifted for days and weeks without food and water. Others made land in countries that did not want the refugees and sent them on their way after providing some supplies. Many individuals were captured by the police while trying to escape, jailed, and tortured, only to try again when they were released. Success, for many, meant months or years in refugee camps.

Most of these refugees eventually found homes in the United States, Canada, France, and Australia. Canada played an important role in settling a large number of the refugees (who were dubbed "the Boat people" by the Western media), taking over 10 per cent of the 2 million refugees (made up mostly of Vietnamese, but also including Cambodians and Laotians) (Buckley 2008, 27). Canada sponsored this large number of refugees due to a number of factors. Significant changes to immigration legislation in 1978 (Bill C-24) made it possible to streamline qualified immigration applicants, regardless of their nationality (whereas previously legislation favoured immigrants from Europe). Additionally, the Progressive Conservative government showed great courage under Prime Minister Joe Clark and Secretary of State for External Affairs Flora MacDonald in announcing a special "matching formula" that allowed one additional refugee to be admitted for every one that was sponsored by a non-governmental group (Lavoie 1989, 20). As a result, more than 7,600 private groups were organized: they sponsored more than half of the 59,000 refugees who arrived between 1979 and 1982 (Buckley 2008, 29; Dorais and Richard 2007, 26).

The number of refugees who arrived in the late 1970s and early 1980s was sufficient to support the founding of religious associations and, with time, to finance the purchase or construction of buildings to serve the Vietnamese Buddhist communities. Many of the first temples in major Canadian cities started as lay organizations. Eventually, these communities sponsored monastics to come to Canada and take up residence in the temples that they had created. The next stage resembled cell-splitting: monastics were sponsored, or recruited and trained, and then went off to form their own temples, taking a portion of followers with them, and the process often repeated itself in the new temple. The number of temples in Canada increased quickly, until today there are approximately fifty-five.[11] The majority are located in the Greater Toronto Area and Montreal, although they can be found in urban centres across the country, from Quebec City to Victoria.[12]

Scholars who have documented the growth of Buddhism in Canada have mentioned the striking tendency for divisiveness and the establishment of competing organizations in the overseas Vietnamese diaspora (Dorais 2006; McLellan 1999, chapter 4). Indeed, disagreements and divisions have been one of the main forces behind Vietnamese Buddhism's rapid expansion, especially in Montreal and the Greater Toronto Area. Most of the temples outside Vietnam are associated with the Unified Buddhist Church of Vietnam (or UBCV), which is the main unifying organization that was created in South Vietnam during the 1960s. After the Communists reunified Vietnam, the UBCV was outlawed and replaced by a state-controlled organization. The UBCV went underground in Vietnam and stayed active as a "unifying" organization overseas, although in most countries where there are significant Vietnamese communities, several competing organizations emerged claiming to represent the UBCV. In Canada, these include Tam Bảo Temple's Union of Vietnamese Buddhist Churches in Canada and the Overseas Unified Buddhist Church of Vietnam in Canada;[13] the latter has three affiliated temples in Montreal.

The most prominent reasons for the lack of unity include: (1) an underlying tradition of temples being largely independent, with an absence of centralized control (Nguyen and Barber 1998, 133); (2) the desire of lay Buddhists to have more control over temple finances and affairs than they had in Vietnam (especially when the temples were established by laity, and monastics were later invited to reside there), and the conviction among monastics that this is an intolerable break from traditional monastic authority (Dorais 2006, 124–5; McLellan 1999, 108, 118); (3) regional differences among Buddhists from the centre, south, and north (who fled when the Communists took over in 1954) (McLellan 1999, 108, 118); (4) lingering political differences regarding what the appropriate response should have been to the war (Dorais 2006, 124–5; McLellan 1999, 108, 118); (5) differences regarding the stance toward the present Communist regime; and

(6) structural issues that have led monks to start their own temples. Once monks have become ordained, they often want to run their own temples independently. The loose organizational structure within Vietnamese Buddhism allows any monk to start his own temple at will and run it without interference. Even when the temple is associated with one of the unifying Vietnamese Buddhist organizations, there are few mechanisms of control, and membership usually means little more than loose affiliation. Under these conditions, striking out on one's own once attaining high enough rank is an attractive option. Monks in Vietnam have built up followings, and there is sometimes competition between the more prominent ones. There were several factions within the Unified Buddhist Church in Vietnam during the war, and these divisions have continued overseas.

BIOGRAPHY OF THÍCH NỮ PHỔ TỊNH

Thầy Phổ Tịnh was born in January 1952 in Nha Trang, in southern Vietnam. Her parents divorced when she was seven years old and, blaming their marital woes on their daughter, abandoned her to her uncle.[14] He was a monk and the teacher of *vinaya* (discipline) at Hải Đức Temple in Nha Trang. He brought her to stay at the temple for nuns, Vạn Thạnh Temple, which was attached to the Hải Đức Temple complex. Because of the common perception that donating to monks is more meritorious than donating to nuns, the nuns made incense sticks by hand in order to support themselves. Nonetheless, Thầy Phổ Tịnh reports that they had more money than the monks because, while monks receive more money, nuns are more frugal.

Life at this time was very difficult for Thầy Phổ Tịnh, but she was happy. There were about sixty nuns living in the temple, and the older nuns pitied her for her situation and were fond of her. Nonetheless, she was not coddled. She recalls that she would sometimes come home late from school and would be beaten. Other punishments included having to go the distance from the gate to the temple on her knees.

When she was twelve she became a novice, undertaking the ten precepts four years earlier than normal. Eight years later she took the full 348 precepts and became a fully ordained nun at the rank of Đại Đức (Reverend).[15] Her uncle, meanwhile, had moved to Saigon while she remained at the nunnery in Nha Trang. Occasionally she would travel to Saigon to bring incense from her temple to her uncle, who by that time was prominent in the Buddhist sangha in the south, under the leadership of Thích Trí Quang. Later Thầy Phổ Tịnh lived in Saigon in order to attend university, eventually receiving a bachelor of science degree.

Her uncle resided at Ấn Quang Temple, the centre of Buddhist activism in the South that rose to prominence during the struggle against President Ngô Đình Diệm's Catholic regime and continued to be politically central for the Buddhist Struggle Movement of the 1960s. The activist Buddhists were working toward a negotiated peace, a democratically elected government, and getting the Americans out of Vietnam. They were labelled Communists by both the government and the Americans. Ấn Quang Temple is still a centre of Buddhist radicalism today and continues to be heavily monitored by the government (Topmiller 2002, 164n82).

After the reunification of Vietnam in 1975, it became increasingly difficult to be a Buddhist monastic. Thầy Phổ Tịnh moved from Nha Trang to Saigon, and her uncle started to plan their escape. According to Thầy Phổ Tịnh, because of her uncle's opposition to the Communists, the government harassed them in various ways, including denying them papers that would allow them to live in the temples and to buy food. They had to live on the donations brought by lay people. At Ấn Quang Temple the police harassed the monks, making life unbearable for them. Thầy Phổ Tịnh describes it this way:

> Every day the Communists came to see, to take a look, you know? And they were very bad. When we lit incense, they would take the incense and throw it away. And they never took their hats off in the temple. They did this every day, so my uncle was really angry. They had guns and everything. For four years it was very bad. Every time my uncle went out to do something they had people follow him to see what he was doing. And even when I came to bring some food, they would always watch. My uncle wasn't an activist; he just did Buddhist ceremonies. At that time the government thought that Buddhism is like cocaine. They tried to destroy Buddhism. So when they saw Buddhist monks, they hated them very much. They saw we wore long robe and said: "you have to save money, not wear a long robe. Cut them shorter!"[16]

They tried to escape a number of times. Lay followers paid owners of small boats in American dollars to help them escape, but they were pursued by the police, and had to abandon their first attempts. Finally, in 1979 they escaped from near the southern tip of Vietnam. They stayed in a temple for one week until their chance came to board the small boat that would take them away, along with thirty-eight strangers. Their experience, like that of many refugees who escaped Vietnam at this time, was harrowing. They stayed on the boat for six days with no food or water and then were shipwrecked on an island. They lived on bananas for thirty days. During this time pirates would land every day looking for women. Thầy Phổ Tịnh and the other women hid in a cave in the mountain whenever pirates were spotted, until they were finally rescued. The experience left a lasting imprint on her, including a persistent unwillingness to eat bananas.

For a year they lived in Pulau Bidong refugee camp in Malaysia, which had a population of 45,000. They stayed at a temple in the camp with a Buddhist monk who went on to lead a temple in Honolulu. Thầy Phổ Tịnh describes life in the camp this way: "Life was terrible. There was no food and not enough water for [the refugees] to drink. Every day they fought together because they had to line up for cans of fish or something." During this time her uncle developed kidney stones. She begged for help, but there were too many people and the doctor could do nothing. Food was rationed; the group with which they had arrived was given one pineapple to be divided among them, but she asked that they give the whole thing to her uncle to help him pass the stones. In return, she gave them all the fish meant for her and her uncle. As a vegetarian, the only food available to her was canned peas and rice. She added peas to bananas on her list of food she would never willingly eat again.

While they were in the refugee camp they received many invitations from monks in the United States. However, Thích Thiện Nghị felt that he would upset people if he picked one over another. A monk named Thích Phước Huệ, who was in Hong Kong at the time but is now in Sydney, advised Thích Thiện Nghị: "Go somewhere that has no Buddhist monks, because the Buddhist people there will need you. Don't go to the United States." So, they decided to go to Canada. The government turned down their initial application on the grounds that they spoke neither English nor French.

Eventually they were sponsored by Liên Hoa Temple in Brossard (across the river from Montreal), which was the first Vietnamese temple to be founded in Canada. The lay members who founded the temple were compelled to take in these two monastics in 1980 at the insistence of their master, Thích Tâm Châu, who had worked with Thích Thiện Nghị in Saigon before 1975.[17] Thích Tâm Châu had come from the north when the Communists took over, and led the faction within the Unified Buddhist Church that supported the war against the Communists at all costs, including tolerating the American presence, in opposition to the faction opposed to the American presence, led by Thích Trí Quang (Topmiller 2002, 7). Thích Thiện Nghị had been aligned with Thích Trí Quang, and so there are stories that Thích Tâm Châu had only reluctantly become involved with sponsoring the uncle and niece. McLellan suggests that Thích Thiện Nghị threatened to seek support from the Catholics if Thích Tâm Châu refused to help them (1999, 232n8). Thầy Phổ Tịnh told me that he helped because they had been friends and worked together in Saigon before 1975.

There were difficulties between the community at Liên Hoa Temple and the new monastics they had sponsored. The community at the temple consisted primarily of people from the north, and there were tensions right from the beginning. According to Thầy Phổ Tịnh, they did not want the temple to be dragged into political battles and sternly warned the newly arrived monastics not to make trouble. They believed that because Thích Thiện Nghị had been aligned with Thích Trí Quang he could therefore not be trusted. Thích Trí Quang was believed by some to be a Communist due to the role that he played in leading a Buddhist uprising against the Kỳ regime in South Vietnam in 1966, and had been opposed to Thích Tâm Châu.

Another difficulty, Dorais (2006, 124) suggests, is that a lay community had founded the temple and they were not willing to relinquish full control to the monastics. In Vietnam, temples are traditionally under the total control of the monastics. However, in the new setting relinquishing control to monastics has been a source of disagreement and divisiveness in a number of cases. As one monk I interviewed in Australia pointed out, it is reasonable for a lay group to not place total trust in a monk until the monk has proven himself trustworthy over a number of years.[18] Other monastics I have interviewed, however, have insisted that monastics have total control, since the monastic sangha is necessarily higher than lay Buddhists.

After three months Thích Thiện Nghị went to a meeting in the United States with Thích Mãn Giác, then leader of the Overseas Vietnamese

Buddhist Association in America (Hội Phật Giáo Hải Ngoại Tại Hoa Kỳ). The community at Liên Hoa Temple thought that he had gone for a meeting with Communists, so when he left they held a meeting and decided that he and Thầy Phổ Tịnh could no longer reside at their temple. Thầy Phổ Tịnh asked that they wait until her uncle's return, but they insisted she pack their bags immediately. Naturally, this decision by the temple leadership created a division in the community. Since this was the first Vietnamese temple and these the first Vietnamese monastics in Canada, many felt that it was unacceptable that they were being treated in this way. There was a big meeting when Thích Thiện Nghị returned and some people (especially southern Vietnamese) denounced the actions of the leaders of the Liên Hoa Temple and put their support behind Thích Thiện Nghị. Many lay Buddhists from south and central Vietnam went with them, putting up money for them to rent an apartment and eventually to buy an old synagogue that was transformed into Tam Bảo Temple.

Thích Thiện Nghị and Thầy Phổ Tịnh built up a new organization, called the Union of Vietnamese Buddhist Churches in Canada (UVBCC).[19] Dorais is correct in identifying Liên Hoa Temple as the "original source" from which many temples in Canada are derived (2006, 127). Nonetheless, the temple founded by Thích Thiện Nghị and Thầy Phổ Tịnh, by training and sponsoring monastics who have then gone on to start other temples, is more directly the source for many of the temples in Montreal, and a number across Canada. Some of these temples remain loosely affiliated with Tam Bảo Temple and the UVBCC, while others separated less amicably. At its height, there were twelve resident novice monks being trained at Tam Bảo Temple (Soucy 1994, 105).[20] One of the biggest projects of the UVBCC has been the building of a monastery in the Laurentians, north of Montreal, called the Great Pine Forest Monastery (Đại Tòng Lâm). This now houses the school where novices are taught, a Buddhist library, and a beautiful sanctuary. Large statues on the grounds depict the life of the Buddha and of other bodhisattvas.

When I started conducting research at Tam Bảo Temple in 1992, Thích Thiện Nghị was very active in efforts to assist in the founding of other temples, in building up the Great Pine Forest Monastery, and in bringing unity to Vietnamese Buddhism in Canada. However, it was immediately apparent that responsibility for the daily running of the temple rested with Thầy Phổ Tịnh, despite official leadership being held by Thích Thiện Nghị.

The division of responsibilities within the temple closely resembled the division within the Vietnamese family, where women were expected to care for the home – and had a great deal of power in this position – while men more often served as the official (but distant) authority and represented the family in the larger community (Soucy 1994; 1996). In a similar way, Thích Thiện Nghị descended from his apartment above the sanctuary in time to perform the Sunday service and give the sermon, but would then retire upstairs, available to those who wanted an official audience with him, mostly about major issues. Thích Thiện Nghị acted as the figurehead of the temple and the association. He was frequently absent, dealing with the affairs of the other temples in the organization and representing them in dialogues with other Vietnamese communities in exile.

Thầy Phổ Tịnh, on the other hand, was mainly concerned with training the novices and ensuring the temple's maintenance. She was very present, both before and after the service, directing people and making sure that everything was running smoothly. She was (and is) charismatic and funny – a forceful presence who garnered support and admiration from the lay community and novice monastics at the temple. People expressed to me that Thầy Phổ Tịnh was more approachable, especially regarding personal issues.[21] This was particularly true for women, who were more prone than men to discuss personal issues and seek guidance.

After suffering a stroke, Thích Thiện Nghị has moved to Australia and returns only periodically. This means that Thầy Phổ Tịnh has assumed practical leadership of the entire organization. In fact, her uncle's withdrawal from the daily life of Tam Bảo Temple started much earlier (Soucy 1994, 113–14). From 1992 to 1994 I observed that Thích Thiện Nghị was increasingly absent from the daily operations of the temple and the Sunday services. While at the beginning he conducted most rituals, he gradually started appearing only to give the sermon and later left even that task to Thầy Phổ Tịnh. The reason for his withdrawal, evidently, was his mounting age combined with his demanding responsibilities to the larger organization. Another important reason may have been that Thầy Phổ Tịnh was being prepared to eventually take over the leadership of the Tam Bảo Temple. However, by her admission, since taking over her uncle's responsibilities she has found maintaining the organization to be very demanding. Thus, while there are still ten temples across Canada affiliated with Tam Bảo Temple, in effect it is only Hoa Nghiêm Temple in Toronto, Tam Bảo

Temple in Montreal, and the monastery in the Laurentians that are directly under the leadership of Thầy Phổ Tịnh.

THẦY PHỔ TỊNH'S ROLE

Although there has been a strong *bhikṣuṇī sangha* (order of nuns) that some estimate has been larger than the *bhikṣu sangha* (order of monks) in Vietnam (Dharma 1988, 156), the *bhikṣuṇī sangha* has not been equal in status to the *bhikṣu sangha*. According to Buddhist monastic rules, nuns of all ranks are expected to bow to monks of any level, and monks always take precedence over nuns. Monks always are given higher status than nuns, a status displayed by nuns following monks in processions and being placed behind monks in rituals. Further, nuns never perform rituals if there are monks present to do so. Almost all the prominent Vietnamese Buddhist figures in Vietnam today are monks,[22] and while there are many nuns, they usually confine themselves to their own temples. A monk always leads public ceremonies if one is present. Thầy Phổ Tịnh explains this lower status on the basis that nuns lack the education essential to performing the services. Karuna Dharma – the abbess of the International Buddhist Meditation Center, founded by Thích Thiên Ân, and an active Buddhist feminist – writes, "A second obstacle is that the Vietnamese bhikkhunis themselves tend to be too shy and retiring" (Dharma 1988, 159). While Dharma's impressions are, I suspect, based partly on Western, Orientalist, stereotypes of the "Asian woman," it is nonetheless true that nuns remain largely in the shadows in Vietnam.[23] For example, in a temple in Hanoi where I have conducted research since 1997, the resident nun, who was by no means "shy and retiring," would nonetheless defer to monks (Soucy 2012), and in a Zen monastery in Hanoi, where I have been doing research since 2004, nuns are always subordinate to monks, always standing behind monks and never taking leadership roles in rituals.

The situation is markedly different in Canada. First, the particular circumstances in Canada, with a scarcity of resources when Vietnamese Buddhists initially arrived and with no established monastic communities, led to Tam Bảo Temple being the residence of both nuns and monks. This has created a situation where a nun has been a leader and a teacher of both monks and nuns out of necessity. However, we must also recognize that, while there were circumstantial imperatives, they might not have led to the same result if not for the unusual personalities involved.

Janet McLellan has pointed out that the prominent position of Thầy Phổ Tịnh rests partly on her level of secular and Buddhist education but also on the support of her uncle, Thích Thiện Nghị. From the beginning Thích Thiện Nghị has been a strong supporter of his niece and of women in general. McLellan points out that Thích Thiện Nghị was supportive of Thầy Phổ Tịnh performing rituals as well as instructing members and organizing activities. McLellan writes, "He feels nuns are needed in Canada and should be used to their full capacity as spiritual teachers, leading religious services, and as administrators, although this attitude causes controversy and dissent" (1999, 117).

Thầy Phổ Tịnh has acted as a positive female role model for the women of her temple. Thus, Tam Bảo Temple upholds the ideal of equality and educates the monks and nuns together. Furthermore, Thầy Phổ Tịnh has acted as one of their teachers, explaining gender inequalities of the past as misinterpretations. Through her, they see the example of a woman who is actively religious and who is in a position of power. She turns the traditional karma-based justification of male supremacy on its ear by pointing out that "if men were more spiritually advanced there would not be so many unenlightened men in the world." She also frequently cites the Buddha's treatment of women as a way to refute culture-based assumptions about gender.

She refuses to believe that a man is higher than her solely by virtue of being male. She explained to me that nuns bow to monks only out of politeness, rather than due to inequality or subservience. Because nuns are often uneducated, they do not understand the real intention of the rule, and it is misinterpreted to mean that nuns of any level must bow to even the most junior monk. She has expressed to me on a number of occasions that she considers gender to be at the root of many of our problems: "My expectation is to translate the rules for women into English and French and to write a book admonishing people to think about gender. I hate gender because it has brought so much suffering. The Buddha said you are in samsara because of gender. If you think too much about gender, it makes you do very bad things. For example, thinking: 'Oh, I am a man, I am number one. You are a woman, you have to do this and this,' causes so many bad actions."

For Thầy Phổ Tịnh, authority is not a matter of gender but of education, and with education should come equality. She has therefore gone to great lengths to gain added legitimacy through a secular education. She is the first Vietnamese nun to receive a master's degree in a North American university. Since then, her responsibilities within her organization have made it difficult to study, although her will to do so is strong. She believes that education is a crucial condition for holding authority, but it is not sufficient. Authority must rest on actions rather than words.

> In Vietnam, lay Buddhists follow monastics unquestioningly because of emotional connection (*cảm tình*), but here they follow because of capacity (*khả năng*). The Buddhist people from other [Vietnamese Buddhist] communities, they told people here they really admire me because they see the Great Pine Forest Monastery. I do everything without asking for help. I never ask people "give me dollars, give me dollars." I just do the work. People see this and give money right away. You have to prove yourself to them by your capacity – not by telling them things. I don't like to tell someone. Right now I am 55 years old, and as I become older I don't like to talk so much. So, the people are really surprised and ask: "why don't you talk to us, why don't you speak to us like before?" I tell them that I am getting older. I want to do things without talking. That is the Buddhist way. The Buddha says you have to keep quiet all the time. Sometimes you need to talk and sometimes you don't. In my case, I need to act, not talk.

Thầy Phổ Tịnh's teachings have a clear influence on the way that women are regarded at Tam Bảo Temple, but she also has an influence in another sense. In trying to shape the ideas of Buddhists at Tam Bảo Temple, she serves as a filter, keeping away those who do not agree with her position.

CHALLENGES

Thầy Phổ Tịnh's presence at Tam Bảo Temple, and the stance that both she and her uncle have taken regarding female leadership and her authority, have been contested on a number of occasions. Indeed, the gender issue has been one factor in both lay Buddhists and monks leaving Tam Bảo Temple and starting other temples in Montreal. Of course, as mentioned earlier, it is not the only reason for monks leaving Tam Bảo Temple. Nonetheless, it has been fairly central, and often the catalyst for schism. There have been disagreements from the beginning about her and her uncle residing in the same temple. Immediately after the separation from Liên Hoa Temple in Brossard, a number of the laity made it clear that they thought it inappropriate for monks and nuns to reside together. They insisted that Thầy Phổ Tịnh move to a nunnery that had been established in the United States, and Thầy Phổ Tịnh was prepared to do so. However, her uncle protested that, since they were relatives, it was unthinkable that there would be any sexual relations between them and so refused the demands of the laity. In her words, "My uncle said no. We are from the same family. We cannot do something bad. That is a Vietnamese tradition. Uncles cannot get married with nieces – this is very dirty. But they always think dirty, so some of them left my uncle because of me."

Being one of the first monastics in Canada, it fell to Thầy Phổ Tịnh, with her seniority and her education, to take a leadership role and to train the novices at Tam Bảo Temple. A nun taking such a prominent role in training monks is particular to Vietnamese Buddhism in the diaspora and does not happen in Vietnam.

Because reform movements from the early twentieth century improved the position of women in Vietnam as part of a push for modernization, in contemporary Vietnam it is generally not thought to be a problem for women to be educated and achieve high positions.[24] However, in reality, particularly when the situation is not abstract, Vietnamese men often feel uncomfortable in relationships where women have more social capital. Thus, men are seldom willing to marry women who have more education or earn higher salaries, and consequently parents often discourage their daughters from pursuing ambitions that will create a barrier to what are thought of as women's defining roles: that of a mother and wife.

Within Buddhist contexts, embodied expectations of women's subordination are carried through, and the conservatism of Buddhism in Vietnam further reinforces gender inequality. Nuns are always seated in subordinate positions, always come after monks in processions, and usually play a supportive, rather than dominant, role in Buddhist rituals. This being the case, Thầy Phổ Tịnh's education serves to grant authority, but also poses a challenge in that it threatens monks in the same way that it threatens husbands. She describes her problems in this way:

You know the Vietnamese tradition, especially with the monks. Every monk, after they finish training in the monastery, they want to control themselves in their own temple. They don't want to be under another's control, even though they are young. That is why they don't want to be in contact with me. It isn't only my problem either. In [another Vietnamese temple in Montreal] an important and senior monk has also trained Buddhist monks who then don't want to be under his control. That is a big problem for him. Besides, with me, they think I am a woman and I also have a higher education than them, so they don't want to talk to me. My problem with them really comes down to education.

Because some monks have been uncomfortable with female leadership, Thầy Phổ Tịnh's presence has led to schism. In the past, Tam Bảo Temple has sponsored monks from refugee camps and from Vietnam, with the intention of building up the sangha in Canada. However, Thầy Phổ Tịnh has found the results of these ventures to be disappointing, largely because the monks arrive with inflexible notions of gender and of the relative positions of monks and nuns. Many are unprepared to follow the leadership of a nun. A couple of monks who were sponsored from Vietnam demanded that Thầy Phổ Tịnh leave the temple when they arrived. Although she was willing to leave, her uncle refused, so they left to start temples of their own. She says, "Buddhist monks I sponsored from refugee camps; they tried to oppose me. I don't know what happened. Even though I tried to be very kind with them, in their minds, they cannot erase their preoccupations about gender. I told them: 'You teach Buddhists – men and women – to be equal, but you cannot apply it. That is very contrary.' So, they don't like me. Sometimes I suffer."

Another monk started as a novice at Tam Bảo Temple, but when he achieved the rank of *Đại Đức* (reverend) he told Thích Thiện Nghị that he would stay only if Thầy Phổ Tịnh left. He also has gone on to start a temple elsewhere in Montreal. In this way, Tam Bảo Temple has acted as a seed temple for the proliferation of Vietnamese Buddhist temples in Montreal. In her words:

So they left, but we still had other new Buddhist people come in. About three years later, in 1993, a group of Buddhist young people – mostly men – tried to start activities with the non-religious [Vietnamese] community, which is very political.[25] But my uncle said no. So they tried to separate again and form another group. They try to establish Huyền Không Temple, you see? At the same time, I sponsored two monks. A couple of others talked to them about me. And two of them tried to force a decision that I should leave. So I said, "Ok, if you don't have enough good cause to stay with me, I will go. I don't mind." From that time I vowed I would never sponsor Buddhist monks [from Vietnam]. I will accept someone from here into the temple to become a monk, but not from Vietnam, nor from refugee camps, because they always listen, but they don't see. I told them, you have to see before you listen. Another monk I accepted to become a monk here in Montreal. He became a monk after three years and achieved the rank of Đại Đức. But he hated me because he followed the two other monks. And he asked my uncle, if my uncle needs him to stay with him kick me out. So my uncle said, "No. She's my niece. I cannot let her out. If you feel that way you can leave." And he left to establish another temple.

An indication of the unwillingness of monks to accept her seniority comes through in a controversy over terminology used to designate the ranks of monks and nuns. Monks are usually referred to in written form and in introductions with their rank preceding their name. The monastic ranks are: (1) Pre-initiands (*chú tiểu*), usually children who enter the monastery for education and may or may not decide to continue when they reach the age of twenty; (2) Novice (*Sa Di*); (3) Reverend (*Đại Đức*), attained after twenty years in the sangha; (4) Venerable (*Thượng Tọa*) attained after thirty years in the sangha, and; (5) Most Venerable (*Hòa Thượng*), which is the highest rank and is attained after fifty years in the sangha. There is no rationalized system of examination or test to rise from one rank to the next and, instead, seniority depends on how many years one has been a monastic. This coincides with the general understanding in Vietnamese society that age confers status and seniority. However, Thầy Phổ Tịnh, with the support of Thích Thiện Nghị, insisted that nuns should be addressed in the same way as monks and be allowed to wear the same coloured robes. Thầy Phổ Tịnh explains that many monks do not want to refer to nuns by their rank, as they would a monk, instead preferring to call them a generic term – *sư cô* – which means simply "nun," or *sư bà*, which means "senior nun." This position causes a great deal of friction with other Buddhist monks:

OK, so if you are a man they will call you "Đại Đức," but if you are a woman, they don't want to call you "Đại Đức," they call you "sư cô." If I'm older they would call me "sư bà." But that is not good. It still depends on gender. In Buddhism, they are Buddhist monks, so they should leave behind these outside ideas. So, the reason the monks in the U.S. and here don't want to speak with me is because the Buddhists at my temple called me "Đại Đức," and now "Thượng Tọa." If the Buddhist lay people here followed outsiders in calling me "sư cô," they would be in trouble with me right away. But the Buddhist people here go to other temples and say "ok, my master – or Đại Đức – at Tam Bảo Temple taught us this way, the monks there will hate me right away." Women are not allowed to be called "Đại Đức." But from the Buddha – when the Buddha was alive – men and women were the same level.

Senior monks living in the West have also had difficulty with the issue of gender. Thầy Phổ Tịnh pointed out that one famous Vietnamese monk, who has both Western and Vietnamese followers, is inconsistent in separating men and women when the followers are Vietnamese, but talking about equality with his Western followers. She accuses leading monks in North America of being hypocritical, saying gender-positive things but refusing to put it in writing: "[One senior monk] talked to some of my members from this community, he said, 'ok every time I meet her I will call her "Đại Đức," but if she is gone I have to call her "sư cô."' So, it is opposite, you know? But my view is that, as a leader, when you talk you should do the same. If I tell something to you, I will do it."

The issue of Thầy Phổ Tịnh being a leader, and outranking (or being of equal rank to) monks at other temples, has also been an obstacle to bringing unity to the various unifying organizations: "The most important thing now is the gender. You know, according to Buddha's teaching, we try to erase discrimination. However, in theory it is OK, but in practice they don't want to. So if they were back under my uncle's control they would agree to unite, but only if I left. If I'm here they don't want to be a part of it. So I told my uncle that if they are willing, he should try to unite them and I will leave. I can live by myself, its OK."

In the early 2000s, after Thích Thiện Nghị's stroke, it fell to Thầy Phổ Tịnh to assume leadership of the UVBCC. However, the autonomy of temples means that the strength of any unifying organization depends largely on the charisma and respect accorded to the leader. Thích Thiện Nghị had been a well-respected monk with a relatively senior position as a teacher of *vinaya* at the Buddhist university in Saigon. He was able to build up the UVBCC largely through his social capital and his charisma. However, organizations that are started by charismatic founders can usually find continuity only through replacing one charismatic individual with another or, as is more usually the case, through a process of normalization and institutionalization.[26] The process of assuming overall leadership from Thích Thiện Nghị has been difficult for Thầy Phổ Tịnh. Her uncle returns periodically, and he is still the nominal head, but he is not likely to recover his health sufficiently to reassume full leadership. When I was last doing research in 2006, people would still refer to Thích Thiện Nghị as their master, but effective leadership was in the hands of Thầy Phổ Tịnh.

Thầy Phổ Tịnh has found that she cannot maintain a strong connection with all the affiliated temples across Canada. She told me that they expect her to visit each one at least once a month, which she feels is too demanding. This is especially the case since she finds that Hoa Nghiêm Temple – the large temple in Toronto that has the closest association with Tam Bảo Temple – has many problems and demands a great deal of her attention. The effort that she is required to exert in order to maintain authority is likely much greater than it was for her uncle.

The organization has been nominally maintained, but the absence of Thích Thiện Nghị as a centralizing force has weakened it. The Great Pine Forest Monastery, however, is thriving. Thầy Phổ Tịnh says that all the monks around Montreal willingly go to their monastery in the Laurentians because it is currently being run by one of her male disciples, a monk named Thích Pháp Thán. Because he is a monk, they have no problem getting along with him. This is true, she explains, within Vietnamese society as a whole. Even women tend to prefer to be taught by monks rather than nuns. As a result, while monks can rest somewhat on the fact that they are male, she has to rely more on her qualities and virtues as a teacher and monastic.

CONCLUSION

Thầy Phổ Tịnh, Thích Thiện Nghị, and Tam Bảo Temple have had a profound effect on Vietnamese Buddhism in Canada. Because of their uncompromising stand regarding gender issues and their attempts to accommodate changes to make a sangha viable in Canada, some monks have left Tam Bảo Temple to start their own temples. This has had the overall effect of increasing the presence of Vietnamese Buddhism in Canada. Thầy Phổ Tịnh and Thích Thiện Nghị have also had an effect on the roles of monks and nuns in Canada, at least within the affiliated temples across Canada.

Thầy Phổ Tịnh has been studying for her doctorate in California for the past few years. However, she has remained president of the Unified Buddhist Church of Vietnam in Canada and in charge of Hoa Nghiêm Temple in Toronto and the Great Pine Forest Monastery, while Tam Bảo Temple is being run by one of her monastic disciples, Thích Pháp Tánh. Thus, in spite of her absence, little has changed in terms of her authority in the organization, the monastery, and the two main temples in Montreal and Toronto. Nonetheless, she is busy, and it is a challenge to maintain her presence in Canada while continuing to study and teach in the United States.

There are a number of converging factors that have led to Thầy Phổ Tịnh's successful leadership. Thích Thiện Nghị showed immense foresight and leadership by insisting on gender equality in his organization. This has combined with a broader societal context in Canada that differs from Vietnam's, in that gender equality is a major element of public discourse and there is a greater recognition of women's equal capacity. However, Thầy Phổ Tịnh's leadership would surely not have become a reality had it not been for her charismatic leadership abilities and her indomitable spirit, her drive for gender equality, and her efforts to solidify her authority by striving to be educated and to lead by example. Her example as a female monastic leader will doubtless have a lasting effect on the shape that Vietnamese Buddhism will take in Canada.

NOTES

1   At the time, she was at the monastic rank of Đại Đức (reverend) and had the name Thích Nữ Quảng Oanh ("Thích" is standard for all Vietnamese monastics and "Nữ" denotes that she is a nun.) Her name was changed when she advanced to the rank of Thượng Tọa (venerable). I refer to her as "Thầy" (teacher), following the practice of

the Buddhists at Tam Bảo Temple. "Thích" is the transliteration of Śākya (the surname of the Buddha), which all monastics adopt in Vietnam.

2 The Vietnamese word for a Buddhist temple, *chùa*, was generally translated as "pagode" by French scholars during the colonial period in order to draw a distinction with non-Buddhist structures that are called "temples." Scholars who write about Vietnamese religion, including myself, often adopt this practice, calling it "pagoda," but in this essay I use "temple" for the sake of conformity with other chapters in this volume.

3 As of the summer of 2011, she has been working on a doctorate and teaching meditation in California, although I am not sure where she is studying, when she started, or when she expects to finish (Thầy Phổ Tịnh, email correspondence with the author, April 2012).

4 Victor Hori, email communication with the author in 2012.

5 From an interview with a monk at Tam Bảo Temple, conducted in 2006.

6 To my knowledge, there is only one biographical account of a Vietnamese Buddhist nun in the West: *Dam Luu: An Eminent Vietnamese Buddhist Nun* (Thich Minh Duc 2000). In Vietnamese, I am aware of only one collection of monastic biographies that includes nuns (four out of 141 entries describe female monastics) (Thích Thanh Từ 1992).

7 This is not to say there are none. Cheng Yen, the founder of Tzu Chi, is one example, but the exceptionality of her case illustrates my point.

8 See V. Hori (2010a) and Soucy (2010) for critiques of the bias against "ethnic" Buddhists.

9 In fact, most have played down their previous association with Tam Bảo Temple, and it would have been awkward and likely unfruitful to dig into these old disputes.

10 While the first Vietnamese students arrived as early as 1950 and 1951, the number of students arriving increased in the 1960s due to the Colombo Plan scholarship program (Dorais 1987, 16; 1988, 168–9; Lavoie 1989, 8).

11 This number comes from my ongoing list of contacts that I have derived from English and Vietnamese websites as well as the contact books of some temples. This number does not include meditation groups who follow Thích Nhất Hạnh's organization, Tiếp Hiện – Order of Interbeing.

12 There are no Vietnamese temples in Atlantic Canada due to the small size of communities there. Only Halifax has a sizeable community, but with a total of around five hundred individuals (many of whom are Christian), there are still not enough Vietnamese to start a temple (Soucy 2013).

13 Giáo hội Phật giáo Việt Nam Thống nhất tại Canada and Giáo hội Phật giáo Việt Nam Thống nhất hải ngoại tại Canada, respectively.
14 Thích Thiện Nghị is Thầy Phổ Tịnh's father's mother's brother's son.
15 There are four monastic ranks, which are described later in the essay.
16 Except where noted, all quotations from Thầy Phổ Tịnh were taken from two interviews that lasted two hours each in the summer of 2006. The conversations were in both English and Vietnamese. The quotations have been translated into English where necessary and the English has been edited for the sake of clarity.
17 Thích Tâm Châu was residing in France at the time, but has since relocated to Montreal.
18 Thích Quảng Ba, interview with the author in Canberra, Australia, September 2011.
19 The UVBCC was founded in 1988, with Thích Thiện Nghị as president, with the understanding that Venerable Thích Nguyên Tịnh would be in charge of Western Canada, while Thích Thiện Nghị would take care of the East. Today there are ten temples in Canada that are associated with the UVBCC, although association with the UVBCC does not override the essential autonomy of individual temples, and association is often nominal.
20 By 2006 Thầy Phổ Tịnh reported that there were ten temples in the association for which she was responsible.
21 It should be noted that in Vietnamese stereotypes, fathers are strict, distant, and the authority in the house, while mothers are primary caregivers and seen as compassionate and closer to their children.
22 Sister Chân Không of the Order of Interbeing is a notable exception, although technically she does not live in Vietnam, and it could be argued that she would not have her present renown if she had stayed in Vietnam.
23 There are, of course, exceptions. Dam Luu in the United States is one and another is Sister Chân Không, who has long held a prominent position in Thích Nhất Hạnh's organization.
24 For more on the movement to improve the status of women in Vietnamese society in the early twentieth century, see Marr (1981, chapter 5). For more on the sometimes ambiguous position of women in Vietnam, see Gammeltoft (1999), and Drummond and Rydstrøm (2004).
25 By "political" she is likely referring to anti-Communist activity, but may also be referring to a tendency for internal contestation and infighting.
26 As, for example, Lang and Ragvald (1998) described a spirit-writing cult in Hong Kong in the early twentieth century, which transformed into a mass-worship cult in the years following the death of the founder.

15

Leslie Kawamura: Nothing to Add, Nothing to Take Away

JOHN S. HARDING

We had gathered in San Francisco in November 2011 for the annual meeting of the American Academy of Religion (AAR) and its usual busy schedule of meetings, interviews, panels, and presentations. On the last evening of the conference, however, the pace slowed down. A group of scholars, colleagues, family, and friends congregated to commemorate a popular and influential scholar, Dr Leslie Kawamura. Dr Kawamura, who was born in Alberta in 1935, had passed away on 10 March 2011. The program featured words he had spoken just before he died and a photo in which he is dressed in Buddhist vestments, with a *wagesa* – the stole worn by a Jōdo Shinshū (Pure Land) Buddhist priest – over a black robe (see illustration 12). The back of the program listed sponsoring academic groups and the names and institutional affiliations of the panel's chairperson and ten speakers. The panelists included prominent scholars of Buddhism and two students who had been especially close to Kawamura and were editing his festschrift. Kawamura's wife, Toyo, provided the quotation at the top of the program: "Everything is perfect. Nothing to add. Nothing to take away. It is all good." She said that her husband had uttered these words to her and their daughter, Nao, just before his death.[1]

The memorial panel resounded with stories about Kawamura's scholarship, humour, dedication, friendship, mentoring, breadth and depth of knowledge, support of junior colleagues, and generosity to students. Kawamura's final words seemed strikingly appropriate for the remarkably complete life and work described by his friends and colleagues. Prompted by reflections offered by the esteemed scholars who spoke before me – Charles Prebish, John Holt, Charles Willemen, Dan Lusthaus, Ken Tanaka, and A. Charles Muller – I recalled a diverse array of interactions with Leslie Kawamura during the first year I met him that indicated the range of his activities and contributions.

I thought back to May 2004, when most of the former Numata scholars flew back to Calgary to attend the Numata Chair 15th Anniversary Symposium. In addition to enjoying the uniquely intimate format of this conference, I was struck by these eminent Buddhologists' praise of Dr Kawamura as an exceptionally competent steward of the Numata Chair in Buddhist Studies. Later that month, I began to realize the extent of Dr Kawamura's support for his graduate students: he drove a group of students from Calgary to the 2004 Congress of the Humanities and Social Sciences in Winnipeg and back, more than 1,300 kilometres each way, in his well-used minivan. I joined the group at a Chinese restaurant during the conference and noticed that he paid everyone's bill following the convivial meal. After these initial encounters with Dr Kawamura, I was surprised to see him as Rev. Leslie Kawamura in ministerial regalia at the early July ceremonies celebrating the seventy-fifth anniversary of the rural Buddhist temple where he was born.[2] Conversations with Leslie Kawamura during this and subsequent Jōdo Shinshū events revealed his candour and concern for the tradition's survival in Canada. Months later, Dr Kawamura lectured in my introductory Buddhism course. My students responded enthusiastically to his humor and approach, which was neither reverent nor dry but instead unpredictable, insightful, and engaging. In that same year, I witnessed Leslie Kawamura in his several roles as scholar, facilitator of academic interaction, advisor of graduate students, teacher of undergraduates, and as a Buddhist priest and practitioner with lifelong ties to the local Jōdo Shinshū community.

Practitioners, priests, scholars, and sympathizers have nurtured the growth of Buddhism in Canada and contributed to the larger global currents that have shaped and sustained it. Leslie Kawamura stands out as an especially influential Buddhist pioneer in and beyond Canada, who dedicated himself to cultivating both the ministerial and the academic fields. This chapter reflects on a Buddhist life in which these ministerial and academic strands of Buddhism intertwine and uses the example of Rev./Dr Kawamura as a lens through which to analyse the difference, and at times tension, between the roles of priest and scholar. Leslie Kawamura's skilful navigation of the various challenges and expectations presented by both roles demonstrates one way that this tension can be overcome and invites contemplation about how these roles can conflict with or complement each other. For the most part, I will use the title Rev. Kawamura in the section that explores the ministerial role and Dr Kawamura in the section on the academic role, and Kawamura throughout.[3]

MINISTER – REV. KAWAMURA

Leslie Kawamura served as a minister of Jōdo Shinshū, also known simply as Shin Buddhism. Shin is the largest school of Buddhism in Japan and the oldest sect of Buddhism in Canada. It was also the dominant form of Buddhism in Canada for approximately sixty years, from the opening of the first temple in Vancouver in 1905 until the new influx of immigrants from Asia that began in the late 1960s (Harding 2010; Watada 2010). Given the importance of this tradition to the development of Buddhism in Canada, there are many figures who merit attention. Among these, Rev. Yutetsu Kawamura, Leslie's father, has been recognized through awards in his own lifetime, such as the Order of Canada in 1984 and an honorary doctorate at the University of Lethbridge in 1987.[4] His extensive service is also the subject of the documentary film *The Travelling Reverend* (Ohama 2000). Their ministerial paths have been linked from Leslie Kawamura's birth in the Raymond Buddhist Church on 7 July 1935, where his father was the resident minister. Almost seventy years later, father and son participated in the seventy-fifth anniversary service at that temple, on 4 July 2004. Despite this clear connection between Reverends Kawamura, when Leslie Kawamura was preparing an autobiographical chapter for a book I edited, *Studying Buddhism in Practice*, he attributed his ministerial role as much to his mother, Yoneko, as to his father.[5] He was not able to complete these reflections before his death, so there is an absence of information on his early life. Therefore, this section focuses more on Rev. Kawamura's adult life, from his work with youth and the Buddhist Churches of America (BCA) in the San Francisco Bay area in the 1950s to his role in the final five years of his life revitalizing Shin as Director of the Living Dharma Centre for the Jodo Shinshu Buddhist Temples of Canada.

In the intervening years, Kawamura moved to Kyoto, Japan, in 1958 to pursue Buddhist Studies at Ryukoku University, in preparation for ordination and a career as a Shin minister. Rev. Kawamura was awarded a master of arts degree in Buddhist history at the Nishi Honganji affiliated Ryukoku University in 1961, but extended his Buddhist studies for another three years in Japan. For his second MA, Kawamura pursued a more academic focus, this time at Kyoto University where he earned a master of arts degree in Buddhist philosophy in 1964 under the supervision of Gadjin Nagao, who became the ranking scholar of Buddhist studies in Japan.[6] Oscillating between academic and religious roles, Rev. Kawamura returned to Raymond, Alberta, as its minister in 1964. Despite his strong academic and ministerial credentials and the support of many in the community who were eager to have him as their minister, others opposed his appointment. This division later widened into an institutional split within Buddhism in Alberta (examined in the section on "Innovation and Division" below), which led Rev. Kawamura to offer his letter of resignation from the Buddhist Churches of Canada (BCC) in 1969. A few years later, Nishi Honganji headquarters in Japan suspended his official status as a minister. These difficulties with religious authorities coincided with Kawamura's renewed interest in academic study. By the beginning of the 1970s, Rev. Kawamura decided to pursue doctoral studies at the University of Saskatchewan, where he earned a PhD in Far Eastern Studies in 1976 under the supervision of the Buddhologist Herbert Guenther. Dr Kawamura then began his thirty-five-year career as a professor of Buddhist Studies at the University of Calgary. Although the pendulum had swung back to scholarship and teaching, he continued to cultivate Buddhist practice and to minister informally for several decades until his official reinstatement by Honganji authorities and appointment in 2006 as the director of the Living Dharma Centre for the Jodo Shinshu Buddhist Temples of Canada.

Bridge between Countries, Cultures, Languages, and Generations

Rev. Kawamura's role in bridging several gaps between East and West began with his birth. He was born in the temple where his father was the resident minister, replicating the Japanese pattern of hereditary transmission in which the resident priest of a Shin temple expects to pass on the temple to his son. At the same time, this temple was in rural Alberta, which was a strikingly different environment for a Shin priest: Buddhism had a marginal position in Canadian society; lay members, rather than a temple family, owned the "Buddhist Church," affecting hereditary succession;

Christian forms were adopted, including the use of terms like "church" and "minister" as well as Sunday services, Dharma school for children, sitting in pews, and singing hymns.[7] Because Kawamura was born in Canada, a *nisei* (second-generation) descendant of Japanese immigrants, and received training on both sides of the Pacific Ocean, neither the Japanese Shin forms nor Canadian variants were foreign to him.

The context – 1935 southern Alberta – was also significant. Six-and-a-half years after Kawamura's birth, Japanese residents of Canada were forcibly relocated away from the West Coast to internment camps or to work on sugar beet farms in southern Alberta. Raymond's Buddhist population swelled in 1942 with this influx, resulting in Raymond's temple becoming central to the organization and history of Buddhism in Canada in that era. Kawamura's life spans the hardships of the 1930s and 1940s as well as different types of challenges and opportunities in subsequent decades, when Buddhism began to be established in universities but struggled to survive intergenerational transitions. Kawamura served as a bridge between Japanese immigrants and their Canadian descendants, between the early pressure to assimilate and the transition to multiculturalism. At home in either Japan or Canada, fluent in Japanese and English, fully trained as both scholar and minster, he was the right person, born at the right place and time, to help establish Buddhism in Canada.

Leslie Kawamura's life and work also bridge the recurring typology for academic scholarship on Buddhism in the West that often divides the field into Asian/ethnic and Western/convert. His entire life took place on the border between Asian/ethnic and Western/convert. This typology continues to dominate the discussion.[8] However, the problems in applying such categories as "immigrant" and "convert" in the West beyond the first generation are illustrated in Kawamura's case, since he was neither immigrant nor convert. Richard Seager introduced a third category, "Asian Americans, primarily from Chinese and Japanese backgrounds, who have practiced Buddhism in this country for four and five generations" (Seager 1999, 9–10), but this does not entirely fit either. Kawamura's undergraduate study of Western philosophy and interaction with the Beat "Dharma Bums" in the San Francisco Bay area in the 1950s demonstrates characteristics from all three categories without being captured by any one.[9] Nevertheless, the ethnicity, country of origin, and country of Buddhist ministerial training remain relevant points of contention that speak to perceptions of the strengths and limitations of religious leaders for Buddhist communities that have become established in North America.

Japanese Overseas Priests in Canada vs Canadian Ministers

Although it has the deepest roots in Canadian soil, Shin Buddhism shows signs of distress. Its influence is waning and its population is aging. But there are signs of vitality as well, and under Rev. Kawamura's direction, the Living Dharma Centre nurtured renewal of the tradition with special attention to youth engagement. Discussions about the ability of Shin to survive and thrive typically hinge on strategies to retain members and their offspring and to attract others, including large numbers in North America who have a general interest in Buddhism but no specific connection to Jōdo Shinshū. At times, these conversations about connecting with a broader audience raise issues regarding the relative advantage of being a native-born Buddhist minister fluent in English rather than a priest born and trained in Japan. Currently, training to become a Jōdo Shinshū minister can begin in North America but must be completed in Japan, which poses language and cultural challenges for non-Japanese applicants. For a priest trained in Japan, the challenges work in the other direction because, after several generations, relatively few Japanese-speaking members remain in North American Shin congregations.

The earliest Shin ministers were all born and trained in Japan. Although Rev. Yutetsu Kawamura was born in Japan and believed that the strengths of first-generation Japanese (*issei*) priests matched well with ministering to Japanese immigrants, he also saw that this background would be inadequate for subsequent generations and for growth beyond the Japanese community. He therefore advocated recruitment of non-Japanese ministers who could help Buddhism take root and continue to spread in North America (Y. Kawamura 1997, 49–50; Harding 2010, 153–4). Leslie Kawamura connected with both aspects of his father's vision for ministerial directions in North America. That is, he became a Canadian-born minister fluent in English and in Canadian cultural references and he supported the training and assignments of Caucasian ministers in Alberta.[10]

Honpa Buddhist Churches of Alberta, supported by both father and son, hired the first two Caucasian Shin ministers in Canada, James Burkey for over two years in the early 1970s and then June King for a longer term from the late 1970s to early 1980s (LDJCA 2001, 93). Leslie Kawamura was proud of these milestones. In an article describing changes within Shin Buddhism in Alberta, he wrote in reference to the hiring of Rev. Burkey that the Honpa Buddhist Church's "acceptance of a Caucasian minister to administer to the needs of the congregation – a first in the whole history of Buddhism in Canada – is a landmark in Canadian Buddhism" (1978, 50). Moreover, Kawamura added, "the second minister to join, and who contributes yet another landmark, is Reverend June King. She is the first woman to serve any of the Buddhist organizations in Canada" (1978, 50). This more progressive vision for fostering increasing vitality within the tradition in Canada's religious landscape, and the willingness to act upon innovative ideas, marked Rev. Kawamura's ministerial attitude.[11] This endeared both father and son to many lay members who agreed that the tradition should adapt to its time and environment but alienated others, including some fellow ministers and members of central authority in Japan.

Innovation and Division

In fact, in this case, innovation and alienation of authority are inextricably linked. During this pivotal time for the Buddhist community in southern Alberta, the Kawamuras, as well as the Honpa Buddhist Churches of Alberta that they helped establish, were central to the innovations as well as the schism. The Honpa Buddhist Churches of Alberta's decision to hire Burkey and King illustrates its progressive stance. But because the Honpa Buddhist Churches of Alberta held authority over the placement of ministers *only as a result of* separation from the Buddhist Churches of America (BCA), this innovation is also linked to that schism. Before the formation of this separate Honpa organization in 1965, the Nishi Honganji headquarters in Japan had ultimate authority with regard to ministers, and the BCA administered such decisions for Canada and the United States (except for Hawai'i, which was and continues to be its own district with dozens of temples). Then in 1965, the two Kawamuras helped create Honpa Buddhist Churches of Alberta, which rejected the authority of the BCA and its Japanese headquarters. Honpa remained independent until 1982. Meanwhile, in 1967 the Buddhist Churches of Canada (BCC) took over this administrative role from the BCA within Canada (Harding 2010, 143). By 1982, the Honpa Buddhist Churches of Alberta joined the Buddhist Churches of Canada, which meant that authority for hiring and placing ministers reverted to Honganji headquarters and BCC administration (Watada 1996, 185). The more local and progressive, but separate, Honpa Buddhist Churches of Alberta organization was reabsorbed into the global network headquartered in Japan.

Conflicting accounts, reluctance of some to discuss past tensions that continue to resonate today, and the rapidly changing circumstances and divisions as congregations decided which group to join make it difficult to concisely characterize the seventeen-year history of the Honpa Buddhist Churches of Alberta. Consistent with Ama's chapter in this volume about conflict among early Shin Buddhists in Canada, problems in Alberta included personal animosities, which were at times exacerbated by regional allegiances carried over from Japan and by the mother temple's uncertainty about how best to resolve local tensions.[12] Significantly, neither difference of religious belief nor even of practice was central to the schism. Instead, interpersonal issues and differences of opinion about the role and authority of ministers versus lay board members appear to have been at the forefront along with generational differences and diverse perspectives on how Shin could best develop in Canada. Anthropologist Carlo Caldarola notes that these problems seemed rooted in "personality conflicts," "generational differences," and issues of tradition and lay control over ministers (Caldarola 2007, 12). Although Caldarola offers little detail, his account is valuable as an assessment from an academic who was on the scene at that time but not a party to the conflict.

In contrast to Caldarola, *Bukkyo Tozen: A History of Jodo Shinshu Buddhism in Canada 1905–1995*, provides considerable detail but comes across as rather one-sided in the chapter that recounts what Japanese headquarters called the "Alberta Problem" (Watada 1996, 173). In this source, we learn that Shin authorities attempted interventions beginning on 8 March 1965, when Bishop Hanayama (head of the BCA) met with leadership from the Alberta Buddhist Churches and the Buddhist Foundation of Canada "to discuss ministerial matters" (Watada 1996, 174). Watada describes Bishop Hanayama's distress at that first meeting and his decision to request that Rev. Yutetsu Kawamura be transferred to Waimea, Hawai'i, in order to defuse the hostility (1996, 174). Both Reverends Kawamura then "resigned as ministers" of the Buddhist Foundation of Canada, and "formed their own organization" with supporters from "the Raymond and Coaldale Churches and the Southern Alberta Sunday School Teachers League" (Watada 1996,

174). The description in *Bukkyo Tozen* suggests that animosity was directed toward Rev. Yutetsu Kawamura in particular and emphasized reports of the conflict critical of both Kawamuras. Rev. Leslie Kawamura was upset by the portrayal in *Bukkyo Tozen,* and reported that for the sake of relations within the Shin community he reluctantly decided not to file a lawsuit for what he characterized as a libelously misleading account.[13]

Toyo Kawamura reiterated the accounts of tensions at the time of the split, ongoing harm from that animosity, and frustration with how the conflict is represented.[14] She concurs that intense animosity was directed at Yutetsu Kawamura and explains that Leslie Kawamura strongly supported the decision that his father go to Hawai'i for his own protection. Although Leslie's parents reported that the years in Hawai'i were rewarding, Canada was home, and the animosity left scars that never fully healed.[15] Toyo Kawamura indicated that misinformation from one side of the original dispute in combination with a lack of continuity among administrative officials in Japan, which required rebalancing the account of events after each personnel change, has contributed to the persistence of views that are critical of Rev. Yutetsu Kawamura and his supporters. In fact, I encountered critical views in Japan during an October 2011 interview with Rev. Tokunaga Michio, an influential scholar and administrator at Nishi Honganji headquarters in Kyoto. He asserted that Honpa members were too confrontational and that "Yutetsu Kawamura was too strong; he criticized Honganji policy."[16] Moreover, according to Tokunaga, problems persisted in Alberta long after reunification. For example, when the Monshu, the religious leader of Jōdo Shinshū, travelled from the Nishi Honganji headquarters in Japan to Alberta approximately twenty years ago, divisions were still evident. Rather than a unified reception, "when I accompanied Monshu there, in the small town, we had two celebration parties"; Yutetsu Kawamura's "members agreed with him, that's why, two celebration parties, two ordination ceremonies in that small town."[17] Tokunaga's criticism was directed to Yutetsu rather than Leslie Kawamura, and did not directly address which Honganji policies Yutetsu Kawamura critiqued.

In contradistinction, Leslie Kawamura's own account points to local power struggles and disparate models for ministerial leadership and autonomy (L. Kawamura 1978). Rev. Kawamura describes a dysfunctional organization vulnerable to the whims of the lay chairman in the mid-1960s when he returned to Canada from Japan. "In principle, the Alberta Kyoku was a worthy organization, but in practice, it was a ballpark for those who vied for power and prestige ... A president was elected from among the delegates and he acted as the chairman and spokesman for the group. Because the Kyoku had no constitution to guide it in its policies, on many occasions, the chair took it upon itself to veto anything he did not favour personally ... this meant that the Alberta Kyoku could function effectively provided that the chairman was an honourable man, but if he were not then the Kyoku would be inefficient" (L. Kawamura 1978, 47).

Kawamura also describes how the separation allowed the Honpa members to push ahead innovations such as support for English-speaking ministers.

> [T]he Honpa Buddhist Church of Alberta was now in a position to make plans for the future. One of the issues that it had to confront was the creation of ministers. Because aid from either the mother temple in Kyoto or the Buddhist Churches of Canada was not forthcoming, the Honpa Buddhist Church of Alberta established a scholarship fund to educate anyone interested in becoming a minister.[18] Unlike the old Alberta Kyoku, the Honpa Buddhist Church of Alberta was aware that unless Buddhism could be discussed in the English language, it would become a dead issue in Canada and in Alberta. So long as the *Issei* (first generation) congregation remains, there would be a need for a Japanese-speaking minister, but when the future is considered, the only medium which would be understood by a Caucasian or a *Nisei* or *Sansei* (third generation) congregation would be English. Thus, in the view of the Honpa Church, the destiny of Buddhism in Alberta lies in the creation of English-speaking ministers. (1978, 50)

Although Leslie Kawamura's service was unstinting, his relationship with central authorities was tense at various times in his life and in both of his careers. He was not shy about expressing disgust with top administrative figures at the University of Calgary or voicing disagreement with the direction for Jōdo Shinshū in Canada, whether the decisions were made by local officials or by Nishi Honganji headquarters in Japan. His wife, Toyo, confirmed that he was frustrated with "feudal and hierarchical central authority at Honganji without ears for his innovation."[19] She also acknowledged that his confrontational and short-tempered reaction to what he perceived as counterproductive and intransigent authority led to his resignation and disrobing. It was only after more than three decades that he was fully reinstated when central authorities finally came around to soliciting rather than rejecting his approach and asked him to become the director of the Living Dharma Centre (LDC).[20]

The LDC is charged with revitalizing Shin through education, "not only as an intellectual pursuit" but in an effort "to create a deeper understanding and appreciation of Jodo Shinshu Buddhism as a way of life throughout Canada"[21] – a highly appropriate role for Rev. Kawamura. He was able to state his terms at the outset and was free to try innovative methods to engage interest and to support communities. He did this not from a central administrative office but by travelling and visiting all temples as the director of the now decentralized Living Dharma Centre.[22] Rev. Kawamura promoted this new model of the LDC, not as "focused in a particular location," but "as a 'living' system within Canada. In other words, the Living Dharma Centre is centred in each follower of the Nembutsu."[23] The LDC organizes retreats for youth and sponsors talks that are then made available through the Living Dharma Centre YouTube channel.[24] As director of the LDC, Rev. Kawamura was able to renew the contemporary, educational, and engaging approach that had met resistance early in his career. His reinstatement and administrative appointment belatedly vindicated Rev. Kawamura's view that innovations were necessary to overcome alienation of the young generations even at the cost of estranging some more conservative members.

SCHOLAR – DR KAWAMURA

It is not unusual for a Buddhist priest or minister to study his or her own tradition, including through formal academic training and participation in academic discussions. But even here, Dr Kawamura is atypical. His university studies focused first on philosophy rather than religion. Even after turning toward graduate work and scholarship in Buddhism, he is best known for work outside of the Jōdo Shinshū tradition in which he was raised. He has focused on Buddhist philosophy and psychology with an emphasis on the Yogācāra school, using Tibetan sources (although his expansive interests and contributions went well beyond this). Dr Kawamura was a pioneer in his research, in his contributions to a host of international organizations, in his leadership in establishing Buddhist Studies in Canada, and in his skilful combination of personal and professional dedication to the tradition, which led students to approach him in relation to both capacities.

Scholarship

Dr Kawamura is widely acknowledged for the excellence of his academic writing as well as for his thorough reading and philological analysis of texts in various Buddhist languages. He credited, and attempted to replicate, the philological training he received from Gadjin Nagao in Japan and Herbert Guenther at the University of Saskatchewan. He described the multi-year, and at times multi-decade, projects required to really "read" a text according to Nagao, his teacher at Kyoto University. Not only does one need to carefully read the Buddhist text in its original language (or more than one language for texts with Tibetan and Chinese variants), but all commentaries written about that text as well. Such a reading project, particularly if combined with translating the text oneself and writing a commentary on it and its commentaries, can stretch out indefinitely. Dr Kawamura had the training, ability, patience, and dedication to do this level of Buddhological scholarship and to train students at the University of Calgary to read and understand Buddhist texts. His students often told stories about the language tutorials he held, which he often gave one-on-one, in addition to his other courses.

Dr Kawamura published ten books and many more journal articles and book chapters during his thirty-five-year academic career. His close bond with G.M. Nagao, his mentor and the supervisor of his MA in Buddhist philosophy at Kyoto University, is evident in the volume of Nagao's collected papers that Kawamura translated and edited, *Mādhyamika and Yogācāra: A Study of Mahāyāna Philosophies* (Nagao 1991). These essays are widely read by Western students seeking clarity on Mādhyamika and Yogācāra, which are notoriously difficult branches of Buddhist philosophy. Kawamura's *The Bodhisattva Doctrine in Buddhism* (1981) includes an essay by Nagao and another by Kawamura's PhD supervisor, Herbert Guenther. Dr Kawamura edited this volume, which stems from a conference he organized at the University of Calgary in 1978, just two years after taking a teaching position there. The essays indicate the wide scope of the conference, with sections on India, Tibet, China, and Japan and chapters by Lobsang Dargyay, Lewis Lancaster, Hisao Inagaki, Yün-hua Jan, Minoru

Kiyota, Arthur Basham, Turrell Wylie, Peter Slater, and Leslie Kawamura himself. This project, and many others, illustrates Dr Kawamura's interest, skill, and success in connecting scholars and organizing conferences. Along with Keith Scott, Dr Kawamura edited *Buddhist Thought and Asian Civilization: Essays in Honor of Herbert V. Guenther on His Sixtieth Birthday* (1977). He translated some works with Guenther, such as *Mind in Buddhist Psychology* (Guenther 1975), while he took on other translation projects, such as *Golden Zephyr* (1975), on his own.

Dr Kawamura clearly expressed his appreciation for and debt to Nagao and Guenther, but the breadth of his academic interests had begun to take form even before the influence of these great Buddhologists. Before coming to Nagao at Kyoto University, Kawamura had earned a master's degree in Buddhist history at Ryukoku University and before that had studied philosophy in the San Francisco Bay area. There he attended two undergraduate institutions in California – San Mateo College, a community college where he earned an associate's degree, a two-year certificate completed before a bachelor's degree, in philosophy; and San Francisco State University, where he continued his studies of Western philosophy, earning his bachelor of arts degree in 1958. These studies in Western philosophy were already in dialogue with Buddhism since Kawamura engaged in conversations with the Dharma Bums, attended lectures by D.T. Suzuki, and carried out his own work with the youth group movement of the Buddhist Churches of America (BCA).[25] In the autobiographical sketch that Dr Kawamura sent to me in late 2009, he briefly reflected on his time in California in the 1950s. "I plan to detail out my life as a student of Buddhism starting from my early desire to become a 'philosopher' and hence my major in Philosophy with a concentration on epistemology and logic, especially, because my time in California led me to the debate in logic taking place between UC Berkeley and Stanford University (which UC logicians called 'the farm' a term quite familiar to me as a farm worker making my yearly tuition fees in the field of a Southern Alberta farm), and because of my direct contact with the 'Dharma Bums' (especially with the poet Gary Snyder, who has a book of poems dedicated to me)."[26]

Kawamura was in Berkeley at the same time as the Beats in the 1950s and his study in Kyoto from 1958 to 1964 coincided with Gary Snyder's Zen training in that same cultural capital of Japan. In an email exchange with me, Gary Snyder noted that he got to know Leslie Kawamura while visiting

Lethbridge after his time in Japan rather than from Japan or earlier days in Berkeley. Snyder did recall close interaction with the Imamura family, in particular, during the time he spent with "Jodo Shin temple people in Berkeley."[27] This was likely a key forum for the contact with Snyder and other Dharma Bums to which Kawamura alluded. Rev. Kanmo and Jane Imamura hosted many gatherings at their home, including Friday evening study groups, which served as the point of encounter and lively conversation among Buddhist practitioners, ministers, and scholars as well as the Beat Dharma Bums, such as Gary Snyder and Philip Whalen (Varvaloucus 2012; Schneider 2011). Their son, Rev. Ryo Imamura, reflects on the many connections of Buddhist scholars and practitioners, including Snyder, Kawamura, and Suzuki, through the discussions his parents held in Berkeley. "My father was quite a progressive and open-minded priest, who opened up the doors of his temple in Berkeley to everyone. He offered study classes and discussion groups, which were attended by scholars and students from East and West. In addition to distinguished Buddhist teachers from Asia such as D.T. Suzuki, Hajime Nakamura, Lama Tada, Hirofumi Ueda and Ryugyo Fujimoto, the discussion groups regularly included Western Buddhists such as Alan Watts, Jack Kerouac and Gary Snyder as well as many of our Jodo Shinshu scholars and ministers such as Taitetsu and Tetsuo Unno, Leslie Kawamura, and Haruo Yamaoka."[28] Leslie Kawamura's participation in these discussions further suggests that his life had mirrored several stages of Buddhism in North America even before his training and studies in Japan.

During his studies in Japan, Kawamura earned money by teaching English, which is how he met Toyo. She recounts going to English classes each week, meeting Leslie Kawamura, and at first being reluctant about the prospect of marriage at a relatively young age. In describing Kawamura's persistent courting, Toyo added that "he is just so stubborn about these things."[29] They married six months before Kawamura was scheduled to return to Canada. Although Rev. Kawamura returned to a ministerial role in 1964, Toyo remained an important influence in his scholarly life, consistently encouraging an academic career as preferable to a ministerial path. Kawamura was strongly interested in further study but also concerned about the implications of leaving his daily role as a Shin minister to pursue a PhD. Toyo acknowledged that Kawamura was an excellent minister in Raymond, but she thought that personal animosities that had been directed at his father would also hamper his ability to perform in his ministerial role in southern Alberta.[30]

In an interesting connection dating back to his father, Leslie and Toyo Kawamura went to the University of Wisconsin in Madison to visit Richard Robinson, the founding professor of the first program of Buddhist Studies in North America. Robinson was born in the small town of Carstairs, Alberta, and did his BA at the University of Alberta in Edmonton. Even before his graduate studies and influential academic career, Robinson used to travel south to Raymond to learn about Buddhism from Rev. Yutetsu Kawamura. Robinson, in turn, invited Leslie Kawamura to study Buddhism as part of Wisconsin's groundbreaking doctoral program in Buddhist Studies. However, due to Robinson's unexpected death, among other reasons, Leslie Kawamura decided to pursue his PhD in Far Eastern Studies at the University of Saskatchewan with the Buddhologist Herbert Guenther.

Kawamura had met Guenther in the early 60s through Nagao while studying at Kyoto University, where Guenther gave a talk. Guenther impressed Kawamura with the breadth and depth of his academic knowledge, and Guenther's proximity, in the adjacent prairie province, may also have been a draw. Kawamura had learned to read texts closely with Nagao (at times focusing on just a few sentences a day), and extended his philological training with Guenther, where he improved his speed and ability to grasp the whole text. Toyo, who offered the above "slow and focused" versus "fast and comprehensive" characterization of the difference in philological methods, told a story about Guenther's first task for Kawamura. Kawamura was to find a specific term in a long Tibetan sutra. He struggled all weekend. On Monday morning, he had to report sheepishly that he could not find it. Guenther then acknowledged that it was not there, but the exercise got Kawamura reading the full text both closely and quickly. Dr Kawamura's academic training was shaped by these scholars in particular, and he remained motivated to provide a similarly excellent education to his own students.

Organizations and Networks

Dr Leslie Kawamura founded, co-founded, participated in, and supported many Canadian and international organizations for the study of Buddhism, the study of particular strands of the tradition, and Asian Studies more generally. Despite his frank criticism of several senior administrators at his home institution, he was awarded the Order of the University of Calgary in 2010, following up on the President's Award for Internationalization in 2004. These awards recognized the many contributions he made to Religious Studies, Buddhist Studies, Asian Studies, the Numata Chair, and other services to the university. Dr Kawamura remained at the same institutions for his entire career, from 1976 (the year he finished his PhD and chose the University of Calgary over the University of Alberta) until his death in 2011.

Virginia Tumasz, Head of the Department of Religious Studies at the University of Calgary, details some of Dr Kawamura's service through an online page, "In Memoriam of Dr. Leslie Kawamura," which is linked to the departmental website. Along with noting his rapid rise to full professor and department head by 1983, she lauds his role in securing funds to establish the Numata Chair at the University of Calgary and lists a range of scholarly organizations that he founded, or in which he served in an executive role at a formative time: the Canada Mongolia Society (1974), the International Association for Buddhist Studies (1977), the North American Association for Buddhist Studies (1977), the Society for Tibetan Studies in Alberta (1981), the International Association of Shin Buddhist Studies (1982), and the Buddhism Section of the American Academy of Religion (AAR), "all of which seek to promote the study of Buddhism and Asian cultures in the academy."[31] Although an extensive list, it does not include his service to the Canadian Asian Studies Association and the Canadian Society for the Study of Religion. Moreover, Dr Kawamura's leadership roles in international organizations (for example, the twenty-five years he served as Canadian representative and board member of the International Association for Shin Buddhist Studies) demonstrate that he was prominent in larger international networks as well as central to the academic growth of Buddhism in Canada.

Dr Kawamura's networking initiatives extended beyond formal organizations. The Numata Chair 15th Anniversary Symposium at the University of Calgary in May 2004, which combined papers with meals and even an excursion to Banff, was an intimate gathering. All the participants came together for every paper and every meal, and almost all travelled together in the same bus for the excursion. Sustained conversation and camaraderie created an atmosphere that is rare at larger conferences, which usually include multiple simultaneous panels, attendees bouncing back and forth from one panel to the next, and less opportunity for extensive exchanges.

Dr Kawamura organized the Numata Symposium for Buddhist Studies in Canada at the University of Calgary on 4 April 2009 (see illustration 13). In essence, he invited all scholars working on Buddhism in Canada (and a few working in the United States) to gather and share information about their work and their programs. Institutions with graduate programs could indicate who was there and what opportunities they offered students. Scholars at smaller schools would better know where to direct their students for graduate work. Scholars with shared interests might strike up a joint project. There was no particular agenda beyond creating a space and opportunity for interaction, which could then lead to many possibilities. The approximately twenty scholars of Buddhism who made the trip to Calgary for the symposium demonstrated the growth of Buddhist Studies in Canada and the success of Dr Leslie Kawamura's ambition to "put 'Buddhist Studies' on the Canadian map."[32]

As Sensei and Colleague

Dr Kawamura's death released an outpouring of praise and fond recollections in memorial services, hallway conversations, email exchanges, and online postings of condolences. Many invoked Dr Kawamura in his role as *"sensei,"* a term for an esteemed teacher (fitting for both his academic and ministerial roles). For example, on 11 March, Rev. Toshihide Numata, chairman of Bukkyo Dendo Kyokai – Society for the Promotion of Buddhism, Tokyo, Japan, posted: "Kawamura Sensei was a pioneer in the field of Buddhist Studies in North America and we are deeply grateful for his many years of leadership and direction of the Numata Program at the University of Calgary. His lifelong dedication of sharing the Dharma with his students and those he came in contact with will be his lasting legacy for years and years to come." Also, a co-president of Kelowna Buddhist Temple expressed sadness "to hear of the untimely passing of Kawamura Sensei. We express our deep gratitude for his guidance and propagation of the Buddha Dharma through the Living Dharma Center." Other expressions of condolence came from friends, Shin members, students, students who had become scholars in their own right, and scholars describing his lasting influence, such as James A. Benn, a scholar of medieval Chinese religions at McMaster, who wrote: "My condolences on the sad loss of a man who exemplified the true balance of wisdom and compassion. I had the greatest respect for Dr. Kawamura as a scholar and friend. He did so much for Buddhist Studies throughout the world and especially in Canada. We shall not see his like again."[33]

Even more striking than the praise for Dr Kawamura's scholarship and leadership in various organizations and initiatives are comments of appreciation for his extraordinary generosity and commitment to students. Dr Kawamura mentored at least eight PhD students and more than a dozen MA students. A number of his former students have pursued successful academic careers both in Asia and North America, at least two have pursued ministerial or monastic religious paths, and some, like Dr/Rev. Kawamura himself, have combined religious and academic pursuits. In our interview, Toyo Kawamura reaffirmed that her husband was "very grateful to his teachers so that is why he [was] so good to his students. Because that was his way of paying back the kindness he received. He was just extremely good to his students." She went on to describe how students from various parts of the world began flying back to Calgary as soon as they heard he was in the hospital and likely would not live much longer. She was touched that they came back and amazed by some of the stories she then heard for the first time as students prepared eulogies and discussed his kindness and influence. She related the story of one student who was going to have to drop out of the program because she could not pay her rent. Dr Kawamura replied "no" and paid her rent for the rest of the year. To another he gave airfare to visit a temple in California that was of interest for the student's research. A third related how he had helped the student move house, and so on.[34]

During his final days in the hospital, Toyo told Leslie that a festschrift for him would be coming out and that a number of his students had quickly booked flights and were on their way, including the two who were editing the collection of essays written in his honour. Although Leslie Kawamura passed away before most had arrived, Toyo quickly arranged for the funeral so that the students could attend. Here, too, she expressed how touched she was by the outpouring of grief: a monk and former student indicated that he had not cried at his own father's death but wept at the news of Dr Kawamura's passing. Dr Sarah Haynes, another former student, describes the extraordinary compassion he showed for his students' "overall well-being" – beyond tireless efforts to assist their academic success. "When news spread of Leslie's death his former graduate students from around the world gathered in Calgary to discuss what exactly it was that made him such a special man and teacher. It was unanimous, Leslie was more than a mentor; he was a father figure to many of us" (Haynes 2011, 8).

The festschrift about which Toyo reminded her husband is entitled *Wading into the Stream of Wisdom: Essays Honoring Leslie Kawamura*, edited by Sarah Haynes and Michelle J. Sorensen (2013). Both editors of this festschrift spoke at the memorial panel for Dr Kawamura at the AAR annual meeting the following November. In fact, I turned to Sarah Haynes in response to a question about how Leslie Kawamura understood the two roles of scholar and practitioner. In an email exchange shortly after Kawamura's death, she replied that "for Leslie, as a scholar-practitioner, it was all about the bodhisattva ethic. About embodying compassion and manifesting that when he interacted with his colleagues and students. If one thing became clear to me this past week, especially in emails from former students and colleagues, Leslie showed compassion and generosity to most everyone."[35]

COMBINING ROLES

Leslie Kawamura integrated parts of both roles but also distinguished between his primary area of academic work and his own tradition. He trained for, and contributed to, both vocations – at times simultaneously but often consecutively. The combination of vocations challenges certain assumptions of scholars, such as myself, who are cautious about the pairing of religious practice with scholarship about religion.[36] Although in our *Introduction to the Study of Religion*, Hillary Rodrigues and I argued for the importance of clarifying the distinction between one's role as a scholar and as a practitioner or adherent of a tradition, there has been productive crossover between these roles from the origins of Buddhist Studies through current debates in the field.[37] Leslie Kawamura exemplified a successful synthesis. Moreover, there are surprising connections between the first two Buddhist Studies programs in North America and the rural, southern Alberta temple where he was born. Richard Robinson, founder of the first program (at the University of Wisconsin – Madison) began his studies of Buddhism with Leslie Kawamura's father at the temple in Raymond. The previous minister at that same temple, Rev. Shingo Nagatomi, was the father of Masatoshi Nagatomi, who founded the Buddhist Studies program at Harvard, which was the second in North America (Harding 2010). Like Masatoshi Nagatomi, Leslie Kawamura became a scholar of Buddhism after following his father's ministerial training. Many scholars of Buddhism who did not grow up in the tradition also became adherents before they became scholars. Leslie Kawamura was certainly conscious of his dual role, and conscientious about his conduct on both paths. In his plans for the chapter he had intended to write for *Studying Buddhism in Practice*, Kawamura framed his reflections in terms of a life as "a Jōdo Shinshū minister and a scholar of Buddhist Studies."[38]

The theme of balancing both roles also emerged in tributes and comments of condolence that followed Kawamura's death. For example, Ken Tanaka's message highlighted this theme along with Leslie Kawamura's centrality to a number of academic organizations:

> I send my condolences personally as well as on behalf of the International Association of Shin Buddhist Studies as president of this academic association. Dr. Kawamura was not only a long time member of the Steering Committee but served as chair of two international meetings of our association held at University of Calgary. He was scheduled to be the keynote speaker at the upcoming August 5–6 conference in Kyoto. We deeply regret that we will not be able to have him share with us his insights accumulated over half a century of professional work. We shall miss his leadership and his beaming smile. On a personal note, I had always looked up to him as one of my elder colleagues who paved the way for those of us interested in both the academic and spiritual sides of Buddhist Studies.[39]

Balancing these dimensions was the topic of the first Leslie S. Kawamura Memorial Lecture, "Toward a Meaningful Study of Buddhism," delivered by Jonathan A. Silk on 20 September 2011. Before he died, Dr Kawamura had invited Jonathan Silk to come to the University of Calgary, so the speaker and topic were particularly appropriate.

Problems of Blurred Boundaries

A longstanding issue in religious studies concerns the relative advantages and limitations associated with observations made by religious "insiders" versus "outsiders." On the one hand, "insiders" may have access to experiences or understandings of their own tradition beyond the grasp of "outsiders." On the other hand, "outsiders" may be better positioned to view a religious tradition more objectively. Theology has been primarily conducted by insiders for other insiders, with the intention of prescribing certain interpretations or actions based on shared assumptions and sources of authority within the tradition. However, the academic study of religion emphasizes open access to all and the merit of value-neutral analysis that is not beholden to assumptions or claims of authority from within any religious tradition. Just as normative views of the religious "insider" can lead to bias or ignoring certain topics, so too hostility, or even excessive polite reserve, from the religious "outsider" can limit rigorous and thorough academic analysis of religious traditions.

Critical analysis is not synonymous with criticism of religion. But as with all academic endeavours, academics must be able to criticize conventional understanding, whether of other scholars or of practitioners within a religious tradition. Academic training demands that scholars strive for relative neutrality, openness, and freedom from presupposition in addition to depth and breadth of knowledge and specific linguistic, theoretical, and methodological disciplinary training. This model has clear advantages, particularly in comparison to theological polemics that disparage other traditions from a stance of certainty about the truth of one's own religion. Although the move to more objective engagement with various religious traditions has provided space for the study of Buddhism in universities, there are diverse opinions about the extent to which this neutral and objective position is possible or desirable. Some scholars in recent decades have argued that a fully objective, neutral stance is an unattainable ideal but nonetheless worth approaching to the extent possible. Others do not agree that it is an ideal at all and instead advocate identifying one's subjectivity and related social and cultural location. There has also been a growing movement advocating the benefits of bringing a Buddhist perspective to scholarship about the tradition and scholars' participation in constructing normative Buddhist theology. These movements will be discussed below, but first it may help to clarify the perceived problems with blurred boundaries between ostensibly objective scholarship and subjective religious commitment.

Concerns about problems associated with dual academic and religious commitments, as opposed to potential benefits, are common to discussions of theory and method in Religious Studies in general. They are by no means particular to Buddhism, but naturally arise in discussing a figure such as Leslie Kawamura. In fact, the poster for the Inaugural Leslie S. Kawamura Memorial Lecture, delivered by Jonathan Silk, frames the issue well: "One of the key hallmarks of academic study is its – ideally – disinterested, neutral and objective standpoint. When dealing with religious traditions in particular, such distance can be hard to maintain, with the siren call of advocacy sometimes not far in the distance. Indeed, most academic programs and departments of Religious Studies began, and many remain, theological. In such a framework, how can a tradition like Buddhism be presented, rendering it meaningful to both Buddhist and non-Buddhist audiences while maintaining a neutral and disinterested standpoint?" (Silk 2011) This question will elicit various answers.

One response comes from Bruce Lincoln, whose "Theses on Method" (Lincoln 1996, 225–7) articulates a position advocating stricter disciplinary norms for the study of religion quite separate from theological concerns. I would like to call particular attention to four of his thirteen theses in abbreviated form:

5 Reverence is a religious, and not a scholarly virtue.
9 Critical inquiry need assume neither cynicism nor dissimulation to justify probing beneath the surface, and ought to probe scholarly discourse and practice.
12 Although critical inquiry has become commonplace in other disciplines, it still offends many students of religion, who denounce it as "reductionism." This charge is meant to silence critique ... the refusal to ratify its claim of transcendent nature and sacrosanct status ... may be regarded as heresy and sacrilege by those who construct themselves as religious, but it is the starting point for those who construct themselves as historians.

13 When one permits those whom one studies to define the terms in which they will be understood, suspends one's interest in the temporal and contingent, or fails to distinguish between "truths," "truth-claims," and "regimes of truth," one has ceased to function as historian or scholar.

Lincoln makes clear that religion cannot be exempt from critical analysis; nor can scholarly discourse about religion be exempt. This view challenges the scholarly credentials of certain conflations between religious commitment and academic study. Leslie Kawamura's rigorous scholarship, openness, qualified irreverence, and separation between his primary academic specialty in Yogācāra and ministerial role within Shin Buddhism mitigated the pitfalls expressed in these theses. He did write about his own tradition as well, but his academic work has not suffered from a lack of critical analysis or from an attitude of reverence getting in the way of asking difficult questions about the leadership, vitality, and future of his tradition. As previously noted, the Jōdo Shinshū hierarchy found him, if anything, too critical. However, Kawamura was at ease in both roles and his confidence and competence in both areas were accompanied with great care for the rigour of his scholarship and for the vitality of his Jōdo Shinshū community.

Potential of Complementary Dimensions

Alongside increased attention to the need for greater disciplinary clarity that emphasizes separation between critical academic study and normative religious commitment, there has been a countervailing increase in general awareness of many scholars' Buddhist practice and an interest in more fully incorporating Buddhist perspectives into their scholarship. The anthology *Buddhist Theology: Critical Reflections by Contemporary Buddhist Scholars* (Jackson and Makransky 2000) signals a maturation of this development. The issues had already been discussed in journals and panels at academic conferences including the American Academy of Religion in 1996. Roger Jackson asserts that the term Buddhist theology, despite objections that it may strike some as borrowed from Western religions and peripheral to Buddhist concerns, is appropriate when properly contextualized

(R. Jackson 2000). "Buddhist theologians of pre-modern Asia were an élite within an élite" and although few in numbers, these literate scholar-monks' intellectual reflections on their tradition were "a persistent and prestigious part of what Buddhists did ... virtually everywhere in Asia that the monastic tradition spread" (R. Jackson 2000, 5–6). Jackson recounts shifts within the tradition in relation to modernity, secularization, ideological challenges to traditional cultures, a growing lay orientation, and the transformation of Buddhism into a truly global tradition (R. Jackson 2000, 7–8). Consequently, there has been a de-centring of Buddhist theology from Asian monasteries to a variety of venues. These include universities, both in Asia and the West, linked to the contemporary movement among *Buddhist* scholars of Buddhist Studies to participate in contributing to, rather than merely studying, Buddhist theology (R. Jackson 2000, 8–13). Buddhist Studies scholar John Makransky advocates for Buddhist theology, noting its access to "a fuller understanding of Buddhism" as well as "the potential of Buddhist experience to shine new light upon a host of contemporary cultural and religious concerns" (Makransky 2000, 18–19).

On the role of the Buddhist scholar-practitioner in the West, Charles Prebish has been ahead of the curve. In his 1999 book *Luminous Passages: The Practice and Study of Buddhism in America*, he includes a chapter on the "Silent Sangha" of Buddhist practitioners in the academy. He analyses changes in academic training, in the willingness among scholars to acknowledge their Buddhist practice, and in a growing self-reflective literature on this issue from the mid-1990s.[40] Prebish asserts: "In the absence of the traditional 'scholar-monks' so prevalent in Asia, it may well be that the 'scholar-practitioners' of today's American Buddhism will fulfill the role of 'quasi monastics,' or at least treasure troves of Buddhist literacy and information, functioning as guides through whom one's understanding of the Dharma may be sharpened. In this way individual practice might once again be balanced with individual study so that Buddhist study deepens one's practice while Buddhist practice informs one's study" (1999, 199).

Leslie Kawamura excelled on both fronts, although he also navigated around potential hazards – real or perceived – in this dual role. Prebish's description of what the role could, and perhaps should, be for a Buddhist scholar-practitioner fits well with his own interaction with Leslie Kawamura. At the tribute panel to Dr Kawamura at the 2011 AAR meeting, and in the *Buddhadharma: The Practitioner's Quarterly Online* article by

Danny Fisher that same year, Prebish very eloquently expressed his esteem for Leslie Kawamura as a person and scholar who served as just such a "treasure trove" of Buddhist knowledge, not to mention a paragon of collegiality. Prebish describes the time he held the Numata Chair of Buddhist Studies at the University of Calgary in 1993 as one of "the most exciting and rewarding" periods in his career primarily because of his time and conversations with Kawamura: "It didn't matter whether it was Vinaya or Vimalakirti, monasticism or meditation, the discussions were lively and free-spirited. It reminded me of similar occasions I'd experienced when visiting Masatoshi Nagatomi at Harvard two decades earlier. With Leslie, as with Nagatomi, I was absolutely astounded at the breadth of his knowledge and learning. He simply knew things that I never would have imagined he knew" (Fisher 2011). In that same interview, Prebish elaborated on Kawamura's influence on his own work, on Asian Studies and Buddhist Studies at the University of Calgary, and on various international academic organizations. He articulated how Kawamura served as a model steward of the Numata Chair, a consummate scholar and colleague, and "the most astounding mentor of graduate students I have ever met. It was always exciting to watch Leslie re-connect with his former students at conferences, and to know that it was his selfless efforts that helped to carve out careers for these brilliant young scholars. For me, he was the true embodiment of wisdom and compassion, and Buddhist Studies is far greater for his work and his civility" (Fisher 2011).

In short, Leslie Kawamura exemplifies an ideal scholar-practitioner in support of Prebish's scholar-monk analogy. Although I think the analogy needs to be adjusted to better account for ongoing influence from Asia, including global flows that may continue to provide scholar-monks and otherwise influence Western and Asian developments, Prebish's assessment of Leslie Kawamura's contributions, balance, and example are compelling.

CONCLUSION

This chapter is not an exhaustive biography of Leslie Kawamura, his life and his works. There have been several forums already for reflection from friends, family, students, and colleagues ranging from memorial services at the University of Calgary to the already mentioned Memorial Panel and Reception in Dr Leslie Kawamura's honour at the 2011 American

Academy of Religion annual meeting in San Francisco. The stories and insights at each event reinforce themes of Kawamura's selfless dedication, humour, blunt honesty, knowledge, kindness, and rigorous scholarship. The festschrift volume, *Wading into the Stream of Wisdom: Essays Honoring Leslie Kawamura* (Haynes and Sorensen 2013) includes new essays from seventeen scholars – many of whom are former students or holders of the Numata Chair of Buddhist Studies at the University of Calgary. That volume and others will continue to reflect on Leslie Kawamura's profound influence and will be better positioned to analyse the ongoing contributions of his scholarship through his own works, his students, and the scholarship of colleagues worldwide.

The focus of this chapter has been to reflect on Kawamura's skilful cultivation of academic and ministerial realms – fields that are at times carefully separated in the academy for the relatively recent discipline of Religious Studies and at other times carelessly mixed in ways that may mislead readers, students, and other travellers through either realm. Kawamura was not careless, nor was he content to cultivate only one of these fields and let the other lie fallow. His stewardship of both is remarkable and worthy of reflection as a way to think through tensions and pitfalls that have accompanied the growth of Buddhist Studies in recent decades. I am certainly not suggesting that all scholars and ministers should follow his example; it is quite reasonable to have commitments to only one side of this combination. However, I would assert that his care for students is exemplary for any teacher, his rigour is inspirational for any scholar, and his openness to change is worthy of reflection for any minister.

NOTES

1   Toyo Kawamura, interview with the author in Calgary, Alberta, 16 September 2011.
2   See Harding (2010, 134–5).
3   In this chapter, references to Kawamura or Rev. Kawamura will always be designations for Leslie Kawamura. References to Leslie's father, Rev. Yutetsu Kawamura, will include the given name, Yutetsu, for clarity.
4   See The Governor General of Canada (n.d.).
5   Unfortunately, due to illness, Leslie Kawamura did not have an opportunity to write that autobiographical chapter. He had briefly sketched the contents in a document

that he sent to me by email on 30 November 2009. In this précis he makes the intriguing reference to "my mother's influence on 'designing me' into a Jōdo Shinshū Minister" along with an indication of "early childhood experiences that may have led me into the life of a Jōdo Shinshū minister and a scholar of Buddhist studies."

6   See Jonathan Silk's obituary for Gadjin M. Nagao in *The Eastern Buddhist* (Silk 2005).
7   See Harding (2010, 160–1n1).
8   See V. Hori (2010a); Soucy (2010); and both the introduction and chapter 1 in the current volume.
9   Toyo Kawamura, interview with the author, Calgary, 16 September 2011. She described his time with the Dharma Bums while he was pursuing undergraduate studies in Western philosophy, and indicated that at the same time he had been very involved with the San Francisco Buddhist Church and the youth group movement of the Buddhist Churches of America (BCA). These groups crossed paths on occasion.
10 Leslie Kawamura's trajectory resonated with that of Takashi Tsuji, the first Canadian-born minister who later became bishop of the BCA. Both were *nisei* who welcomed innovation and broader membership. Like Rev. Kawamura, Rev. Tsuji also "advocated the desirability of opening the sangha for the purpose of propagating the Buddhist teachings to more non-Japanese members" and saw the need to move beyond "an ethnic organization if it is to become a vital religious organization" (Kashima 2007, 324). The link with Rev. Tsuji's path reemerges at the end of Rev. Kawamura's ministerial career when, as director of the Living Dharma Centre, he was appointed to a leading role within the national Shin organization.
11 For reflections akin to Dr Kawamura's from another scholar of religion, see the similarly blunt assessment by Dr George Tanabe Jr (2010).
12 Although some tensions appear to express regional biases from Japan, this was by no means always the case. For example, Yutetsu Kawamura emigrated from Shiga Prefecture in the Kansai region of Japan's main island, Honshu. However, his dedication to and strong popularity among the Okinawan settlers in Coalhurst and Hardieville provide a counter-example to the enduring influence of such regional tensions.
13 Leslie Kawamura, email message sent to author on 16 November 2009 as well as personal conversations with the author from 2004 through 2010.
14 Toyo Kawamura, interview with the author in Calgary, 16 September 2011 and a follow-up phone conversation, 10 September 2012.
15 Toyo Kawamura, phone conversation with the author, 10 September 2012.
16 Tokunaga Michio, interview with the author at the Honganji International Center in Kyoto, Japan, 12 October 2011.
17 Ibid.

18 Fredrich Ulrich was a recipient of this scholarship, studied at the Institute of Buddhist Studies in Berkeley, California, was ordained as a Jōdo Shinshū priest, and later became the Resident Minister of the Manitoba Buddhist Temple, a position he has held for the past fifteen years.
19 Toyo Kawamura, interview with the author in Calgary, 16 September 2011.
20 Ibid.
21 See Jodo Shinshu Buddhist Temples of Canada (2010).
22 These observations reflect points that arose in personal conversations between Leslie Kawamura and the author from shortly before he received this appointment in 2006 through 2010.
23 Jodo Shinshu Buddhist Temples of Canada (2010).
24 See http://www.youtube.com/user/livingdharmacentre?ob=0&feature=results_main. Videos include commemorative ceremonies, festivals, messages from the Monshu (the head abbot in Japan), and talks given by ministers and scholars. For example, there are a number of contributions by Mark Unno and Jeff Wilson, who are scholars of Buddhism also capable of speaking to ministerial concerns consistent with the mission of the LDC.
25 Toyo Kawamura, interview with the author in Calgary, 16 September 2011.
26 Leslie Kawamura, from the document he prepared in anticipation of contributing a chapter to the volume *Studying Buddhism in Practice* (Harding 2012).
27 Gary Snyder, email message to the author, 30 January 2012.
28 From Rev. Ryo Imamura's comments in 2008 when he was minister of the Buddhist Church of Florin in Sacramento, California (Imamura 2008, 2).
29 Toyo Kawamura, interview with the author in Calgary, 16 September 2011.
30 Ibid.
31 See Tumasz (2011).
32 Leslie Kawamura, from the document he prepared in anticipation of contributing a chapter to the volume *Studying Buddhism in Practice* (Harding 2012).
33 Notes of condolence, "Condolences for the family of 'KAWAMURA – Rev. Dr. Leslie Sumio,' posted to McInnis & Holloway Funeral Homes online obituaries and condolences page at http://www.mhfh.com/kawamura-%E2%80%93-rev-dr-leslie-sumio/.
34 Toyo Kawamura, interview with the author in Calgary, 16 September 2011.
35 In addition to the 15 March 2011 email exchange, I reference this quote in the interview; see Fisher (2011). See also reflections and obituary contributions written by Sarah Haynes such as her post to the widely read H-Buddhism listserve in the days immediately after Leslie Kawamura's death as well as her tribute, "A Pioneer in the

Canadian Buddhist Landscape: Remembering Rev. Dr. Leslie Kawamura" in the *Canadian Journal of Buddhist Studies* (Haynes 2011).

36 There is no intent to disparage religious practice. Buddhist practices, and practices in the academic study of religion, are the two foci of my *Studying Buddhism in Practice* (Harding 2012). However, I am typically uncomfortable with insiders' normative claims encroaching on academic assertions. Although one's religious practice (or lack thereof) can compromise one's scholarship, the two roles can enhance each other as well, as in the case of Leslie Kawamura.

37 See, for example, the volume *Buddhist Theology* (Jackson and Makransky 2000), as well as the presentations by scholar-practitioners referenced in note 24.

38 Leslie Kawamura, from the document he prepared in anticipation of contributing a chapter to *Studying Buddhism in Practice* (Harding 2012).

39 Ken Tanaka on 13 March 2011. Posted to McInnis & Holloway Funeral Homes online obituaries and condolences page at http://www.mhfh.com/kawamura-%E2%80%93-rev-dr-leslie-sumio/ and accessed March 14, 2011.

40 See Cabézon (1995); Eckel (1994); Gómez (1995); Lopez (1995); and Nattier (1997).

Bibliography

Abbott, Elizabeth. 1999. *A History of Celibacy*. Toronto: HarperCollins
Adachi, Ken. 1991. *The Enemy That Never Was: A History of the Japanese Canadians*. Toronto: McClelland and Stewart
Adams, David. 1992. "Joseph Beuys: Pioneer of a Radical Ecology." *Art Journal* 51, no. 2: 26–34
Administrative Committee of Wat Nong Pah Pong. 2010. "A Response to the 30th December 2009 Article 'Monks Target Western Clergy.'" http://www.dhammlight.com/official/Response_to_30_Dec_Article_02_01_10
Ahir, D.C. 1999. *Vipassana: A Universal Buddhist Technique of Meditation*. Delhi: Sri Sat Guru Publications
Ahmed, Syed Jamil. 2006. "Tibetan Folk Opera: Lhamo in Contemporary Cultural Politics." *Asian Theatre Journal* 23, no. 1: 149–78
Aitken, Robert. 1984. *The Mind of Clover: Essays in Zen Buddhist Ethics*. San Francisco: North Point Press
Akamatsu, Renjō. 1893. *A Brief Account of Shin-Shiu (The True Doctrine Sect of Japan)*. Kyoto: Buddhist Propagation Society
Ama, Michihiro. 2011. *Immigrants to the Pure Land: The Modernization, Acculturation, and Globalization of Shin Buddhism, 1898–1941*. Honolulu: University of Hawai'i Press
Amaro (Bhikkhu). 2001. "Theravada Buddhism in a Nutshell." In *Broad View, Boundless Heart*, edited by Ajahn Pasanno and Ajahn Amaro, 36–53. Redwood Valley, CA: Abhayagiri Buddhist Monastery. http://abhayagiri.ehclients.com/pdf/books/Broad_View.pdf
Amstutz, Galen. 1997. *Interpreting Amida: History and Orientalism in the Study of Pure Land Buddhism*. Albany: State University of New York Press
Anālayo. 2003. *Satipatthāna: The Direct Path to Realization*. Birmingham, UK: Windhorse

Anand, Dibyesh. 2000. "(Re)imagining Nationalism: Identity and Representation in the Tibetan Diaspora of South Asia." *Contemporary South Asia* 9, no. 2: 271–87

Anderson, Benedict. 1983. *Imagined Communities: Reflections on the Origin and Spread of Nationalism*. New York: Verso

– 2005. "I Like Nationalism's Utopian Elements." Interview by Lorenz Khazaleh, 15 December. http://www.culcom.uio.no/english/news

Anderson, Leon. 2006. "Analytic Autoethnography." *Journal of Contemporary Ethnography* 35, no. 4: 373–95

Antliff, Allan. 2005. "Rewind: The Mr. Peanut Mayoralty Campaign of 1974." *Canadian Art* (Fall). http://www.canadianart.ca/art/features/2006/05/11/399

Appadurai, Arjun. 1996. *Modernity at Large: Cultural Dimensions of Globalization*. Minneapolis: University of Minnesota Press

Arnold, Grant. 2008. "Kate Craig: Skin." *Western Front Research Library* (October). http://front.bc.ca/research/texts/10

Arslanian, Varant. 2005. "Leaving Home, Staying Home: A Case Study of an American Zen Monastery." MA thesis, McGill University

Art for Tibet Canada Benefit Event Committee. 2011. "Art for Tibet Canada: Call for Submissions." 25 August. http://sftcanada.wordpress.com/2011/08/25/art-for-tibet-canada-call-for-submissions

Arunaratanagiri Buddhist Monastery. 2011. *The Collected Teachings of Ajahn Chah*. 3 vols. Harnham, UK: Aruna Publications

Asad, Talal. 1986. *The Idea of an Anthropology of Islam*. Washington, DC: Georgetown University

Attygalle, Randima. 2009. "Where East Brings Solace to the West." *The Nation Eye* 8 (February). http://www.nation.lk/2009/02/08/eyefea7.htm

Avatamsaka Monastery. n.d. http://www.avatamsaka.ca/index.html

Bagnall, Janet. 1981. "Quebec to Probe Cult Children." *Montreal Gazette*, 6 November, 1

Bailey, Greg, and Ian Mabbett. 2003. *The Sociology of Early Buddhism*. Cambridge: Cambridge University Press

Banana, Anna. n.d. "A Report by Canadian Mail-Artist Anna Banana on the Postal Activities of Angela and Peter Netmail." http://www.netmailart.de/english/story/text2.html

Bangkok Post. 2009. "Thai Monks Target Western Clergy." 30 December

Bao, Jiemen. 2005. "Merit-Making Capitalism: Re-territorializing Thai Buddhism in Silicon Valley, California." *Journal of Asian American Studies* 8, no. 2: 115–42

Barnhill, David L. 1990. "Bashō as Bat: Wayfaring and Antistructure in the Journals of Matsuo Bashō." *Journal of Asian Studies* 49, no. 2: 274–90

Bartholomeusz, Tessa J. 1994. *Women under the Bo Tree: Buddhist Nuns in Sri Lanka*. Cambridge: Cambridge University Press

Barua, D. Mitra (Bhikkhu), 2010a. "Temporary Ordination for the Benefit of Oneself: A Diasporic Appropriation." Unpublished paper presented at Buddhism and Diaspora Conference, University of Toronto Scarborough, 14 May

– 2010b. "Dhamma Education: The Transmission and Reconfiguration of the Sri Lankan Buddhist Tradition in Toronto." PhD diss., Wilfrid Laurier University

– 2011. "Temporary Ordination for Character Transformation: A Diasporic Practice with Transnational Connections." *Journal of Global Buddhism* 12:51–68 http://www.globalbuddhism.org/12/mitra11.pdf

Batchelor, Stephen. 1998. *Buddhism without Beliefs: A Contemporary Guide to Awakening*. New York: Riverhead Books

Baumann, Martin. 2001. "Global Buddhism: Developmental Periods, Regional Histories, and a New Analytical Perspective." *Journal of Global Buddhism* 2: 1–43

– 2002. "Protective Amulets and Awareness Techniques, or How to Make Sense of Buddhism in the West." In Prebish and Baumann, *Westward Dharma*, 51–65

Bechert, Heinz. 1966. *Buddhismus, Staat und Gesellschaft in den Ländern des Theravada Buddhismus*. Vol. 1. Frankfurt am Main/Berlin: Alfred Metzner/ Otto Harrassowitz

– 1984. "Buddhist Revival in East and West." In *The World of Buddhism*, edited by Heinz Bechert and Richard Gombrich, 273–85. London: Thames and Hudson

Bell, Catherine. 1998. "Performance." In *Critical Terms for Religious Studies*, edited by Mark C. Taylor, 205–24. Chicago: University of Chicago Press

Bell, Sandra. 2000. "Being Creative with Tradition: Rooting Theravada Buddhism in Britain." *Journal of Global Buddhism* 1: 1–23

– 2002. "Scandals in Emerging Western Buddhism." In Prebish and Baumann, *Westward Dharma*, 230–42

Bennett, Nelson. 2010. "Misconceptions Plague Plan: Expansion Won't Affect ALR: Architect." *Richmond News*, 16 December. http://www.richmond-news.com/life/Misconceptions+plague+plan/3539857/story.html

Berger, Peter. 1990. *The Sacred Canopy: Elements of a Sociological Theory of Religion*. New York: Anchor Books

Bergman, Rob. 2011. *Windsor Crossing*. Podcast. 2 January. http://www.wcrossing.org/default.aspx?page=3352&item=80

Berkwitz, Stephen C. 2003. "Recent Trends in Sri Lankan Buddhism." *Religion* 33: 57–71

Bernstorff, Dagmar, and Hubertus von Welck, eds. 2003. *Exile as Challenge: The Tibetan Diaspora*. New Delhi: Orient Longman Private Limited
Bethune, Brian. 2006. "Noah Richler: In Search of Nowhere." *Maclean's*, 6 September. http://www.macleans.ca/culture/books/article.jsp?content=20060911_133164_133164
Beyer, Peter. 1994. *Religion and Globalization*. London: Sage Publications
– 2006. *Religions in Global Society*. London: Routledge
– 2010. "Buddhism in Canada: A Statistical Overview from Canadian Censuses 1981–2001." In Harding, Hori, and Soucy, *Wild Geese*, 111–23
Bhushan, Nalini, Jay L. Garfield, and Abraham Zablocki, eds. 2009. *TransBuddhism: Transmission, Translation, Transformation*. Amherst: University of Massachusetts Press
Binning, Amy. 2012. "Situating Sati Saraniya: Discourses on Gender and Legitimacy in Theravada Buddhism." Honours thesis, McGill University
Birken Forest Monastery. 2005. "Birken Forest Monastery: Our First Ten Years 1994–2004."
Blackburn, Anne M. 2010. *Locations of Buddhism: Colonialism and Modernity in Sri Lanka*. Chicago: University of Chicago Press
Blum, Mark L., and Shin'ya Yasutomi, eds. 2006. *Rennyo and the Roots of Modern Japanese Buddhism*. New York: Oxford University Press
Blum, Michael L. 2009. "The Transcendentalist Ghost in EcoBuddhism." In Bhushan, Garfield, and Zablocki, *TransBuddhism*, 209–38
Bodhi (Bhikkhu). 2009a. "Formalities of the Law, Qualities of the Heart: A Response to Thanissaro Bhikkhu, Letter of Nov. 13, 2009." Posted by Judy Pham, 26 November. http://livingdharma.webs.com/apps/blog/show/2204490-ven-bhikkhu-bodhi-formalities-of-the-law-qualities-of-the-heart
– 2009b. "Socially Engaged Buddhism and the Trajectory of Buddhist Ethical Consciousness." *Religion East and West* 9, no. 10: 1–23
Bodian, Stephen. 1989. Review of *Zen Center: Portrait of an American Zen Community*, video, produced by Anne Cushman. *Yoga Journal* 89 (July/August): 90
Bond, George D. 1988. *The Buddhist Revival in Sri Lanka: Religious Tradition, Reinterpretation and Response*. South Carolina: University of South Carolina Press
– 1996. "A.T. Ariyaratne and the Sarvodaya Shramadana Movement in Sri Lanka." In Queen and King, *Engaged Buddhism*, 121–46
Bookchin, Murray. 1987. "Social Ecology versus Deep Ecology: A Challenge for the Ecology Movement." Originally published in *Green Perspectives: Newsletter of the Green Project Program*, 4–5. http://ruby.fgcu.edu/courses/twimberley/EnviroPhilo/Bookchin.pdf

Borup, Jorn. 2004. "Zen and the Art of Inverting Orientalism: Buddhism, Religious Studies and Interrelated Networks." In *New Approaches to the Study of Religion*. Vol. 1, *Regional, Critical, and Historical Approaches*, edited by Peter Antes, Armin W. Geertz, and Randi R. Warne, 451–88. New York: Walter de Gruyter

Boucher, Sandy. 1988. *Turning the Wheel: American Women Creating the New Buddhism*. San Francisco: Harper and Row

Brahmavamso, Ajahn (Bhikkhu). 1997. "Vinaya Monks and Women Nuns and Men." Newsletter, *The Buddhist Society of Western Australia*, July–October. http://www.dhammatalks.net/Books6/Ajahn_Brahm_Vinaya_Monks_and_Women_Nuns_and_Men.htm

– 2009a. "Open Letter to All from Ajahn Brahm on the Excommunication by Wat Pah Pong." http://www.dhammalight.com/personal/AjahnBrahmOpenLetter.html

– 2009b. "On the Bhikkhuni Question, an interview by Nissara Horayangura." http://www.buddhanet.net/budsas/ebud/ebdha353.htm

– 2011. "Relations with the Wat Pa Pong Sangha Worldwide." *Dhammaloka Buddhist Centre, Operated by the Buddhist Society of Western Australia*, 18 November. http://www.dhammaloka.org.au/home/item/1157-relations-with-the-wat-pa-pong-sangha-worldwide.html

Bramadat, Paul, and David Seljak, eds. 2005. *Religion and Ethnicity in Canada*. Toronto: University of Toronto Press

Buckley, Brian. 2008. *Gift of Freedom: How Ottawa Welcomed the Vietnamese, Cambodian, and Laotian Refugees*. Renfrew, ON: General Store Publishing House

Buddhajahn, Ven. Somdet. 2009. "Some Key Remarks Made by Ven. Somdet Buddhajahn in a Meeting with a Delegation from Wat Nong Pah Pong on 17 Nov. 2009." Administrative Committee of Wat Nong Pah Pong Sangha

Buddhist Channel, The. 2009. "Notification of the Wat Nong Pah Pong Sangha decision to revoke the status of a branch monastery." http://www.buddhistchannel.tv/index.php?id=70,8660,0,0,1,0

Buddhist Churches of America, ed. 1998. *Buddhist Churches of America: A Legacy of the First 100 Years*. San Francisco: Buddhist Churches of America

Buddhist Dictionary, n.d. http://buddhistdoor.com

Buddhist Fellowship. 2009. "Excommunication of Ajahn Brahm for performing Bhikkhuni Ordination in Australia." http://www.buddhistfellowship.org/cms/index.php?/General-News/excommunication-of-ajahn-brahm-for-performing-bhikkhuni-ordination-in-australia.html

Buddhist Peace Fellowship. 1991. "Buddhist Teachers and Sexual Misconduct." *Buddhist Peace Fellowship Newsletter* (Spring, Summer, Fall)

Bunting, Madeleine. 1997. "The Dark Side of Enlightenment." *The Guardian*, 27 October. http://www.fwbo-files.com/guardian_article_v2.htm

Bureau of Justice Statistics. n.d. "Deaths of Prisoners under Federal Jurisdiction, by Sex and Cause of Death, 1999–2008." http://bjs.ojp.usdoj.gov/index.cfm?ty=tp&tid=194

Burnet, Jean. 1979. "Myths and Multiculturalism." *Canadian Journal of Education* 4, no. 4: 43–58

Butler, Katy. 1983. "Events Are the Teacher." *CoEvolution Quarterly* 4: 112–23

Cabézon, José Ignacion, ed. 1992. *Buddhism, Sexuality and Gender*. Albany: State University of New York Press

– 1995. "Buddhist Studies as a Discipline and the Role of Theory." *Journal of the International Association of Buddhist Studies* 18, no. 2: 231–68

Cadge, Wendy. 2004. "Gendered Religious Organizations: The Case of Theravada Buddhism in America." *Gender and Society* 18, no. 6: 777–93

– 2005a. "Lesbian, Gay, and Bisexual Buddhist Practitioners." In *Gay Religion*, edited by Scott Thumma and Edward R. Gray, 139–52. Walnut Creek, CA: AltaMira Press

– 2005b. *Heartwood: The First Generation of Theravada Buddhism in America*. Chicago: University of Chicago Press

Caldarola, Carlo. 2007. "Japanese Cultural Traditions in Southern Alberta." In *Sakura in the Land of the Maple Leaf: Japanese Cultural Traditions in Canada*, edited by Carlo Caldarola, Mitsuru Shimpo, K. Victor Ujimoto, and Ban Seng Hoe, 5–72. Gatineau, PQ: Canadian Museum of Civilization Corp.

Calverley, Donna. 2010. "Adult Correctional Services in Canada, 2008/2009." *Juristat* 30, no. 3: 3–32

Campbell, Patricia Q. 2010. "Transforming Ordinary Life: Turning to Zen Buddhism in Toronto." In Harding, Hori, and Soucy, *Wild Geese*, 187–209

– 2011. *Knowing Body, Moving Mind: Ritualizing and Learning at Two Buddhist Centers*. Oxford: Oxford University Press

Canadian Centre for Justice Statistics. 2004. *Adult Correctional Services in Canada 2003–2004*. Ottawa: Statistics Canada

Carbine, Jason. 2005. "*Shwegyin Sasana*: Continuity, Rupture, and Traditionalism in a Buddhist Tradition." In Engler and Grieve, *Historicizing "Tradition" in the Study of Religion*, 145–74

Casey, Noah. 2002. "The True Buddha School: A Field Research Report on the Chan Hai Lei Zang Temple." *Montreal Religious Sites Project*. http://mrsp.mcgill.ca/index.htm

Chan, Victor. 2003. "A Tale of Two Cities." In Bernstorff and von Welck, *Exile as Challenge*, 101–6

Chandler, Stuart. 2004. *Establishing a Pure Land on Earth: The Fo Guang Buddhist Perspective on Modernization and Globalization.* Honolulu: University of Hawai'i Press

Chandrasekera, Swarna. 2001. *Teaching Buddhism to Children: A Curriculum Guide to Dhamma School Teachers.* Mississauga: Halton-Peel Buddhist Society

Chapman, John. 2007. "The 2005 Pilgrimage and Return to Vietnam of Exiled Master Thích Nhất Hạnh." In Philip Taylor, *Modernity and Re-enchantment*, 297–340

Chūgai Nippō (Japan) [Chūgai Daily Bulletin]. 1925

Chui, Tina, Kelly Tran, and Hélène Maheux. 2009. "2006 Census: Immigration in Canada: A Portrait of the Foreign-born Population, 2006 Census: Findings." *Social and Aboriginal Statistics Division, Statistics Canada.* http://www12.statcan.ca/census-recensement/2006/as-sa/97-557/index-eng.cfm

Cohen, Andrew. 2007. *The Unfinished Canadian: The People We Are.* Toronto: McClelland & Stewart

Cohen, Anthony P. 1985. *The Symbolic Construction of Community.* London: Tavistock Publications Ltd

Coleman, James William. 2001. *The New Buddhism: The Western Transformation of an Ancient Tradition.* New York: Oxford University Press

Collected Teachings of Ajahn Chah, The. 2011. 3 vols. Harnham, UK: Aruna Publications

Corless, Roger. 2000. "Gay Buddhist Fellowship." In Queen and King, *Engaged Buddhism in the West*, 269–79

Correctional Service Canada. 2006. *Religious and Spiritual Accommodation in CSC Institutions.* Ottawa: Correctional Service Canada

– 2010. *Use of Force Annual Report, 2009–2010.* Ottawa: Correctional Service Canada

– 2011. "Correctional Service of Canada (CSC) Response to the Office of the Correctional Investigator's Deaths in Custody Study, the Correctional Investigator's Report: A Preventable Death and the CSC National Board of Investigation into the Death of an Offender at Grand Valley Institution for Women." http://www.csc-scc.gc.ca/text/pblct/rocidcs/grid2-eng.shtml

– n.d. "Incidents of Violence." Internal Correctional Service Canada. http://www.cancrime.com

Criminon International. http://www.criminon.org

Crowe, Paul. 2010a. "Chinese Religions." In DeVries, Baker, and Overmyer, *Asian Religions in British Columbia*, 249–74

– 2010b. "Universal Buddhist Temple (世界佛教會): Embracing a Myriad Dharmas." *Canadian Journal of Buddhist Studies* 6: 89–115

Cuevas, Bryan J. 2003. *The Hidden History of the Tibetan Book of the Dead.* Oxford: Oxford University Press

Culadasa, Upasaka. 2010. "Stronghold August 15 – Rites & Rituals." *Dharma Treasure.* Podcast. http://dharmatreasure.com/2010/08/dharma-talks/stronghold-august-15

Cushman, Anne, producer, Lou Hawthorne, director. 1987. *Zen Center: Portrait of an American Zen Community*, video. Albuquerque: Miracle Productions

The Dalai Lama, His Holiness. 2005. *The Universe in a Single Atom: The Convergence of Science and Spirituality.* New York: Morgan Road Books

Dalailama.com. n.d. "Awards & Honors: 2000–2010." The Office of His Holiness the Dalai Lama. http://www.dalailama.com/biography/awards-honors

Darlington, Susan M. 2009. "Translating Modernity: Buddhist Response to the Thai Environmental Crisis." In Bhushan, Garfield, and Zablocki, *Trans-Buddhism*, 183–207

Denzin, N.K. 1997. *Interpretive Ethnography: Ethnographic Practices for the Twenty-First Century.* Newbury Park, CA: Sage

Despland, Michel. 2005. "Tradition." In Engler and Grieve, *Historicizing "Tradition" in the Study of Religion*, 19–32

DeVido, Elise A. 2007. "'Buddhism for This World': The Buddhist Revival in Vietnam, 1920 to 1951, and Its Legacy." In Philip Taylor, *Modernity and Re-enchantment*, 250–96

– 2009. "The Influence of Chinese Master Taixu on Buddhism in Vietnam." *Journal of Global Buddhism* 10: 413–58

DeVries, Larry, Don Baker, and Daniel Overmyer, eds. 2010. *Asian Religions in British Columbia.* Vancouver: University of British Columbia Press

Dezeuze, Anna. 2004. Review of *Robert Filliou, Génie sans Talent*, Villeneuve d'Ascq, France, Musée d'Art Moderne Lille Metropole. *Papers of Surrealism* 2: 1–10. http://www.surrealismcentre.ac.uk/papersofsurrealism/journal2/acrobat_files/dezeuze%20review.pdf

dhamma.org. 2011. "Vipassana Meditation." http://www.dhamma.org

Dharma, (Bhikṣuṇī Dr) Karuna. 1988. "Nuns of Vietnam." In *Sakyadhītā: Daughters of the Buddha*, edited by Karma Lekshe Tsomo, 154–9. Delhi: Sri Satguru Publications

Dharma Drum Mountain Vancouver Center. n.d. "About Us." http://www.ddmba.ca

Dharma Realm Buddhist Association. 1996. 宣演正法萬佛城 [Xuanyan zhengfa: Wanfo cheng – Propagating the Dharma: The City of Ten Thousand Buddhas]. Ukiah, CA: Dharma Realm Buddhist Association and the City of Ten Thousand Buddhas

Dib, Kamal, Ian Donaldson, and Brittany Turcotte. 2008. "Integration and Identity in Canada: The Importance of Multicultural Common Spaces." *Canadian Ethnic Studies* 40, no. 1: 161–87

Diebel, Linda. 2007. "When Rights Collide with Freedoms." *Toronto Star*, 28 May. http://www.thestar.com/news/article/218355--when-rights-collide-with-freedoms

Diehl, Keila. 2002. *Echoes from Dharamsala: Music in the Life of a Tibetan Refugee Community*. Berkley and Los Angeles: University of California Press

Do, Hien Duc. 2006. "Reproducing Vietnam in America: San Jose's Perfect Harmony Temple." In *A Nation of Religions: The Politics of Pluralism in Multireligious America*, edited by Stephen Prothero, 79–93. Chapel Hill: University of North Carolina Press

Donnenfield, David. 1997. *Changing from Inside*. Onalaska, WA: Pariyatti Digital Editions

Dorais, Louis-Jacques. 1987. *Exile in a Cold Land: A Vietnamese Community in Canada*. New Haven, CT: Yale Southeast Asian Studies

– 1988. "Cold Solitude and Snowy Peace: The Indochinese in Quebec City." In *Ten Years Later: Indochinese Communities in Canada*, edited by Louis-Jacques Dorais, Kwok B. Chan, and Doreen M. Indra, 165–88. Montreal: Canadian Asian Studies Association

– 2006. "Buddhism in Quebec." In Matthews, *Buddhism in Canada*, 120–41

Dorais, Louis-Jacques, and Éric Richard. 2007. *Les Vietnamiens de Montréal*. Montreal: Les Presses de l'Université de Montréal

Doris, David T. 1998. "Zen Vaudeville: A Medi(t)ation in the Margins of Fluxus." In Ken Friedman, *The Fluxus Reader*, 91–135 http://researchbank.swinburne.edu.au/vital/access/manager/Repository/swin:9624

Dorjee, Tenzin, and Howard Giles. 2005. "Cultural Identity in Tibetan Diaspora." *Journal of Multilingual and Multicultural Development* 26, no. 2: 138–57

Downing, Michael. 2001. *Shoes outside the Door: Desire, Devotion and Excess at the San Francisco Zen Center*. Washington, DC: Counterpoint

Doyle, Tara. 2003. "Liberate the Mahabodhi Temple: Socially Engaged Buddhism *Dalit* Style." In Heine and Prebish, 249–80

Drummond, Lisa, and Helle Rydstrøm, eds. 2004. *Gender Practices in Contemporary Vietnam*. Singapore: Singapore University Press

DuBois, Fletcher, Erik de Maaker, Karin Polit, and Marianne Riphagen. 2011. "From Ritual Ground to Stage." In Grimes, Hüsken, Simon, and Venbrux, *Ritual, Media, and Conflict*, 35–62

Dumoulin, Heinrich. 1979. *Zen Enlightenment: Origins and Meaning*. Translated by John C. Maraldo. Boston: Weatherhill

– 2005. *Zen Buddhism: A History*. Volume 2. Translated by James W. Heisig and Paul Knitter. Bloomington: World Wisdom

Durkheim, Emile. 2001. *Elementary Forms of Religious Life*. Oxford: Oxford University Press

Dutt, Sukumar. 1957. *The Buddha and Five After-centuries*. London: Luzac and Co.

Eckel, Malcolm David. 1994. "The Ghost at the Table: On the Study of Buddhism and the Study of Religion." *Journal of the American Academy of Religion* 62, no. 4: 1085–110

Edelstein, Scott. 2011. *Sex and the Spiritual Teacher: Why It Happens, When It's a Problem, and What We All Can Do*. Boston: Wisdom Publications

Egan, Kieran. 2003. "What is Curriculum?" *Journal of the Canadian Association for Curriculum Studies* 1, no. 1: 9–16

Eldershaw, Lynn. 2010. " Shambhala International: The Golden Sun of the Great East." In Harding, Hori, and Soucy, *Wild Geese*, 236–67

Engler, Steven, and Gregory P. Grieve, eds. 2005. *Historicizing "Tradition" in the Study of Religion*. Berlin: Walter de Gruyter GmbH & Co

Fairview bukkyō seinenkai, ed. 1930. *Otakebi* [The Roar]. Vancouver: Uchida shoten

Falk, Nancy Auer. 2001. "The Case of the Vanishing Nuns: The Fruits of Ambivalence in Ancient Indian Buddhism." In *Unspoken Worlds: Women's Religious Lives*, edited by Nancy Auer Falk and Rita Gross, 196–207. Belmont, CA: Wadsworth

Farber, Don, and Rick Fields. 1987. *Taking Refuge in L.A.: Life in a Vietnamese Buddhist Temple*. New York: Aperture

Fenn, Mavis L. 2008. "Buddhist Women in Canada: Researching Identity and Difference." In *Buddhist Women in a Global Multicultural Community*, edited by Karma Lekshe Tsomo, 171–7. Malaysia: Suki Hotu Dhamma Publications

– 2012. "Canadian Buddhist Women: Multicultural Connections." Unpublished paper presented at the Sakyadhita conference, *Canadian Women in Buddhism: Connect Support Share*, 15 September. http://www.sakyadhitacanada.org/conference-review.html

– 2013. "Buddhism." In *World Religions: Canadian Perspectives (Eastern Traditions)*, edited by Doris Jakobsh, 156–203. Toronto: Nelson Education

– 2014. "Sakyadhita Canada: Branching Out." *Canadian Journal of Buddhist Studies* 9: 131–41

Fenn, Mavis L., and Kay Koppedrayer. 2008. "Sakyadhita: A Transnational Gathering Place for Buddhist Women." *Journal of Global Buddhism* 9: 45–79

Ferranto, Matt. n.d. "Moticos and Mail Art: A History." http://www.spareroom.org/mailart/mis_2.html

Fields, Rick. 1992. *How the Swans Came to the Lake: A Narrative History of Buddhism in America*. Boston: Shambhala

– 1998. "Divided Dharmas: White Buddhists, Ethnic Buddhists, and Racism." In Prebish and Tanaka, eds, *The Faces of Buddhism in America*, 196–206

Filliou, Robert. 2004. "Robert Filliou, July, 1973." In *Artists Talk: 1969–1977*, edited by Peggy Gale, 250–61. Halifax: Press of the Nova Scotia College of Art and Design

Fisher, Danny. 2011. "'All about the Bodhisattva Ethic': John Harding and Charles Prebish remember Dr. Leslie Kawamura." *Buddhadharma: The Practitioner's Quarterly Online*, 17 March. http://shambhalasun.com/news/?p=19818

Fleischman, Paul. 1995. *Karma and Chaos*. Seattle: Vipassana Publications

Forest Sangha. n.d. "Forest Sangha." http://forestsangha.org

Freiberger, Oliver. 2006. "Early Buddhism, Asceticism, and the Politics of the Middle Way." In *Asceticism and Its Critics: Historical Accounts and Comparative Perspectives*, edited by Oliver Freiberger, 235–58. Oxford: Oxford University Press

Friedman, Ken. 1990. "Getting Into Events." In Ken Friedman, *Fluxus Performance Workbook*, 4–6
- ed. 1990. *Fluxus Performance Workbook*. Trondheim: El Djarida
- 1998. "Fluxus and Company." In Ken Friedman, *The Fluxus Reader*, 237–53. http://researchbank.swinburne.edu.au/vital/access/manager/Repository/swin:9624
- ed. 1998. *The Fluxus Reader*. New York: Academy Editions
- 2009. *99 Events: 1956–2009*. New York: Stendhal Gallery. http://www.fluxusheidelberg.org/kenfriedman99eventscatalog.pdf

Friedman, Lenore. 1987. *Meetings with Remarkable Women: Buddhist Teachers in America*. Boston: Shambhala

Friz, Anna. 2007. "Send Us Your Art's Birthday Presence! Traces of Art's Birthday Networks at the Western Front 1989–2007." Western Front Research Library, February. http://front.bc.ca/research/texts/3

Gammeltoft, Tine. 1999. *Women's Bodies, Women's Worries: Health and Family Planning in a Vietnamese Rural Community*. Surrey, UK: Curzon

Gangadharan, Seeta Peña. 2009. "Mail Art: Networking without Technology." *New Media Society* 11: 279–98

Garcia, Joseph. 2008. "Postulations on the Fragmentary Effects of Multiculturalism in Canada." *Canadian Ethnic Studies* 40, no. 1: 141–60

Garfield, Jay L. 2009. "Translation as Transmission and Transformation." In Bhushan, Garfield, and Zablocki, *TransBuddhism*, 89–103

Gethin, Rupert. 1998. *The Foundations of Buddhism*. Oxford: Oxford University Press

Giddens, Anthony. 1990. *The Consequences of Modernity*. Cambridge: Polity Press
- 1991. *Modernity and Self-Identity*. Stanford, CA: Stanford University Press
- 2002. *Runaway World: How Globalisation Is Reshaping Our Lives*. London: Profile Books Ltd

The Globalist. 2005. "Pope John Paul II and Globalization." 5 April. http://www.theglobalist.com/StoryId.aspx?StoryId=1268

Globe and Mail. 2012. "Nathan Cullen on Why He Wants to Lead NDP," video, 14 March. http://www.theglobeandmail.com/news/politics/video-nathan-cullen-on-why-he-wants-to-lead-ndp/article2368972

Goenka, S.N. 1987. *Discourse Summaries.* Igatpuri: Vipassana Research Institute

– 1994. *Sayagyi U Ba Khin Journal.* Igatpuri: Vipassana Research Institute

– 2000. "Universal Spirituality for Peace." *United Nations Millennium Peace Summit,* 29 August

– 2006. *The Gem Set in Gold.* Onalaska: Vipassana Research Publications

Goldberg, Natalie. 2004. *The Great Failure: My Unexpected Path to Truth.* New York: Harper Collins

Gold Buddha Monastery. 2004. *Red Lotuses Abound in the Valley of a Thousand Mountains, Twenty Years of Fellowship with GBM: Commemorating the 20th Anniversary of Gold Buddha Monastery.* Vancouver: Gold Buddha Monastery

Gombrich, Richard, and Gananath Obeyesekere. 1988. *Buddhism Transformed: Religious Change in Sri Lanka.* Princeton: Princeton University Press

Gómez, Luis. 1995. "Unspoken Paradigms: Meanderings through the Metaphors of a Field." *Journal of the International Association of Buddhist Studies* 18, no. 2: 183–230

Gouin, Margaret. 2010. *Tibetan Rituals of Death: Buddhist Funerary Practices.* New York: Routledge

Government of Canada. 1992. "Corrections and Conditional Release Act, S.C. 1992, c. 20." http://laws-lois.justice.gc.ca/eng/acts/C-44.6/FullText.html

Governor General of Canada, The. n.d. "Order of Canada: Yutetsu Kawamura, C.M." http://www.gg.ca/honour.aspx?id=876&t=12&ln=Kawamura

Grieve, Gregory P. 2005. "Histories of Tradition in Bhaktapur, Nepal: Or, How to Compile a Contemporary Hindu Medieval City." In Engler and Grieve, *Historicizing "Tradition" in the Study of Religion,* 269–82

Grieve, Gregory P., and Richard Weiss. 2005. "Illuminating the Half-Life of Tradition: Legitimation, Agency, and Counter-Hegemonies." In Engler and Grieve, *Historicizing "Tradition" in the Study of Religion,* 1–18

Griffiths, Rudyard. 2009. *Who We Are: A Citizen's Manifesto.* Toronto: Douglas & McIntyre

Grimes, Ronald L., ed. 1996. *Readings in Ritual Studies.* Upper Saddle River, NJ: Prentice Hall

– 2011. "Ritual, Media, and Conflict: An Introduction." In Grimes, Hüsken, Simon, and Venbrux, *Ritual, Media, and Conflict,* 3–34

Grimes, Ronald L., Ute Hüsken, Udo Simon, and Eric Venbrux, eds. 2011. *Ritual, Media, and Conflict.* New York: Oxford University Press

Guenther, Herbert V., and Tshe-mchog-gliṅ Ye-śes-rgyal-mtshan. 1975. *Mind in Buddhist Psychology*. Translated by Herbert V. Guenther and Leslie S. Kawamura. Volume 3 of *Tibetan Translation Series*. Emeryville, CA: Dharma Publishing

Gunaratana, Henepola. 1985. *The Path of Serenity and Insight*. Delhi: Motilal Banarsidass

Gunaratne, K.S. 1986. "Buddhist Education for Children." *Toronto Buddhist* 8, no. 1: 11–12

Gyatso, Sherab. 2003. "Of Monks and Monasteries." In Bernstorff and von Welck, *Exile as Challenge*, 213–43

Hallisey, Charles. 1995. "Roads Taken and Not Taken in the Study of Theravāda Buddhism." In Lopez, *Curators of the Buddha*, 31–61

Hansen, Peter H. 1996. "The Dancing Lamas of Everest: Cinema, Orientalism, and Anglo-Tibetan Relations in the 1920s." *American Historical Review* (June): 712–47

Harding, John S. 2008. *Mahāyāna Phoenix: Japan's Buddhists at the 1893 World's Parliament of Religions*. New York: Peter Lang

– 2010. "Jodo Shinshu in Southern Alberta: From Rural Raymond to Amalgamation." In Harding, Hori, and Soucy, *Wild Geese*, 134–67

– ed. 2012. *Studying Buddhism in Practice*. London: Routledge

Harding, John S., Victor Sōgen Hori, and Alexander Soucy. 2012. "Buddhism in Canada." In *2600 Years of Sambuddhatva: Global Journey of Awakening*, edited by Oliver Abenayaka and Asanga Tilakaratne, 509–24. Colombo, Sri Lanka: The Ministry of Buddhasasana and Religious Affairs, Government of Sri Lanka

– eds. 2010. *Wild Geese: Buddhism in Canada*. Montreal & Kingston: McGill-Queen's University Press

Hardy, Robert Spence. 1850. *Eastern Monachism*. London: William and Norgate

– 1853. *Manual of Budhism* [sic]. London: Partridge and Oakey

Harris, Clare. 1999. *In the Image of Tibet: Tibetan Painting after 1959*. London: Reaktion Books

– 2006. "The Buddha Goes Global: Some Thoughts towards a Transnational Art History." *Art History* 29, no. 4: 698–720

Hart, William. 1987. *The Art of Living: Vipassana Meditation as Taught by S.N. Goenka*. New York: Harper Collins

Harvey, Peter. 1990. *An Introduction to Buddhism: Teachings, History and Practice*. Cambridge: Cambridge University Press

Hayashi, Rintarō. 2000. "Kuroshio no hateni [At the end of Kuroshio Currents]." In *Canada iminshi shiryō* [The records of the history of Japanese immigration to Canada], edited by Toshiji Sasaki and Tsuneharu Gonnami, 8: 1–355. Tokyo: Fuji shuppan, reprint

Hayashi, Yukari, Barrie McLean, and Hiroaki Mori, directors. 1994. *The Tibetan Book of the Dead: The Great Liberation*, film. Montreal: National Film Board of Canada

Hayes, Bob. 1967. "Pointe Claire Hears New Generation Views." *Montreal Gazette*, 1 December, 10

Hayes, Richard. 1995. "Androgyny among Friends." http://www.unm.edu/~rhayes/afterpat.pdf

Haynes, Sarah. 2010. "A Relationship of Reciprocity: Globalization, Skilful Means, and Tibetan Buddhism in Canada." In Harding, Hori, and Soucy, *Wild Geese*, 321–45

– 2011. "A Pioneer in the Canadian Buddhist Landscape: Remembering Rev. Dr. Leslie Kawamura." *The Canadian Journal of Buddhist Studies* 7: 7–8

– 2013. "The Re-imagination of Tibet: Ritual Adaptation in the Tibetan Diaspora." In *Re-imagining South Asian Religions: Essays in Honour of Professors Harold G. Coward and Ronald W. Neufeldt*, edited by Harold Coward, Ronald W Neufeldt, Pashaura Singh, and Michael Hawle, 155–70. Leiden: Brill

Haynes, Sarah, and Michelle J. Sorensen, eds. 2013. *Wading into the Stream of Wisdom: Essays Honoring Leslie Kawamura*. Berkeley, CA: Institute of Buddhist Studies and BDK America

Hearth Foundation. n.d. "About Us." http://www.hearthfoundation.net/joomla1.5/about-us.html

Heine, Steven, and Charles Prebish, eds. 2003. *Buddhism in the Modern World*. Oxford: Oxford University Press

Helbling, Jerry. 2004. "Interview with Christopher Queen, Harvard University, Center for the Study of World Religions." *Echo Chamber Project*, 18 June. http://www.echochamberproject.com/queen

Henderson, Anne, director. 1991. *A Song for Tibet*, film. National Film Board of Canada

Henry, Patrick, ed. 2001. *Benedict's Dharma: Buddhists Reflect on the Rule of Saint Benedict*. New York: Riverhead Books

Hickey, Wakoh Shannon. 2010. "Two Buddhisms, Three Buddhisms, and Racism." *Journal of Global Buddhism* 1: 1–25. http://www.globalbuddhism.org/11/hickey10.pdf

Hirota, Dennis, Hisao Inagaki, Michio Tokunaga, and Ryushin Uryuzu, trans. 1997. *The Collected Works of Shinran*. 2 vols. Kyoto: Jodo Shinsu Hongwanji-ha

Ho, Jackie. 2010. "Administrative Processes of a Modern Buddhist Organization: Changing Roles of the Sangha in the True Buddha Calgary Pai Yuin Lei Zang

Temple." Unpublished paper presented at the University of British Columbia conference, *Buddhism in Canada: Global Causes, Local Conditions*. Vancouver, British Columbia, 15 October

Hobsbawm, Eric, and Terence Ranger, eds. 1983. *The Invention of Tradition*. Cambridge: University of Cambridge Press

Holt, John C. 1981. *Discipline: The Canonical Buddhism of the Vinayapitaka*. Delhi: Motilala Banarsidass

– 2004. *The Buddhist Viṣṇu: Religious Transformation, Politics and Culture*. New York: Columbia University Press

Hori, Victor Sōgen. 1994a. "Teaching and Learning in the Rinzai Zen Monastery." *Journal of Japanese Studies* 20, no. 1: 5–35

– 1994b. "Sweet and Sour Buddhism." *Tricycle* (Fall): 48–52

– 2003. *Zen Sand: The Book of Capping Phrases for Koan Practice*. Honolulu: University of Hawai'i Press

– 2010a. "How Do We Study Buddhism in Canada?" In Harding, Hori, and Soucy, *Wild Geese*, 12–38

– 2010b. "Western Buddhism, the Ethnic Religion." Unpublished keynote address presented at *Buddhism and Diaspora Conference*. University of Toronto, Scarborough, 14–16 May

Hori, Ichirō. 1962. *Nihon shūkyō no shakaiteki yakuwari* [The social roles of Japanese religions]. Tokyo: Miraisha

Hot Facts. 2008. "2006 Census Profile of Richmond." Richmond, BC: City of Richmond, 3 April. http://www.richmond.ca/discover/demographics/Census2006.htm

Hotz, Michael, ed. 2003. *Holding the Lotus to the Rock: The Autobiography of Sokei-an, America's First Zen Master*. New York: Four Walls Eight Windows

Houle, René. 2011. "Recent Evolution of Immigrant-Language Transmission in Canada." *Component of Statistics Canada Catalogue no. 11–008–X Canadian Social Trends*. 7 June. http://www5.statcan.gc.ca/access_acces/alternative_alternatif.action?l=eng&loc=/pub/11-008-x/2011002/article/11453-eng.pdf

Houston, Serin, and Richard Wright. 2003. "Making and Remaking Tibetan Diasporic Identities." *Social & Cultural Geography* 4, no. 2: 217–32

Huber, Toni. 2001. "Shangri-la in Exile: Representations of Tibetan Identity and Transnational Culture." In *Imagining Tibet: Perceptions, Projections, and Fantasies*, edited by Thierry Dodin and Heinz Rather, 357–72. Somerville, MA: Wisdom Publications

Hughes, Aaron. 2005. "The 'Golden Age' of Muslim Spain: Religious Identity and the Invention of a Tradition." In Engler and Grieve, *Historicizing "Tradition" in the Study of Religion*, 51–74

Hurst, Lynda. 2007. "Multiculturalism Policy Falling behind the Times." *Toronto Star*, 29 May. http://www.thestar.com/article/218666--multiculturalism-policy-falling-behind-the-times

Hutcheon, Linda. 1988. *The Canadian Postmodern: A Study of Contemporary English-Canadian Fiction*. Toronto: Oxford University Press

Iino, Masako. 2002. "BC shū no bukkyōkai to nikkei Canadajin community [Buddhist temples and Japanese Canadian community in British Columbia]." *Tokyo daigaku amerika taiheiyō kenkyū* [The University of Tokyo America and Pacific Studies] 2: 45–61

Ikuta, Shinjō. 1981. *Kanada bukkyōkai enkakushi* [A history of Japanese Buddhist temples in Canada]. Toronto: Buddhist Churches of Canada

Imamura, Ryo. 2008. No title. http://florinbuddhist.org/home/docs/Oct2008a.pdf

Insight Meditation Society. n.d. "Does IMS Have an Ethics Committee?" *FAQ about Retreats*. http://www.dharma.org/meditation-retreats/faq

Iwaasa, David. 1978. "Canadian Japanese in South Alberta: 1905–1945." In *Two Monographs on Japanese Canadians*, edited by Roger Daniels, 1–97. New York: Arno Press

Iwamura, Jane. 2011. *Virtual Orientalism: Asian Religions and American Popular Culture*. New York: Oxford University Press

Jackson, Peter A. 1989. *Buddhism, Legitimation, and Conflict: The Political Functions of Urban Thai Buddhism*. Singapore: Institute of Southeast Asian Studies

Jackson, Roger R. 2000. "Buddhist Theology: Its Historical Context." In Jackson and Makransky, *Buddhist Theology*, 1–13

Jackson, Roger R., and John J. Makransky, eds. 2000. *Buddhist Theology: Critical Reflections by Contemporary Buddhist Scholars*. London: RoutledgeCurzon

Jacob, Luis. 2002. "Golden Streams: Artists' Collaboration and Exchange in the 1970s." Centre for Contemporary Canadian Art, Canadian Art Database. http://www.ccca.ca/c/writing/j/jacob/jaco01t.html

Jakobsh, Doris R., ed. 2013. *World Religions: Canadian Perspectives (Eastern Traditions)*. Toronto: Nelson Education

Jodo Shinshu Buddhist Temples of Canada. 2010. "Living Dharma Centre." http://www.bcc.ca/ldc.html

Jones, Noa. 2008. "If I'm Lucky They Call Me Unorthodox." *Shambhala Sun*. http://www.shambhalasun.com/index.php?option=content&task=view&id=1542

Jorgensen, John. 1987. "The 'Imperial' Lineage of Ch'an Buddhism: The Role of Confucian Ritual and Ancestor Worship in Ch'an's Search for Legitimation in the Mid-T'ang Dynasty." *Papers on Far Eastern History* 35: 89–133

Kabilsingh, Chatsumarn. 1991. *Thai Women in Buddhism*. Berkeley: Parallax Press

Kanter, Rosabeth Moss. 1972. *Commitment and Community: Communes and Utopias in Sociological Perspective*. Boston: Harvard University Press

Kaplan, Janet A., Bracken Hendricks, Geoffrey Hendricks, Hannah Higgins, and Alison Knowles. 2000. "Flux Generations." *Art Journal* 59, no. 2: 6–17

Kashima, Tetsuden. 2007. "The Buddhist Churches of America: Challenges for Change in the Twenty-first Century." In *Shin Buddhism: Historical, Textual, and Interpretive Studies*, edited by Richard K. Payne, 321–40. Berkeley: Institute of Buddhist Studies and Numata Center for Buddhist Translation and Research

Katz, Jonathan. 1999. "John Cage's Queer Silence; Or, How to Avoid Making Things Worse." *glq: A Journal of Lesbian and Gay Studies* 5, no. 2: 231–52

Kawamura, Leslie S., trans. 1975. *Golden Zephyr; Nāgārjuna: A Letter to a Friend BShes-pa'ispring-yig (Suhrllekha) Mi-pham'Jam-dbyangs Rnam-rgyal Rgyamtsho. The Garland of White Lotus Flowers; a Commentary on Nāgārjuna's A Letter to a Friend BShes-spring Gi Mchan-grel Padma-dkar-po'i Phreng –ba*. Emeryville, CA: Dharma Publishing

– 1978. "Changes in the Japanese True Pure Land Buddhism in Alberta – A Case Study: Honpa Buddhist Church in Alberta." In *Religion and Ethnicity*, edited by Harold B. Barclay, Harold G. Coward, and Leslie S. Kawamura, 37–55. Waterloo, ON: Wilfrid Laurier University Press

– ed. 1981. *The Bodhisattva Doctrine in Buddhism*. Waterloo, ON: Wilfrid Laurier University Press

– 1984. *A Buddhism Primer: Buddha – Dharma – Sangha*. Calgary, AB: distributed through University of Calgary Press

– 2006. "Buddhism in Alberta." In Matthews, *Buddhism in Canada*, 30–42

Kawamura, Leslie S., and Keith Scott, eds. 1977. *Buddhist Thought and Asian Civilization: Essays in Honor of Herbert V. Guenther on His Sixtieth Birthday*. Emeryville, CA: Dharma Publishing

Kawamura, Yūtetsu. 1988a. *Kanada alberta shū cowboy song no sato* [The hometown of cowboy songs in Alberta, Canada]. Kyoto: Dōbōsha

– 1988b. *Kanada bukkyo shi (1936–1985)* [A history of Buddhism in Canada, 1936–1985]. Kyoto: Dōbōsha, reprint

– 1997. *The Dharma Survives with the People: Memoirs of Yutetsu Kawamura*. Published privately

Kenney, Jason. 2009. Speaking notes for the Honourable Jason Kenney, P.C., M.P., Minister of Citizenship, Immigration and Multiculturalism. "Good Citizenship: The Duty to Integrate" at Huron University College's Canadian

Leaders Speakers' Series. http://www.cic.gc.ca/english/department/media/speeches/2009/2009-03-18.asp

Kertzer, David I. 1996. "Ritual, Politics, and Power." In Grimes, *Readings in Ritual Studies*, 335–52

Kimura, Yukiko. 1988. *Issei: Japanese Immigrants in Hawaii*. Honolulu: University of Hawai'i Press

King, Sallie. 2005. *Being Benevolence: The Social Ethics of Engaged Buddhism*. Honolulu: University of Hawai'i Press

King, Winston. 1980. *Theravada Meditation: The Buddhist Transformation of Yoga*. University Park: Pennsylvania State University Press

Kirk, David. 2008. "Profile: Birken Forest Monastery." *Buddhadharma: The Practitioner's Quarterly* (Spring). http://www.thebuddhadharma.com/issues/2008/spring/index.php

Kitsilano bukkyō seinenkai, ed. 1935. *Butsuda sōritsu jisshūnen kinen tokushūgō* [The tenth-year special anniversary booklet of "The Buddha"]. Vancouver: Kitsilano bukkyō seinenkai

Kiyozawa Manshi. 2002 [1892]. "*Shūkyōtetsugaku gaikotsu* [The Skeleton of a Philosophy of Religion]." In *Kiyozawa Manshi Zenshū* vol. 1. Tokyo: Iwanami shoten

Kjolhede, Bodhin. 2000. "Afterword." In *The Three Pillars of Zen: Teaching, Practice, and Enlightenment*, edited by Phillip Kapleau, 375–89. New York: Anchor Books

Kobayashi, Audrey. 1989. "The Early History of Japanese Canadians." In *Spirit of Redress: Japanese Canadian in Conference*, edited by Cassandra Kobayashi and Roy Miki, 81–8. Vancouver: JC Publications

Kodama, Shiki. 2005. *Kinsei shinshū to chiiki shakai* [Early modern Shin Buddhism and local communities]. Kyoto: Hōzōkan

Kohn, Richard J. 2001. *Lord of the Dance: The Mani Rimdu Festival in Tibet and Nepal*. Albany: State University of New York Press

Koppedrayer, Kay, and Mavis Fenn. 2006. "Buddhist Diversity in Ontario." In Matthews, *Buddhism in Canada*, 59–84

Kramer, Joel, and Diana Alstad. 1993. *The Guru Papers: Masks of Authoritarian Power*. Berkeley: Frog Publications

Kreinath, Jens, Jan Snoek, and Michael Stausberg, eds. 2006. *Theorizing Rituals: Classical Topics, Theoretical Approaches, Analytical Concepts*. Leiden: Brill

Kunz, Jean Lock, and Stuart Sykes. 2010. *From Mosaic to Harmony: Multicultural Canada in the 21st Century*. Policy Research Initiative, Government of Canada

Kuroda, Shintō. 1893. *Outlines of the Mahāyāna as Taught by Buddha*. Tokyo: Bukkyō gakkuwai

Lachs, Stuart. 1994. "Coming Down from the Zen Clouds: A Critique of the Current State of American Zen." http://lachs.inter-link.com/docs/ComingDown fromtheZenClouds2.pdf
– 2002. "Richard Baker and the Myth of the Zen Roshi." http://www.terebess.hu/english/lachs.html#baker
Lachs, Stuart, and Vladimir K. 2010. "The Aitken-Shimano Letters." *The Zen Site*. http://www.thezensite.com/ZenEssays/CriticalZen/Aitken_Shimano_Letters.html
Lai, David Chuenyan. 1988. *Chinatowns: Towns within Cities in Canada*. Vancouver: University of British Columbia Press
– 1991. *The Forbidden City within Victoria*. Victoria: Orca Books
Lai, David Chuenyan, Jordan Paper, and Li Chuang Paper. 2005. "The Chinese in Canada: Their Unrecognized Religion." In Bramadat and Seljak, *Religion and Ethnicity in Canada*, 89–110
Lai, Whalen. 1982. "The Search for the Historical Śākyamuni in Light of the Historical Jesus." *Buddhist-Christian Studies* 2: 77–91
Laliberté, André, and Manuel Litalien. 2010. "The Tzu Chi Merit Society from Taiwan to Canada." In Harding, Hori, and Soucy, *Wild Geese*, 295–320
Lama Chhimi Kinley. n.d. *Pema Lingpa Treasure Vajrayana Buddhist Center*. http://pemalingpa.ca/Weekly_Notice.htm
Lang, Graeme, and Lars Ragvald. 1998. "Spirit-Writing and the Development of Chinese Cults." *Sociology of Religion* 59, no. 4: 309–28
Latulippe, Hugo, and François Prévost, directors. 2008. *Ce qu'il reste de nous*, film. Montreal: National Film Board of Canada
Lavoie, Caroline. 1989. "Dispersal and Concentration of the Vietnamese Canadians: A Montreal Case Study." MA thesis, McGill University
Law, Judith. 1991. "The Religious Beliefs and Practices of the Vietnamese Community in Britain." Community Religions Project Research Paper (New Series). Leeds: University of Leeds, Department of Theology and Religious Studies
LDJCA History Book Committee. 2001. *Nishiki: Nikkei Tapestry: A History of Southern Alberta Japanese Canadians*. Lethbridge: Lethbridge and District Japanese Canadian Association
Leary, Mark R. 1999. "Making Sense of Self-Esteem." *Current Directions in Psychological Science* 8, no. 1: 32–5
Ledi Sayadaw. 1999. *The Manuals of Dhamma*. Igatpuri: Vipassana Research Institute
Levine, Sarah. 2004. "Dhamma Education for Women in the Theravada Buddhist Community of Nepal." In *Buddhist Women and Social Change*, edited by Karma Lekshe Tsomo, 137–53. Albany: State University of New York Press

Lewis, Brian. 2010. "Roadblock Rises on Highway to Heaven, Temple Expansion: Neighbours Worry about the Precedent the 'Buddha Disneyland' Will Set for the Area." *The Province*, Vancouver, 26 September, A8–A9

Lewis, James, and Olav Hammer, eds. 2007. *The Invention of Sacred Tradition*. Cambridge: University of Cambridge Press

Lin, Irene. 1999. "Journey to the Far West: Chinese Buddhism in America." In *New Spiritual Homes: Religion and Asian Americans*, edited by David K. Yoo, 134–68. Honolulu: University of Hawai'i Press

Lincoln, Bruce. 1996. "Theses on Method." *Method & Theory in the Study of Religion* 8: 225–7

Lindberg Falk, Monica. 2008. *Making Fields of Merit: Buddhist Female Ascetics and Gendered Orders in Thailand*. Seattle: University of Washington Press

Liogier, Raphaël. 2010. "Buddhism and the Hypothesis on Individuo-globalism." Unpublished keynote address presented at *Buddhism in Canada: Global Causes, Local Conditions*. University of British Columbia, 15–17 October

Liu, Tannie. 2005. "Globalization and Chinese Buddhism: The Canadian Experience." PhD diss., University of Ottawa

– 2010. "Globalization and Modern Transformation of Chinese Buddhism in Three Chinese Temples in Eastern Canada." In Harding, Hori, and Soucy, *Wild Geese*, 270–94

Liu, Yunchang (Jack). 2010. "Western Challenge: The Arrival of Buddhist Forest Tradition in Canada." Unpublished paper presented at the conference, *Buddhism in Canada: Global Causes, Local Conditions*. University of British Columbia, 16 October

Logan, Jennifer J. 2010. "'There's No Place Like Home': A Snapshot of the Settlement Experiences of Newcomer Tibetan Women in Parkdale, Toronto." MA thesis, York University

Lopez Jr, Donald S., ed. 1995. *Curators of the Buddha: The Study of Buddhism under Colonialism*. Chicago: University of Chicago Press

– 1998. *Prisoners of Shangri-la*. Chicago: University of Chicago Press

– 2002. "Introduction." In *A Modern Buddhist Bible: Essential Readings from East and West*, edited by Donald S. Lopez, vii-xli. Boston: Beacon Press

Lozoff, Bo. 1985. *We're All Doing Time*. Durham, NC: Human Kindness Foundation

Luu, Tuong Quang. 2011. "Changes and Challenges to Vietnamese Buddhism in Australia." In *Buddhism in Australia: Traditions in Change*, edited by Christina Rocha and Michelle Barker, 134–9. London: Routledge

Madanayake, Bandu. 2010. "Sri Lankan Buddhism in British Columbia." In DeVries, Baker, and Overmyer, *Asian Religions in British Columbia*, 124–40

Maha Boowa Nanasampanno, Bhikkhu. 2004. *Venerable Acariya Mun Bhuridatta Thera: A Spiritual Biography*. 2nd ed. Translated by Bhikkhu Dick Silaratano. Udon Thani Province, Thailand: Forest Dhamma of Wat Pa Baan Taad

Makransky, John J. 2000. "Contemporary Academic Buddhist Theology: Its Emergence and Rationale." In Jackson and Makransky, *Buddhist Theology*, 14–21

Malone, Calvin. 2008. *Razor-wire Dharma*. Somerville, MA: Wisdom Publications

Marr, David G. 1981. *Vietnamese Tradition on Trial, 1920–1945*. Berkeley: University of California Press

Masters, Jarvis Jay. 1997. *Finding Freedom: Writings from Death Row*. Junction City, CA: Padma Publishing

Matthews, Bruce, ed. 2006. *Buddhism in Canada*. New York: Routledge

Maull, Fleet. 2005. *Dharma in Hell: The Prison Writings of Fleet Maull*. Boulder: Prison Dharma Network

McDaniel, Justin. 2006. "Buddhism in Thailand: Negotiating the Modern Period." In *Buddhism in World Cultures: Comparative Perspectives*, edited by Stephen C. Berkowitz, 101–28. Santa Barbara: ABC-CLIO

McLellan, Janet. 1999. *Many Petals of the Lotus: Five Asian Buddhist Communities in Toronto*. Toronto: University of Toronto Press

– 2008. "Themes and Issues in the Study of North American Buddhists and Buddhism." In *North American Buddhists in a Social Context*, edited by Paul David Numrich, 19–50. Boston: Brill

McMahan, David L. 2008. *The Making of Buddhist Modernism*. New York: Oxford University Press

– ed. 2012. *Buddhism in the Modern World*. London: Routledge

Menahemi, Ayellet, and Eilona Arie. 1997. *Doing Time, Doing Vipassana*, film. Karuna Films

Merton, Thomas. 1992. *The Monastic Journey*, edited by Patrick Hart. Kalamazoo, MI: Cistercian Publications

Métraux Daniel A. 1996. *The Lotus and the Maple Leaf: The Soka Gakkai Buddhist Movement in Canada*. Lanham, MD: University Press of America

Michaels, Axel. 2006. "Ritual and Meaning." In Kreinath, Snoek, and Stausberg, *Theorizing Rituals*, 247–61

Miller, Lisa. 1999. "Inside the Competitive New World of Prison Ministries." *Wall Street Journal*, 7 September, B1

Milman, Estera. n.d. "Artifacts of the Eternal Network." Alternative Traditions in the Contemporary Arts. http://sdrc.lib.uiowa.edu/atca/subjugated/two_4.htm

Milner Jr, Murray. 1994. *Status and Sacredness: A General Theory of Status Relations and an Analysis of Indian Culture*. New York: Oxford University Press

Mitchell, John, and Vincent Trasov. n.d. "Mr. Peanut for Mayor Campaign." http://front.bc.ca/performanceart/events/1922

Morris, Michael, and Vincent Trasov. n.d. "Colour Bars and Colour Research." http://vincenttrasov.ca/index.cfm?pg=cv-pressdetail&pressID=9

Mrozik, Susanne. 2009. "Robed Revolution: The Contemporary Buddhist Nun's (*Bhikshuni*) Movement." *Religion Compass* 3, no. 3: 360–78

Mukpo, Gesar, director. 2009. *Tulku*, film. Montreal: National Film Board of Canada

Mullins, Mark. 1987. "The Life-Cycle of Ethnic Churches in Sociological Perspective." *Japanese Journal of Religious Studies* 14, no. 4: 321–34

Mumola, Christopher J. 2005. *Suicide and Homicide in State Prisons and Local Jails*. Washington, DC: Department of Justice

Murai, Tadamasa. 1998. "*Dainiji sekai taisenmae no minami alberta Nikkei shakai: Sono seisei to hatten no kiseki* [The society of Japanese Canadians in southern Alberta before World War II: Traces of its formation and development]." *Imin kenkyū nenpō* [The Annual Bulletin of Immigration Studies] 4: 45–64

Nafekh, Mark, and Yvonne Stys. 2004. *A Profile and Examination of Gang Affiliation within the Federally Sentenced Offender Population*. Ottawa: Correctional Service of Canada

Nagao, Gadjin. 1991. *Mādhyamika and Yogācāra : A Study of Mahāyāna Philosophies (Collected Papers of G.M. Nagao)*. Edited, collated, and translated by Leslie S. Kawamura in collaboration with G.M. Nagao. Albany: State University of New York

Nanakirti Himi, Ganegama. 2008. *Bauddha Daham Pasal Adhyapanaya ha Daham Guruwaraya* [Buddhist religious education and Dharma teacher]. Dehiwala, Sri Lanka: Buddhist Cultural Centre

Nanamoli, Bhikkhu, and Bhikkhu Bodhi. 1995. *The Middle Length Discourses of the Buddha: A New Translation of the Majjhima Nikaya*. Kandy, Sri Lanka: Buddhist Publication Society

Nanayakkara, Sanath. 1997. *Buddhism: A Graduated Course (Step One & Step Two)*. Dehiwala, Sri Lanka: Buddhist Cultural Centre

Nandy, Ashis. 2000 [1988]. *The Intimate Enemy: Loss and Recovery of Self under Colonialism*. New Delhi: Oxford University Press

Nattier, Jan. 1997. Review essay of *Curators of the Buddha: The Study of Buddhism under Colonialism*, edited by Donald. S. Lopez Jr. *Journal of the American Academy of Religion* 65, no. 2: 469–85

– 1998. "Who is a Buddhist? Charting the Landscape of Buddhist America." In Prebish and Tanaka, *The Faces of Buddhism in America*, 183–95

Negru, John (Karma Yönten Gyatso). 2009. *A Rosary of Precious Offerings to Enrich the Mind being a collection of annotated photographs of Vajrayana shrine offerings*. PDF e-Book: Sumeru-books. http://www.sumeru-books.com/downloads/Sumeru%20Press%20Release%20-%20Rosary.pdf

New Canadian, The (Vancouver), 1939, 1941

Nguyen, Cuong Tu. 1995. "Rethinking Vietnamese Buddhist History: Is the Thiền Uyển Tập Anh a 'Transmission of the Lamp' Text?" In *Essays into Vietnamese Pasts*, edited by K.W. Taylor and John K. Whitmore, 81–115. Ithaca, NY: Southeast Asia Program, Cornell University

Nguyen, Cuong Tu, and A.W. Barber. 1998. "Vietnamese Buddhism in North America: Tradition and Acculturation." In Prebish and Tanaka, *The Faces of Buddhism in America*, 183–95

Nguyễn Lang. 2000 [1973]. *Việt Nam Phật Giáo Sử Luận*, vol 1–3 [History of Buddhism in Vietnam]. Hanoi: Nhà Xuất Bản Văn Học

Nishimura, Eshin. 1987. Review of *The Mind of Clover: Essays in Zen Buddhist Ethics*, by Robert Aitken. *Eastern Buddhist* New Series 20, no. 1: 142–4

Norbu, Khyentse, director. 2002. *The Cup*, film. Festival Media

– 2005. *Travellers and Magicians*, film. Zeitgeist Films

Obeyesekere, Gananath. 1970. "Religious Symbolism and Political Change in Ceylon." *Modern Ceylon Studies* 1: 43–63

– 1972. "Religious Symbolism and Political Change in Ceylon." In *The Two Wheels of Dhamma: Essays in Theravada Tradition in India and Ceylon*, edited by Bardwell L. Smith, 58–78. Chambersburg, PA: American Academy of Religion

Ohama, Linda, writer, director. 2000. *The Travelling Reverend*, film. White Pine Picture. Episode for *Scattering of Seeds* series

Olcott, Henry S. 1881. *The Buddhist Catechism*. Madras: The Theosophical Publishing House

Oliver, Ian P. 1979. *Buddhism in Britain*. London: Rider and Co.

Orme-Johnson, David W., and Richard M. Moore. 2003. "First Prison Study Using the Transcendental Meditation Program: La Tuna Federal Penitentiary, 1971." In *Transcendental Meditation in Criminal Rehabilitation and Crime Prevention*, edited by Kenneth G. Walton, David Orme-Johnson, and Rachel S. Goodman, 89–95. London: Routledge

Paññāsiha, Madihe (M.N. Thera). 1995. "Dhamma Schools and Their Development." *The Buddhist: Dhamma Schools Centenary Issue*. 66, no. 2 (June–July): 4–5

Parks, George A., et al. 2003. "The University of Washington Vipassana Meditation Research Project at the North Rehabilitation Facility." *American Jails Magazine* (July/August). http://www.prison.dhamma.org/amjarticle.pdf

Patten, Lesley Ann, director. 2003. *Words of My Perfect Teacher*, film. ZIJI Film & Television

Payutto (Phra Dhammapitaka Bhikkhu). 2001. "Where Women Stand." Interview by Sanitsuda Ekachai. *Bangkok Post*, 22 September

Pearlman, Ellen. 2002. *Tibetan Sacred Dance: A Journey into the Religious and Folk Traditions*. Rochester, VT: Inner Traditions

Perkins, Stephen. n.d. "Utopian Networks and Correspondence Identities." *Alternative Traditions in the Contemporary Arts*. http://sdrc.lib.uiowa.edu/atca/subjugated/two_5.htm

Phillips, Jenny, ed. 2008. *Letters from the Dhamma Brothers: Meditation behind Bars*. Onalaska, WA: Pariyatti Publishing

Pittman, Don A. 2001. *Toward a Modern Chinese Buddhism: Taixu's Reforms*. Honolulu: University of Hawai'i Press

Placzek, James A. 1981. "The Thai Forest Tradition: Local and International Aspects." In *Southeast Asia: Women, Changing Social Structures, and Cultural Continuity*, edited by G.B. Hainsworth, 156–85. Ottawa: University of Ottawa Press

– 2011. "Bhikkhuni Ordination in Theravada Buddhism and Its implications for the Thai Forest Tradition in Canada." Paper presented at a conference of the Canadian Council for Southeast Asian Studies, University of Toronto, 14 October

Placzek, James A., and Ian Baird. 2010. "Thai and Lao Buddhism in British Columbia." In DeVries, Baker, and Overmyer, *Asian Religions in British Columbia*, 107–23

Placzek, James A., and Larry De Vries. 2006. "Buddhism in British Columbia." In Matthews, *Buddhism in Canada*, 1–29

Port, Dosho. 2013. "The King is Dead, Thank God: Reflections on New Training Models for Zen in the Global Culture." *Sweeping Zen*. 2 March 2013. http://sweepingzen.com/the-king-is-dead-thank-god-reflections-on-new-training-models-for-zen-in-the-global-culture

Prebish, Charles S. 1975. *Buddhist Monastic Discipline: The Sanskrit Prātimokṣa Sūtras of the Mahāsāṃgikas and Mūlasarvāstivādins*. University Park: Pennsylvania State University Press

– 1979. *American Buddhism*. North Scituate, MA: Duxbury Press

– 1999. *Luminous Passage: The Practice and Study of Buddhism in America*. Berkeley: University of California Press

– 2002. "Studying the Spread and Histories of Buddhism in the West: The Emergence of Western Buddhism as a New Subdiscipline within Buddhist Studies." In Prebish and Baumann, *Westward Dharma*, 66–81

– 2003. "Varying the Vinaya: Creative Responses to Modernity." In Heine and Prebish, *Buddhism in the Modern World*, 45–73

Prebish, Charles S., and Martin Baumann, eds. 2002. *Westward Dharma: Buddhism beyond Asia*. Berkeley: University of California Press

Prebish, Charles S., and Kenneth K. Tanaka, eds. 1998. *The Faces of Buddhism in America*. Berkeley: University of California Press

Preece, Rob. 2009. *The Courage to Feel: Buddhist Practices for Opening to Others*. Ithaca: Snow Lion Publications

Prison Dharma Network. n.d. "Prison Dharma Network." http://www.prisondharmanetwork.net/

Prochaska, James. 1997. "The Transtheoretical Model of Health Behavior Change." *American Journal of Health Promotion* 12, no. 1: 38–48

Prothero, Stephen. 1996. *The White Buddhist: The Asian Odyssey of Henry Steel Olcott*. Bloomington: Indiana University Press

Quan, Douglas. 2012. "Federal Government Ends Part-Time Contracts with Minority-Faith Prison Chaplains." *National Post*, 5 October. http://news.nationalpost.com/2012/10/05/federal-government-ends-contracts-with-minority-faith-chaplains/

Queen, Christopher. 2000. "Introduction: A New Buddhism." In Queen, *Engaged Buddhism in the West*, 1–31. Boston: Wisdom Publications

– 2004. "Interview with The Echo Chamber Project." 18 June. http://www.echochamberproject.com/queen

Queen, Christopher, and Sallie King, eds. 2000. *Engaged Buddhism: Buddhist Liberation Movements in Asia*. Albany: State University of New York Press

Rahula, Walpola. 1978. "The Problem of the Sangha in the West." In *Zen and the Taming of the Bull: Toward the Definition of Buddhist Thought*, edited by Rahula Walpola, 55–70. London: Gordon Fraser

Raines, John, ed. 2002. *Marx on Religion*. Philadelphia: Temple University Press

Rao, Ursula. 2006. "Ritual in Society." In Kreinath, Snoek, and Stausberg, *Theorizing Rituals*, 143–60

Rapaport, Al, and Brian D. Hotchkiss, eds. 1998. *Buddhism in America: Proceedings of the First Buddhism in America Conference*. Rutland, VT: Tuttle Publishing

Reed-Danahay, Deborah E. 1997. "Introduction." In *Auto/Ethnography: Rewriting the Self and the Social*, edited by Deborah E. Reed-Danahay, 1–17. Oxford: Berg

Ricard, Matthieu, director. 1998. *The Spirit of Tibet: A Journey to Enlightenment*, film. Montreal: National Film Board of Canada

– 2003. *Monk Dancers of Tibet*. Boston: Shambhala

Richler, Noah. 2006. *This Is My Country, What's Yours?* Toronto: McClelland & Stewart

Roberts, Julian V. 2005. *Public Opinion and Corrections: Recent Findings in Canada*. Ottawa: Correctional Service Canada

Robertson, John. 2011. "Semiotics, Habitus and Music in the Transmission of Tibetan Culture in Toronto." MA thesis, Liberty University, Lynchburg, Virginia

Robertson, Roland. 1995. "Glocalization: Time-Space and Homogeneity-Heterogeneity." In *Global Modernities*, edited by Mike Featherstone, Scott Lash, and Roland Robertson, 25–44. London: Sage
- 2009. "Anti-Global Religion?" http://www.oxfordhandbooks.com/view/10.1093/oxfordhb/9780195137989.001.0001/oxfordhb-9780195137989-e-59
Rocha, Christina. 2012. "Buddhism and Globalization." In McMahan, *Buddhism in the Modern World*, 289–303
Rodrigues, Hillary, and John S. Harding. 2009. *Introduction to the Study of Religion*. London and New York: Routledge
Rorty, Richard. 1999. "Introduction: Relativism: Finding and Making." In *Philosophy and Social Hope*, xvii–xxxii. New York: Penguin Books
Rosales, Esperanza. 2009. "Search for the Spirit." http://www.frieze.com/shows/review/search_for_the_spirit
Roy, Patricia E. 2003. *The Oriental Question: Consolidating a White Man's Province, 1914–41*. Vancouver: University of British Columbia Press
Rutledge, Paul. 1985. *The Role of Religion in Ethnic Self-Identity: A Vietnamese Community*. Lanham, MD: University Press of America
Ryan, Phil. 2010. *Multicultiphobia*. Toronto: University of Toronto Press
Safran, William. 1991. "Diasporas in Modern Societies: Myths of Homeland and Return." *Diaspora: A Journal of Transnational Studies* 1, no. 1: 83–99
Said, Edward. 1979. *Orientalism*. New York: Vintage
Sākyadhitā. n.d. "Become a Member of Sakyadhita International." *Sākyadhitā: International Association of Buddhist Women*. http://www.sakyadhita.org/home/join_us.html
Sale, Kirkpatrick. 1986. "The Forest for the Trees." *Mother Jones* 11, no. 8: 24–33 and 58
Samuelson, Marlene, James Carmody, Jon Kabat-Zinn, Michael A. Bratt. 2007. "Mindfulness-based Stress Reduction in Massachusetts Correctional Facilities." *The Prison Journal* 87, no. 2: 254–68
San Francisco Zen Center. n.d. "Ethics and Reconciliation Council." http://www.sfzc.org/zc/display.asp?catid=1,5,13&pageid=766
Sangharakshita, Bhikkhu. 2008 *Anagarika Dharmapala: A Biographical Sketch* (online edition). Kandy, Sri Lanka: Buddhist Publication Society. http://www.bps.lk/olib/wh/wh070-p.html#Honolulu:MeetingwithMrs.MaryE.Foster
Saper, Craig J. 1998. "Fluxus as a Laboratory." In Ken Friedman, *The Fluxus Reader*, 136–51. http://researchbank.swinburne.edu.au/vital/access/manager/Repository/swin:9624
- 2001. *Networked Art*. Minneapolis: University of Minnesota Press
Sapers, Howard. 2010. *Annual Report of the Office of the Correctional Investigator*. Ottawa: Correctional Investigator

Sasaki, Toshiji. 1999. *Nihonjin Kanada iminshi* [A history of Japanese immigration to Canada]. Tokyo: Fuji shuppan

Sasaki, Toshiji, and Tsuneharu Gonnami, eds. 2000. *Kanada iminshi shiryō* [The records of the history of Japanese immigration to Canada]. 11 vols. Tokyo: Fuji shuppan

Sasson, Vanessa, ed. 2012. *Little Buddhas: Children and Childhoods in Buddhist Texts and Traditions*. Oxford: Oxford University Press

Saturday Citizen. 1975. "Buddhist Group Considers Setting Up Ottawa Temple," 8 February, 29

Sava, Sharla. 1996. "As if the Oceans Were Lemonade: The Performative Vision of Robert Filliou and the Western Front." MA thesis, University of British Columbia

– n.d. "Determining the Cultural Ecology: Ray Johnson and the New York Corres Sponge Dance School of Vancouver." Centre for Contemporary Canadian Art, Canadian Art Database. http://www.ccca.ca/c/writing/s/sava/savo01t.html

Schedneck, Brooke. 2011. "Constructions of Buddhism: Autobiographical Moments of Western Monks' Experiences of Thai Monastic Life." *Contemporary Buddhism*, no. 2: 327–46

Schneider, David. 2011. "Lives Well Shared: The Friendship of Philip Whalen and Gary Snyder." *Tricycle* (Summer): 66–9, 114–17. http://www.tricycle.com/feature/lives-well-shared

Schrempf, Mona. 1994. "Tibetan Ritual Dances and the Transformation of Space." *Tibet Journal* 19, no. 2: 95–120

Schwartz, Ronald D. 1994. *Circle of Protest: Political Ritual in the Tibetan Uprising*. New York: Columbia University Press

Seager, Richard Hughes. 1999. *Buddhism in America*. New York: Columbia University Press

– 2011. Review of *American Buddhism as a Way of Life*, edited by Gary Storhoff and John Whalen-Bridge. *Journal of Global Buddhism* 12: 47–9

Senauke, Alan. 2008. Interview on *Progressive Religious Voices*. Podcast. 19 May. http://progressiveandreligious.org/podcasts/

Sharf, Robert H. 1993. "The Zen of Japanese Nationalism." *History of Religions* 33, no. 1: 1–43

– 1995. "Buddhist Modernism and the Rhetoric of Meditative Experience." *Numen* 42 no. 3: 228–83

Shea, Tusa. 2001. "Representing the Eternal Network: Vancouver Artists' Publications, 1969–73." MA thesis, University of Victoria

Sherpa, Ang Tsherin. 2011. "For the Preservation of Thangka Art." http://tsherin.com

Shils, Edward. 1981. *Tradition*. Chicago: University of Chicago Press

Shinpo, Mitsuru. 1996. *Kanada imin haisekishi: Nihon no gyogyō imin* [A History of the exclusion of Japanese immigrants in Canada: Fishery immigrants from Japan]. Tokyo: Miraisha

Shiu, Henry. 2010. "Buddhism after the Seventies." In Harding, Hori, and Soucy, *Wild Geese*, 84–110

Shneiderman, Sara. 1999. "Appropriate Treasure? Reflections on Women, Buddhism, and Cross-Cultural Exchange." In *Buddhist Women across Cultures: Realizations*, edited by Karma Lekshe Tsomo, 221–38. Albany: State University of New York Press

Sidor, Ellen S., ed. 1987. *A Gathering of Spirit: Women Teaching in American Buddhism*. Cumberland, RI: Primary Point Press

Silk, Jonathan A. 2005. "Gadjin M. Nagao (1907–2005) and His Buddhist Studies." *The Eastern Buddhist N.S.* 37, no. 1–2: 294–7

– 2011. "Toward a Meaningful Study of Buddhism." The Inaugural Leslie S. Kawamura Memorial Lecture. Delivered at the University of Calgary, 20 September

Silver, Warren. 2006. "Crime Statistics in Canada." *Juristat* 27, no. 5. http://www.statcan.gc.ca/pub/85-002-x/85-002-x2007005-eng.pdf

Singer, Wendy. 2003. "The Dalai Lama's Many Tibetan Landscapes." *The Kenyon Review* (Summer/Fall): 233–56

Snodgrass, Judith. 2003. *Presenting Japanese Buddhism to the West: Orientalism, Occidentalism and the Columbian Exposition*. Chapel Hill: University of North Carolina Press

– 2009a. "Discourse, Authority, Demand: The Politics of Early English Publications on Buddhism." In Bhushan, Garfield, and Zablocki, *TransBuddhism*, 21–41

– 2009b. "Publishing Eastern Buddhism: D.T. Suzuki's Journey to the West." In *Casting Faiths: Imperialism and the Transformation of Religion in East and Southeast Asia*, edited by Thomas D. Dubois, 46–72. Basingstoke: Palgrave Macmillan

Sole-Leris, Amadeo. 1986. *Tranquility and Insight: An Introduction to the Oldest Form of Buddhism*. Boston: Shambhala

Sona, Ajahn. 2006. "Observations from the Forest." *Ehi Passiko* 1 (May)

Soucy, Alexander. 1994. "Gender and Division of Labour in a Vietnamese-Canadian Buddhist Pagoda." MA thesis, Concordia University

– 1996. "The Dynamics of Change in an Exiled Pagoda: Vietnamese Buddhism in Montréal." *Canberra Anthropology* 19, no. 2: 29–45

– 2010. "Asian Reformers, Global Organizations: An Exploration of the Possibility of a 'Canadian Buddhism.'" In Harding, Hori, and Soucy, *Wild Geese*, 39–60

– 2012. *The Buddha Side: Gender, Power and Buddhist Practice in Vietnam*. Honolulu: University of Hawai'i Press

– 2013. "Outpost Buddhism: Vietnamese Buddhism in Halifax." *Canadian Journal of Buddhist Studies* 9: 107–28
Spirit Rock. 2012. "Teacher Code of Ethics." http://www.spiritrock.org/page.aspx?pid=315
Spivak, Gayatri, and Sarah Harasym. 1990. *The Post-Colonial Critic: Interviews, Strategies, Dialogues*. New York: Routledge
Statistics Canada. 2003. "2001 Census: Analysis Series Religions in Canada." http://www12.statcan.ca/english/census01/Products/Analytic/companion/rel/canada.cfm#growth
– 2006. *Census* (a). "Visible minority groups, 2006 counts, for Canada and census metropolitan areas and census agglomerations - 20% sample data."
– 2006. *Census* (b). "Population and Dwelling Count Highlight Tables, 2006 Census." http://www12.statcan.gc.ca/census-recensement/2006/dp-pd/hlt/97-550/Index.cfm?TPL=P3C&Page=INDX&LANG=Eng
– 2010. "CMA profile: Vancouver: Vancouver's Visible Minority Population Could Double by 2031: New Population Projections." 9 March. http://www42.statcan.gc.ca/smr09/smr09_018-eng.htm
Storhoff, Gary, and John Whalen-Bridge. 2010. "Introduction: American Buddhism as a Way of Life." In *American Buddhism as a Way of Life*, edited by Gary Storhoff and John Whalen-Bridge, 1–12. Albany: State University of New York Press
Stryk, Lucien. 1985. *On Love and Barley: Haiku of Basho*. New York: Penguin
Sugunasiri, Suwanda. 2001. *Towards Multicultural Growth: A Look at Canada from Classical Racism to Neo-Multiculturalism*. Toronto: Village Publishing House
– 2006. "Inherited Buddhists and Acquired Buddhists." *Canadian Journal of Buddhist Studies* 2: 103–42
– 2008. *Thus Spake the Sangha: Early Buddhist Leadership in Toronto: Kwang Ok Sunim, Bhante Punnaji, Samu Sunim, Tsunoda Sensei, Zasep Tulku Rimpoche*. Toronto: Nalanda Pub. Canada
Sujato (Bhikkhu). 2007. "A Painful Ambiguity: Attitudes toward Nuns in Buddhist Myth." Santi Forest Monastery, Bundanoon, Australia. http://www.buddhanet.net/budsas/ebud/ebdha330.htm
– 2010a. "Bhante or Ajahn?" Sujato's Blog. http://sujato.wordpress.com/2010/03/23/bhante-or-ajahn/
– 2010b. "Sects and Sectarianism: The Origins of the Three Existing Vinaya Lineages: Theravada, Dharmaguptaka, and Mulasarvastivada." In *Dignity and Discipline: Reviving Full Ordination for Buddhist Nuns*, edited by Thea Mohr and Ven. Jampa Tsedroen, 29–38. Boston: Wisdom Publications
Sumedho (Bhikkhu). 2006. "On Strong Roots." *Forest Sangha Newsletter*, no. 77

Susila Himi, Kompitiye Sri. 1995. *Sri Lankave Daham Pasel Adhyapanaya* [Dharma school education in Sri Lanka]. Colombo: S. Godage saha Sahodarayo

Suzuki, D.T. 1938. *Zen Buddhism and Its Influence on Japanese Culture*. Kyoto: Eastern Buddhist Society

Swearer, Donald. 1989. "Buddhism in Southeast Asia." In *Buddhism and Asian History*, edited by Joseph Kitigawa and Mark Cummings, 107–29. New York: Macmillan

Sweeping Zen. n.d. http://sweepingzen.com/?s=eido+shimano&cat=s&Search=Search

Tairiku Nippō (Vancouver), 1925–26

Takata, Toyo. 1983. *Nikkei Legacy: The Story of Japanese Canadians from Settlement to Today*. Toronto: NC Press

Tanabe, George Jr. 2010. "Heresy and the Future of Japanese Buddhism in Hawaii." *Patheos* website, 5 July. http://www.patheos.com/Resources/Additional-Resources/Heresy-and-the-Future-of-Japanese-Buddhism-in-Hawaii.html

Tanaka, Kenneth K. 1998. "Epilogue: The Colors and Contours of American Buddhism." In Prebish and Tanaka, *The Faces of Buddhism in America*, 287–98

Tathaaloka, Ayya. 2007. "Glimmers of a Thai Bhikkhuni Sangha History." Ayya Tathaaloka's blog, 21 December. http://www.myspace.com/ayyatathaaloka bhikkhuni/blog/340063946

Taylor, Charles. 1995. "Two Theories of Modernity." *The Hastings Center Report*, 25, no. 2: 24–33

– 2007. *A Secular Age*. Boston: The Belknap Press of Harvard University Press

Taylor, J.L. 1993. *Forest Monks and the Nation-State: An Anthropological and Historical Study in Northeastern Thailand*. Singapore: ISEAS

Taylor, Keith. 1992. "Pagan." In *The Cambridge History of Southeast Asia*, volume 1, part 1, edited by Nicholas Tarling, 164–7. Cambridge: Cambridge University Press

Taylor, Philip. 2001. *Fragments of the Present: Searching for Modernity in Vietnam's South*. Crows Nest, NSW, Australia: Allen & Unwin

– ed. 2007. *Modernity and Re-enchantment: Religion in Post-Revolutionary Vietnam*. Singapore: Institute of Southeast Asian Studies

Terakawa, Hōkō, ed. 1936. *Hokubei kaikyō enkakushi* [The history of the Buddhist mission of North America]. San Francisco. Hongwanji hokubei kaikyō honbu

Thanissaro (Bhikkhu), trans. 2007. *Bhikkhu Pāṭimokkha: The Bhikkhus' Code of Discipline*. http://www.accesstoinsight.org/tipitaka/vin/sv/bhikkhu-pati.html

– 2009. "On the Validity of the Bhikkhuni Ordination." http://www.dhammalight.com/vinaya/ThanissaroBhikkhu_13-11-09.htm

Thibeault, François. 2006. "Constructing Ethnoreligious Identities: Inheritance and Choice in Two Theravada Buddhist Organizations around Montréal." Unpublished paper
Thich Minh Duc. 2000. "Dam Luu: An Eminent Vietnamese Buddhist Nun." In *Innovative Buddhist Women: Swimming against the Tide*, edited by Karma Lekshe Tsomo, 104–20. Richmond, Surrey: Curzon Press
Thich Nhat Hanh. 1967. *Vietnam: Lotus in a Sea of Fire*. New York: Hill and Wang
Thích Thanh Từ. 1992. *Thiền Sư Việt Nam* [Zen masters of Vietnam]. Ho Chi Minh City: Thành Hội Phật Giáo TP. Hồ Chí Minh
Thich Thien An. 1975. *Buddhism and Zen in Vietnam in Relation to the Development of Buddhism in Asia*. Rutland, VT: Charles E. Tuttle Company
Thomas, Claude. 2004. *At Hell's Gate: A Soldier's Journey from War to Peace*. Boston: Shambhala
Thompson, Chris. 2011. *Felt: Fluxus, Joseph Beuys, and the Dalai Lama*. Minneapolis: University of Minnesota Press
Thornhill, Arthur. 1998. "'Impersonality' in Bashō: Neo-Confucianism and Japanese Poetry." In *Self as Image in Asian Theory and Practice*, edited by Roger T. Ames with Thomas P. Kasulis and Wimal Dissanayake, 341–56. Albany: State University of New York Press
Thrangu Monastery Canada. 2010. "Why a Monastery in Canada?" 28 December. http://thrangumonastery.org/the-monastery/why-a-monastery-in-canada/
– 2011. "Monastery I: Why a Monastery in Canada?" 4 January. http:/thrangumonastery.org/the-monastery/monastery-i/
– n.d. "Thrangu Monastery Canada" booklet, distributed at Grand Opening
thuong-chieu.org. n.d. "Thiền viện Dưới sự Giáo hóa của Hòa Thượng Thích Thanh Từ [Zen monasteries under the instruction of the Most Venerable Thích Thanh Từ]." *Thiền tông Việt Nam* [Vietnamese Zen Sect]. http://www.thuong-chieu.org/uni/CacThienVien/CacThienVien.htm
Tiradhammo (Bhikkhu). 2002. "The Challenges of Community." In Prebish and Baumann, *Westward Dharma*, 245–54
Tisarana Forest Monastery. n.d. "Discipline and Conventions of Theravada Buddhist Renunciate Communities: A Guide for the Western Sangha." Perth, ON: Tisarana Forest Monastery. http://tisarana.ca/dics/dis-conv.htm
Tiyavanich, Kamala. 1997. *Forest Recollections: Wandering Monks in Twentieth-Century Thailand*. Honolulu: University of Hawai'i Press
– 2007. *Sons of the Buddha: The Early Lives of Three Extraordinary Thai Masters*. Boston: Wisdom
Todd, Douglas. 2010. "'Nice' Buddhism Growing in Canada, with Rivalry." *Vancouver Sun*, 8 May. http://blogs.vancouversun.com/2010/05/08/nice-buddhism-growing-in-canada-with-rivalry/

Topmiller, Robert J. 2002. *The Lotus Unleashed: The Buddhist Peace Movement in South Vietnam, 1964–1966.* Lexington: University of Kentucky Press

Trasov, Vincent. "Mr. Peanut." http://vincenttrasov.ca/index.cfm?pg=menu&filter=Mr.%20Peanut

True Buddha School. n.d. *True Buddha School: Cultivation and Meditation Booklet.* Taiwan: True Buddha School

Tsunemitsu, Kōnen. 1964. *Nihon bukkyō to beishi* [A history of Japanese Buddhism in America]. Tokyo: Bukkyō Times

– 1973. *Hokubei bukkyō shiwa: Nihon bukkyō no tōzen* [History and anecdotes of Japanese Buddhism in America: The eastward transmission of Japanese Buddhism]. Tokyo: Bukkyō dendō kyōkai

Tumasz, Virginia. 2011. "In Memoriam of Dr. Leslie Kawamura." http://www.ucalgary.ca/numatachair/In_Memoriam_Dr._Leslie_Kawamura

Turpie, David. 2001. "Wesak and the Re-creation of Buddhist Tradition." MA thesis, McGill University. http://mrsp.mcgill.ca/reports/pdfs/Wesak.pdf

Tweed, Thomas A. 1999. "Night Stand Buddhists and Other Creatures: Sympathizers, Adherents, and the Study of Religion." In *American Buddhism: Methods and Findings in Recent Scholarship*, edited by Duncan Ryūken Williams and Christopher Queen, 71–90. Richmond: Curzon Press

– 2002. "Who Is a Buddhist? Night Stand Buddhists and Other Creatures." In Prebish and Baumann, *Westward Dharma*, 17–33

Tworkov, Helen. 1989. *Zen in America: Profiles of Five Teachers.* San Francisco: North Point Press

– 1991. Editorial, "Many Is More." *Tricycle: The Buddhist Review* 1, no. 2: 4

Ueda Makoto. 1983. *Modern Japanese Poets and the Nature of Literature.* Stanford: Stanford University Press

Unno, Taitetsu. 2000. "Constructive Buddhist Theology: A Response." In Jackson and Makransky, *Buddhist Theology*, 386–404

Van Auken, Phil. n.d. "Ten Ways Prison Ministry Promotes Church Growth." http://business.baylor.edu/phil_vanauken/Prison.htm

Varvaloucas, Emma. 2012. "Remembering Jane Imamura." *The Tricycle Blog*, 30 January. http://www.tricycle.com/blog/remembering-jane-imamura

Vásquez, Manuel A., and Marie Friedman Marquardt. 2003. *Globalizing the Sacred: Religion across the Americas.* New Brunswick, NJ: Rutgers University Press

Verchery, Lina, director. 2007. *The Trap/la trappe*, film. Montreal: National Film Board of Canada

– 2011. "Avatamsaka Buddhist Monastery in Calgary, Alberta." Unpublished paper presented at the colloquium, *The Consecrated Life in Canada: What Future?* McGill University, 24 August

- 2013. "Buddhism before 'Buddhism': The Avatamsaka Sagely Monastery and New Perspectives on Globalized Buddhism in Canada." Unpublished paper presented at *Conference on the State of the Consecrated Life in Contemporary Canada*. Concordia University, Montreal, 26 January

Vipassana Research Institute. 1994. *Sayagyi U Ba Khin Journal*. Igatpuri: Vipassana Research Institute

Wallace, B. Alan, ed. 2003. *Buddhism and Science: Breaking New Ground*. New York: Columbia University Press

Walmsley, Roy. 2008. *World Prison Population List*. 8th ed. London: International Centre for Prison Studies

Wat Pah Nanachat Sangha. 2009a. "Statement by the Wat Pah Nanachat Sangha explaining the decision of the Wat Pah Pong Meeting on November 1, 2009, to exclude Bodhinyana Monastery, Perth Australia, and Ajahn Brahmavamso from the group of Wat Pah Pong monasteries. An appendix to the official letter issued by Wat Nong Pah Pong." http://www.watpahnanachat.org

- 2009b. "The Gathering of Elders, Dec. 2009." http://www.forestsangha.org/index.php?option=com_content&view=article&id=385&Itemd=8
- 2009c. "Why Ajahn Brahmavamso was excluded from the Wat Pah Pong Sangha." *The Buddhist Channel*, 5 November. http://www.buddhistchannel.tv/index.php?id=70,8661,0,0,1,0

Watada, Terry. 1996. *Bukkyo Tozen: A History of Jodo Shinshu Buddhism in Canada 1905–1995*. Toronto: Hasting Park Foundation Press and the Toronto Buddhist Church

- 2010. "Looking East: Japanese Canadians and Jodo Shinshu Buddhism, 1905–1970." In Harding, Hori, and Soucy, *Wild Geese*, 62–84

Watson, Scott. 1992. "Hand of the Spirit: Documents of the Seventies from the Morris/Trasov Archive." Centre for Contemporary Canadian Art, Canadian Art Database. http://www.ccca.ca/c/writing/w/watson/wat003t.html

- 2006. "Transmission Difficulties: Vancouver Painting in the 1960s." http://transmissiondifficulties.vancouverartinthesixties.com/print/01
- n.d. "Transmission Difficulties: Vancouver Painting in the 1960s." http://transmissiondifficulties.vancouverartinthesixties.com/print/01

Weeraratne, D. Amarasiri. 1998. "Revival of the Bhikkhuni Order in Sri Lanka." *The Island*, Colombo, Sri Lanka, 4 April. http://www.buddhanet.net/e-learning/history/nunorder.htm

Welch, Chuck. 1993. "Corresponding Worlds: Debate and Dialogue." In *Eternal Network: A Mail Art Anthology*, edited by Chuck Welch, 186–97. Calgary: University of Calgary Press

Western Elders Council, Forest Sangha. 2009. "Where We Are Now." 19 November. www.dhammalight.com/official/pdf/where_we_are_now/pdf

Wherry, Aaron. 2012. "'Bogus refugee claimants receiving gold-plated health care benefits.'" *Maclean's*, Monday, 16 July. http://www2.macleans.ca/2012/07/16/bogus-refugee-claimants-receiving-gold-plated-health-care-benefits

Whitney, Kobai Scott. 2002. *Sitting Inside: Buddhist Practice in America's Prisons*. Boulder, CO: Prison Dharma Network

Wijayaratna, Mohan. 1990. *Buddhist Monastic Life*. Cambridge: Cambridge University Press

Wijesundara, Himale. 2008. "The West End Buddhist Centre Dhamma School: Then & Now." In *Dhamma School: West End Buddhist Centre*, no editor, 16–28. Mississauga: Westend Buddhist Centre

Wilden, Anthony. 2001. *System and Structure: Essays in Communication and Exchange*. London: Routledge

Wilson, Jeff. 2009. "Mapping the American Buddhist Terrain: Paths Taken and Possible Itineraries." *Religion Compass* 3, no. 5: 836–46

– 2011. "What is Canadian about Canadian Buddhism?" *Religion Compass* 5, no. 9: 536–48

Wimbush, Vincent L., and Richard Valantasis, eds. 1995. *Asceticism*. New York: Oxford University Press

Woodcock, George. 1975–76. "Dragons, Mandalas and Secret Writings." *Artscanada* 8

Yeh, Emily T. 2007. "Exile Meets Homeland: Politics, Performance, and Authenticity in the Tibetan Diaspora." *Environment and Planning D: Society and Space* 25: 648–67

Yesaki, Mitsuo. 2003. *Sutebusuton: A Japanese Village on the British Columbia Coast*. Vancouver: Peninsular Publishing Company

Yeshe Tsogyel. 1978. *The Life and Liberation of Padmasambhava*. 2 vols. Translated by Kenneth Douglas and Gwendolyn Bays. Berkeley: Dharma Publishing

Yifa. 2002. *The Origins of Buddhist Monastic Codes in China: An Annotated Translation and Study of the Chanyuan Qinggui*. Honolulu: University of Hawai'i Press

Yip, Andrew K.T., and Sharon Smith. 2010. "Queerness and Sangha: Exploring Buddhist Lives." In *Queer Spiritual Spaces: Sexuality and Sacred Places*, edited by Kath Browne, Sally R. Munt, and Andrew K.T. Yip, 111–38. Farnham, Surrey: Ashgate

Yoo, David K. 2000. *Growing Up Nisei: Race, Generation, and Culture among Japanese Americans of California, 1924–1949*. Urbana: University of Illinois Press

Young, Charles H., and Helen R.Y. Reid. 1938. *The Japanese Canadians*. Toronto: University of Toronto Press

Zen Center of Denver. n.d. "The Diamond Sangha Teachers Ethics Agreement." http://www.zencenterofdenver.org/ethics_statement.aspx

Zen Studies Society. 2011. "Transcript of the Announcement Made on July 2nd at Dai Bosatsu Zendo." http://hoodiemonks.org/PDFs/20110705_ZSS_Announcement.pdf

– n.d. *Newsletter*. Spring: 2–3. http://www.zenstudies.org/images/ZSSNewsltr11.pdf

Contributors

MICHIHIRO AMA is assistant professor of Japanese at the University of Alaska, Anchorage. The focus of his scholarship is Buddhism in modern Japan with an emphasis on transnational studies and literary criticism. He is the author of *Immigrants to the Pure Land: The Modernization, Acculturation, and Globalization of Shin Buddhism, 1898–1941* (University of Hawai'i Press 2011). He is also guest editor for the special issue on "Natsume Sōseki and Buddhism" in *The Eastern Buddhist* 38 (2007). His articles include "Shin Buddhist Women in America" (2011), "Transcending Death in *Departures* (*Okuribito*) – A Case Study of Film, Literature, and Buddhism in Modern Japan" (2010), and "Shifting Subjectivity in the Translation of Shinran's Texts" (2005). Ama is currently working on a book project, tentatively titled *The Awakening of Fiction: Literature and Buddhism in Modern Japan*.

D. MITRA BARUA received his PhD (2011) from the joint Laurier-Waterloo program on religious diversity in North America. Since 2011, he has been teaching South Asian religions and philosophies at the University of Saskatchewan, Canada. His recent publications include "Buddhism for a Multicultural Society: Redefining Buddhism for a New Canada-born Generation," in *Buddhism: Contemporary Studies* (2010), and "Temporary Ordination for Character Transformation: A Diasporic Practice with Transnational Connections," in *Journal of Global Buddhism* (2011). From historical as well as contemporary perspectives, Mitra is interested in understanding what Buddhism looks like in minority contexts. He is currently transforming his dissertation into a monograph, provisionally entitled *Weaving Ola and Maple Leaves Together: Sri Lankan Buddhists in Toronto*.

PAUL CROWE received his PhD in Asian Studies from the University of British Columbia in 2005. His graduate research focused on Daoist inner alchemy and was based on readings of eleventh- to thirteenth-century Daoist and Buddhist canonical texts and literati (*ru*) texts. He is an associate professor in the Department of Humanities at Simon Fraser University where he also directs the David See Chai Lam Centre for International Communication and teaches for the Asia-Canada Program. Since commencing his position at SFU in 2006, in addition to continued classical textual work, he has begun researching and publishing on modern Chinese Buddhist and Daoist institutions in Canada and Hong Kong with a view to better understanding the relationships between migration, religion, and identity.

MELISSA ANNE-MARIE CURLEY is assistant professor of Japanese religions at the University of Iowa. Her research focuses on modern Japanese Buddhism and the ways in which the Buddhist imagination is shaped by the forces of modernism, nationalism, and cosmopolitanism. Recent publications include "Shinshū Studies and the Legacy of Liberal Thought" in Ugo Dessì's *The Social Dimension of Shin Buddhism* (Brill 2010) and "Zen-Boy Ikkyū" in Vanessa R. Sasson's *Little Buddhas* (Oxford 2013). With Victor Sōgen Hori, she edited *The Kyoto School: Neglected Themes and Hidden Variations*, the second in Nanzan's Frontiers of Japanese Philosophy series.

MAVIS L. FENN is the chair of the Department of Religious Studies at the University of Waterloo. She teaches courses in Asian religions with a focus on Buddhism. Her recent research is centred on Buddhism in Canada, women in Buddhism, and the International Association of Buddhist Women (Sākyadhitā). Her articles have appeared in the *Journal of Buddhist Ethics*, *Journal of Global Buddhism* (with Kay Koppedrayer), as well in *Buddhism in Canada* (with Kay Koppedrayer), edited by Bruce Matthews; *The Encyclopedia of Buddhism*, edited by Damien Keown and Charles S. Prebish; *Religion and Social Justice*, edited by Michael D. Palmer and Stanley M. Burgess; and *The World's Religions*, edited by Peter B. Clarke and Peter Beyer.

KORY GOLDBERG completed his doctorate in religious studies at the Université du Québec à Montréal. He currently teaches courses on education, religion, ethics, and the environment in the Humanities Department at Champlain College in St-Lambert, QC. He has published articles on Buddhist pilgrimage in peer-reviewed journals and edited volumes, and has co-authored with his wife, Michelle Décary, *Along the Path: The Meditator's Companion to the Buddha's Land* (Pariyatti Press 2009). When not teaching, writing, or travelling, he can be found raising his organic vegetables and children.

JOHN S. HARDING received his PhD from the University of Pennsylvania. He is an associate professor in the Religious Studies Department and the coordinator of Asian Studies at the University of Lethbridge, Canada. Research interests include Japanese Buddhism, the cross-cultural currents that have shaped the global circulation of Buddhism in the last 150 years, and issues of theory and method in religious studies. He is the author of *Mahāyāna Phoenix: Japan's Buddhists at the 1893 World's Parliament of Religions* (2008), the co-author with Hillary Rodrigues of *Introduction to the Study of Religion* (2009) and *The Study of Religion: A Reader* (2013), the co-editor with Victor Sōgen Hori and Alexander Soucy of *Wild Geese: Buddhism in Canada* (2010), and the editor of the volume *Studying Buddhism in Practice* (2012).

SARAH F. HAYNES earned her PhD at the University of Calgary and is associate professor of Asian religions in the Department of Philosophy and Religious Studies at Western Illinois University. The focus of her teaching and research is Tibetan Buddhist ritual and Buddhism in the West. Her publications include "A Relationship of Reciprocity (*Wild Geese*, McGill-Queen's 2010), "An Examination of Jack Kerouac's Buddhism: Text and Life" (*Journal of Contemporary Buddhism* 2007). Her current research projects relate to the adaptation of Tibetan ritual practices in the diaspora, and to Jodo Shinshu communities in Alberta and Utah.

VICTOR SŌGEN HORI received his PhD in Western philosophy in 1976 from Stanford University. The same year, he was ordained and thereafter spent thirteen years as a monk in the Rinzai Zen monastery system. He returned to North America in 1990 and in 1993 joined the Faculty of Religious Studies of McGill University, where he is presently associate professor in Japanese Religions. Research interests include Zen Buddhism, Buddhism in the West, Kyoto School of Philosophy, and Japanese Religion. Publications include *Wild Geese: Buddhism in Canada*, co-edited with John S. Harding and Alexander Soucy (McGill-Queen's University Press 2010); *Zen Sand: The Book of Capping Phrases for Zen Kōan Practice* (University of Hawai'i Press 2003); *The Wheel and the Web: Collected Papers of the Teaching Buddhism Conference*, co-edited with Richard P. Hayes and Mark Shields (Curzon Press 2002); *The Ten Oxherding Pictures: Lectures by Yamada Mumon Roshi* (University of Hawai'i Press 2004).

JACKIE LARM is a PhD candidate at the University of Edinburgh. The focus of her thesis is Kagyu Samye Ling, "the first Tibetan Buddhist centre established in the West," where she researched its residents' approaches to community, authority, environmentalism, gender, and bioethical debates. She is also fascinated with questions surrounding identity formation and negotiation among members of contemporary communities, especially diasporic communities. Undoubtedly, the latter research interest was first connected to her parentage – her father was born in Hong Kong and immigrated to Canada 1969, while her mother and maternal grandfather were born in the Prairies. The stories of these two separate waves of Chinese immigrants drove her to examine who she believed she was. Jackie's interest in identity was further fuelled by the Tibetan Buddhist presentation of emptiness. Jackie currently lives in Richmond, British Columbia, and calls Thrangu Monastery her "home" centre.

PAUL MCIVOR is a volunteer in the Ontario correctional system. His research interests are Buddhism and religious practice in corrections (in Canada, the United States, and internationally) as well as spiritual conversion experiences. He holds a BA in religious studies and Japanese studies from the University of Toronto and an MA (cum laude) in religious studies from the University of South Africa.

JIM PLACZEK travelled extensively in Southeast Asia during the 1960s, and worked in Thailand for seven years. During that time he met some of the early Western disciples of Ajahn Chah and has since followed the historic spread of this group globally. His academic degrees are in psychology (BA, University of Windsor), linguistics (MA, University of British Columbia), and Southeast Asian culture history (PhD, also UBC). He has taught courses on Southeast Asia and on Thai language in the Vancouver area at UBC, Langara College, and Capilano University. After retiring from Langara (last seven years as chair of the Asian Studies Department), he is now serving as Community Coordinator at the Center for Southeast Asian Research at UBC, and works on the early culture history of Southeast Asia (e.g., domestication of rice) and contemporary issues such as the ordination of female monks in Theravada Buddhism, the evolution of the Association of South East Asian Nations, and the South China Sea disputes.

ALEXANDER SOUCY is an associate professor at Saint Mary's University, Halifax, and the chair of the Religious Studies Department. He is the author of *The Buddha Side: Gender, Power, and Buddhist Practice in Vietnam* and several articles on Vietnamese Buddhism and gender. He also co-edited *Wild Geese: Buddhism in Canada* and has published several essays on Buddhism in Canada, particularly relating to Vietnamese Buddhism. Along with John Harding and Victor Hori, he has been active in promoting the study of Buddhism in Canada by organizing conferences and conference panels on the subject. His current research looks at transnational Vietnamese Buddhism and the rising popularity of Zen in Vietnam.

ANGELA SUMEGI is associate professor of humanities and religion at Carleton University. She was born and raised in Jamaica, immigrating to Canada with her family in 1962. She lived and studied in south India for five years (1981–86), two of which were devoted to Sanskrit language study as a Fellow with the Shastri Indo-Canadian Institute. Sumegi's doctoral thesis was completed at the University of Ottawa in 2003 and published under the title *Dream Worlds of Shamanism and Tibetan Buddhism* (SUNY Press 2008). Her most recent publication is *Understanding Death: An Introduction to Ideas of Self and the Afterlife in World Religions* (Wiley-Blackwell 2013). Current research interests focus on religious approaches to death as well as Indo-Tibetan Buddhism in contemporary indigenous and Western contexts. She is also the founder and director of a Canadian charity that supports Tibetan refugee children in India.

Index

abbey. *See* monastery
abbot: Chinese, 171; Japanese Pure Land, 57–8, 74n3, 382n24; Thai and Thai Forest, 102, 107, 109–10, 113–14, 116, 122–3, 322, 324, 326; Tibetan, 134, 148n5, 227; Vietnamese, 8, 333
Abhayagiri Forest Monastery, 102–3, 107, 109–10, 113, 323, 326, 330
Abhidhamma, 178, 320–6, 329, 332n4
abuse of power, 165, 188–90, 192
academic, 22, 313, 317, 397; approach to Buddhism in the West, 4–5, 10, 28
activism, 31, 34
adaptation, 11, 18, 20, 28, 50, 150; Chinese, 151–2, 166, 167; Goenka, 79, 87, 94–5; Japanese Pure Land,150, 361; modernity, 38; not needed, 153–5, 159; prison life, 253; Sri Lankan, 205–6, 220–1, 223; Theravada, 101, 108, 113, 121, 330; Tibetan, 137, 139, 144, 146–7, 227, 229, 238, 241–3, 287, 290, 292, 295, 307; Vietnamese, 33, 51, 328, 334; Zen, 284, 287
aesthetics, 268–70; Zen, 279
Ajahn Brahm, 113–18, 125
Ajahn Chah, 102–26, 126n2; lineage, 323–6

Ajahn Pasanno, 102, 103, 107, 326
Ajahn Sona, 102–26
Ajahn Sumedho, 106, 107, 112–13, 116, 123, 124, 126n1
Alberta Kyoku, 363–4
altars, 48, 63, 71, 234, 235, 240, 295, 296
Amaravati Monastery, 107, 112, 326
American Academy of Religion (AAR), 355, 370, 373, 377
American Buddhism, 6, 25, 27, 30, 33, 37, 38, 47, 194, 282, 285, 378
Amitābha, 57, 63, 68, 73, 234, 239
ancestor worship, 7, 48, 68–9, 138, 187, 197n18, 231, 244n2
Anderson, Benedict. *See* imagined community
Ang Tsherin Sherpa, 299, 301
Ấn Quang Temple (Ho Chi Minh City), 49, 339
Appadurai, Arjun, 13, 14
architecture, 40, 135, 147, 158, 270
ascetic, 80, 193, 283, 313; attitude, 182–4, 104–5, 196n15; discipline, 175, 185, 187
authenticity, 43, 141–2, 240–1, 242, 297, 301; arbiters of, 254; claims of, 300; of ethnic Buddhism, 7; vs inauthenticity, 4–5, 7, 10–12, 30, 294; and

lineage, 243; of Thrangu Monastery, 130, 134, 136, 144, 145,147; and tradition, 142, 147, 289; of Western Buddhism, 30
authority, 11, 187–94; in Asian monasteries, 240–2, 337, 346, 361, 364
autoethnography, 226
Avatamsaka Monastery (Calgary), 181, 185, 186, 189, 197n19
Avataṃsaka Sutra, 21, 269
Ayya Khema, 317, 318, 322, 324, 327
Ayya Medhanandi, 178, 325

Baker, Richard, 173, 179, 190–1, 195n5
Ba Khin, U (Sayagyi), 79, 81–3, 96n7
Bardo Thodol (Tibetan Book of the Dead), 233–8, 240, 302
Bashō, 267–8
Baumann, Martin, 5, 6, 7, 51n1, 140, 231
Beatniks, 10, 27–8, 50
bhikkhu. See monk
bhikkhuni. See nuns
bias. *See* subjectivity
Birken Forest Monastery, 101–10, 118, 122, 123, 125–6, 126n2, 324–25
Bishop Masuyama. *See* Masuyama
Bodhgaya, 22, 135
Bodhinyana Monastery (Perth, Australia), 114, 116
bodhisattva, 57, 215, 216, 264, 295, 342, 373
British Columbia, 59, 66, 75n6, 76n20, 77n34, 125, 129, 157, 160–3, 274, 323; Chinese Buddhism in, 151–2; racial tensions, 150; Thai Forest Tradition in, 101–10, 118, 122, 123, 125; Vipassana in, 79, 84, 90, 91, 93, 100n28
Buddha, the, 52n12, 86, 97n14, 208, 221; biography, 43–4, 98n14, 196, 209–11, 213, 216; as example, 16, 84, 174, 188, 209; historical, 44; idealized, 11, 123; lineage, 52, 136, 242; offerings to, 138, 214, 238; and ritual, 229, 239; Sakyamuni, 11, 44, 70, 71, 234; Siddhartha, 10, 261n15; statue, 87, 131, 135, 139, 187, 188, 234, 300, 342; take refuge in, 46, 59, 60, 84, 213, 235; teaching method, 202, 209, 218; teachings, 79–83, 87, 95, 108, 115, 118, 124, 178, 212, 222, 229, 331; and *vinaya*, 110–12, 113, 118, 120–1; and women, 110–11, 113, 313–15, 345, 346, 350
Buddhadharma. *See* dharma
Buddha Light International Association. *See* Fo Guang Shan
Buddhism: in Asia, 9–11, 15, 30, 42, 241, 274, 283; Asian distortion of, 11; Asian/ethnic vs Western/Convert, 4–7, 11–12, 28, 46, 50, 145, 149n9, 156, 231, 232, 359; categories, 5, 9, 11–12, 20, 26, 28, 33–6, 46, 47, 92, 232, 359; characteristics, 16, 27, 31, 32, 38, 41, 47, 328, 359; communication, 12, 20, 21, 25, 28, 41, 42, 50, 51, 96, 129, 133, 248, 284; delineating, 36, 41, 43; ethnic, 6–7, 8, 9, 20, 33–6, 47–8, 55, 92, 145, 334, 353n8; globalization of, 8, 11, 38, 229; globalized, 26, 50; inauthentic vs authentic, 4–5, 7, 10–2, 30, 294; modernization of, 10, 11, 12, 15, 17, 19, 38, 64, 378; "New," 9, 10–11, 16, 27, 30, 31, 37, 194; original, 11, 30, 32, 43, 52n13, 86, 115, 120–1, 229, 230; orthodox, 42, 44, 151, 153, 154, 163, 170, 241, 315; as religion, 42–4; study of Buddhism in Canada, 3–5, 26, 27, 285; traditional vs modern, 4, 6, 7–10, 11, 28, 44, 136–7, 143–6, 231, 287; transmission, 25, 37, 58, 135, 141, 204,

207–9, 220–1, 269, 284, 358; unity, 15; in the West, 4, 5, 7, 8, 10, 11, 16, 23–4n1, 28, 31, 33, 46, 50, 51n5, 52n15, 95, 110, 145, 194, 313, 328, 330, 334; as world religion, 42–4. *See also* American Buddhism; Buddhist reform movements; Canadian Buddhism; Global Buddhism; Humanistic Buddhism; modern Buddhism; popular culture; Protestant Buddhism; Pure Land; science; *Shin Bukkyō*; Western Buddhism

Buddhist churches: Alberta, 36–2; of America (BCA), 73, 74n2, 357, 367, 381n9; Buddhist Mission of North America (BMNA), 55, 74n2; of Canada (BCC), 358, 364. *See also* Honpa Canada Buddhist Mission

Buddhist globalism, 15, 16, 37, 40–1, 51; characteristics, 41–7; and individualism, 45–7; influence, 38; and modernity, 44–5; outward looking, 41–2; and parochialism, 39, 50; as process of hybridization, 38; and "world religions," 42–4

Buddhist localism, 39, 40, 41, 45, 46–50

Buddhist parochialism, 39–40, 46–50, 51

Buddhist reform movements, 15, 30, 38, 40, 50; and authenticity, 43; China, 10, 40; and Christianity, 42; and colonialism, 44; and education, 49; influence, 17, 27, 32, 49; Japanese, 27, 37; lay involvement, 22; permeation, 10; and publications, 41; Sri Lankan, 15, 203, 223, 320; Taiwanese, 40; Thai, 105, 117; transnational, 15, 28, 41, 49; Vietnamese, 10, 27, 36, 37, 48–9; and women, 319. *See also Shin Bukkyō*

Buddhist Relief and Compassion Tzu Chi Foundation. *See* Tzu Chi Merit Society

Buddhists: Asian American, 5, 359; Caucasian, 153, 154, 156, 159, 204, 328, 360–1, 364; demographics, 5, 51n5, 67, 95, 169; elite, 5, 44, 92, 378; evangelical, 5, 92; immigrant/refugee, 5, 39, 56, 220, 221; modernist, 6, 7, 8, 9, 10, 17, 27, 48, 86, 231, 232; reform movements, 9–10, 17, 22, 27, 30, 32, 37, 38, 41–2; traditionalist, 6, 7, 140, 231; types of, 16, 28, 231; white, 5, 32, 34, 46, 51, 51n5, 52n10, 52n11, 134, 185. *See also* conversion

Buddhist Studies, 22, 209, 373, 378–9

Burian, Anna. *See* Dhammadinna

Burma (Myanmar), 15, 19, 56, 80, 96n1, 96n7, 97n13, 120; Goenka and, 79, 82; meditation movement in, 80–2; nuns in, 110, 127n17, 315, 316

Cage, John, 269–70, 272, 275–6, 284–5

Canadian Buddhism, 26–33, 51n2, 232, 244

catechism, Buddhist, 9, 41, 203

categories. *See* Buddhism

Catholicism, 9, 14, 87, 182, 192, 320, 339, 341

celibacy, 16, 20, 174–5, 179, 181, 184, 193, 194

Ceylon. *See* Sri Lanka

'chams (Tibetan ritual dance), 21, 131, 289, 291–3, 296, 298, 302, 307n9

Chandrasekera, Swarna, 23, 205

Chân Không, Sister, 22, 354n22, 354n23

chanting, 71, 119, 183, 186, 234; Chinese, 153, 157, 171n8; Goenka, 83–4, 87, 91–2, 97n11; melody, 143; merit, 80; Sri Lankan, 204, 212–13; Tibetan, 135,

228, 233, 235, 240, 293; Vietnamese, 35, 36, 46, 48
chaplains, 36, 245–62
Cheng Yen, 8, 22, 319, 353n7
children, 56, 69, 160, 297, 298, 317, 324, 349, 354n21; Asian/Western, 5; language transmission, 160, 162; teaching, 7–8, 20, 23, 63, 90, 201–31, 316, 323, 359. *See also* Japanese Canadian, *issei, nisei, sansei, yonsei*; Sunday school
China, 10, 15, 115, 140, 169, 187; Buddhist reform in, 10, 27; immigrants from, 20, 133, 161, 170, 170n1; nuns in, 111, 315, 318; representatives from, 15; and Tibet, 287, 304, 307, 307n6, 309n26
Chinatown, 151, 153, 158, 170n1, 172n15
Chödrön, Pema, 22. *See also* Gampo Abbey
Christianity, 9, 14, 55, 86, 258, 286; and colonialism, 14, 316; evangelism, 223; influence on Buddhism, 42, 150, 202, 223, 240, 359; Japanese Christians, 64, 65, 69, 76n20; missionaries, 9, 14, 27, 43, 81; as model for religion, 9, 42, 44; prison outreach, 262, 265; Vietnamese Christians, 353n12
clergy and laity, 19, 40, 56, 60, 66, 67, 70, 119, 120, 122, 132, 177, 194, 331, 362
Coleman, James William, 10–11
colonialism, 12–15, 42–4, 80, 259, 315; as catalyst for reform, 18, 39, 42, 95, 202, 223; hegemony, 27, 44, 81
communication, 12, 13, 25, 41, 42, 125, 129, 272; network, 277–8; transnational, 28, 50, 162. *See also* religion as
compassion (*karuṇā*), 209, 228, 261, 296; Amida's, 73; Avalokiteshvara, 295; as Canadian stereotype, 29; and children, 208, 354n2; and the Dalai Lama, 290, 291; Dhammadinna, 322; development of, 87, 98n17, 211, 331n2; of Leslie Kawamura, 372, 373, 379; places of, 137; practice of, 189, 259; and vegetarianism, 25
conflict: Shin Buddhist, 55, 56, 57, 60, 64, 66, 362, 363; Vietnamese, 337–8, 341–2, 346–51
Confucianism, 42, 115, 187, 197n18, 268
conversion, 87, 254; concept of, 232; experience of, 227, 265
counterculture, 21, 27, 50, 257, 268

Dalai Lama, 140–1, 252, 261, 287, 295, 303, 304, 309n25; and China, 296, 306, 309n26; Engaged Buddhism, 91; and female ordination, 117, 318; honorary citizenship, 25; interfaith dialogue, 42; persona, 258–9, 290–1, 305; and science, 45; Tibetans and, 287, 289–92, 297, 304; visit to Toronto, 302, 308n16. *See also* science
dasa sil mata, 127n17, 316–17, 319, 320, 322, 331n1, 332n4
death, 225–44; rituals, 264
deep ecology, 282–3, 285–6
democracy, 17, 31, 47, 58, 89, 115, 281
devotion, 35, 98n16, 185, 229, 235, 317; literature, 251; practices, 35, 80; rituals of, 6, 8, 9, 231, 232, 235; and superstition, 7, 33
dhamma, 80–4, 86, 89–91, 94–5, 97n8, 104, 106, 111, 119, 122; education, 202–4. *See also* dharma
Dhammadinna, Anagarika, 21–2, 107, 313–22, 332n4

Dhamma Giri (Mumbai), 83, 89
Dhammayuttika Nikaya. *See* Thai Forest Tradition
dharma, 51n1, 131, 142, 148n3, 150, 153, 171n6, 230, 237, 330, 371, 378; Buddha, dharma, sangha, 46, 194, 235; Buddhadharma, 20, 158, 171n6, 174, 199, 230, 234, 378; Dharma Bums, 359, 367–8, 381n9; dharma centre, 130, 227–8; dharma heir, 157; Dharma master, 171n4, 171n6; dharma name, 72, 75n7; dharma position, 269, 272; dharma practice, 86, 91, 189–90, 193; dharma school, 359; dharma talk, 25, 43, 152, 154, 186, 197n19, 199, 229–30, 233, 236; dharma teaching, 134; false dharma, 148n3; Living Dharma Centre, 357–8, 360, 365, 371, 381n10; Prison Dharma, 248, 250–1, 253, 261. *See also dhamma*
Dharma Drum Mountain, 148n4, 157–8
Dharmapala, Anagarika, 9, 15, 22, 27, 41, 320
Dharma Realm Buddhist Association, 153, 185–6
diaspora: Sri Lankan, 202, 205, 209, 214, 220–1, 224; Tibetan, 17, 21, 287–92, 295–8, 301–7, 307n4, 309n25; Vietnamese, 8, 49, 337, 347
disaster relief, 8, 319
doctrine, 45, 58, 86, 230, 253–4
donations, 108, 111, 122, 131; book donations for prisoners, 248, 251; to build temple, 62, 69, 102; at courses, 89, 91; for membership, 138; at memorial service, 62, 71; to nuns, 315, 328, 339; online, 136
Durkheim, Émile, 257, 266n12

ecology: art and, 284; cultural, 282, 286; deep, 282–3, 285–6
ecumenism, 42, 48, 233. *See also* interfaith
education, 10, 23, 131, 160, 298, 315, 330, 349, 365; Buddhist, 201–24, 331, 345; and Buddhist reform, 49; institutions, 186, 248; modern, 7, 49; religious, 258; secular, 22, 345; and women, 316–17, 318, 319, 344, 346, 347–8
egalitarianism, 17, 80, 85–6, 88–9, 268, 330
England, 106, 107, 110, 112, 114, 116, 117
enlightenment, 73–4, 87, 192, 229, 237, 291; the Buddha's, 11, 48, 84; and Buddhist globalism, 45; as a goal, 45, 46, 48, 73, 84, 108; and meditation, 46; Western focus on, 31, 47; women and, 314, 315
Enlightenment, the, 44
equality, 211, 305, 345–7, 350; gender equality, 31, 47, 115, 164, 165, 242, 352
ethics, 137, 211, 219; Buddhist ethics, 180, 216; code of ethics, 174; secular ethics, 218; Zen ethics, 268, 270. *See also* morality; *śīla*
ethnicity, 6, 33, 56, 95, 214, 225, 260, 359
ethnocentricism, 6, 16, 30

family, 8, 41, 62, 68, 91, 111, 138, 158, 177, 209, 215–16, 225, 227, 230, 232–4, 236, 240, 260, 314, 316, 355, 379, 382n33; extended, 204; family religion, 69, 187; family resemblance, 17, 40; Imamura family, 368; and immigration, 160, 164; lineage, 52n9, 68; physician, 323; renounce family, 331n4; temple family, 358; Vietnamese family, 343, 347

fate, 35, 98n17. *See also* karma
feminism, 96, 242, 344
Filliou, Robert, 267, 269, 271–6, 281, 283, 284
fishermen, 63, 70–1
Fluxus, 21; and Buddhism, 272–3, 276; and Zen, 267, 269–73, 275, 285, 286
Fo Guang Shan, 7–8, 38, 40, 42, 49, 319
Foster, Mary E., 22
Friedman, Ken, 269, 270, 272, 273, 274, 276, 277, 278, 284
funeral, 20–1, 71, 111, 225–44, 372

Gampo Abbey, 22, 134, 148n7, 177
gender, 22–3, 98n18, 113, 152, 180, 182, 345; binary gender system, 285; equality, 88–9, 115, 165, 242, 318, 331n2, 352; inequality, 345–8; in New Buddhism, 31, 47; roles in Buddhist temple, 31, 51, 346, 350, 352; transgendered, 257
generation, 124, 160, 161, 170, 360; Canadian-born, 223; first, 204, 214, 215, 220–1; fourth, 306; *issei*, 56, 57, 64, 67, 69, 72–4, 230–1, 360, 364; issues, 5, 359, 362, 365; *nikkei*, 64–5, 67, 69; *nisei*, 56, 67, 72, 230–1, 359, 364; *sansei*, 67, 230, 231; second, 206, 215, 224n1, 307n4; third, 306; transmission between, 20, 144, 147, 162, 187, 201, 204, 206–9, 220, 221, 230; *yonsei*, 230–1
Giddens, Anthony, 12, 143, 146
Global Buddhism, 10, 15–18, 30, 36, 37, 38, 49
globalization, 11–14, 94, 162, 241; of Buddhism, 8, 11, 38, 229; and communication, 162; definition, 12–13; effect on Buddhism, 12, 22, 39; and local, 18, 94; networks, 15, 50; of religion, 14, 20, 38, 39, 42–4; as social, 13; women 20, 22, 257
glocalization, 18, 44
Goenka, Satya, 19, 79, 82–4; and Buddhism, 84, 86, 87; organizational oversight, 89; and religion, 84, 86–7; teachings, 85, 87; view of meditation, 79, 80
Gold Buddha Monastery (Vancouver), 153–4, 171n8, 185, 186–7
Government of Canada, 29, 51n3, 63, 67, 71, 131, 163, 216, 258, 288, 335, 336
Great Pine Forest Monastery, 342, 346, 351, 352
Guenther, Herbert, 358, 366, 367, 369
Gunaratne, Bhante, 102, 103, 107, 110, 118, 123, 124, 126n4
Gyatso, Gonkar, 299, 300–1

Halifax (Nova Scotia), 51, 176, 177, 233, 303, 353n12
Hawai'i, 57, 59, 68, 361, 363
Heng Chau (also Ch'au), 154, 171n7, 185, 186
Heng Sure, 154, 171n7, 185, 186
hermitage, 203, 315, 320; Arrow River, 177; Birken, 101, 103, 107, 177, 324; Little Heron Zen, 328; Sati Saraniya, 178, 325
Higashi Honganji. *See* Honganji
Hippies, 27, 50
Ho Chi Minh City. *See* Saigon
Honganji, 57–8, 59, 362, 363; division, 19, 56, 58, 59, 62, 64, 74n3; Higashi, 19, 56, 58, 61–4; Nishi, 19, 56, 58, 59, 61, 63–7, 73, 358, 361, 363, 364; reconciliation efforts, 60; sends priests to Canada, 59, 60, 62
Hong Kong, 91, 96n7, 163, 354n26; immigrants from, 133, 142, 158, 161, 170

Honpa Canada Buddhist Mission (HCBM), 55, 60–6,
Hsüan Hua, Master, 153, 185–6
Humanistic Buddhism, 7, 10, 27, 40
hybridity, 33, 38, 232, 301

identity, 80, 143, 153, 160, 207, 233, 284; Asian, 193; Buddhist, 201, 208, 209, 244n1; Canadian, 5, 18–19, 29–30, 129, 134, 137, 152, 168–9, 208, 277; and children, 208, 209, 213, 215; Chinese, 155; creating, 296; cultural, 27, 29, 103, 155, 164; ethnic, 16, 70, 159, 231; hybrid, 5, 226; Japanese, 230; lack of, 166; national, 26–8, 60, 170, 276; negotiating, 287, 295, 297, 299, 304; public, 158; queer, 275–6, 285; regional, 69, 74; scholar-practitioner, 226–7, 234, 373, 378–9; self-, 143, 258; sexual, 276; Shin Buddhist, 60, 69–70, 73; Sri Lankan, 103, 201, 204; Theravada, 112, 213–14, 219; Tibetan, 287–8, 291, 292, 296, 299–301, 304, 306; Vietnamese, 36
imagined community, 29, 33, 169, 304
immigrant, immigration, 140, 174, 231, 323, 391; adaptation of, 151, 166–7; Chinese, 153–6, 185–6; demographic change, 152, 160–1; immigrant Buddhism, 39, 155o, 205, 220–1; Japanese, 55–7, 59–60, 66–9, 72–4, 230, 357–60, 397, 406, 411; language, 160–2; laws, 66, 174, 336; Minister Kenney, 29, 166, 401; and multiculturalism, 29, 51, 151, 155, 165, 168, 170; Sri Lankan, 202, 205; Thai, 178
individualism, 31, 212; and Buddhism, 17–18, 31, 41, 45–7; 52n15, 231; and modernity, 12; and Trúc Lâm, 48;

and Vipassana, 80, 84, 86, 88; in the West, 214; and Zen, 190
inmates, 245–65
insider/outsider, 55; insider perspective, 226, 235, 383n36; outsider, 68, 228, 350; religious insider, 375
insight meditation. *See* meditation
institutionalization: of authority, 80, 351; education, 203; of lay nuns, 316; of meditation, 81; of religion, 192, 314
insularity, 16, 159, 162, 167
interdependent cooirigation, 272, 273, 283
interfaith, 20, 42, 76, 240. *See also* ecumenism
Internet, 13, 96, 129, 148, 162–3, 173, 192, 195n6; blog, 176; stereotypes, 306; websites, 134, 157, 186, 228, 298, 299, 323, 328
issei. See Japanese Canadians
Izumida, Junjō, 61–3, 75n8

Japan, 9, 15, 132; Buddhist reform in, 9, 13, 27; expansionism, 60; immigrants from, 5, 55–7, 59, 60, 67, 230, 359; influence of, 37; modernization, 58; monasteries in, 182, 187, 190, 191, 196n13; nationalism, 65; nuns in, 111, 315; relations with Canada, 66; studying in, 34, 49, 357, 358, 360, 367, 368; Zen in, 286
Japanese-Canadian: internment of, 29, 359; *issei*, 56, 57, 64, 67, 69, 72–4, 230–1, 360, 364; *nikkei*, 64–5, 67, 69; *nisei*, 56, 67, 72, 230–1, 359, 364; *sansei*, 67, 230, 231; *yonsei*, 230–1
Jayantā. *See* Johannesen, Shirley
Jōdo Shinshu (Japanese Pure Land Buddhism), 22, 55, 57, 155, 162, 355–7,

360, 363–5, 374, 377; Christianizing Shin Buddhism, 150; Higashi Honganji, 19, 56, 58, 61–4; Honpa Buddhist Churches of Alberta, 360, 361–4; Honpa Canada Buddhist Mission (HCBM), 55–6, 61, 62, 63–4, 65–7, 72; Nishi Honganji, 19, 56, 58, 60–7, 73; Shin Buddhism, 55–74. *See also* Kawamura

Johannesen, Shirley, 21, 22, 313, 321, 322, 323, 325–30

Karma (*kamma*), 6, 7, 45, 52n12, 211, 218, 219, 231, 236, 238, 315, 345
Karma Kagyu: centres, 140–1; lineage, 129–30, 133–4, 148n5
Karmapa, head of Karma Kagyu lineage, 131, 134, 141–2, 148n5
Karuna Dharma, 344
Kawamura, Leslie, 355–80
Kawamura, Toyo, 355, 363–4, 368–9, 372–3
Kawamura, Yutetsu, 55, 357, 360, 362–3, 369, 381n12
Kenney, Jason, 29, 166–7, 172n4
Kyoto, 61, 66–7, 75n7, 77n30, 357–8, 363–4, 366–7, 369, 374, 381n16

laity, 46, 64, 73, 82, 87, 126, 174, 203, 268, 292, 330; Chinese, 154–5, 156, 158, 183; emphasis in Buddhism in the West; 31, 47, 194, 231, 331; female, 319; Fourfold Sangha, 318; lay centres, 20, 177, 183; lay nun, 316; lay teachers, 6, 8, 79, 205, 327; leadership, 77n35, 225, 239, 327, 363; reform Buddhism's orientation toward, 9, 36, 206, 315–16, 378; set up temples and organizations, 31, 65, 75n6, 153, 336, 337, 341, 358; support from, 60, 66, 116, 119, 122, 315, 317, 334, 339, 340, 343, 347, 350, 361; teachers, 125, 313, 325, 326, 329; at Thrangu Monastery, 131, 133, 135, 136, 138, 139, 140, 146; Vietnamese, 22, 342, 346; Vipassana and, 80–3, 86, 91, 92; women, 313, 314, 316, 317, 318, 327, 330. *See also* clergy; *dasa sil mata*; volunteers

Lama Pema Tsewang. *See* Pema Tsewang
lamas, 132, 238, 243
language, 26, 32, 56, 115, 117, 133, 135, 151–2, 159, 167–8, 170, 185–6, 333; Asian, 252; Buddhist, 366; Buddhist religious, 219, 229; Chinese, 154–5, 159; English, 34, 304; European, 58, 186; first, 160, 162; Goenka, 84, 87, 90, 93, 97n10, 97n24; Japanese, 65, 67, 360; multicultural, 138–9; Official Languages Act, 163; Pali, 213; and silence, 272; Thai, 126n2; Tibetan, 132, 289, 294, 298; traditional, 142, 145; transmission of, 162, 169; Vietnamese, 252; Zen, 268, 275, 284
leader/s, 7, 22, 42, 44–6, 48, 51n3, 99n25, 110, 131, 134, 137–8, 143, 146, 176–7, 182, 193; activist, 49; Ajahn, 126n6; Buddhist, 1, 4, 23, 34, 91, 159, 170, 185, 193, 202; exiled, 141; female, 22, 334–8; first generation, 270; lay, 8, 22, 77n35, 79, 125, 327; leadership, 3, 8, 25, 57, 80, 113–14, 124, 129, 154–6, 158, 171n7, 174, 190, 192–3, 203, 259–60, 287, 339, 350–2, 362, 365, 370–2, 374; lineage, 110, 114, 117, 125; religious, 360, 363; spiritual, 134
Ledi Sayadaw, 80, 81
Liên Hoa Temple (Montreal), 340–2, 347

Ling Yen Mountain Temple (Richmond, British Columbia), 154–5, 163, 171n9, 185
liturgy, 213, 228, 237, 240, 305
localism, 18, 37–40, 46–8
localization, 11, 18, 23, 44, 50, 69, 94; Buddhist, 15, 51
Lotus Light Temple (Vancouver), 153
loving-kindness (*mettā*), 85, 97n11, 213, 232, 236, 323

magazines, 162; Buddhist, 174; *FILE*, 273, 280; *Shambhala Sun*, 174, 229; *Tish*, 276; *Tricycle*, 6, 174, 261; *Viên Giác*, 8–9
Mahayana, 17, 122, 96n7, 318; nuns, 111, 114, 124; sutras, 91, 235; and Theravada, 122, 123, 124, 318
mandala, 21, 131, 293–4; painting of, 274; principle, 135; sand, 293, 299
mantra/s, 235, 240, 293
Maplehurst Correctional Complex, 245–54
marriage, 179, 368; ceremony/ritual, 120, 243; intermarriage, 109, 231
Masuyama, Bishop, 65–6, 67, 76n23
materialism, 12, 86
McMahan, David, 10, 17, 38, 294, 308n4
meals: community, 318, 356, 370; rules, 16, 127n9, 183, 186, 189, 333
media, 170; Buddhist, 42, 64–5, 261; controversy, 116, 156; shaping identity, 29, 168, 169; about Tibet, 288, 291, 306
meditation: in 1960s, 321; and activism, 106, 261; ascetic practice, 183; centres, 4, 6, 7, 15, 174–95; for children, 204, 213; classes, 298; and Dhammadinna's students, 322–9; and enlightenment, 210; essential part of Buddhism, 21, 213, 235; and Fluxus, 270, 273, 280; image of Buddha, 11; insight meditation, 80, 157, 183, 211. 80, 85, 86, 174; instruction, 98n14, 111, 134, 321, 329, 330, 353; Karuna Dharma, 344; lack of, 35; mindfulness, 34, 121, 213, 229, 255, 263, 323, 324; modernist emphasis, 6, 7, 11, 15–16, 46–8, 180–1, 194, 231, 232, 252; and new Buddhism, 31; in prison, 246, 248–50, 252–5, 261–4; and psychology, 330; retreats, 322, 326, 327; as scientific, 46; sessions, 9, 132, 140, 156, 157; sexual misconduct and, 174–5, 184, 192–3; and stress reduction, 252, 255, 262, 323–4; teachers, 157, 174, 229; Thai Forest Tradition and, 16, 19; Thích Nhất Hạnh and, 34, 353; Tibetan, 17, 293, 298; in Vietnam, 35; Vipassana, 19, 79–96, 97n13, 99n25, 322; in the West, 17, 20, 31, 46, 227–8, 321; women and, 104, 317, 318; Zen, 156
merit (*puñña*), 228, 338; accumulation, 85, 131, 138, 229, 238, 239; chanting for, 80; dedication, 233, 236; rituals, 231–2, 233, 315; traditional, 6, 7
mettā. *See* loving-kindness
migration, 162, 163, 166, 201, 220; changing dynamics, 151–2, 160; of traditions, 22, 79, 83
mindfulness. *See* meditation
mindfulness-based stress reduction (MBSR), 252, 262, 323
minister: lay minister, 326; Leslie Kawamura, 356–65, 368–9, 371–2, 374, 377, 380, 381n5, 381n10, 381n18, 381n24, 381n28; in Shin Buddhism, 56, 59, 60–7, 69–72, 77n37

minorities, 6, 164, 168; ethnic, 155; faith, 245, 260, 265; visible, 161, 172n18

missionaries, 232, 251; Buddhist, 19, 31, 41–2, 157, 324; Christian, 9, 14, 27, 42, 43, 81, 296. *See also* proselytization

modern/ist/ized Buddhism, 5, 6, 8, 15, 16, 17, 19, 31, 32, 36, 38, 91, 181, 44–5, 194; characteristics, 15, 31, 32, 41, 48, 231; in Sri Lanka, 208, 315; in Thailand, 19, 27; Theravada, 221–2, 321. *See also* Dharmapala; Fo Guang Shan; Goenka; Suzuki, D.T.; Taixu; Thai Forest Tradition; Thích Nhất Hạnh; Thích Thanh Từ; Trúc Lâm; Vipassana

modernity/modernism, 12, 38, 41, 44–5, 74, 144, 192, 230, 300; definition, 38, 41, 231; discourses, 17, 45; and individualism, 12, 45–7; interpretations, 299; and meditation, 46, 80, 193, 231; and rationalism, 17; and religion, 42, 44–5, 47, 192; representation as, 300; and secularization, 14, 44, 378; and tradition, 4, 6, 7–10, 11, 28, 44, 136–7, 143–6, 231, 287; Western, 38, 45, 86, 145; world view, 12, 79; and Zen, 37. *See also* Buddhism, modernization of

modernization: in Asia, 9, 10, 12, 15–16, 44, 347, 378; critiques, 229–230, 300; equivalent to Westernization, 4; of Japan, 58, 60; of Thailand, 105; theory, 44–5; and *vinaya*, 119–20; *See also* Buddhism, modernization of

monastery: Birken Forest, 18, 19–20, 101–26, 324–5; Gold Buddha, 153–4, 158; Great Pine Forest, 342, 344, 346, 351, 352; Thrangu, 129–48

monasticism: forest practice, 19, 104, 118, 119–20, 122; Goenka, 82, 86, 91; and meditation, 35, 46; sex scandals, 20, 175, 177, 182, 183; and Tibetan dance, 287, 291–7; Western de-emphasis, 16, 31, 194, 321, 326, 329–30; and women, 110, 111, 314, 316, 344

monastics, relationship with laity, 19, 40, 56, 60, 66, 67, 70, 119, 120, 122, 132, 177, 194, 331, 315, 317, 341, 346, 362

monks, 112–13; in Asia, 228, 330, 338, 339; forest, 19, 105–8, 121–4; and meditation, 80–1; ordination, 34, 241; and rules, 6, 16, 146, 187–8; sex scandals, 20, 175, 177, 178–9, 182, 184; teaching children, 206; Tibetan, 132, 133, 135–6; in West, 31, 33, 49, 102, 158; and women, 317, 334, 344, 347–51

Montreal: Tam Bảo Temple in, 22, 333, 337, 342, 343–4, 346; Tzu Chi in, 8, 176, 326; Vietnamese Buddhism in, 9, 18, 31, 32, 35, 40, 48, 340, 348, 349, 351, 352, 354n17; Vipassana in, 89

morality, 183, 202, 210, 253; discipline, 60; education, 204, 207, 211, 218, 298; justification, 14; principles, 60; prison outreach, 253, 259, 260, 261; responsibility, 188. *See also* ethics; *śīla*

Morris, Michael, 273, 274, 275, 276, 278, 281–4

movies, 287, 291, 302–4, 305, 307, 308n21

multiculturalism, 20, 93, 94, 95, 160, 284, 298, 331, 359; and Buddhism, 25, 32, 79, 138, 202, 216, 217, 223, 296; critique of, 51n3, 164–8, 172n22; policy in Canada, 29, 51n3, 151–2, 155, 163, 170, 208, 215–16

Myanmar. *See* Burma

Nagao, Gadjin, 358, 366–7, 369
Nalanda University, 49; College, 322; Monastic Institute, 135
nationalism, 32, 36, 167, 169; and Buddhism in Asia, 36, 44, 65, 105, 304; and Buddhism in the West, 30; Canadian, 29; and identity, 26–8, 60, 170, 276
newspapers, 62, 162, 165, 176, 196n7
nirvana (nibbana), 57, 73, 85, 211, 219, 222
nisei. See Japanese Canadians
Nishi Honganji. See Honganji
novices, 87–8, 127n18, 188, 254, 332n4, 333, 338, 342, 343, 347, 348, 349; ordination, 21, 316, 317, 320
nuns, 7; Buddha's reluctance, 117, 119, 124–5, 178, 242, 313–14; celibacy, 20, 74–5, 184; changes in West, 31, 92, 327; Chinese, 7, 91, 153–4, 163, 181, 185–6, 189, 319; history of ordination, 21, 110–15; inequality, 22, 319, 325, 331, 334, 338, 344–5, 347, 348–9; "lay nun," 317, 318; nunnery, 91, 316; ordination lineage, 21, 313–14, 315–18, 322, 325; and rules, 154, 175, 177, 189; sex scandals, 16, 20, 179, 181, 184–5; *sīladharā*, 112–13, 118, 127n17; Thai Forest, 16, 178; Theravada 107, 213, 313–32; Tibetan, 131, 137, 317; Vietnamese, 328, 333–54. See also Cheng Yen; Dhammadinna; Thích Nữ Phổ Tịnh

objectivity, 6, 28, 29, 32, 33; scientific, 80; and the study of religion, 375, 376. See also subjectivity
offerings (ritual), 138, 214, 228, 233–5, 238–9
Olcott, Henry Steel, 9, 15, 27, 42, 203

Order of Interbeing, 22, 45, 52n10, 353n11, 354n23
ordination, 108, 187, 357, 363; female, 19, 21, 22, 101, 110–18, 124–5, 242, 313–31, 331n2; ritual, 241; temporary, 8; training, 189; of trees, 241; validity, 120, 123; and *vinaya* rules, 120, 314; of Westerners, 34, 102–3, 108–9, 124
Orientalism: reverse, 296, 305, 307, 309n28; scholarship, 11, 43; and Tibet, 291, 296, 304; and women, 344. See also Oriental Monk
Oriental Monk, 290–1, 305
orthodoxy, 42, 44, 151, 152, 153, 154, 170, 241, 315
orthopraxy, 43, 241
Ottawa, 7, 21, 23, 225, 227, 230, 233, 240, 278
outsider, 68, 228, 375

Padmasambhava, 291–2, 307n8
painting, 127n14, 274, 287, 298, 299, 300, 307
Pali canon, 52n13, 112, 115, 119, 125, 127n17, 210, 221–2, 236, 313, 317, 320
Pali language, 80, 87, 96n2, 97n11, 98, 102, 121, 126n2, 126n6, 142, 196n15, 204, 210, 212–15, 218, 320
Pali Text Society, 44, 224n4
paññā. See wisdom
Parkdale, Toronto, Ontario, 287, 288, 296–8
parochialism, 14, 16, 48; Buddhist, 39–41, 46, 47–51
Pāṭimokkha, 119, 125, 178
Pema Tsewang, Lama, 130, 131–2, 135, 138, 139
philosophy, 27, 58, 264, 320, 359, 365, 367, 381n9, 381n9; Buddhist, 132, 142, 157, 204, 212, 213, 227, 228, 323n4, 358,

366; Mahayana, 17; public, 151, 165; Tibetan 132, 142
pilgrimage, 22, 185–6, 196n16
pluralism, 20, 217, 219
poetry, 50, 70, 251, 267–8, 275, 276, 367
Po Lam Buddhist Association (Chilliwack, British Columbia), 91–2, 94, 99n26
popular culture, 29; Buddhism in, 25, 299; Tibet and, 288, 299, 300; Zen and, 21, 25, 50
postmodernity, 96, 277
prayer, 9, 135; book, 9; flags, 294; in funeral 233, 234–5, 236, 240; for luck, 7; retreat, 132; Tibetan, 135, 143
Prebish, Charles, 51n1, 89, 123, 355, 378–9
precepts, 46, 60, 85, 175, 184, 193, 229, 257, 338; and celibacy, 20, 84–5, 178–82; defining a Buddhist, 92; Dharmaguptaka, 196n11; five, 84, 92, 99n27, 111, 183; and teaching children, 204, 208, 212, 213, 214, 218–9; ten, 112, 127n17, 316, 338; Theravada, 19, 174, 175, 178–9, 196n11; and women, 111, 174, 189, 196n11, 316
priests, 290, 355; Christian, 65, 87, 194; Hindu, 97n8; Shin, 58, 61, 62, , 69, 72, 74n4, 75n7, 356, 358, 360, 368, 382n18; Zen, 190, 194
prisons, 21, 84; outreach 245–65
proselytization, 5, 232, 252. *See also* missionaries
Protestant Buddhism, 9, 27, 208, 223, 315
psychology, 45, 365; Buddhism in psychotherapy, 229, 328, 330; Western emphasis, 47, 88, 228, 330. *See also* psychotherapy

psychotherapy, 194, 229, 248, 328, 330. *See also* psychology
publications: on Buddhism in Canada, 3–4, 39; Buddhist dictionary, 8; Buddhist Publication Society, 321–2, 334–5; on Buddhist women, 331n2; magazines, 8–9; as a public act, 256; and reform movement, 39; on sexual misconduct, 174. *See also* magazines; newspapers
puñña. *See* merit
Pure Land, 57, 60, 64, 73, 234, 237; ancestor worship and, 69, 239; Chinese, 40, 156, 157; Japanese, 19, 55, 355; as metaphor, 240; temples, 129; Tibetan, 234, 237, 239, 240; Vietnamese 9, 35. *See also* Jōdo Shinshu
purity, 39, 210, 219, 221, 296, 314, 315

Quebec, 247, 326, 329; immigrants in, 287, 335, 337; and self-government, 164, 276; Vipassana in, 79, 84, 89, 90, 93
queer, 275, 285

racism, 30, 52n5, 55, 150, 151
radicalization, 257–8
rankings: Ajahn Brahm, 115; monastic, 115, 188, 303, 338; nuns, 344, 350; Thích Nữ Phổ Tịnh, 338, 352n1; Thrangu Rinpoche, 130, 133; Vietnamese, 348–9, 354n15
rationalism, 17–18, 124, 203, 216, 219, 241; Buddhism and, 6, 7, 9, 15, 16, 44, 48, 80, 85, 231; and education, 49, 207, 212, 349; irrationality, 7, 14; and modernization, 14, 17, 44
Raymond Buddhist Church, 55, 72, 76n20, 78n39, 357, 359, 362, 374

recitation. *See* chanting
reductionism, 29, 376
reflexivity, 28, 226
reform, 38, 42; in Asia, 10, 15, 27–8, 30, 32, 36–7, 40, 43–4, 49, 50, 105–6, 223; discourses, 39; extent, 9; global Buddhism, 17, 41, 46, 48; lay involvement, 315; movements, 10, 17, 22, 27, 49, 30, 32, 36, 37, 38, 41, 42, 43, 49, 203, 347; reformers, 10, 22, 41, 49, 117, 319, 320; and women, 111, 319, 347
Reformation, 44, 46
refugees, 5, 34; government policy, 29, 51n3; Tibetan, 287–9, 300, 306; Vietnamese, 34, 36, 335, 336, 340, 348, 349
reincarnation, 7, 35, 45, 52n12, 131, 218, 295, 303, 314, 315; and funerals, 237, 238, 239; and modern Buddhism, 45, 218, 219, 231. See also *tulku*
religion, 6; and art, 299; and change, 32; China and, 140; as communication, 20, 51; and culture, 287–8, 299, 301, 302, 303, 304; dissatisfaction with, 28, 52n11; family, 69; folk, 243, 244n2, 268; and globalization, 14, 42; and individualism, 46; and politics, 288, 299, 301, 302, 303, 306, 308n21; vs practice, 7, 86; re-enchantment, 14; and ritual, 243; scholarship of, 373, 375, 376, 377, 383n36; and science, 16, 86; and secularization, 14; vs spirituality, 87, 192; theories of, 42, 150, 257, 263, 266n12. *See also* Buddhism as; Christianity, as model for; globalization of religion; modernity and; world religion

Renjian Fojiao. See Buddhism, Humanistic
renunciation, 119; women, 316, 317, 325, 331
retreat, 8, 103, 104, 132, 134, 137, 176, 249, 271, 321, 323, 328, 329; centre, 89, 102, 131, 148n7; meditation, 82, 175, 183, 322, 326–7; rains, 123; solitary, 125, 157; youth, 365
rhetoric, 29, 74n1, 166–8, 172n24, 187, 217, 223, 306
Richmond (British Columbia), 19, 129, 131–2, 137, 140, 148n4, 154–6, 161, 171n9, 171n12, 172n20, 185
ritual: death, 20–1, 225–43; and globalism, 45–6, 87, 150, 328; and merit, 43; and monastic life, 175, 182, 188, 193; Pure Land, 9; sacred, 228, 240, 292; tantric, 228, 292; and teaching children, 204, 214, 215; Tibetan, 131, 132, 135–6, 138–9, 142, 145–7, 288, 292, 295, 304–5; and traditional/modern, 6, 8, 9, 11, 16, 35; and women, 112, 115, 156, 344–5, 347
romanticism, 17, 137, 142, 190; of Tibet, 291, 296, 303, 305
Ryukoku University, 72, 357–8, 367

sacredness, 134, 135, 228, 240, 241, 251, 376; sacred performance, 291–8; sacred sites, 135, 213, 214, 314
saddhā, 210–1
sādhanā, 132, 133–4, 140
Saigon, 49, 335, 338, 339, 341, 351
Sākyadhitā (Daughters of the Buddha), 21, 317, 318–19, 322, 327–8, 330, 331n2, 332n11
Sakyamuni. *See* Buddha
samādhi, 84, 210, 214, 217, 221

San Francisco, 55, 58, 66, 70, 73, 76n23, 285, 355, 357, 359, 367
San Francisco Zen Center, 173, 174, 191, 195n5, 321
Sangha: Asian institution, 315; as Buddhist refuge, 46, 84, 194, 208, 213–14, 235; female, 313–14, 316, 318–19, 344; Forest Sangha 17, 105–6, 188, 325; laity/monastic relations, 81, 89, 92, 341; in monastery, 138; in ritual, 232–3, 235, 240; in West 189, 348, 349
Sangharakshita, 22, 182, 193
sansei. *See* Japanese Canadians
Sasaki Jōshū, 195n6
Sasaki Senjū, 59–60
Sasaki Sōkei-an, 3, 23n1
Saskatchewan, 93, 329; University of, 247, 358, 366, 369
Sati Saraniya, 178, 196, 324–5
Sayadaw. *See* Ledi
Sayagyi U Ba Khin. *See* Ba Khin
schism: in Shin Buddhism, 56, 62, 66, 69, 361–2; in Thai Forest tradition, 116, 124–5; in Vietnamese Buddhism, 347–8
scholar, 9, 23, 27–8, 33, 47, 91–2, 105, 163, 175, 231, 261, 270, 292, 315, 319, 331, 337, 355, 365, 367–9, 375, 377; and administrator, 363; and friend, 372; and globalization, 13, 15; Indian, 259; Japan, 358; and minister, 359; and monk, 81, 114, 320–1, 378–9; Numata, 356, 371, 380; Pali, 119; and priest, 58, 356; ritual studies, 241; scholar and practitioner, 20, 226, 234, 368, 373, 378–9; scholarly, 119, 144, 185, 226, 368, 370, 376; Tibetan, 134; in West, Western, 5–6, 30–1, 44, 46, 296
scholarship, 28, 105, 125, 359, 366; Buddhist, 285, 366; critical, 31; objective, 376; Orientalist, 11, 43, 296; and practice, 358; rigorous, 377, 380; on Vietnamese Buddhism, 34–5. *See also* studies
schools, 7, 83, 93, 168, 180, 371; Dhamma school, 202–5, 207, 220, 223; missionary, 42; residential, 29; school of Buddhism, 52n9, 318; for women, 316. *See also* Sunday school
science, 80, 96, 192, 219, 226; compatibility with Buddhism, 7, 9, 10, 15, 16, 31, 42, 45, 52n14, 219; Dalai Lama and, 42, 45; Humanistic Buddhism and, 7, 10; meditation and, 46, 79, 80, 83, 85, 86, 94; "modern Buddhism" and, 16; reform Buddhism and, 7, 9; religion and, 16; *Shin Bukkyō* and, 9; social, 6, 14, 165, 226; Vipassana and, 79, 83, 85, 86, 94, 96
scripture, 210, 235; authority, 222; emphasis on, 114; as rational, 120, 121
Seager, Richard, 5, 359
sectarianism, 64; non-sectarianism, 61, 80, 85–7, 158, 323, 329
secular, 60, 77n34, 79, 83, 92–4, 177, 183, 202, 230, 243, 259, 293, 318, 331n2, 333, 345–6; secularism, secular world view, 20, 80, 85–6, 212, 218, 219, 223; secularize, secularization, 86, 252, 255, 300, 328
segregation, sex, 179, 180–2
sexism, 11, 16, 112
sex scandals, 17, 18 20, 173–95
sexuality: in art, 275–6; in prison, 253, 256, 257, 270; rules, 84, 120, 123, 257; sensuality, 85, 179, 217, 222
Shaku Sōen, 9, 27, 41
Shambhala, 22, 134, 141–2, 261; crisis, 174; in Halifax, 51, 176, 177, 303. *See*

also Chödrön, Pema; Gampo Abbey; Trungpa, Chögyam Rinpoche
Shambhala Sun. See magazines
Shangri-la, 291, 300, 304–6, 307n6, 308n17
Sheng Yen, 157–8
Shiga prefecture, 59, 63, 69, 76n15, 77n33, 381n12
Shin Buddhism. *See* Jōdo Shinshū
Shin Bukkyō, 9, 27
Shinran, 57, 63, 68, 70, 71, 73
shrines, 98n16, 111, 131, 135, 141, 151, 170n1, 214, 233; Shinto, 68
Siddhartha. *See* Buddha
sīla, 84, 210, 221, 263. *See also* ethics; morality
sīladharā. See nuns
Sitavana. *See* Birken Forest Monastery
Snodgrass, Judith, 11, 30, 43, 44
Snyder, Gary, 282, 285, 367–8, 382n27
Soka Gakkai, 5, 42, 52n10
solidarity, 62, 150, 151–2, 155, 159, 163, 172n15, 289, 305
spiritual: counselling, 91, 93; country, 291; development, 20, 45, 72, 81, 95, 105, 119, 202, 210–18, 221, 222, 330; guidance, 72, 129; longings, 192; and mundane, 60; needs, 143; orientation, 56; practice, 59–60, 86, 91, 121, 130, 197n20, 228–9, 237; in prison, 246, 247–8, 251–65, 323; protection, 97n11; qualifications, 148; questions, 50; relationships, 181; vs religion, 85; seeker, 79, 83, 227, 326; spirituality, 85–7, 143, 192; teachings, 119; women and, 314, 318, 320, 322, 324, 327, 331n2, 345
Sri Lanka, 21, 43, 56, 81, 128n22, 315; Buddhist revival in, 9, 15–16, 27, 96n7, 101, 203, 223; dhamma education in, 42, 202–3; Dhammadina and, 320, 321, 324; immigration from, 323; nuns in, 315–16, 318–19, 322; ordination in, 114, 120–1; women in, 316–17, 330. *See also dasa sil mata*
stereotypes, 165; of Asia, 8, 12, 188, 193; 344; of Canadian identity, 29–30; of Tibet, 290–1, 299
studies: of Buddhism in Canada, 3–4, 26–7, 33, 285; Buddhism in the West, 145; of philosophy, 359; religion, 375–6, 383n36; of ritual and practice, 227, 228, 238; of Tibetan community in Canada, 305–6. *See also* scholarship
subjectivity, 28–32, 33, 64, 152, 226, 252, 272, 334, 353n8, 375–6, 381. *See also* objectivity
Sugunasiri, Suwanda, 3, 51n3, 156
Sumegi, Angela, 20, 23, 227
Sunday school, 63, 70, 75n7, 150, 202, 203, 207, 214, 215, 223, 362
superstition, 7, 9, 14, 31, 39, 43, 105
Surrey (British Columbia), 102, 103, 104, 323
sutras, 91, 178, 233, 251, 369; Avataṃsaka Sūtra, 269; chanting, 35–6, 46, 48, 71, 91, 92; Great Heart of Wisdom Sutra, 233, 235; The Larger Sutra of Immeasurable Life, 57; Mettā Sutta, 233; studies, 204
Suzuki, D.T., 22, 31, 37, 41, 191n21, 269, 367, 368
symbolic capital, 262–3
symbols, 145, 146, 150, 182, 214, 235, 239, 307; Buddhist, 25, 43, 105, 214, 236, 240; of Canadian identity, 25, 167–8; nationalist, 29, 36, 167, 168; in prison, 256, 258, 265; Tibet, 228, 288, 290, 294, 295–7, 301, 305–6

sympathizers, 92, 319, 356

Taga, Gijin, 62–5, 69
Tairiku Nippō, 62, 63, 65
Taiwan, 7–8, 49, 127n15, 141; Buddhist organizations in, 8, 40, 140, 153, 154, 157–8, 163, 248; immigrants from, 170; nuns in, 111, 114, 154, 319, 325; reform movements, 17; Vipassana in, 97n1
Taixu, 10, 15, 27, 37, 40, 41, 319
Tam Bảo Temple (Montreal), 32, 333, 337, 342–4, 351; division, 346–8, 352, 353n9; female leadership at, 334, 335, 343, 346, 347; nuns at, 344–5, 350; sponsoring monks, 348
Taylor, Charles, 14, 44
technology, 8, 13, 18, 19, 97n10, 323
temple, 83, 101, 175–6; Burmese, 323; Chinese, 7–8, 20, 40, 148n4, 150–63, 170n1, 171n9, 171n11, 171n14, 183, 184–5; community, 255, 256; decisions, 15; ethnic, 5, 9, 49; ethnography of, 4, 227–8, 330; Japanese, 55–7, 59–72, 77n35, 148n4, 174, 356, 357–74, 382n18; lay involvement, 31, 315, 341, 342; monastics at, 184; offerings to, 238; practices, 7, 292; Second Life, 149n10; Sri Lankan, 20, 102, 103, 203, 204, 214, 224n1; stereotype, 7; Thai, 189, 322, 325; Tibetan, 232, 237, 238; traditional, 6, 9; Vietnamese, 8–9, 31–9, 43–50, 51, 252, 328, 333, 336–8, 339, 340–52, 353n2, 353n12, 354n19, 354n20; women, 319, 320, 325; Zen (Chan), 34, 91, 188, 227. *See also* Tam Bảo; Thrangu
tensions: racial, 150–2; religious, 40, 74, 139, 301, 341, 363
textbooks, 7, 203, 214, 224n1, 224n3

texts, 15, 150, 236, 243; canonical, 86, 98n14; 119, 121, 126n6, 178, 196; commentary, 16; practices, 80, 132, 135, 153, 235, 238, 241; in prison, 249, 251–2, 260; reinterpretation of, 86, 121, 221, 242; in ritual, 236, 237–8, 238; Shin, 58; study of, 16, 104–5, 119, 227, 231, 366, 369; of women, 315
Thai Forest Tradition, 16–17, 27, 38, 104–5, 107, 324, 326; and Ajahn Brahm, 114; in Canada, 18, 19, 101, 177; connection to Birken, 105; internationalized, 107; lineage, 107; monasteries, 178, 181, 186, 189, 196n8, 324–5; in the West, 117, 125
Thailand, 15, 17, 27, 56, 106; Buddhism in, 107, 112, 114, 122; immigration from, 323; monks in, 105, 118; nuns in, 110–11, 114, 117, 118, 124, 127n154, 128n22, 316, 325; Vipassana in, 96
Thammayut Nikaya. See Thai Forest Tradition
thangkas, 131, 275, 294, 298–9, 300
therapy, 86, 87, 88, 96, 98, 98n17, 262. *See also* psychology
Theravada, 4, 23, 34, 108, 113, 119, 123, 202, 209–10, 212–13, 214, 218, 221–2; in America, 56, 121, 321, 330; in Britain, 142; in Canada, 232, 313, 323–5, 329; discipline, 109; education, 201–24; and Forest Tradition, 19, 127n18, 101–28; Goenka, 79–100; Great Council, 121; identity, 212–14, 219; immigrants, 205; and Mahayana, 122, 124; meditation, 79; monks and monasteries, 96n7, 102, 108, 122, 142; Pali scholarship, 221; reformer, 320; teaching, 118; *vinaya*, 119–20, 127n15, 196n11, 317–19; in the

West, 108; women in, 23, 101, 107, 110–12, 114, 124, 313–2

Thích Mãn Giác, 34, 49, 341

Thích Nhất Hạnh, 8, 22, 34–7, 45, 47–9, 252, 259, 261; and ecumenism, 42; followers, 32, 52n10; as missionary, 31; as reformer, 41; and socially engaged Buddhism, 10, 91

Thích Như Điển, 8

Thích Nữ Phổ Tịnh, 22, 333; biography, 338–44; challenges to, 348; education, 333, 344, 345, 346, 352, 353n3; gender inequality, 344–5, 348, 350; leadership, 334, 351; role model, 345; support of Thích Thiện Nghị, 345, 346–7, 349

Thích Tâm Châu, 341, 354n17

Thích Thanh Từ, 36, 37, 46, 47–9, 353n6

Thích Thiên Ân, 33–4, 35–6, 37, 41, 47, 48, 49, 344

Thích Thien Nghị, 49, 333, 340–3, 351, 354n14, 354n19; stroke, 334, 350; support of nuns, 345, 348, 349, 352

Thích Trí Quang, 339, 341

Thiền Viện Linh Sơn (Montreal), 9

Thrangu Monastery: constituency, 140–1, 149n9; description, 129, 130–4, 148n4; sacred, 134, 180–1, 147; traditional, 130, 134–5, 142, 143, 145, 147; untraditional, 136, 137, 144, 145

Thrangu Rinpoche, 129, 130, 131–6, 139–40, 148n1, 148n2, 148n3, 148n7

Thrangu Tibetan Buddhist Monastery (Richmond, British Columbia), 19, 129–48

Tibet, 15; Buddhism, 9, 17, 129–48, 173, 196n11, 227, 229, 234, 252, 321, 365; and China, 287, 304, 307, 307n6, 309n26; diaspora, 17, 287–307; nuns, 196n11, 242, 317, 318, 319; representations of, 287–307; rituals, 225, 228, 233–40, 242–3, 288; stereotype, 21; temple, 232, 237, 271. See also *Bardo Thodol*; 'chams; Dalai Lama; Thrangu; Trungpa

Tiếp Hiện. *See* Order of Interbeing

Tokyo, 49, 157, 371

tolerance, 76n20, 124, 165, 170, 217, 246

Toronto, 7, 8, 25; Buddhists in, 32, 51n3, 75n7, 201, 202, 204, 206–8, 220–1, 230; demographics, 20, 161–2, 205, 217, 223; multiculturalism in, 215, 216; prison outreach in, 249; temples in, 20, 40, 148n1, 176, 184–5, 224, 252, 253, 328, 330, 337, 343, 351, 352; Tibetans in, 287–8, 296–9, 302, 305–6, 307n1, 308n21

traditional, 18–19, 30, 33, 35, 38–9, 49, 129–30, 134, 137, 141–4, 153, 289, 335; Asian, 4, 11, 179, 181, 193; ethnic, 9, 11, 35–6, 47, 50, 145; form and content, 134–5; identity, 143; image, 134, 141, 144; indigenous, 12; invented, 29, 36, 52n9, 137; Judeo-Christian, 86–7; monastic, 82–3, 129–30, 134, 136; reform, 15; return to, 16–17; Theravada, 23, 315, 318, 325, 330; traditionalist, 6, 8, 140, 145–6, 231; traditional vs modern, 4, 7–24, 44, 136, 287; untraditional, non-traditional, 136, 138, 232, 242. *See also* Goenka; Forest Tradition; Thrangu Monastery

transformation, 11, 27, 29, 30, 170, 242, 268, 301; agents of, 6; of character, 210, 218; global, 46, 50, 232, 378; multiple conversations, 14; ongoing, 150; originates in Asia, 27, 30, 31; process, 28; of rituals, 225, 241, 242;

social, 84, 285; of Vietnamese Buddhism, 37, 47; in the West, 41, 48, 50
transmission, 25, 37, 58, 241; of Buddhism, 20, 25, 58, 89, 269, 284, 285, 297, 315; of disease, 174; intergenerational, 162, 201, 202, 204, 206–9, 220–1, 224n1, 358; language, 160, 162–3, 169; lineage, 135, 148n3, 187; qualifications for, 141
transnationalism, 12; artistic movements, 267; Asian reform, 15, 28, 41, 50; Buddhist, 26, 37, 50, 335; Chinese, 41; connections, 15; prison programs, 261; restrictions, 74; Vietnamese, 37, 335; Vipassana, 93
Tricycle. See magazines
Triple Gem, 84, 97n11, 208, 212, 213, 214
Trúc Lâm, 36, 37, 46, 47–8, 50
Trungpa, Chögyam Rinpoche, 22, 31, 41, 173, 176, 303
Tsomo, Karma Lekshe, 317, 318
Tulku, 130, 303
Tung Lin Kok Yuen, 126n1, 156, 157
Tu Viện Huyền Không (Montreal), 9
Tweed, Thomas, 33, 38, 92
Tzu Chi Merit Society, 8, 22, 38, 319, 353n7

Union of Vietnamese Buddhist Churches in Canada, 337, 342, 354n13
universalism, 79, 80, 83, 85–9, 93, 94, 167, 219

values, 375; Asian, 284, 314; Buddhist, 118, 207, 208, 211–16, 220–1, 268; Canadian, 112, 167, 169, 202, 217, 284; equality, 112; monastic, 315; moral, 298; religious, 69; Western, 112, 113
Vancouver, 103, 104, 130, 276, 281, 282, 286; and art, 273–5, 277–80, 282, 320; Chinatown, 151, 153; Chinese, 20, 140, 161, 171; Japanese, 55, 56, 59, 60–7, 69–70, 73, 77n33, 77n34; Riot (1907), 71; temples in, 7, 8, 59, 148n4, 153, 154, 156, 157, 158, 185, 186, 357
Vancouver Island, 55, 65, 79, 91
vegetarianism, 21, 25, 94, 100n29, 122, 131, 154, 186, 254, 340
Viên Giác. See magazines
Viên Giác Temple (Hanover, Germany), 8
Vietnamese: abbot, 8; 33, 51, 328, 333, 334; Buddhists in Canada, 4; Buddhists in Montreal, 9, 18, 31, 32, 35, 40, 48, 340, 348, 349, 351, 352, 354n17; chanting, 35, 36, 46, 48; Christians, 353n12; community conflict, 337–8, 341–2, 346–51; diaspora, 8, 49, 337, 347; family, 343, 347; identity, 36; immigrants, 33; laity, 22, 342, 346; language, 252; monastic ranking, 348–9, 354n15; Pure Land Buddhism, 9, 35; refugees, 34, 36, 335, 336, 340, 348, 349; schism, 347–8; temple, 8–9, 31–9, 43–50, 51, 252, 328, 333, 336–8, 339, 340–52, 353n2, 353n12, 354n19, 354n20; transnationalism, 37, 335; Zen (*Thiền*), 34–5, 36–7, 47–8. *See also* Buddhism; Tam Bảo Temple; Trúc Lâm; Union of Vietnamese Buddhist Churches in Canada
vinaya, 16, 178, 196n11, 338, 351, 379; interpretation, 30, 50, 119–24, 127n18, 128n23; and nuns, 124, 127n17, 317–19, 332n7; and sexuality, 178, 180, 182–3, 186; Theravada, 101, 108, 112, 113, 127n15
vipassana, 79, 252, 262, 321; Dhammadinna, 320, 321–2, 326. *See* Vipassana Meditation Movement

Vipassana Meditation Movement: egalitarian, 80, 85–7, 88, 89; history, 79–4, 89, 90, 92–6; non-sectarian, 80, 85–9; as secular reform, 38, 79, 85–7, 94–5; teachings and practices, 84–5, 88–9, 90–2. *See also* meditation, science

volunteers, 9, 91–2, 132, 133, 203, 331; chaplains, 36; meditation instructors, 84, 88, 93, 99n21, 99n22, 99n23, 99n27; prison outreach, 245–61, 265; relief work, 8

vows: Amida's, 57; breach of, 146; monastic, 174, 175, 177, 182–4, 189; *sannyasi*, 320; Shin Buddhism, 73; Vipassana, 84

Wat Abaghiri. *See* Abhayagiri Forest Monastery
Wat Bodhinyana, 114, 116
Wat Nong Pah Phong, 107, 114
Watts, Alan, 285, 368
Weber, Max, 14
West End Dhamma School (Mississauga, Ontario), 205, 210, 211
Western Buddhism, 2–38, 47, 50–1, 52n12, 116, 145, 193, 232, 252, 261, 335
Westernization, 4, 44
Wild Geese, 3, 4, 5, 8, 22, 23, 26, 27, 33, 38, 159, 177, 223
wisdom (*paññā*), 84, 85, 210, 221

world religion, 14, 41, 42–4, 47, 179
World's Parliament of Religions, 58, 75n5
worship, 48, 141, 143, 156, 167, 213–14; ancestor, 7, 68–9, 187, 197n18; cult, 191, 354n26; goddess, 35; guru, 190; ritual, 239, 243

yoga, 298, 320, 321, 323, 326, 328–9; prison programs, 248, 249, 253
Yogācāra, 365, 366, 377
yonsei. See Japanese Canadians
youth, 215; and education, 202, 204–5; and language, 162; Tibetan, 296–7, 298

Zen, 273, 367; appropriation of, 21, 25, 277, 280; and art, 21, 268–70, 272, 275, 283, 284, 286; awakening, 24n1; centre, 173, 174, 176, 180, 195n2, 195n6, 253, 321, 328; Chinese (Chan), 157; 171n13; ecology, 285; master, 173, 189–92, 195n5, 197n20, 268; meditation, 80, 156, 272; monastery, 187, 196n13, 344; monk, 3, 9, 180; poetry, 50, 267–8; Rinzai, 34, 268, 196n13; Sanbo Kyodan, 249; and sex scandals, 173, 180, 190–2; Sōtō, 156; students, 180, 197n21; temple, 34, 227; Vietnamese, 34–5, 36–7, 47–8. *See also* Trúc Lâm